FROMMER'S
DOLLARWISE
BRAZIL
MICHAEL UHL

□

1989–1990

Published by Prentice Hall Trade Division
A Division of Simon & Schuster, Inc.
Gulf + Western Building
One Gulf + Western Plaza
New York, N.Y. 10023

ISBN 0-13-217761-7

ISSN 0899-2827

Manufactured in the United States of America

Text design: Levavi & Levavi, Inc.

*Although every effort was made to ensure the accuracy
of price information appearing in this book,
it should be kept in mind that prices
can and do fluctuate in the course of time.*

CONTENTS

MAPS

For Carol and Simon

ACKNOWLEDGMENTS

The author wishes to acknowledge the kind assistance of Fuad Atala, Helen Mosca, and the many other Brazilian and American colleagues who contributed to the preparation of this text.

INFLATION ALERT: In Brazil inflation is rampant. A few years back, the Brazilian government knocked three zeros off the old currency and changed its name from the *cruzeiro* to the *cruzado*. Unless the Brazilian economy undergoes a radical transformation in the near future, it is safe to assume that this process—which has already occurred twice in two decades—will be repeated at some point in the not-too-distant future. Prices in this guide, however, are quoted in American dollars. Dollar prices in Brazil (especially where money is exchanged at the nonofficial rate, a common practice throughout the country) have shown a tendency to remain relatively stable, since of the two currencies, the *cruzado* is by far the weaker. Nevertheless, the trend throughout the world is toward a steady rise in prices. And while the author has made every effort to ensure the accuracy of the information in this guide, the wise traveler will add at least 10% yearly during the lifetime of the book to the quoted prices, in recognition of this general upswing in the annual cost of living to which we have all become resigned, if never reconciled.

A DISCLAIMER: Although every effort was made to ensure the accuracy of the prices and travel information appearing in this book, it should be kept in mind that prices do fluctuate in the course of time, and that information does change under the impact of the varied and volatile factors that affect the travel industry.

DOLLARWISE GUIDE TO BRAZIL

□ □ □

1. WHY BRAZIL?
2. THE FROMMER'S DOLLARWISE TRAVEL CLUB—HOW TO SAVE MONEY ON ALL YOUR TRAVELS

Vast, mysterious Brazil—beyond the confines of Rio de Janeiro and its famous beaches—is a continent-sized nation that is virtually *terra incognita* to most North Americans, even those who routinely travel to distant and exotic corners of the world. Yet despite its seeming remoteness, Brazil is actually a viable destination for a broad spectrum of today's North American tourists, including vacationers, retirees, and part-time adventurers. Whether or not Brazil is right for you is one of the questions this guide will attempt to help you answer. It may just turn out that a well-planned Brazilian vacation could be one of the high points of your world traveling experiences.

1. WHY BRAZIL?

If you were to ask most North Americans what kinds of facts and notions Brazil conjures up in their minds, you would be likely to get the same half dozen responses from one and all. To us Brazil is Third World poverty; the Amazon; the $110-billion foreign debt; Pele, the soccer phenomenon; ultramodern Brasília, the capital; Sónia Braga, a Latin movie goddess; and of course, Rio de Janeiro—especially Rio at Carnival time.

The list seldom extends beyond these well-honed media images. We tend not even to know that Brazilians speak Portuguese, not Spanish. And it's strangely true that we North Americans, during the course of our history, have expressed little curiosity about South America in general. But our disinterest in Brazil is especially intriguing, because like the United States, Brazil is immense and potentially very powerful—and is, as we are, a patchwork of distinct cultures, captivating geographies, and fascinating regional characteristics.

Yet the North American traveler, by and large, has avoided Brazil. Only a dribble of North Americans have really explored Brazil and know something of its vastness, its history, and the place it occupies in the modern world. There are those Brazil aficionados who have been aptly nicknamed "Brazil Nuts." Having discovered Brazil's charms, they keep returning year after year, disdaining all other world destinations for the opportunity of getting to know this single colossus better and better on each successive visit.

What the Brazil Nuts have discovered is that the object of their infatuation may indeed be a Third World country with all the widespread poverty and social problems that unhappy status entails. But beyond the shroud of misery, they have also seen other realities—the emerging and already mammoth industrialized country with world-class cities, and a country of such uncommon natural beauty and fecundity that, among all nations, it best exemplifies the ideal of the tropical paradise on earth, that vision of sensuality and sunshine that world travelers are perpetually searching for. The fact of a favorable exchange rate for those with U.S. dollars or other "hard" currencies makes accessible many pleasures—like eating in the finest restaurants and staying in the most luxurious accommodations—that at home are the prerogatives of only the most affluent.

The allusion to "tropical paradise" may sound like so much promotional hype. Yet what other nation on earth can claim a beachfront of nearly 5,000 miles where the sun shines virtually all year round? Life along coastal Brazil is spent outdoors much of the time in lush tropical surroundings. And every population center—whether big city or fishing hamlet—has its movement, its outdoor scene which the visitor can experience and share in, without fee, and to the limits of individual taste and spontaneity. There are market stalls and craft bargains everywhere, beach culture, promenades at dusk along splendid boulevards, and café society with excellent food and drink found at bargain prices, no matter where you go, down to the smallest main square in the simplest village. Brazil is also a land saturated with the pulsating rhythms of samba: as a musical people, Brazilians have few rivals on this planet.

Beyond the shore stretches interior Brazil, larger in land mass than the continental U.S. For most travelers to Brazil—Americans very much included—beach life is the beginning and the end of their Brazilian adventure. But the Brazil of the interior is where the real adventure begins. These vast internal regions with all their hidden secrets and attractions are only just now becoming hospitable to international tourists, meeting the minimum standards of comfort and ease of transportation that are generally demanded. Brazilians themselves have only recently grasped the potential of their country as a tourist destination to ultimately rival not only the great sunshine spas of the Caribbean and the Mediterranean, but also the remote and romantic backwaters of Asia and Africa—which attract that segment of the world traveling population who want to see "what it's really like" before "it" disappears.

What is this other Brazil beyond the beaches and the shoreline? It's the region known as Amazônia, still very sparsely inhabited, and covering literally half the country with wetlands, river systems, and rain forests. In contrast, it is São Paulo, only one of the country's 23 states, yet an industrial powerhouse producing an amazing 50% of the nation's GNP, and boasting as its capital the world's third-largest city. It is Minas Gerais, where the record of Brazil's gold and mineral boom has been preserved in several historic towns that have been declared "treasures of the world."

Central Brazil seems like the American West of the last century, with the modern world present as only a thin overlay in the form of the airplane, the automobile, and the electrification of its cities and municipalities. Set among this rural antiquity is the Space Age capital, Brasília—Space Age because it was conceived and constructed in the manner one imagines the first planetary colonies will be built—transported section by section from the civilized world to the empty wastelands of the cosmos.

Southern Brazil, a corner bordering Argentina, Uruguay, and Paraguay, is actually somewhat temperate in climate. This region was settled largely by European and Asian immigrants, who today produce the great cash crops of coffee and soybeans, raise the meat cattle, and make the country's beer and wines.

The Northeast is the cradle of Brazilian culture at its oldest. Here the original Portuguese colonials and their African slaves merged with the pre-Columbian natives and formed the *caboclo,* the core stock of the Brazilian race, blending as well the traditions, spiritual values, customs, legends, music, cuisine—even the languages—of three continents into a unified people who have endured the harsh desert-like conditions of the *sertão* for almost five centuries. Bahia, a large state, stands alone at mid-coast. Gateway to the northeast, with its capital at Salvador, Bahia was the center of power and wealth of the south Atlantic during the first three centuries of Brazil's history, and is today a region uniquely influenced by both the aristocratic traditions of the original Portuguese planters and by the popular customs of the descendants of the captive and far more numerous Africans.

Finally there is Rio—the city that is itself synonymous for many world travelers with the very idea of Brazil. Rio has long, and justifiably, been an obligatory stop for any sophisticated traveler whose ambition it is to visit and enjoy all the truly great cities of the world.

That is Brazil: a country populated by Brazilians, as difficult a group to sum up or stereotype as any among the peoples of the world. The American and Brazilian perspectives on life clash or harmonize, according to the personalities of individuals, and because of or despite the sometimes enormous differences in our respective cultures. I can almost guarantee, however, that whatever the differences—the most formidable of which is the language barrier—if you make the slightest effort in Brazil, you will penetrate the somewhat set patterns of the tourist experience and get as much authentic people-to-people contact as you can handle.

IS BRAZIL SAFE?
Brazil has garnered in recent years an undeserved reputation for being a criminally infested country, and therefore a place best to be avoided by the tourist, who is by nature already somewhat vulnerable in any foreign land.

There is indeed crime—far too much crime—in the large Brazilian cities. It is crime based on the eternal clash between the haves and the have-nots. Residents of big cities throughout the world live with the ever-present possibility of being mugged, much as residents of Los Angeles adapt to the inevitability of earthquakes. Rio, São Paulo, and Salvador are no exceptions to this global rule. At the end of the day, the police blotters in every major city of the world will register the daily roundup of robberies and assaults.

Luck and circumstance protect most of us from crime, even in cities where street crime is common. But more important than luck is how one chooses to behave under conditions that are unfamiliar and potentially hazardous. If you are not an urban dweller, and therefore unfamiliar with the rules of being street savvy (or even if you are, and you happen to forget yourself when traveling abroad), here are a few tips that should go a long way toward protecting you from the typical street crime, which is a crime of opportunity:

□ Do not tempt a thief with dangling gold chains or expensive gems or watches.

□ Carry your photographic equipment in a bag—but never bring anything you aren't willing to part with to the beach. The street urchins of Rio, for example, while rarely dangerous to your person, can operate very swiftly—and are difficult to detect, much less capture once the deed is done.

□ If you like to walk the streets at night, do so only where you see throngs of Brazilians taking their nocturnal constitutionals. And even then, you look different than they do, so out of common courtesy—as well as self-protection—don't go out of the way to call attention to yourself.

□ Don't ride the public buses unless you have really gotten to know the city and speak some Portuguese. You could be an easier target in a contained space. Also, buses are sometimes held up in broad daylight, like stagecoaches and trains of yore.

□ At night, travel to and from your hotel by taxi. Someone at the restaurant or nightclub you've gone to will be happy to call you a cab, if there is not already a line of hacks in the vicinity. I give this advice somewhat halfheartedly, since you are much more likely to be ripped off—at least in Rio—by the hordes of dishonest cab drivers than by the street people. Still, even if you end up paying three times what you should, you will at least be assured of getting home safely.

□ Spend some time figuring out the unfamiliar money values before you hit the street. And never flash large wads of cash in public. Do what Brazilians do when at the beach. Tuck the equivalent of a few dollars into your swimsuit. Wet money will buy you a fresh pineapple or a soft drink as readily as dry money.

□ On a positive note, you are in South America and thus are very unlikely to be a target of terrorism in a large department store or at the airport—conditions which travelers to Europe must sometimes confront.

□ If you are unlucky enough to get mugged, don't resist! Give the thief what he wants with as much dispatch as possible. Because what he really wants is to get away from you—with the goods—quickly and with no complications.

□ To be on the safe side, leave everything you don't need with you on a given excursion—including money and documents—in your hotel, preferably under lock and key in your room's individual safe (if there is one), or with the concierge at the desk. Personally, while I have never been robbed, I always carry "thief money" when traveling in any big city (except to the beach). This is the equivalent of $15 to $20 loose in a pocket, to cough up on demand if the occasion ever arises.

□ You will be happy to learn that outside of the three large Brazilian cities mentioned above, crime in Brazil is not a great problem. You can walk virtually anywhere, day or night, within the cities of the interior or in the smaller cities of the northeast like Aracajú, Maceió, João Pessoa, and Natal—where even the beaches at night are not out of bounds. I base my evaluation in this on both personal experience and on the say-so of local officials wherever I have traveled. Nevertheless, you, dear reader, must satisfy yourself as to whether or not a particular place feels secure and comfortable. Local orientation in every case is a must.

DOLLARWISE–WHAT IT MEANS: This is a guidebook giving specific, practical details—including prices—about the hotels, restaurants, nightlife, sights, and shopping opportunities to be found throughout Brazil. The term "dollarwise" means something very different in Brazil than, say, in Europe. Brazil—put quite simply—is more of a value.

The overwhelming majority of all North Americans who visit Brazil annually—some 200,000 according to both the Brazilian government and independent sources—go to Rio only, and remain there during their entire stay. Thus this first edition of *Frommer's Dollarwise Brazil* reflects primarily the touring patterns and preferences of this existing market. Americans tend to come to Rio in groups or with individual package tours, and they stay in luxury or first-class hotels, which cost about half of what equivalent hotels would cost in New York, London, Paris, and other major world cities.

These same American visitors also tend to eat in the top, even gourmet, restaurants. Why? Because, by and large, they can easily afford the best once they have exchanged their dollars for *cruzados,* as the Brazilian currency is called. Some Americans get so caught up in the reality of how far their dollars will stretch in Brazil that they bargain-hunt to the point of obsession and rudeness. The Brazilians don't have to be reminded that we have a higher standard of living and a harder currency than they do. So if you want to "put on the ritz," do so with panache and in a fun-loving way, and the Brazilians you are dealing with will not only enjoy your experience vicariously, but they'll also welcome graciously the jolt of the little extra cash you brought their way.

This guidebook, then, because of both the favorable exchange rate and the existing touring patterns of Americans in Brazil, will tend to concentrate on what, by Brazilian standards, are the medium- to high-priced establishments. In recognition of, and with total sympathy for, those Americans who have come to really trek through Brazil, and who are traveling on restricted individual or family budgets, I have included a number of bargain establishments for many cities. I have avoided the $5- and $10-a-night rooms, but any youthful or seasoned traveler worth his or her salt will have no trouble locating such accommodations. Most airports and bus stations have tourist information counters, and the attending staff will recommend a hotel for your budget, if you arrive in any major city without a reservation. It must be noted, however, that the farther you wander in Brazil from the beaten tourist paths, the less likely you are to find people in service positions who speak English.

AN INVITATION TO READERS:

As the principal destination for Americans, Rio deserves—and will receive in this guide—a great deal more attention than the rest of the country. Nevertheless, this is also a true "Guide to Brazil" in that it attempts to cover all the bases, all the major regions, cities, and sites throughout what is a very large country. Since this is the first edition of the guide, written by a single author under scheduling restraints, I could not hope to have documented everything worth knowing or seeing. Some, indeed many, of you who travel to Brazil over the next two years (after which this guide will be updated) will break ground that I could not. You will go to different restaurants and shows, discover new beaches, bargains, or street scenes. I would like you to consider this guide as your bulletin board for sharing information and experiences with me and other Brazil travelers who will read subsequent, updated editions. Please keep in mind, as well, that no one—no business or individual—has paid to be mentioned in this book. With one or two exceptions (noted in the text), all locales and establishments mentioned herein have been visited personally by the author. I have tried to include only those listings that will stimulate your curiosity, please your palate, and comfort your repose. So please share your experiences —for good or ill—with me, and address all comments to Michael Uhl, c/o Prentice Hall Trade Division, Gulf + Western Building, One Gulf + Western Plaza, New York, NY 10023.

INFLATION DISCLAIMER:

Brazilian inflation is among the worst in the world. Brazilians joke that you can walk into a supermarket and see a product marked at a certain price, and by the time you reach the checkout counter, the price has already risen. The American dollar is somewhat inflation-proof in the Brazilian economy, because the dollar is always strong in relation to the cruzado. So depending on whether the dollar is strong or weak on the world market, you will find prices in Brazil either incredibly cheap or only reasonably so. On the other hand, prices the world over tend to go up faster than personal income.

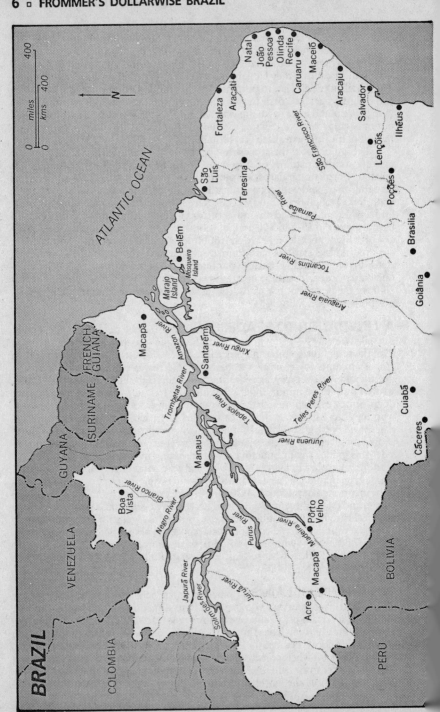

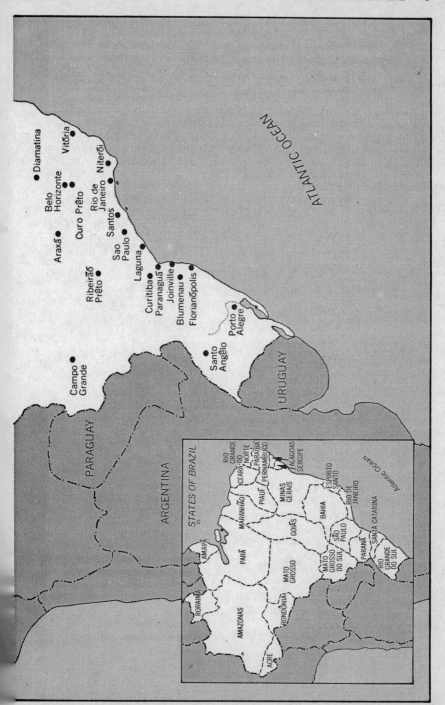

Therefore you may find that costs in Brazil are higher in absolute terms than those listed as of this writing. It is unlikely, however, that in the foreseeable future Brazil will cease to be a bargain destination for American tourists, especially those who travel with group or package promotional air fares.

2. FROMMER'S™ DOLLARWISE TRAVEL CLUB—HOW TO SAVE MONEY ON ALL YOUR TRAVELS

In this book, we'll be looking at how to get your money's worth in Brazil, but there is a "device" for saving money and determining value on all your trips. It's the popular, international Frommer's Dollarwise Travel Club, now in its 27th successful year of operation. The club was formed at the urging of numerous readers of the $-A-Day and Dollarwise Guides, who felt that such an organization could provide continuing travel information and a sense of community to value-minded travelers in all parts of the world. And so it does!

In keeping with the budget concept, the annual membership fee is low and is immediately exceeded by the value of your benefits. Upon receipt of $18 (U.S. residents), or $20 U.S. by check drawn on a U.S. bank or via international postal money order in U.S. funds (Canadian, Mexican and other foreign residents) to cover one year's membership, we will send all new members the following items:

(1) Any *two* of the following books

Please designate in your letter which two you wish to receive:

Frommer's™ $-A-Day® Guides
Europe on $30 a Day
Australia on $30 a Day
Eastern Europe on $25 a Day
England on $40 a Day
Greece (including Istanbul and Turkey's Aegean Coast) on $30 a Day
Hawaii on $50 a Day
India on $25 a Day
Ireland on $30 a Day
Israel on $30 & $35 a Day
Mexico (plus Belize and Guatemala) on $25 a Day
New York on $50 a Day
New Zealand on $40 a Day
Scandinavia on $50 a Day
Scotland and Wales on $40 a Day
South America on $30 a Day
Spain and Morocco (plus the Canary Is.) on $40 a Day
Turkey on $25 a Day
Washington, D.C., and Historic Virginia on $40 a Day

Frommer's™ Dollarwise® Guides
Austria and Hungary
Belgium, Holland, & Luxembourg
Bermuda and The Bahamas
Brazil (avail. Nov. 1988)
Canada
Caribbean
Egypt
England and Scotland
France
Germany

Italy
Japan and Hong Kong
Portugal, Madeira, and the Azores
South Pacific
Switzerland and Liechtenstein
Alaska
California and Las Vegas
Florida
Mid-Atlantic States
New England
New York State
Northwest
Skiing USA—East
Skiing USA—West
Southeast and New Orleans
Southwest
Texas
USA (avail. Feb. 1989)

(Dollarwise Guides discuss accommodations and facilities in all price ranges, with emphasis on the medium-priced.)

Frommer's™ Touring Guides
Australia
Egypt
Florence
London
Paris
Thailand
Venice

(These new, color illustrated guides include walking tours, cultural and historic sites, and other vital travel information.)

Gault Millau
Chicago (avail. Feb. 1989)
France (avail. Feb. 1989)
Italy (avail. Feb. 1989)
Los Angeles
New England (avail. Feb. 1989)
New York
San Francisco
Washington, D.C.

(Irreverent, savvy, and comprehensive, each of these renowned guides candidly reviews over 1,000 restaurants, hotels, shops, nightspots, museums, and sights.

Serious Shopper's Guides
Italy
London
Los Angeles
Paris

(Practical and comprehensive, each of these handsomely illustrated guides lists hundreds of stores, selling everything from antiques to wine, conveniently organized alphabetically by category.)

A Shopper's Guide to the Caribbean
(Two experienced Caribbean hands guide you through this shopper's paradise, offering witty insights and helpful tips on the wares and emporia of more than 25 islands.)

Beat the High Cost of Travel
(This practical guide details how to save money on absolutely all travel items—accommodations, transportation, dining, sightseeing, shopping, taxes, and more. Includes special budget information for seniors, students, singles, and families.)

Bed & Breakfast—North America
(This guide contains a directory of over 150 organizations that offer bed & breakfast referrals and reservations throughout North America. The scenic attractions, and major schools and universities near the homes of each are also listed.)

Dollarwise Cruises
(This complete guide covers all the basics of cruising—ports of call, costs, fly-cruise package bargains, cabin selection booking, embarkation and debarkation and describes in detail over 60 or so ships cruising the waters of Alaska, the Caribbean, Mexico, Hawaii, Panama, Canada, and the United States.)

Dollarwise Skiing Europe
(Describes top ski resorts in Austria, France, Italy, and Switzerland. Illustrated with maps of each resort area. Includes supplement on Argentinian resorts.)

Guide to Honeymoon Destinations
(A special guide for that most romantic trip of your life, with full details on planning and choosing the destination that will be just right in the U.S. [California, New England, Hawaii, Florida, New York, South Carolina, etc.], Canada, Mexico, and the Caribbean.)

Marilyn Wood's Wonderful Weekends
(This very selective guide covers the best mini-vacation destinations within a 200-mile radius of New York City. It describes special country inns and other accommodations, restaurants, picnic spots, sights, and activities—all the information needed for a two- or three-day stay.)

Manhattan's Outdoor Sculpture
(A total guide, fully illustrated with black and white photos, to more than 300 sculptures and monuments that grace Manhattan's plazas, parks, and other public spaces.)

Motorist's Phrase Book
(A practical phrase book in French, German, and Spanish designed specifically for the English-speaking motorist touring abroad.)

Paris Rendez-Vous
(An amusing and *au courant* guide to the best meeting places in Paris, organized for hour-to-hour use: from power breakfasts and fun brunches, through tea at four or cocktails at five, to romantic dinners and dancing 'til dawn.)

Swap and Go—Home Exchanging Made Easy
(Two veteran home exchangers explain in detail all the money-saving benefits of a

home exchange, and then describe precisely how to do it. Also includes information on home rentals and many tips on low-cost travel.)

The Candy Apple: New York for Kids
(A spirited guide to the wonders of the Big Apple by a savvy New York grandmother with a kid's-eye view to fun. Indispensable for visitors and residents alike.)

The New World of Travel
(From America's #1 travel expert, Arthur Frommer, an annual sourcebook with the hottest news and latest trends that's guaranteed to change the way you travel —and save you hundreds of dollars. Jam-packed with alternative new modes of travel that will lead you to vacations that cater to the mind, the spirit, and a sense of thrift.)

Travel Diary and Record Book
(A 96-page diary for personal travel notes plus a section for such vital data as passport and traveler's check numbers, itinerary, postcard list, special people and places to visit, and a reference section with temperature and conversion charts, and world maps with distance zones.)

Where to Stay USA
(By the Council on International Educational Exchange, this extraordinary guide is the first to list accommodations in all 50 states that cost anywhere from $3 to $30 per night.)

(2) Any *one* of Frommer's™ City Guides
Amsterdam
Athens
Atlantic City and Cape May
Boston
Cancún, Cozumel, and the Yucatán
Dublin and Ireland
Hawaii
Las Vegas
Lisbon, Madrid, and Costa del Sol
London
Los Angeles
Mexico City and Acapulco
Minneapolis and St. Paul
Montreal and Quebec City
New Orleans
New York
Orlando, Disney World, and EPCOT
Paris
Philadelphia
Rio (avail. Nov. 1988)
Rome
San Francisco
Santa Fe and Taos (avail. Dec. 1988)
Sydney (avail. Nov. 1988)
Washington, D.C.
(Pocket-size guides to hotels, restaurants, nightspots, and sightseeing attractions covering all price ranges.)

(3) A one-year subscription to *The Dollarwise® Traveler*

This quarterly eight-page tabloid newspaper keeps you up to date on fast-breaking developments in low-cost travel in all parts of the world, bringing you the latest money-saving information—the kind of information you'd have to pay $35 a year to obtain elsewhere. This consumer-conscious publication also features columns of special interest to readers: **Hospitality Exchange** (members all over the world who are willing to provide hospitality to other members as they pass through their home cities); **Share-a-Trip** (offers and requests from members for travel companions who can share costs and help avoid the burdensome single supplement); and **Readers Ask . . . Readers Reply** (travel questions from members to which other members reply with authentic firsthand information).

(4) Your personal membership card

Membership entitles you to purchase through the club all Frommer publications for a third to a half off their regular retail prices during the term of your membership.

So why not join this hardy band of international budgeteers and participate in its exchange of travel information and hospitality? Simply send your name and address, together with your annual membership fee of $18 (U.S. residents) or $20 U.S. (Canadian, Mexican, and other foreign residents), by check drawn on a U.S. bank or via international postal money order in U.S. funds to: Frommer's Dollarwise Travel Club, Inc., Gulf + Western Building, One Gulf + Western Plaza, New York, NY 10023. And please remember to specify which *two* of the books in section (1) and which *one* in section (2) you wish to receive in your initial package of members' benefits. Or, if you prefer, use order form at the end of the book and enclose $18 or $20 in U.S. currency.

Once you are a member, there is no obligation to buy additional books. No books will be mailed to you without your specific order.

CHAPTER 1

GETTING TO AND AROUND BRAZIL

□ □ □

1. TRAVELING TO BRAZIL
2. TRAVELING WITHIN BRAZIL
3. THE ABC'S OF BRAZIL

Flying down to Rio is the way most travelers from the northern hemisphere reach Brazil for the first time. Flights to Brazil take between 5 and 12 hours, depending on where you leave from in North America and where you land in Brazil. Steamship travel, of course, has long vanished from the globe. In its place are the cruise ships that call at half a dozen ports in the course of their two- or three-week sojourns in South America. Rio is a popular one- to two-day stop on many such cruises. Intrepid land travelers with time on their hands have been known to drive to Brazil along the at times desolate Pan American Hwy. I wouldn't deign to advise such seasoned travelers on so brave an undertaking. They certainly have my admiration. Most of us must adapt ourselves in our travels to the great cattle cars of the sky. To their credit, the major airlines that provide Brazil air service have managed to make what could be a long and tedious flight into a diverting and reasonably pleasant experience.

Flying is something Brazilians take quite seriously. A Brazilian comic satirizing his compatriots might even proclaim that "the airplane is sacred in my country." Brazilians are in fact taught that it was their countryman, Alberto Santos Dumont, who "invented" the airplane, thus laying claim to the very world-class Yankee ingenuity that Americans bestow on the Wright brothers. Some superficial probing reveals that a number of other nationalities also have legitimate heroes from the earliest days of aviation. Santos Dumont, who grew up on a coffee plantation in Minas Gerais, was a tireless and driven aviation pioneer who performed most of his experiments in Paris. His daring and brilliant exploits were widely covered in the international press during the early years of this century. A bust or statue of the diminutive aviator, wearing the floppy hat that was his trademark, is a frequent sight at airports throughout Brazil.

1. TRAVELING TO BRAZIL

Finding the right flight to Brazil is not particularly complicated. But first you do have to make several decisions. Do you want to visit Brazil during the peak season, or the low season—or perhaps during Carnival? How long will you want to stay? Do you want to stay only in Rio, or will you travel a bit around the country? Do you want to go with an individual ticket and book all your own land arrangements, or will you want to choose from a wide range of tour packages, which include hotel accommodations, airport transfers, and even some sightseeing excursions? And finally, will you want to go on a regularly scheduled flight, or take advantage of group rates by flying with a charter?

VARIG AIRLINES: Many travelers get their first taste of Brazil the moment they embark from New York, Los Angeles, or Miami on a VARIG Airlines widebody bound for Rio or São Paulo. Not only is VARIG Brazil's flag carrier for all international flights to Brazil from abroad, including the United States and Canada, but the airline is also the country's principal and most popular domestic carrier as well. In a poll taken by the prestigious *Folha de São Paulo* daily newspaper in May 1987, Brazilian air travelers expressed their preference for flying VARIG over the company's two major rivals, Transamerica and VASP, by a margin of three to one. The respondents held that VARIG was safer, provided better in-flight service, and was more reliable in its scheduling. VARIG's international reputation is also built on safety, performance, and comfort. Flight attendants orchestrate the nine-hour passage from New York, for example, with such skill that what could be a difficult flight on many airlines passes quickly and pleasantly.

Flights

VARIG offers more flights from the U.S. and Canada to more cities in Brazil than any other airline. In the U.S., the VARIG **toll-free reservations number** is 800/468-2744.

To Rio/São Paulo, VARIG has a daily nonstop flight from New York's John F. Kennedy International Airport at 8 p.m. (flight time: 9 hours and 15 minutes), and daily nonstop service to Rio from Miami at 9 p.m. (flight time: 8 hours and 15 minutes). There are five VARIG flights weekly to Rio from Los Angeles: nonstop on Tuesday and Friday; via Lima, Peru, on Wednesday and Sunday; and via Panama City on Saturday (flight time is about 12 hours). In addition, there are VARIG flights from Montréal to Rio on Thursday and Sunday, departing at 5 p.m. with one stop in Toronto (flight time: 13 hours and 15 minutes).

To Manaus, VARIG has a Wednesday nonstop flight from Miami at 6:15 p.m., with a flight time of 5 hours and 15 minutes.

To Belém, Recife, and Salvador, there is a nonstop VARIG flight from Miami on Sunday at 4 p.m., taking 6 hours to Belém.

Disclaimer

The listings here are meant to give Brazil-bound travelers some idea of their flight options. Please be advised, however, that all flights and flight times listed here are subject to change. Furthermore, negotiations have been going on for some time to add additional flights from the U.S. In the near future, for example, travelers to Brazil can expect to have much more direct access to the fabulous beaches surrounding many northeastern cities, like Natal and Forteleza. Check with VARIG or your travel agent for up-to-date flights and schedules while you are still in the early planning stages of your trip to avoid any unpleasant surprises.

VARIG Air Pass

The VARIG Air Pass is the best option for air travel inside Brazil for those who wish to visit destinations other than the principal gateway cities. The pass *must* be purchased outside Brazil before you go, and details are available in the next section ("Traveling Within Brazil"), from VARIG, or from your travel agent.

THE COMPETITION: Pan American Airways is the only U.S. airline with regularly scheduled flights to Brazil. Pan Am flies daily nonstop from New York's JFK and Miami to Rio and then on to São Paulo. At press time, departures from New York were at 10:15 p.m., and from Miami at 11:45 p.m., although (as always) these are subject to change. And of course, the airline has many connecting flights from major U.S. cities to both New York and Miami.

LEAST EXPENSIVE "REGULAR" FARES: Currently your cheapest option with all regularly scheduled airlines flying to Brazil are the APEX fares.

APEX Fares

On VARIG, APEX tickets are valid for a stay in Brazil from 21 days to three months. Travel dates in both directions must be reserved at the time of purchase, with a $100 penalty assessed for either changes or cancellations. And reservations must be made 14 days in advance of desired flights.

VARIG divides its year into three price seasons: Carnival, peak, and low. Low season occurs between January 1 and May 31 (excluding Carnival time), and between August 16 and November 30. Peak season covers June 1 to August 15, and December 1 to December 31. The difference in ticket prices during these two periods, however, is not great. For example, a low-season ticket from New York to Rio at press time cost $885, while a high-season ticket between the same two cities was $985, only $100 more. There are no APEX tickets available during Carnival.

Note that low season for air fares is the high season for prices in Brazil, because that's when Brazilian summer occurs. In other words, it may make more sense, depending on your individual needs and schedule, to pay the extra $100 on the "high-season" air fare and benefit from the "low-season" internal prices in Brazil from roughly April through November.

Economy Fares

The next cheapest individual rates for VARIG are the 30-day excursion fares. With this kind of ticket you must stay a minimum of 7 days and a maximum of 30 days. These fares, too, are divided into peak- and low-season tariffs, but your return reservations may be left open. The low-season economy fare from New York to Rio in early 1988 was $1,079, while the high-season ticket cost $200 more, or $1,279, which was also the price for an excursion ticket during Carnival. Normal economy tickets good for one day to one year cost $1,530, or $765 one way. All ticket prices include a $13 airport and exit tax.

GROUP AND CHARTER FARES: Group and charter flights generally offer the cheapest air fares of all. For the names and telephone numbers of ticket wholesalers, see Chapter XIV; or contact VARIG reservations and ask for the tour desk.

AN ORGANIZATION AND A PUBLICATION: One U.S. organization and a U.S. government publication may be of help to you as you plan your air travel to Brazil.

The Brazilian American Cultural Center

For a $20 membership fee, you can join BACC, the Brazilian American Cultural Center, 20 W. 46th St., New York, NY 10036 (tel. 212/242-7837, or toll free 800/222-2746). BAAC offers some of the cheapest charter prices available to Brazil, from as little as $564 round trip from Miami in 1988, to cite one example. The membership fee also includes a subscription to *The Brasilians*, the organization's lively monthly newspaper. BACC will also secure your visa for Brazil for a fee of $5. You request them to send you a visa application; then you mail them your passport (valid for at least six months from your date of departure), one two-by-two-inch passport photo, the filled-in application, and a check or money order in the amount of $5. They will then secure the visa through the Brazilian consulate in New York.

Flyer's Rights

A booklet called *Air Travelers' Fly Rights* is published by the U.S. government. It is available for $2.75 per copy from the Superintendent of Documents, U.S. Government Printing Office, Washington, DC 20402. Order Stock No. 003–006–00106–5.

2. TRAVELING WITHIN BRAZIL

BY AIR: The best option for North Americans who want to travel around Brazil by air is the **VARIG Air Pass.** It must be purchased outside Brazil before you depart, and is available in two versions, both add-ons to your international flight to Brazil on VARIG. For $250 you may add four cities in Brazil for travel within a 14-day period. The $330 air pass allows unlimited air travel within Brazil for 21 days. The time limits do not begin until you use the air pass for your first domestic flight.

BY BUS: Beyond flying, Brazilians who don't own a car—the vast majority, that is—do their traveling by bus. Every major city has its *rodoviária,* usually a major terminal with direct or indirect bus connections to every corner of the country. Bus travel is slow and inexpensive. The most comfortable buses are called *leitos,* which have reclining seats and tend to make fewer stops than the common bus. For those who have the time and the inclination to rough it, bus travel through Brazil is highly recommended. There is no better way to see the country, or to gain exposure to the widest possible range of the day-to-day Brazilian reality.

BY TRAIN: There is little travel by train in Brazil, although what there is is fairly inexpensive and reasonably comfortable. There are a few daily trains on the run between Rio and São Paulo, but travel by train to other cities is sparse. For example, there are only two trains each week between Rio and Belo Horizonte, and the trip takes 13 hours. You'd generally do better by bus.

BY CAR: Both renting a car in Brazil and bringing your own car into the country present problems for the driver. Let's take a quick look.

Car Rentals

There are car-rental agencies in most airports and in all major cities. Car rental is not recommended for most short-term visitors to Brazil: there are just too many rules to learn in too short a time to make the experience worthwhile. For example, how do you find fuel on Sundays when most filling stations are closed? You'd be better off renting a car with a driver if you want to do any serious touring. The cost isn't much more than a standard car rental, and you can leave the responsibility of driving to a professional. Note that gas prices are roughly double the U.S. rate per gallon, with the state-subsidized alcohol fuel slightly less than double.

Bringing Your Own Car into Brazil

If you're planning to bring your own car, here are three useful organizations you may wish to contact for information about Customs regulations, insurance, and road travel in Brazil:

American International Underwriters, 105 Maiden Lane, New York, NY 10005, for information on Brazilian automobile insurance for your car; and **Automovel Clube do Brasil,** Rua do Passeio 90, and **Touring Clube do Brasil,** Avenida Gen. Severiano, in Botafogo (tel. 295-7440), both in Rio.

3. THE ABC'S OF BRAZIL

The Introduction and the first two chapters of this guide are designed to provide a general orientation to Brazil—everything from the history and culture to the food and public transportation.

These ABCs get down to details. What follows is an alphabetical listing of categories with information about those mundane elements and institutions of daily life on which we all depend—especially since we tend to take them for granted. We all know what the drinking age is in our own community, what time the post office opens and closes, and we don't think twice about plugging in the toaster whether we know anything about voltage or not. These ABCs provide a ready reference to help inform you about how these aspects of daily living function in Brazil.

More specific information related to Rio, and to the other larger Brazilian cities, is contained in orientation sections or introductory comments to be found in the respective chapters on each of these destinations.

BABYSITTERS: The very best hotels offer babysitting services. You can expect to pay in the vicinity of $5 per hour, perhaps even more. Remember, you are hiring a bilingual babysitter, not a neighbor's teenage daughter or son. Otherwise, you must pretty much resolve to have the kids with you, unless they're old enough to go to the pool or game room by themselves. For this reason, if you're planning to travel with children, you'd be best off selecting a self-contained resort where there are likely to be both programs for children and babysitting when required. Fortunately, there are many such resorts throughout Brazil, and families may travel to even the large cities like Rio, São Paulo, and Salvador and find such accommodations no farther away than the municipal outskirts.

CIGARETTES: American cigarettes were once fashionable in Brazil, but have all but disappeared from most counters where tobacco products are sold. Shops in all the better hotels sell American cigarettes, as do the top restaurants. Brazilian cigarettes appear to be of comparable quality, however, and are priced at around 50¢ a pack. There is little antismoking consciousness in Brazil, so nonsmokers should prepare themselves for the assault. It would be most surprising, however, if some Brazilian smoker in your company should refuse to extinguish his cigarette when asked to do so politely. A total stranger will probably be less accommodating.

CLIMATE: Most of Brazil lies immediately to the south of the equator. What seasonal variation exists can be found in the temperate south, where temperatures can hover around the freezing mark at night and early in the morning—but only in the deep winter months of July and August. Winter afternoons in the south will often be sunny and warm, even beach weather. Generally the climate runs from comfortably tropical along the coast to unbearably humid and sticky in parts of the interior and the Amazon. Along the tourist coast—from Santos

(São Paulo) in the south to Fortaleza (Ceara) in the north—the mercury ranges from a low of 65°F to a high of 95°F. Strong ocean breezes on the northern beaches often mitigate the heat, if not the burning power, of the tropical sun.

CREDIT CARDS: American Express, Diners Club, and VISA are most in evidence. Remember that you will charge your purchase in cruzados but you will pay in dollars, computed at the official rate. In other words, using a credit card could end up costing you between 20% and 50% more, depending on the relative position of the dollar to the "official" cruzado at a given moment. (See "Currency.")

CRIME: Little can be added to my comments in the Introduction, under the heading "Is Brazil Safe?"

CURRENCY: The Brazilian currency is the **cruzado,** abbreviated **$CZ,** a new designation since a 1986 monetary reform replacing the longstanding cruzeiro. Comments on Brazil's inflation and the relative position between the dollar and the cruzado, from the consumer's point of view, can be found in the Introduction under the heading "Inflation Disclaimer."

Changing money in Brazil can be something of an art. There is an "official exchange rate," the *câmbio oficial,* and a semilegal "black market rate"—*o paralelo,* or the parallel money market. Both rates are published daily in the economic sections of the major Brazilian daily newspapers, so dispel the notion that trading in this black market will involve you in some risky or unacceptable practice. Banks and the cashiers of most hotels trade at the "official rate," which is generally at least 20% less than the *paralelo.*

How, then, does the tourist trade at the more advantageous parallel rate? Don't worry, because as sure as the sun shines in Brazil, you will be approached by someone wishing to buy your dollars, probably as soon as you alight from Customs with your baggage in hand. It may be your tour guide or the person sent to transfer your group from the airport to the hotel. It may be the doorman or the bellboy, and most assuredly the porter behind the concierge desk. Assuming you know the current parallel rate (having glanced at the Brazilian daily during your in-coming flight), you may still expect to exchange at three to four points below the rate listed in the paper. Why? Well, changing money is a sideline for many people in the service sector of the tourist business. In general, these small-scale money traders are not dealing with huge sums of money. They therefore attempt to negotiate the lowest possible rate in order to maximize their profit margin. You may be able to haggle for a point or two. The key to these negotiations, however, is knowing the current parallel rate.

It generally doesn't make sense to change more than $100 or $200 at a time. The parallel rate seldom drops, and you can do some serious hanging-out on that limited amount of money. The more money you exchange, however, the better rate you ought to find. If you are not comfortable changing money with your bellhop in the corridor of a five-star hotel, there are many businesses—travel agencies, boutiques, and the like—that trade in the parallel money market. Someone in the hotel or with your tour company will gladly indicate the address of a shop near your hotel. (They are probably getting a commission!) Go there with your cash or traveler's checks and your passport, and exchange your money in a suitable business environment. Traveler's checks, incidentally, trade at a point or two lower than cash, though who can argue with the good sense of traveling with as little hard currency as possible, unless you are traveling deep in the interior where traveler's checks and credit cards are just so much useless paper and plastic.

The most important thing to remember when exchanging money at the parallel rate is that even if you receive a lower rate than that published in the newspaper, you are still getting a better deal than if you exchanged at the official rate.

Note that in the Brazilian reckoning of money, commas and periods are used exactly opposite from North American usage. One thousand six hundred cruzados is written as $CZ 1.600, while one cruzado and fifty centavos appears as $CZ 1,50.

CUSTOMS REQUIREMENTS: Besides clothing and personal belongings, tourists entering Brazil may bring one of each of the following items: a radio, a tape deck, a typewriter, film, and cameras. You are further allowed to bring to Brazil items totaling $300 as gifts, including any liquor or cigarettes you purchase at the duty-free shop, and to return with $400 worth of Brazilian merchandise, not including certain craft items which are duty free.

DENTISTS AND DOCTORS: Luxury and first-class hotels generally have physicians on call. For any emergency care, dental or medical, it would be wise to consult with a member of the diplomatic mission of your country of origin.

DOCUMENTS FOR ENTRY: A visa is required for U.S. citizens wishing to visit Brazil. Passports, valid for at least six months from the intended date of arrival, must carry a visa for Brazil. Tourist or transit visas, generally processed within one working day, are obtained from the nearest Brazilian consulate in the U.S. One passport-size photograph, along with your round-trip ticket and a duly completed and signed application form, are required for the free visa, valid for 90 days (for tourists) or 10 days (transit). Citizens of the U.K. and Canada are not required to have visas.

DRUGSTORES: In the large cities, there are many *farmácias* and *drogarias,* often open late into the night. Your hotel staff or a friendly cab driver will know the address of an all-night drugstore if one is required. To be quite frank, prescription drugs are not as tightly regulated in Brazil as they are in the U.S. For a fee of, say, $5—supposedly to pay a doctor for the necessary paperwork after the fact—you can often get those antibiotics or sleeping tablets you neglected to bring with you. Brazilian medications are manufactured by the familiar multinational pharmaceutical companies, so the brand names will be recognizable.

ELECTRICITY: What we refer to as "house current"—110 volts A.C.—is rare in Brazil. Rio is said to be wired with 110, but my impression nonetheless is that there are a considerable number of 220-volt lines throughout the major hotels as well. Bathrooms in these hotels usually provide an alternate house current receptacle suitable for electric shavers, but not hairdryers. The top hotels often provide "hard-wired" hairdryers as an extra bathroom feature. Bring the necessary 220-volt converter if you have any equipment you wish to run (slide projector, hairdryer, tape player, etc.), and always check with the hotel staff before plugging in anything. Some hotels provide these transformers or adapters for guests. Adding to the confusion is the widespread use of 127-volt current in cities like Salvador, Manaus, and Curitiba. Be particularly careful where there is no running hot water and showers are equipped with visible electric hot-water heaters. People have been known to get electrical shocks in such showers if the heaters are inadequately grounded.

EMBASSIES AND CONSULATES: All foreign embassies are of course located in the capital, Brasília, in the interior. Since most foreign travelers make Rio their headquarters in Brazil, many governments have established consulates there to service the needs of their citizens, including those of the following English-speaking countries: **United States,** downtown (Centro) at Avenida Presidente Wilson 147 (tel. 292-7117); **Canada,** also in the Centro section at Rua Dom Geraldo 35 (tel. 233-9386); the **U.K.,** in Flamengo at Praia do Flamengo 284, on the second floor (tel. 552-1422); and **Australia,** in Botafogo at Rua Voluntários da Pátria 45, on the fifth floor (tel. 286-7922).

ETIQUETTE: Generalizing about etiquette is a somewhat meaningless exercise. One could fairly suggest, though, that Brazilians are—or can be—more formal and more ceremonial than Americans. The Portuguese language itself retains both the formal mode of address (*o senhor, a senhora*) as well as the familiar form (*você* or *tu*, depending on the region). American brashness and straight talking can at times grate on Brazilians. The culture gap is based to some degree on Brazilian hypersensitivity to gradations of social class in their country, which have no functional counterpart in largely middle-class America. Needless to say, it is up to the individual traveler to unravel in a given situation the mysteries of cross-cultural differences.

FILM: Photographic film for most modern cameras is widely available throughout Brazil, as is tape for video cameras, especially in the larger cities. Film, however, is not one of the bargain items in Brazil, and can be priced at double the U.S. amount. Many photo bugs bring all the film they will need, and store it in their hotel refrigerators to keep it fresh. Unless you are on an extended vacation, it's probably best to delay processing until you get home. Very rarely will you be restricted in the use of your camera, and then, generally only in museums and churches. If you are with a tour group, your guide will inform you where restrictions are in effect.

FOOD AND DRINK: See Section 3 in Chapter II, following.

GAS: See Section 2, "Traveling Within Brazil," above in this chapter.

HAIRDRESSING: All luxury and first-class hotels have their own—sometimes unisex—hairdressers. Most American travelers in Brazil will therefore not have to leave their hotels when seeking a shampoo, a haircut, or styling. These facilities at the top hotels, like restaurants and bars, are generally open to the public. Standard barbershops seem to be well concealed in Brazil, although your hotel staff will be able to direct men who want to treat themselves to the luxury of a cheap and close shave done the old-fashioned way. Prices for beauty and barbershop services vary from hotel to hotel, but are generally 30% to 50% cheaper than in the U.S.

HITCHHIKING: While not illegal in Brazil, nobody does it. Over 20 years ago, however, the author hitchhiked throughout central Brazil with pretty fair success.

HOLIDAYS: Principal holidays and festivals with their dates are as follows:
　　January 1: New Year's Day—and the feast day of Iemanjá, goddess of the sea, accompanied by much public celebration.
　　February: Carnival, the extended Mardi Gras celebration which brings Brazil to a standstill for at least five days before Ash Wednesday every year.
　　March/April: Good Friday and Easter Sunday.
　　April 21: Tiradentes Day, in honor of the Brazilian republican martyr.

May 1: May Day.

June: Corpus Christi.

June/July: The Festas Juninas, important winter holidays on the feast days of saints John, Peter, and Anthony.

September 7: Independence Day.

October 12: Our Lady of the Apparition.

November 2: All Souls' Day.

November 15: Proclamation (of the Republic) Day.

December 25: Christmas.

Like North Americans in recent years, Brazilians have the habit of celebrating certain holidays not on the official dates, but on the Monday that falls closest to the official date. The *feriadão* (feh-ree-ah-*downg*), or long holiday weekend, is the result, meaning that you may find stores and banks unexpectedly closed if you have only consulted the "official" calendar.

LANGUAGE: Brazilians speak Portuguese, the linguistic legacy of the country's original Portuguese colonizers. The Brazilian accent differs from that of Portugal, much in the same way that American and British English differ. A useful vocabulary list and pronunciation key can be found in the Appendix of this guide. English is spoken by designated staff at the major hotels, specialized tour guides, and at airport information centers. Otherwise it would be fair to say that English—other than pidgin—is not widely spoken throughout Brazil, particularly as you travel any distance from the large urban centers.

LAUNDRY AND DRY CLEANING: Hotels have normal two-day service and a special express service, which costs about 50% more. Hotel laundry service, while convenient, is nonetheless expensive. Travelers with a container of Woolite (in powder form in the event it opens in your suitcase), or some equivalent cold-water soap, and a summer wardrobe of wash-and-wear clothes will be able to avoid high-priced hotel laundry fees. The other option is to find the nearest *tinturaria* (dry cleaner) or *lavandaria* (laundry).

LIQUOR: Like most Americans, Brazilians tend not to be teetotalers. Their beers and wines (the great French burgundies duly excepted) rate with the world's best. **Cachaça,** a potent sugarcane brandy, is widely used in many cocktails, which drinking Americans tend to like very much indeed. Bars open early and many rarely close before dawn. Drinking is generally inexpensive in Brazil, unless you insist on imported scotch, in which case you'll be charged a small fortune. Nearly quart-size bottles of beer, on the other hand, run about 35¢ to 50¢ a bottle. A good Brazilian wine can be had in most restaurants beginning at $6 . . . or less.

LOST AND FOUND: Lost or misplaced items are not necessarily gone forever in Brazil. Chances are, if you go back to the place where you last remember having the item in your possession—bars and restaurants in particular—it will be there waiting for you. Losses in cabs are more problematical, but you can have your hotel make inquiries at the local *delegacia* (police precinct). Report all lost traveler's checks and credit cards to the appropriate organization immediately.

METRIC MEASURES: Some useful conversion figures are listed in the chart below:

Weight

1 kilo (kg) = 2.205 pounds

1 pound (lb) = 0.454 kilos

Length
1 millimeter (mm) = 0.03937 inches
1 meter (m) = 3.281 feet
1 kilometer (km) = 0.621 miles
1 inch = 25.417 millimeters
1 foot = 0.305 meters
1 mile = 1.609 kilometers

Capacity
1 liter = 2.11 pints
1 liter = 1.06 quarts
1 liter = .26 gallons
1 pint = .47 liters
1 quart = .95 liters
1 gallon = 3.8 liters

Area
1 hectare = 2.471 acres
1 sq. kilometer = 0.386 sq. miles
1 acre = 0.405 hectares
1 sq. mile = 2.590 km

Temperature Conversion
$°F = (°C \times 9/5) + 32$
$°C = (°F - 32) \times 5/9$

NEWSPAPERS: The top newspapers are the *Folha de São Paulo, Jornal do Brasil,* and *O Globo.* The *Latin American Daily Post* is an English-language rag published out of São Paulo four days a week, with a Rio edition; it's good for entertainment, real estate, and business news. The very expensive *International Herald Tribune* is available generally only in Rio, São Paulo, and Salvador, as are the *Wall Street Journal, New York Times,* and *Miami Herald,* as well as *Time* and *Newsweek.*

OFFICE HOURS: White-collar business hours are normally from 9 a.m. to 6 p.m. Monday through Friday, with an hour for lunch. Office lunch-hour periods are usually staggered from noon till 3 p.m. Longer hours and obligatory work on Saturday are the rule for most service and nonunion blue-collar jobs.

POLICE: Brazil has a tradition of military rule, under which the police have considerably more power than in the U.S. The presence of the *PMs* (military police) on the street—depending on how they are behaving—can be as ugly as it is reassuring. If you have a problem on the street, it is the local citizen who is more likely to come to your aid than the police. While the cop on the beat will never hassle tourists, they are still best to be avoided.

POSTAL SERVICE: The most convenient way to handle your outgoing mail is to purchase stamps from the reception desk in your hotel, and to have the staff mail your letters and postcards for you. The post office, **Correio** (co-hay-yu), is open from 8 a.m. to 6 p.m. weekdays, and until noon on Saturday.

RADIO AND TELEVISION: Most hotel rooms have music piped in from a handful of local radio stations, with the Brazilian equivalent of elevator music. With your own radio, you ought to be able to pick up some of the best of Brazilian popular and country-style music no matter where you are. Some—but not all—luxury and first-class hotels have satellite dishes that pick up the U.S. Armed Forces Radio and Television Network, which broadcasts the "Today Show," the national news shows on all three networks, CNN newscasts throughout the day, and that big game or prize fight you thought you were going to miss. Brazilian TV is definitely worth tuning in on: the prime-time soaps and miniseries are a major export to Western European countries. Discreet female and male nudity often appears in both commercials and shows.

RELIGIOUS SERVICES: Brazil is primarily a Catholic country—the most populous such in the world, in fact—and every brand of Catholicism flourishes here from the most traditional to the most radical. Protestantism has made its inroads over the years, and most denominations are present in the larger cities. There are small but religiously active Jewish communities in most big cities as well. The other main religious movement in Brazil is the spiritism brought by the Africans, blended with the practices and beliefs of the original natives, and today widely practiced by Brazilians of all backgrounds and races. These religions—known as Macumba, Candomblé, and Umbanda—have also become something of a tourist attraction in recent years, in much the way voodoo, a related cult, has always been in countries like Cuba and Haiti.

REST ROOMS: Brazilians have yet to become overly proprietary about their bathrooms. Restaurants you are not eating in and hotels where you are not staying will nonetheless cheerfully allow you to use the facilities when necessary. There are otherwise few public toilets, and they are best to be avoided anyway, since they tend to be as filthy as the hotel and restaurant bathrooms are clean.

STORE HOURS: The shops in Brazil are open from 9 a.m. to 6:30 p.m. Monday through Friday, and from 9 a.m. to 1 p.m. on Saturday. Shops close as late as 10 p.m. during the month of December. Banks are open from 10 a.m. to 4:30 p.m. Monday through Friday. If the city you are visiting has a shopping center, chances are it will be open six to seven days a week from around 10 a.m. till as late as midnight.

TAXES: There is no sales tax. What you see on the sticker—if there is one—is what you pay. Otherwise one bargains, and that of course is a science that some shoppers thrive on and others find a nuisance. Most hotels charge an across-the-board 10% service tax. So if it says you're paying $70 a night, it's really $77. Please take note that every item appearing on your final hotel bill—long-distance phone calls, room service, laundry—is subject to this 10% tax. Restaurants also add 10%, but in this case it's the whole tip. Depending on the nature of your airline ticket, you may have to pay a token airport tax between internal destinations, and a $10 exit tax when returning home. Taxes and tariffs on items like U.S. cigarettes, imported liquor, and gasoline—at any given time about double what we pay—are all high.

TELEPHONES: Area codes for each Brazilian city or side-trip locale will be found in the beginnings of each chapter or subsection, as appropriate. Local phone calls from your hotel room are generally free. On occasion in the cities you might find a charge for a call you thought was local, say, to the airport, but was actually suburban and subject to a fee. Phone service is good overall, though payphones are a minor nightmare. The main problem is that you must use tokens, and inevitably there is noplace nearby to buy them. Newsstands at airports— and supposedly elsewhere—sell these phone tokens, called **fichas** (*fee*-shas). They come in a five-pack, and are inexpensive. If you're lucky, someone near the phone you want to use will know the nearest place to buy *fichas.* Or better yet, stick to your hotel phone—it's a lot easier. Telephone company offices, called TELERJ, located in airports and at other locations, facilitate phoning from a public space. There are attendants to place the calls for you.

TELEX: Your hotel will send your message, if they have a Telex, and they will notify you as soon as there is a reply.

TIME: In most of the country and in the main (that is, coastal) cities the time is three hours earlier than Greenwich (London) Mean Time. Because Brazil is in the same time zone as North America, there is a maximum of two hours' difference ahead of New York's time.

TIPPING: As with bargaining, there is no mechanical answer to how much or how little you should tip a person rendering a service, be it in an institutional setting like a hotel or restaurant or in some individual context. Brazilians are on the whole light tippers. In a sense there is no such thing as spare change in a country with Brazil's yearly rates of inflation—except for the super-rich. Tourists, of course, are held to a higher standard, and generous tips are always appreciated—though they are by no means expected.

TOURIST INFORMATION: First of all, get as much information as you can before you actually travel. In purchasing this book you have made a good start. Back issues of travel magazines at the library are also recommended.

There is no completely reliable Brazilian source of information in the U.S. for the moment, although this will undoubtedly change if Americans continue to show an increased interest in traveling to Brazil. You might try the **Brazilian Tourist Board, Funtur,** located at 551 Fifth Ave., Room 421, New York, NY (tel. 212/286-9600), but it is often difficult to get information over the phone. If you're in New York City, you could drop in at their offices.

An additional source of information before you depart is the **Brazilian consulate,** located in seven major U.S. cities. Contact the one nearest you: Atlanta—229 Peachtree St. NE, Suite 2420, Atlanta, GA 30303 (tel. 404/659-0660); Chicago—20 N. Wacker Dr., Suite 1010, Chicago, IL 60606 (tel. 312/372-2179); Houston—1333 West Loop South, Suite 11000, Houston, TX 77027 (tel. 713/961-3063); Los Angeles—3810 Wilshire Blvd., Suite 1500, Los Angeles, CA 90010 (tel. 213/382-3133); Miami—330 Biscayne Blvd., 11th floor, Miami, FL 33132 (tel. 305/374-2263); New York—630 Fifth Ave., 27th floor, New York, NY 10111 (tel. 212/757-3080); and San Francisco—300 Montgomery St., Suite 1160, San Francisco, CA 94104 (tel. 415/981-8170).

Most **airports,** including Rio's (which is likely to be your point of entry), have excellent to fair tourist information centers. The one in Rio is excellent at this writing. But if the state government changes—in Rio or in any state—the tourist information apparatus is also subject to change, sometimes for the better, sometimes not. The airport information center could be a high priority for one government and an extravagance for another. In this regard, however, Brazil is stabilizing somewhat, since the country is really promoting tourism and a consensus about the importance of facilitating the way for foreign tourists is growing.

Where they exist, I have included useful telephone numbers and addresses of information centers and booking agencies throughout this guide.

International Distances and Flying Times to Rio de Janeiro

From	Distance (miles)	Air Travel Time (hours: minutes)
Amsterdam	5,921	11:00
Asunción	969	2:00
Bogotá	2,883	5:50
Buenos Aires	1,217	3:10
Caracas	2,813	6:00
Frankfurt	6,239	11:15
La Paz	1,639	3:30
Lima	2,389	5:15
Lisbon	4,807	9:05
London	5,768	10:50
Los Angeles	6,292	12:15
Mexico City	4,767	11:00
Miami	4,269	8:15
Montevideo	1,155	3:00
Montréal	5,457	12:15
New York	4,817	9:30
Paris	5,700	10:50
Quito	3,074	9:15
Rome	5,681	10:50
Santiago	1,981	5:35
Tokyo	11,528	28:00
Toronto	5,134	11:00

Distances from Rio

To	Distance (miles)	To	Distance (miles)
Aracaju	1,233	Maceió	1,405
Belém	2,013	Manaus	2,740
Belo Horizonte	275	Natal	1,707
Brasília	701	Porto Alegre	963
Cuiabá	1,315	Recife	1,528
Curitiba	520	Salvador	1,068
Florianópolis	693	São Luís	1,862
Fortaleza	1,770	São Paulo	266
Goiania	813	Vitória	319
João Pessoa	1,598		

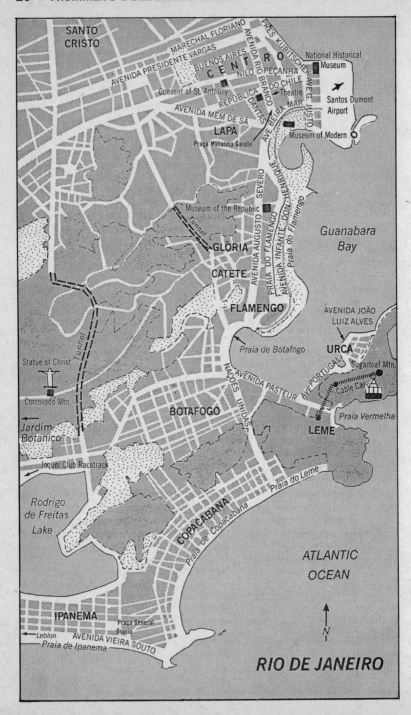

RIO DE JANEIRO

CHAPTER II

BRAZIL IN PERSPECTIVE

□ □ □

1. THE BRAZILIANS
2. BRAZILIAN CULTURE
3. FOOD AND DRINK

Why go to Brazil? The answer can be given in three simple words: Rio de Janeiro. At least that's the place to start. For sheer physical beauty, Rio has no rival among the great cities of the world. In fact, few cities are better equipped to return the traveler's investment of time and money with as much sheer pleasure for the eye, the body, and the spirit. And Rio is just the tip of the . . . well, how about palm tree?

BASIC FACTS: Brazil is divided into five distinct regions: north, northeast, central-west, southeast, and south. The country is the world's fifth largest—larger than the continental United States (not counting Alaska), but smaller than Canada, China, and the USSR. Brazil borders all the nations of South America with the exception of Chile and Ecuador. Brazil's 3,319,666 square miles or 8,511,965 square kilometers cover almost half the continent. Over 70% of Brazil's 135 million inhabitants are under 30 years of age.

Regionalism is the essential reality of modern Brazil. And many of the country's cultural distinctions are based on accidents of geography as much as any other cause. The great rain forests covering much of what is known as Amazônia have proven impossible to conquer along any conventional models of development. Northeastern Brazil is subject to long periods of drought, alternating with less frequent, but equally destructive flooding. The northeastern *sertão* is a parched wilderness of scrub growth, ribbed with rocky ridges and bare mountains, barely hospitable to the rugged millions who make it their home. And yet the region, as with all desert landscapes, has its peculiar fascination and beauty. The coastal lowlands are a narrow strip of land running the length of the coast, once site of the great Atlantic forest, and for centuries the focal point of agriculture, commerce, and industry. Not far inland (often a mile or less) from the coastal strip rise the great plains and high plateaus that characterize much of southern, southeastern, and central Brazil. Here are the most fertile lands, producing much of the world's coffee and cocoa, and vast harvests of citrus fruit and soybeans as well. Much of interior Brazil—where the land is good—continues to be laid out in vast private holdings, or *latifúndia,* which may or may not be in productive use, and are the source of much of the power—and powerlessness—in Brazil to this very day.

Ethnically and racially Brazil is as diverse a nation in its types of peoples as any on the globe. Today only approximately 100,000 pure Indians survive from the millions (estimates range from two to five million) who, in a great variety of subcultures and tribal groups, inhabited the land when the Portuguese arrived in 1500. The mark of these indigenous cultures is visible on the features and in the customs and values of many contemporary Brazilians, who trace some portion of their ancestry from the original inhabitants. After slavery was introduced in the early 16th century, the decendants of Africans soon outnumbered their white overlords. The blending of these two races has produced the sizable mulatto segment of Brazil's population. Western European immigrants—Italians, Germans, Spaniards, for the main part—and the Portuguese (who never stopped coming) came in waves during the 19th and early 20th centuries. They were joined by equally large numbers of Japanese, who began to arrive in Brazil after the turn of the current century.

One reason Brazil manages to feed most of its population is because the country is really a vast greenhouse. Nature provides endless varieties of fruit and seafood, and crop returns are generally very high. It may surprise some to learn therefore that, in addition to being a great agrarian producer, Brazil has the eighth-largest industrial output of the world's nations as well. The south and southeast regions account for virtually all the heavy industry, producing everything from cars and consumer goods to aircraft, weapons, and machinery. No country can boast of greater mineral and gem deposits, much of which, it is believed, have yet to be discovered, much less mined.

For all of its wealth—real and potential—Brazil has always had an economy oriented toward exports, based often on the rising and falling cycles of a single commodity. Even today with its mighty industrial base, much of what Brazil produces must be sold abroad to pay off the astronomical foreign debt of $110 billion, representing loans once believed to offer the miraculous means to the country's rapid development. Instead, Brazil today remains trapped in debt, assuring for the foreseeable future its traditional position as the great country of the future with the perennial economy of a banana republic.

1. THE BRAZILIANS

A "sleeping giant," was how Brazil's romantic poet, Casto Alves, once described his country. All the realities, the expectations, even the stereotypes of the great nation are contained in that simple observation. The Brazilian identity has adapted itself to the image of the "sleeping giant," and so Brazilians never cease to wonder, "When will the giant awaken?"

Since Brazil—because of its size, its parallel New World heritage, its wealth and potential—is inevitably compared with the United States, many Brazilians have come to believe that Brazil ought to "be" like the U.S. Trying to understand why Brazil is *not* like the U.S., and more positively, what grand role the country *is* destined to play in world events, is one of the great preoccupations of both popular and intellectual Brazilian culture.

One might be tempted to respond, "Brazil is fine just the way it is." From the vantage point of the casual visitor, this is certainly a valid perspective. All categories of international travelers to Brazil—sun worshippers and other hedonists, groups and individuals with special interests, free-wheeling adventurers, and business people—can discover and appreciate during even the briefest of stays a distinct and indefinable "Brazilian-ness," those qualities and graces peculiar to any nation that do not demand explanation or require justification. Not surprisingly, even Brazilians are not always conscious of their true uniqueness, nor of the almost mystic appeal their country has for so many visitors, who on arriving home, proclaim rapturously to their friends that "Brazil is the ultimate destination!"

Brazilians, by and large, cannot be so sanguine. They live the reality of an underdeveloped—or at least unevenly developed—country. A portion of the country is modernized on the scale of anything you would find in the most developed of nations; another portion sustains a mass of people under primitive circumstances, and often in misery; and a third portion is virtual wilderness, uninhabited, and perhaps uninhabitable. The most severe consequences of this uneven development in Brazil, both economic and geographical, is the inability of the nation to provide employment and the necessities of life for a large segment of its population. This does not mean that the visitor will be assaulted with an endless panorama of wretchedness and oozing sores. The visual reality, owing perhaps to the luxuriant tropical setting, is seldom harsh even to the most delicate observers. But all will undeniably perceive the tenuous coexistence of two distinct worlds throughout Brazil: a consumer society embracing an elite 30% of the population; and a subsistence society—healthy in many respects, but at the fringes accounting for some of the planet's highest rates of infant mortality and child malnutrition, and a life expectancy far lower than that in the industrialized nations.

It is from this torpor of underdevelopment that seemingly grips their country in endless cycles of economic and political chaos that Brazilians would like their "sleeping giant" to be awakened. How Brazil arrived at this impasse is a complex and intriguing question, for which no simple interpretation exists. As with other nations, however, some insights can perhaps be gleaned from an understanding of the past. Only the thinnest sketch of Brazilian history will be presented here. This is, after all, a guidebook, not a history text. But the outline is here, as are the titles of some suggested reading for those—avid prevacation researchers and armchair travelers alike—who wish to deepen their knowledge of Brazil, and read more widely from the story of its almost 500 years of existence.

A BRIEF HISTORY: The history of Brazil begins largely as an account of the land's colonization by a single dominant culture, the Portuguese, who first came to the eastern coast of South America as commercial explorers in the year 1500. The Portuguese had been pioneering the unknown navigational routes around Africa to India for some years before the expedition under Pedro Álvares Cabral departed from Lisbon on a mission that historians still can't agree about. Did Cabral chart a sweeping curve around the bulge of Africa because he wanted to quicken his circumnavigation of that continent with the help of the prevailing winds in mid-Atlantic? Or was he probing the outer limits of that ocean for some sign of the mythical western route to the Orient? By the beginning of the 16th century the sea route around Africa was no longer a secret. The Portuguese knew they would soon cease to exercise what had begun as a near monopoly on trade along the African coast, not to mention their newly won advantage over Arab traders in the East. Like all the large maritime powers in the Europe of that day, Portugal periodically financed expeditions into unknown waters, seeking easy wealth as well as control over new territories and shipping lanes. But whatever route Cabral was ordered to take, he was still bound for India when he sighted the coast of Brazil in April of that year and claimed the "great island" of Vera Cruz for the crown of Portugal. The first landfall was made in the harbor of Porto Seguro, today a small city to the south of Salvador in the state of Bahia.

The explorers found friendly Tupi Indians, but little in the way of precious wealth. Only a cargo of *pau brasil*, a dyewood much prized in Europe by cloth makers for its reddish hues, could return a profit against the costs of expeditions to Brazil by the early merchant adventurers. Such was the intensity of the trade in brazilwood that the land derived its name from that commercial tree. By the 1530s Portugal had settled on a plan to colonize its new territory, at least to the extent of creating large plantations of sugarcane. European tastes for this new spice and stimulant had been developing for some time. Supply was the main problem. But the establishment of the plantation system on the vast unfarmed tracts of the New World provided the solution not only to the supply of sugar, but to that of tobacco, and ultimately, coffee and cocoa as well.

Administratively, Brazil was divided by the Portuguese Crown into 17 *capitanias,* or captaincies. For 100 years each captaincy functioned as a virtually separate colony, governed by a nobleman (often from afar), but ultimately subordinated to the king of Portugal. The most successful of the early colonies were Pernambuco, and São Vicente (the coast of São Paulo state). Indians were enslaved to work the sugar fields, and when they proved unadaptable, or simply scarce, the practice of importing Africans—who unlike the natives could not simply disappear back into the forests from whence they came—began in earnest. The early planters were more adventurers than colonists, the venture capitalists of their day. They came to the New World to rough it for a few years (though not with their own hands, to be sure) and make their fortunes, delaying or resuming family life until their return to the mother country. So typical was this experience that it was even a subject of early English fiction. Robinson Crusoe, hero of the novel by Daniel Defoe, begins the fatal voyage that will leave him stranded on an uninhabited island for decades, from the port of Salvador (Bahia), where he had been living as a successful tobacco planter in the early 1600s.

From the union of these European adventurers with the native and slave women, a new, uniquely Brazilian race was forming—bred in the New World and tied to it by blood, but taking its organizational and political cues from the dominant Portuguese culture of the male overlords. In time many of the planters could see no reason for returning home, and the Crown itself had shifted its policy to one of genuine colonization, sending out families to accompany their mercantile and military expeditions. Society in Brazil rapidly developed into a hierarchy of three classes: slaves, freemen of mixed race (a kind of soldier and pioneer class), and the local Portuguese who governed, though not without the predictable tensions between their interests and those of the distant Crown.

During the first two centuries of modern Brazil's history, the plantation system gradually spread along much of the fertile coastal area, as great landed estates came to replace the once-dense Atlantic forest. At the same time military expeditions patrolled the offshore waters, and continually added new territories resulting from conquest of the native inhabitants and victories over European rivals who, at various points along the coast, had attempted to establish colonies of their own. The French, for example, occupied an island off what is today Rio de Janeiro but where, at the time, the Portuguese had yet to settle. They were finally defeated by the Portuguese and driven from the southern region after a 12-year occupation. The French later founded the city of São Luís, capital of Maranhão, in the north, but their stay in that region was of even shorter duration. Only the Dutch managed to invade—and hold for 24 years—a significant section of Brazilian territory.

Owing to a legitimate right of succession, the Portuguese Crown in 1580 had passed to the heir of the Spanish throne. For 60 years, until the restoration of its independent monarchy, Portugal—and Brazil—were to be dominions of Spain. In a war with Holland, Spain had denied the Dutch access to Brazilian ports, endangering what had been the preeminent position of the Dutch commercial fleet in the world trade and distribution of sugar. In retaliation, the

Dutch invaded the northeastern coast of Brazil and occupied considerable territory in Pernambuco, Bahia, and other regions to the north. By the time Holland was expelled in 1654, both the Dutch and the English had established sugar plantations throughout the Caribbean, and the favored Brazilian position in the world sugar market was ended. Ironically, the legitimate Spanish claim to much of what is modern Brazil was eroded during the period of Spain's dominion over Portugal. By the Treaty of Tordesillas (1494) papal authority had divided the New World between Spain and Portugal. Portugal's share of South America was actually only the great bulge of Brazil, stretching in a line from Belém, at the mouth of the Amazon, to just west of São Paulo. Internal politics during the late 1500s and early 1600s kept the Spaniards from contesting the expansion into Spanish territory by the explorers and authorities in Brazil, who were, after all, claiming all their conquests in the name of the House of Castille.

Expansion into the vast interior of Brazil was carried on primarily by two groups: missionaries, especially Jesuits; and pioneers, who were called *bandeirantes,* or standard bearers. The missionaries had accompanied the earliest voyages to Brazil, and were ever after caught between the shifting policies of the Crown, now favoring the peaceful conversion, now the conquest of the "heathen" natives. Most churchmen favored the former policy and opposed the enslavement and maltreatment of the natives. Nonetheless the pacification of the Indians by the missionaries, and their concentration into mission settlements, made the natives easy targets for the *bandeirantes,* who, at least initially, were nothing but glorified slave hunters.

The *bandeirantes* were merely the instrument of the oppression and virtual extermination of the Indians. The demand for cheap labor by the gentry (that is, the planter class) not only sanctioned the enslavement of Indians, but provided a solution for another socioeconomic problem as well. For the *bandeirantes* were largely that class of racially mixed Brazilians who were neither fish nor fowl. They were not of the ruling European group, nor were they slaves. The *mamelucos, mulatos,* and *mestiços* (as the various mixtures were called) had to fend for themselves. In great numbers they banded together under the flag of a single leader, to whom they pledged complete fealty, and then penetrated deep into the unexplored interior of the continent, seeking captives, and later mineral riches, but leaving one settlement after another in their paths. They fought the Jesuits, the colonial authorities, and each other, but in the end it was the *bandeirantes* who discovered the El Dorado that the original explorers had sought in Brazil 200 years earlier.

In 1693 gold was discovered in the hills of Minas Gerais. Soon thereafter came the discovery of rich diamond deposits in the same province. Until the beginning of the 18th century Salvador had been the jewel of Brazilian colonial cities, the center of power, commerce, and culture in the south Atlantic of the early Americas. And while Salvador would continue to shine in the course of Brazil's history, a new pole of power was to arise in the booming goldfields of the interior, and events and tastes for the next hundred years, called the Gold Cycle, would be strongly influenced by Vila Rica, known today as Ouro Preto.

Such was the wealth flowing from Brazilian gold and diamond mines during many decades that the coffers of states and the vaults of bankers throughout Europe were filled to overflowing. Here was capital enough to finance an Industrial Revolution, and a world mercantile economy! But much glitter was to be scattered over the varied landscapes of Brazil as well. Architecturally and artistically the flowering of baroque forms in towns and villas throughout Brazil during the course of the 1700s reflected a genuine Belle Époque. Many were the instant fortunes, and the opportunities for displays of pseudo-aristocratic ostentation, in the style of the era: carriages of gold, costumes of golden thread, gold nuggets cast at the feet of visiting performers, among other gestures of great extravagance. Craftsmanship in building and décor was highly prized, and boatloads of artists and artisans migrated from mother Portugal to the colonies in response to this rare and bountiful patronage.

Politics in the mining region became inflamed by the ideas of revolutionary republicanism that were then sweeping the world. But whereas the events of 1776 in the United States and of 1789 in France caused in those countries the overthrow of monarchic governments, the republican rebels in Brazil failed. The Inconfidência Mineira, the Minas Uprising of 1789, with its headquarters in Vila Rica, was crushed by the Brazilian aristocracy, ever loyal to the Crown, with the help of resident Portuguese troops. One principal rebel leader, Tiradentes, whose low social position left him without sympathetic influence in high places, was executed. Other leaders were more fortunate. Tiradentes was hanged, his body quartered and transported by cart as a grotesque warning to republicans in the four corners of the settled land; his head set on a pike in the main square of Vila Rica, which today bears his name.

Much republican ferment stirred within Brazil from the late 1700s and throughout most of the 1800s as well. Rebellions were frequent but always unsuccessful. A single happenstance effecting the fortunes of the Portuguese Crown all but ensured that the establishment of a republic in Brazil was to be forestalled for some time. The sudden arrival of the royal family from Portugal in 1808, fleeing in advance of Napoleon's occupation of Lisbon, brought to Brazil not only the power of the throne, but thousands of the empire's aristocrats of highest rank. This solid aristocratic block gave new tenor to the economic grip of the great land barons, which is where the real power traditionally lay in Brazil, and in many ways still does to the current day. The exiled Portuguese monarchy ruled its overseas empire from Rio de Janeiro—till then a relatively sleepy harbor compared with Salvador—for the brief span of a dozen years. In 1820 Dom João VI resumed the throne his mother had been forced to abandon in Portugal, leaving behind a royal seed, his son Pedro, to serve as regent in a land now viewed as being equal in importance with the mother country.

Weakly, the Portuguese Parliament tried to reassert its control over government and finances of the now-powerful colony. But the Brazilian aristocracy was jealous of its own power, and soon influenced Pedro to declare independence, crowning the young prince as Brazil's first Emperor. After ten years Pedro I abdicated and returned to Portugal, but he in turn left his young son, also Pedro, to allow the continuation of the royal line. Pedro II, following a decade of corruption under a government of regents and general popular unrest, was declared Brazil's second emperor in 1840, at the age of 14. Pedro II, a somewhat modern man with many liberal and progressive ideas, managed to reign fairly peacefully for the next 50 years, when he was suddenly deposed in 1889, and the Republic was finally installed by military men, who have since created their own tradition of rule in the country. Pedro II had a great interest in the political and literary works originating in the United States of his day, and was particularly fond of Hawthorne and the New England transcendentalists, like Emerson and Bronson Alcott. The emperor, visiting the U.S. in his later years, made a pilgrimage to the Concord burial ground where many of the bards he admired were laid to rest.

Economically, as the flow of gold and diamonds began to diminish, other natural or agricultural products rose in importance in both regional and national terms. Coffee was first introduced from French Guiana in 1727, and became a crop that ultimately spurred the expansion of plantations beyond the current state of Rio de Janeiro, deep into São Paulo and other southern and central territories. Coffee wealth was the basis on which the current industrial and agricultural power of São Paulo was built. The rubber cycle began in the mid-19th century. Brazil had a virtual monopoly on rubber—the tree was found in great numbers only in the Amazon. But the rubber trees occurring in nature were spread out some distance one from another. Large numbers of individual tappers were needed to gather the latex, which was collected by boat, and thus the banks of the great river for many leagues were tamed and settled. Out of the rubber wealth grew the cities of Manaus and Belém, which also saw their periods of grandeur.

The production of all Brazilian wealth depended largely on slave labor until that institution was finally abolished in 1888, one principal cause of Pedro II's downfall. Both the longevity of the slave system, and the utter failure of the early Brazilian Republic to integrate the blacks into the productive economy thereafter, can account for the disparity in wealth and class privilege that still characterizes modern Brazil. The Republic engaged for years thereafter in the extension of its administrative power throughout the country, but was chronically without the necessary reforming zeal that would have gradually transformed Brazil from a semifeudal to a modern agrarian/industrial state consistent with the country's potential. In many ways the very feudal mentality of most rural Brazilians—including the peons attached to the vast estates of the north and northeast regions—made even the extension of central republican rule a task of considerable difficulty.

Driven somewhat mad by years of marginal existence, ignorance, and neglect, many rural inhabitants viewed the new state as a virtual anti-Christ. One of the most bizarre episodes of Brazilian history occurred when masses of religious zealots from all over the northeast fled to Canudos, an abandoned ghost town in the barren interior of Bahia, under the influence of the fanatic Antônio Conselheiro, to avoid the sacrilege of civil matrimony and other abominations that the new federal government was imposing on the populace. It took three increasingly major military expeditions to destroy the millennarian village, and but for a handful of survivors, all of its inhabitants.

The task of consolidating federal power in Brazil occupied the first 30 years of this century. But the process of orderly transition through democratic means from one government to another was never firmly established. Presidents were elected or appointed and deposed in revolving succession, depending on the course of various regional political crises and revolts. One of the great romantic rebellions occurred when military reformers under Carlos Prestes formed an armed column which crisscrossed the interior of Brazil and the frontiers of neighboring South American countries for several years. The Prestes column failed to rally their phlegmatic countrymen to revolutionary fervor, and so it disbanded. Prestes himself later came to head the Brazilian Communist Party, at first allied to the Soviets and later to the Chinese. Today an anachronistic folk hero well into his 80s, he survives in relative political obscurity. A military strongman, Getúlio Vargas, with fascist leanings, seized power in a 1930 coup following a decade of continuous rebellion. Vargas's rise was a classic reflection of the confrontation between left and right that was taking place throughout Europe in those years, culminating in the Spanish Civil War. Under Vargas, Brazil would later enter World War II on the Allied side, participating in the Italian Campaign. During the war an American base was established near the city of Natal as a resupply depot for the North African Campaign (Africa is relatively close to Brazil from that point on the northeastern coast). To one degree or another, Vargas maintained his control of the government until his suicide in 1954, when a new era, for better and for worse, was inaugurated in Brazilian politics.

RECENT TIMES: With the election of Jucelino Kubitschek de Oliveira, a medical doctor from Minas Gerais, in 1956, it seemed that a new spirit of democracy was dawning in Brazil. The political conditions of these past 30 years, however, have proved as volatile and unpredictable as they had been at any other time since the departure of Dom Pedro II. Jucelino (in recent years, Brazilian presidents and politicians of benign visage are referred to by their first names; heavies, particularly generals, whose image is always that of a stern father, are spoken of by their last names) played Augustus to the Caesar of Getúlio Vargas. Leaving untouched the essential social and economic deficiencies affecting the Brazilian majority, Jucelino launched an awesome program of development at the top. In one bold stroke he built the moonscape capital of Brasília, shifting the locus of governmental power from its traditional east-coast moorings to the sparcely inhabited interior. The new road to Brasília then continued northward through a swath cut from the jungle on to Belém, the delta city of the Amazon River. Foreign investments multiplied, as did borrowed capital, for Jucelino was determined to give particular impetus to the country's industrial development. Jucelino's was a vision of grandeur, mixed with a childlike insistence on instant gratification. Leaving the government in disastrous financial straits, Jucelino had, with his impulsive changes, accomplished much. His legacy of financial instability has also had far-reaching consequences.

Succeeding Jucelino in 1961 was the eccentric nationalist Jánio Quadros, who had gained a reputation for being a cost-cutter as mayor, and then governor of São Paulo. Brazilians of all political stripes still shake their heads in disbelief when recalling the bizarre, short-lived presidency of this strange politician, who arose again recently from virtual obscurity and was once again elected mayor of São Paulo. Jánio, it was rumored, spent hours watching Hollywood westerns in the basement of the Presidential Palace. He found the Federal Congress intractable, and could not adapt his tone of autocratic righteousness to the horse-trading idiom of the legislature. Jánio's fierce pride in Brazil translated into a foreign policy of nonalignment, a popular stance until he offended the right by praising the Cuban Revolution and presenting Ché Guevara with a medal in Brasília. After slightly more than six months, Jánio resigned, hoping, it was said, that Congress would beg him to resume his post. It didn't.

The man in succession, Vice-President João Goulart, was feared. He was a protégé of Getúlio Vargas, charismatic, given perhaps to a left-leaning brand of populism. After some struggle, the succession was allowed, as the Congress showed an uncharacteristic faith in the viability of democratic institutions to right themselves during crises. Goulart's presidency had the same impact on the military in Brazil during the early 1960s as did that of Socialist Salvador Allende on the Chilean army ten years later. It was enough to imagine that Goulart would disturb rural feudalism with his modest proposals for land reform, or concede certain power to labor unions, or limit the power of foreign investors, to send shock waves through the circles of power. On April 1, 1964, a bloodless military coup d'état took place—encouraged avidly by the American government—and for the next 20 years Brazilians would be ruled by the "generals" who subjected both their opponents and the populace at large to varying degrees of repression and cruelty.

Brazil during this extended period of military dictatorship was a saddened country. Despite its historical tale of woe, Brazilians had always managed to feel good about where they lived, and to squeeze much joy from the sensual pleasures of their climate and from a bountiful nature. They had also become accustomed to speaking their minds on political matters. During the military dictatorship, newspapers were censored and political debate ceased, both in public meetings and as heated café conversation, for no one could be sure who they could trust. The military leaders ruled by intimidation, but for a while at least, they really did make the economy hum. Economic growth was so high that Brazil was widely noted by advocates of Western-style development as a success story among underdeveloped countries. The Oil Crisis of 1973 sharply stemmed Brazil's forward economic motion. The resultant and sudden jolt to the mobility of a growing middle class—including many technical and industrial workers—ultimately created broad popular pressure for a return to democracy. The relaxing of tensions was gradual, but by 1979 a general amnesty was declared and a series of open elections occurred in quick succession. Brazilians have yet to elect their first civilian president, though a civilian currently holds the office, having been selected by an electoral college heavily influenced by the military. This fact notwithstanding, a fascinating and critical moment in Brazilian politics is currently in progress. A Constituent Assembly has been convened, representing both the traditional power structures and some threads of Brazilian society heretofore excluded from the political process, organized labor in particular. The exciting task of this body is to write a new constitution, and to attempt, once again, to establish ground rules for a stable representative democracy in Brazil.

2. BRAZILIAN CULTURE

The story of Brazilian culture is considerably brighter than that of the country's political and economic history. This is, of course, good news to those tourists who are going not to live there, but for a brief escape from their own pressing realities. Tourists need only sample the very best of Brazil and its captivating popular culture: beach and café life, music and dance, tropical ambience and wildlife, crafts, and above all, food. Brazil can also be appreciated, vicariously, through selected readings from its excellent letters and literature.

BEACH CULTURE: The good life throughout much of Brazil is associated with the sun, the beach, and good beer at a reasonable price. The one great leveler of all economic distinction in Brazil, in fact, is a sunny day at the beach. On weekends in Rio—and in the other coastal cities as well—everyone flocks to the beach when the weather is right. And the weather is seldom wrong. Half the crowd on the beach will be moving at a furious pace, consumed in some variety of sporting activity: pickup soccer games, body and board surfing, volleyball, jogging, exercise, and *frescobol,* a paddleball game played by two people. The other half will be completely at rest, surrendering to the totally passive act of getting a perfect tan.

Vendors stroll up and down the strands all day, offering delights to eat and drink. There are small boys selling *picolés,* popsicles of tropical fruit flavors. Strong shirtless men carry pineapples or coconuts, which they open or slice on demand with the razor-sharp machetes they carry slung at their sides. Others hawk cold beer and soda from Styrofoam coolers, or sell hats and tanning lotion to shield the sun, or mats to lie on, or cotton kites to fly, often cut in the shape of the ubiquitous *urubu,* that big black buzzard you will see throughout Brazil—ugly to look at but quite beautiful in flight.

Never far from the beach—and frequently right there on the sand with you—will be a food stand where snacks are sold, or a restaurant under some rustic covering with tables and chairs, selling *frutos do mar* (seafood) typical of the area you are visiting. These are the outdoor parlors of Brazilian beach culture, where friends and family entertain themselves and each other in convivial bliss, with food and drink and conversation, watching the panorama of sky, sea, and virtual human nudity that surrounds them—the Brazilian bikini is somewhat akin to the emperor's new clothes in the Hans Christian Andersen tale.

CAFÉ SOCIETY: The other great leisure activity in Brazil that is relatively accessible to all is the outdoor café. Throughout Brazil every neighborhood, every town square, every beachfront avenue will offer some popular spot for indulging the incomparable pleasure of communing with surrounding society from the vantage point of a chair in an outdoor café. There are outdoor cafés to fit every pocketbook and every mood in the large cities. And in the smaller towns, often a single establishment in a village square, illuminated by a few strings of naked lightbulbs, will serve as a meeting place for all the town's inhabitants. *"Da um chopp"* ("Bring me a draft") is the perpetual cry of thirsty patrons who demand an endless flow of cold beer to lubricate the animated café chatter. Side dishes (*porções*) stream in continuous succession from the kitchen, with plates of french fries, bits of roasted meat, or *salgadinhos* — uniquely Brazilian appetizers of meat, shrimp, chicken, cheese, or eggs, all encased in a crust or batter. On the weekends, and in the evenings beginning with Thursday night, the cafés often stay jammed until the wee hours. There is probably no better way to experience the raw energy of Brazilian culture than from within the ambience of an outdoor café.

MUSIC AND DANCE: Brazilian music has had wide influence throughout the world in recent decades. From the classical compositions (especially for the guitar) by Heitor Villa-Lobos, to the suave and lyrical bossa nova of Tom Jobim and João Gilberto, to the intoxicating rhythms of the *batucada* (played by the Afro-Brazilian drum-and-percussion bands, or *baterias*) that give the samba its universal trademark, Brazilian music has finally gotten the global attention it deserves. Brazilian vocalists like Milton Nacimento and Gal Costa today routinely give concerts in major venues like Carnegie Hall or Lincoln Center in New York City, and it is hardly a rare occurrence to find a Brazilian percussionist working in many jazz and Latin bands both in the U.S. and around the world.

In Brazil itself, music is everywhere. There are piano bars with accomplished musicians in the many hotels and restaurants. Discos offer the best of international and Brazilian hits and standards. *Gafieiras* (traditional dance halls) have recently revived in popularity among lovers of the Big Band sound in nightclub settings. Intimate clubs offer the best in Brazilian folk and country music, with its clear ties to the melancholy ballads of the Iberian Peninsula, filtered through regional Brazilian life and times. Chamber music and recitals are frequent occurrences in salons and theaters. Many poolside and luncheon restaurants hire trios to serenade their guests with traditional Brazilian favorites. It's not infrequent in these places for an individual or couple to suddenly spring to their feet and begin to dance in the wild and pulsating steps of the samba. Music has a way in Brazil of continually drawing people from smaller circles into larger and larger groups, showering feelings of goodwill in every direction. Street bands of percussionists are also not uncommon, and few events can match the excitement of a public rehearsal of a bonafide Carnival band preparing for that yearly pre-Lenten extravaganza when all of Brazil becomes an outdoor dance hall for at least five days.

ARCHITECTURE AND ART: There is, to be sure, some very exciting work being done in both painting and carving, but you have to really search it out. The artistic face presented to the tourist in attractions like street fairs, and in many of the most visible galleries, is superficial — and often just plain tacky. This vision of Brazilian art is somewhat disappointing. Much of the work is technically dull, meant strictly to decorate, not illuminate or startle. Even the primitives tend to be very derivitive, as if their creators, too, had already seen the unself-conscious oils depicting the dramas of daily life that once flowed from places like Haiti 20 years ago, and decided to copy rather than elaborate a style suitable to their own realities. Woodcarving is quite popular in Brazil, but the results are often clunky, lacking any gracefulness in design, as if the value in the work were in the species and volume of the wood itself.

Nor are there great public collections of modern or classical art in Brazil compared with the museums of Europe or the United States. There are, however, a number of unique smaller exhibits, the Chácara do Céu in Rio and the Fundação Oscar Americano in São Paulo for example, both of which are the former homes of wealthy art patrons whose private collections are on display. The one great event of the Brazilian art world of international significance is the Bienél—the biannual art exhibition that takes place in São Paulo during odd years, which attracts not only the best of Brazilian art, but wide participation as well from artists throughout the world.

Before the modern era, Brazilian artisans and artists produced mostly sacred art, works reflecting themes of strictly religious significance. The vast quantity of sacred art throughout the country, whether found in its original church setting or housed in one of many national or regional museums devoted to the genre, is generally of much greater interest to the visitor than the contemporary art scene. The baroque period in particular, throughout the 18th century, was the great epoch of Brazilian art and architecture which, given the times, took the form of elaborately carved altars and images, great allegorical panels painted on church ceilings and walls, finely wrought silver and gold ceremonial accoutrements, and of course, the elegant structures of the churches and dwellings themselves. Of special note are the sculptures of Antônio Francisco Lisboa scattered among the historical cities of Minas Gerais, though concentrated primarily in Congonhas do Campo. The museums of sacred art in São Paulo and Salvador are first rate. But my personal favorite is the tiny church museum lovingly maintained by a single curator in the interior city of Goiás Velho (see Chapter VIII for details).

The Brazilian architectural patrimony from the colonial and baroque periods is unique in all the Americas for its stunning simplicity and elegance, as well as for the sheer numbers of structures and neighborhoods that have been preserved and restored throughout the country. The historical cities of Olinda (five miles from Recife) and Ouro Preto are considered to be "world treasures" by UNESCO, as is the Pelurinho section of Salvador. Virtually every city in Brazil, however, has its historical architectural relics, some even more pristine than those mentioned above, like Goiás Velho, Paraty, Belém and João Pessoa, because they have yet to be commercially exploited and promoted as major tourist attractions. Indeed virtually everywhere curious visitors wander throughout this immense country, they are bound to discover some sampling of antique churches, homes, or buildings, dating from at least the 18th century. Some of the old structures moreover were built a hundred years before the Pilgrims settled in North America. Special-interest travelers, lovers of history as seen through its preserved buildings, will be particularly rewarded by their travel in Brazil beyond the beaches of Rio.

CRAFTS:
Crafts in Brazil are also a mixed bag. As with the art scene, you often have to ignore the "official" displays—the weekly "hippie" fairs and artisan centers—in favor of popular markets and roadside stands, where the less touristy kinds of items can be found. Much is made, for example, of Brazilian leather and needle crafts, but an amateur's eye can often easily see that the craftsmanship in assembly and design just isn't there. The biggest collections of schlock goods are usually found at the state- or city-subsidized centers, like the Mercado Modelo in Salvador or the Sunday Hippie Fair in Rio's Ipanema neighborhood. Not all the official crafts centers are tourist traps, however. Some notable exceptions are the state-sponsored craftshop in Cuiabá, Mato Grosso (which is close to a steady sup-

ply of well-made baskets and pots by the state's large Indian population), the attractive artisan galleries in the tourist office in Aracajú, and the Asian Fair in the Liberdade section of São Paulo. The soapstone containers and figures found throughout Minas Gerais, particularly at the craft center in Belo Horizonte, are quite attractive, but very brittle and even when well packed tend to travel badly. Municipal markets, like those in Aracajú, Natal, and São Luís, are better bets for finding truly unique and often useful craft items—hammocks, rugs, rustic cutting boards, and handmade tools. The *ver-o-peso* market in Belém (and its counterpart in Manaus) is a veritable bazaar, fascinating as much for its general active waterfront ambience as for the hundreds of fetish objects and potions on sale there.

While not strictly speaking craft items, the general shopping scene for clothes, shoes, and gemstones of excellent quality—with modest price tags by North American standards—is a popular activity among international visitors.

NATURE AND WILDLIFE: A quick visit to Rio's Botanical Gardens and Zoo may be as close as most visitors will be able to get to the flora and fauna of Brazil. But even this cursory exposure is recommended and will convey some sense of the country's unique animal and plant life. True nature aficionados will want to construct a more demanding itinerary for exploring sections of the Amazon or the Pantanal, a great wildlife reserve in the country's south-central region. Special tour operators can fashion excursions to the needs of the most adventurous nature travelers, taking you far from the beaten tourist paths to remote and untrammeled areas for field study and exploration. Special-interest tours for birdwatchers and flower enthusiasts, including orchid lovers, are also available. But no matter where your itinerary takes you in Brazil, you are likely to be immersed in an attractive environment, provided to a large extent by the kind of tropical beauty that only nature can provide.

LANGUAGE: The language of Brazil is Portuguese, an Indo-European language of the Romance group, all members of which derive more or less directly from Latin. When spoken slowly, Brazilian Portuguese can be moderately intelligible to speakers of Spanish or Italian, its closest relatives in the Romance group. Nonetheless there are many distinctions in syntax and pronunciation between Portuguese and those two, and all the other languages to which it is more or less closely related, including English. I will give one relatively technical example on pronunciation.

As with French, Portuguese uses many nasalized vowel sounds. These particular sounds are not found so prominently in most Western languages, and so they present obstacles for many wishing to learn spoken Portuguese. To complicate matters, sometimes these nasal vowels occur in combination, forming so-called nasal dipthongs. Take the Portuguese word for bread, *pão* (the tilde accent over the *a* indicates the nasal element). A reasonable facsimile for this sound in English occurs in words like *found*. The *ou* in this word represents a pairing of two English vowels, a dipthong in linguistic jargon. And the air which produces this sound is expelled through the mouth. When nasalized, the same sound in Portuguese is expelled through the nose. In other words, the mechanical trick is to train the muscles of your inner mouth to route certain sounds through the nasal passages rather than out the mouth.

There are many other distinct elements which impart to Brazilian Portuguese its exotic sound. Some of these are covered briefly in the Appendix. Many other resources are available for anyone who wants to study Portuguese before traveling. In addition to phrase books and taped lessons which can be bought or ordered through bookstores, there are often classes at local colleges or language institutes. Practically speaking, a few hours invested in learning some Portuguese before traveling to Brazil—especially for those traveling beyond the main tourist routes—can make your trip a lot smoother, if only because you could understand something quite simple being told to you by a bus driver or waiter. A reading knowledge of Portuguese is easily achieved by anyone who knows Spanish, and useful for gaining access to the country's lively and intelligent newspapers and magazines.

LITERATURE: Until the middle of the 19th century Brazilian writers told their stories in the manner of their mentors, in that florid, biteless style then fashionable in the *belles lettres* of Portugal. A more unified Brazilian identity began to emerge during reign of Dom Pedro II in the last century, and from that time Brazilian literature began to reflect reality in a style of its own, more direct and representational. Every generation since then has produced remarkable fiction. The great book of Brazil, however, remains a work of nonfiction, *Os Sertões*, or *Rebellion in the Backlands,* by Euclides da Cunha, a stunning account of the downfall of millennarian Antônio Conselheiro and his followers, and their destruction by the new republican government in the interior town of Canudos.

Readers of novels have long accompanied the boom in Latin American fiction that began with the successful translation of Colombian Gabriel García Marquez's *The One Hundred Years of Solitude,* and opened the American book market to other greats of Latin American literature, including many Brazilians. From the earlier fiction came new translations of Machado de Assis, who captured with considerable grace the ennui of bourgeois life in Rio during the latter part of the last century. Brazilian fiction written during the first half of this century is vastly underrepresented among republished translations, however. Some essential names from this period are Raquel de Queiroz, Graciliano Ramos, José Lins do Rego, Vianna Moog, and Eric Veríssimo, all of whom mined the modernist vein, transforming material from life and folklore into vivid, realist prose.

In a category by himself, publishing since the 20s and today a veritable institution in Brazil, is the novelist Jorge Amado. Avon has published a great many of Amado's novels in recent years, including *Gabriela, Clove and Cinnamon, The Violent Lands,* and *Dona Flor and Her Two Husbands.* Within Brazilian society Amado has received all honors, and despite his long-standing ties to the world Communist movement, political bigotry does not tarnish his stature as Brazil's literary laureate and cultural hero, even among the most stolid conservatives. Reading a few good Amado novels before visiting Salvador in Bahia is a painless way to get your cultural introduction to this region of Brazil, and at the minimum provide some kind of background against which to compare your own impressions.

Avon also publishes the zany, pointed social satires of Márcio Souza, a Brazilian "new left" activist during the days of the military dictatorship and now a successful novelist and playwright. *The Emperor of the Amazon* got Souza banned in his native Amazônia by the very governor his novel satirized. *Order of the Day* is a novel parodying the Brazilian penchant for joining mystical sects, and is written in the format of a sci-fi thriller. As yet untranslated is the *Flying Brazilian,* Souza's touching fictionalized life of Brazilian aviator Alberto Santos Dumont. Two other Avon paperbacks that give a flavor of Brazil's contemporary fiction are Ivan Ângelo's *The Celebration,* a scathing portrait of decadence in a middle class that made great social gains during the recent dictatorship, and *Sergeant Getúlio,* by João Ubaldo Ribeiro, a novel of brilliant malevolence gaining the highest critical praise internationally that makes Stephen King's *The Shining* seem like a Mother Goose tale. This introduction to Brazilian literature merely scratches the surface, but every book mentioned in this précis has the advantage of being available from American publishers, and is therefore likely to be in library systems as well. Another excellent source of Brazilian prose and poetry is the mail-order distributor Luso-Brazilian Books, 3 Nevins St., Brooklyn, NY 11217, which will send you a free catalog on request.

3. FOOD AND DRINK

It's not easy to get a bad meal in a Brazilian restaurant. Culinary skills and food quality seem consistently high in public eating establishments of varying price ranges throughout the country. To be sure, cooking styles and basic ingredients change, sometimes very radically, from region to region. If tastiness and absence of indigestion are two reasonable criteria on which to judge restaurant food, Brazilians in this field rate extremely high. Not that the food is fancy, and certainly it's often far from delicate. But it is virtually always well prepared, served in generous portions—platters or stew pots groaning with succulent meats or brimming over with a dozen varieties of fin and shell fish—and always accompanied by numerous delightful side dishes.

When dining in Brazil, you'll need to pace yourself. The breakfasts served by most tourist-quality hotels (included in the price of your room) can be lavish, so tempting to many that any idea of a formal, sit-down lunch at midday is quickly abandoned. The two-meal diet—breakfast and dinner—is a common response among international tourists to the abundance of food in the meals put before them. Another useful strategy to consider is the single-meal-for-two option. Say, two or three people go to an average-priced restaurant for lunch. The ambience is comfortable, tables covered in white starched linen, and the waiters, while not formal, are pros in their own right, well trained and helpful. You order one serving of breast of chicken, sautéed in some sauce of the cook's invention. The platter arrives with enough meat, rice pilaf, mashed potatoes—usually two starchy foods, good news to carbohydrate fans—and everyone fills their plate. You order separately a large hearts-of-palm salad and whatever side dishes you might want, plus beer or freshly squeezed fruit juice, and finally coffee, and the bill comes to about $3 apiece.

A New York food critic, spoiled (enviably, I might add) by a regular diet of meals at the world's finest restaurants, severely panned a gourmet restaurant in Rio that locals held in high regard. And indeed haute cuisine is not the forte of the Brazilian kitchen. In the ethereal world of French cooking, an also-ran establishment that most mortals would find perfectly acceptable does not get much respect. Brazil's French restaurants have flourish and style, but there is seldom a genuine delicacy in their dishes. But the point is not to seek in Brazil food you could only find in New York or France. Instead turn your imagination in the direction of the best in home-cooking. Then imagine eating this fare twice a day in a great variety of seafoods, pastas, poultry, or meat, with side dishes of rice, beans, potatoes, and greens, not to mention a whole lot of delicious foods you've never heard of. That's Brazilian cooking, with its emphasis on heartiness and taste, and it's likely to keep your palate in a state close to ecstasy during your stay in Brazil. Bom apetite!

BRAZILIAN FOOD: Meals fall roughly into two categories: traditional dishes and international dishes. One traditional dish, **feijoada**—a pork and black-bean stew—is routinely eaten every Saturday throughout the country by rich and poor alike. Thus two styles of feijoada have emerged, a fancy buffet style with all the ingredients (including prime cuts of beef and pork) served separately, popular with hotels, and the more funky home-style feijoada served stew-like from a single cauldron preferred by the more traditional restaurants. The traditional accompaniments of feijoada are white rice, **feijão** (black beans), **couve** (shredded kale), orange slices, and **farinha** (manioc flour). International dishes are those bearing familiar names, like veal milanese or beef Stroganoff, made especially appetizing because they are prepared by some typically competent Brazilian cook, and because any number of side dishes from rice and beans to farofa or pirão can add the inimitable ingredients that make any Brazilian meal truly Brazilian.

Farofa is totally unique to Brazil. Flour ground from the manioc root is fried in oil. Bits and pieces of many things, from egg to tortoise meat, may be added to the pan, and the dish arrives at the table looking like a sawdust pilaf. Its taste is positively addictive, especially when used to soak up juice from black beans or to thicken pirão or vatapá. A dictionary defines **pirão** (found in Bahia and throughout the Northeast) as "manioc mush." Doesn't sound appetizing? It is. Mixing pirão with rice and farofa, all accompanying a seafood stew and a well-chilled cold beer, is eating pleasure at the tropical best. **Vatapá** is a staple of Bahian cuisine, one of the most distinct in all Brazil.

Food is definitely a drawing card for Salvador, capital of Bahia state. Vatapá, xim xim de galinha, and moquecas are the centerpieces of Bahian cooking. **Vatapá** is also a kind of mush, made from bread dough, cashew nuts, and dried shrimp, while **xim xim** (pronounced approximately "shing shing," the final letter, however, being a nasal vowel, not a consonant) is a chicken dish prepared with native herbs. **Moquecas** are fish stews, and all three dishes are spicy, and cooked in the strongly flavored **dendé,** or palm oil.

"Cozinha Mineira" is how the food of Minas Gerais is known, one of two regional cuisines of any complexity that can rival the uniqueness of the Bahian fare. The food in most other regions and cities, including Rio and São Paulo, is often called international, and would be more accurately described as "general Brazilian." In both Rio and São Paulo, traditional Brazilian food has become just one more specialty like Italian or Japanese food. But there is little room for complaint about the eating in either of these culinary capitals. Southern Brazil is cattle country, and justly prides itself on its **steak** and mixed-grill houses. The **rodízio,** or round-robin way of serving all the beef, chicken, turkey, and pork you can eat carved right at your table, is the southern culinary tradition that evolved from this prosperous animal husbandry. Exotic river **fish** and even game are commonly eaten throughout Amazônia. Beyond these distinctions, there is always some dish or snack or desert unique to each place that is routinely offered to visitors for their satisfaction and approbation, and these items will be mentioned in turn according to their proper place in the narrative.

No discussion of typical Brazilian food would be complete without mention of **canja,** an excellent chicken soup, as hearty and healthful as any you will ever taste.

The couvert is a common feature of most restaurant meals. It means cover, and usually includes bread and butter, a little pâté, and some hard-boiled quails' eggs. The couvert, which generally costs a dollar or two at moderately priced restaurants, is optional and may be refused.

THE FRUITS FROM BOTH LAND AND SEA:
Without exaggeration there are a hundred varieties of edible fruits that are either native to Brazil or were adapted to its fertile soil. Buffet breakfasts at the top hotels offer a fresh selection daily, minimally including **pineapple,** several types of **melon** and **bananas,** and **mango.** The more exotic fruits, like **caju** (each of which bears a single cashew nut), **tamarind,** and **breadfruit,** along with dozens of new varieties to discover, can be purchased from vendors and at open markets on the streets. If you express enough curiosity at any given stand, the vendor is very likely to offer a slice for you to taste. Practically any bar, lunch counter, or restaurant you stop at will include freshly squeezed orange juice on its menu. A dozen other varieties of fruit

juices, pure or in combination, can be had at juice bars popular throughout the country.

The bounty in fruit throughout Brazil is only matched by the abundant catches from the seas of **frutos do mar**—shellfish, fin fish, shrimp, crab, lobster, and octopus—a steady harvest seemingly without end, from the omnipresent ocean along the coast and from the many river systems inland. One island city—Floriánopolis, capital of Santa Catarina state—has a large inland lake where restaurants serve a round robin of dishes, all shrimp prepared in a variety of ways.

BRAZILIAN BEVERAGES: In addition to the **fruit juices** already mentioned, Brazil produces a popular soft drink, **guaraná,** made from a berry of the same name. Other international soft drinks like Pepsi, Coke, Fanta, and so forth are widely available. **Mineral water,** plain or carbonated, is a common sight at Brazilian meals, as tap water tends to be avoided for direct consumption. Ask for *agua mineral,* either *sem* or *com gaz* (with or without fizz).

The most popular alcoholic beverages are **beer** for most occasions, wine at meals, and a cocktail called a caipirinha, made from **cachaça** (a potent sugarcane brandy), crushed fresh limes, and sugar over ice. Brazilian brewers can hold their own with any of the great beer makers worldwide. Brand names like Antarctica and Brahma are most popular, and cast American beer in a poor light when compared for body and taste. A .75-liter (18-oz.) bottle of Brazilian beer costs roughly 60¢ in most bars and cafés. Brazil also has a flourishing **wine** industry, which, like the breweries, is located in the South, heavily populated by descendants of German and Italian settlers. An excursion in the wine-growing areas, with obligatory stops for tasting along the way, is an ideal way to visit Rio Grande do Sul, Brazil's southernmost state, bordering Uruguay and Argentina. In restaurants, Brazilian domestic wines are comparable in price to their California equivalents purchased retail. Imported wines, French in particular, are steeply priced, as are imported whiskies—some brands of scotch fetch in the vicinity of $10 per drink.

The better grades of cachaça can also be drunk pure, like cognac. Sippers of whisky might find this inexpensive drink an adequate substitute, though pinga, as the drink is also called, which can be quite smooth, has none of whisky's smoky taste. Northeasterners from the countryside refer to cachaça as honey, or *mel.* The welcoming drink for those on package tours will most certainly be a **caipirinha.** Once discovered, many drinkers will ask for nothing else for cocktails or when café-hopping. Caipirinhas are also *de rigueur*—only for those who enjoy alcoholic beverages of course—when eating the Brazilian national dish, feijoada. That is, until the end of the meal, when the other national drink, coffee, is served.

Brazil is, and has been for some time, a major world producer of **coffee** beans. Brazilians drink their *cafezinhos* (little coffees) frequently throughout the day, in demitasse cups and usually quite sweet. For those who like black unsweetened coffee, ask for *café sem açúcar* (the *em* in *sem* is a nasal vowel, but if you say "sang," you will be understood; the *ç* in *açúcar* is pronounced like an *s*). Coffee with milk can be hard to come by after breakfast, when Brazilians drink their own version of café au lait, *café com leite* (*leite* is pronounced lay-chee). Great boxes of Brazilian coffee can be purchased in the airport duty-free shops before returning home, as can bottles of cachaça.

CHAPTER III

SETTLING INTO RIO

□ □ □

Rio has long been a mecca for sun worshippers and escapists of every stripe. The city has enjoyed this status for over 50 years. Initially, however, Rio was primarily an exotic destination for South American sophisticates and international jet-setters. Most North Americans' first view of Rio was as a playground for swells, the perennial image of the city as depicted in a handful of Hollywood movies, where the plot involved some faction of the Cole Porter set in the act of "putting on the ritz." But the era when only the super-chic in their first-class steamship cabins, or at the other end of the travel spectrum, foot-loose adventurers who wandered the world in tramp freighters, dared dream of visiting Rio are long gone by. Group travel and package flights have brought dreamy, steamy, and somewhat distant Rio within the reach of today's typical globetrotter whose ambitions are to "see the world," or at least its principal cities. And Rio, distinguished for its physical beauty, its sublime beach culture and café society, and its unique brand of urbane sensuality, must certainly be counted among them.

1. ORIENTATION

Rio de Janeiro is capital of a state with the same name, located roughly midway down the eastern coast of Brazil. We forget sometimes how much farther to the east South America is than our own continent (and how close to Africa!). Looking at a world map, and drawing a line longitudinally north, Rio de Janeiro would be positioned in the Atlantic somewhat equal with Cape Farewell in Greenland. So much for longitude. The city's latitude, however, places it foresquare in the Tropic of Capricorn, with emphasis here on the word "tropic."

Two-thirds of the way down the somewhat elongated coastal state, the relatively unbroken shoreline jogs radically inland. So strong was the water's current at this great indentation that the first Portuguese explorers believed they had sailed into the mouth of a great river estuary. Since their discovery was made on New Year's Day, they called the place January River or Rio de Janeiro. Later explorers would discover that what was initially thought to be a river was really a vast bay, which the natives called Guanabara.

It is along the western shore of Guanabara Bay, and along the sandy regions of the open sea to the south, that the city of Rio de Janeiro was planted and has since grown into a sprawling metropolis of nine million inhabitants. Since the coastal mountain range comes virtually to the edge of the sea in this region, the city's growth in many areas has been limited to narrow strips of alluvial lands, earth and sand deposited along the base of the mountain range by beating waves and tidal action over the centuries. It is this juxtaposition of mountains—some lush with tropical vegetation, others barren and volcanic—with an endless and majestic seascape that accounts for Rio's reputation as a city of extraordinary natural beauty.

Modern Rio, internally, is divided into a southern and a northern zone—**Zona Sul** and **Zona Norte.** Separating the two zonas is a downtown area called the **Centro.** The area of interest to international visitors is the Zona Sul, where the best beaches, nightspots, sights, lodgings, restaurants, and shops are found. The Centro is also of interest, particularly for its historic buildings, but also for some fine and traditional restaurants, many cultural activities, like theater, concerts, film, and bistros, and for its block upon block of popular retail stores. There is nothing wrong with the Zona Norte. It is, for example, what Brooklyn and the Bronx are to Manhattan in New York City, a vast blue-collar community with many fine neighborhoods, and with many pockets of poverty as well, and these, in the case of Rio, are on a scale of a Third, not a first-world country. In years to come, guidebooks will no doubt begin to reveal the attractions and mysteries of the Zona Norte, for there are popular nightspots, bars, and restaurants that only the cognoscenti frequent. Some tourists approach the fringes of the Zona Norte these days when going to Maracanã Stadium for a soccer match, or penetrate more deeply to visit the rehearsal sites of the great working-class samba clubs, which provide the mass spectacles around which Rio's unrivaled Carnival is organized. But the Zona Sul is still where 90% of the action is. Plus it possesses something the bay-bordered and interior northern zone will never have—some of the finest ocean beaches in the world.

THE BAIRROS OF RIO:

The *bairros* (*bye*-whos) are Rio's many neighborhoods. From the point of view of the transient visitor, the two most important bairros are **Copacabana,** with its justly famous strand and the city's highest concentration of fine hotels, and **Ipanema,** with Rio's best restaurants and boutiques, and its own beach of world renown. **Leme,** an extension of the Copacabana, and **Leblon** connected to Ipanema, are two other *bairros* close to the center of tourist activities. Slightly more remote are the oceanfronted neighborhoods of **Vidigal** and **São Conrado,** where two of the city's most elegant resort hotels are located.

Farther out along the ocean coast is the bairro of **Barra da Tijuca,** a 15-mile stretch of beach developing rapidly into a site of residential condominiums and sprawling shopping malls. Beyond Barra is Rio's only remaining stretch of pristine, still somewhat sparsely populated ocean beach, **Recreio dos Bandeirantes,** where shantytowns and weekend homes of the well-to-do stand side by side—a perfect place to escape the city's other swollen weekend beaches.

Other bairros of Rio that readers of this guide will become familiar with in the course of the narrative are **Botafogo** and **Flamengo,** the once fashionable

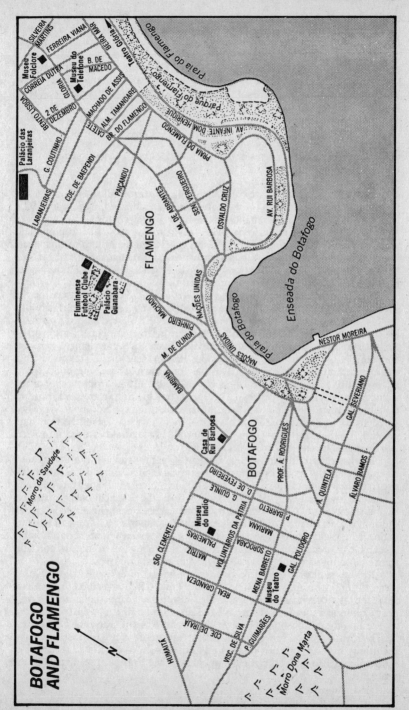

BOTAFOGO AND FLAMENGO

bayfront neighborhoods, still the center of yachting in Rio, and home to some exceptionally good gourmet and seafood restaurants. **Larangieras, Gloria, Catete,** and **Lapa** are neighborhoods that all have their individual charms and attractions, and are closer in to the Centro, Rio's modern and active commercial and cultural downtown hub. **Cosme Velho,** jumping-off point for the ascent to **Corcovado**—affording from its summit one of the most extraordinary views you will ever get of any city—and **Santa Teresa** are two vest-pocket neighborhoods, off the beaten track, where many houses of Rio's past eras are preserved. The **Parque Nacional da Tijuca** is Rio's great inner city national park, set among the slopes of various connected hills and mountains. **Gávea** offers golf and shopping, and **Urca** is a quietly elegant neighborhood at the foot of Sugar Loaf Mountain, the other spectacular promontory offering for its part a view of Rio from the edge of the sea.

HISTORY: Before there were bairros, the region surrounding Guanabara Bay was a great forest inhabited by indigenous tribes. On January 1 in the year 1502, a fleet under Portuguese command sent to survey the territorial discoveries of Âlvares Cabral, and thought to have been navigated by the Italian explorer and enigmatic historical figure, Americo Vespucci, entered the mouth of Guanabara Bay. A halfhearted attempt to set up a permanent camp failed, and for years thereafter subsequent Portuguese explorers—including Magellen—used the harbor for safe anchorage during their various expeditions.

The French knowingly poached on Portuguese New World territory in search of a colonial empire of their own, in what was already by the early 1500s a rapidly shrinking world. The Huguenot admiral Villegaignon landed a formidable troop of soldiers in 1555—and subsequently large numbers of colonists— on several islands near the mainland in Guanabara Bay. A settlement here was christened Coligny. In 1567 the tenacious French were forcibly removed from their beachhead, part of which today is the downtown Santos-Dumont Airport, by troops under Brazil's governor-general, Mem de Sá, who from the city of Salvador in the northeast supervised Portugal's strategic dominance over production for a new and growing world sugar market. During the bloody siege pressed by Mem de Sá against the French interlopers, a fort was established on high ground in what is now downtown Rio, and this stronghold evolved into Rio's first Portuguese colony, São Sebastião do Rio de Janeiro.

Rio has rewarded handsomely the hard-fought victory of the Portuguese, having been at the center of important historical events in Brazil since the city's rise to national dominance in the mid-1700s. Although the French returned and sacked the town in 1711, Rio had already become the principal port for Europe-bound shipments of gold from nearby Minas Gerais. Having finally eclipsed Salvador in importance, Rio became the colony's capital in 1763. Most of what remains from the layout of that city can be found close to the waterfront, notably several old churches and monasteries, the Praça XV (square) of colonial administrative buildings, and the Passeio Público, Rio's first public park.

Rio was suddenly thrust into world prominence after the Portuguese monarchs, fleeing the Napoleonic wars, settled there in 1808 and ruled their empire from the city for a span of 13 years. That historic accident implanted the only post-Columbian monarchy to actually take root and flourish in the New World, forestalling the establishment of a republic in Brazil until nearly the 20th century. The royal presence, however, led to the creation of many basic institutions— including printing, till then suppressed in the colony—which had the effect of modernizing Rio and other Brazilian cities to the European standards of the times.

Brazil's relatively enlightened monarch, Pedro II, who ruled during much of the 19th century, made Rio his home, and nearby Petrópolis in the mountains, the site of his summer palace. The residences of Dom Pedro and his family, along with other collections of royal memorabilia, are open to the public. Rio experienced tremendous growth during Dom Pedro's reign, but nothing compared with what has occurred in this century. Even until well into the 20th century, bairros like Copacabana and Ipanema were fishing villages and summer hideaways. The spread of the city always seemed to outdistance the development of its basic services, from paved roads to sanitation. And such remains the case today in the outlying areas, and even in the inner-city shanytowns, the *favelas,* most of which, however, were removed in recent years from the fashionable neighborhoods.

In 1960 Rio—part of a city-state then called Guanabara—surrendered its status as Brazil's capital to the new interior city of Brasília. Guanabara itself was finally dissolved in 1975, and Rio was reinstated as capital of the State of Rio de Janeiro, whose previous capital, Niterói is located on the bay's opposite shore. The two cities are connected by a causeway bridge nine miles long. While no longer the political center of the country, nor even its largest and most economically powerful city, Rio and its *Cariocas* (as its residents are known) still exercise enormous influence over Brazilian affairs, both popular and public.

TOURIST INFORMATION: This guide, of course, is an indispensable reference to the life and attractions of Rio de Janeiro, and much that is of interest in the city's environs as well. After reading it, accompanied by consultations with knowledgeable friends and travel professionals (agents and tour guides, that is), you should know pretty much what there is to see and do before you get to Rio. These sources cannot tell you, however, who will be appearing at a particular jazz or samba club during your stay, nor what the hottest or newest discos, bars, and restaurants are at precisely that moment. There will be, moreover, unforeseen, and unavoidable gaps in this guide that will require you to find information elsewhere. Here are some useful suggestions on where to get that information.

The state and the city promotional arms are named TurisRio and Riotur respectively. TurisRio maintains an **information center** with a highly animated and competent staff at Rio's International Airport, on Ilha do Governador (Governor's Island), a 30- to 45-minute drive from most areas in the Zona Sul. If you don't have a hotel reservation, they can help you. They can also give you basic transportation information: where to catch the airport bus, how to get to Petrópolis, Búzios, Paraty, or other destinations, popular or personal, within the Estado do Rio, the state of Rio, as most Brazilians call it. These are the first people to take your questions to when you land.

Both **TurisRio** (tel. 221-8422 or 225-4512) and **Riotur** (tel. 297-7117) maintain offices downtown at Rua da Assembléia 10. And they both distribute printed materials on a variety of excursion options. Riotur also maintains branches in much-frequented locations like Pão de Açúcar (Sugar Loaf Mountain), Avenida Pasteur 520, in Urca, near the entrance to the cable car (open from 9 a.m. to 7 p.m.); at the overlook on Corcovado Mountain; in the downtown bus station, Estaçao Rodoviária Novo Rio, at Avenida Francisco Bicalho 1 (tel. 291-5151, *ramal,* or extension, 143), located in São Cristovão, slightly to the north of the downtown area (open from 6 a.m. till midnight); and the Marina da Glória, in Flamengo Park (tel. 205-6447), open from 9 a.m. to 5 p.m. English and other major Western languages are spoken at these locations. Riotur's 580-8000 number is a **multilingual information service** operating 24 hours a day.

Another valuable number to have is that of the **tourist police,** Poltur, in the event you are ripped off. Poltur, where English is spoken, is located in Leblon on Avenida Huberto de Campos 315, at the intersection of Afranio de Melo, near the Scala nightclub (tel. 259-7048). It's open 24 hours a day, seven days a week.

Maps are available, for a fee, at most of the above-mentioned information centers, or they can be purchased at local bookstores and newsstands, including those at the airport and bus station. For car travel, buy a copy of the *Quatro Rodas,* a Brazilian road guide complete with a country map, or consult with the Touring Clube do Brasil, with its own building downtown near the waterfront on the Praça Mauá. Maps in Brazil tend to be attractive, but stylized and often incomplete. I would be indebted to anyone who writes with information about a source of good maps in Brazil.

The **principal sources of information** for most tourists, once settled in the city, are the desk staff at their various hotels. The hotel *portaria* is where you will deposit and retrieve your room key, pick up messages, and find out about local hot spots and tours. Just remember that while the portaria staff can really be a most immediate and valuable source of informant, and their services will cost you nothing, chances are your informant will receive a commission if you accept his recommendation. And while their recommendations are generally quite sound, porters have been known to steer people away from certain choices in favor of others to guarantee their fees. The porters, by the way, will also be a key source for finding out where to change money at the quasi-legal black-market rate.

There are a number of **publications** that can be consulted for current cultural listings. Rio's daily newspapers all have entertainment sections, the best of which can be found in the *Journal do Brasil* and *O Globo.* While they are obviously written in Portuguese, it isn't too hard to retrieve basic information like movie titles, locations, and times, and who may be appearing in what club or concert. Hotels also often provide guests with English language publications, like *Rio This Month* in *TV Guide* format, or the *Daily Post,* which appears four times weekly.

TRANSPORTATION: Public transportation in Rio—mostly a network of buses—is quite extensive. Most tourists, though, are likely to get around the city by cab or on transportation provided by a tour company for a particular excursion.

Airport Transfers

If your package or ticket does not include airport transfers—where a tour company van or hotel car is there to meet you—you have several options for getting to your hotel. The **luxury car service** of two airport companies, Cotramo and Transcopass, is the most costly, and the most hassle-free. You pay a fixed rate, calculated according to neighborhood zones: figure $15 to $20 to get to Copacabana or Ipanema. With **metered taxis,** you will have to negotiate a price, which will probably be less expensive. The modern and comfortable cars of the luxury services, plus the professional mien of their drivers, make this the recommended option. A Greyhound-style **bus,** called the frescão (because it's air-conditioned), leaves for the Zona Sul about every half hour. While the bus costs only about $1 and stops near all the major hotels, you may not care to drag your suitcases that extra block or two when you've just arrived. The route taken by the frescão will skirt closer to downtown than your private cab, and the ride can be an interesting first orientation to the city. The **public bus**—actually a series of buses

—from the airport to the city or beach areas is even more of an adventure, which only the most intrepid will need to experience.

Taxis

There are three varieties of cabs in Rio. Most plentiful are the **common metered cabs,** small cars painted yellow, which are hailed from the street or from official taxi queues throughout the city. The meter has two flag settings, labeled 1 and 2. The no. 2 setting adds 20% to the fare and is used after 11 p.m., on Sundays and holidays, when outside the old city limits, or when climbing particularly steep inclines, like the access road to Corcovado. Meters are seldom calibrated to keep up with Brazil's inflation. The meter reading, instead, is used as a base, and the true price is calculated by reference to the *tabela,* an official table of updated equivalents that should be posted on the vehicle's rear window. Brazilians usually quote the meter figure aloud, and look closely over the driver's shoulder while he consults his own copy of the tabela. Thus do Cariocas themselves try to keep from being overcharged by Rio's notorious meter hacks, who have become particularly devious as a result of runaway inflation and the high cost of fuel.

The second type of cab is the **radio taxi,** which can be hailed on the street or called for by phone. One reliable company is **Coopatur** (tel. 290-1009). The fare of a radio taxi seems to be roughly twice that of a metered cab when both are playing by the official rules. Radio-cab drivers will often try to sign on with you for your entire stay, which, if the price and the driver are agreeable, can be a beneficial relationship to both parties.

Finally, there are the **luxury cabs** already referred to. Most first-class hotels have a fleet of these cars and the fare is generally four times what a metered cab ought to cost. The exorbitant price of the private cars makes the inevitable hassles with metered cab drivers all the more frustrating, since on occasion you can feel stranded between options, all of which are unacceptable.

Buses

Adding to the frustration is the fact that, for most tourists, riding the public buses, even the frescãos, is not recommended. The public buses—which are virtually free from the standpoint of a tourist's purse—are crowded, driven maniacally, and too often, since they are targets for roving bandits, dangerous. That being said, the odds of a safe bus ride are still overwhelmingly in your favor. And if you've got the desire, buses can take you to virtually every corner of the city for next to nothing. Some of the best routes are those that follow the seaside avenues. Bus stops are indicated by signs with the word "Ônibus," but buses must be flagged, since there are no automatic stops except at the beginning and the end of the lines. You enter the rear of the bus and get off from the front. Travel with a lot of small change, since fare takers will not accept large bills, and often don't even have change for smaller ones. Buses marked "Metro" go to the subway station in Botafogo, while those indicating "Castelo" go downtown. It is generally possible to ride the bus hassle-free along the beachfront, say, from one end of Ipanema beach to the other end of Leblon. The open-sided buses called *jardineiras* exist for this purpose.

The downtown terminal for the air-conditioned special buses is **Menezes Cortes,** Rua São José (tel. 224-7577). Here you can not only board a frescão back to the Zona Sul after a day in the Centro, but also catch buses to Petrópolis, Teresópolis, and other side-trip destinations within the state.

Subways, Trains, and Rio's Last Streetcar

The **subway** goes no farther into the Zona Sul than its terminal station in Botafogo, but this is the best means of public transportation for getting around in downtown Rio. To take advantage of this thoroughly clean and modern system, you must first get to the Botafogo station by either cab or bus. From there the many stops within the city will bring you within close range of your downtown destination. Change from linha 1 (line 1) to linha 2 (line 2) at the Estácio station for the bus terminal in São Cristovão or Maracanã Stadium. Another important line 1 stops in the Centro are Cinelândia, for the Teatro Municipal and the Sala Cecília Meirelles. This is also the closest stop to the in-town Santos Dumont Airport, where you get the air shuttle to São Paulo or any number of air taxi services to resorts like Búzios.

The Carioca stop places you near the terminal point of Rio's only remaining streetcar line, the **bonde,** which makes the dramatic ride over the *arcos,* the arched structure of an 18th-century aqueduct, to the historical hillside neighborhood of Santa Teresa. The *bonde,* which is ridden by thousands of commuters daily, is nevertheless the most dangerous of all Rio's public transports. Despite the presence of special police, the open-sided trolleys are vulnerable to hit-and-run assaults by roving street urchins. One way to enjoy the streetcar ride with a minimum of fear is to ride in the section of the car that is protected by wire mesh, bearing in mind the necessity for carrying as few valuables as possible.

Few **passenger trains** leave Rio for out-of-state destinations. But there are still trains running to the relatively nearby cities of São Paulo and Belo Horizonte. The Dom Pedro II train station is located in the Centro off Praça Cristiano Ottoni (tel. 233-4090 or 233-3277).

Car Rentals

You are probably best off limiting your patronage to Hertz, Avis, or Budget. Then, if something goes wrong—as not infrequently occurs in the case of cars rented throughout South America—there will be someone nearby to whom you can forward your complaints. Hertz (tel. 398-3162) and Avis (tel. 398-3083) have locations at the international airport, and all three companies have outlets in Copacabana: Hertz, Avenida Princesa Isabel 334 (tel. 275-4996, or toll free in Brazil 011/800-8900); Avis, Avenida Princesa Isabel 150 (tel. 542-4249, or toll free in Brazil 011/800-8787); and Budget, Avenida Princesa Isabel 250 (tel. 275-3244). The Avenida Princesa Isabel is a principal access route in Copacabana between the Centro and the northeastern shore in one direction and the city's southern beaches and southwestern shore in the other.

PRACTICAL FACTS:

In a **medical emergency**—or any other, for that matter—the first place you should turn to for help is your hotel staff, if at all possible under the circumstances. Many hotels have physicians on duty or on call. During regular business hours, your consulate is also a reasonable place to turn for advice on medical care, and for doctor or dentist referrals. (see "Embassies and Consulates" in Section 3 of Chapter I.)

The **Rio Health Collective,** Avenida Ataulfo de Paiva 135, Suite 1415 (tel. 511-0949), refers travelers to English-speaking doctors in every area of medicine.

Among the hospitals offering emergency care in Rio 24 hours a day are the **Hospital Miguel Couto,** Rua Bartolomeu Mitre, Leblon (tel. 274-2121), and the **Hospital Souza Aguiar,** Praça da República 610, Centro (tel. 296-4114). Telephone operators at these hospitals are not likely to speak English, however. Private clinics will more probably have staff and doctors who do speak English and other languages. One conveniently located clinic is the **Centro Médico Ipanema,** Rua Anibal Mendonça 135, in Ipanema (tel. 239-4647).

Private **ambulance** services include the Clinic Savior (tel. 227-6187 or 227-5099) and Pullman (tel. 236-1011 or 257-4132).

In the event you require a **dentist** for emergency treatment and you are unable to obtain a reference from your hotel or consulate, try **Clínica de Urgência,** Rua Marquês de Abrantes 27, in Flamengo (tel. 226-0083), or **Dentário Rollin,** Rua Cupertino Durão 81, Leblon (tel. 259-2647).

There are 24 hour-a-day **drugstores** (*farmácias* or *drogarias*) operating in neighborhoods throughout Rio. Again, check for the most convenient location through your hotel staff. All-night drugstores are not scarce, and prescription drugs—while this perhaps ought not to be the case—are fairly easy to obtain without the necessary paperwork. See "The ABCs of Brazil" in Chapter 1.

The **telephone area code** for Rio is 021. The telephone system in Brazil is generally reliable, but not without its glitches. Dial tones will sometimes be elusive, transmissions weak, broken connections not infrequent—the system is about 80% there. If you can avoid making long-distance phone calls from your hotel room, your billing rates will be roughly 50% lower. Like room-service food, telephone calls and every other service you purchase within the hotel will be priced at a premium. Your hotel will not charge for local calls, however. Wherever you call from, however, you may now dial direct, both within Brazil and internationally.

Telephone centers—quieter and more comfortable than street payphones —are in locations throughout the city. There are centers open 24 hours in Copacabana at Avenida Nossa Senhora de Copacabana 462, in the Centro at Praça Tiradentes 41, in the Novo Rio bus terminal, and at the international airport. Other centers with fixed schedules are in Ipanema at Rua Visconde de Pirajá 111 (open from 6:30 a.m. to 11 p.m.), in the Santos Dumont Airport (open from 6 a.m. to 11:30 p.m.), in the downtown Menezes Cortés bus terminal (open on weekdays from 6:30 a.m. to 10:30 p.m.), and at Barra Shopping, in Barra da Tijuca (open from 10 a.m. to 10 p.m. daily except Sunday).

Payphones require *fichas,* slotted slugs which can sometimes be hard to come by, even if the public apparatus itself is in functioning order. Try to find a newsstand or a tobacconist who may sell the tokens, or if you plan to use the payphone system a lot, stock up at a telephone center.

There are numerous branches of the **post office** located throughout the Zona Sul. Avenida Nossa Senhora de Copacabana, which runs parallel to the oceanside Avenida Atlântica the length of Copacabana beach, has two postal branches, at nos. 540 and 1298. In Ipanema there is a branch in the principal square, Praça General Osório. Post office hours tend to be from 8 a.m. to 5 p.m. weekdays, on Saturday till noon. The post office at the international airport is open 24 hours a day. Postcards and letters can also be mailed through the porter's desk of your hotel.

RIO'S HOTEL SCENE: Rio, in case you've missed the point, is a beach town.

The best hotels, a good portion of the entertainment and shopping scenes, and the preponderance of popular eating spots are all located in the beach neighborhoods of the Zona Sul, particularly in Copacabana, Leme, Ipanema, and Leblon. Slightly more remote, but compensatingly luxurious and self-contained, are two resort hotels in the beachside neighborhoods of Vidigal and São Conrado. It makes no sense to stay in one of the many hotels located downtown, the Centro. There is virtually no residential life downtown, and so the streets tend to be empty after dark, except in the immediate vicinity of the Teatro Municipál or other nightspots. You may want to play downtown some nights, but all except the most confirmed inner-city buffs and students engaged in their rites of passage with budget to match will want to wake up to the smell of salt water and the sound of the surf. The best crash-pad lodgings for backpackers, students, and other budget

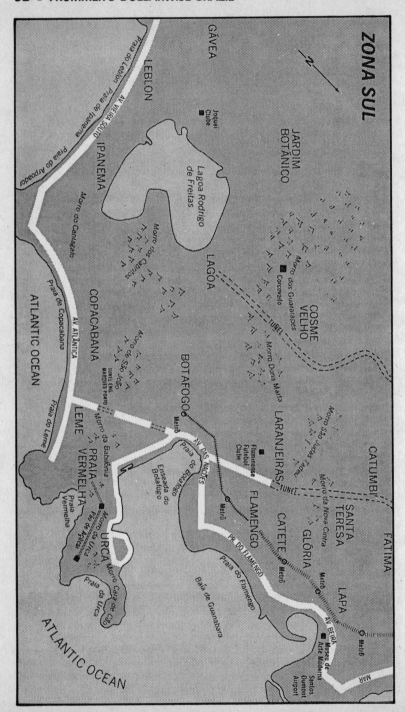

tourists can probably be found in Flamengo, where the backstreets are appropriately threadbare and the location is advantageous, close to both the Centro and Copacabana.

For the past 15 years Hans Stern, one of Rio's most successful jewelers, has collected data on how North American tourists organize their Brazilian vacations. He has concluded that 90% of all North Americans come to Rio and travel nowhere else in the country. Of this population, another 90%, according to Stern's estimate, arrive with a group or an individual package. These group and package arrangements to Rio are popular because what you get, practically speaking—low air fare, first-class beach hotel, prearranged tours and transfers—is often competitively priced with comparable tours to say Rome or Greece. The same deal you get with a package to Rio would cost you twice as much if you pieced it together yourself. For scores of reasons, it is lamentable that most North Americans visiting Brazil don't get to see more of the country. This limited curiosity about greater Brazil will undoubtedly change in the years to come with the expansion of tourist facilities in many of the country's other sunny, historical, or adventurous locations. But it must be said that, as of this writing, only about three dozen hotels in Brazil cater to the tourist trade from Canada and the United States—and most of these are located in Copacabana.

It is *not* wise to arrive in Rio without a hotel reservation. Since most visitors apparently wish to stay on the beach in Copacabana or Ipanema, and since there are no longer potential construction sites in these bairros for new seaside hotels—barring the unforeseen demolition or reconversion of an existing luxury apartment building—the number of available rooms is limited. During the peak season—in the summertime from Christmas until after Carnival, and in the winter during the July school holiday, and on holiday or special-event weekends throughout the year—Rio's hotels easily fill to capacity. Even during the so-called off-season in Rio, if you arrive without a reservation, you are unlikely to secure a satisfactory room—for example, one in a prime location with a view of the beach. You may have to settle for a perfectly nice room but several blocks from the strand. This may not be the end of the world, but if your expectation of a Rio vacation includes a view of Copacabana's magnificent sweeping curve, you may be disappointed.

Hotels in Four Price Ranges

Copacabana's most expensive and desirable rooms are to be found in the handful of five-star hotels located on the Avenida Atlântica, opposite the beach. Next in priciness are the smaller and generally less elaborate four- and three-star hotels that also front the sea. Moderately priced hotels, some of which are considerably more modern and comfortable than their Avenida Atlântica counterparts, are found off the beach on side streets and back avenues. There are even, happily, a few hotels that can be considered in the budget range.

Every hotel reviewed in this guide includes breakfast in its daily rate, with perhaps one or two exceptions that will be duly noted. And breakfast can vary from a sumptuous buffet or room service with the works at no extra charge (on the deluxe level) to the hearty bread, cheese, and bananas of a budget establishment. Most hotels add a 10% service surcharge to their bills, which will apply to package clients only when they purchase extras like midnight room service, poolside drinks, restaurant meals, and so forth. A characteristic attraction of Rio's hotels is that you can stay in the best room in town for much less than what a room of comparable quality would cost in New York, London, or Paris. With the package rate reductions further cutting the price quoted at the reception desk by up to an additional 30%, Rio delivers a lot of comfort in its lodgings at wholesale prices.

Bidets and Mini-bars

There is certain standard equipment in most of Rio's tourist hotel rooms. Bathrooms generally have bidets, a reminder of the continental influence in Brazil. The mini-bar was almost certainly American inspired, and it is not one of our most admirable cultural contributions. Even the most underrated rooms contain these little refrigerators now, stocked with overpriced beverages and snacks. It's easy to beat the mini-bar monopoly, however. Do a little shopping at the food store in your hotel's neighborhood and stock the refrigerator with your favorite items—which will cost you a quarter of what the hotel wants to charge you. Your rooms may also contain a small private strongbox called a *cofre*. There is a daily fee for its use at most hotels, and the key may be obtained at the reception desk.

2. COPACABANA AND LEME

Copacabana and Leme are the names given to a seven-kilometer- (4¼-mile-)long, cove-shaped beach just south of the entrance to Guanabara Bay and to the residential neighborhoods that embrace it. Three-quarters of the beach belongs to the Copacabana end, one of the world's most densely populated neighborhoods, according to the local claim. Leme beach, at the opposite end of the mushroom-cap curve, is a tiny, quiet neighborhood, one of Rio's most charming. The beach is an unobstructed wide stretch of white sand and rugged, pounding surf. The boundary line of the two neighboring bairros is the wide Avenida Princesa Isabel, which tunnels under a mountainous spine and goes on toward Botafogo and the Centro. Rio is wrapped in an environment of natural beauty—a beauty which beguiled and fascinated Darwin 150 years ago, and has been little disturbed, perhaps even complemented, by the numberless habitations humans have tucked into its topographical folds over the years. Watching the sun go down over Copacabana from some perch high above the ground, and seeing the electric lights begin to sparkle in the dark of a clear southern sky and streak along the empty strand and up and down the neighboring mountains, few will avoid surrender to a subversive reflection on the infinite value of pure idleness.

DELUXE HOTELS: The **Rio Palace,** Avenida Atlântica 4240 (tel. 521-3232), is about the number-one choice for visiting North Americans in Rio. The staff, whose marketing director is a native Michigander, actively pursues the American tourist market. Independent of this possible attraction for some, the Rio Palace is above all one of the most comfortable and best-situated hotels in all of Rio de Janeiro. Two tall U-shaped towers in brown-hued tones of stone and glass occupy the farthest corner of Copacabana, opposite the beach's end which borders a historical site, a diminutive and still-active military fort. (Out of the old barracks, a group of young lieutenants marched in open rebellion one morning in 1922 and confronted a superior government force about halfway up the beach, where several of their number were killed; an imposing statue of the fallen youths today marks the spot.) The hotel is also within five minutes' walking distance of Rio's other premier beach, Ipanema.

All 418 rooms at the Rio Palace have sheltered balconies, half of which face an interior court and overlook a swimming pool; the other half give some eye-filling views of the surrounding sea. The terrace at poolside is probably one of the most popular spots in Rio to languish in the noonday heat, or to soak up evening cocktails and pay tribute to the setting sun. Excellent food is served in the Atlantis restaurant, off the pool. And here, in the morning a groaning breakfast buffet is set up with pastries, fruits, juices, meats, and cheeses, along with chafing dishes of bacon and eggs. Coffee and milk are served piping hot directly at your table. As

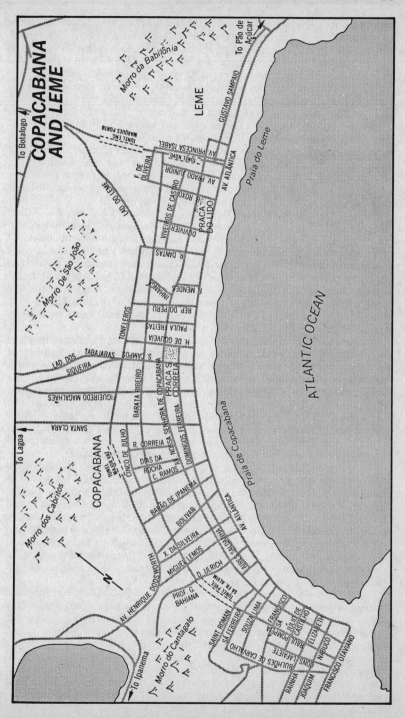

you look out beyond the terrace wall, you'll see the madcap scene of Rio's early-morning exercise mania unfolding on the beach below, as walkers, joggers, and bike riders share the wide, beach-long sidewalk with its famous mosaic pattern of undulating black lines against a sea of white. The Le Pre Catalan is the hotel's principal restaurant, contributing to the Rio version of haute cuisine.

The rooms are large and offer every comfort in tasteful furnishings. Each contains an elegant bath with shower and tub, a mini-bar, individually controlled air conditioning, and a color television set featuring a CNN satellite channel and regularly scheduled English-language movies. Tariffs are $140 to $180 for singles, $160 to $200 in two twin-size beds or a queen-size bed. A favorite congregating place, day or night, is the lobby bar, near the hotel's entrance. The Horse's Neck Bar and the Palace Club, a private nightclub, are perennial nightlife favorites for visitors and residents alike. Other services include indoor parking, a health club, and conference rooms, and an auditorium where shows feature international talent—including Frank Sinatra on one occasion.

The **Copacabana Palace Hotel,** Avenida Atlântica 1702 (tel. 255-7070). Before the era of the high-rise five-star hotels, this was the best address in Rio, and many travelers still hold to that opinion. Thanks to recent multi-million-dollar renovations the Riviera-style grand hotel is guaranteed a bright place in Rio's pantheon of hotels for years to come. The Copacabana Palace doesn't market to package tours, but the hotel does a brisk business with individuals, groups, and conventions. The well-heeled who can afford to pick their friends tend to favor this horizontal plazzo over the less formal atmosphere of the newer fine hotels. And who is to gainsay their choice? A suite at the Copacabana Palace is still a way to treat yourself royally when staying in Rio.

Like a fancy centerpiece, the Copacabana Palace stands near the midpoint of the beach, a favorite rendezvous for gays. Today the seven-story building of carved stone has been combined with a more modern ten-story annex—which may soon be added to if a zoning battle is resolved in the hotel's favor. A circular drive leads past several elegant shops (jewelers, florist, bookstore) into a lobby which conveys a European-style reserve, almost a club-like atmosphere. To one side of the hotel is the glassed-in and casual Pergula restaurant, behind which spreads one of Rio's largest swimming pools, with outdoor tables, chairs, and waiter service. The Bife de Ouro restaurant is one of Rio's finest without the pyrotechnic flashiness of French service, and prices are very reasonable.

Among the 222 rooms and suites, those along the front of the building are smallish but bright, furnished in mahogany. Armchairs and sofas are newly upholstered in fine floral-patterned fabrics, and baths are tiled, though small. Singles are $160 and doubles cost $200. Suites, for $300 nightly, are sizable and luxuriously appointed, with a totally separate sitting room. Baths in the suites are mostly large and old-fashioned in white porcelain and tiles, with a pedestal sink and free-standing tub. All units have TV with cable and king-size or twin beds, high ceilings; most are without balconies, but are air-conditioned. The Copacabana Palace offers numerous other amenities, such as parking, room service, and an in-house beauty salon.

The **Ouro Verde,** Avenida Atlântica 1456 (tel. 542-1887), is refined and efficient, a perennial favorite of corporate travelers, journalists, and aesthetically demanding clients in general. Lacking a pool and other required amenities like hairdressers and saunas that would qualify the four-star hotel for official deluxe status, the Swiss-run Ouro Verde nonetheless has few peers in the city for quality of service and the general tastefulness of its rooms and public spaces. The Ouro Verde Restaurant, located on the mezzanine overlooking the beach, is one of Rio's most popular, serving finely turned meals on linen-covered tables made elegant by silver candlesticks, china, and crystal.

There are 66 rooms, all uniquely furnished, with fine wooden pieces. Graceful watercolors decorate the walls. Embroidered towels embellish the modern combination baths. Rooms with covered verandas face the ocean, and all accommodations include TV, mini-bar, and air conditioning. Singles range from $75 to $95; doubles, $95 to $115. A reservation well in advance is an absolute necessity.

The Ouro Verde is located beyond the Copacabana Palace in the direction of Leme, but is still close to the central stretch of the beach. Most of the buildings along Avenida Atlântica are 12 stories high, in conformity with the neighborhood's longstanding zoning regulations, and house the apartments of a very fortunate minority. Built for the most part over the past 50 years, many are curvaceous in the deco style. Others are more straightforward, like the 12-story Ouro Verde. A barrier of plants separates a street-level bar from the distractions of the street. The small lobby stands at the bottom of an atrium which rises all the way to the roof. The architectural details are rich in marble and highly polished hardwood moldings and trim. An enclosed miniature garden at the rear of the lobby is the picture of a Portuguese *quintal,* an old-fashioned backyard. Off the lobby are formal sitting and reading rooms with club furnishings and tapestries. The clientele is all word-of-mouth; the hotel does not advertise, and does not accept groups.

The posh **Meridien,** Avenida Atlântica 1020 (tel. 275-9922), occupies one corner of the intersection where Avenida Princesa Isabel leads to downtown Rio, at the boundary between Copacabana's red-light district and the staid, family neighborhood of Leme beach. The Meridien is Leme's only luxury hotel, and is a favorite of European tourists. With its 37 floors of glass and steel, the Meridien is a portent of the architectural change bound one day to transform the skyline of this famous strand. The hotel has two fine restaurants: on the ground floor, the Café de la Paix; and on the roof, the St. Honoré, with its reputation for gourmet dishes and one of the city's great panoramic views. The lobby is all business, designed not for lingering but to funnel guests and visitors efficiently to various facilities, including a bar, a shopping arcade, a small movie theater, computerized conference rooms, and the popular disco, Régine's, open only to guests and private members.

Modern in every way, the 497 rooms are decorated in bright pastel shades, with ultramodern furnishings. There are no balconies. The ample windows are sealed and equipped with blackout draperies. All rooms offer satellite color TV with movies, modern baths, safe-deposit boxes, and mini-bars. Singles start at $170; doubles at $180.

One of the Meridien's best assets is its location in Leme. This section of the beach is pleasantly quiet, especially on weekdays. The surrounding area is just the perfect scale for getting to know well a single neighborhood in Rio during a relatively brief stay. Both on Avenida Atlântica and the parallel Avenida Gustavo Sampaio, a block from the ocean, are several attractive hangouts and some excellent restaurants: the tiny Shirley's specializing in fish, and the touristy but tasty Mariu's churrascaria, where grilled meats are served *rodízio* style—as much as you can eat for a fixed price. All the necessary neighborhood stores and services can be found among Leme's few backstreets: a pharmacy, newsstand, stand-up corner bar, laundry, and more. There always seems to be some movement in Leme on both of its principal avenues, but it, too, along with the light auto traffic, is on a diminutive scale appropriate to the limited size of this special little corner of the city.

UPPER-BRACKET HOTELS: The **Miramar Palace Hotel,** Avenida Atlântica 668 (tel. 247-6070), is a near neighbor of the Rio Palace, on the southern end of the beach. Here where the fort sits, a point jutting into the sea forms a slight protective pocket from the relentless beating of the South Atlantic. A half dozen fishing boats are still hauled to the sand at this spot, an appealing anachronism in the otherwise seamless urbanity of Copacabana. The Miramar has surveyed this prospect for some time, and has a venerable reputation. The large glassed-in café and bar at the edge of the sidewalk has long been a favorite place to hang out for some refreshment along the avenue.

The lobby, reached through an entrance on a side street, is strictly functional, and the two smallish elevators are slow. A stylish staircase leads to a mezzanine and a better-than-average restaurant with a wide-angle window view of the beach scene across the avenue. The 150 rooms are quite comfortable, almost homey, not at all fancy in their décor. All the in-room basics and extras are there: full bath, TV, temperature control, and mini-bar. Still, one gets the feeling of a Copacabana from a bygone age, one not too distant perhaps, but past nonetheless. Even the service is somewhat premodern, as the staff exhibits a kind of good-natured friendliness that can't be taught in hotel training seminars.

Of special mention is the doorman of many years, a tall, erect, smartly uniformed man with the easy air of a scoundrel-prince from the other side of the tracks, like the hero from the classic film *Black Orpheus*. Even the maids seem to be having a good time at the Miramar. Other amenities include a tea room (taking afternoon tea is fashionable in Rio), the rooftop Ponto do Comando bar with an open-air deck, and a third-floor coffeeshop above the restaurant, which is visible from the lobby through a central atrium. Standard singles are $70 and doubles are $77; beachfront rooms adding about 25% to the price. Off-season rates —April through September—are $52 single and $60 double.

The **Leme Othon Palace,** Avenida Atlântica 656 (tel. 275-8080), is one of ten Rio hotels in the Othon group—nine of these are located in Copacabana, and six are on the beach. It is midway into Leme, the quiet beach, and therefore probably has the best objective location of any hotel along the seven-kilometer (4½-mile) strip. Of the 193 rooms in this large rectangular block, approximately a third offer ocean views. Rooms are adequately furnished, but otherwise nondescript. They do have covered balconies, however. All rooms have television, air conditioning, and mini-bars, plus baths with separate tubs and showers.

Entrance to the lobby is on a side street. A second-floor restaurant is reliable for lunch, or as a fallback for the odd evening a guest might prefer to stay close to home. The Leme Pub offers live music, and a ground-floor coffeeshop recalls a saloon in Portugal with its typical blue and white tiles. The Leme Palace has the experience and capacity to handle large groups reliably. Singles cost $93 to $103, and doubles run $121 to $134, depending on location.

The **Lancaster,** Avenida Atlântica 1470 (tel. 541-1887), also an Othon hotel, occupies one of those smart deco buildings (this one is a converted apartment house) that grace this famous ocean avenue. Narrow and small, the building's white façade sports a rack of curved balconies. Near the Ouro Verde and Copacabana Palace, the Lancaster offers a suite-size room as its standard accommodation. The hotel was recently renovated, giving the furnishings a correct, if unspectacular, facelift. Enter the lobby past a sunken sidewalk bar. Off the lobby a small game room houses a first-class table-soccer game. The Lancaster restaurant is quite small, almost family scale, perfectly suitable for breakfast (included in the tariffs) and for light meals.

The Lancaster's rooms are divided by partitions into a sitting area with TV, couch, table, and chairs, and a sleeping area with a modern bath. Only the front rooms have balconies. Rooms elsewhere overlook an interior court, and seem a bit dreary for lack of light; they also have sleeping areas that are slightly smaller than those on the avenue. The hotel's 70 rooms are priced according to location.

Interior singles are $68 and interior doubles run $75, while deluxe front rooms range between $94 and $104. Special services include a car-rental agency, babysitting, and free use of beach towels and umbrellas. Children under 8 stay in their parents' room free.

Luxor Continental, Rua Gustavo Sampaio 320 (tel. 275-5252). The Luxor chain has four hotels in Rio, three of which are in Copacabana or Leme. The Continental is not on the beach, but it occupies a prized location. This principal backstreet of Leme is a genuine neighborhood, complete with colorful street life, shops, and restaurants. The beach is only a block away. Recently redecorated, the 19-story Continental has adopted the color scheme of the other Luxor properties, making free use of vibrant and fiery shades of orange, red, and yellow.

The 123 rooms are smaller than average, and half the baths lack tubs, but all have bidets and some have phone extensions. Only the corner rooms offer narrow views of the beach through spaces in between neighboring buildings. Otherwise the hotel looks out onto backstreets and nearby hills. There are TVs and stocked mini-bars in all rooms, which are also air-conditioned. The 320 Restaurant and Poty Bar are available for dining and drinks, to the accompaniment of live piano music. The Carmelo coffeeshop occupies the mezzanine, and has its own entrance. Singles run $54, $62, and $71; and doubles, $60, $69, and $79.

The **Plaza Copacabana,** Avenida Princesa Isabel 263 (tel. 275-7722), located on the Copacabana side of the furiously busy eight-lane access road, is an 18-story four-star hotel about two blocks from the beach. Behind the lobby is a multilevel lounge with a restaurant overlooking an atrium which rises to an unusual domed ceiling. The 165 high-ceilinged rooms are comfortably furnished, and include TV, mini-bars, and air conditioning. This would be a convenient hotel for those whose interests or business took them frequently to the Centro while in Rio—from this location the Botafogo Metro station is just a short cab or bus ride away. Perhaps because of its location, so near the tunnel and on the fringes of the Copacabana red-light district, the Plaza is not as expensive as the typical four-star hotel. Single rooms range in cost from $50 to $60, and doubles are $70 to $80. An added incentive is that the hotel does not include the usual 10% service charge in the rates, so you pay 10% less than at most other hotels.

The **Olinda,** Avenida Atlântica 2230 (tel. 257-1890). Café-style tables and chairs occupy the sidewalk at the hotel's entrance, and are surrounded by potted plants and hedges for privacy. The Olinda also has a small but old-fashioned lobby complete with overstuffed armchairs and table lamps. A three-star hotel fronting the sea at this central location along the Copacabana beach, the Olinda is somewhat a bargain. The 100-room hotel also has a restaurant and a beauty parlor. Rooms are airy, comfortable, and cheerfully undistinguished in décor. All contain what are the requisite amenities in every hotel rated by the Brazilian tourist board, including TV, mini-bar, and air conditioning. Rooms facing the beach begin to be competitive in price with the better hotels in the area. Staying here costs between $50 and $77 for a single, and $55 to $102 for a double.

The **Hotel California,** Avenida Atlântica 2612 (tel. 257-1900). This hotel with the felicitous name will remind some people of the recent popular song with the same title. A further distinguishing mark of the 12-story Mediterranean-style building is its location smack dab at the midpoint of the lengthy concave avenue. The closest the hotel comes to reflecting a West Coast image, however, is the bright sidewalk bar you pass at the lobby entrance, with its striped slatted chairs and tables, and multicolored umbrellas. Otherwise, the 117-room hotel has a somewhat European atmosphere, and caters to a repeat clientele of vacationers and business people alike.

The rooms are very pleasant, with homey furnishings and balconies. A few deluxe rooms facing the ocean feature huge verandas with two entrances. Accommodations have large tile baths with pedestal sinks and enormous tubs, plus the ubiquitous TV and mini-bar. All rooms are air-conditioned, but those in beachfront accommodations may get the same effect more naturally—especially on the upper floors—by trapping the cool breezes off the ocean through an open balcony door. Some single rooms are quite small, and if they don't face the street, a bit dark as well. The Le Colonial restaurant specializes in both Brazilian and international meals. In addition to the marble-lined lobby, the other public spaces include a lounge, meeting rooms, and a pub with cigarbox-style paneling. The hotel, one of the Othon group, provides guests with umbrellas and towels for the beach. The prices parallel those of its companion hotel, the Lancaster, with singles for $68 to $94, and doubles for $75 to $104.

The **Luxor Copacabana,** Avenida Atlântica 2554 (tel. 257-1940), is also centrally located along Copacabana's sweeping curve. This early version of the glass-and-steel structure is unusually thin, and offers the unique feature of balconies with its side rooms and excellent views of the ocean. The reason for this architectural option is that the building next door sits back on the sidewalk considerably farther than the hotel, creating a welcome jog in the straight line of the long sidewalk promenade.

A predominance of natural woods—particularly jacarandá, or Brazilian rosewood—in the furnishings, bedboards, and trims give the rooms a very masculine look. Natural plank floors stand out sharply against the bright primary colors of the décor, giving the rooms a feeling of both warmth and vitality. Lamps, ashtrays, and wall decorations are of modern design, as are the bathroom fixtures. Not all baths have tubs, but all have showers and bidets, as well as wall-phone extensions.

Front rooms have glassed-in balconies, and breakfast nooks complete with table and chairs. Corner suites that face the ocean are quite large and have spacious verandas filled with potted plants. There is excellent shopping in the boutiques on nearby side streets, and behind the hotel on Avenida Nossa Senhora de Copacabana. The hotel's terrace is home to the Fogareiro bar and restaurant. The Luxor Copacabana's 123 rooms are divided into three categories—standard, superior, and deluxe—depending on size, location, and decorative appointments, and will cost you, $68, $77, or $89 for a single, and $75, $86, or $99 for a double.

The **Rio Othon Palace,** Avenida Atlântica 3264 (tel. 255-8812), toward the southern end of Copacabana beach, is Othon's flagship, a 30-story brown-glass landmark that towers high above the other buildings along the strip. The tower is spaced between its neighbors in such a way that every one of the 606 rooms offers at least a partial water view. Call the Othon semi-deluxe. It has all the five-star amenities, and caters heavily to package-tour operators. Many Americans spend their stays very enjoyably at the Othon Palace.

The atmosphere is one of constant motion, and the public areas—the tiny pool, the rooftop bar—have a worn-out look in places. Unlike the other large beachfront hotels, the Othon Palace lacks transitional space between the sidewalk and the lobby, which subjects guests to a gauntlet of hustlers right up to the entrance.

All the rooms have balconies, and they have been recently redecorated with tasteful streamlined furnishings. Bathrooms are lined in marble, and accommodations provide in-house video and multilingual TV channels. The rooftop Skylab bar opens to a sundeck with a small open-air pool. The Skylab is one of the hotel's most popular drawing cards, attracting a steady flow of local residents as well as guests. Small wonder, as the bar is aptly named. This is the best closeup view of the hills behind Copacabana, where you can see quite dramatically how narrow a strip of land the neighborhood occupies between the coastal mountains and the sea. And you can also get a glimpse of life on the rising slopes, where even the favelas are somewhat prosperous.

The Estância Restaurant on the third floor serves churrasco (steaks and grilled meats, Brazilian style) and is worth a try for its panoramic view of the beach. Breakfast is served in lavish buffet style in the Samambaia coffeeshop, also on the third floor. Other facilities include an "underground" disco in the basement, and a small health club on the roof. Singles cost from $130; doubles, from $150.

The **Luxor Regente,** Avenida Atlântica 3716 (tel. 287-4212), is the largest of the Luxor hotels in Rio, and is close to the Ipanema end of the beach. The hotel's façade of windows assures that all front rooms are bright during the day. These glass walls are all equipped with full-length blackout curtains to keep out unwanted early-morning rays and noise, however. Rooms are spacious, decorated in Brazilian colonial style, with gallery-white walls. Hotel service includes: the Forno e Fogão Restaurant, where the fare is very satisfactory. Rates here are equal to those at the Luxor Copacabana: standard rooms are $68 single and $75 double, superior rooms run $77 and $86, and deluxe rooms go for $89 and $99.

The **Copacabana Praia,** Rua Francisco Otaviano 30 (tel. 521-2727), was recently built right behind the Rio Palace, a short walking distance from both Copacabana and Ipanema beaches. This very small hotel houses only 55 rooms, all of which face the front and have balconies. The staff is friendly and caters with equal grace to individual clients and small groups, many of whom are from the States. Rooms are fully equipped with TVs, mini-bars, and individual thermostats. There is a small dip pool and sundeck on the roof, and a sauna as well. The Pícollo restaurant/bar serves international and local food. Singles begin at $50; doubles, at $55.

The **Real Palace,** Rua Duvivier 70 (tel. 541-4387), was built in 1984 on this side street two blocks from the beach. If the rooms are compared with, say, the Lancaster, they are much smaller, half as attractive, and almost twice the price. The 60 accommodations have TVs suspended from the ceiling, hospital style, plus mini-bars and combination baths. At $150 for two, suites are the hotel's best bet. They are much more elegant, and offer three times the space of the standard rooms. Suites have private saunas, shower with water massage, and two rooms—one with two large double beds and the other with leather armchairs and a couch, and a glass-topped table with four comfortable chairs. There is a small rooftop dip pool and a restaurant serving Spanish food. Singles are $90; doubles, $100.

MEDIUM-PRICED HOTELS: The **Acapulco,** Rua Gustavo Sampaio 854 (tel. 275-0022), is a moderately priced alternative to the Meridien or the Leme Palace for those wishing to stay in Leme, and who want to experience the vest-pocket atmosphere of a backstreet neighborhood and still be only a block from the beach. The deluxe double-occupancy rooms, costing $50 a night, are large with smallish beds and have balconies facing the street, where the rear of the towering Meridien dominates but does not darken the skyline. Even the smaller rooms off the front have a comfortable appearance, and have good, functional baths, mini-bars. TVs, and air conditioning. Other features in this 123-room hostelry are parking facilities, a restaurant, and a coffeeshop. Singles are $35, and doubles run $40 to $50, breakfast included. The Acapulco does not charge 10% for service, which adds to its genuine bargain status.

The **Rio Copa,** Avenida Princesa Isabel 370 (tel. 275-6644), is only a stone's throw from the tunnel leading to the center of the city, and three blocks from the beach. The hotel is relatively new, with double-glazed windows that effectively soundproof the rooms from the traffic below. Accommodations are spacious, with Scandinavian furnishings and baths with showers, plus mini-bars and TVs.

The hotel is totally air-conditioned. The view above the muted din of the street is of Copacabana's rooftops, and is wide and appealing. Luxury doubles offer half again as much space as the standard rooms, but the L-shaped design and narrow dimensions of the sitting area make the space impractical. Other hotel features include executive meeting rooms, the Le Baron restaurant, Le Princesse bar, and a coffeeshop open 24 hours a day. Prices begin at $55 for a single and $60 for a double. Deluxe rooms are priced at $85.

Right before the tunnel on the Leme side are two private alleyways that are worthy of a quick peak if you find yourself walking in or near this stretch of the avenue. If you identify yourself at the security gate as a curious tourist, you may walk past the rows of charming houses to the end of the alley and climb the stone stairs. You will be climbing the leeward slope of a hill on whose opposite face is the infamous Favela de Babilonia, a shantytown of folkloric stature once memorialized in a poem by Elizabeth Bishop. The stairs rise several flights. The view from the top is confined to rooftops, but you will also suddenly be in close contact with the dense green vegetation that covers the hill, much the way it must have long before the New World was colonized.

The **Debret**, Rua Almirante Goncalvez 5 (tel. 521-3332), also a converted apartment building, with 98 guest rooms, actually sits on Avenida Atlântica but has its entrance on this side street. The hotel's intimate lobby, adorned with sculpture and paintings, invites lingering. The rooms in the Debret are really a cut above Rio's other three-star hotels in comfort and in the quality of furnishings, fixtures, and décor, which is formal colonial. The front rooms (actually in this case, the side rooms) view the ocean. Room service is available 24 hours, and all rooms have TVs and mini-bars. You pay $55 for a single room and $78 for a double.

The Debret is obviously named for the romantic and naturalistic French painter Jean-Baptiste Debret, whose paintings and graphics provide a rich visual chronicle of early-19th-century life in Brazil. Debret came with a team of French artists who were invited to Brazil by Dom João VI, the prince regent who had fled Lisbon from Napoleon's advancing armies in 1808. Debret lived in Brazil for many years, and helped found the Brazilian Academy of Fine Arts. His work emphasizes popular scenes from that age in amazing detail, the dress and habits of masters, slaves, and Indians, as well as depicting some important events in Brazilian history. Several printed collections of his work exist, and are worth scrutinizing in a library or bookstore.

The **Copacabana Sol**, Rua Santa Clara 141 (tel. 257-1840). While beyond Rua Barata Ribeiro, the third major avenue in from the seaside Avenida Atlântica, this hotel is still only a five- to ten-minute walk from the beach, and for the price, you may find the stroll worth the savings. The surrounding neighborhood is filled with good, inexpensive restaurants, and the street life is relatively quiet, yet colorful, with open-air markets and many sidewalk vendors.

The hotel is new and quite attractive in appearance, and offers features not usually required of a three-star hotel, including restaurant, bar, parking, and room service. Accommodations are large and well furnished, with TV, mini-bar, and air conditioning. The hotel has 70 rooms: singles range from $40 to $43, doubles run $42 to $45, and some very attractive suites go for a very reasonable rate of $60.

The **Bandeirantes Othon**, Rua Barata Ribeiro 548 (tel. 255-6252), with 96 guest rooms, is a relatively small hotel built more for commercial travelers than for tourists. This stretch of Rua Barata Ribeiro has less charm than the area around Rua Santa Clara, farther to the north. The rooms are comfortable, however, and its location three blocks from Copacabana beach makes it a fair choice for budget-conscious travelers who like modern surroundings. The hotel has a coffeeshop and bar, and offers limited parking as well as 24-hour room service. Singles range from $33 to $39; doubles, $43 to $47.

The **Castro Alves,** Avenida Nossa Senhora de Copacabana 552 (tel. 257-1800). Facing the Praça Serzedelo Correira, this small Othon hotel bears the name of Brazil's most beloved poet. Public plazas are rare in Copacabana, making this small park a welcome patch of green along this street of shops, apartments, and eating spots, one block from the water. There is a McDonald's on the next street, but it's rumored among Americans that they don't quite have the taste right on the Big Mac's special sauce. Next to the hotel, however, is a branch of La Mole, a chain of Italian restaurants with a reputation for good and inexpensive dishes. Hotel patrons also eat their buffet-style breakfast on the pleasant La Mole premises. The hotel has 76 rooms, all containing TVs and mini-bars. Other than room service, there are few other amenities provided by the hotel, where a single will cost you $46, and double occupancy is $62.

The poet Castro Alves was Brazil's answer to Lord Byron, a total romantic given to the self-destructive melancholia and bohemian lifestyle made popular by the English poet of that mid-19th-century age. His passion for life was unrepressed in his verse, though he was cut down prematurely by consumption when only 24 years old. Alves was a great lover of his country's natural beauty, a confirmed republican, and one of the most committed voices of his time against slavery.

The **Trocadero,** Avenida Atlântica 2064 (tel. 257-1834), is located at the corner of Rua Paula Freitas, two-thirds of the way down the Copacabana strip. Part of the Othon group, the Trocadero has been a favorite among traditional beach hotels for many years. While not cramped, the rooms aren't terribly spacious. Standard rooms facing the hotel's interior are actually larger than the deluxe front accommodations, which have good sea views but no balconies. All rooms have old-fashioned baths with porcelain fixtures, plus TVs, mini-bars, and writing desks.

Redecorating is overdue throughout the entire hotel, as the public spaces are beginning to look a bit shabby. Yet one senses that the clientele might prefer this old-slipper ambience over the sometimes polyester slickness of more modern second-class hotels. Next to the lobby entrance is a sidewalk café, behind a partition of shrubs, with access to an inside bar through a separate door. The Moenda restaurant is one of the few eateries left in Copacabana where real Brazilian food is served, including the funky moqueca fish stews of Bahia. Standards of service remain high at the Trocadero, which is similar to the Miramar in its personalized touch. Some of the hotel's 120 rooms—depending on location—can still be a bargain, given the beachfront location, as singles start at $60, and doubles, at $66.

The **Copacabana Hotel Residência,** Rua Barata Ribeiro 370 (tel. 256-2610). Travelers of the American highways have long been familiar with motels offering "efficiency" accommodations, which always include a refrigerator and stove, along with some pots, plates, and eating utensils. The idea was that you could stop in an area of interest for several days and—especially when traveling with children—you could economize on food by preparing your own meals.

The term for such units in Brazil is "apart-hotel," generally two-room suites with bath and kitchenette. This one, the Copacabana Hotel Residência, is well located in a nice side-street quarter, and is far more modern than the old roadside cabins reminiscent of family travel in the U.S. A sitting room with attached kitchenette and a separate bedroom add spacious comfort to normal single-room hotel accommodations. There is even a separate laundry sink for washing out clothes and bathing suits. In addition to parking facilities, the hotel has a small pool, an exercise room, and a sauna. The price, at $40 per night, could make the hotel's location, three blocks from the beach, an acceptable sacrifice.

The **Riviera,** Avenida Atlântica 4122 (tel. 247-6060), is half a block from the Rio Palace and its large neighboring arcade of chic boutiques, and the Cassino Atlântico. The nicest rooms in the Riviera face the beach. The excellent location at this tranquil end of the strand compensates somewhat for the generally worn appearance of the lobby and other public spaces, and the sparseness of the room furnishings. The hotel is frankly overdue for a full renovation. On the other hand the guest rooms—all with combination baths, TVs, and mini-bars—are very moderately priced, starting at $43 for a single, and ranging from $52 to $61 for a double. The hotel also has room service, a restaurant, and a sidewalk bar.

The small **Praia Lido,** Avenida Nossa Senhora de Copacabana 202 (tel. 541-1347), near the Rua Duvivier cross street, is another option for the budget-minded, or to be kept in mind as an alternative for beach-area lodgings when the better hotels are booked. The lobby to the 51-room hotel is found up a flight of stairs. Here, an adequately furnished double room with basic amenities like bath, TV, mini-bar, and air conditioning can be had for $44 a night. A small suite, with private sauna, is priced at a daily rate of $50.

The **Rishon,** Rua Francisco Sá 17 (tel. 247-6044), is located on a side street very close to Copacabana beach. This small hotel has large and comfortable rooms, with TV and mini-bar service. On the roof is a small dip pool and an ample sundeck. The hotel also provides room service, and houses a restaurant/bar as well, where food prices are considerably less than those charged at beachfront hotels only half a block away. Singles range from $40 to $45, and doubles run $45 to $50.

THE BUDGET RANGE: The budget-range hotels in Copacabana tend to be simple backstreet affairs with a limited number of rooms, quite happy to maintain their status of informality in the shadow of the neighborhood's more elegant establishments. Always clean, they are the best bet for that small minority of North American travelers who come to Rio each year without pre-packaged accommodations. You pay less at these hotels, and while you will not experience the inner life of a resort with its many luxuries, large and small, you will likely get a step or two closer to the average Brazilian reality.

The **Martinique,** Rua Sá Ferreira 30 (tel. 521-4552), half a block from Copacabana beach, is every bit as comfortable as many more highly rated hotels, at half the price. The hotel is also located in the same desirable environs as the Rio Palace and the Miramar hotels, accessible by foot to both Ipanema and Copacabana. The beds are smaller than those I usually like in hotels and tend to prefer in my own home. For a large person, a small bed can be a big factor in choosing a hotel room where he expects to spend seven or eight nights. The hotel has a nice little lobby and a bar. Room service is also provided. A double room costs $37 per night.

The **Excelsior,** Avenida Atlântica 1800 (tel. 256-1950), is a large beachfront hotel on the same block as the Copacabana Palace. Once undoubtedly a fashionable hotel, this Horsa group property is well broken in, but not without its charms. You enter from a side street into a spacious lobby where on one end a pleasant bar overlooks the ocean. A stairway leads to the mezzanine restaurant, also with a wrap-around view of the beach scene, where a business buffet lunch is served daily.

The location and size of the 184-room Excelsior make the hotel popular for groups in the budget range. Rooms are larger than those in hotels constructed in more recent years. Furnishings are plain, but comfortable, and decorative prints brighten the walls. Tiled baths have large porcelain tubs. The good service and discount rates compensate for the somewhat-dreary wood-paneled corridors. Staying at the Excelsior costs $35 to $40 for a single and $45 to $60 for a double.

The **Hotel Diplomat** is on the Praça Demétrio Ribeiro at No. 103 (tel. 295-8282), set in from Avenida Princesa Isabel, across the street from the Suppertopf Restaurant. This is another very informal, small hotel with a good location for anyone who wants to be at the beach, but who needs quick access to downtown. Like other hotels in this area, it is but a short cab ride to the Metro stop in Botafogo. Plain and simple, with no frills, the rooms nevertheless do have TVs and mini-bars. Singles are $35 and doubles run $45 to $50.

The **Biarritz**, Rua Aires Saldanha 54 (tel. 255-6552), is on a narrow avenue that runs for around ten blocks between and parallel to Avenida Atlântica and Nossa Senhora de Copacabana. The Biarritz sits a short block from the beach, right behind the Othon Palace. The marble entrance and stately awning suggest more elegance than you will find inside. Beware also of the small beds. Otherwise, there are 29 modest but acceptable rooms, and a public TV salon. Room service is also provided. The price for a double room is $38.

The **Copa Linda**, Avenida Nossa Senhora de Copacabana 1144 (tel. 225-0938), is located in a building near the corner of the cross street Rua Bolívar on this busy commercial avenue. The reception desk is located on the building's second floor, up an unassuming flight of stairs. The 21 rooms are very small, very kitsch, very cheap—$18 for a double—and close to the beach.

The **Angrense**, Travessa Angrense 25 (tel. 255-3875), is located at the far end of a dead-end lane which is entered from Avenida Nossa Senhora de Copacabana about 100 feet in from Rua Santa Clara. This stripped-down boarding house is a suitable choice for unbearded youths and superanuated bohemians alike. Many of the 36 rooms have neither baths nor air conditioning, but cost less than $20 per night.

Grande Hotel Canada, Avenida Nossa Senhora de Copacabana 687 (tel. 257-1864), also near the busy Rua Santa Clara intersection, is a 72-room two-star hotel. The rooms have been recently redecorated, and while agreeably nondescript, can be had for as little as $17 a night for a single and $20 for a double. Some of the better rooms are more expensive, up to $45 for a double. The hotel also has an American bar (a euphemism for a smallish alcove equipped with a traditional bar and stools). There is also a public TV room and room service.

Among Rio's two-star beach hotels, the **Toledo**, Rua Domingos Ferreira 71 (tel. 257-1990), is a cut above the average. This quiet street is half a block from Avenida Atlântica, which it parallels. In all there are 54 accommodations, some of which are unusually large. Single rooms are $35 and doubles are $39, a very good value considering the space and comfort. The hotel has a coffeeshop and bar.

The **Apa**, Rua República de Perú 305 (tel. 255-8112). Another choice in a quiet corner of the neighborhood, the strangely named Apa is a three-star hotel with two-star rates. And while the rooms are furnished in early Salvation Army, the beds are full-sized twins, a rare offering for a hotel in the bargain range. There are 54 relatively large rooms, all of which have TVs and mini-bars, priced from $24 for a single to $35 for a double. Services include parking, a coffeeshop, and round-the-clock room service. The Apa is about a five-minute walk from the Trocadero section of the beach.

3. IPANEMA AND LEBLON

Rounding the Apoador Point and at a right angle to Copacabana are the even-longer ocean beaches of Ipanema and Leblon. At the point itself is the sizable spit of sand actually called Apoador Beach, long a favorite of surfers. Ipanema then stretches on until the overflow canal of a nearby lagoon makes a natural separation between it and the continuing beach, from here designated Leblon until the abrupt end of the cove at the base of two mountain peaks called Os Dois Irmãos, (The Two Brothers).

Unlike Copacabana, which is bounded on three sides by mountains, Ipanema and Leblon occupy an isthmus between the ocean and the immense inland lagoon called the Lagoa Rodrigo de Freitas, but known to all as simply Lagoa. Both neighborhoods are more modern than Copacabana, having really come into their own over the past 30 years. With some exceptions (notably the beachfront hotels) the buildings along this strip of beach tend to be no more than five stories high, in accordance with long-standing zoning regulations. Many of these buildings, furthermore, only contain as many apartments as there are floors, giving some idea of the high social status of their inhabitants. Ipanema and Leblon are the neighborhoods of Rio's elite, with its trendiest boutiques, most *in* restaurants, and hottest discothèques.

The chart-busting pop song "The Girl from Ipanema," by the late poet Vinícius de Morais and the very much alive musician Antônio Carlos Jobim, probably did as much to promote tourism in these neighborhoods as any other single factor. And still there are relatively few hotels in Ipanema and fewer still in Leblon, both of which retain their primary characteristic as residential neighborhoods. They attract few tourists and have only a thin veneer of tourist trappings.

In Ipanema, the avenues of principal interest are the oceanfront Avenida Vieira Souto, which turns into Avenida Delfim Moreira on the Leblon end of the beach. Ipanema's main shopping thoroughfare is Avenida Visconde de Pirajá, two blocks from the beach, along which are located some of the most fashionable boutiques, gemstone emporiums, and shoestores in the city. Avenida Ataúlfo de Paiva is the main commercial street in Leblon, lined with the more day-to-day kinds of shops and services. Running along the Ipanema side of the overflow canal and a narrow green space called Alah's Garden (Jardim de Alah) is Avenida Epitácio Pessoa, which then winds around the right bank of the Lagoa. On the Leblon side of this boundary between the neighborhoods is Avenida Borges de Madeiros, encircling for its part the Lagoa's opposite shore.

A DELUXE HOTEL: The **Caesar Park,** Avenida Vieira Souto 460 (tel. 287-3122), is not only the best hotel along fashionable Ipanema beach, but one of the top deluxe establishments in the entire city. Service at the Caesar Park combines the cool efficiency one associates with European hotels with the easygoing informality so typical of Brazilians. Seen from the outside, the concrete, rectilinear structure is not impressive as an architectural object. But inside, attention to detail is the Caesar Park trademark. Everywhere, from the well-polished wood-paneled elevators to the walls in all public areas, are touches of decorative finish —prints, watercolors, posters—contemporary pieces that are both pretty and beguiling to the eye.

This pampering carries over to the accommodations, which are light, spacious, filled with well-stuffed furniture, and finished with the best of paints and fabrics in subtle tones reminiscent of an autumn marshland. The elegant baths are equipped with such extras as terrycloth bathrobes, scales, hairdryers, bathing lotions, and even aftershave for men. Such thoughtful items—which are provided only in Rio's finest hotels—add an element of home comfort which goes a long way toward eliminating some of the inevitable starkness of hotel life. Accommodations also include large-screen color TVs with satellite and closed-circuit video channels, mini-bars, and individual air-temperature controls.

The public spaces are even more attractive than the rooms. A rooftop pool, where breakfast is served daily, offers the best view of any hotel in Rio, a 360°

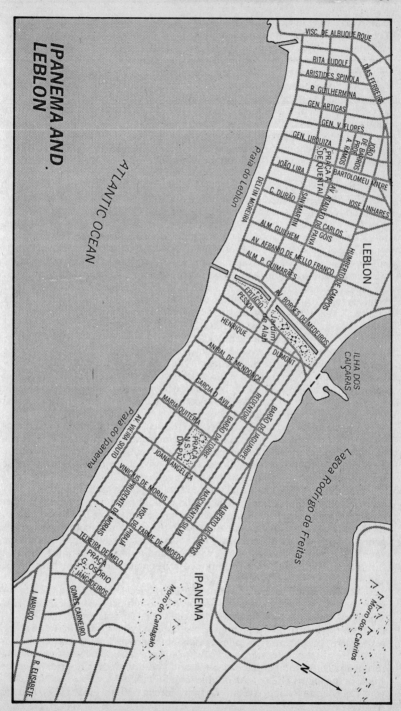

panorama taking in Corcovado and the Lagoa basin, the beaches of Ipanema and Leblon, and the Mist-shrouded Dois Irmãos and Pedra da Gávea (Lookout Rock) mountains. This latter peak is a launching pad for hang gliders, which on occasion land on the sand near the hotel, a jolting experience if you don't see the flyer's approach and the two of you are suddenly sharing the same beach towel.

One floor below the rooftop terrace is the justly respected Petronius restaurant, specializing in fine seafood dishes. Along the corridor leading to Petronius are a series of giant tanks displaying tropical fish and crustaceans gathered from local waters. The Mariko Sushi bar is also located on this floor. If your group or package offers the 221-room Caesar Park as an option, pay the premium and grab it. It will still be cheaper than paying the normal rates, which range from $160 to $180 for singles and $180 to $200 for doubles.

UPPER-BRACKET HOTELS: The **Sol Ipanema,** Avenida Vieira Souto 320 (tel. 227-0060), is located near the cross street Vinícius de Morais, named for the poet and lyricist who wrote "The Girl from Ipanema." The Garota de Ipanema pub and café, which the poet frequented, is a popular daytime hangout, one block from the hotel. Rio's most fashionable shops are also nearby.

The Sol Ipanema has 90 rooms on 15 floors, which are decorated in Brazilian earth tones with a generous use of rosewood throughout. Bahian tapestries add texture and folkloric themes to the general ambience. All rooms have TVs, air conditioning, and well-stocked mini-bars. As for the small dip pool and sundeck found on the roof, a bellhop was heard to comment that "No one comes up here." When asked why, he simply pointed to the gorgeous Ipanema beach down below and right across the street. Other features include a restaurant and bar, as well as parking facilities. Rates are $90 for a single and $100 for a double.

The **Praia Ipanema,** Avenida Vieira Souto 706 (tel. 239-9932), is under the same management as the Sol Ipanema. The 105 rooms are more slickly decorated than at the companion hotel, with bold designer colors for walls and fabrics. Most rooms have token balconies which are too small for comfortable sitting. But they do add to the room's ocean view, and allow the option of natural ventilation by leaving open the balcony door.

A dip pool on the roof is suitable for children, while a sundeck and bar provide a pleasant outdoor environment for evening cocktails. The La Mouette restaurant occupies the hotel's mezzanine with its own ground-level view of the local beach surroundings. Additional features are a lobby bar and and in-house hairdressing salon. Single rooms cost $85 nightly, and doubles run $105.

The **Everest Rio,** Rua Prudente de Morais 1117 (tel. 287-8282), is a 169-room hotel found on a tree-lined avenue one block from the water, directly behind the Caesar Park. While given a deluxe rating by the Brazilian tourist board, the Everest does not invite comparison with the city's finest hotels. The hotel's general appearance is streamlined and modern, but not luxurious. Rooms are very light, sporting floor-to-ceiling windows and functional Scandinavian-style furnishings. All rooms are air-conditioned and contain combination baths, TVs, and mini-bars.

The Everest offers special rates to business travelers who are in the city for more or less prolonged stays, and so there are often many longtime residents among the hotel's guests. The hotel does offer many first-class amenities, including a rooftop terrace 23 stories high with a stunning view from Corcovado to the sea. Other special features include a reasonably priced restaurant serving international fare, three bars located variously throughout the hotel, executive meeting rooms and convention facilities, a sauna, and a beauty parlor. The price range for single occupancy is $82 to $90; doubles cost $89 to $99.

The **Marina Palace,** Avenida Delfim Moreira 630 (tel. 259-5212), like the

Everest, ought to rate four rather than five stars, falling short of the luxury standards set by the Rio Palace, the Caesar Park, and two or three of Rio's other hotels. It is, however, the best hotel on the Leblon end of the beach. Leblon is even more residential than Ipanema, but among its numerous avenues and side streets are scattered many attractions in the form of shops, restaurants, clubs, and bars.

The Marina Palace also seems strikingly close to the mountain peaks of Gávea as they are seen from the rooftop pool area, which is spread with lounging chairs for sunbathing and also has a bar. The second-floor Bistro da Praia is quietly gaining in reputation among locals as a fine eating spot. The ocean view from the window seats is especially dramatic. The hotel's 163 bedrooms are adequate in every way, but lack the sparkle of other five-star hotels, and the large windows in the rooms are inexplicably sealed. Television sets with satellite channels, mini-bars, and air conditioning are standard in all units, as are full tile baths. Other hotel services include meeting and banquet facilities, indoor parking, a coffeeshop, and a sauna. Rates are $128 for singles, $142 for doubles.

The **Marina Rio,** Avenida Delfim Moreira 696 (tel. 239-8844), is a smaller and less expensive version of the Marina Palace, and is located a block farther down the beach. Both hotels are under the same management, and guests at the Marina Rio may, for no extra charge, use all the facilities of its larger companion hotel. The accommodations of the Marina Rio are functional and roomy, also with sealed windows and without balconies. All 70 rooms, of course, are air-conditioned, contain suitable baths, and have TVs and mini-bars. Hotel services are limited to a second-floor restaurant and piano bar. Single rooms cost $90 nightly, and doubles run $100.

MEDIUM-PRICED HOTELS: The **Apoador Inn,** Rua Francisco Otaviano 177 (tel. 247-6090), is one of only two hotels in Rio where access to the beach does not involve crossing a heavily trafficked avenue. Located on a promenade overlooking Apoador beach, this hotel of only 50 rooms has become a particular favorite among repeat visitors to Rio. The 15 oceanfronting rooms are especially desirable accommodations.

While by no means fancy—many rooms in fact provide only cot-sized beds—there is a cozy familiarity about this hotel that justifies use of the term "inn" in its name. Many guests hang out, day and night, at the small coffeeshop restaurant on the premises, with its unusually closeup view of the beach and the sea. The Apoador offers special discounts to "firms, diplomats, and airline personnel." Advance reservations are an absolute necessity for ocean-view rooms, which cost $57 for doubles. Other rooms are priced at $35 per double occupancy.

The **Atlantis Copacabana,** Rua Bulhões de Cavalho 61 (tel. 521-1142), its name notwithstanding, is located closer to Ipanema than to Copacabana. The Atlantis is a brand-new hotel in a very attractive building, located on a quiet street. Given a three-star rating, the hotel is really closer to a first-class establishment, considering its general appearance and many facilities. The room dimensions are average, but well appointed with all the comforts. There is a rooftop sundeck with pool, and two bars, one an appealing spot off the lobby, and another a piano bar called the Gaivota (Seagull), where light meals are also served. In all, the hotel has 87 rooms and suites. Singles are priced between $43 and $50 while doubles go for $45 to $56.

Rio-Ipanema Hotel Residência, Rua Visconde de Pirajá 66 (tel. 267-4015), is an apart-hotel option for Ipanema, which faces the neighborhood's principal square, the Praça General Osório. On these spacious grounds the Hippie Fair (or Feirarte, as it is officially called) is mounted every Sunday. The daily street life around the plaza is one of Rio's most colorful scenes. In addition to many stands of familiar and unfamiliar fruits and vegetables, there are multitudes of sidewalk vendors selling everything from household knick-knacks to items of personal toiletry. Among the most interesting displays are the strange assortment of roots, barks, and dried plants spread on wide patches of the sidewalk, and used for flavoring foods, and for a host of medicinal teas and home remedies.

The ultramodern residence hotel overlooking this appealing hurly-burly scene offers two-room apartments with large verandas that front on the plaza for $65 per night double occupancy, or two-bedroom units at $75, with an additional 35% for one extra person.

THE BUDGET RANGE: The **Ipanema Inn,** Rua Maria Quitéria 27 (tel. 287-6092). Also around the corner from the Caesar Park is this 56-room hotel, owned by the same group as the Apoador Inn several blocks away. The Ipanema Inn's front rooms offer an oblique view of the seas. Given its side-street location, the higher the floor, the better the view. Like the Apoador, the rooms are simple in the tradition of a real beach hotel. With singles beginning at $35 a night and doubles at $38, the hotel is definitely a reasonable option for anyone who is beach- and budget-minded at the same time. Television sets in the rooms are optional, but all rooms do have mini-bars, telephones, and private baths. There are also a small bar and a souvenir shop in the hotel. The souvenirs include fossil fish amulets, lacquered piranhas, and Brazilian tarot cards.

The **Vermont,** Rua Visconde de Pirajá 254 (tel. 247-6100), is several doors in from the corner of Rua Vinícius de Morais. This 54-room hotel is in the heart of Ipanema's most fashionable shopping area, and two blocks from the beach. The atmosphere is spartan, but all the basics are there, including bathrooms, TV, and mini-bar. The hotel also has a bar and offers room service. Singles are priced between $27 and $29; doubles run $30 to $33.

The **Carlton,** Rua João Lira 68 (tel. 259-1932), is found on a tree-lined backstreet in Leblon. The atmosphere in Leblon is very sedate, and this mood is reflected in the Carlton, a beacon of shabby gentility in a sea of affluence. The 50 accommodations are roomy and comfortable. All are air-conditioned, and contain combination baths, TVs, and mini-bars. The hotel also has a coffeeshop restaurant and a bar. Rates begin at $35 for a single and $39 for a double.

4. VIDIGAL AND SÃO CONRADO

These two areas are further stretches of Rio's Atlantic ocean beachfront. Vidigal was once a shantytown that has been transformed into a chic cliffside and canyon neighborhood of the well-to-do. São Conrado in the early '60s was still a remote, even primitive beach. Today high-rises and condominiums dominate the skyline, but the beach is still among the most popular in the city.

DELUXE HOTELS: The **Rio Sheraton,** Avenida Niemeyer 121 (tel. 274-1122), is Rio's only genuine resort hotel, set on an outcropping of rocks behind a small, private beach in Vidigal. This is the city's other hotel where you can take a dip in the ocean without crossing a street. A sprawling complex, the hotel's public areas stretch from roadside to shoreline six stories down.

There are advantages and disadvantages involved in staying at the Sheraton. Unlike the other beach neighborhoods already described, there is no street life here among the hills and cliffs of Vidigal. You are dependent on transportation to get from here to anywhere else in the city. And transportation is of the usual varieties, with the usual associated problems: unsafe buses, hustling cab drivers, hassle-free but overpriced hotel cars. The advantages are that once you are at the Sheraton, you don't necessarily have to go anywhere else—a boon to those travelers who crave the womb-like atmosphere of a truly self-contained resort.

Millions were spent in recent years to repair what had been a reputation for shoddiness. The hotel now sparkles, and the rooms are warm and well decorated. The lobby is of cathedral proportions, but rectilinear and modern, sheathed in brown tinted glass. Full of movement, the lobby seems like a busy crossroads, with people coming to and from the arcade of shops, the One Twenty-One bar, or one of the service desks. Three flood-lit tennis courts and an equal number of freshwater pools are distributed on several levels of the spacious grounds. Also for the fitness-minded are a health club and sauna. In all, there are seven restaurants and bars within the Sheraton complex, including Valentino's, where fine Italian cuisine is served. The Casa da Cachaça is a bar specializing in cocktails made with Brazil's native sugarcane brandy, cachaça.

The Sheraton can boast 617 rooms, which are trimmed out in fine hardwood and appointed with attractive rugs and wall hangings. The use of brass lamps and huge TVs recessed in bookshelves adds to the comfortable den-like atmosphere. All rooms have tile combination baths and balconies with dramatic ocean views. The units in the five-story wings are much larger than those in the 26-floor main tower. Rates range from $125 to $160 for single rooms, and $140 to $200 for doubles.

The **Inter Continental,** Avenida Prefeito Mendes de Morais 222 (tel. 322-2200). This just might be Rio's most luxurious hotel, but it suffers from some of the same disadvantages as the Sheraton. The Inter (as it is called) occupies a place in the moonscape of condominiums that is São Conrado. The spirit of orderly architectural harmony that guided the growth of Copacabana and Ipanema seemed to have vanished as development spread along the shore to São Conrado and Barra da Tijuca. Both beaches lack in their surroundings any of the intimate scale that we associate with neighborhoods. The buildings glitter, but the streets are cold. The background, of course, is the unceasing natural beauty of the Rio mountains and seascapes.

The inner environment is everything in high-rise heaven, and the Inter does not disappoint. The lobby is elegant, lined with stylish shops. But the real hotel life centers around a geometrical arrangement of pools, lounging chairs, and outside eating areas. This is the most insulated and sensuous poolside in Rio. On those many days when weather permits, the skies over the Inter are filled with the soaring antics of hang-glider enthusiasts, who launch themselves from Lookout Rock, cheek-by-jowl with the hotel. Across the road is the lovely São Conrado beach, somewhat abandoned on weekdays, and destitute of such services as roadside food stands and vendors, except on the weekends when it's a very popular and animated spot.

Accommodations in the hotel are among the best in Rio: spacious, with comfortable sitting areas, and balconies that let you get closer to the natural surroundings. The décor is cool and stylish, with well-designed and original Brazilian furnishings, and the walls are covered with textured paper. The baths are in stone and marble, fully equipped with robes and lotions, while the rooms all have individually controlled air conditioning, TVs, and mini-bars.

Liberally distributed throughout the hotel are numerous lounges, bars, and restaurants, including the Monseigneur, with French cooking and service, and the new Alfredo di Lello's, for fresh pasta dishes. The Papillon discothèque is a favorite nightspot for the younger set, especially on weekends. A bar off the lobby has a satellite TV and features major U.S. sporting events. The Inter is extremely popular with American travel groups, and is often included as an option in the most expensive packages. Charges for singles range from $125 to $165, and for doubles, $135 to $175.

UPPER-BRACKET HOTELS: The **Nacional,** Avenida Niemeyer 769 (tel. 322-1000), part of the Horsa group with hotels throughout Brazil, is a 26-story glass-and-steel cylindrical tower designed by Oscar Niemeyer, principal architect for the country's ultramodern capital, Brasília. The hotel has pretentions to luxury, but the poor upkeep makes it more suitable for the convention trade, which the Nacional pursues over the conventional tourist down on a package and looking for splashy digs in a five-star resort.

The most striking feature of the pie-shaped rooms is the view. Niemeyer's design democratically distributes a dramatic slice of the natural surroundings to virtually all rooms. Accommodations are brightly decorated, but not up to the quality of other five-star hotels. All units have a TV and a mini-bar, and are air-conditioned. The ground-level pool area is large and appealing. A private tunnel leads under the roadway to São Conrado beach. The hotel has several restaurants and bars, and a host of other guest and convention services. There are 520 rooms in the Nacional, and rates for singles begin at $90; for doubles, at $105.

The **São Conrado Palace,** Avenida Niemeyer 776 (tel. 322-0911), is a hotel that will begin to figure more and more in the future for medium-priced tour packages. Jokingly referred to as the Favela Palace, the allusion has nothing to do with the hotel's construction or interior comforts. It's the location that a lot of locals poke fun at, right there at the foot of Rio's largest working-class hill town. The population of the Rocinha favela is said to number some 600,000. But while Rocinha may be no place to walk around unaccompanied, it is a bona fide neighborhood, albeit mostly of the urban poor—not a den of thieves and desperados. Such elements may be there, but their presence is just as disturbing to the majority of the favela's residents as it is to outsiders.

The São Conrado Palace occupies a hollow among several clusters of lowland high-rises close to the shore. Still, guests must ride a hotel shuttle bus the short distance to the São Conrado beach. The shuttle, which also makes runs to Copacabana and Ipanema, is furnished free of charge and operates on a regular schedule. Inside, the hotel is of genuine four-star quality, brand new and generously spacious in both its rooms and its public areas. Accommodations are large and furnished with good, simple taste, similar to first-class wardrooms on cruise ships. Understated but well-chosen prints personalize the units, which are equipped with balconies, baths with lots of elbow room, TVs, mini-bars, and air conditioning. Beyond the large, somewhat institutional lobby is a ground-level pool area that rivals those at most of the best hotels. Potted trees and umbrellas give the veranda a secluded air. Other features are a bar and a restaurant. In all there are 160 rooms, beginning at $55 for a single and $80 for a double.

5. BARRA DA TIJUCA

Only 25 years ago Barra da Tijuca, an extension even farther southward of Rio's magnificent shoreline, was virgin beach, surrounded by summer homes and squatters' shacks. Since the late 1970s, however, Barra has been the site of rapid development all along the 15-km- (9-mile-) long beach. Today the strands are lined with mammoth high-rise buildings, mostly condos, built on the reclaimed swamplands that edged the sea. A long shallow lake separates the development along the shore from that inland, where in addition to more residential complexes are some of the largest supermarkets and shopping centers in South America, and quite probably the world. Surrounding the lake are the remaining marshlands, which serve as a habitat for wildlife. In the morning sky it is common to see large birds spread their wings and soar high above the protected marsh.

Barra tends to be popular with tourists from the southern cone of South America—Argentines, Urugayans, Chileans—who come to sun in Rio during their winter or to shop for bargains all year round. So common is this latter experience that a favorite Carioca nickname for their Spanish-speaking neighbors is

"Da me dos." In other words, since the merchandise is either rare or cheap by the tourist's standards, they are often overheard saying "Da me dos" ("give me two.") Barra's hotels fill to capacity on at least two occasions during the year, Carnival and the Grand Prix Formula One race held in the spring at the nearby auto track.

Perhaps the visitors from the southern cone are quite happy staying out in Barra because they are not anywhere near as hampered by the language barrier, and are thus able to get around town with a fair amount of ease. Most first-time North American visitors are not usually content to be in Barra. It's just too far from the action of Ipanema and Copacabana, a good half-hour cab ride away. Some tour packages offer very good deals, however, if you stay in Barra, where hotels are new but still relatively inexpensive. For those who already know Rio somewhat, Barra could be a very tempting base, especially if you have a car.

The **Tropical Barra,** Avenida Sernambetiba 500 (tel. 399-0660), an attractive three-star hotel, is frequently offered as a choice in the least expensive package tours to Rio. The hotel sits across the boulevard from the beach and its 86 accommodations are modern and comfortable. The Tropical Barra also offers such amenities as its own restaurant and bar. Single rooms begin at $35; doubles, at $39.

The **Rio Hotel Residência,** Avenida Sernambetiba 6250 (tel. 325-4519). Somewhat typical of the apart-hotels in Barra, the Rio Hotel Residência caters to vacationing families and corporate people on extended stays. The 270 two-bedroom apartments include a sitting room and large balcony/terrace, plus full kitchen and bath. They rent for $150 per night, not accounting for discounts that might apply. Sports facilities include two squash courts, tennis and volleyball courts, and a large swimming pool. The hotel is further distinguished by the presence of the La Petit Paris French-style restaurant, a nice addition to this somewhat suburban zone with its still-considerable allotment of wide-open spaces.

Also prominent on the lodging landscape in Barra are the many **motels.** At least in Rio, motels rent by the hour (and overnight), and are used strictly by lovers for their assignations. Some are truly outlandish in the opulence of their décor, worthy of a visit as cultural artifacts if for no other reason. The most famous of these pleasure palaces, VIP's, is located in Vidigal, set among the chic villas that are nestled in the folds of the mountains.

6. GLÓRIA AND FLAMENGO

These are two contiguous neighborhoods along the entrance to Guanabara Bay on the Rio side. The beaches at the mouth of the bay are polluted and no longer suitable for swimming, a singular example of humans' relentless fouling of their own nests. The island-filled bay and its environs are still beautiful to look at and definitely worth a day trip on one of the many excursion boats. But the environment of the bay's marine life has been all but obliterated by the dumping of human and industrial waste.

Both Glória and Flamengo are close in to the city, and serviced by subway. Some 30 years ago these were still fashionable neighborhoods. Hollywood stars and heads of state all stayed at the Hotel Glória, and Flamengo, with its enormous apartments, was the residential preference among many of the city's most affluent citizens. Fickle fashion has moved the center of action farther down the beach, but both neighborhoods are bearing up well. In fact the grand old apartments are once more in great demand because of the shortage of good housing in the city's highly speculative real estate market.

As mentioned elsewhere, there are numerous hotels of the simplest variety throughout the backstreets of Flamengo. If you're on the lookout for rock-bottom prices, it's preferable to stay in this section than downtown, because you will be in a residential area, as opposed to in the city, which tends to empty after business hours.

The **Glória,** Praia do Russel 632 (tel. 287-8282), with its 700 rooms, is Brazil's largest hotel, and is very popular with the tour operators who package the least-expensive trips to Rio. In the past the Hotel Glória was on a par with the Copacabana Palace, attracting a jet-set clientele from all over the world. Today, with most tourists to the city wanting beachfront accommodations, the Glória has accepted its role as a mass-market alternative for those who want the scale of a full-size hotel and all its services, but at discount prices.

Set close to the sidewalk, the massive white stone building in the grand style overlooks—approximately a quarter of a mile across a wide park—a section of Flamengo beach and the harbor. From here the historic downtown square, Praça XV, is about a 20-minute walk, though this is not recommended. The most direct route hugs the main thoroughfare, and there are no sidewalks in places. Subway access is rapid and direct, on the other hand. Rooms at the Glória are comfortable, but with no pretensions to luxury. The hotel's buildings curve around small but well-landscaped grounds, including a rock garden and an attractive pool area with surrounding patio. A second pool has been added, and the hotel's two restaurants have recently been reorganized and redecorated. There are several bar environments, a breakfast room, and a sauna, among other facilities. Rates range from $76 to $108 for a single, and $92 to $138 for a double, which are discounted considerably for group travelers.

The **Novo Mundo,** Praia do Flamengo 20 (tel. 225-7366). This 40-year-old hotel, also facing Flamengo beach, has 200 air-conditioned rooms that are clean and well tended, all with baths, TVs, and mini-bars. The hotel has a restaurant, parking facilities, a barbershop, and an American bar. Singles start at $15, and doubles begin at $20.

CHAPTER IV

RIO'S RESTAURANTS

□ □ □

Compared with the rest of Brazil, Rio is one of the country's most expensive cities. Yet restaurant food in the *Cidade Maravilhosa* is still a bargain for most North American visitors. Eating *bom e barato* (well and cheap) is, after all, a national Brazilian pastime that few visiting travelers will disdain. Most entrees in the vast majority of restaurants—the exception is almost inevitably a fancy lobster or shrimp dish—seldom go higher than $10, and many a good deal less. A typical meal at a good restaurant, including domestic beer or wine, dessert, and service, will rarely exceed $20. The service charge of 10% is always included with the bill. You can also leave a few small bills on the table to sweeten the tip, but this is completely discretionary.

Fancy Food, Local Drinks. Rio also has its share of fancy and expensive restaurants. These tend to offer French-style cooking and service, and to be located in the best hotels. But even if your taste runs to gourmet meals, or you just want to splurge, the bill will seem modest when compared with a comparable eatery in other major world cities. The trick to dining economically in Brazil, even in the chic-est places, is to stay away from imported beverages, which can cost you two to three times more than you're used to paying at even the most expensive bars and restaurants back home. The most commonly accepted credit cards at better restaurants are American Express, VISA, and Diners Club.

Skip Lunch. With the generous breakfasts included in the price of your room at virtually all the hotels mentioned in this guide, many travelers will feel the need for only a light snack at lunchtime. Rio abounds in small cafés, fast-food emporia (both of the home-grown and multinational variety), juice bars, and traditional lunch counters. You can eat very well in Brazil at these simple establishments. Many of these snackbars will be described in more detail at the end of this section.

Surf and Turf. Brazilians are big meat and seafood eaters, as the country and coastal waters are supplied with an abundance of both commodities. Most restaurants I will mention offer extensive meat and seafood menus. "Extensive" is perhaps too weak a word to describe menus that not infrequently offer a choice of 30 to 50 items. Even specialty restaurants like churrascarias outdo themselves in the variety of their dishes. The phrase "all you can eat" takes on new meaning in a churrascaria that serves its food *rodízio* style. Rodízio means that the various cuts of meat are served on skewers in an endless round right at your table. As for fish, fin and shell varieties alike, seafood lovers will find in the Brazilian selection of *frutos do mar* an unprecedented cornucopia of delights. Even where seafood is not featured, at least several varieties of fish filet and a number of shrimp dishes will most likely be included on the menu. Brazilians retain the European dining option of having both fish and meat courses in a single meal. The steaming fish stews, served in general only at seafood restaurants, are firmly in the tradition of the brimming and succulent mariscadas found throughout Spain and Portugal. As for fin fish, each region can boast a fresh catch of several species that are the favorite of local palates, prepared in a variety of ways, familiar and unique. The impression that Brazil is a moveable feast is quite intended. A great many satisfactory meals have led to this author's unmitigated praise for Brazilian cooks and the solid, tasty, and very digestible meals they consistently produce.

1. COPACABANA AND LEME

There are restaurants of every category densely packed inside the borders of this great district. Dress is never formal, even where the service is ceremonial. Neither jacket nor tie is required for men dining in Rio, except in one or two business restaurants downtown. The Copacabana area is particularly informal, as people constantly drop into the many restaurants on the way to or from the beach.

THE UPPER BRACKET: The **Le Pre Catalán,** Avenida Atlântica 4240 (tel. 521-3232), is a fine French restaurant serving nouvelle cusine for lunch and dinner. Though it's ensconced discreetly on the premises of the Rio Palace Hotel, you need not enter the hotel to get to the restaurant, which is serviced by a separate elevator right before the main entrance to the lobby. Elegant décor, imaginative cuisine, and service with a flourish combine to maintain the restaurant's reputation as one of Rio's best. Supervision of the fare is in the hands of a highly regarded French chef, who maintains very consistent standards of quality in the preparation of many complex and subtle dishes.

Two people can dine and fully indulge their culinary passions, eating several courses, drinking both cocktails and wine, and still escape for only slightly more than $100 between them. One may also dine quite satisfactorily for less, or try the fixed-price lunch menu, a bargain at around $12, including dessert but not beverage. The cushioned banquettes and large tables encourage an abundant meal, consumed at a civilized pace. Part of the enjoyment involves allowing ample time to take in the surrounding *mise en scène* among animated fellow diners and to observe the staff in its perpetual state of formal attentiveness. Periodically, at the signal from a captain, in unison waiters lift the silver covers from the principal dishes when they arrive at a given table.

You may order from a fixed-price dinner menu, which includes appetizer, entree, and dessert, for around $25, or choose from a wide selection of à la carte suggestions. For a first course, you might have duck or rabbit, each in its own delicate sauce, followed by an even more elaborate and succulent entree of lobster, large shrimp, or a prime cut of lamb or beef. A soufflé or a plate of mixed pastries and a strong cup of aromatic Brazilian coffee will round out the meal— in all, a memorable culinary experience. Reservations are necessary, especially if you want to eat after 10:30 p.m., which is the normal hour for Brazilians to dine. Lunch served from noon to 3 p.m., and dinner is after 7:30 p.m.

Le Saint Honoré, Avenida Atlântica 1020 (tel. 275-9922), is located at the opposite end of Copacabana beach in the equally swank Hotel Meridien. In contrast to Le Pre Catalán, which is draped and mirrored like a French salon, and seemingly sheltered from the outside world, Le Saint Honoré is wrapped in windows and occupies the top floor of its hotel, 37 floors high. By day the restaurant is bathed in natural light, and at night the grand panorama of curvaceous Copacabana beach and its surrounding mountains is projected on the glass against a starlit sky and a shimmering sea.

Delicate seafood dishes are a specialty of the St. Honoré's kitchen. But whatever you sample in this fine restaurant—from the delectible hors d' oeuvres served before the meal to something suitably rich from the dessert tray—you will be satisfied with both the quality and the value. Entrees begin at $15. Lunch is also served at the St. Honoré, and at $12 for selections from the set menu, you can't go wrong.

Ouro Verde, Avenida Atlântica 1456 (tel. 542-1887). Spoken of in Rio with a praise bordering on reverence, the Ouro Verde has no trouble living up to its exhalted reputation as one of Rio's finest traditional French restaurants. Climb the stairs from the lobby of the Ouro Verde Hotel to the mezzanine. The relatively small room displays elegantly set tables, each with silver candlestick, silver salt shaker, and pewter pepper mill to complement the starched-linen covers and the fine settings of crystal and china. A select few of these tables line the front wall beside large windows that admit welcome ocean breezes along with a wide view of the beach.

The food and impeccably professional service soon direct your attention away from the seating arrangements and the view. Daily at lunch there is a cold buffet with a choice of some dozen platters, including salad niçoise, various pâtés, smoked meats and cold cuts, vegetables, and greens. The price: $8. Typical specialties served at both lunch and dinner are shrimp sautéed in whisky ($12), shredded veal in cream sauce with hash browns ($5.50), and rolled beefsteak, filled with diced, sautéed onions and sweet pickle, smothered in a deep brown gravy ($7.50). For dessert there is diplomatic pudding—a concoction of bread, raisins, and liquor. Open daily from noon to midnight.

For over 30 years **Le Bec Fin,** Avenida Nossa Senhora de Copacabana 178 (tel. 542-4097), has been one of Rio's shining culinary institutions. While not cramped, seating is intimate, in subdued and comfortable surroundings. As in all good French restaurants, emphasis is on the food. Entrees range from $10 to $25, lobster and duck being particular specialties. Open daily for dinner only, from 8 p.m. to 2 a.m.

MEDIUM-PRICED RESTAURANTS: The price range for meals in this category is fairly broad, starting as low as $6 for simple fish dishes and going no higher than $20 for the most expensive plates.

Overlooking the street through gauzy curtains and narrow blinds at ground level in the Copacabana Palace is an unheralded but excellent steakhouse, the **Bife de Ouro,** Avenida Atlântica 1702 (tel. 255-7070). There are curved banquettes and large potted plants to screen the views from table to table. On the walls are the large canvases of artist Jorge Guinle Filho, explosions of powerful colors that are true to their tropical inspiration.

This unusually pleasant interior does not overshadow the good food, however, which is very reasonably priced. Appetizers, including creamed soups and smoked fish, are between $2 and $6; fish dishes range from $8 to $15; and no beef or steak dish is more than $10. Figs flambé over ice cream and coffee brewed at your table add the final touches to an epicurean meal. The service at the Bife de Ouro is just right, attentive but not solicitous. The lunch and dinner menus are the same. Open for lunch from noon to 4 p.m. and for dinner from 7 p.m. to midnight. The other restaurant at the Copacabana Palace is the Pergula, a more informal day-room environment for lunch and light meals, overlooking both the street and the hotel's magnificent pool area.

Well into Leme is **Mariu's,** Avenida Atlântica 290 (tel. 542-2392), the only churrascaria along this oceanside avenue. The restaurant occupies the first two floors of a modern building, and overlooks the beach through a façade of plate glass. Inside, Mariu's serves its barbecued fare round robin or *rodízio* style, the cuts including, sirloin, lamb, loin of pork, sausages, and smoked ham. You can eat as much as you want, but leave some room for the many side dishes of salads, french fries, farofa, cold asparagus, and hearts of palm. Its beachfront location makes Mariu's a more expensive choice than the average churrascaria, but for $15 a person, depending on your bar bill, meat eaters can eat and drink divinely. Open daily from 11 a.m. to 2 a.m.

Shirley's, at Rua Gustavo Sampaio 610 (tel. 275-1398), is the epitome of a neighborhood restaurant. Tucked into the space of a small storefront, the restaurant only has a dozen tables. And the perpetual line for seating underscores the popularity of this primarily Spanish-style seafood establishment. A typical fish plate costs between $4 and $5, while lobster dishes run about $13. Open daily from noon to 1 a.m. No credit cards.

Suppertopf, Avenida Princesa Isabel 350 (tel. 275-1896), is a German restaurant set back in an arcade not far from the tunnel entrance that leads from Copacabana to downtown Rio. The attractive rathskeller atmosphere is conducive to what one does in a typical German beer garden: drink suds and eat dishes like schnitzel and sauerkraut, the food in this case being largely of Bavarian origin. Entrees cost between $5 and $15. Open from noon to 3 a.m. No credit cards.

The **Café de la Paix,** Avenida Atlântica 1020 (tel. 275-9922), is the Meridien Hotel's everyday restaurant, located at street level where the hotel's guests eat their buffet-style breakfast. The Café de la Paix is also open for lunch and dinner, serving a variety of tasty meals from club-style sandwiches to omelets and steaks. The brasserie ambience is very pleasant, with a view of the beach, and is suitable for both casual meals and business lunches. You will pay between $4 and $15 for most menu items. Open for lunch from noon to 3 p.m., and for dinner from 7 to 11 p.m.

A Marisqueira, Rua Barata Ribeiro 232 (tel. 237-3920). Offering over two dozen fish dishes, this Portuguese-style seafood restaurant is in one of Copacabana's most genial backstreet environments. If you want something really light, try the caldo verde, that wonderful and traditional Portuguese soup made from purée of potato and filled with crispy kale and slices of country sausage. Here, $7 to $8 entrees are the rule. There is a branch of A Marisqueira in Ipanema as well, at Rua Gomes Carneiro 90 (tel. 267-9944). Open daily from 11 a.m. to 1 a.m.

The **Pomme d'Or,** Rua Sá Ferreira 22 (tel. 521-2548), not far from the venerable Miramar, is also a perennial favorite among local residents who are fond of French cooking at reasonable prices. The restaurant occupies a large, attractive space and offers a list of daily specials from $7 to $12, while the most expensive dish on the menu, lobster, is $20. Open daily from noon to 2 a.m.

Enotria, Rua Constante Ramos 115 (tel. 237-6705), is several blocks in from the beach, near the corner of Avenida Barata Ribeiro. This tiny, and newly renovated, restaurant serves some of the best Italian food in Rio. All pastas and breads are baked daily in the Enotria's own kitchen. At the gourmet shop next door, which is under the same management as the restaurant, you can buy take-out for those midnight snacks back in the hotel. The Enotria offers daily specials from a fixed-price menu as well as à la carte selections. Some dishes include tortelli di porri (cheese-filled tortellini), giamberoni ai pinoli (shrimp in cognac with pinoli nuts), and for dessert, pera a la Cardinali (chilled stewed pears, with ice cream and strawberry mousse). The prices range between $8 and $20. The Enotria is open only for dinner, and reservations are suggested. Closed Sunday.

Jardim, Rua República de Perú 225 (tel. 235-3263), another neighborhood institution, has been a reliable steakhouse for many years. If anything, the restaurant has just gotten more and more informal with age, giving less and less attention to décor. The result is refreshingly provincial and confirms the notion that the consumption of barbecued meat does not require fancy surroundings. The word *jardim* means garden, and there is a small open-air sitting area that is particularly pleasant at night. Service here is à la carte, not *rodízio.* For a selection of meats, which are cooked within view over charcoal pits, try the mixed grill. Prices, between $8 and $15, reflect both the quality of the meats as well as the status of the restaurant. Open daily from 11 a.m. to 1:30 a.m.

Atlantis, Avenida Atlântica 4240 (tel. 521-3232). Adjacent to the pool on the terrace of the Rio Palace Hotel, the Atlantis functions as an all-purpose quality restaurant for both lunch and dinner. Guests of the hotel also use the Atlantis as a breakfast room in the morning. With a wide-ranging menu, the restaurant can serve practically anything from sandwiches to full-sized meals: inside the restaurant itself, on the terrace overlooking Copacabana beach, or at poolside tables. On Saturday the Atlantis features a formal feijoada, and on Sunday, a brunch. Many meals are in the $6 to $12 range, including a fixed-price luncheon menu. Open from 6 a.m. to 1 a.m.

BUDGET-RANGE CHOICES: The **Arosa,** on Rua Santa Clara (tel. 262-7638), is a classic—a clean, well-lighted place that was once an abundant species of restaurant throughout Copacabana, but now is sadly all but extinct. So thank your stars for the Arosa. It's the kind of place you could dine at regularly, in between those weekly binges at more pricey restaurants. The interior is paneled in light-toned woodwork, and the spacing among the tables is very generous. The menu features meat, chicken, and seafood dishes, with most entrees falling in the $3 to $5 range. A delicious pan-fried filet of fish with a pilaf of white rice costs $4. Open daily from 11 a.m. till midnight.

A Polônia, Rua Hilário de Gouveia 116 (tel. 237-7378), is located between Avenida Nossa Senhora de Copacabana and Avenida Barata Ribeiro, offers pirogis, stuffed cabbage, and borscht right here in Rio. These Eastern European flavors provide a nice change of pace for dinner or weekend lunch. Open Tuesday to Friday from 6 p.m. to 1 a.m., and on Saturday and Sunday from noon to 2 a.m. Soups cost between $1.25 and $2, while entrees are priced from $4 to $5.

Boninos, on Avenida Nossa Senhora de Copacabana at Rua Bolívar (tel. 262-7638), is an old-fashioned tea room and restaurant. The backroom is a pleasant air-conditioned salon, ideal for a quick afternoon pick-me-up. In front is a lunch counter, serving ice-cream sundaes as well as coffee, tea, and diverse snacks and pastries. Most items on the menu are priced between $2 and $3, while shrimp platters run up to $10. Open from 8 a.m. to midnight.

Da boca pra dentro, Rua Almirante Gonçalves 50. This is a typical-looking hole-in-the-wall lunch counter like those found throughout the streets of Copacabana. Except in this case the quick and easy snacks are vegetarian salads and sandwiches. Very inexpensive, from 50¢ to $1.50.

Botiquins, juice bars, pizza parlors, and fast-food establishments abound among the side streets of Copacabana. A **botiquim** is usually a bar with a small counter where patrons stand for a quick nip of *pinga* (cachaça), a beer or soft drink, or a cup of cafezinho. Depending on its size, the botiquim may also have a grill for turning out a mixto sandwich (grilled cheese and ham) or some similar eat-on-the-run specialty.

The **juice bars** are less common than botiquins but never more than a few blocks from any given point in the neighborhood. Having a *vitamina* (an instant dose of vitamins) in the form of a squeezed or blended fruit drink is an old Carioca tradition—especially the morning after a binge on the town without the benefit of much sleep. A great variety of fruits is usually in season at all times of year.

Several chains of **pizzarias** (really simple Italian restaurants) are located throughout the city. A branch of Bella Blu is at Rua Siqueira Campos 107. Pizza Pino's is at Rua Constante Ramos 22, and the Bella Roma can be found at Avenida Atlântica 928. Pizza, spaghetti and meatballs, lasagne, and so forth. Generally open from 10 a.m. to midnight, or later on weekends.

For fast food, a **Bob's** or a **Gordon's**—and now a **McDonald's**—is always somewhere in the vicinity. There is some novelty in Brazilian junk food, for those who may be curious.

Last—and probably best—are the **galetos,** the barbecued chicken counters that also usually offer a variety of grilled meats as well.

2. IPANEMA AND LEBLON

This is *the* restaurant district of Rio de Janeiro, where people go to see and be seen, or where gourmands maintain their perpetual vigil for the latest in new wave culinary artistry.

THE UPPER BRACKET: The **Petronius,** Avenida Vieira Souto 460 (tel. 287-3122), is the pride of the Caesar Park Hotel. The Petronius is a picture of swank in its décor and of romance in its mood—banquettes divided by etched panels of glass, and a grand piano on a raised platform between an alcove bar and the dining area, the formal air and attire of the staff, and the starlit Ipanema night seen through windows high above the beach.

The Petronius specializes in seafood served in a manner that only French cuisine could inspire. The fish in pastry or the soufflé of codfish (unbelievably good) are samples of the imaginative presentations that emerge from the kitchen. The Petronius may have the further distinction of being the only restaurant in Rio that serves its martinis with a pimento-stuffed green olive. As for dessert, the little goblets of chocolate filled with liqueur and topped with whipped cream require no additional commentary. An excellent and expensive restaurant. Expect to spend $40 to $50 per person for a no-holds-barred bout of feasting. Open for dinner only, from 6 p.m. to 1 a.m.

Equinox, Rua Prudente de Morais 729 (tel. 247-0580). On those two days yearly when the day and night are of equal length—that is, on the two equinoxes—this very chic and very "in" restaurant sees fit to change its menu. The production of nouvelle cuisine as featured at the Equinox is an endless series of performances. The chef at the Equinox must be a relentless student of world cookery, and certainly his menu recognizes no national boundaries. His creations are inspired by both East and West. They are also expensive, around $30 a person, but that will likely include drinks or wine.

The Equinox seems to function as a tavern for a very smart set of local gentry who come to exchange the news of the day with their peers, and perhaps further a pet interest or two. But the atmosphere is by no means closed and the house treats all its guests admirably. Particularly attractive are the intimate dining alcoves, with their touches of fresh flowers and fine works of art. There is a pianist to entertain nightly in the downstairs bar. For drinks or for dinner, served upstairs in this two-story house, the Equinox opens daily at 5 p.m., with dinner service beginning after 7:30 p.m. and continuing until closing at around 2 a.m. Reservations are suggested.

MEDIUM-PRICED RESTAURANTS: Let's start with the rooftop restaurant at the Caesar Park Hotel, **Tiberius,** Avenida Vieira Souto 460 (tel. 287-3122). As Shecky Green might comment, "With a view like that, how bad can the food be?" Not only Rio's best rooftop view, but good standard Brazilian fare from appetizer to entree. Lunch will cost somewhere in the $10 to $15 range. It's open daily from 7 a.m., when breakfast service begins there for hotel guests, until 11:30 p.m.

    Le Streghe, Rua Prudente de Morais 129 (tel. 287-1369). The name means witch in Italian, an allusion to the artful brewing up of new wave cuisine Italian style, the trademark of the Le Streghe. To satisfy himself that a given dish embodies a particular taste from Italy, the owner will sometimes amuse Customs officials with suitcases filled with cheese or herbs on his return from visits to his old homeland. Le Streghe is one in a trio of nightspots under the same roof, a former private house across from Ipanema's main square, the Praça General Osório. In addition to the restaurant there is a popular piano bar, and the Calígola discothèque.

    The food is very good, as the kitchen turns out some delicious variations using familiar basics like veal and pasta. Noshing before the meal can mean sampling the prosciutto or eating delicate breaded crab legs. Prices are quite reasonable given the quality of the meals: veal dishes run about $8 to $10, pastas are between $4 and $5, and the shellfish dishes are priced somewhat higher. Open for dinner from 7:30 p.m. till 2 a.m. Reservations are recommended.

    Grottammare, Rua Gomes Carneiro 132 (tel. 287-1596). Guests staying in hotels at the Rio Palace end of Copacabana can easily walk the several blocks to the Grottammare, a popular Italian seafood restaurant. Simply head down Rua Francisco Sá, which after several blocks turns into Rua Gomes Carneiro after you have crossed the Avenida Bulhões de Cavalho. The restaurant specializes in salads, pasta dishes, and grilled fish—whatever species turn up daily in the nets of the fishermen who supply the Grottamare. Seafood dishes are priced between $8 and $15, while pastas and salads generally run $5 to $6. Open every night for dinner from 6 p.m. until the last customer leaves in the early morning, and on Sunday at noon for lunch, as well.

    Via Farme, Rua Farme de Amoedo 47 (tel. 227-0743). A block or so from both the beach and the popular Garota de Ipanema bar is this restaurant which emblazons its menu with the slogan: "La Vera Cuccina Italiana—Genuine Italian Cooking." The Via Farme's popularity since opening four years ago attests to the veracity of that claim. Diners may choose from a varied menu that includes traditional meat, fish, and pasta dishes as well as pizza. Meals are priced between $3.50 and $15. Open daily from noon until 2 a.m. or later, depending on business.

    Trattoria Torna, Rua Maria Quitéria 46 (tel. 247-9506), a short walk from the Caesar Park Hotel, is an attractive Italian restaurant with traditional checkered tablecloths. If candles in empty straw-wrapped bottles of chianti were added to the table settings, the ambience would resemble those intimate Italian restaurants of New York's Greenwich Village in the '60s. Pasta dishes average $2.50, while fish plates are $6 and up. Open daily from 11:30 a.m. till 2 a.m.

    Mediterrâneo, Rua Prudente de Morais 1810 (tel. 259-4121). This festive-looking eatery with a definite flavor of the Mediterranean shore occupies the first and second floors of a corner house. Divided rooms and balconies provide separate areas for intimate dining amid nautical bric-a-brac and polished woodwork.

It's generally crowded, so reservation or not, you will probably have to wait a few minutes for a table. For a filling and satisfactory meal, try the spaghetti Mediterrâneo, a concoction of pasta and fresh seafood, including giant shrimp, mussels, fish, and squid. With a couple of draft beers to wash it all down, the meal will cost you about $13, including service. Mussel and fish dishes run between $6 and $10, while lobster can cost as much as $20. Open from noon to 2 a.m. daily.

The **Mistura Fina,** Rua Garcia D'Ávila 15 (tel. 267-6596), is ideal as a supper club, or for an evening of music and drinks. A popular dish in the downstairs restaurant is the flank steak with potatoes gratiné for about $6, or steamed clams in orange sauce for around $12. The restaurant is open daily from noon till 3 a.m. The Mistura Up, offering live music (a pianist or a small group playing light jazz), opens at 6 p.m. and—at least on weekends—doesn't close until dawn.

Lord Jim, Rua Paul Redfern 63 (tel. 259-3047). From Lord Jim's, on the last street in Ipanema before crossing into Leblon, the British lion holds forth in this genuine public house re-created in the tropics. Boisterous and rowdy in a good-natured way, the weekend crowds exercise their Anglo-Saxon nostalgia for pub life to the tune of endless rounds of good English bitters, kidney pie, and a rousing game of darts. 'Ey what? Lord Jim's is the crossroads and meeting ground for Rio's English colony and therefore a favorite attraction for many visitors to Rio from the diverse countries of the English-speaking world. In addition to the traditional English fare—roast beef, Yorkshire pudding, fish and chips—tea is served daily from 4 until 6:30 p.m. Closed Monday, both pub and restaurant are open between 4 p.m. and 1 a.m. Tuesday through Saturday, and for lunch on Sunday from 11 a.m. till the normal closing hour of 1 a.m.

Saborearte, Avenida Bartolomeo Mitre 297 (tel. 511-1345), in Leblon, is more new wave than nouvelle, as the emphasis here is on the novelty of food combinations, deriving only remotely from any tradition of French cooking. All the dishes are therefore unusual—some quite tasty, others less successful. Such are the risks in all experimental arts, whether in the theater or in the kitchen. The menu, furthermore, changes frequently, and is likely to be completely different by the time this guide comes into circulation. A few of the more interesting recent selections were the boi de manço appetizer of sun-dried beef, a Brazilian version of prosciutto, very tender and with a sweeter taste. The cream of manioc and cheese soup was excellent—a truly new taste. The trout lightly baked in its own juices was quite delicate. With beer, dessert, and tip, the cost was about $15 per person. Open daily for dinner from 8 p.m. till 1:30 a.m., and for lunch on Sunday after midday.

Antônio's, Avenida Bartolomeo Mitre 297 (tel. 294-2699), directly next door to Saborearte, is a long-standing hangout for the arty set. The cooking is French and the atmosphere very appealing. Most meals are in the $8 to $10 range. Open daily from noon to 3 a.m.

Un, Deux, Trois, Avenida Bartolomeo Mitre 123 (tel. 239-0198), another Leblon favorite, is a good choice for both dinner and dancing. The restaurant, however, is separate from the nightclub, and separate reservations are required for both establishments. Fare is of the highly palatable standard Brazilian type labeled "international" in restaurants throughout the city, and ranges from $7 to $15 per entree. The nightclub features dance-band music and a supper-club environment. Open daily for dinner from 7 p.m. till 2 a.m., and for lunch on weekends after noon. There is a reasonably priced feijoada served every Saturday. The nightclub remains open till the wee hours on the weekends.

Caneco 70, Avenida Delfim Morais 1026 (tel. 249-1180). On the Leblon stretch of the beach at the corner of Rua Rainha Guilhermina, the Caneco 70 offers the advantages of being both an outdoor café and a popular restaurant. A large open space, it is an ideal lunch and beverage spot in between sessions in the sun. Or for a genuinely funky feijoada, come here on Saturday, when another national dish, cozido is also served, a beef-and-vegetable stew originating in the northeast. Both dishes cost about $6, and as the waiter explains, "Um da pra dois" ("One serving is enough for two"). For a more quiet meal, the second-floor terrace is suggested. Open daily from 10 a.m. till 4 a.m.

Antiquárius, Rua Aristides Espinola 19 (tel. 274-2595), is perhaps the best Portuguese restaurant in Rio. It specializes in bacalhau, (codfish), that denizen of northern Atlantic waters with its grotesque visage and flaky, delicate meat. For perhaps two centuries before the Plymouth colony took root in Massachusetts Bay, fishermen from Brittany, the Azores, and the coast of France and England plied the waters off Maine and Nova Scotia and filled their bottoms with this one fish prized above all others in the Europe of that day. No country today upholds the tradition of codfish cookery more than Portugal. But the fish must be imported to Brazil, and so its cost is always more than steak, and sometimes priced with shrimp and lobster. Maine lobstermen, who often discard this unwanted interloper from their traps, would be surprised to learn how much a good codfish will fetch in Brazil. The Antiquárius offers many codfish dishes, including the standard Portuguese concoction, many times more appetizing than its basic ingredients of bacalhau, scrambled eggs, and potatoes would imply. The cost is about $12. Other daily specials, primarily seafood, are listed at $8, $10, and $15. Open daily from noon till 2 a.m. It's popular, tiny and crowded, so reservations are a necessity.

Around the corner from the Antiquárius is Avenida Gen. San Martín, a number of restaurants are located between Rua Rita Ludoff and Rua Gen. Artigas, including the **Helsingor,** Avenida Gen. San Martín 983 (tel. 294-0347). The real treat at this Danish restaurant is the Sunday smörgåsbord, a buffet of cold meats, fish and vegetable salads, cheeses and pâté, bread, and of course, Scandinavian crackers. The Helsingor also fills the gap in the Rio restaurant scene for a first-class sandwich-and-salad restaurant. Prices on the varied menu range from $4 to $10. Open Tuesday through Saturday, for dinner only, from 6 p.m. till 1 a.m., and on Sunday for lunch and dinner from noon till closing. No credit cards accepted.

The third large avenue in from the beach is Avenida Ataulfo de Paiva, recommended for its street life, a variety of shops and services, and a number of snack shops and restaurants, like the **Real Astoria,** at no. 1235 (tel. 294-0047). The Real Astoria offers Spanish specialties in the $5 to $8 range, and looks like an attractive place to eat. It's open daily from 11:30 a.m. to midnight.

JAPANESE RESTAURANTS: There are several Japanese restaurants in the Ipanema/Leblon area. Two reliable choices are:

Tatsumi, Rua Dias Ferreira 256 (tel. 274-1342), for sushi, sashimi, and sake on a backstreet in Leblon. For $10 you can fill yourself to blissful satisfaction, if raw fish and tempura are to your taste. And that includes dessert, plus a few rounds of flavorful Japanese beer. Open weekdays for dinner from 7 p.m. until 1 a.m., and on weekends for both lunch and dinner, from 2 p.m. until the last customer pays his bill.

Mariko Sushi Bar, Avenida Vieira Souto 460 (tel. 287-3122), is the top-of-the-line sushi bar at the Caesar Park Hotel, expensive and elegant. Open for lunch and dinner daily.

BARGAIN FOOD IN IPANEMA/LEBLON: Typical of the excellent lunch counters found throughout the city are the **Chaika** and the **Padaria Ipanema,** both on Rua Visconde de Pirajá, near the Praça da Paz square. You may just want

to pick up one of those delicious loaves of bread you've been eating at breakfast in your hotel for a picnic on the beach. Or you may want to take a quick lunch break from a shopping spree in the nearby boutiques. In that case, either at the counter or in a booth, the perfect snack to satisfy both your palate and your schedule is a plateful of tasty, inexpensive salgadinhos. These are the little pies and pastries filled with cheese, chicken, minced meat, egg, or shrimp that cost between 25¢ and 50¢ each.

Don't forget the **Garota de Ipanema** outdoor café on nearby Rua Vinícius de Morais, the very popular daytime hangout, for a cooling, freshly squeezed cup of orange juice or a well-chilled glass of draft beer. Other Ipanema options for informal and inexpensive eating are the **Pizza Palace,** Rua Barão de Torre 340; the **Rio Nápoli,** Rua Teixeira de Melo 53; and **Bonis,** a fast-food emporium on the corner of Rua Henrique Dumont and Rua Visconde de Pirajá.

There is a vegetarian restaurant in Ipanema, the **Natural,** at Rua Barão da Torre 117 (tel. 267-7799).

In Leblon, both **Bela Blu,** Rua General Urquiza 107, and **La Mole,** Rua Dias Ferreira 33, have branches of their pizzarias.

For Vietnamese food, try **Le Viet Nam,** Avenida Afranio de Melo Franco 131 (tel. 239-4491), also in Leblon.

3. OTHER BEACH LOCALES

IN AND AROUND SÃO CONRADO: There are a number of fine restaurants that make a spin out to São Conrado worth the effort. For those staying at one of the São Conrado hotels, these restaurants are the perfect option for evenings when you don't feel like hopping a cab to Ipanema or Copacabana.

Oasis, Praça de São Conrado (tel. 252-5521), is not far from the Inter-Continental Hotel on the road that goes to Barra da Tijuca. You won't find a better churrascaria (barbecue house) in Rio than the Oasis, where the meat is served rodízio style. Proof of this statement is the fact that the Oasis is a favorite of the Cariocas themselves. Like most churrascarias, the restaurant is large, plain, and simple—the white tablecloths are the one concession to décor.

To begin the rodízio ritual at the Oasis, the tables are covered with side dishes: fried bananas, potato salad, hearts of palm, tomatoes, lettuce, chips, fried manioc, farofa, and various condiments and sauces. The meat starts arriving immediately, carried on skewers by waiters who are moving constantly from table to table. The agility of the waiters is their trade as they carve the juicy slices with unerring dexterity directly onto your plate. Try to convince the waiters (against the tide of their generous impulses) that you really *do* want tiny slices on the first round. That way you can try everything that interests you and select more carefully from the endless offerings that follow, until you say "uncle" and call for your bill. Among the alcoholic beverages, good Brazilian beer is the proper accompaniment, with perhaps a shot of *pinga* (cachaça) as an apéritif. Mineral water —both with and without carbonation—aids the digestion, say Brazilians, who always have a bottle or two open on their tables. They should know. For about $10 a person, you can have as good a churrasco blow-out at the Oasis as anywhere in Rio. There is a sister Oasis located downtown at Rua Goncalves Dias 56, (tel. 252-5521). In São Conrado the hours are 11 a.m. till midnight daily. And in the Centro, weekdays only, from 11 a.m. till 4 p.m.

Neal's, Estrada da Barra da Tijuca 6250 (tel. 399-3922), is Rio's American restaurant. Actually, Neal (the owner), lately of New York City, has two establishments with the same name, one in Botafogo at Rua Sorocaba 695 (tel. 266-6577), and this one with a Barra da Tijuca address, though it's very close to the São Conrado end of this neighborhood. By cab from Copacabana through the Dois Irmãos tunnel, the ride takes about 20 minutes. The brand-new Neal's is a structure open on four sides, ultramodern, and yet, with its textures and abundance of vegetation, the perfect tropical temple for a Saturday night out. Rock music, video tapes, and American chow, with that inevitable Brazilian flavor, attract crowds on the weekends to the large tables for the platters—hamburgers, ribs, large salads, etc., priced between $8 and $15. Open daily for lunch and dinner, from noon to 1 a.m. weekdays, later on weekends.

Monseigneur, in the Hotel Inter-Continental at Avenida Prefeito Mendes de Morais 222 (tel. 322-2200), is an upper-bracket French restaurant. While it may not be strictly required, men might feel more comfortable in a jacket and tie as a complement to the formality of the décor and service. The seating is warm and posh, and tables richly set. For the originality and quality of its food the Monseigneur has few rivals among the city's fine French restaurants. The duck and veal are prepared very well in rich, tasty sauces. The desserts—like warm chocolate bonbons filled with ice cream—are equally excellent. For a moderate binge you will spend about $40 per person at the Moseigneur, including beverage. Ladies, by the way, are presented with a long-stemmed rose on leaving the establishment. Open daily from 7 p.m. to 1 a.m.

Alfredo di Roma, also at the Hotel Inter-Continental (tel. 322-2200), is a classy pasta house with its roots in Italy at the original Alfredo's, where the fettuccine dish by the same name was said to have been created. Naturally, all the pasta is made fresh on the premises. The restaurant is bright and overlooks the hotel's pool terrace and the peaks of the Pedra da Gávia mountain. Pasta dishes of numerous varieties predominate on the menu, which also offers a selection of chicken, veal, and seafood choices as well. You'll spend $15 to $20 per person for a full meal, including drinks. Open for lunch daily from noon till 3 p.m. and for dinner from 7:30 till 11:30 p.m.

El Pescador, Praça São Conrado 20 (tel. 322-0851), is a very reputable seafood restaurant, another eating option for guests staying at the hotels in São Conrado. The restaurant's dining terrace is recommended, weather permitting. Frutos do mar (fruits of the sea) from local waters are served in a great variety of ways, but you can also dine on typical Spanish dishes and mixed barbecue grill. Portions at the El Pescador are especially generous. Most prices are between $7 and $15. Open from noon to midnight daily, it's located in the same complex as the popular discothèque, Zoom.

BARRA AND BEYOND: The segment of Barra beach closest to São Conrado is most developed. After the first six kilometers (3½ miles) or so, the remainder of the 20-kilometer (12 mile) beach becomes more and more sparsely settled— an undeniably short-term state of affairs given the pace at which all of Rio's remaining virgin coast is being developed for tourism and luxury apartments. This first stretch of Barra, however, is a landscape of high-rise complexes, usually centered on a fair chunk of real estate, and often separated by an equally generous space from its neighboring structures. Across Avenida Serambetiba is the beach. On the edge of the sand, many trailers and stands cater to weekend bathers with an ample selection of food and beverages, but there is no sidewalk life. It is the land of shopping malls—some of the largest in the world—magical commercial hamlets offering entertainment as well as access to hundreds of shops. There is still something of an urban-frontier look about Barra. Scattered among these condo fortresses are a handful of very good restaurants, to the relief of both beachside residents and the seasonal tourists as well, who have the option to dine well locally.

Le Petit Paris, Avenida Serambetiba 6250 (tel. 385-5776), a fine little French restaurant, is attached to the Rio Hotel Residência, Barra's newest apart-hotel. You may eat voluminously for $20 per person from a first-rate menu of appetizers and entrees. The chef's special veal and the shrimp encased in pastry were lovely, especially in the context of an endless flow of appetizers, breads, drinks, and wine. Open for dinner Tuesday through Saturday from 8 p.m. till 1 a.m., and on Sunday for lunch, after midday, as well as dinner.

Rodeio, Avenida Alvorada 2150 (tel. 325-6163), is not a rodízio, but is considered by many residents the best barbecue restaurant in Rio. Avenida Alvorada is a principal thoroughfare in Barra, running perpendicular to the beach. The Rodeio is not cheap—about $20 per person with beverage for some fine cuts of meat plus the usual barbecue house trimmings. Nearby is the mall-colossus Barra Shopping, and the equally cavernous Carré Four supermarket. Open weekdays from noon to 3 p.m. and 7:30 p.m. to 1:30 a.m., on weekends from noon to 1:30 a.m.

Beyond Barra is yet another string of beaches continuing down the so-called Costa Verde (Green Coast) for a dozen miles or so until reaching Rio's suburban city limits. First comes Recreio dos Bandeirantes, a favorite retreat for weekenders, those with vacation homes, and day-trippers too, who come out to enjoy the unblemished beach. The lone restaurant across from the six-kilometer- (3½-mile-) long beach is the **Ancora,** open daily from 9 a.m. till midnight. Prainha comes next, refuge of the middle class, as well as a favorite spot for surfers. Finally there is Grumari, end of the line, virtually deserted on weekdays, and home to the rustic beach bar, the **Vista Alegre,** a roadside favorite with a great view down the coast, if you happen to find yourself in the vicinity.

About an hour's drive from Rio's Zona Sul, some 50 km (31 miles), is the **Pedra da Guaratiba beach,** well beyond Barra da Tijuca in the direction of Angra dos Reis. Two restaurants in this region have become famous in recent years, attracting a steady stream of weekend gourmets.

The first is **Cândido's,** Rua Barros de Alarcão 352 (tel. 395-2007). Simple in appearance, Cândido's has retained for a decade a reputation as one of the finest seafood restaurants in or around Rio. The santolas, a variety of crab imported from Chile that are considered a great delicacy, are priced at about $40 per kilo. The lobster stew, a Bahian-style moqueca, costs $15, while the crab version of the moqueca is $5. Also available are a variety of shrimp and fish dishes in the $8 to $12 range. Open Tuesday through Friday for lunch and early dinner from 11:30 a.m. till 7 p.m.; on weekends, to 11 p.m.

Quatro Sete Meia, Rua Barros de Alarcão 476 (tel. 395-2716), is the other. This Canadian-Brazilian co-production also features seafood moquecas, but is much smaller than its nearby rival, Candido's. The 476 (which is what *quatro sete meia* means) has seatings for meals, and reservations are therefore quite imperative. The open-air terrace offers a fine view of a coast very active with fishing craft. Expect to spend $20 to $25 per person at this rustic gourmet haven by the sea. Open Friday through Sunday from 1 to 11 p.m.

About 20 kilometers (12 miles) before reaching Pedra da Guaratiba is the fishing town of **Barra da Guaratiba,** where some 30 restaurants have sprung up in recent years as local outlets for the abundant daily catch from the sea. First among equals is **Tia Palmeira,** sitting at the top of an incline with a private parking lot, offering a single fixed meal for all patrons at about $10 for adults and half price for children 8 or under. A typical meal might include, for beginners, fried shrimp, pastel de camarão (small shrimp turnovers), and mussels. Entrees could be fried filet of fish and a baked dish of marinated fish, plus **bobó de camarão** (a shrimp paste), vatapá, pirão, rice, and octopus farofa. For dessert, a cavalcade of fresh fruits along with varied sweets of coconut, melon, banana, and jack fruit (jaca).

Two other choices for Barra da Guaratiba come to me by word of mouth, the **Legal Cantinha da Tia Penha,** roughly translated as Aunt Penha's Groovy Little Corner, and the **Barraca da Baiana.** At Tia Penha's, lines form on the weekend —patrons are given numbered tickets to maintain the rule of first come, first served—to savor the risotto of cuttlefish ($3 a plate) or the moqueca of octopus ($5 a serving). The Barraca da Baiana (really a roadside stand) specializes in pasteis, those incomparable turnovers in light pastry filled with delights from the sea.

4. THE LAGOA

An immense Lagoon, the Lagoa Rodrigo de Freitas occupies much of the center ground between the *bairros* of Copacabana and Ipanema. On the margins of the Lagoa, as the district is always referred to in conversation, are some of Rio's most exclusive houses and apartment buildings—and a number of its better bars and restaurants as well. The restaurants listed here tend to be of the upper-bracket variety.

Antonino, Avenida Epitácio Pessoa 1244 (tel. 294-2699), is quiet elegance by the shaded banks of a lagoon. At night the glass façade at Antonino's always seems bathed in shimmering sepia tones, adding to the experience of dining there. Even the solemn formality of the waiters seems an anachronism, albeit a pleasant one. From the font of this genteel sensibility, Antonino's has managed to maintain the consistently high standards of its kitchen. Here you will eat the familiar dishes, including spring lamb or badejo (sea bass), cooked to perfection. With appetizer, dessert, and beverage, the bill comes to about $25 per person. Open daily from noon to 2 a.m.

The backroom at the **Castelo da Lagoa,** Avenida Epitácio, Pessoa 1560 (tel. 287-3514), is a clubhouse for one of Rio's best-known society journalists and his circle, primarily actors and actresses. The restaurant's décor is even a little flashy in a Hollywood sense, but the prices are reasonable and the food reliable. The vichyssoise, followed by grilled langostino (a kind of saltwater crayfish), makes for a tasty lunch, especially if you have time to linger in the tranquil atmosphere of a table in the outdoor patio. A full lunch or dinner can be had for between $20 and $25 per person. At dinner the restaurant tends to fill up, and the movement of customers is constant between the restaurant and the attached Chico's Bar, where there is always a solid jazz group to entertain in what is one of the most popular bars for singles and couples in Rio. The restaurant is open daily from 11 a.m. till 5 a.m. the next morning.

Guimas, Rua José Roberto Macedo Soares 05 (tel. 259-7996), is one of the hottest small restaurants in Rio, with only a dozen or so tables. It's almost impossible to get a seat without waiting for an hour. The ambience is bistro-like with contemporary graphics and posters announcing art exhibitions or plays filling the walls. Each table is set with a cup of crayons, for doodling on the paper table cover. Guimas serves the latest in Brazilian nouvelle cuisine in large portions. Typical are the linguine with smoked whitefish, and the spicy scalloped chicken served with beets. With drinks, dessert, coffee, and tip, expect to spend about $13 a head. Guimas, despite its popularity, is not a household word among Rio's cab drivers. It's not far from the Jardím Botânico end of the Lagoa. Ask your driver to call ahead for directions, if possible (he can call from the porter's desk if you're leaving for the restaurant from your hotel). The cab ride from Copacabana ought to be in the $3 to $4 range. Open for dinner only, from 7 p.m. till 1:30 a.m. daily.

Troisgros, Rua Custodio Serrao 62 (tel. 226-4542), also on the Jardím Botânico end of the Lagoa, near Botafogo, is operated by a French chef who was formerly with Le Pre Catalán at the Rio Palace Hotel. The chef personally supervises the creation of all meals, and so his menu is limited and includes a set plate from appetizer to dessert, which changes from day to day. Expect to spend around $35 per diner. Open from Monday through Saturday for dinner from 7:30 p.m. to midnight.

5. FLAMENGO AND BOTAFOGO

Flamengo and Botafogo were the fashionable beachfront neighborhoods during the early 20th century until the '50s. As desirable residential areas, they have undergone a revival in recent years as well, because of the high rents demanded for much smaller apartments in other districts. There are a fair number of fine restaurants to be found in both these *bairros*, especially tucked away on the backstreets, but also overlooking the Baia da Guanabara. The nearby beaches have long been replaced by the ocean beaches from Leme onward as desired swimming and tanning spots.

Clube Gourmet, Rua General Polidoro 186 (tel. 295-3494), another chef-owned upper-bracket eatery, has an unimposing exterior on a narrow backstreet in Botafogo across from an old cemetery. Inside, the converted town house is smartly decorated and informal. Typical of the dishes is the veal Margherita, flavored with tomato and cheese, and leg of lamb, delicately spiced and cooked in white wine. A soufflé of maracujá (a mango-like fruit) is popular for dessert. The menu is prix fixe, and a full meal will cost about $40 per person, wine included. Open for lunch every day except Saturday from noon to 3 p.m., and for dinner daily from 8:30 p.m. to 1 a.m.

Maria Tereza Weiss, Rua Visconde de Silva 152 (tel. 286-3098), which features "Brazilian" food, is located in a large old manse on a winding tree-lined road in the heart of Botafogo. Senhora Weiss is the author of several standard cookbooks on Brazilian fare, and many of her personal creations grace the menu. This, at least, is one restaurant in the city where you can order black beans with any meal. The tasty turtle bean has inexplicably disappeared from the menus of many regular day-to-day restaurants. This would be an ideal choice for a Saturday feijoada. Entrees range between $7 and $15. Open from noon to 1 a.m. every day except Monday.

The **Sol e Mar,** Avenida Repórter Néstor Moreira 11 (tel. 295-1947), can be found on the same dock where the Bâteau Mouche excursion boats are boarded. These are the day-trip cruises that sightsee among the islands of Guanabara Bay. The Sol e Mar (Sun and Sea) is a Spanish-style seafood restaurant, very expensive for full dining. A large deck sticks out over the bay, and from it you can appreciate one of the best closeup views of Pão de Açúcar from sea level in Rio. This is a most peaceful spot to enjoy a drink or a light meal either before or after a night on the town. The Bâteau Mouche Bar, behind the restaurant, offers live music nightly for dancing and listening. Open daily from 11 a.m. till 3 a.m.

Laurent, Rua Dona Mariana 209 (tel. 266-3131). Formerly the head chef at the St. Honoré, the owner opened his own fine restaurant in 1986 here in the heart of Botafogo. Once a large and lovely private house, the many rooms add intrigue and intimacy to the dining experience. The food is superb, and special attention is given to soups and salads. With a drink or wine, plus one of the rich tarts or other pastries for dessert, expect to spend approximately $30 to $35 per diner. Open Monday through Saturday from 8 p.m. to midnight. Reservations suggested on weekends.

The **Barracuda,** Marina da Glória (tel. 265-4641), is nestled dockside among the moorings of pleasure cruisers and yachts bordering the neighborhoods of Flamengo and Glória. You actually have to drive onto the wharf through a guarded gate to get to the restaurant. Dining is inside and there is no particular view of any note, but the décor is appropriately nautical. The Barracuda is one of the only seafood restaurants in town where you can order a mixed seafood barbecue served on a skewer. The apple salad is also an unusual and welcome accompaniment. A lunch of seafood for two, including appetizers and a couple of rounds of caipirinhas to wash it all down, will cost perhaps $40 in all. Reservations for lunch are suggested, as the restaurant's proximity to downtown makes it a favorite spot for business luncheons. Open daily from noon to midnight, though it closes an hour or so earlier on Sunday nights.

Café Lamas, Rua Marquês de Abrantes 18 (tel. 205-0799), located on a backstreet in Flamengo, is one of Rio's oldest restaurants, though no longer at its original site. The interior is reminiscent of the popular Lisbon cafés, which no doubt served as model and prototype for a style of public eatery now disappearing from the scene in Rio. The Lamas keeps café hours, making it a convenient choice for afternoon lingering or early-morning meals—breakfast or supper, depending on whether you've just gotten up or haven't been to bed yet. The food is standard quality fare, and very reasonable, in the $3 to $7 range, with a varied menu including the usual snacks, meat, chicken, and fish dishes. Open daily from 6:30 a.m. to 4 a.m.

6. CENTRO

The restaurant scene downtown, from the tourist's point of view, is actually somewhat of a novelty. The whole Centro is packed with places to eat, of course, catering primarily to the lunchtime needs of the thousands who work there. The variety runs the gamut from simple *galetos* (barbecued chicken stands) to some fine clubs and restaurants, including the few places in Rio where men are required to wear jacket and tie. Many downtown restaurants don't even serve dinner, and are closed for the weekends. Those places that remain open at night and on Saturday and Sunday usually provide other attractions, in most cases their location or some historical significance. They are not just tourist attractions, however, because you are just as likely to find residents as well as nonresidents in them.

THE UPPER BRACKET: The **Café do Teatro,** on Avenida Rio Branco, in the Teatro Municipal, Rio's grand old Opera House. The restaurant's Doric columns and walls of mosaic tiles make you wonder if perhaps you haven't stumbled onto the stage setting for one of the classical productions. The food is also classically international, as the Café do Teatro is under the stewardship of the same group that owns and operates Antonino's on the Lagoa. It's open only for lunch on weekdays, from noon till 3:30 p.m. and the prix-fixe menu at about $12, with beverage and dessert, is a reasonably economical choice. Take note that no credit cards are accepted.

The **English Bar,** Rua do Comércio 11 (tel. 224-2539), is a popular choice among business people who work downtown and who want to eat well without traveling to the more fashionable areas. Prime rib of roast beef is a favorite meal here, but the menu is fully international, offering French, Spanish, and Portuguese specialties as well. Entrees are in the $8 to $15 range, and a full meal can easily cost you $25 per person. Open weekdays only from noon till 4 p.m. for lunch, and until 8 p.m. for cocktails.

La Tour, Rua Santa Luzia 651 (tel. 242-3221). A revolving carousel of a restaurant 34 stories above it all, La Tour makes one full turn every hour. Yes, it *is* a bit of a tourist trap—the food is nothing special and too expensive at that—so have something simple like grilled filet of fresh fish. But the view is stunning, a wholly different perspective on Corcovado and Pão de Açúcar than that from the

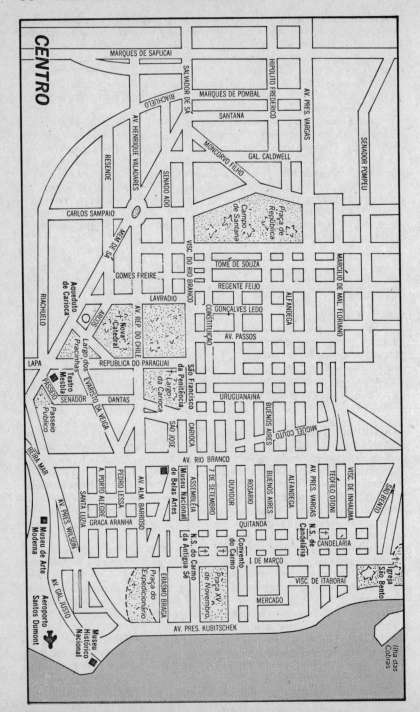

various perches in Copacabana or Ipanema, plus a panorama of Guanabara Bay as well. For any full dinner or lunch from the international menu, expect to pay $20 a head. Open noon to midnight daily.

THE MEDIUM RANGE: The **Café Nice,** Avenida Rio Branco 277 (tel. 240-0490), is a stone's throw from the American consulate and the Pan Am offices, both of which are on nearby Avenida Presidente Wilson. The Café Nice is found below ground level, down a flight of stairs in an office building on this the second largest of Rio's two major boulevards (the first is Avenida Presidente Vargas). Café Nice serves two distinct functions: during the day it is a popular spot for business lunches, but at night it's transformed into an equally popular singles bar and disco playing live music, sometimes rock, sometimes samba. Meals are priced in the $4 to $12 range, and drinks (domestic drinks that is) are inexpensive. Open daily from 11:30 a.m. to midnight (till dawn on Friday and Saturday).

At one point some years back, the **Alba Mar,** Praça Marechal Áncora 184 (tel. 240-8378), was about to be closed. A dozen waiters decided to pool their resources and buy the place, forming a partnership that still endures. The restaurant has been operating since 1933 in the last remaining cast-iron and leaded-glass building—an octagonal tower—of what was once the dockside municipal market. It's a short walk from Praça XV, and should be considered as a lunchtime option during a visit to this historic square. Be careful on the walk: there are few sidewalks once you get close to the water's edge, and the traffic is relentless. Eating at the Alba Mar will not necessarily be the culinary high point of your stay in Rio. But the view of the waterfront and the bay from the third-floor windows will more than compensate for the simple seafood fare. Typical entrees run between $5 and $15. Open from 11:30 a.m. till 10 p.m.; closed Sunday.

The **Colombo,** Rua Gonçalves Dias 32 (tel. 231-9650), is a genuine fin-de-siécle café, opened in 1894 and an unchanging Carioca landmark in a city that has shed its skin a dozen times since this café was built. It's a favorite spot for munching salgadinhos or pastries with a steaming cup of cafezinho or an ideal setting for an afternoon spot of tea. Fortunately the art nouveau décor is made of stone and crystal or you might be tempted to eat that too. The second-story gallery encircles an oval opening above the café's ground floor, and is an ideal setting for a downtown luncheon. The Colombo's prices are only slightly higher than other typical cafés, which means it remains an economical choice. Open Monday through Friday only, from 6:30 a.m. till 8:30 p.m.

The **Bar Luís,** Rua da Carioca 39 (tel. 262-1979), is another traditional and informal lunch spot, a favorite of the journalists and editors who work in the nearby offices of book publishers and periodicals. Founded in 1887, it is even more venerable than the Colombo, though the atmosphere is more saloon-like than continental. The Rua da Carioca is also one of Rio's oldest, where an annual costume festival takes place in the second week of August every year. The Bar Luís offers good solid German eats—veal Holstein, wurst and kraut, kassler—for between $4 and $9 a meal. Open from 11 a.m. till midnight; closed Sunday.

LUNCH COUNTERS AND PÉS SUJOS: There are innumerable *galetos,* *leitarias* (luncheonettes) and *pés sujos* scattered throughout the labyrinth of downtown streets. *Pé sujo* is a slang name for those lovable greasy spoons that even the most discerning gourmets love to eat in from time to time, usually for the bar life as well as some snack food that is unavailable elsewhere.

For Bahian-style food, try the **Oxalá,** a lunch counter in the Cinelândia section at Rua Francisco Serrador 2 (tel. 220-3035). The counter is Loja 1 (Store 1) inside a gallery of shops. All the Bahian specialties, from moqueca seafood stews to vatapá and xim xim de galinha, are served up in simple and large portions.

Open during business hours, Monday through Saturday. Meals range between $4 and $8.

Among the most popular *pés sujos* (literal translation is "dirty feet") to be found downtown are: **Arco do Telles,** Travessa do Comércio 2, open till 8 p.m. weekdays only. The specialty here is calf's foot, for $1. The **Ocidental,** on Rua Miguel Couto at the corner of Marechal Floriano, is open Monday through Saturday till 11:30 p.m., and the treat here is fried sardines, about 75¢ a dozen. The Farão, at Rua do Lavradio 192, open till 11 p.m. daily except Sunday, serves a mean cabeca de galo (rooster head) soup, made with kale, manioc flour, and two eggs. The **Tangara,** Rua Álvaro Alvim 35, is the place for batidas—blended drinks made with cachaça and tropical fruits—for less than 50¢, including one made from jilo, an edible variety of deadly nightshade or belladonna.

7. SANTA TERESA

One very special restaurant in the neighborhood called Santa Teresa, which sits in the hills overlooking the Centro, is the **Bar do Arnaudo,** Rua Almirante Alexanrino 316 (tel. 252-7246). An excursion to Santa Teresa is described in the next chapter, and the best choice for lunch for anyone taking this excursion is this delightful and slightly bohemian hangout specializing in food from the northeast. Carne seca, carne de sol (sun-dried jerky) and sarapatel (minced sweetbreads) are the typical dishes. No meal costs more than $4. But the way to try everything, including dessert and plenty of beer—for less than $10—is to order the large portion appetizers called *pratos diverso* on the menu. Open Wednesday through Sunday from noon till 10 p.m.

RIO: WHAT TO SEE AND DO

□ □ □

While Rio is primarily a city to be enjoyed as a spa by day and as a feast or party by night, it's also a great shopping center and a city of numerous environmental and cultural attractions. Rio can further lay claim to hosting what even P. T. Barnum would have had to acknowledge is the real "greatest show on earth," the annual street Carnival with its cast of tens of thousands. Droves of international visitors are lured to Rio each year specifically to take part in this extraordinary week-long celebration.

1. THE TOP SIGHTS

There are at least two sightseeing excursions that most people, regardless of their differences, are guaranteed to enjoy. Such is their fame that even 150 years ago, in the 1830s, Charles Darwin could write in his journal during the voyage of the *Beagle:* "Everyone has heard of the beauty of the scenery near Botafogo." He was referring to Corcovado and Pão de Açúcar. From these two heights—especially Corcovado—Rio can be seen for miles around in all directions. The views reveal the city's general layout, the contours of its 90km (56-mile) shoreline, along with all its principal man-made and topographical features. Of the latter, Darwin humbly noted that "every form, every shade so completely surpasses in magnificence all that the European has beheld in his own country, that he knows not how to express his feelings."

The vistas and scenery praised by Darwin are still there for you to see today. No matter how much Rio develops, nothing seems to diminish or obscure the beauty of its natural setting. But the Rio of today is also a vastly different place from the sleepy South Atlantic town visited by the great naturalist in the 1830s, one that provides all the urban distractions that we would expect to find in one of the truly great cities of our own day. And depending on one's particular interests, each of the places or groups of places described here—whether historical site or formal garden, inner-city forest or bayscape, art museum or jewelry exhibition—has its special recommendations.

CORCOVADO: A giant statue of Christ the Redeemer stands with outstretched arms on the summit of Corcovado, or Hunchback Mountain, 2,400 feet above sea level, and dominates the landscape in Rio. During the day, but particularly at night when the statue is bathed in floodlights, the landmark can be seen clearly from many points in the city, stretching from Ipanema to the Centro and beyond. Photographs of the statue overlooking Rio have become almost synonymous with the city itself. But Corcovado was a beloved landmark in Rio, as Darwin's remarks demonstrate, long before the monumental statue was constructed.

Initial access to the peak was along a road that followed the ridgeline from the Alto da Boa-Vista, an ascent that required more leisure time than most of Rio's citizens could afford. To democratize the experience of the renowned view, Dom Pedro II ordered the construction of a passenger train, completed in 1885, that could carry a group of sightseers to the summit and back in a short time. Initially a steam engine, and later Brazil's first electric train, the railroad has been modernized many times in the last century, and the climb today can be accomplished in only 20 minutes.

The imposing statue of the Cristo Redentor, Christ the Redeemer, was conceived as a fitting monument to mark the centennial of Brazilian Independence in 1921. The project was underwritten by thousands of donations collected in churches throughout the country. Finally, in 1931 the statue was completed. Constructed of reinforced concrete and coated with soapstone, the massive figure with the welcoming arms rises 120 feet above a spacious observation platform, and weighs over 1,000 tons.

The view from this observation deck is truly unforgettable. Make sure you have a map along to help you identify what you are seeing. Trace the shoreline from deep within the bay all the way to Leblon. In a single glance embrace all of Lagoa and Jardim Botânico. Perhaps you'll even see the mounts circling the field at the Jocqui Club racetrack. Study Ipanema and Copacabana at a distance and then focus on the nearby backstreets of neighborhoods like Botafogo, Laranjeiras, and Cosme Velho. Let your eyes hike from the buccolic highlands of Santa Teresa across the ancient aqueduct into the heart of downtown, where the buildings assume the disorienting scale of an architectural model. Watch the small planes circle close to that conical wonder at the mouth of Guanabara Bay, the Pão de Açúcar mountain, and then sweep across the harbor near Flamengo as they land at Santos Dumont Airport. Then face away from the city and wonder at the enormity and the denseness of the surrounding forest that literally creeps to the very edges of Rio's most civilized corners. From the summit of Corcovado, all of Rio's disjointed parts fall into place, and the city suddenly becomes knowable in a way that could not be imagined before.

The best time to make the ascent is in the afternoon around 4 or 5 p.m., when the sun is already low on the horizon and the light is evenly distributed above the landscape. Try to organize your visit to Corcovado on the clearest possible day as well. But even if you are forced to make your visit when the weather is overcast, don't fail to make the ascent on that account. The sensation of being above the clouds can be very powerful in and of itself, even if the panorama is somewhat obscured by the ocean mists.

Getting There

A number of options are available for reaching the top. But first you must decide if you want to go by yourself or with an organized tour. If by yourself, take a public bus or cab to the Cosme Velho train station. Bus 583 leaves from Copacabana, and a number of buses leave from the downtown Menezes Cortes bus terminal. The **train**—which climbs sometimes at a 30° angle and has a tractor system similar to that of a roller coaster—leaves every 20 to 30 minutes from 8:30 a.m. to 6:30 p.m. and costs approximately $2.25 round trip. The last returning train from the summit leaves at 7 p.m. The train ride is a worthwhile excursion in its own right, as it crosses deep ravines with their own dramatic views, and cuts intimately through the dense tropical vegetation on the surrounding slopes. There are a number of stops along the route to the top where residents who live on the hillside get on and off, so you get to see something of local life along the way as well.

You may also choose to go by **cab or private car** all the way to the top along the paved road that zigzags up the slopes. This is the most expensive option, but also the most convenient, especially if time is a factor. The arrangement you make with your driver usually includes his waiting for the return trip. Tour lines offer organized bus tours, some of which go directly to the top while others take you to and from the Cosme Velho train station. (The names of various tour companies are given toward the end of Section 2 of this chapter.) These bus tours leave from your hotel and operate on fixed schedules, generally costing around $20. The buses are accompanied by a tour guide who points out the sights, usually in four or five different languages, and answers your questions.

A Stop at the Mirante Santa Marta

Many tours stop at the Mirante Santa Marta before climbing all the way to the top. From this vantage point 1,200 feet above the ground, both Corcovado and Pão de Açúcar can be seen, and you get a closer view of the surrounding neighborhoods. Some tours, especially the smaller groups traveling by van, will also make a quick detour near the train station to a nearby cobblestone courtyard called the **Largo do Boticário** to view the façades and setting of some lovely old town houses with wooden balconies and pan-tile fronts. While of no particular historical significance, the courtyard is a graceful residential cul-de-sac, entered through a metal archway, where gas lamps, a central fountain, shady trees, and its own babbling brook add to the charm. If the artist is receiving, visit the studio of painter Augusto Rodrigues, near the entrance to the Largo. There is also an antique shop where English is spoken.

PÃO DE AÇÚCAR: Sugar Loaf Mountain is the eternal counterpoint to Corcovado. While the Hunchback Mountain occupies an inland setting and is covered with lush vegetation, Pão de Açúcar stands virtually naked, a huge cone-shaped hunk of metamorphic rock composed primarily of granite, quartz, and feldspar that clings to the very shoreline of the great bay. Whether you are observing Pão de Açúcar from Corcovado or vice versa, the visual pleasures are equally stunning.

No roads lead to the summit of Sugar Loaf. Either you ride the cable cars or you climb—and most visitors choose the way of least resistance. The sleek gondolas, made from hardened aluminum and wrapped in acrylic windows, can carry over 1,000 passengers an hour on their two-stage ascent. The first ride takes you to the top of the Morro da Urca (Urca Hill), the neighboring peak, and a second car completes the journey to Sugar Loaf itself. During both legs of the climb you are suspended in mid-air for approximately three minutes. It is reassuring to note that there has never been an accident.

The name *pão de açúcar* is of uncertain origin. Some say the mountain was named by the Portuguese, who compared its shape with that of the ingots or "loaves" of raw sugar that were shipped to market from the refineries. A more esoteric—and probably romantic—theory holds that the name derives from the Tupi Indian phrase *pau-hn-acugua,* meaning a remote hill that is high and pointed. Yet it is undoubtedly true that the hill was made less remote when the first cable car system was installed in 1912, a simple affair of wooden carriages that remained in service until the more high-tech system in current use was inaugurated in 1972.

The first recorded ascent by a climber was that of an Englishwoman in 1817. Many more followed, until all faces of the mountain were conquered. Today, climbing the Pão de Açúcar is a weekly event, as the safety lines of enthusiasts can be seen dangling from the rocks on any clear day. A more gentle ascent—but still a vigorous hike—can also be arranged, chaperoned by the organization that runs all the concessions on the mountain. As with Corcovado, however, the main reason for visiting Pão de Açúcar is for its unique view of bay and city. A sundown excursion is particularly exciting, for there is no better place to see the illuminated city after dark.

While Pão de Açúcar's altitude is only 1,300 feet (roughly the same height as New York's World Trade Center), the unique location of the huge rock gives it a virtually unobstructed view of much of the city. As is also the case when visiting Corcovado, it is extremely useful to have a map along to help you distinguish one feature or area from another. Of special note is the closeup view of Botafogo harbor, and the full visual sweep of the 15-km- (9-mile-) long bridge that connects Rio with its companion city, Niterói, begins on the opposite shore of the bay. Just south of Niterói begins another unbroken shoreline which includes the pristine beaches of Piratininga, Itaipú, Itacotiara, and Itaipuaçu. Both the mouth of the bay and the coast beyond Niterói can best be viewed from the garden walk on the far side of the hill.

In addition to its function as an overlook, the Pão de Açúcar complex is also home to various entertainment programs, several bars, and even a restaurant, most of which are actually located on the Morro da Urca. Every Monday night from about 10 p.m. till midnight the samba school Beja Flor presents a cabaret version of Carnival with colorful costumes, music, and dance in a covered amphitheater. The show costs $10 a ticket. Live performances of top singers and musicians are also staged in the amphitheater, known as the Concha Verde (the Green Shell) on weekend nights, which in Brazil means Thursday through Saturday.

Getting There

Getting to Pão de Açúcar is considerably less involved than going up to Corcovado. Here, in fact, is one excursion where a bus ride may be entirely appropriate. Take bus 511 from Copacabana or bus 107 from downtown to the Praia Vermelha station, Avenida Pasteur. Or take a cab, which from Copacabana ought to cost no more than $3 or $4. Then just climb the stairs to the ticket office, pay the fee, and ride to the top. The cars function from 8 a.m. till 10 p.m. on a continuous basis if the demand is heavy, or at 30-minute intervals when traffic is light. Cars also function later to accommodate those attending special events. There is a gift shop in the boarding station for film or souvenirs, and a tourist information center, open during business hours only. For **information** about the shows, climbing excursions, or any number of other activities and special events, call either 541-3737 or 295-2397.

Urca

While in the area, don't fail to walk or ride through the neighborhood of Urca, nestled at the foot of the hill of the same name. Urca is just a handful of streets seemingly unattached to the rest of the city, not particularly elegant, but with private houses and a shady, small-town feeling. Residents there must feel themselves among the most privileged in all of Rio, being so close to the principal zones of the city yet in so private and tranquil a setting overlooking both ocean and harbor.

THE BEACHES: Beaches in Rio are as basic an ingredient of daily life as food and shelter. And on the weekend the beaches are life itself. Rio's coast is 130 km (80 miles) long, and dozens of beaches dot the shoreline from one end of the city to the other. There are 23 beaches on Governor's Island alone, the island in the Zona Norte where the international airport is located. There are no bad beaches in Rio, only beaches that keep getting better the farther you go from the center of town. There are bay beaches and ocean beaches, but—in the Zona Sul, at least—only the latter are good for swimming. The Cariocas have gone and gummed up this part of the bay and now it's too polluted for bathing. This is a dilemma all too familiar to many Americans who live in cities where the urban waterways have likewise been so thoughtlessly fouled. But until a Brazilian Pete Seeger arises in Rio to help spark a campaign to clean up the bay, take your dips in the ocean.

General Information

The ocean surf is often very powerful in Rio, and the **undertow** can be treacherous. Be careful not to overextend yourself, especially if you're unfamiliar with or out of practice playing in heavy waves. Experienced ocean bathers will find the bodysurfing rugged and exciting, while swimmers must look for the most protected coves or await calm seas in order to practice their crawls. Where the waves are high, you will usually find surfboarders. They're fun to watch and they keep to well-defined areas, but it's best to be alert when flying surfboards are in the air.

During the week, especially in Copacabana and Ipanema, the beach attracts a fair crowd of fitness buffs from the time the sun comes up till it's time to go off to work. Then for the remainder of the day—at least during the **off-season** (April through June and August through October)—the beaches remain sparsely peopled. Even Copacabana and Ipanema are quiet during these months, but for a few nannies with preschoolers, and the usual crowd of bon vivants. Tourists also come to Rio during the off-season, by choice or necessity. They may also be found weekdays on the major beaches, gathered in small pockets on the sand in front of their respective hotels. Thus you can always tell the Rio Palace crowd from that of the Othon, the Copcabana Palace, or the Meridien, but only during those months when the daytime crowd is light and the scene subdued. There are always a few vendors on Copacabana as long as there's someone to sell to, and many of the trailer cantinas on the beach side of Avenida Atlântica also remain open throughout the year.

The **high season** for tourism in Rio coincides with those months when Cariocas themselves are on vacation or holiday. The summer school holiday extends from Christmas through February (and into early March for Carnival when Ash Wednesday falls late on the calendar). July is the month-long winter school holiday. And while November, December, and March are not holiday months in Brazil, the tourist business remains strong in Rio at those times as well. Rio's beach life is at its richest and most intense on a daily basis during this high season.

On **weekends**, regardless of the season, as long as the sun is shining in Rio's obliging climate, capacity crowds will flock to the beaches from all over the city, providing a rare common ground for the mingling of Brazil's two vastly separate economic realities. And when it's crowded, no matter what beach you go to or where you sit, at least three minor sporting events will be taking place in the vicinity of your umbrella (supplied by your hotel, or rented from a beach vendor). The game might involve a dozen men—of all ages—playing pickup soccer. Or it may be a hard-fought game of volleyball, one of the best-loved sports in Brazil. Almost certainly you will see the fast-paced *fréscobol*, where two friends use large wooden paddles to smash a rubber ball back and forth in the air. Despite the apparent chaos and the blanket-to-blanket crowds, a convivial atmosphere reigns, and only rarely do the energies of one activity spill over into those of its neighbors. When the ball (or player) rolls onto your blanket, just throw it (or him) back.

Stepping gingerly among the reclining bodies are the scores of **vendors,** who will offer you food and drink, souvenirs or beach mats, sun hats, and sun screen. The vendors seem like characters from a kind of *Three Penny Opera* by the seashore: colorful in person, and admirable in the dogged pursuit of their peddler's trade. Sometimes the vendors sing or use noisemakers, less to entertain than to penetrate the somnambulant state of the sunbathers they hope to attract as clients. Cries of *sorvete* (ice cream), *agua de coco* (coconut water), *amendoins* (peanuts), and *cerveja bem gelada* (well-chilled beer) can be heard from one end of the strand to the other as long as the sun is shining.

All of Rio's beaches are public, and none contains bathhouses or changing rooms, much less rest rooms. (When the need arises, cross the avenue to the nearest restaurant; the better the restaurant, the better the rest room.) Rio by day is strictly a come-as-you-are town. In the beach neighborhoods, people parade around everywhere in **bathing suits** all day. Women often use sarongs to cover their swimsuits when going to or from the beach, but you're just as likely—and strikingly—to see men and women traveling about in just their bikinis. The *fio dental* worn by many women translates as "dental floss," a graphic metaphor for how this swimsuit fits behind.

Only the principal beaches have **lifeguards,** and none too many at that. There is also a very discreet police presence on those beaches, like Copacabana, most frequented by tourists, usually a pair of patrolling young officers dressed in mufti (tank top, shorts, and baseball cap) who only stand out when you suddenly realize that the object hanging from their waists is a revolver. The cops are there primarily to intimidate the urchins. Many of the children are said to be homeless, and they likewise patrol the beaches for targets of opportunity in their hit-and-run banditry. If they don't see a camera or wallet, they'll run off with your sneakers. There are also street children on the sidewalks, hanging out at the outdoor cafés, usually selling peanuts or chewing gum or candies. The best way to deal with them when they surround your table is to smile and buy something from one of them, or just make a small donation to their cause—survival.

The Best of the Beaches

I'll begin with **Flamengo,** first beach of the Zona Sul, and closest to downtown Rio. You might check it out if you're at the Hotel Glória or the Novo Mundo. As a bay beach, swimming is not advised, but it's fine for sunbathing. The surroundings are pleasant, and you have all of Flamengo Park behind you to explore. The kids might like the tractor-pulled train that tours the park, and the large playground.

Botafogo beach is next along the shore, a tanning spot primarily for local residents of this still-charming neighborhood, Rio's most fashionable throughout much of the 19th century.

Near the Pão de Açúcar cable-car station is the football-field-length **Praia Vermelha,** a somewhat-protected ocean beach said to be popular with swimmers. A morning here could be tied in with a stroll around Urca, the nearby vest-pocket neighborhood, and maybe a day trip to Sugar Loaf for lunch or a drink.

Leme and **Copacabana** are the first real pearls in the chain. Wide, sandy ocean beaches at their best, they are remarkably clean—considering the use they get—and the South Atlantic here always seems to provide a moderately frothy sea.

Apoador, Ipanema, and **Leblon** form the next stretch of shoreline going down the coast, brimming over with its variety of scenes, from teenyboppers to tourists. Neighborhood residents still predominate along this strand, with each family or group occupying its own piece of the turf. Ipanema, in particular, is always an exciting beach, an endless swirl of activity, of which the bold preening of young beauties in the scantiest of bikinis lends more than a thread of legitimacy to the "Girl from Ipanema" story.

São Conrado (or **Pepino,** the beach's traditional name) can teem with activity on the weekends, yet be virtually deserted Monday through Friday. Close to the deluxe Inter-Continental resort hotel, the beach is the official landing strip for hang-glider enthusiasts, who sweep down from the surrounding mountains. The Gávea golf course runs along much of São Conrado beach. Interested golfers who wish to play the course may make arrangements through their hotel, but for weekdays only.

After São Conrado, the suburban and more remote beaches begin with a great sand reef some 20 km (12½ miles) long known as **Barra da Tijuca.** Barra is definitely a weekend beach, one of the most frequented in the city. If you're ever looking for a condo along a beach that is serene enough during the week and wildly active on the weekends, Barra is the place.

Recreiro dos Banderantes (or just Recreiro, as locals refer to the beach) is a community of summer and weekend houses, one of the last that remains in Rio proper, right on the ocean. Some blocks in Recreiro are fully developed with houses—villas really, with gardens and swimming pools—occupying every lot. Other blocks contain only a single dwelling or two. The many empty house lots are the flattened remains of white sandy dunes, alive with beach vegetation. There are also large empty expanses of this sandy scrub land still undeveloped, especially the land nearest the hilly parts of the neighborhood. In an hour's walk through these sandy fields you can reap two dozen varieties of wildflowers, thistles, and exotic seed pods, the delicate products of an ocean-bounded ecosystem. A good deal of the land in Recreiro is still occupied by the poor, whose colorful shantytowns manage to seem so appealing from the outside and at the same time so forbidding. One does not enter the *favela* world easily in Brazil.

Beyond the high rock formations at the end of Recreiro beach is the small strip of sand known as **Prainha**—Little Beach. You have to drive over those rocks to get to Prainha, a beachhead for the middle class against the tide of the masses they fear is about to sweep over them from the city's remote and crowded slums. The last beach, **Grumari,** approaches the city line, and is the most undeveloped stretch of ocean beach that Rio still possesses. From here you can move on the explore the southern shores of the state, along the lovely Costa Verde (the Green Coast), which is described in the next chapter.

PARQUE NACIONAL DA TIJUCA: The Tijuca National Park must be one of the largest—if not *the* largest—inner-city parks in the world. The park is an immense forest growing on the slopes of the Serra da Carioca (Sierra Carioca) that cuts across the center of metropolitan Rio, dividing the Zona Norte from the Zona Sul. Stretching at one end from the Mirante Dona Marta, which overlooks the neighborhoods of Laranjeiras and Botafogo, to the Alto da Boa Vista and the Floresta da Tijuca at the other extreme, the park is a voluminous natural preserve of vegetation typical of the Atlantic forests that once lined the eastern coast of Brazil. Most (but not all) of the vegetation is second growth. The park was once the neighboring estates of early aristocrats and planters. These same slopes a hundred years and more ago were mostly cleared and covered with plantation crops of coffee and sugarcane.

The park is etched with several major arteries, many smaller roads, and numerous paths and trails. A pleasant half-day, or even an all-day, excursion can be made in the park. A typical itinerary might be a long orientation drive, lunch at one of the two isolated restaurants, and at least one stop to cool off in the cascades of water that fall from the rocky walls at various locales along the sides of the roads. Make sure you bring suitable dress and a towel so you can take to the water.

There are entrances to the park at the most extreme points throughout the city. So when you're traveling from one neighborhood to another, you can trade the urban backdrop for a tranquil green space by routing your drive through the park, if you don't mind taking the extra time. If you were downtown, for example, you would drive through Santa Teresa, and then continue up the mountain chain into the park via Cosme Velho and Corcovado. From there, you could drive the whole length and breadth of the park, and emerge through the gate in Jardim Botânico, on the far shore of the Lagoa district. On this drive you would pass two of the park's most famous overlooks. The first is the **Vista Chinesa,** with its Chinese Pavilion, a poignant memorial to immigrants from China of the last century who were settled in the vicinity on what were at that time tea plantations. Up the road, the **Mesa do Imperador** (the Emperor's Table) was once a favored picnic spot for the family and court of Dom Pedro I. From both heights you will have an unparalleled view of the city's southern sectors. The park is so vast that there are even entrances to it from as far away as São Conrado and Barra da Tijuca.

From Copacabana or Ipanema, the most direct route to the **Floresta da Tijuca** (Tijuca Forest), a separate entity within the national park with many points of interest, is to enter the park in São Conrado and follow signs to the **Alto da Boa Vista,** where there is a formal common, the Praça Afonso Vizéu and an English tavern called the Robin Hood. The entrance gate to the Floresta is off this plaza. Heading straight on, you pass the **Cascatina de Taunay,** a small waterfall named for the baron whose estate once occupied these lands. Farther on is the tiny **Capela Mairynk,** a delightful sample of an old rural chapel in pastel-pink and white with a reproduction of the original altar panels painted by Portinari (the originals were added to the depleted collection of the Modern Art Museum). The chapel is popular for society weddings, but has been closed to the public of late.

Past the chapel, the road divides and forms a series of loops through the remainder of the grounds. The two park restaurants are to be found beyond this point. If you fancy international food like curried shrimp or chicken Maryland, turn off to the left for **Os Esquilos** (the Squirrels; tel. 258-0237), open for lunch only, from 11 a.m. to 7 p.m. daily except Monday. To the right is a more rustic Brazilian restaurant called **A Floresta** (tel. 258-0183), where hummingbirds flit among the rafters, open from noon to 8 p.m. Both restaurants are favorite luncheon spots for locals when they want a respite from the swelter and motion of the city. Beyond the A Floresta restaurant the road continues to **Bom Retiro,** where it ends and a trail leads to the **Pico da Tijuca** (Tijuca Peak), at an altitude of over 3,000 feet.

HISTORICAL RIO: Rio has no "old town" per se. Yet there are numerous monuments to its past scattered throughout the downtown section and surrounding areas. And there are several architectural relics that date, in whole or part, from the early 17th century. Of primary interest are several churches and monasteries, a few palaces and government buildings, the city's oldest parks and public squares, and one or two blocks of buildings where the architectural integrity of a particular era is more or less preserved intact. What follows are several itineraries for walking tours that can be accomplished in only a few short hours, yet provide you with a genuine opportunity to glimpse a little bit of Rio's past and its present at the same time.

Since most sites of historical interest are located downtown, it would be wise to get some picture in your mind of how the center city is laid out. The two major boulevards are named **Avenida Rio Branco** (running north-south) and **Avenida Presidente Vargas** (which runs east-west). These two grand avenidas are products of 20th-century urban renewal. First came Rio Branco (originally Avenida Central), which was conceived and executed in order to embellish the city with a fin-de-siècle elegance typical of large European capitals—and to avoid being outshined by the beautification of its major rival in South America, Buenos Aires. Before the city's expansion westward into what were at that time the rural and fishing communities of Copacabana and Ipanema, Avenida Rio Branco was the Champs-Élysées of Rio, along which were arrayed the city's most fashionable cafés and shops. It was also along Rio Branco that the great samba schools first paraded at Carnival time. Avenida Presidente Vargas wasn't built until the 1940s, but it, too, was to transform the face of the city.

Many of the city's older buildings and narrow streets were demolished when these two thoroughfares were constructed, and old neighborhoods were also destroyed, emptying downtown Rio of its former residential populations. The two wide avenues intersect dramatically at a point that at one time was near the center of the old colonial city. It is therefore in the vicinity of this intersection that most of the buildings, streets, and plazas of historical interest can still be found—those narrow lanes and cobblestone squares that, through good fortune as much as good planning, were spared from the wheel of progress.

Getting Downtown

Getting to the Centro from the Zona Sul is relatively easy. Take a cab by all means, if that is your preference. The *frescão* air-conditioned buses or the public buses heading for "Castelo" can take you directly to the Menezes Cortes terminal on Rua São José very close to where this tour begins. But remember that Rio also has a modern and safe subway system that runs from Botafogo with many downtown stops. You can get to the Botafogo station by cab or bus. Regardless of your mode of transportation, the best place to begin your tour is probably Praça XV, near the waterfront.

A Prelude

For the purposes of this tour, however, I will assume you are riding the subway. Get off at the **Cinelândia** stop. Cinelândia means movieland, and there are several fine old movie palaces in this area. Films tend not to be dubbed, but play in their language of origin, with subtitles in Portuguese. This is also the neighborhood for downtown singles bars, both gay and straight.

When you alight from the train, follow the exit signs to Rua Santa Luzia and head in the direction of the waterfront. At the end of this street at no. 490 is the **Igreja Santa Luzia** (tel. 220-4367). This gem of the baroque era, built in 1752, was freshly painted recently in striking stucco blue, and there is no better example of that golden age in the city than this delightful little church. Patrons of Saint Luzia celebrate her December 13 feast day by washing their eyes in the church's holy water, believed to possess miraculous properties.

Breaking for Lunch

If you were thinking of lunch at the **Alba Mar,** the seafood restaurant occupying the old octagonal market depot on the wharf, you would cross the wide

Avenida Presidente Antônio Carlos at this point and walk toward the water. On the way, you will pass the **Museu Histórico Nacional,** Praça Rui Barbosa (tel. 240-7978), open Tuesday through Friday from 10 a.m. to 5:30 p.m. and on weekends and holidays from 2:30 to 5:30 p.m. This is the National History Museum, which is housed in a squat fortress-like building, sections of which date from 1603, while most of the structure dates from the late 1700s. The museum's collection of paintings, furnishings, maps, and artifacts guides the history buff from Brazil's discovery in 1500 until the creation of its first republic. The building, which also contains the Military Museum, has been closed for thorough remodeling in recent times, but it is scheduled to reopen sometime in 1988.

The Tour

Continue on in a northerly direction from here, winding your way through the labyrinth of heavily trafficked streets until arriving at **Praça XV**—probably the best point of departure if you have arrived downtown by cab. The orientation from this distinguished landmark is relatively easy, and with the aid of a reasonable map, you can strike off in the direction of any of the sights mentioned in this section. Another good reason to begin at the Praça XV is that the square is a total environment from the past, with several colonial buildings that are open for inspection.

Praça XV is Rio's oldest square. From here the governing viceroys administered all of Brazil, and their residence, constructed in 1743, was converted into the Royal Palace when Dom João and his family made Rio the seat of their empire in 1808. Originally called the Praça do Paço (Plaza of the Court), the name was changed following the Proclamation of the Republic on November 15, 1889. Here also in the preceding year, Princesa Isabel, eldest of Dom Pedro II's children, signed the document that abolished slavery in Brazil, the principal event leading to the downfall of the monarchy. The buildings today are used as exhibition and concert halls, and include a permanent photo display of both visual and historical interest.

Among the antiquities to be seen in the immediate vicinity of the Praça XV are two churches across the busy **Rua 1 de Março.** The old cathedral, **Nossa Senhora do Carmo da Antiga Sé** (1752), was used first by Carmelite monks, and it became the Royal, then the Imperial, chapel, and finally cathedral of the city (it has now been replaced by the ultramodern Nova Catedral, near the Largo da Carioca). The 1822 coronation of Dom Pedro I as Brazil's first emperor took place in the old cathedral, which contains a golden rose given to Princesa Isabel by Pope Leo XIII. Next door is the quaint **Convento do Carmo,** connected to its church by Rio's only remaining public oratory under the tiled roof of an arch hewed from stone. The altar and much of the carving, including the portals, are by the important 18th-century sculptor Mestre Valentim da Fonseca e Silva, the illegitimate son of a Portuguese nobleman and a slave.

Recrossing the Rua 1 de Março, opposite the north side of the square, enter the lane called the **Travessa do Comércio.** The arch above your head, the **Arco do Telles,** also dates from the 1700s. The narrow colonial street is all charm, from the wavy cobblestone pavement to the flat-fronted houses with their wrought-iron balconies and large wooden doors. This route takes you right by the door of a popular *pé sujo* (greasy spoon), the Arco Telles, located at no. 2. Check out the chalkboard menu as you stroll by—this may be the restaurant surprise you've been looking for.

From here you can explore the surrounding cross streets, like the **Rua do Ouvidor,** which has a degree of lore associated with it. It is a street that has appeared in Brazilian literature. *Ouvidores* were petty colonial officials who worked for the Crown, and as such, bedeviled the people of that era with their authority and their corruption. Today it's a banking street. Going in the direction of the bay, you will come to no. 35, the diminutive **Igreja Nossa Senhora da Lapa dos Mercadores** (the Merchants' Church of Our Lady of Lapa), built in 1750 and well worth a peek.

For blocks around on both sides of Avenida Rio Branco, which the Rua do Ouvidor crosses, there are shop-filled streets that are tempting whether you're in the mood to browse the merchandise or just want a distracting walk and some inner-city atmosphere. At some point, though, turn right on nearby Rua Quitanda and walk until you reach Avenida Presidente Vargas where you will see the **Igreja Nossa Senhora de Candelária,** a treasure that was earmarked for demolition in the avenue's initial construction plans. Fortunately a sober judgment saved the church, which remains on a little plaza of its own in the center of the avenue. Donations from sailors built this church in 1775 to commemorate a terrible shipwreck, scenes from which are vividly depicted by panels on the church's dome. Outside, behind the church, Avenida Vargas stretches beyond view in the direction of São Cristóvão and the Zona Norte. This was also the starting point for the Carnival parades that took place after the construction of the enormous avenue, until 1984 when an official parade ground was inaugurated on the other side of town.

Two other sites of historic interest are located on this end of Avenida Rio Branco, the **Praça Mauá,** and old dockside square that has seen its share of history, and an early monastery, the **Mosteiro do São Bento.** Return to the intersection of Rio Branco with Presidente Vargas and before turning away toward the bay, look down the length of Rio Branco for a long view of the imposingly winged War Memorial in the distance. Then, walk to the Praça Mauá for a quick inspection of the still-active pier, and return along Rio Branco to Rua Dom Geraldo at the opposite end of which is the São Bento Monastery. The monastery complex is an unadulterated example of early-17th-century church and convent architecture, dating from the mid-1600s and built on the side of a *ladeira,* a steep incline overlooking the bay. To enter the monastery, take the elevator at no. 40— and you must be appropriately dressed (no shorts or halters). Enjoy a moment of quiet meditation on the lovely grounds and visit above all the rococo chapel with the gold-leaf interior. Look also for the 17th-century paintings of Friar Ricardo do Pilar, including *O Salvador (The Savior),* which hangs in the sacristy.

The Largo da Carioca

This is Carioca Square, a crossroad for street life in the city (there is a Metro stop right on the square). The first thing you will probably want to do when you get here is to check out the vendors and the entertainers who fill the square and line the neighboring blocks.

On a low rise overlooking the largo is the **Convento do Santo Antônio** and its church, built between 1608 and 1615 and notable for the decorative use of *azuleijos,* those white Portuguese tiles that are hand-painted using only the color blue. Directly next door is the **Igreja São Francisco da Penitência,** on the corner of Rua Uruguaiana, a street noted for its bargain shopping. The church, which was built in 1773, is of the later baroque period, with an elaborately carved wooden altar and ceiling murals by José de Oliveira that are worth pondering.

Heading east toward the Avenida Rio Branco, you will see the **Teatro Municipal,** a small-scale replica of the Paris Opéra, set back on the Praça Floriano. This is Rio's temple of high culture, which has hosted the Brazilian arts as well as many international performers since opening in 1909. Check the box office while you're here to see if there's something going on you'd like to see. And also check out the **Café do Teatro,** if only to ogle the movie-epic décor.

Practically across from the theater at Avenida Rio Branco 199 is the **Museu Nacional de Belas Artes,** the Museum of Fine Arts (tel. 240-0160), Rio's most important art museum. The collection of Brazilian paintings provides a comprehensive visual account of the country's artistic development, and of its social and cultural history as well. Of contemporary interest is the painting *Café* by the Brazilian modernist Cândido Portinari. The museum is open Tuesday and Thursday from 10 a.m. to 6:30 p.m., on Monday and Wednesday from noon to 6:30 p.m., and on Saturday, Sunday, and holidays from 3′ to 6 p.m. There is an admission charge.

On to Lapa

Continue on down Avenida Rio Branco—you're going toward the War Memorial now—until you come to Rua do Passeio. Turn in here toward the neighborhood of Lapa. On the left you will pass the **Passeio Público,** Rio's oldest park, which once began at the waters edge before landfill pushed back the bay. The park is a bit of a no-man's-land at this point, in need of some care and regular tending, but its basic look is captivating because the landscaping dates from 1775 when public gardens reflected a very different view of nature than they do today.

When you reach the **Largo da Lapa,** look for the **Sala Cecília Meirelles,** a concert hall, at no. 47. This is a favorite place to hear classical orchestral and chamber music in Rio. A little farther along, at Avenida Mem de Sá 15, is the **Asa Branca** *gafieira,* a musical hall of a different type which is described more fully in the section on nightlife. The Asa Branca building is one of many in the neighborhood dating from the middle of the last century that have had their exteriors lovingly restored. Lapa was once a bohemian quarter and hub of Rio's cabaret life. Something of that era seems to linger in the air, making Lapa a delightful place for an unstructured stroll.

If your consumer curiosity is piqued, drop in at the Mesbla department store, Brazil's largest chain, and look around. Make sure you check out the store's rooftop restaurant.

From the Largo da Lapa, walk up Avenida República do Paraguai and cross under the aqueduct, officially the **Aqueduto da Carioca,** but known simply as **os arcos** (the arches). To remedy the shortage of fresh water within the city proper, the aqueduct was begun in 1724, linking the springs of hilly Santa Teresa with a public fountain in what is now the Largo da Carioca. Since 1896, when tracks were laid, the Lapa arches have shouldered a **trolley-car line,** the only one that still functions in Rio. Today passengers follow the ancient route of the water from the terminal on the Avenida República do Chile, near the Largo da Carioca, up through the winding streets of Santa Teresa.

The large conical dome that dominates the horizon beyond the arches is not a nuclear power plant, though use of this design in an urban setting seems grimly in pace with the times. What is strange, however, is that the city's **Nova Catedral** (New Cathedral), on Avenida República do Chile just above the Largo da Carioca, should have assumed such a shape. The building is massive, the exterior segmented by four huge stained-glass windows, and it has a standing-room capacity of 20,000 worshippers. Personally, I would feel as if I were delivering my prayers through the funnel of a jet turbine to the Great Engineer in the sky (we all have our biases, and when it comes to churches, mine is for the baroque of stone, timber, and plaster over the high tech).

The Nova Catedral stands on flattened terrain that was once a hill, the Morro do Santo Antônio. In Rio, urban renewal and slum clearance has on several occasions taken the form of removing the entire hill occupied by a *favela,* or poor neighborhood, and using the earth for landfill somewhere else, usually a nice upper-class neighborhood. Thus did the hill of Santo Antônio become the *aterro* (landfill) of Flamengo Park, which was completed in 1960.

From the Largo da Carioca you can take the subway in either direction, depending on the next environment you wish to explore. Nowhere else in Rio, however, will you get as concentrated a sampling of historical sights and exhibitions as is available in the vicinity of the Largo da Carioca and the Praça XV. Many of the remaining museums and miscellaneous sights can best be visited individually, or in the case of the next itinerary, the Zona Norte, possibly linked to other excursions of interest. There is the **Feira Nordestinho** every Sunday morning from 6 a.m. till 1 p.m. in São Cristóvão, an old neighborhood of the Zona Norte close to downtown. Other attractions that could bring you to the area are a visit to an **escola de samba** (samba school) rehearsal, or a soccer game at **Maracanã Stadium.**

The Zona Norte

There are several points of interest in and around São Cristóvão. Take the subway to the São Cristóvão stop, where you will be visiting the nearby **Quinta da Boa Vista,** a royal residence for all of Brazil's monarchs. The pink-and-white mansion was built in 1803 by a wealthy Portuguese colonial named Lopes, and bestowed on Dom João VI and the royal family when they arrived in 1808. Dom João was the architect of Brazil's major cultural institutions, including the country's first museum, now installed in the old palace. The entrance hall to the museum contains the Bêndego meteorite, which was discovered in the state of Bahia in 1888, perhaps the world's largest at almost 12,000 pounds. Displayed throughout are all the elements of a natural history museum as they pertain to the Brazilian experience: birds, mammals, reptiles, insects, plants, minerals, prehistoric relics, and artifacts of the country's various indigenous cultures. There is a separate **Museu de Faúna,** a museum of Brazilian fauna, at the Quinta da Boa Vista as well. The National Museum (tel. 264-8262) is open Tuesday through Sunday, from 10 a.m. to 4:45 p.m.

The **Jardim Zoológico** (the Zoo) is located on the grounds of the Quinta da Boa Vista—which means, incidentally, the country house with the nice view. The grounds are what you would expect from what was once a private royal park, including an elegantly geometric garden filled with sophisticated marble statuary. Brazil has many birds and animal species that are not found in North America, or even elsewhere on its own continent. Those who plan a trip from Rio to the Amazon region will have ample opportunity to view these creatures. If not, Rio's zoo is a very good place for an introduction to the country's unique birds and animals. There are capybaras and boas, jaguars and monkeys, tapirs and toucans, and much, much more. The zoo is open from 8 a.m. till 4:30 p.m. every day except Monday.

Although the **Igreja Nossa Senhora da Penha,** in Penha, is distant from downtown, true lovers of church architecture, as well as adventurous train buffs, might find the trip worthwhile. Our Lady of Penha sits high on a hill, where 365 steps cut from the rock ascend to the church door. Some penitents make the climb on their knees in a gesture of atonement or thanksgiving (a funicular transports those who cannot or do not wish to negotiate the steps). Inside the church are hung crutches and plastic facsimiles of body parts, the votive offerings of those who have been delivered by the intercession of Our Lady from their suffering. This particular form of devotion seems peculiar to the Roman church in the Portuguese- and Spanish-speaking countries.

If you don't go to Penha by cab or car, you could try the suburban train, the Leopoldinha line. Pick up the train at the Barão de Mauá Station in São Cristóvão, or take it all the way to the Penha neighborhood.

Between Downtown and the Zona Sul

If you had headed back toward the Zona Sul from your downtown tour, you could make a stop at the Glória subway station and visit the octagonal church called **Nossa Senhora da Glória do Outeiro** (Our Lady of Glory on the Knoll). This famous society church, built in 1714, is located behind the Glória Hotel at Praça da Glória 135 (tel. 225-2869), and is open to the public Monday to Friday from 8 a.m. to noon and 1 to 5 p.m. Emperor Pedro II was married in Our Lady of Glória, and his daughter, the Crown Princess Isabel, was baptized there. The Glória's interior also contains carvings by Mestre Valentim, most notably the main altar. Access to the church's collection of sacred art can be arranged by contacting one of the priests. On August 15 the church is ablaze with decorative lights in honor of the Feast of the Assumption, and provides a striking sight against the darkened background of the surrounding mountains.

If you want to get a closer look at the War Memorial, the **Monumento dos Mortos da II Guerra,** this would be a good opportunity. Walk from the church to the Praça Paris, a park that was indeed laid out in Parisian style with formal hedges, fountain, and reflecting pools. Do not attempt to cross the Avenida Beira Mar—instead locate the nearest underpass or overpass. Please keep in mind that pedestrians are always in season from the point of view of any Carioca who is behind the wheel of a—usually speeding—automobile. There is a small museum next to the War Memorial that explains Brazil's role in the Italian campaign during World War II.

Toward downtown from the memorial, but still in Flamengo Park, is the **Museu de Arte Moderna** (the Modern Art Museum; tel. 210-2188), or MAM as it is known locally. The building and the grounds are of more interest than the collection, much of which was destroyed by a fire in 1978. The MAM is in the process of reaquisition of works, and is used primarily as a site for visiting exhibitions. It's open Tuesday through Sunday from noon to 6 p.m. Films are shown daily, and there is also a reliable restaurant on the premises.

Opposite the Catete subway stop at Rua do Catete 179 (entrance on Rua Silveira Martíns) is the **Museu da República** (Museum of the Republic), which occupies the Catete Palace, formerly the official residence of Brazil's presidents until the transfer of the country's capital to Brasília in 1960. Getúlio Vargas committed suicide here in 1954 while still in office, and the bedroom where his body was found has been preserved. The collection begins where the National History Museum leaves off, with the founding of the Republic. There are exhibits of presidential memorabilia and furnishings. The grounds of the palace, planted with towering royal palms, and the impeccable garden are also open to the public —or will be when the restoration work that has been going on since 1984 is completed. Till then, there are two guided tours each month. To reserve a place, or to find out if full operations have been resumed, call either 225-4302 or 265-9747.

THE MUSEUMS OF FLAMENGO AND BOTAFOGO:

On Avenida Rui Barbosa, across from no. 560 at the southern end of Flamengo Park, is the **Carmen Miranda Museum** (tel. 551-2597). The Portuguese-born chanteuse and one-time Las Vegas headliner helped put Brazil on the map for many Americans in the '30s and '40s with her Latin rhythms and outrageous hats of dangling fruit and full-skirted *baiana* costumes, many of which are on display in this small tidy collection. Open Tuesday through Friday from 11 a.m. to 5 p.m., and on weekends and holidays from 1 to 5 p.m. The Flamengo station is the closest subway stop to this section of the park.

There are a number of smaller museums in Botafogo that are worth a visit if you've got the time. Near the Botafogo subway stop is Rua São Clemente, where at no. 134 you will find the **Museu Casa de Rui Barbosa** (tel. 286-1297, extension 45), the house of the remarkable statesman and jurist that has been opened to the public since 1930. Author of Brazil's first constitution after the founding of the Republic, Rui Barbosa was also a lifelong abolitionist. In his zeal to obliterate the memory of the cruel institution, Barbosa ordered all official records and documents relating to slavery destroyed following the emancipation. This action was strangely out of place from a man who could read in seven languages and who devoted his life to scholarship. Barbosa's library of over 30,000 volumes is open to the public, as are the many rooms of this rambling pink mansion. Open Tuesday through Friday from 10 a.m. to 4:30 p.m., and on weekends and holidays from 2 to 5 p.m.

The **Museu do Índio** (Indian Museum) is located off Rua São Clemente some blocks farther into Botafogo at Rua das Palmeiras 55 (tel. 286-8799). This exhibition of Indian artifacts is small but intelligently displayed. After an hour's study of the photographs and cultural objects, you'll have a fairly good idea of the diversity of Brazil's tribes and the manner in which they lived. Particularly beautiful are the items of dress and adornment that were expertly crafted from the raw material of nature—feathers, bones, shells, and noble hardwoods—into headdresses, jewelry, and various practical utensils for eating or storing food. Tapes of native language and music are also available, and there is an inventory of films that document the contemporary lives and struggles of Brazil's remaining Indians. Open weekdays from 10 a.m. to 5 p.m.; closed weekends.

SANTA TERESA: If you want to get a representative taste of old Rio and you only have a limited time available after visiting the obligatory sights of Corcovado and Pão de Açúcar, go to Santa Teresa. This hilly neighborhood close to the center of town was settled early in Rio's history, primarily by the well-to-do who sought the elevation as a refuge from the heat and noise below. The architectural integrity of the neighborhood is remarkable. Private homes, some extremely lavish, and small commercial buildings preserve a pre-20th-century scale throughout the area, and picturesque narrow streets wind dramatically among the rising slopes.

The main attractions in Santa Teresa, beyond the place itself—which merits a long drive, or better yet, a good old-fashioned constitutional—are a restaurant called the Bar do Arnaudo, and a museum, the Chácara do Céu, the former private residence of a wealthy industrialist that houses the art treasures of his rich and selective collection.

In the past, when one wanted to introduce a friend to the charms of Santa Teresa, there was no question that the way to get there was via the old **bonde,** the streetcar trolley that leaves from near the Largo da Carioca and rides above Lapa along the old aqueduct. But the *bonde,* especially where tourists are concerned, has been the object of considerable controversy in recent years. Gangs of young marauders have apparently found the trolley an easy target for their muggings, and the incidents are said to have occurred with alarming frequency in recent years. Because the trains were open on all sides to allow for the constant boarding and getting off while the train remained in motion, they were particularly vulnerable to these lightning assaults. Today sections of the trains have been closed off by wire mesh, and police now ride shotgun to discourage the bold assailants, who have always operated in broad daylight. The trains, moreover, are always packed, and the citizens of Rio, in growing outrage at the street crime epidemic, have been increasingly coming to the aid of assault victims, a case where the remedy is at times more ugly than the offense.

It is difficult to make a judgment as to whether a tourist ought or ought not to ride the *bonde,* though I'm tempted to answer in the affirmative, if for no other reason than that the train's bad reputation has made the authorities and passengers more alert, a condition that is not favorable to thievery. Nevertheless, tourists often stand out, and in the minds of the muggers, are likely to represent fairly risk-free targets. In conclusion, I personally believe that one can ride the *bonde* these days without great risk if you keep a low profile, leave your valuables in the hotel, and follow the lead of the thousands of passengers who ride the train daily without incident.

If you opt for the experience of the trolley ride, ask the driver to leave you off in the vicinity of the **Chácara do Céu Museum,** Rua Murtinho Nobre 93 (tel. 224-8981). The walk is somewhat circuitous, and will take you down one of the many stairways cut into the hillside, but the museum sits on a rise at the end of this dead-end street, and there are signs that indicate the way. By bus, take the no. 206 or 214 from the downtown bus terminal, Menezes Cortes, to Rua Dias de Barras and follow the signs. The word *chácara* in Portuguese conveys the image of a gentleman farmer's country home, and *céu* means sky or heaven. This former home of the industrialist Raymundo de Casto Maia, however, has more of the Bauhaus about it than the barnyard. The home is very modern, and the grounds are landscaped and beautiful, but urban in their inspiration, not rural.

The modernist influence pervades the mansion in its design, its furnishings, and its art, one of the best small collections of impressionist and modern paintings in the country. While of a later vintage, the collection here has a force similar to that of the Frick in New York City, but on a much reduced scale of grandeur. The studies of Don Quixote in colored pencil by Cândido Portinari occupy an entire room. The work of other greats, Brazilian and foreign, are distributed throughout the mansion. They include canvases by Di Cavilcanti, Monet, Degas, Matisse, Miró, Modigliani, and Picasso. The library is the warmest room in the house, which almost seems to have been conceived as a gallery rather than as part of a dwelling. A large ground-floor space is given over to some very whimsical exhibitions, as in 1987 when bathroom interiors of the past—complete with all the fixtures—were juxtaposed with those of the present. Prints, catalogs, and postcard reproductions of the collection are sold in the lobby. The museum is open Tuesday through Saturday from 2 to 5 p.m., and on Sunday from noon till 4:30 p.m. If you arrive by cab, make sure you have your driver wait, since it will be difficult to hail a cab in this vicinity for the return trip.

The **Bar do Arnaudo,** Rua Almirante Alexandrino 316 (tel. 252-7246), is the perfect place for refreshments or lunch before wandering over to the Chácara do Céu. The bar is located near the **Largo de Guimarães,** Santa Teresa's main square, also easily accessible by trolley or bus. The bar is a traditional rendezvous for artists whose works are often displayed on the walls. This is nonetheless a family-run restaurant, featuring the country-style food of the northeast where the owners grew up. The food is so good that it's hard to choose a single platter from the menu. Instead, ask Dona Georgina to serve you a little bit of everything in the large-portion appetizers. Open from noon till 10 p.m., daily except Monday and Tuesday.

JARDIM BOTÂNICO: A visit to the Botanical Garden must certainly rank high on the list of activities for nature lovers and birdwatchers. The gardens were the pet project of Dom João VI, who ordered the initial plantings soon after arriving from Portugal in 1808. This was the age that inspired the greatest naturalists who ever lived, including Baron Von Humbolt, and subsequently, Darwin. Dom João was clearly caught up in the naturalist vision of his day, which combined mercantile practicality with a dreamy romanticism. The garden was created as both a nursery for the adaptation of commercially desirable plants and as a great temple to nature, suitable for private walks and meditations. One has only to study the famous painting that depicts Humbolt and his native guides deep in the Amazon forest of the late 18th century to grasp the power of that melancholy vision. It was in this age that man discovered nature as the spiritual counterweight to the rise of materialism and the advances of science that everywhere accompanied the political and industrial revolutions raging in the midst of the old order. The naturalist, after all, was merely cataloguing the very nature that mankind has now embarked on destroying, while the creator of parks and gardens went about the task of both enshrining nature in discreet patches and of cultivating the merchandizable plants that were culled from the naturalist's store.

The conscious motivation for Dom João VI no doubt had more to do with the challenges of growing spices and fruits introduced from the East Indies— nutmeg and cinnamon, breadfruit and avocado. From the West Indies came many species of palm trees that were not indigenous to Brazil. No one driving by the great wall of the Jardim Botânico in Rio can fail to be moved and impressed by the 100-foot-high royal palms that stand at the periphery of the garden like sentinels and line the avenue at the main entrance. Along with these, the garden is filled with thousands of equally archetypal trees and plants; its 340 acres divided between "natural" stands and more cultivated groves. The native plants are particularly fascinating, like the Régia Victória, a water lily native to the Amazon with a giant pad up to 20 feet in diameter, and the orchids, with their intoxicating aromas that saturate the air. As for birds, there have been some 140 sightings, including occasional flocks of toucans, a creature that must have the most beautiful eyes of any on the planet.

Getting there by bus is relatively easy. It borders the Avenida Jardim Botânico, a principal thoroughfare from Gávea to Botafogo, where it becomes the Avenida São Clemente. Many bus lines travel this route, like those marked "via Jocqui" or "Jardim Botânico." The garden is open daily from 8 a.m. till 6 p.m., and there is a small admission charge.

GUANABARA BAY: For those who wish to be not just *in* the water, but also *on* it, there are several boat excursions available. The **Bâteau Mouche** has been plying the waters of the bay for many years, and offers cruises every day but Monday, leaving from Botafogo, adjacent to the Rio Yacht Club (Iate Clube), Avenida Repórter Néstor Moreira 11 (tel. 295-1997). The Bâteau Mouche has three different daily cruises. For about $25 there is a cruise that leaves the dock at 9:30 a.m., and crosses the mouth of the bay where it calls at Piratininga beach for a swim and lunch, and returns—sweeping close to Copacabana when the sea permits—at 1:30 p.m. An afternoon boat leaves at 2:30 p.m. and cruises up the bay, under the Rio–Niterói bridge and on to the island of Paquetá, returning at twilight to catch a view of the illuminated city. The cost of the afternoon cruise is approximately $18. The third cruise is an all-day affair that combines both itineraries for $30.

Paquetá has been a popular weekend and tourist destination for many years. No motor vehicles are allowed on the island, but you may hire a horse and carriage for about $5 an hour, or for $1 an hour there are bicycles for rent. Since Paquetá is quite small, these modes of transportation are completely adequate for getting around. The island has several beaches and hotels and is crowded on the weekends, but quiet during the week. Once a pristine fishing village, Paquetá has lost some of its allure since its heyday as a summer colony 30 years in the past. But it is an island in a beautiful bay, and accessible by inexpensive ferry service. The ferry leaves from Praça XV downtown, and costs 50¢ each way for the 1½-hour trip. Regularly scheduled ferries leave about every two to three hours Monday through Saturday between 5:30 a.m. and 11 p.m., and from 7 a.m. till 11 p.m. on Sunday. There is also a hydrofoil service that leaves every hour on the hour from 8 a.m. till 5 p.m. from the same dock, making the trip in a third of the time, and for only $1 each way during the week, $3 on weekends.

Boat Rental: A variety of craft, from windsurfers to cabin cruisers may be rented through private agencies and owners. For more information, either visit or call the **Marina da Glória** (tel. 285-2247).

MARACANÃ: Maracanã is the name of Rio's legendary soccer stadium, built

to hold as many as 200,000 people. Sports fans are the only ones likely to spend their time in Rio at a soccer match. But since soccer is Brazil's middle name, the true sports fanatic is very likely to be tempted for the opportunity to see the game played at its very best, in that free-wheeling, individual style that has made Brazilian players both feared and admired by their opponents throughout the world. The game of the week takes place on Sunday at 5 p.m.

There is a subway station at Maracanã, and you could go there on your own and be assured of getting a ticket. But given the size of both the stadium and the crowds, I strongly suggest that you book a tour for this particular activity. The cost will be somewhat higher than if you did it on your own, but you'll be assured of the best and most comfortable seats, transportation to and from your hotel, and most important, a reliable escort who will help you negotiate the large crowds and the unfamiliar turf. Most tour companies provide game packages to Maracanã, which can usually be booked through your hotel.

Maracanã Stadium is also used to host super-concerts and other special events. Frank Sinatra has performed there, and the pope once said Mass in Maracanã before a crowd of 180,000. In addition to its soccer field, Maracanã also has a total sports complex, with facilities for Brazil's other professional or Olympic sports, including swimming, volleyball and basketball. The gymnasium, called the Maracanazinho (Little Maracanã), holds 20,000 people and also serves as a concert hall for top names in music from home and abroad.

GEMSTONE AND JEWELRY WORKSHOP TOUR: One of the great vis-

ual attractions in Brazil—beyond her natural grandeur and historic patrimony—are the dozens of varieties of gemstones that are scooped from the country's mineral-rich earth. You don't have to fancy finished jewelry to appreciate the mystical attraction of the brilliant colored crystals, known as semiprecious stones for decades, but now—given their value and scarcity—referred to more appropriately as gemstones. In recognition of their general appeal, the H. Stern company has organized a tour of their lapidary workshops which allows you to witness craftsmen as they cut and polish the stones, design and construct their settings in gold and silver, and assemble the finished jewelry into rings, necklaces, and bracelets. The tour takes about 15 minutes and is conducted in one of seven different languages with the use of headphones. Don't forget to visit the small museum on completion of the tour to see some of the world's largest uncut gemstones, and the fascinating displays of polished gems as well, particularly the dozens of tourmalines in their many varieties of shapes and colors.

The free tour takes place during business hours in the **H. Stern Building,** located in Ipanema at Rua Visconde de Pirajá 490. H. Stern will even provide you with round-trip transportation—by private car or taxi—between the workshop and your hotel. Just contact a representative at one of the company's many outlet stores in hotels throughout Copacabana or elsewhere in the city, and arrangements for the tour will be made in a prompt and obliging manner. Clearly the tour is a form of sophisticated promotion, and the company would naturally like to attract your business. After completing the tour, you will be invited to a jewelry showroom or a large and well-stocked souvenir shop, but there is absolutely no pressure to buy. Anyone with the slightest curiosity about gemstones— where they come from, how they are mined, and how they are milled into priceless stones—will definitely find the H. Stern tour of great value.

2. THE BEST OF THE REST

For those with even more time to get acquainted with Rio, the following museums and activities have much to offer.

OTHER MUSEUMS: The **Museu do Palácio do Itamarati** (Itamarati Diplomatic Museum) Avenida Marechal Floriano 196, Centro (tel. 291-4411). Itamarati is the name still used when Brazilians refer to their Foreign Service, once housed in this palace when Rio was the country's capital. Initially a private residence, the palace was built in 1854 and later served as official home for Brazil's presidents from 1889 to 1897. The museum's collection consists of tapestries, old furnishings, and other historical artifacts, some of which relate to the life of Brazil's most distinguished foreign minister, the Barão do Rio Branco, who was a major force in South American diplomacy during the 19th century. Open Tuesday through Friday from 11:30 a.m. till 4:30 p.m.

The **Museu da Cidade** (City Museum), Estrada de Santa Marinha, Parque da Cidade, Gávea (tel. 322-1328), is located on the grounds of what was formerly a private estate and is now a well-tended public park. The City Museum documents both the development of Rio and the central role the city has played in the history of Brazil. The displays are laid out chronologically by century, and there is a special room devoted to a collection of pharmaceutical objects. Open Tuesday through Sunday and holidays from noon to 4:30 p.m.

There is a special collection of woodcarvings located on the Morro da Urca on the way up to Pão de Açúcar, called the **Museu Antônio de Oliveira** (tel. 541-5244), open daily from 9 a.m. to 6 p.m. The hundreds of carvings depict life in colonial Brazil and early Carnival scenes.

The **Museu de Foclore Edson Carneiro** (Museum of Folklore), Rua do Catete 181, Catete (tel. 285-0891), is a separate collection of craft goods, musical instruments, and items from everyday life located at the Museum of the Republic. Open Tuesday to Friday from 11 a.m. to 6 p.m., and on weekends and holidays from 3 to 5 p.m.

For an introduction to Brazilian classical and folk music, visit the **Museu da Imagem e do Som** (Sound and Image Museum), Praça Rui Barbosa 1 (tel. 282-0309, extension 181). The museum also houses a noncommercial movie theater, and numerous photographs and modern paintings. Open Monday through Friday from 2 to 6 p.m.

Near the Gávea Golf Club in São Conrado is the **Vila Riso,** Estrada da Gávea 728 (tel. 322-1444 or 322-0899), a restoration of a colonial era *fazenda* (farm). Employees don colonial garb, and will take you on a 3½-hour tour, including lunch, for $20. The tour takes you through the old-fashioned gardens and presents a medley of Brazilian theatrical music dating from the 1860s to the First World War. Lunch is buffet style, and includes feijoada and churrasco. You must make a reservation to take this tour, which is offered on Tuesday only, from 12:30 till 4 p.m., though there is talk of adding additional days during the high season if the demand warrants. Arrangements will also be made for pickup and return to your hotel.

ACTION AND AMUSEMENTS: Rio has a small but animated amusement park, the **Tívoli,** along the shores of the Lagoa, open on Thursday and Friday from

2 to 8 p.m., on Saturday from 3 to 11 p.m., and on Sunday from 10 a.m. to 10 p.m.

Next door is the city's only open air drive-in theater, and across the street is the racetrack called the **Jocqui Club.** Fans of the ponies will enjoy the grandstand restaurant (tel. 297-6655 for reservations) along with the races, which take place every Monday and Thursday night and on Saturday and Sunday afternoons. Handicappers should check the sports pages of the *Jornal do Brazil.* The track only costs about 25¢ to enter, $1 for the enclosed grandstands. Bets are taken for win (*vencedor*) and place (*place*) only.

Rio also has a **Planetarium,** Rua Padre Leonel Franca (tel. 274-0096), located in Gavea, for those who are interested in a formal presentation of the Rio starscape.

TAKING THE TOURS: Rio has many companies that package tours, big and small, and may in general be booked directly through your hotel. Some typical tour packages are:

Corcovado and the Tijuca Forest, taking in all the major overlooks, including Corcovado, the principal attractions of the forest and the beaches of Barra, Leblon, and Ipanema.

Pão de Açúcar and City Tour, including the beaches of the Zona Sul, Sugar Loaf, and downtown sights like the Lapa aqueduct, the sambadrome, and Maracanã Stadium.

Rio by Night might include a big production show and a tour of several nightclubs and discos.

If you're looking for this type of guided tour, the first place to inquire is at the **porter's desk of your own hotel.** Many hotels actually provide their own buses and itineraries.

Other companies that are reliable and experienced are **South American Turismo, Ltda.,** Avenida Nossa Senhora de Copacabana 788, sixth and seventh floors (tel. 255-2345); **Kontik-Franstur,** Avenida Atlântica, 2316 A (tel. 237-7797); and **Gray Line,** Avenida Niemeyer 121, Suite 208 (tel. 274-7146).

For a more custom-tailored tour, contact **Expeditur,** Rua Visconde de Pirajá 414 (tel. 287-9697). Expeditur specializes in tours to the Amazon and Pantanal, but also has a fleet of vans and tour guides in Rio who can give you a more personalized view of the city. "Projecto Roteiros Culturais" (Cultural Tour Project) offers high-brow tours of museums, colonial and imperial Rio, and the Botanical Garden, and can be contacted at their round-the-clock number (tel. 322-4872) or at their offices in Copacabana, Rua Santa Clara 110, Suite 904. Daytime tours are generally in the $20 range, and tours by night run twice that amount or more, since they tend to include a show with drinks, and sometimes dinner.

TWO GOOD BOOKS: There is an excellent book of photographs of "Old Rio" available in most good bookstores. The title is **O Rio Antigo do Fotógrafo Marc Ferrez** ($15) and contains over 200 photos of Rio taken between 1865 and 1918. Another book, significantly more esoteric, but wonderful also for its illustrations, city plans, and photographs, is **Evolução Urbana do Rio de Janeiro** ($7) by Maurício de A. Abreu, about Rio's urban growth from colonial times to the present. Both books are in Portuguese only.

3. THE SHOPPING SCENE

Rio is a giant marketplace, filled with shops and shopping malls, souvenir stores and street fairs. Shopping in Rio can be a search for bargains in clothes or shoes at a fashionable boutique near your hotel. Or it can be an opportunity to explore up-close the popular culture by wandering from stall to stall at one of the open-air markets that are regularly scheduled at various points throughout the city. But whether you approach shopping as an end in itself, or as a means to explore Rio off the beaten track, you are likely to find many items that will please your eye and tempt your purse.

Because of Brazil's status as a developing nation, many items that U.S. residents purchase there, including gemstones and jewelry, may be duty free. A list of exempt items can be obtained from the U.S. Customs Service. Shops in Brazil tend to be open Monday through Friday from 9 a.m. till 6 or 7 p.m., and on Saturday until 1 p.m. Shopping malls generally remain open till 10 p.m. Most, but not all, stores are closed on Sunday, which is a day for street fairs at several locations in the city.

ARTS AND CRAFTS:
The **Hippie Fair,** or Feirarte as it is also known, occupies every inch of the spacious Praça General Osório in Ipanema on Sunday all year round. At about 9 a.m. the artists and artisans begin to mount their booths and displays, and they remain there throughout the day until sunset. Paintings and woodcarvings occupy one large section, and as is generally the case with open-air art markets, you have to search carefully for anything original among all the dross. There are many stalls selling costume jewelry, predominantly silver pieces, but also bone, beads, and of course, gemstones, both loose and in settings. Leather goods are also much in evidence, primarily belts and handbags, as well as wallets, sandals, and portmanteaux. Check the stitching before making any leather purchases. Other items of interest are handmade toys and cooking utensils, hammocks, and musical instruments. Most of the vendors know enough English to be able to bargain. Never accept the first price, unless you just can't imagine getting it any cheaper.

The **Feira do Nordeste** (Northeast Fair) is the other Sunday street market of major interest. Much less artsy than its counterpart in Ipanema, the Northeast Fair caters more to the everyday needs of working people and is also somewhat of a weekly popular festival. Many of the stalls sell food typical of Brazil's northeastern states, and there are always many groups and individuals playing regional music as well. While the Hippie Fair may be a more suitable place to buy souvenirs for friends and family, you should think of the Northeast Fair as a cultural event, and a very entertaining one at that, although you will no doubt find something to purchase in the hundreds and hundreds of booths that spread out in all directions. The fair's one drawback is its location in the Campo do São Cristóvão on the Zona Norte side of downtown, near the National Museum at the Quinta da Boa Vista. The most direct route is by cab through the Rebouças Tunnel, the same centrally located tunnel you will take to get to Corcovado. The Northeast Fair is open from 6 a.m. till 6 p.m., on Sunday only.

ANTIQUE MARKETS:
There is a weekly antique market, **Feira de Antiguidades,** on Saturday from 9 a.m. to 5 p.m. near the Praça XV, downtown. Among the more transportable items are stamps, coins, and antique weapons. The Passeio Público **stamp and coin markets** are on Sunday mornings. A smaller **antique fair** of more recent vintage also takes place on Sunday in Barra da Tijuca on the grounds of the Casa Shopping Mall from 10 a.m. to 6 p.m. The well-regarded **Rodeio Churracaria** is also located in Casa Shopping, by the way.

More serious antique buffs might want to take in an auction. There are several convenient **auction houses** in Ipanema and Copacabana, like the Investirarte, located in the Cassino Atlântica mall, attached to the Rio Palace Hotel. Check the Saturday and Sunday editions of the local newspapers *O Globo* or *Jornal do Brasil* under *"Leilao,"* the Portuguese word for auction.

STREET MARKETS: Open-air fruit and vegetable markets take place throughout Rio's neighborhoods on a rotating basis. They usually begin at dawn and are over around midday. For color, smell, and general kaleidoscopic crowd activity, nothing in the day-to-day world of the Cariocas surpasses these markets as public spectacles. Every minute you spend at one of these markets is an education, whether to study and taste the produce or to watch the hearty *favelodos* as they dismantle the stalls and load them on the festively painted flat-bed trucks. The whole event has the energy of a circus coming to town. And when the tents have moved on, all that's left is the strong odor of spoiled produce embedded in the pavement that awaits the arrival of the sanitation trucks.

In **Copacabana,** there are open-air markets on Wednesday on Rua Domingos Ferreria, on Thursday on Rua Belford Roxo and Rua Ronald de Carvalho (close to Avenida Princesa Isabel), and on Sunday on Rua Decio Vilares (near the Praça Edmundo Bittencourt). **Leme** has its market on Monday on Rua Gustavo Sampaio. The **Ipanema** street markets are on Monday on Henrique Dumont, on Tuesday at Praça General Osório, and on Friday at Praça da Paz. And the **Leblon** market is on Thursday on Rua General Urquiza.

FLOWER MARKET: The center of the flower market is downtown on the Praça Olavo Bilac, off Rua Gonçalves Dias, near the Rua Uruguaiana Metro stop. For fancy floral arrangements or corsages, there is a flower shop at the Copacabana Palace Hotel on Copacabana beach.

Generally, it is forbidden to enter the U.S. with botanical or agricultural products from abroad. But there is at least one plant that U.S. Customs allows, the **pau d'agua.** At some point during your stay in Brazil you are bound to see someone at a flower stall or on the street selling what looks like the segmented and leafless limb of a tree. These are *pau d'aguas,* or water sticks. You take it home, stick it in water, and it sprouts into the most amazing tropical plant—the waxy, palm-like fronds grow right out of the stalk in great profusion.

THE FASHION SCENE: Many travelers to Rio, particularly women, find the city's clothing fashions much to their tastes and very pleasantly affordable when compared with prices at home. The principal street for fashions is **Rua Visconde de Pirajá,** in Ipanema, which is lined with boutiques from one end to the other. Many fine shops are also located on the side streets of both Ipanema and Leblon. The main items of interest are formal and sports apparel, shoes and sandals, and swimwear. The favorite fabrics for dresses and outfits—generally in the $30 to $100 range—are cotton, linen, jersey, and silk. Acrylic knit dresses, ideal for traveling, are also quite popular. Tops, skirts, and pants made of smooth and often multitoned leather, are more expensive. Well-made sandals and pumps of many styles costs between $10 and $20, while highly styled dress shoes in soft, sculpted leather are between $50 and $75.

For women's clothing try **Mariazinha,** Rua Visconde de Pirajá 365A, next to the **Forum,** a gallery of several shops, including **La Bagagerie, Elle et Lui** for both sexes, and **Soft Shoes** for footwear. Also in this block, across from the Praça da Paz, there is a VARIG-Cruzeiro airline office and a **Casa Piano** câmbio which changes money at the black-market rate. Going in the direction of Leblon is the **Galeria 444,** between Rua Maria Quitéria and Rua Garcia, an arcade of shops and galleries, including **Bum Bum** for bikinis and beachwear, and **Benneton** with men's and women's apparel. The Brazilian airline VASP has a ticket office in 444.

AN ARTIST'S STUDIO: For an opportunity to see some interesting primitives and woodcarvings, and possibly meet a charming pair of international artists, visit the studio of **Batista and Mady,** Rua Pacheco Leão 1270 (tel. 227-8702 or 294-6715 for an appointment).

SOUVENIRS: Brazil, like any other country, has what would have to be considered its traditional souvenirs. Typical of the *tchotchkes* are butterfly trays, carvings, stuffed snakes, and of course, T-shirts.

The most typical of all Brazilian souvenirs is the **figa,** a good luck charm in the shape of a fist with the thumb between the second and third fingers, available in a variety of materials from carved wood and stone to silver. According to tradition, however, the charm is only potent if you have received the figa as a present. It is therefore a nice, simple gift for the folks back home.

Most of the souvenir trade is centered in Copacabana, between Rua Paula Freitas and the Praça do Lido, primarily along Avenida Nossa Senhora de Copacabana. Look for **Macumba Souvenir** and **Liane.** Other popular souvenir shops are **Foclore,** Avenida Atlântica 1782, for Indian artifacts, and **Copacabana Couros e Artesanatos,** Rua Fernando Mendes 45A, for leather goods, especially in crocodile.

It should be mentioned that **Avenida Nossa Senhora de Copacabana,** which runs parallel to the ocean one block in, is the major shopping street in the Copacabana neighborhood. Copacabana, with its 300,000 residents, has been called a ghetto for the rich, and in Rio it's billed as the most densely populated neighborhood in the world. This street is a scene of animated street life from early in the morning till late at night, and contains shops of every type, including its own share of fancy boutiques. To experience and enjoy in full, you should stroll along one end to the other.

DOWNTOWN SHOPPING: While you are walking around downtown, you'll certainly want to poke your head into any number of stores that strike your fancy. For the opposite of Ipanema chic, wander over to **Rua Uruguaiana** and its surrounding streets, and you'll see many clothing stores, and perhaps score a real bargain. At Rua do Rosário 155 is **Kosmos,** a shop specializing in old engravings and prints of the city, like those of Jean Baptist Debret, the French artist who has left an amazing pictoral record of early-19th-century Rio.

THE SHOPPING CENTERS: Over the past ten years the shopping-mall phenomenon has exploded throughout Rio. This occurrence doesn't seem to have reduced the consumer movement in neighborhood shops, but rather to have added a new dimension to the city's shopping habits. The malls, for example, tend to open later than most neighborhood shops. They also provide free and ample parking, which is always a challenge in heavily populated areas like Ipanema and Copacabana.

Barra Shopping, Avenida das Américas 4666, Barra da Tijuca, is said to be the largest shopping center in South America. Barra Shopping houses 322 shops, all under the same roof. In addition to large department stores like Sears and Mesbla, there are dozens of restaurants and lunch counters, and even an amusement center with rides and video games for the children. Barra can also boast Rio's only ice-skating rink. Shuttle buses run between 40 of the major hotels and the shopping center on a fixed schedule. The first bus leaves from Leme at about 10:15 a.m., and the final bus of the evening returns at 9 p.m. For details on scheduling, check at the porter's desk of your hotel. Barra is about a 30-minute cab or car ride from Copacabana, and stores are open from 10 a.m. till 10 p.m. Monday through Saturday. Entertainment and recreational areas are open seven days a week from 10 a.m. till midnight.

Carrefour, Avenida das Américas 5150, right next door to Barra Shopping, is a gigantic supermarket and home center. Any one with a passion for large supermarkets, and sufficient time in Rio to warrant the visit, ought to visit Carrefour just for the experience. Row after row of edible commodities, fresh, packaged, and canned, will dazzle your eyes and set your mouth watering. Students of labels and packaging techniques will thrill to the overwhelming selection of goods to browse and admire. On a practical note, pick up a few large bottles of mineral water or beverage of your choice to stock the fridge in your hotel room rather than paying those outrageous mini-bar prices. Open from 8 a.m. to 10 p.m. Monday through Saturday. While you're there, especially if you're feeling a bit nostalgic, check out the branch of the "golden arches."

Casa Shopping, Rua Alvorado 2150, in Barra da Tijuca, is the newest shopping center in Rio. Tiles, tubs, wallpaper, and furnishings—everything you need for home design is here in many shops that all have first-floor entrances on the street. There are also numerous restaurants, including the famous Rodeio, and several cinemas. The open-air antique fair also takes place here on Sunday. Store hours are the same as at Barra Shopping.

Shopping da Gávea, Rua Marquês de São Vicente 52, Gávea. Gávea is an inland neighborhood bordered by Leblon and the Jocqui Club racetrack. Because of the Catholic University there, it is somewhat a college neighborhood. Rua Marquês de São Vicente is a main drag, a westward extension of Avenida Jardim Botânico. Shopping da Gávea is a very toney mall, with high-fashion shops, art galleries, and show rooms of designer furnishings. Of special interest is the branch of **John Somer,** Brazilian manufacturers of fine pewter, the word for which in Portuguese is *estanho* (literally, "tin," the principal metal used to make the product).

Rio Design Center, Avenida Ataúfo de Paiva 270, Leblon, is where Cariocas go when they want the latest in home decorations and designer furnishings.

Rio Sul, Avenida Lauro Muller 116, in Botafogo, is the closest full-size shopping center to Copacabana, located on the other side of the Tunel Novo at the end of Avenida Princesa Isabel. In addition to the many boutiques, there is a toy store and a branch of both Mesbla and Lojas Americanas, the Brazilian equivalent of Woolworths. Rio Sul also operates a free bus service to and from many major hotels, and is open Monday through Saturday from 10 a.m. till 10 p.m.

GEMSTONES: Brazil is said to produce 90% of the world's colored gemstones. Furthermore, the low cost of labor in Brazil means that stones and finished jewels purchased in the country are 20% to 40% cheaper than comparable products elsewhere. For this reason, and because of the stones' intrinsic beauty, visitors to Brazil are often excited by the prospect of finding attractive gemstones, set in traditional jewelry or by themselves, to carry home as investments and as remembrances of their trip. The visitor in Rio, the country's gemstone capital, can be forgiven for thinking that practically all Brazilians deal in gemstones, so aggressively are the precious rocks marketed to arriving tourists. This misconception can make the task of a reliable gemstone purchase that much more difficult. Assuming you are not a gemological expert, how do you know you are getting a stone that's worth what you're paying for it? In fact, how do you know if you're even getting the stone you think you're paying for?

These potential dilemmas can best be remedied by purchasing your stones and jewelry from one of Rio's major gem dealers, who stand behind their products and provide buyers with certificates of appraisal and other safeguards like credit, exchange, or repurchase guarantees. The two largest and best-known jewelers in Brazil are the H. Stern Company and Amsterdam Sauers, the Hertz and

Avis of Brazilian gemstones. Both enterprises are vertically integrated companies, which means that they handle all phases of the gemstone operation from mining through retailing. You won't have any trouble finding retail outlets for either company. Their stores are located at the airports, in all the major hotels, and at many other points throughout the city.

Brazilian jewelers offer all the world's precious stones at reduced prices, including diamonds, rubies, and sapphires. But the best deals are to be had on those gems that come from Brazil's own mines. These are amethyst, aquamarine, citrine, emerald, opal, topaz, and tourmaline. The price per carat of a given stone depends on numerous factors, not the least of which is its visual beauty—a quality that is difficult to guage. In general, the fixed criteria of a gem's worth are based on a stone's color (both its shade and degree of transparency) and on its clarity or absence of flaws. In some cases, however, as with cat's-eye tourmalines or star sapphires, the flaw is considered intrinsic to the stone's beauty and value. The major characteristics for each of the Brazilian stones—including what some believe are their healing and mythical properties—are listed below:

Amethyst is the most highly prized quartz variety of gemstone. Colors range from pale lilac to rich purple. Believed to protect against blood disease and drunkenness, the amethyst signifies purity and is the birthstone for February.

Aquamarine, next to emerald, is the most highly prized of the beryls. It ranges from pale to deep blue, the price often depending on the depth of its shading. Frequently free of flaws, the aquamarine is said to calm the nerves, and to revive a lagging marriage. Sailors have long worn the stone as protective amulets. Aquamarine is the birthstone for March.

Citrine is quartz that grades from smoky brown to deep yellow. It looks like precious topaz, but costs far less, so you must be particularly careful when purchasing the latter stone. Still, the citrine is beautiful in its own right, and is believed to have powers to aid failing eyesight. It is the birthstone for November.

Emerald is the most valuable of the beryls, and has been in fashion for millennia. A fine stone of good color—deep green with no tint of blue or yellow—and flaw free can cost $50,000 a carat. Emeralds are believed to strengthen the memory and to protect against temptation and seduction. The emerald is the birthstone for May.

Opal, composed of silicone oxide, is called the queen of gems. The most popular are white with fireflies of red, gold, blue, purple, and green. The rarest and costliest are black, harlequin patterned. The opal is considered bad luck, unless it is your birthstone, which it is for those born in October.

Topaz is brilliant and sparkling. The most important color range is from yellow to brown, with rich sherry-brown the most expensive—up to $1,000 a carat. The gem also comes in pink (the rare imperial topaz) and in blue, which is becoming increasingly popular as aquamarines get more and more expensive. Said to heal insomnia, the topaz is also to be worn as a ring to guard against untimely death. The topaz is the birthstone for November.

Tourmaline comes in virtually any color you can imagine, but the most popular is emerald green. Some crystals have two or three color bands. These are called watermelon tourmalines because they are almost always green on the outside and pink in the center. Tourmalines are believed to attract goodwill and friendship, and are the alternative birthstone for October.

In all, there are about 90 different types of gemstones, though only 20 are of particular interest to jewelers. The names of some of these other stones you may see offered for sale are garnet, agate, hermatite, and amazonite.

The headquarters for **H. Stern and Company** is the modern 18-story building in Ipanema at Rua Visconde de Pirajá 490 (tel. 259-7442). The company, founded by Hans Stern, a refugee from Nazi Germany and a brilliant success story, now has 170 stores and retail centers throughout Brazil and in 13 countries worldwide—including New York City, at 645 Fifth Ave. (tel. 212/688-0300), which exists primarily to service North American clients who have made their purchases in Brazil. Stern makes the following warranty for his products: "If we say something is perfect, it is perfect. If we say it is genuine, it is genuine." See the Gemstone and Jewelry Workshop Tour information in Section 1 for details on the company's free tour of its workshops.

Amsterdam Sauer, Rua Mexico 41 (tel. 220-8332), is H. Stern's closest competitor. The company also has many outlets throughout Rio, including those at the Rio Palace, Meridien, and Caesar Park Hotels. The New York office, at 580 Fifth Ave. (tel. 212/869-5558), does no retail business, but services North American clients and handles the company's export business. Founder Jules Roger Sauer's background is remarkably similar to that of Hans Stern, (he also just managed to flee Europe on the eve of World War II). Sauer is the author of the excellent illustrated book *Brazil: Paradise of Gemstones,* which is printed in seven languages including English (available in bookstores throughout Rio for about $10).

4. Rio's Nightlife

Do Cariocas ever sleep? This is a question you may find yourself asking after spending any time at all in Rio de Janeiro. Practically any night of the week, no matter where you are in the city, the restaurants are filled and the clubs and bars are jumping. *Movimento* the Brazilians call it—motion. *Movimento* plays as important a role in the daily life cycle of Cariocas as the *praia* (the beach). During the week, of course, there is not as much *movimento* as there is on the weekends, when favorite nightspots are filled to the rafters and pulsating with the *papo* (table talk) and steamy rhythms of whatever music happens to be occupying the same air space as the animated conversation.

And music is as inevitable an ingredient of Rio's nightlife as are sand and surf to the makeup of a beach. If there is no band around to make the music for them, Brazilians will make their own. Key chains, match boxes, the edge of a table—whatever. These are the instruments that Cariocas will employ for the spontaneous *batucadas* (rhythm jams) that break out from table to table wherever Cariocas gather to let down their hair.

And song. Brazilians love to sing—especially the great samba tunes of yesterday and today. They love to "join in," whether at clubs or concerts, the lack of inhibition being practically universal in this country of Carnival, where people of all backgrounds are taught from childhood to feel free about singing and dancing in public.

Things don't really begin to happen at night in Rio until after midnight. After work, people go home to *tomar banho e descansar* ("take a shower and rest up") for the long night's festivities ahead. By around 10 p.m. the restaurants and clubs slowly begin to fill, and most of them then remain open until the last customer toasts the dawn for the final time. Sunday and Monday nights are the slowest, depending on the time of year. Tuesday and Wednesday are so-so. By Thursday night the clubs are jumping all over town. Friday and Saturday nights are out-a-sight.

LIVE MUSIC: As if to tune you up for the night ahead, most deluxe and first-class hotels have small samba groups circulating in their restaurants and at poolside during lunch. And at cocktail hour in the hotel bars there is usually a piano player to take your requests.

Restaurants that are also clubs feature cabaret-style shows with music and dance. And nightclubs offer supper along with their full-blown stage productions.

Samba and jazz clubs take up the slack during the wee hours, and the main discos and dance halls also feature live bands, and you are sure to find a place suitable to your particular brand of foot stomping.

Finally, there is a new rage sweeping all of Brazil, called *karoaké* (Japanese for "empty stage"), where you and the other guests provide the entertainment.

Traditionally, many nightclubs in Rio admitted couples only, though this is no longer a hard-and-fast rule. You should check at the porter's desk of your hotel as to whether or not a particular club allows singles to enter. All clubs with live music charge an "artistic cover," generally between $3 and $8, and sometimes a minimum as well. Nightclubs are more expensive, beginning at $10 and going up to $50 for organized tours, which include dinner and a drink or two.

Samba

When Antônio Carlos Jobin and João Gilbeto wrote the tune *"Só Danço Samba"* ("I Just Dance Samba") they were expressing the almost-universal preference of their countrymen for a music and dance form that is truly Brazilian. But the samba also owes much to drum rhythms brought from Africa by the country's original slaves. This music had a religious significance, used in the spiritist rituals that are known today as *candomblé, macumba,* and *umbanda.* Drum music is central to the frenetic supplications pressed upon the gods to descend and take possession of the faithful who worship them. As each devotee is "mounted" by his or her god, they whirl and swoon until falling to the ground in a state of blissful exhaustion. The samba is the secular and popular form of music and dance that has evolved from the chanting and gyrations of these religious practices.

Samba is also the centerpiece of Carnival. If you go to Rio during Carnival, you will experience samba in its most magnificent manifestations. If, however, your trip to Rio occurs during some other time of the year, you can still sample the samba culture in a more or less authentic form, depending on time, degree of interest, and individual taste.

The **Clube do Samba,** Estrada da Barra 65, is located in the heart of Barra da Tijuca's motel district, in a large, white cinderblock building. Inside, the décor is kept to a minimum. There are café-style tables and chairs, and a spacious dance floor. Only beer and a few snacks are served. A nontouristy club, the Clube do Samba was started by musicians affiliated with several major samba schools, the huge neighborhood clubs that participate in the yearly Carnival parade. People come to hear and see the great *sambistas* of the past and present, including Alcioni, Beth Carvalho, and João Nogueira. The clube is open on Friday and Saturday nights only, and the show begins around 11 p.m. or later, but there is dancing to the *baterias* (the samba percussion bands) till dawn if the crowd is there and willing.

The **Escolas de Samba** (samba schools) rehearsals are another nontouristy way to check out the samba scene. To date, only **Beja Flor** has scheduled rehearsals in the Zona Sul, on Saturday at 9:30 p.m. in Lagoa, near the drive-in theater. But to get the real flavor of the samba schools, you must see them rehearse in their own spaces, all of which are located at various points in the Zona Norte. The most convenient from the Zona Sul are **Mangueira,** in the Palácio do Samba, Rua Visconde de Niterói, near Maracanã Stadium (tel. 234-4129), Friday through Sunday at 10 p.m.; and **Salgueiro,** Silva Teles 104 in Tijuca (tel. 246-8604), on Saturday at 10 p.m. Both rehearsal spots are relatively close to downtown.

Jazz

Jazz is alive and well, and living in Rio. Whether your preference is for be-bop, modern, or Latin, you're likely to find a group playing somewhere in the city that suits your tastes, especially if you're willing to make the rounds of the various clubs. Check the entertainment section of the local newspapers under *"Música para Ouvir"* (listening music) for name-groups—Brazilian and international—that are making the scene.

Jazzmánia, Rua Rainha Elizabeth 769, in Ipanema (tel. 227-2447), is considered one of the best jazz clubs in Rio. Located over the Barril 1800, a large beachfront café, Jazzmánia always features some top talent from the Brazilian or international jazz milieu. Here you can saturate yourself with the most sophisticated modern jazz being played in the world today.

At **Chiko's Bar,** Avenida Epitácio Pessoa 1560, in Lagoa (tel. 267-0113), every night of the week there's a combo playing, for this is one of the most popular bars in town for both couples and singles. You may not know the musicians' names, but the music is hot and professional. If you stick around until the early-morning hours, you may witness a real old-fashioned jam session, as jazzmen drift in from their gigs all over town and play at their best for their friends and themselves. You can also eat a full dinner at Chiko's, or dine in the attached Castelo da Lagoa restaurant.

Canecão, Avenida Venceslau Brás 214, in Botafogo (tel. 295-3044), opposite the Rio Sul Shopping Mall, is really a concert hall that plays host to both pop entertainers and well-known jazz ensembles. Canecão can seat over 2,000 people, and is a supper club as well. In addition to the featured act, there is also continuous music.

O Viro de Ipiranga, Rua Ipiranga 54, in Laranjeiras (tel. 225-4762). Housed in a 200-year-old building, lovingly restored with exposed brick and beams, O Viro de Ipiranga is on a backstreet in this neighborhood behind Flamengo. A different type of music is featured every night of the week, from rock to jazz. On Monday nights you can hear *chorinho,* guitar and flute music that has been characterized as a cross between Dixieland and ragtime, Brazilian style.

People, Avenida Bartolomeu Mitre 370, in Leblon (tel. 294-0547), has a glitzy, new wave interior and is a favorite nightspot for dance and music. It's located down the block from the Saborearte restaurant.

Some of the other restaurants and clubs where live jazz can be heard regularly are **Eqinox,** Prudente de Morais 729 in Ipanema (tel. 267-2895); and in Lagoa, at the **Cattleman,** Avenida Epitácio Pessoa 864 (tel. 259-1041), and **Biblo's,** Avenida Epitácio Pessoa 1560 (tel. 267-0113).

The bars at the Rio Palace, Meridien, and Sheraton Hotels also feature live jazz on a regular basis.

DANCING: Those who like to get their exercise on the dance floor will find ample opportunity in Rio to cut a rug in whatever tempo and style suits their mood or taste. There's no sense showing up at any of these spots much before 11 p.m. Most clubs will remain open till 2 a.m. on slow days, and till dawn on the weekends.

Cheek-to-Cheek

The **Asa Branca,** Rua Mem de Sá 15, in Lapa (tel. 252-4428), is a throwback to the Big Band era of the 40s. The warm-up house band gets the patrons in the mood for the big show, usually some major Brazilian talent. The place opens at 10 p.m., and the show begins about midnight.

The **Bâteau Mouche Bar,** Avenida Repórter Nestor Moreira 111, in Botafogo (tel. 295-1997), is a supper club for those who prefer the foxtrot over flash dancing.

Carinhoso, Rua Visconde de Pirajá, 22 (tel. 287-0302), is on the Copacabana end of Ipanema. There is a restaurant and two bands nightly.

Un, Deux, Trois, Avenida Bartolomeu Mitre 123, in Leblon (tel. 239-0198), has a restaurant downstairs and a supper club with orchestra upstairs. You must make separate reservations on weekends if you want to dine and dance.

Disco

Café Nice, Avenida Rio Branco 277, Centro (tel. 240-0490), by day an executive lunchroom, becomes a swinging supper club and disco by night. It's not an "in" place on the tourist agenda, which is why Adam Carter of Brazil Nuts in Brooklyn, N.Y. —who accompanies tours to Rio—likes to take his groups there. It's a singles spot for Brazilian men and women, the music is first rate, and the food is good and inexpensive.

Biblos, Avenida Epitácio Pessoa 1484, in Lagoa (tel. 521-2545), in addition to being a place to hear music, is also a disco and a meeting place for singles.

Calígola, Praça General Osório, in Ipanema (tel. 287-1369) was Rio's No. 1 disco in 1987. Located on the bottom floor of the same building that houses the Le Streghe Italian restaurant, the dance floor at Calígola is designed like a pit in the Colisseum, and surrounded by columns and other details to recall Imperial Rome.

Help, Avenida Atlântica 3432, in Copacabana (tel. 521-1296), has the reputation of being a wild spot, for a mostly younger crowd and hungry single males who feast on the B-girls who hang out there.

Zoom, Praça São Conrado 20, in São Conrado (tel. 322-4179), is the newest disco popular with the younger set. It's informal but not quite as raunchy as Help. It occupies the same building as the Pescador Restaurant.

In the same vein is **Circus,** Rua General Urquiza 102, in Leblon (tel. 274-7895), located above the Bella Blu Pizzaria.

Gafieiras

Gafieiras are old-fashioned dance halls. The best are those that retain their links to the popular culture and attract a cross section of social and economic classes. The bands play all the old standards, Brazilian and otherwise, and you wouldn't expect to see any of the musicians playing at society weddings.

Among the best are **Estudantina,** Praça Tiradentes 79, Centro (tel. 232-1149), open Thursday through Saturday; **Forro Forrado,** Rua do Catete 235, in Catete (tel. 245-0524), open Thursday through Sunday; and the **Elite Club,** Rua Frei Caneca 4, Centro (tel. 232-3217), open Friday through Sunday nights. Gafieiras generally open around 10 p.m., and cost about $1 at the door.

PIANO BARS: Almost all the major hotels, including the Inter-Continental, Caesar Park, Miramar, and Othon Palace have piano bars, where you can enjoy your drinks in an environment where music is confined—at least during the week—to the background.

PRIVATE CLUBS: These are discos, generally quite popular, which restrict entrance to members or those who acquire temporary membership through their four- or five-star hotels.

Of all the private discos, the **Hippopotamus,** Rua Barão da Torre 354, in Ipanema, was the hottest spot recently, followed by the **Palace Club** in the Rio Palace Hotel and **Régine** in the Hotel Meridien.

VIDEO BARS: If drinking in a bar and screening tapes from MTV is your kick, try the brand-new American bar, **Neal's,** Avenida Barra da Tijuca 6250 (tel. 399-6577). Neal's old location offers the same American fare, with videos, at Rua Sorocaba 695 in Botafogo (tel. 266-6577). **Crepúsculo de Cubatão,** in Copacabana at Rua Barata Ribeiro 543 (tel. 235-2045), is a new wave haunt with old films and videos.

TOURIST SHOWS: It's hard to tell whether the following shows are actually popular with the tourists or not. They are passed off as authentic portraits, in song and dance, of everything folkloric in Brazil, from Carnival to candomblé. And though these shows are created for and aggressively marketed to the tourist, the impressarios then turn around and claim: "This is what the tourists want." Needless to say, you'll find few locals at these shows (other than those, of course, who are performing in them). It is, sadly, as close as many tourists get to Brazilian culture. They're not to my taste, but if you like big productions à la Vegas and Atlantic City, here they are—though, to be frank, they're not even that good.

At the **Scala I & II,** Avenida Afránio de Mello Franco 292, in Leblon (tel. 239-4448), the show is like something left over from the heyday of Batista's Cuba: gaudy, tawdry, and slightly amateurish, but with none of the raunchy eroticism those pre-Castro spectacles were renowned for. There is a fair amount of topless nudity, usually confined to the *mulatas,* many of whom are indeed strikingly beautiful. For $50 you get the show plus dinner and transportation. If you go at all, it's advisable to skip the meal and the tour, and just go on your own to catch the show. The Scala II, on the other hand, is a showcase on occasion for top Brazilian and international talent. The show begins around 11 p.m. and lasts for about two hours, after which there is dancing till 4 a.m.

The **Beja Flor** Carnival show at Pão de Açúcar every Monday night has already been described in the section on Rio's sights. Compared with Carnival, or a genuine samba school rehearsal, however, the show has all the drama and authenticity of a TV game show.

The other big production shows are **Oba-Oba,** Rua Humanitá, 110, in Botafogo (tel. 286-9848), and **Plataforma 1,** Rua Adalberto Ferreira 32, in Leblon (tel. 274-4022).

KARAOKÉ: This is a craze which has ignited throughout Brazil. The house provides the music (mostly tapes, but sometimes live) and you provide the song. Karaoké clubs can be found in most of the country's major cities. In Rio the clubs to try are **Canja,** Avenida Ataufo de Paiva 375, in Leblon (tel. 511-0484); **Limelight,** Rua Ministro Viveiros de Castro 93, in Copacabana (tel. 542-3596); and **Manga Rosa,** Rua 19 de Fevereiro 94, in Botafogo (tel. 266-4996).

CONCERTS, OPERA, AND BALLET: The **Teatro Municipal,** Praça do Floriano, Centro (tel. 210-2463), stages all three during its year-round season. Check newspapers for current programs.

Other venues for classical music are the **Sala Cecília Meirelles,** Largo da Lapa 47, Centro (tel. 232-9714), and the **Sala Nicoláu Copérnico,** Rua Padre Leonel Franca 240, in Gávea (tel. 274-0096), in the Planetarium.

For dance, classical and modern, there is the **Teatro Villa-Lobos,** Avenida Princesa Isabel 430, in Leme (tel. 275-6695).

GAY NIGHTLIFE: Much of gay male nightlife centers around the **Galeria Alaska,** Avenida Nossa Senhora de Copacabana 1241, where there are several bars and a drag (transvestite) theater. A section of the beach in Copacabana that is popular with gays fronts the Copacabana Palace Hotel, while in Ipanema it's the stretch of beach between Rua Farme de Amoedo and Rua Vinícius de Moraes. There are additional gay bars and discos in the vicinity of Cinelândia, the downtown movie theatre district.

RED LIGHT AND EROTICA: Rio's most respectable red-light district is located in Copacabana off Avenida Atlântica, between Avenida Princesa Isabel and the Praça Lido. These blocks contain numerous pick-up bars, some of which, like the **Erotika,** Avenida Prado Junior 63 (tel. 237-9370), have erotic stage shows. Single men sitting at night in cafés along this section of Avenida Atlântica will almost certainly be approached by streetwalkers.

5. Carnival

No other country in the world has a national holiday as elaborate or as all-consuming as Carnival in Brazil. Nor as long! For over a week, all normal activity grinds to a halt throughout the country as Brazilians everywhere, from the tiniest backwater hamlet to the most sophisticated urban centers, take to the streets to reenact a pre-Lenten ritual that has been celebrated with a special zeal in Brazil for over a hundred years. And nowhere is the event staged with more panache or grandeur than in Rio de Janeiro—so much so, in fact, that for many non-Brazilians, the city and the event are fused into a single reality.

The official time span for the revelry is only four days, from Friday evening until noon of Ash Wednesday, which generally falls in mid to late February, though rarely in early March. But in actuality the organized festivities are spaced over at least a two-week period. And for those who are its principal participants —members of the neighborhood associations called **Escolas de Samba**— Carnival is virtually a year-long preoccupation. In August each *escola* settles on the theme it will enact through song and dance during the Carnival parades. By November, intense rehearsals are in full swing, and the associations' seamstresses are working overtime to create costumes consistent with the chosen theme for as many as 4,000 members. The theme songs also have to be written, and recordings are aired by Christmas so that the public already has them committed to memory by the time Carnival rolls around.

The parades are the yearly celebration's most formal element. And they are certainly tremendous spectacles. Each year the samba schools attract thousands of visitors to Rio, and their performances are beamed over television to every corner of Brazil with all the hype and pomp of the Super Bowl.

But Carnival is not merely a commercial creation for the consumption of tourists and TV audiences. Carnival is a state of mind that infects the entire culture. Or better, it is a state of collective mindlessness, because it's anything but cerebral. All Cariocas—excepting those killjoys who yearly flee the city to escape the madness—take to the streets by day and attend the mass parties by night. These may be the ritzy, glitzy balls of the elite, or the frenzied dances of the poor, held in tin-covered pavilions in the most wretched of *favelas.* No matter! The spirit of total release from the psychological prisons of daily existence—whatever the social class of the participant—is what unites all the citizenry in a momentary utopia of euphoria and abandon. For many, the letdown is swift and inevitable. As the song "Manhã de Carnival" ("Carnival Morning"), from *Black Orpheus* puts it, "Tudo se acabar na segunda-feira" ("On Monday [following Ash Wednesday], everything comes to an end") and it's back to business as usual for another year. But then again, it really isn't the end, but the beginning. There's always next year's Carnival to look forward to.

STREET CARNIVAL: A strong argument can be made that the best part of Carnival is also its simplest, most accessible element—dancing through the streets in the company of perfect strangers. Life affords few opportunities to be linked with fellow humans who are not of one's acquaintance in such moments of uncensored goodwill. After this experience, the evasions of daily life (the avoidance of eye contact in elevators, for example) will seem just that much more absurd.

The streets of Copacabana, Leme, Ipanema, and Leblon—to name only those neighborhoods where most foreign visitors are lodged during Carnival—are a constant swirl of activity from early in the afternoon until dawn. Mornings, in contrast, are silent and calm, not only in these *bairros,* but throughout the rest of the city as well. Even during Carnival people have to sleep sometime. After lunch, which may have to be in your hotel since many of your favorite restaurants will be closed, the pockets of revelers begin to form. On designated blocks, **bandas** (the traditional neighborhood bands) take up their positions as the evening draws near. Then the bands begin to play and march through the streets, attracting hundreds of revelers in their wake. Some people are dressed in *fantasias* (as costumes are called), others not. There are no dress codes. Many men are in drag; others play the fool. Women wear next to nothing and vamp as if their lives depended on the most erotic displays imaginable. Many people dress in beach wear or shorts—which are reasonable choices given the high temperatures and humidity of the Brazilian summer.

The basic dance step of the samba is not difficult. Essentially you jump up and down with your hands above your head to the driving rhythm of the percussion bands. As for the more complex steps, just watch and imitate. Who knows, you might be a natural. The one thing you can't do is stand around and watch shyly from the sidelines. The only human behavior—other than violence, of course—that is frowned upon during Carnival is timidity. And remember, you don't need a ticket to be a part of Carnival in the streets: it's one worthwhile experience that's completely free.

The best-known *bandas* and their jumping-off points are as follows: the **Banda do Leme,** on Rua Gustavo Sampaio, behind the Meridien Hotel; the **Banda da Vergonha do Posto 6** (the Shameful Band from Post 6), near the Rio Palace Hotel; and the **Banda de Ipanema,** Praça General Osório, site of the weekly Hippie Fair. Practically every block in these neighborhoods has its own band, however, and there's nothing to prevent you from hopping from one to another for as long as your energy holds out.

THE BALLS: The traditional Carnival balls are to the upper and middle classes what street carnival is to the *povo*—the people. The other distinctions are that the balls require tickets—from as little as $15 to as much as $100 per person—and their general atmosphere is even more lavish and erotic than anything taking place on the streets. Some participants at the balls wear costumes of extraordinary complexity and beauty, costumes whose costs can range into the thousands of dollars. Most participants, however, wear as little as possible. Nudity or near nudity is the order of the night. Ballrooms are swollen to capacity with revelers dancing back-to-back and belly-to-belly, and the music never stops until morning. These events are not for the prudish—you will get no fair hearing if your bottom is pinched. The major balls are as follows:

The **Hawaiian Ball** is the event that kicks off Carnival each year. It takes place on Friday night a week before Carnival at the Iate Clube do Rio de Janeiro, Rio's Yacht Club, on Avenida Pasteur in Botafogo, where tickets may be purchased directly. The celebrants spend much of the evening outdoors dancing under the sky on the club's beautifully landscaped grounds.

On Thursday night—a day before official Carnival begins—one of the city's most traditional balls, the **Vermelho e Preto** (the Red and Black) is hosted by Flamengo, Rio's most popular soccer club. While relatively cheap at about $30 a couple, the ball has a reputation for being among the raunchiest of them all.

The **Pão de Açúcar Ball,** perhaps Carnival's most fashionable, takes place on Friday night high above the city on Urca Hill. Tickets may be purchased for approximately $75 per person at the office of the event's organizers at Rua Vicconde de Pirajá 414, Room 909, in Ipanema (tel. 287-7749).

Other traditional balls, like the **Champagne Ball** and the **Gala Gay** (one of several homosexually oriented events), are scheduled in Rio's major showcase houses, like the Scala in Leblon or the Help discothèque in Copacabana. Travel agencies specializing in booking the Carnival trade are the best sources for where these events will be scheduled in a given year.

Most of the major hotels, like the Copacabana Palace's **Golden Room Ball** on Monday night, produce their own spectaculars for those who want to celebrate close to home.

THE PARADES: The **Passarela do Samba** is Carnival's main event. On Sunday and Monday nights, the year's 16 most prominent **Escolas de Samba**—the voluntary samba clubs that tend to be integrated into the very fabric of all Rio's blue-collar and *favela* neighborhoods—compete for first prize in the spectacular parades staged downtown in the **Sabódromo.** Tickets are required to view the parades in this special stadium that was inaugurated in 1984. And several grandstands are reserved exclusively for tourists, whose tickets are usually included in the packages they purchase at home before arriving in Rio. Otherwise, tickets are sold at offices of the Bank of Rio de Janeiro (BANERJ) in locations throughout the city; the main branch is downtown at Avenida Nilo Pecanha 175 (tel. 224-0202). The best source of information on all Carnival activities is the event's major sponsor, **Riotour** (tel. 232-4320). As a last resort, tickets may be purchased from scalpers who buy them by the lots when they first go on sale, and later do a land-office business with the tourists. Needless to say, a scalper's ticket will cost you more than face value. But remember, you shouldn't accept their first offer; a good round of bargaining can be as satisfactory to a scalper as a high markup.

The parades are scheduled to begin on each of the two evenings at 7 p.m., but they rarely get off before 9 p.m. and can run until noon of the following day. The logistics involved in coordinating the productions are awe-inspiring. The schools can each involve the participation of 3,000 to 4,000 members organized into as many as a hundred separate components.

Each school's performance conforms to an *enredo*—a theme which is generally political or patriotic—and tells a story as the dancers and musicians strut their stuff in the 45 minutes allotted per school.

Each parade begins with the **abre-ala,** a float that is the sampler or title page of the whole ensemble, followed up by the **comissão de frente,** traditionally the school's directors and honchos who, rather than dance, would execute a series of formal salutations to the audience. Many schools have departed from the traditional use of the *commissão* component in recent years, using it to showcase celebraties or even to create laughs—as when one school put burros in its front line. Next comes the body of the school, with everyone in lavish *fantasia,* the costume that reflects its theme.

From here the school is divided into its various components, the group's dancers who whirl and twirl in unison, including the **ala das baianas,** the women in the traditional costumes of Bahia; the flag bearer and dance master, a couple who execute a formal choreography; individual dancers and musicians, whose steps will knock your socks off if anything does; and the **bateria,** the percussion band with the force of a locomotive, numbering as many as 300 musicians, that drives the whole machine. Each element in the parade is judged and given a score. The winner then appears for a curtain call at the victory parade scheduled for the Saturday after Ash Wednesday. This is Carnival's finale.

The Passarela do Samba is only one of several official competitions. The less important schools, called *blocos,* parade along Avenida Rio Branco practically all week long. Some can number as many as 10,000 participants in a single, joyous spectacle of mass celebration. Others, like the *frevo* and *rancho* schools, reenact regional or historical versions of Carnival. These events are free and very crowded, so leave your valuables in the hotel.

The best way to reach downtown during Carnival—when traffic crawls, at best, at a snails's pace—is to take the Metro, which runs 24 hours a day during this period only. It's perfectly safe, and cheap, but don't forget to purchase round-trip tickets so you don't have to stand on line for the return.

6. Special Events

A number of other special events or activities take place in Rio throughout the year. Some of the more interesting from a visitor's point of view are these:

FESTA DE IEMANJÁ: The Feast of Iemanjá turns New Year's Eve into a genuine pagan celebration, a homage to the goddess of the sea whose worship was introduced to New World culture by its African inhabitants. The celebration takes place on virtually all of Rio's beaches, most notably in Copacabana and Ipanema. The white-garbed celebrants begin to arrive on the beaches during the day to mount their endless circles of candles and the altars of offerings—from flowers to cosmetics—that will be cast upon the waves at midnight in the hope that they will be acceptable in the sight of Iemanjá, the mother of all. Whether as a participant or an observer, this unique celebration is a memorable experience.

FESTAS JUNINAS: June is the month that Catholic Brazil celebrates the feast days of its favorite saints, Anthony (June 13), John (June 24), and Peter (June 29). Parties are held primarily in private clubs and at home. The predominant theme is a recognition of Brazil's peasant culture and the rural experience in general. Children dress up in their versions of country costumes, and barbecues and bonfires are also typical elements of these celebrations. If you're in town during these times, you can try to have your hotel arrange an invitation for you at a private club. The low-key parties are typical of Brazilian home comfort and hospitality, and are a very pleasant way to get closer to the culture for anyone who cares to.

MACUMBA: Macumba is the name of the spiritist religion as it is practiced in Rio and its environs. In Bahia you will hear the term *candomblé,* while in São Paulo the term *umbanda* is used. All of these practices are similar, if not entirely the same in all their rituals.

Many tour agencies in Rio include a macumba rite in their list of sightseeing activities. The tourist should be aware, however, that these events are not genuine. Anyone who has a genuine interest in witnessing or learning more about macumba should try to strike up an acquaintance with a true practitioner—and these are not lacking in the city—and try to tag along informally. Only in this way are you likely to get a look at the real thing, which is not only impressive as a religious ceremony, but allows you to hear some of the most inspired drum music you will ever hear in your life.

CHAPTER VI

NEARBY EXCURSIONS FROM RIO

□ □ □

1. DAY TRIPS
2. COSTA DO SOL
3. COSTA VERDE

Cariocas themselves, at least those who have the means, seldom spend the weekends or holidays in Rio. The beaches of Copacabana and Ipanema tend to fill up rapidly on Saturday and Sunday, a scene which can be quite pleasing and exciting to the tourist, but less appealing to the full-time resident. Travelers spending more than a week in or around Rio might easily include one of the following side trips in their itinerary. To escape the crowds, people generally head—depending on the season—in one of three directions. The two nearby beach options are the Costa do Sol and the Costa Verde. Those seeking relief from the hottest days of summer in January and February might opt, however, for the mountain regions, rather than the shore, where the heat and the action during the high season can be quite intense.

In any event, all of the locales described in this chapter are year-round destinations, more or less frequented depending on the season. Lodging and food prices tend to accompany the highs and lows of the season. The relative isolation and calm of the low season (most of the year) will cost you less than during those times of the year when the spas fill up with vacationers: summer, winter school vacation during the month of July, and some major holidays (see "The ABCs of Brazil" in Chapter I). The choice, then, is between the people-scene of the high season, when the clubs are jumping, or the privacy-scene of the low season, when you can have the towns and beaches much more to yourself. So as not to give a totally misleading impression, however, there is always *something* going on in most of these destinations, especially on the weekends, throughout the year.

1. Day Trips

NITERÓI: A short ferry ride away, Niterói, the former capital of the State of Rio de Janeiro, is Rio's sister city across the bay. Ferries and hydrofoils leave regularly from the dock near Praça XV in downtown Rio. There is also frequent bus service across the bay bridge, leaving from the Rodoviária Novo Rio in São Cristóvão.

Bus 33 from the Niterói ferry terminal will take you to the bay beaches of **Icaraí, São Francisco,** and **Jurujuba.** The ride is picturesque, but the beaches (like those on the other side of the bay) are less than pristine. There is a beautiful view of the Rio shoreline, however, especially from the beaches known as **Adam** and **Eve** (Adão and Eva). Beyond Jurujuba is the 16th-century fort (*fortaleza*) of **Santa Cruz,** one of Brazil's oldest fortifications, open daily from 8 a.m. till 4 p.m.

Bus 38 from the ferry terminal carries passengers to the spectacular ocean beaches of **Piratininga, Itaipú,** and **Itacoatiara,** about a 45-minute ride from Niterói. In Itaipú, there is an archeology museum in the ruins of the 18th-century convent of Santa Teresa. To the east of Niterói and its nearby beaches lies the Costa do Sol, which is described in Section 2.

PETRÓPOLIS: When Cariocas want to exchange the seaside landscape for the mountains, this is one of the closest and most popular destinations. The tradition was started by Pedro I, who bought a farm there in the 1830s, and was continued by his son, Pedro II, who so loved the more temperate climate in Petrópolis that he moved the country's capital there during the summer months, or during those times when Rio was rife with disease and epidemics. Much of the court followed the emperor's example, so there are many mansions with large gardens left from the empire period in a town that is today a mixture of modern textile plants and narrow cobblestone streets. Petrópolis is only 66 km (41 miles) from Rio, reached by a dramatic climb along a steep mountain road with many stunning views of the surrounding mountains and valleys.

The Sights

The first sight of general interest, just before entering Petrópolis, is **Quitandinha,** once Brazil's most fashionable casino, before gambling was abolished in 1946. Today the place is a middling resort, slated to become an apart-hotel sometime in the near future. But the grounds and the buildings in the grand Norman style are worthy of a look for the old Hollywood-esque glamour they still reflect.

In the town itself, there is the emperor's former palace, now the **Museu Imperial** (Imperial Museum), which houses the crown jewels and other royal possessions, including an early telephone given to Pedro by Alexander Graham Bell. In appearance the palace remains much as it was during the occupancy of the imperial family. The museum is open Tuesday through Sunday from noon to 5:30 p.m.

The **Palácio Cristal** (Crystal Palace), Praça da Confluência, was built by Dom Pedro II's son-in-law, the Conde D'Eu, a Frenchman who imported the structure from his native country to house the great flower exhibition of 1884. Petrópolis is still known for its nurseries today. Flower lovers should visit **Florália,** on Estrada do Alcobaca, just outside town, to see the permanent exhibition of orchids. Florália is open from 9 a.m. to 5 p.m. daily, and cuttings (called *mudas* in Portuguese) may be purchased.

An architectural oddity, the house of Brazilian aviation pioneer **Santos Dumont,** Rua do Encanto 124, is open Tuesday through Friday from 9 a.m. to 5 p.m., and from 11 a.m. to 5 p.m. on weekends. Dumont had this house built at a time in his life when mystical obsessions had outdistanced his earlier scientific curiosity. He believed, for example, that he should always lead with his left foot when walking up stairs. The staircases in his houses were built deliberately narrow to accommodate this eccentricity. Nevertheless, Dumont was a man of indubitable genius, and many displays of his inventions in the house attest to this fact.

Cotton knitwear is the principal product of industrial Petrópolis, and reasonable bargains can be had on *malhas* ("*mahl*-yaz"), as the garments are called, along the Rua Teresa.

Buses leave Rio for Petrópolis frequently from the downtown Menezes Cortes Bus Terminal, and the cost is minimal, about $3 each way.

Where to Eat

Full tea is served from 8 a.m. till 10 p.m. at the **Florália** restaurant, on Rua Maétro Otâvio Maul, which includes tea, toast, honey, jam, and cakes for $2.

A good dish of trout with peanuts can be had for $10 at **La Belle Meunière,** Estrada União Industrial 2189 (tel. 21-1573), ten kilometers (six miles) from the center of Petrópolis.

Within the town, the best restaurants are to be found on Rua João Pessoa and Rua do Imperador.

TERESÓPOLIS: Centered around Teresópolis is the **Parque Nacional da Serra dos Órgãos** (Sierra of the Organs National Park), so named because the surrounding mountains have the appearance of a pipe organ. The huge park boasts numerous trails to hike and peaks to scale.

Teresópolis is located beyond Petrópolis, 95 km (58 miles) from Rio. On the way, be sure to stop at the **Mirante do Soberbo,** an overlook with a panoramic view of the Guanabara Bay and the surrounding peaks, including the **Dedo de Deus** (God's Finger), a prominent rock formation rising to an elevation of several thousand feet. There are many ponds and waterfalls in the park for bathing, and stable horses may be rented there at the **Pracinha do Alto.**

The night and street life in Teresópolis itself is centered around the area known as **A Várzea.**

As is the case for Petrópolis, the Teresópolis buses leave regularly from Rio's downtown bus station. Many tour companies offer day-trip excursions that take in both towns and their environs.

Where to Eat

The **Taberna Alpina,** Rua Duque de Caxias 131 (tel. 742-0123), offers a good Spanish-style codfish plate for $8. For inexpensive "international" food, try **Ângelo,** on the Praça Higino da Silveira (tel. 742-0007).

NOVA FRIBURGO: High in the mountains, approximately 150 km (93 miles) from Rio, is Nova Friburgo, a town originally settled by Swiss immigrants, and today a favorite summer retreat for Cariocas wishing to escape the summer swelter of the city. Many chalets in the **Cônego** suburb still attest to the influence of European colonization, as does the elegant layout of the city's principal squares.

An energetic and steep climb up to the **Pico da Caledônia** offers a magnificent view of the valley, the city to one side and a lake district to the other. A different perspective can be viewed from the **Moro da Cruz,** reached by cable car from the Praça dos Suspiros.

Near Friburgo are two small towns that were only electrified in 1984 and retain the ambience of rural Brazil. First is **Lumiar,** 36 km (22 miles) away, reached from the Rio–Friburgo highway by exiting at Mury. A further 6 km (3½ miles) along on a dirt road is **São Pedro.** Both towns are hospitible to visitors. You can also take a dip in the local swimming hole, the *poço feio* (the Ugly Well).

Nova Friburgo is a three-hour bus ride from Rio.

Where to Eat

There are more than 30 quality hotels and inns in the region. Most offer full board for guests, and their restaurants are also open to the public.

TRÊS RIOS: A number of agencies are now offering white-water rafting expeditions along the Rio Paraibuna, about 1½ hour's distance from Petrópolis. The rafting takes you over numerous small falls—some with drops of up to 15 feet—and takes about 4½ hours to descend the river. The excursion, which costs about $50 per person, including transportation and lunch, can be booked in Rio through **Klemperer Turismo** (tel. 252-8170), or through their main offices in Petrópolis, Avenida Afrânio de Mello Franco 333 (tel. 0242/43-4052).

ITACURUÇA: This beach resort town is actually the first stop along the **Costa Verde**. Only 82 km (51 miles) from Rio's Barra da Tijuca, a trip to Itacuruca can also be considered a legitimate one-day excursion. One favorite activity is to cruise the clear blue waters of Sepitiba Bay in a coastal sloop (called a *saveiro*) and visit some of the many offshore islands. The transparent waters are excellent for snorkeling to see the many colorful varieties of tropical fish that make the bay their home. In Rio, **Sepetiba Turismo**, Avenida Nossa Senhora de Copacabana 605 (tel. 235-2893), offers a cruise of the bay from 10 a.m. till 4:30 p.m. which embarks from Itacuruca on Saturday, Sunday, and Monday. The cost is about $15, which includes fruit on board and lunch on the Ilha de Jaguanum, but drinks are separate. Transportation by bus to and from your hotel can also be arranged by the tour agency.

Where to Eat

On the way to Itacuruça you will pass **Pedra de Guaratiba,** where two of Rio's most popular out-of-town restaurants are located. **Cândido's** and **476** (for details, see Chapter IV).

2. Costa do Sol

East and to the north of Rio, along the shoreline, are a number of towns that have come to be known collectively as the Costa do Sol. The Sun Coast begins at the beaches in the vicinity of Niterói, passes through Búzios, the best-known of its resort towns, and goes on to its most distant point, Macaé, 187 km (116 miles) from Rio. For this first edition, I will only report in depth on Búzios. The names of other spots will be listed, however, with a brief account of their attractions and major accommodations.

BÚZIOS: Once a rustic fishing village, **Armação dos Búzios** (the official name in full) is now most often referred to as the St. Tropez of Brazil. Ironically, it was the French actress, Brigitte Bardot who really put Búzios on the map. Bardot, one of the most popular international stars of the 50s, sought in Búzios a refuge from publicity during frequent vacations to Brazil. In her wake, many others among the rich and famous began to "discover" Búzios, transforming the simple coastal hamlet into one of the chicest of all Brazilian summer colonies and side-trip destinations. The town sits on a small peninsula, approximately 170 km (105 miles) from Rio de Janeiro, and is most easily accessible by car, cab, or even air taxi.

Getting to Búzios

If you were going to rent a car at all in Brazil, this might be the time to do it. Not only will you be able to explore the whole length of the Costa do Sol on your way to and from Búzios, but once you've settled in there, you'll find it very convenient to have your own transportation for getting around from beach to beach or restaurant to restaurant. Your hotel in Rio can provide a **private car and driver** for the 2½-hour drive, or you can hire a **radio cab** to take you there as well. Needless to say, the cab will not wait, but you will be required to underwrite the cost of its return to Rio nonetheless—in all, a very expensive proposition. Finding a cab to take you back could be a problem, but not an insurmountable one.

A number of **tour agencies** make the run between Rio and Búzios on a regular basis. Ekoda, for one, provides a full range of tours and services to tourists who wish to visit Búzios and its beaches. **Ekoda** may be contacted in Rio at Avenida Rio Branco 277 (tel. 240-7067), or in Búzios at Rua José Bento Ribeiro Dantes 22 (tel. 0246/23-1493).

Still another option is to take a **bus** for about $2 from Rio to nearby Cabo Frio, which is only a 30-minute cab ride into Búzios. A public bus also runs between the two locales, and when combined with the bus from Rio this is by far the cheapest way to get to the spa. If you have reservations at one of the better inns, they will sometimes arrange to meet you in Cabo Frio, especially if more than one person is involved.

The fastest way to get to Búzios is by **air taxi.** One company, **Costair,** makes the trip in about 40 minutes, leaving from Rio's downtown Santos Dumont Airport and landing in Búzios on a dirt strip in the middle of a great marsh. The flight is worth it alone for the closeup view of Pão de Açúcar as the plane negotiates the curve of Guanabara Bay on takeoff and landing. The view on the way down the coast isn't half bad either.

Where to Stay

At the entrance to the Búzios peninsula, on the bank of a narrow river, is the reception center for the island resort of **Nas Rocas** (tel. 0246/23-1303, or 251-0001 in Rio for reservations). A seven-minute ride by trawler takes you across the inlet to the private island where coffee exporter and hotel impressario, Umberto Modiano has created a tamer version of the Club Med–style resort. Nas Rocas occupies the entire island, which can be circled by footpath at a comfortable pace in no more than 45 minutes. Nas Rocas is totally self-contained, providing lodging, all meals, aquatic sports from windsurfing to snorkeling, tennis, and a variety of organized activities from pool games to exercise classes, and even a schooner for island-hopping and tours of the coastal beaches.

There are 80 two-room suites in 40 separate and attractive bungalows, which overlook the inlet or the open sea. Each suite has a large veranda, bath with shower, mini-bar, color TV, and air conditioning. The daily rate *per person,* including all meals, is $70. Food is served buffet style, with a minimum of two main dishes—usually fish and meat—and all the trimmings.

The grounds on the island are resplendent with flowers. Every season has its blossoms. The decorative plants are all imported to the island from the mainland, and are lovingly tended by Sr. Hélio, the principal gardener, who receives ample assistance from many of the resort staff of 240 workers. The primitive, native growth on the nonlandscaped sections of the island is equally attractive. Botonists, whether professional or amateur, are welcome to tag along with Sr. Hélio, who will be happy to share his knowledge of Brazilian flora as he makes his daily rounds.

Taxi and bus transportation are available to take you into Búzios, which is actually ten kilometers (six miles) farther down the peninsula. Or you can rent a dune buggy, a very popular mode of transportation in these parts. To get to Búzios proper from Nas Rocas, you cross over a single-lane bridge with an extremely acute curve in the shape of a camel's hump. Then you pass through the village of **Manguinhos,** a ramshackle affair not without its charm—really a strip of houses, cafés, stores, and markets. The 27 beaches of the area (or is it 36? No one seems to know for sure!) begin in this municipality, where off the road and up a winding hill is the **Barracuda** (tel. 0246/23-1314), one of the best *pousadas* (inns) in the region. There are 21 rooms at the Barracuda, in gorgeous vine-covered bungalows, very comfortably furnished with all the amenities. Each bungalow has an attached terrace with hammock overlooking the water. The daily rate per double, including breakfast, is $66. The inn has a particularly attractive pool and patio area, and the much-praised Tartaruga beach is over the hill about 200 meters (650 feet) away.

Another ten minutes down the road brings you to the center of the old fishing village, still somewhat intact, but surrounded by some of the fanciest boutiques, restaurants, and inns this side of Ipanema. One local lady, a British expatriate, attributed to Búzios the character of St. Tropez of 20 to 30 years past. "Totally disorganized," she claimed, by which she meant informal and not overly self-conscious as yet of being the great watering hole of the society set.

Society is here, to be sure. Many of the well-heeled from Rio have summer homes in Búzios. Sr. Modiano, of Nas Rocas, for example, has a beautiful spreading house on the beach, the crown jewel of his 2,500-acre estate, where over the next five years he is planning to build Búzios's first real hotel, a full-scale boat marina, and a new airport that will accommodate medium-size passenger jets.

The principal center of Búzios from the standpoint of its greatest concentration of fashionable shops, fine restaurants, and first-class *pousadas,* is the **Amação,** a term which loosely designates an area of several blocks, but primarily the establishments found on and around the Rua das Pedras. The street has another official name, but is known traditionally as the Street of Stones because of its unusual paving surface. Most of the streets in Búzios that are not simply dirt roads are paved with cobblestones. But on the Rua das Pedras you'll still see the colonial-era paving method of using large, thick flagstones, which stick up at every imaginable angle, forcing all vehicles to amble slowly down this long block at the speed of a walking horse.

On this colorful, if perilous, street is the **Estalagem,** an inn, restaurant, and music bar, the property of an American rock and jazz bassist, Bruce Leitman. In season there is live music at the Estalagem every night, and in the off-season, only over the major holiday weekends. The inn has only eight rooms off an open courtyard, each painted brightly in white with blue.

Other top-rated inns—some 50 in all—can be found scattered among the surrounding hills and beaches, which are for the most part a 15-minute to half-hour walk from the Amação.

Beyond the Amação area is the undeveloped point of the Búzios peninsula, and some of the most beautiful and unspoiled natural beach environments you will find in this part of Brazil. Unlike Cape Cod, say, or other U.S. Atlantic Ocean-beach communities for that matter, which are essentially flat with contiguous networks of elevated dunes, Búzios is hilly with lush vegetation. The vistas in the hills beyond the town are breathtaking in spots, and uniformly beautiful. Try to arrange for a car with a very good suspension system when touring these backroads and undeveloped areas of Búzios—or at least prepare yourself for a jolting ride.

Where to Eat

Búzios is considered a Brazilian culinary capital second only to São Paulo and Rio, though on a much smaller scale to be sure. The original **Le Streghe** is located in Búzios on the Rua das Pedras, and you can get the same fine Italian food there as at the companion restaurant in Ipanema. **Au Cheval Blanc,** an excellent French restaurant, is located several doors down on the same block. Also serving French cuisine is the inn **La Chimere,** on the Ossos beach.

Búzios also has many less fancy eating establishments, as is befitting a beach town, including the usual array of cabañas on the beaches serving fresh seafood at reasonable prices.

As for the nightlife, most of the clubs and bars are concentrated within several blocks of each other. You won't have any trouble finding the latest "in" spot once you are there.

OTHER COSTA DO SOL DESTINATIONS: One could devote many weeks in Brazil just getting to know the stretch of coastline and string of beaches between Niterói and Macaé. The main route to follow is RJ 106, which is picked up outside of Niterói. The road runs north of the *lagos fluminenses,* great lagoons high in saline content from which the region's principal product, salt, is harvested.

At Bacaxa there is a turnoff that leads to **Saquarema,** a resort town surrounded by beautiful beaches where Brazil's surfing championships are held annually. There are many inns in the area, and the **Pousada do Holandés,** Avenida Vila Mar 374, on the Praia de Itauna, comes highly recommended.

The next major port of call along RJ 106 is **Araruama,** which fronts the immense lagoon of the same name. Here, in contrast to Saquarema, the waters are calm and the sands said to possess medicinal properties.

Cabo Frio, one of Rio's most traditional weekend spots, is worth a detour. It is the region's largest town, filled with restaurants, hotels, and many campsites on or near neighboring beaches. After Cabo Frio—which means Cape Cold, a historical reference to the cool climate that has attracted Cariocas for generations— RJ 106 turns abruptly north toward the small port town of **Barra de São João,** where there is a church dating from 1630, the Capela de São João Batista, and the birthplace of poet Casimiro de Abeu, whose house is now a museum and library.

Farther on is the tranquil village of **Rio das Ostras,** renowned for its shellfish, and finally **Macaé,** a municipality that stretches from the ocean to the nearby mountains, embracing in between a historical district of colonial era plantations.

3. Costa Verde

The Costa Verde (Green Coast) is below Rio to the south and west, and stretches along the Rio–Santos highway (BR 101) to the town of Parati near the border with the state of São Paulo, some 300 km (185 miles) away. Green is far too pedestrian a word to describe the spectrum of colors that envelop the traveler along this route, now curving and winding over mountainous terrain clad in every shade of luscious jungle vegetation, now hugging the shores of the island-cluttered bays whose waters glisten with such subtle tones that only a brilliant colorist would dare to give them names. Call them green if you must, even emerald in a burst of promotional zeal. But in the end, the eye will register a thousand variations.

Sit where you will in car or bus on this journey. You will not miss the show. There are no obstructed views, so total is the spectacular scenery in which you are immersed. On one side are the hills and rock outcroppings that in places reach their extremities, dripping with verdure, to the very edges of the water. Elsewhere this same swollen topography has been cleared into rolling pastures and cultivated fields. Frozen on their surfaces, in the form of ancient corrals and *fazenda* houses, is the vision of an agricultural past. In some places only the scent of the sea is present, so you breathe the more deeply and savor the pleasing, salty

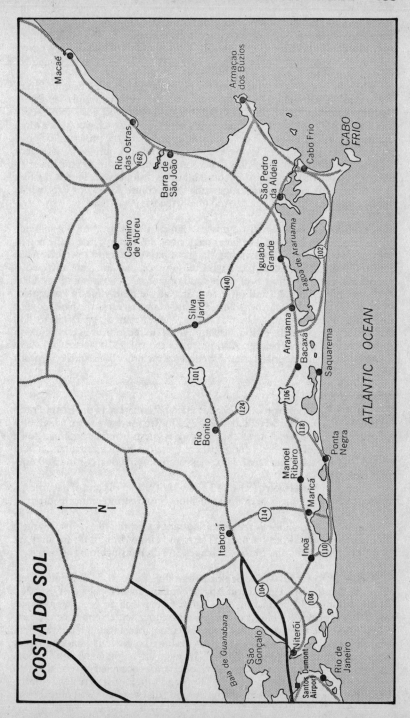

COSTA DO SOL

freshness of the air. But water is rarely out of sight for long as you speed by the succession of graceful coves with their impeccable strands, the horizon of the sea everywhere interrupted with a numberless multiplication of islands in every size and shape. And you think, "I must stop here on the way back, no there . . . oh, but definitely there."

The true miracle of this landscape is that it continues even beyond Parati, virtually to the gates of the belching industrial zone that surrounds São Paulo. The whole journey to São Paulo along the Rio–Santos road takes about seven hours, taking only pit stops into account. A week by stagecoach would be a more reasonable pace. Here we will only take the trip as far as the preserved colonial town of Parati. In Chapter IX, on São Paulo, we will work our way back as far as the beach resort of Ubatuba. Rio's Costa Verde segment of this excursion is divided into three distinct environments, and three major towns. First is the Baia de Sepitiba, with the town of Mangaratiba. Next comes Angra dos Reis, which embraces the Baia da Ilha Grande. And finally there is Parati itself.

MANGARATIBA: What distinguishes Mangaratiba is not the town so much as its surrounding beaches. The great scenery of the Costa Verde really begins from this point onward. The fact that Mangaratiba is not a resort town may make it all the more attractive to those who value peace and quiet on uncrowded beaches more than the hoards of people and organized fun of resort areas. Or if you want, have your cake and eat it too. Stay at the nearby **Frade Portogalo,** about 20 km (12 miles) farther south, and use Mangaratiba as the base for your unstructured explorations. There is a daily ferry from Mangaratiba to **Ilha Grande,** the largest of the offshore islands, which in the mornings continues on to Angra dos Reis (see below). Also nearby is the village of **Itacuruça,** where *saveiro* cruises may be booked for exploration of the other 36 islands of Sepitiba Bay.

Where to Stay

On the Rio–Santos road at the kilometer 71 marker is the **Hotel Frade Portogalo** (tel. 0243/65-1022, or 267-7375 in Rio for reservations), high on a hill overlooking the bay. A novel chair lift carries guests from the pool area down to a little village of attached condos, where there is a French restaurant, a boat marina, and a beach. There are 80 first-class accommodations, costing $60 double occupancy.

The luxury **Hotel Pierre** (tel. 0243/788-1560), on the Island of Itacuruça, is reached by a five-minute boat ride, and includes breakfast and dinner in its rate of $90 double.

Another island choice is the **Hotel Jaguanum,** on the Ilha de Jaguanum, a 30-minute boat ride from Itacuruça. The island affords beautiful surroundings for walks and bathing, and the hotel charges $60 double, including all meals.

ANGRA DOS REIS: While Sepitiba Bay offers more than 30 islands to explore, the Baia da Ilha Grande, off Angra, contains an archipelego of over 300 islands, including the fascinating Ilha Grande from which the bay takes its name. Angra is one of Brazil's oldest towns, in continuous settlement since the early 1500s. There are numerous relics from the colonial past, though they are scattered about in this hillside town which has declined considerably since its heyday as a great port and agricultural center. The main attraction is the **Ilha Grande.** The large island was once a pirate colony, but is today occupied by several fishing hamlets and a Brazilian penal colony. The island's interior is virtually uninhabited, covered by a tropical forest which rises and falls over somewhat hilly terrain.

This is the ideal place for trekking overland from one hamlet to another, and for camping in seclusion on the beach of a suitable cove.

Where to Stay

The **Pousada Mar da Tranquilidade** (tel. 0243/288-4162) is located in Abraão, the principal hamlet on Ilha Grande, and the point of debarkation for the ferryboat. The inn, charging $30 for double occupancy, is attractive and clean, the best option on the island for those not wishing to camp or find simpler accommodations in one of the fishing hamlets. Reservations are necessary. Angra is a wonderful place to visit for island-hopping or camping on the beaches, but it is not the place to lodge yourself in a hotel when Parati is only an hour or so down the road.

Embarking from the port of Angra at noon on Monday and Friday, however, is the **Frade Mar,** a floating four-star hotel aboard a large schooner. The sailing ship, with 12 first-class cabins and semiprivate baths, cruises the bay, making several ports of call—including Ilha Grande—and offers a wide range of aquatic sports from fishing to windsurfing. Reservations are made at the central number for the Frade Hotel chain in Rio (tel. 267-7375).

PARATI: The only blemish along the road from Angra to Parati is Brazil's first nuclear power plant, near Cunhambebe, the very existence of which sends shudders up the spines of Brazilian ecologists who worry about the potential for radioactive pollution of the nearby waters. Other than that, the scenery is the same delicious ensemble of sea and mountains that characterized the earlier stage of the journey, a visual backdrop that is never tiresome.

You'll enter Parati through an access road, and the scene along it is typical of rural Brazil everywhere. There are always groups of shirtless men hanging out in front of the many open-fronted commercial shops, while others are driving by in a variety of conveyances, from rickety trucks to horsecarts to bicycles. The side streets are all unpaved, and bare-bottomed toddlers play in the mud while their mothers with babes in arms sit in the open doorways. These are the folk that Brazil's history has always left in its wake, even in a town like Parati, which was always relatively prosperous, a veritable power during colonial days, and a thriving tourist attraction today.

The Story of Parati

Parati's harbor was deep enough and just the right scale for ships of the colonial days, which called there often to load their holds with precious stones and gold from nearby Minas, and later the coffee and sugarcane that was cultivated so successfully on the surrounding hills. The cane cultivation led to the creation of an ancillary industry, the production of *aguardente de cana,* the archaic name for what is today generally known as *pinga* or *cachaça*. Actually, cachaça was originally distilled from honey, while only *cana* or *pinga* came from sugarcane alcohol. Parati in any case, became the *pinga* capital of Brazil, and is still considered to produce the highest quality sugarcane brandy in the country.

The heart of Parati today is a seven-square-block area set on a jutting neck of land between harbor and river, that might easily have been plucked from the mid-1700s and placed in the present, so authentic is the preservation of its buildings and streets. Development ceased in Parati when a new road was laid in 1723 from the mine fields and plantations of Minas to Rio that bypassed the once-active port. And so Parati slept for almost two and a half centuries in virtual isolation from the rest of the country. But it never decayed, sustaining itself on local agriculture, fishing, and as always, on the production of *pinga*. A new road connecting the town to Angra in the 1950s opened Parati anew, first to artists and bohemians, who were captivated by the tranquility and ambience of the place, and lately to the casual tourist.

The Sights and Festivals

The historic core of Parati has now been declared a national monument by Brazil and a world treasure by UNESCO. Motor-vehicle traffic has been banned from its narrow, stone-paved streets. Many of the historical buildings are private homes, but a fair number also house shops and inns, though the air of commercialization remains extremely faint despite the obvious gentrification. Parati is so genuine in its every detail that even the effete bohemian would still feel at ease here, and the artist no less inspired.

It hardly bears mentioning that one must visit Parati in the daytime, although I highly recommend an overnight in one of the superb inns. It doesn't take more than a couple of hours to see the entire town, including the delightful slave's church, the **Igreja do Rosário** (1725), on the Rua do Comércio across from the post office. Note the black face of the statue of St. Benedict.

The harbor is very quiet, and at the dock are moored the colorful fishing craft that today carry tourists on excursions around the bay.

There are several interesting festivals held in Parati every year. The most important is the **Festa do Divino,** a religious festival of great significance in Portuguese culture dating from the 13th century, and preserved in Parati from its own colonial past. The festival culminates on Pentecost Sunday, after ten days of diverse events, sacred and profane, including medieval pageantry with songs and processions, craft fairs and sporting competitions. The **Festival da Pinga,** a kind of Brazilian Oktoberfest, takes place from the 22nd to the 24th of August. Holy Week and Carnival are two other important periods of celebration.

The Bay and Environs

Numerous *saveiros* also cruise the waters off Parati to take in a panorama of sights that can best be viewed from the sea. Parati was protected by several strong fortifications, which remain as a historical testament to the days when a million tons of gold were shipped from its wharves. It is also claimed that there are, in all, 65 islands and 300 beaches that may be visited in the vicinity of the town.

Also visible from the water, at Boa Vista, is the steam-driven mill of the Quero Essa *pinga* factory.

The schooner **Soberano da Costa** makes a daily cruise of the bay, which includes stopovers for swimming, leaving at noon and returning at 4:30 p.m. Two *pinga* factories, the **Engenho Murycana** and the **Engenho Querro Essa,** both located on colonial *fazendas,* may be visited by land.

Staying the Night in Parati

Within its historic district Parati offers lodgings in some of the most attractive inns to be found anywhere in all of Brazil. The **Estalagem Mercado de Pouso.** Rua Dona Geralda 43 (tel. 0243/71-1114), occupies an extreme corner of the town, with its back to the wharf and the splendid Santa Rita Church to its front. The inn has 19 rooms and five suites, all under thick-beamed ceilings with views of interior gardens, or in ateliers over the tile rooftops of neighboring buildings—in all, an extraordinarily beautiful interior environment. The rate for double occupancy is $40 for a room and $55 for a suite.

The Frade's **Pousada Dom João** is located at the other extreme end of the town at the Rua do Comércio 01 (tel. 0243/71-1205), near the river and behind the Igreja Nossa Senhora dos Remédios. With 40 rooms, the inn also has a swimming pool and a gorgeous outdoor patio and garden. Reservations are made in

Rio (tel. 267-7375), and transportation is offered by the Frade company, which provides regular bus shuttle service from Rio to all of its hotels along the Costa Verde. The cost per night is $50 for a double room.

Two other choices in the same price range, and with similar luxurious accommodations and amenities, are the **Pousada Padieiro,** at the opposite end of the Rua do Comércio at no. 74 (tel. 0243/71-1139); and the **Pousada do Ouro,** Rua da Praia 145 (tel. 0243/71-1378).

For a budget choice, the **Hotel Solar dos Geránios,** Praça da Matriz (tel. 0243/71-1550), is a Swiss-run inn occupying a building with much of the original interior intact, including a massive stone stairway that leads to a second-floor corridor with a number of very simple rooms without baths. The inn is also filled with antique furnishings, collected by the owners and left in their unfinished state, a condition that strangely enhances their aesthetic appeal. Double accommodations are $15 the night.

For **camping,** there is the nearby Praia do Jabaquara.

Eating in Parati

All the better inns in Parati, including those listed above, have their own excellent restaurants. For a good home-cooked Brazilian meal of steak or chicken breast with all the usual side dishes, try the **Restaurante Santa Rita,** across from the Igreja Santa Rita at the corner of Rua da Matriz. For $4 or $5 per person, including beverage, you can eat simply but extremely well.

A fancier choice is the **Restaurante Ancoradouro,** Rua Dona Geralda 345 (tel. 71-1394), around the corner from the Pousada Mercado do Pouso. The menu is international, and entrees fall in the $5 to $10 range.

The **Do Lixo Ao Luxo,** on Rua do Comércio (tel. 71-1124), is a combination bar, restaurant, and antique shop. The name means "From the Garbage to the Rich," and the colonial-era goods, including cast-iron cooking stoves, are certainly expensive and very beautiful.

Tourist Information

The old jail house, next to the Igreja Santa Rita, has a desk where you can get a program of the latest happenings in town, and also a gift shop with some attractive and well-made craft items. It's open daily from 9 a.m. till 4 p.m. (tel. 71-1256).

CHAPTER VII

MINAS GERAIS AND THE HISTORICAL CITIES

□ □ □

1. BELO HORIZONTE
2. SABARÁ
3. CONGONHAS
4. OURO PRETO
5. AROUND MINAS

The name Minas Gerais means General Mines, a rather prosaic term for a state that has contributed so much not only to Brazil's public coffers, but also to the country's artistic, architectural, and political heritage. Geologically, Minas—as the state is called for short—is both favored and ancient. Folded among the layers of its mountainous surface is one of the world's largest reserves of iron ore, so many billions of tons as to make numbers irrelevant and boggle the imagination. Iron, along with cattle and coffee production in the western and northern plains, are the real wealth of Minas today, but it was gold and gem fever that fed the territory's initial exploration and settlement from the late 1600s until well into the 19th century.

Minas also produces much of the Brazil's harvest of precious stones. In this case, the word "harvest" is no metaphor. Early on in the colonial days, stories began to circulate that the beryllium crystals known since ancient times as emeralds were strewn all over the rocky ground in that unexplored region, just waiting for the courageous to go there and gather them up. Minas's reputation as the "Land of the Emeralds" spurred many adventurers to penetrate its forbidden terrain, where the Indian culture still dominated, in search of this easy wealth. The problem was, it was actually the less valuable gemstones that were out in the open, so that what the first pioneers, the *bandeirantes,* took for emeralds were really green tourmalines. Even today a high percentage of Brazil's precious stones are chipped from the surface rocks (if not found actually lying at their feet) by individual prospectors, not mined on an industrial scale. One result is that no one can begin to approximate the size of a given year's production, or the amount of wealth it generates.

It would take many more generations before Brazil's great emerald deposits would be discovered. But when the *bandeirantes* wound their way up the valley of the Rio das Velhas, they found a substance with a duller sheen but an even better market. Nuggets of pure gold, which washed from shallow deposits in the hills of the Serra da Mantiqueira and the Serra do Espinhaço, could be panned from this and other rivers by the bucketful in a single day, or scratched with minimal labor from right beneath the crust of the earth. Instead of emeralds, by 1693 the pioneers had stumbled onto the greatest gold deposits the world had ever known. Some 25 years later it was discovered that Minas also contained diamonds, so vast in quantity that they could be found clinging to the roots of bushes that were plucked from the ground.

From that time on, sugar would no longer be king in Brazil, nor Salvador the center of the country's power and culture. This was the beginning of the Gold Cycle that was to last 100 years. Fortune hunters flocked to Minas by the tens of thousands, and in their wake came the artists and artisans who spun gold into baroque opulence, creating the great art and architectural treasures that adorn the "*cidades históricas,*" the historical cities of Minas, to which thousands today still flock to visit and admire.

1. BELO HORIZONTE

Belo Horizonte is Brazil's third-largest city, with a metropolitan population approaching 3,000,000 inhabitants. Known as "B.H." ("bay-a-*gah*") or Belo, it was a planned city, constructed in a spacious valley and inaugurated in 1897 as the state's capital to replace Ouro Preto, which had outgrown its pinched-in boundaries. Today B.H. has the graceful appearance of a provincial center, the grid-like organization of its streets broken up by ample shade trees, architectural diversity, and the gentle rising and falling of the terrain. The urban core of the city is belted by the **Avenida do Contorno,** which encircles its periphery and greatly enhances the movement of traffic from one neighborhood to another. The principal boulevard, **Avenida Alfonso Pena,** divides the city at its middle, and at dead center an enormous green space, the **Parque Municipal,** occupies 200 of B.H.'s choicest acres. There is about B.H. an unmistakable air of sophistication and dignity that one comes to associate with residents of this remarkable state. And while the beachless city is not promoted heavily as a destination for tourists, it is not lacking in urban amenities, which take the form of animated café life and excellent eating.

TRAVELING TO B.H.: Belo Horizonte is 250 miles (403 km) from Rio de Janeiro, roughly the distance between New York and Boston. The main artery is the 040 highway, which goes via Petrópolis. A traveler with two weeks or more to spend in Brazil might want to consider the following itinerary. Stay the first week in Rio, and then rent a car and head north toward Minas. Spend the first day and night in the vicinity of São João del Rei and Tiradentes. Then travel on to B.H. and use the city as a base for side trips to the principal historical cities, with a possible overnight in Ouro Preto. To return, leave the car at the airport in B.H. and fly back to Rio for your last night or two in the country.

Those with less time to spare can still take in the historical cities by flying the air shuttle, called the **Ponte Aérea** (literally, air bridge) from Rio's international airport to B.H., a flight that takes only 50 minutes. The cost of a round-trip ticket is less than $100. Then contact a local agency directly at the airport and book a standard bus tour. You can see all the sights—somewhat hurriedly to be sure—in a day and a half, and be back in Rio within 48 hours. Normally I would not consider recommending such a frenetic sightseeing pace for anyone in Brazil (that is, in Rio) on a limited stay. But the baroque wonders of Minas are so spectacular that I will suspend my better judgment in this and a handful of other special cases.

Those visitors planning to wander a bit more widely through the country are encouraged to purchase the VARIG Air Pass, a detailed description of which can be found in Chapter I. Long-distance **buses** also arrive regularly in B.H. from most of Brazil's major cities. At $4 one way, the standard bus is the cheapest mode of transportation from Rio to B.H., and the journey takes about seven hours. The more comfortable *leito*, with reclining seats, costs roughly double that amount and is particulary recommended for night travel. There is also frequent bus service from B.H. to all the nearby historical cities, and fares are minimal.

Travelers partial to **railroads** can reserve passage for about $30 each on the twice-weekly train from Rio.

Belo Horizonte is now serviced by two **airports,** with most out-of-state flights landing at Lagoa Santa some 39 km (24 miles) from the city.

Turminas, the state's tourist authority, runs an information counter at the airport, or you can check in at their main offices, Rua Mar de Espanha 745, in the Santo Antônio neighborhood (tel. 344-4572).

THE SIGHTS: While there are no "must see" sights in B.H.—the city is a place where it's simply nice to just hang out—there are numerous museums, parks, and points of interest for those who are so inclined.

You won't find the name **Savassi** on a city map (at least it hadn't yet appeared at press time), but the name indicates four square blocks where the best dining and nightlife in B.H. are to be found. Most of the restaurants listed below are located in the Savassi.

The best way to get a quick visual orientation of the city and its environs is to visit the **mirante** (the overlook) in the neighborhood of Mangabeiras, reached by following Avenida Alfonso Pena east (the direction away from Pampulha). The overlook occupies one corner of a park with picnic and recreational facilities. But the trip out here is really for the vista of the surrounding mountains which, row after row, seem to stretch on to infinity.

The futuristic suburb of Pampulha was, in effect, a prototype of Brasília, promoted, designed, and constructed by virtually the same cast of characters who were to later create the new Brazilian capital. The principal in both cases was the then mayor of B.H., and later president, Jucelino Kubitschek, who in 1939 enlisted some of the country's most creative talent, including architect Oscar Niemeyer, landscape artist Roberto Burle Marx, and painter Cândido Portinari. The project involved the transformation of the area surrounding an existing reservoir into a modern residential and recreational district. The plans included the building of a chapel, sporting clubs, restaurants, and a casino. The **Capelinha de São Francisco de Assis,** designed by Niemeyer and decorated with *azuleijo* tiles and murals by Pontinari, considered now to be some of the artist's masterworks, remained unconsecrated for years, a reaction to both the aesthetic modernism and the leftist political views of the artists by the city's conservative clergy. The casino was converted into the city's **Museum of Modern Art,** Avenida Octacílio Negrão de Lima 16585 (tel. 443-4533), open daily from 8 a.m. to 6 p.m., after gambling was outlawed in Brazil following World War II. As with most of the project's buildings, this, too, was designed by Niemeyer, and the gardens were laid out by Marx. Pampulha lies about ten kilometers (six miles) to the west of the city, a 20-minute ride by cab or car, and is also reachable by frequent bus service.

The **Museu de Mineralogia** (Mineralogy Museum), Rua da Bahia 1149 (tel. 212-1400, extension 359), is in an old municipal building (ca. 1910), one of the few examples of Manueline neo-Gothic architecture in Brazil. Some 98% of the 2,500 samples on exhibit come from the mines and hills of Minas Gerais. There are four exhibition rooms with displays of dozens of minerals and gemstones, organized according to their geological families. For those who can read Portuguese, there are printed explanations of the minerals' chemical composition, occurrence in nature, uses, and the locations of major veins within the state, in Brazil, and in the world. Open daily from 8:30 a.m. to 5:30 p.m.; free admittance.

The **Museu Histórico** (History Museum), on Rua Bernardo Mascarenhas (tel. 212-1055, extension 289), in the Cidade Jardim residential neighborhood, occupies the only structure—an old *fazenda* house—that remains from the days when Belo Horizonte was known as Arraial do Curral D' El Rey. Built in 1833, the adobe house is itself an integral part of the exhibit, most of which documents the process of the new city replacing the old settlement. Open Tuesday through Sunday from 10 a.m. to 5 p.m.

The **Centro de Artesanato Minero** Avenida Alfonso Pena 1537 (tel. 222-2544), is the place to go for well-made and reasonably priced craft items gathered from all over the state. The Craft Center is located close to the major hotels in the Palacio das Artes on the edge of the Municipal Park. Very modern and well organized, the shop features the best of Minas's soapstone statuary (lovely but very difficult to transport without breaking), yellow tinware, baskets, rugs, and woodcarvings, all of exceptionally high quality and imaginative design. The shop is open Tuesday through Saturday from 9 a.m. to 9 p.m., and on Sunday and Monday from 9:30 a.m. to 1:30 p.m.

WHERE TO STAY: Strangely, for a city as charming as Belo Horizonte, the hotel scene is a little disappointing. In reality the city has only one hotel that could be said to meet the highest international standards, and that, ironically, is located ten miles out of town in Contagem, Brazil's third-largest industrial district. I don't mean to imply that the hotels are in anyway uninhabitable, but they are lacking in the finer details of décor and maintenance. Not attempting to be deliberately funky, they at times cross that fine line into the realm of bad taste. B.H.'s downtown hub is relatively small, and all the hotels tend to be within walking distance of each other and of the principal transportation terminals serving the airport.

The Upper Bracket

Belo's best hotel is the **Brasilton,** Rodovia Fernão Dias at km 365 (tel. 031/351-0900), actually located about 25 minutes from downtown in the heavily industrialized suburb of Contagem. The hotel was no doubt built as an oasis for traveling business people. And really, while the location is somewhat bizarre, the hotel's internal environment is so pleasant that you won't care or notice for a minute that you are surrounded by industrial enterprises (which are not on a particularly gigantic scale, in any event). There are also plenty of trees, stores, and open spaces in the vicinity—it's not the cold and smelly industrial-park look of the New Jersey Turnpike by any means.

The handsome white stucco façade of the two-story Brasilton suggests a stylized pueblo, square in shape, where most of the 143 rooms overlook the pool and landscaped patio of a large interior courtyard. Off the central yard are the enclosed public spaces, including a smartly decorated lobby, restaurant, and various discreet seating environments. The medium-sized rooms all have small balconies, along with full baths and self-service mini-bars. Sports facilities at the hotel include tennis, volleyball, and soccer courts, as well as a sauna and a recreational game room. Overall, the Brasilton conveys a relaxed and resort-like atmosphere, despite its popularity among corporate clients as a venue for business meetings and weekend seminars. Rates are $60 to $70 for singles, and $70 to $80 for doubles; the more expensive rooms front poolside.

The **Othon Palace,** Avenida Alfonso Pena 1050 (tel. 031/226-7844), is Belo's only five-star hotel, and by far the best of the downtown selection. The Othon is a fully equipped high-rise in the shape of a concave cylinder, which faces the Municipal Park. The hotel's public spaces are decorated in marble and tiles, with earth-tone colors predominating. Rooms are large, with big windows and separate sitting areas. All have color TV, mini-bar, and modern bath. An outdoor pool (which can be heated when the mercury dips) is located on the 25th floor, along with a dining terrace. The principal restaurant, serving international cuisine, and the bar are on the third floor. Standard rooms are $70 single and $75 doubles, while deluxe rooms (located on the higher floors) run slightly higher, from $78 to $84.

The Medium Range

The **Terminal Center Hotel,** Avenida Amazonas 1445 (tel. 031/337-9555). The entrance is actually around the corner on Rua Rio Grande do Sul, and the large, brand-new building is located across from the *Terminal Turístico* JK, the bus terminal for the airport bus (the *executivo*). The hotel is slated to provide 450 rooms, but only the first few floors are currently in operation, while the remainder are still being fitted out. The standard double runs about $55 and is quite small, if cozy and well furnished, with all the necessities from bath to TV and mini-bar. Larger rooms run to $70 for two.

The **Hotel Del Rey,** Praça Alfonso Arinos 60 (tel. 031/222-2211). The 200-room Del Rey is located across the street from the Museum of Mineralogy. Single rooms range from $39 to $46, and doubles run $45 to $53, according to their location.

The **Real Palace Hotel,** Rua Espírito Santo 901 (tel. 031/224-2111), is another of B.H.'s four-star hotels with a three-star appearance. The 256 rooms here cost slightly more than the comparable Del Rey. Standard rooms are the best buy: $50 for one and $57 for double occupancy. These rooms are on the lower floors, but they are similar in size and detail to the so-called luxury rooms, which are priced between $67 and $77.

The **Wembley Palace,** Rua Espírito Santo 201 (tel. 031/201-6966). The 105 rooms here are good sized, and better furnished than those of rival hotels in the same category. The luxury rooms have a separate sitting area. Standard rooms start at $40 single and $50 double, with larger deluxe rooms priced at $10 more per night.

The **International Plaza,** Rua Rio de Janeiro 109 (tel. 031/201-2300). Any of the 105 rooms here would be a perfect setting for a "Saturday Night Live" satire on bedrooms of Latin American military dictators. The suite is worth seeing as a cultural artifact in its own right—the décor is so gaudy, it's almost camp. The suite has two large separate rooms, an out-of-date TV in each; furnishings include overstuffed, plush couches and chairs, and fabrics that would have made Liberace blush. Both the suites and the standard rooms have small balconies. If you get the suite, make sure it faces the front of the hotel. Rooms begin at $40 for singles and $50 for doubles. The suites cost $80 per night.

The Bargain Range

In many ways the following hotels are superior to their more pretentious rivals, if for no other reason than that the rooms are about half the price, while most of the services, including a restaurant, are still provided.

The **Plaza Palace,** Rua Rio de Janeiro 147 (tel. 031/201-3048), a 63-room hotel charges $18 for a single and $21 for a double.

The **Hotel Esplanada,** Avenida Santos Dumont 304 (tel. 031/222-7411), has 130 rooms and is also located near the bus station where you catch the airport bus. Rooms with bath are called *apartamentos,* and are priced at $12 to $15 a night. The simpler rooms, called *quartos,* have neither attached bathrooms nor TVs, but at $6 to $10 nightly, are very adequate for those on a limited budget or who would rather spend their money on something other than a hotel room.

The **Ambassy Hotel,** Rua dos Caetés 633 (tel. 031/201-0222), offers 72 spacious rooms with the usual amenities, except TVs are optional and may be rented for a fee. The old triangular building at a busy intersection of the downtown shopping district has a certain charm. Rooms cost $13 for one and $19 for two people.

The **Hotel de Minas,** Rua São Paulo 331 (tel. 031/201-6280), is more like an old transient hotel you'd expect to find near the bus or train station in practically any city in the world. There are 19 very serviceable and clean rooms with baths which cost $6, $8, and $9, depending on size. The building is centrally located, a walkup with no elevator, and rooms have no phones, mini-bars, or televisions, which may strike the fancy of those quite willing to deprive themselves of such amenities in exchange for a cheap nightly rate.

WHERE TO EAT IN BELO: One needs no other justification for traveling in Minas Gerais than the opportunity to sample the state's superb cuisine, **comida Mineira,** popular throughout Brazil, but best in the kitchens of its origin. The favorite ingredients of a meal in Minas are pork, black beans, kale, and a cornmeal mush called **angu.** Two dishes you are sure to encounter everywhere throughout the state are **tutu com linguiça e couve,** a dish of country sausage, mashed beans, and kale, and **feijão de tropeiro,** a stir-fry of pork and sausage, beans, eggs, and crackling (fried pork rinds). Many of the Mineiro dishes have their origins in the slave and laboring cultures, but have been fine-tuned over the years into the most palate-pleasing of country fare. Another staple found on most tables is **pão de quijo,** little puff balls of soft cheese bread (bet you can't eat just one!). The desserts, like **doce de leite,** and cheese, **quiejo mineiro,** of Minas are also justly celebrated by all Brazilians everywhere. One favorite dessert is to eat the cheese with a slice of **goiabada** (guava paste) on a **pãozinho,** the classic bread roll universally available no matter where you travel in Brazil.

There are many fine restaurants in Belo Horizonte, whether you favor comida Mineira or more familiar international fare. And the *bom e barato* standard (good and cheap) of Brazilian restaurant food is as much in evidence throughout B.H. as in any other region of the country.

The Upper Bracket

Estalagem, Rua Faraiba 696 (tel. 226-5468), is without a doubt one of the best restaurants in B.H. *Estalágem* in Portuguese means inn, in the old-fashioned sense of stagecoaches and highwaymen. But beyond the name and the hand-painted sign with the coach, there is little to connote such a provincial setting. The restaurant is by no means overdecorated in any thematic way; if anything it's understated, tasteful, and elegant, with large linen-covered tables, fine plates and attentive service. The best dishes in the house, like flambé of giant shrimp, plus wine, dessert, and coffee, can be had for $25 to $30 per person.

The Medium and Bargain Range

Chico Mineiro, Rua Alagoas 626 (tel. 224-5604), in the heart of the Savassi, is the place in B.H. to eat down-home, authentic comida Mineira, the country-style food of central Brazil. The principal dishes are tutu, tropeiro, and galinha (chicken). The restaurant's interior is divided into several partitioned rooms, amply paneled in wood, with indirect ceiling lighting and checkered tablecloths. There are also some ten tables outside on the sidewalk. Your meal with beverage and tip will cost between $4 and $7. Chico Mineiro is open Monday through Friday for lunch from 11:30 a.m. to 3 p.m., and reopens at 6 p.m. for dinner until around 2 a.m. On Saturday the restaurant remains open throughout the day, and on Sunday it opens only for lunch, from 11 a.m. till 5 p.m.

Buona Távola, Rua Santa Rita Durão 309 (tel. 222-6027), is an Italian restaurant owned by the proprietor of the Chico Mineiro, and open during the same hours. Fettuccine da casa costs $4, while other pasta and meat dishes range between $3 and $6. The restaurant is quite small, with only about ten tables. But the owner said he was definitely moving soon, so look for this restaurant at a new location. The phone, he said, will remain the same.

The **Trianon,** Rua Alagoas 730 (tel. 226-0006), is a thoroughly charming and fancy delicatessen. Forest green is the predominant color of the trim and furnishings including the Vienna-style marble-topped tables on wrought-iron bases, and green barrel-backed chairs. A large refrigerator counter runs the length of the room, which is part shop for delicacies, wines, and liquors, and part restaurant. German specialties—meats and cheeses—are displayed in the deli counter, and German dishes add a special dimension to an extensive menu, which also contains a particularly long list of appetizers priced between $1 and $4. Meals aren't much more expensive, being mostly in the $3 to $5 range. Hours are 11 a.m. to 2 a.m. seven days a week.

Vitelo's, Rua Cláudio Manoel 1149 (tel. 226-0993), is a genuine steakhouse, lest we forget that in addition to its vast mineral wealth, the state of Minas Gerais is also a major agricultural, dairy, and livestock producer. The management stresses that at Vitelo's the meat is always fresh, never frozen. One favorite dish is the milk-fed veal, at $10 about the most expensive cut in the house. Many meat dishes are served in a way to preserve the integrity of the cut: that is, you can sometimes get a dish—at a fixed price on the menu for two—that will serve up to six people. Guarnições (side dishes) cost extra, so your rice, beans, farofa, greens, and so forth will run you 75¢ to $1.50 per dish. Monday through Saturday lunch is served between noon and 3 or 4 p.m., depending on the crowd. Dinner runs from 7 p.m. till just past midnight, except on Friday and Saturday when the restaurant stays open to 2 a.m. On Sunday Vitelo's only serves lunch, and remains open from noon till 5 p.m.

Cucina Italiana—Província di Salerno, Rua Cláudio de Manoel 981 (tel. 224-2205). A block away from Vitelo's, on the corner of Rua Pernambuco, there is an old house of yellow stucco that has been turned into a pleasant restaurant which specializes in southern Italian cooking. You have a choice of several rooms, which helps create an intimate atmosphere for dining. Open Tuesday to Saturday for dinner from 6 p.m. till 2 a.m., and on Sunday from noon till 5 p.m. for lunch only; closed Monday. The price range is an incredible $2.50 to $5 à la carte, for traditional meat and pasta dishes.

Chez Bastião, Rua Alagoas 642 (tel. 226-5694), is the favorite restaurant of my guide from Turminas, as much for the food as for the animated atmosphere. The food and menu prices are similar to those of Chico Mineiro, which is directly next door. Chez Bastião, however, stays open all day, from 11 a.m. until the last customer is ready to leave, and the same is true on Sunday, except the closing hour is 2 a.m.

The **Tip Top,** Rua Rio de Janeiro 1754 (tel. 337-9713), is located in the Lordes neighborhood, which is contiguous to Savassi. Other than the fact that it's much larger, the Tip Top has the same deli ambiance as the Trianon, and is open during the same hours. The restaurant is very well attended on Sunday evenings in particular, a favorite time for denizens of the city to hang out and relax before the beginning of a new work week.

Also in Lordes is the **Bartolomeu,** Avenida Olegário Maciel 1741 (tel. 335-9686), another popular spot for Belo's café society. A nice feature of the Bartolomeu is that you can call ahead for take-out. The restaurant serves a feijoada every Saturday for $4. Open for dinner only during the week, from 6 p.m. until the movement dies down, and on the weekends from 11 a.m. until the wee hours.

The **Degrau,** Avenida Alfonso Pena 4221 (tel. 225-7362), is what Brazilians refer to as a *restaurante popular,* which translates roughly as a "restaurant for the masses." Located on the way to the *mirante,* right below the Praça do Papa, where an outdoor altar was built for a Mass celebrated by the visiting Pope John Paul II a few years back, the Degrau has a long menu and seating for hundreds. Many young people are attracted by the ambience and inexpensive food. Directly across the street is the **Brunela,** a restaurant that is a mirror image of the Degrau, but with a different name. Both places are open daily from 9 a.m. till 4 a.m.

Tavares, Rua Santa Catarina 64 (tel. 212-6435), located in a back alley off the Praça Raul Soares, is assuredly Belo Horizonte's most unusual restaurant, serving a variety of game meats that are sure to intrigue the true carnivore. Also a "popular" restaurant, the Tavares is well worn but not unclean. A lunch here can be the starting point for an exploration of the downtown shops and open-air markets, one of which takes place daily on the neighboring plaza. The specialties include viado (deer), capibara (a giant member of the rodentia order of mammals, which has been likened to a 200-pound guinea pig), cordorna (quail), and jacaré (alligator).

The **Casa dos Contos,** Rua Rio Grande do Norte 1065, is a meeting place for artists and intellectuals in B.H. Located in the Savassi, the café atmosphere is relaxed and casual.

WHERE TO SWING: There are many good clubs in and around the Savassi, including the **Tropical Clube,** Avenida Cristóvão Colombo 462 (tel. 221-9304), with live music on Monday nights; and the **Tom Marrom,** Rua Inconfidentes 1141 (tel. 224-3728), a singles bar.

For live cabaret, there's the **Cabaré Mineiro,** Rua Gonçalves Dias 54 (tel. 227-5860), with a different show every night, including political theater. Wednesday nights are for *karoaké,* when the audience provides the vocals, singing along to taped musical backup. The bar opens at 6 p.m. daily, and the show begins after 9 p.m. Closed Sunday.

THE HISTORICAL CITIES

For the first 200 years colonists in Brazil had confined their settlements to the country's coastal lands. They had looked on the mountainous interior as impassable and unihabitable. Late in the 17th century, however, word slowly drifted back to the coast that the crude and antisocial slave hunters known as *bandeirantes* had discovered gold in those inhospitable hills. Within a short time the wealth that flowed from those early grub stakes attracted hords of settlers to the virgin territory, and the rude camps of the prospectors were transformed almost overnight into the glittering pinnacles of baroque culture that are known today as the historical cities of Minas Gerais.

The cities we will visit for this first edition are Sabará, Congonhas do Campo, Ouro Preto, and Mariana. These are the cities closest to Belo Horizonte, and

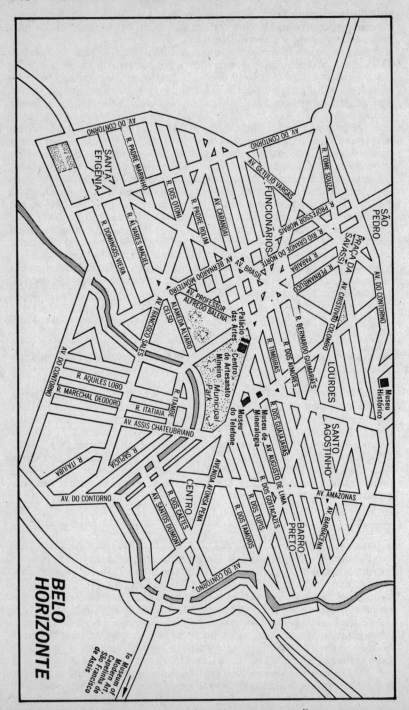

BELO HORIZONTE

therefore most accessible to the majority of international tourists who are likely to visit them, prefering no doubt to fly to the capital of Minas rather than coming to the state by car. A car trip, on the other hand, would take the traveler from Rio first to Sao João del Rei and Tiradentes, which in this edition will only be referred to in passing.

The historical cities of Minas are living tableaux of Brazil's Cycle of Gold which occurred throughout the 1700s, but touched the fringes of two other centuries as well, running from the 1690s to the early 1800s, by which time the auriferous flow from the mines had slowed to a trickle. The principal attractions of the historical cities are the scores of churches, residences, and commercial structures that have been preserved from those times, and the artistry with which the façades and interiors of those churches were decorated by a dozen great artists, most notable of whom were the sculptor Antônio Francisco Lisboa (called Aleijadinho) and the painter Manuel de Costa Atraide. The work of these and many other remarkable artists can be seen in each of the four cities herein described.

Of the cities themselves, Ouro Preto is by far the most important for two related, if contradictory, reasons. As the territory's, and later the state's, capital for 150 years, the town grew to splendid proportions during its reign of power, the hilly streets crowned with one baroque architectural treasure after another. The transfer of its power to Belo Horizonte nearly a century ago, moreover, ensured the preservation of Ouro Preto's characteristic appearance, so that it remains today frozen in a state of near perfection, a veritable living mirror of the period of its former grandeur, little diluted by the developments of the 19th and 20th centuries.

While all the historical cities enjoyed a bountiful prosperity during the Gold Cycle, the heel of Portuguese colonial rule pressed most deeply in Brazil on the backs of the mining towns, whose people were taxed beyond endurance. This oppression in time gave rise to Brazil's first great republican movement, the Inconfidência Mineira, which was hatched and nurtured in Ouro Preto, and ultimately led to the martyrdom of the patriot Ensign Joaquim José da Silva Xavier, known to posterity as Tiradentes. The moving story of Tiradentes's conspiracy and ultimate betrayal is etched into the hearts of all Brazilian schoolchildren. An ample record of this simple man and his movement is also preserved in museums and historical sites, both in Ouro Preto and throughout the entire region.

2. SABARÁ

Sabará is the closest of the historical cities to B.H., only 11 short miles (18 km) from the municipal limits. And what a treasure of the baroque period it is. Sabará contains at least a dozen sites that reward the eye and nurture the imagination. The town is worthy of a full day's visit in its own right.

THE SIGHTS: Whether you arrive by bus or car, you will most likely enter through the mountain pass where Sabará is set in a winding valley, like a jewel among the surrounding slopes, at the point where its two rivers are joined. The principal canal is the fabled **Rio das Velhas,** at one time saturated with gold, and still panned by die-hard prospectors who can even today eke out a living in this anachronistic profession. The other is a tributary called the **Rio Sabará.** The name Sabará, incidentally, is the somewhat twisted adaptation of an Indian word that meant the "Great Rock That Shines," a poetic reference perhaps to the precious metal for which the tribe in question had no use, but that was to ultimately cause its extinction.

The tour begins on **Rua Dom Pedro II,** a street flanked by crooked alleys that most completely preserves the 18th-century flavor of the town. Number 72, known as the House of Dona Sofia, and today the town's library, is a noble example of the grand town houses of the day. The old manor house at no. 200 is the Town Hall, housed in the **Solar do Padre Correia** (1773), once the pride of a wealthy priest, with a private oratory where delicate carved paneling is leafed in gold veneer. The façade of the house was renovated with certain early 19th-century embellishments, like the window balconies with individual iron railings, but in the rear the details of the earlier century are retained around the doors and windows. There you can also see what remains of the stables and the slave quarters. Such architectural details of the past abound in Sabará. As the poet Carlos Drummond de Andrade put it: "It is all inexorably colonial: benches, windows, locks, street lamps." The building may be visited during business hours, Monday through Friday.

Next stop along the same street is the **Teatrinho** (1819), the diminutive theater that was the town's opera house. With only 47 small boxes, the seating area is the same size as the stage. And the acoustics, if you wish to experiment with a note or two, are said to be perfect. Of special interest is the hand-painted curtain with its faded scene of old Sabará by the Austrian artist George Grimm. The theater may be visited Tuesday through Sunday from 9 to 11 a.m. and again after lunch from 1 to 6 p.m.

The nearby Praça do Rosário contains what in Brazil is a rare sight, a church that is totally preserved in an unfinished state. The **Igreja do Rosário** was to be constructed around an existing chapel (1713), and financed by slaves from the pennies they were able to beg as donations. The project begun in 1767, dragged on interminably, and was finally short-circuited by the dispersion of the slaves following their emancipation in 1888. When it was suggested in this century that the thick stone walls ought to be demolished or the church completed, the town historian said the idea was like "sculpting arms for the *Venus de Milo*." The chapel is open daily from 1 to 5 p.m.

The **Museu do Ouro** (Gold Museum) is located in the Intendência, or Smelting House building (1732), on Rua da Intendência. Here a representative of the Portuguese Crown resided with his family and collected the odious tax, called the *quinto*, the one-fifth of all gold mined in Brazil that was sent to the royal coffers in Lisbon. The interior of the museum is arranged like a private house of the period. There are many interesting period paintings, furnishings, religious carvings, and mining and smelting tools of that era. The museum hours are noon to 5 p.m. Tuesday through Sunday.

Among the most important churches to be seen in Sabará is the **Igreja Nossa Senhora do Carmo,** on Rua do Carmo, begun in 1763. The sculptor Aleijadinho played an important role in the decorative finishing of this church. He is responsible for the portal, the pulpits, and the choir loft, and some of his most famous wood statuary occupies niches and altars throughout, including the images of the four Evangelists, and the 12th-century English mystic, St. Simon Stock, whose dying words, "Holy Mary, Mother of God, pray for us sinners now, and at the hour of our death," were incorporated by papal authority into the "Hail, Mary," the principal prayer of the Catholic rosary. The church also contains many beautiful panel paintings, some of which are attributed to Atraide. At Rua do Carmo 153 is the house where, according to custom, Aleijadinho lived during his years in Sabará, from 1770 to 1783.

The **Matriz de Nossa Senhora da Conceição,** begun in 1700 and completed in 1710, is as plain on the outside as the Church of Carmo is ornate. On the inside the opposite is true. Carmo is all simplicity, and Conceição is a festival of lavish carvings, sheathed in gold lamé. Leading to the sacristry is the famous "Chinese Door," which like much of the interior, is said to be the work of artists brought to Sabará from the Portuguese colony of Macau on the Chinese mainland. The church is located out of town, along a road that leads to the Belgo-Mineira steel plant, and can be reached by city bus or a ten-minute cab ride. It may be visited Monday through Saturday from 8 a.m. to 6 p.m., and on Sunday from 11 a.m. to 6 p.m. Also undoubtedly of Chinese influence is the tiny **Capela de Nossa Senhora do O,** slightly farther out along the road to the steel plant. Built in 1698, the church's official name is Our Lady of Maternity (in Portuguese, literally Our Lady of the Expectant Birth). The "O" comes from the initial sound uttered during the recitation of a litany on the feast day of this divine aspect of the Blessed Virgin, celebrated in the days before Christmas since the time of the Council of Toledo in the year 656. Again the unadorned exterior masks the ornate, gold-covered carvings within. And many figures in the panel paintings, including the burros, have almond-shaped, Oriental eyes. Open daily from 8 a.m. to 6 p.m.

3. CONGONHAS

Congonhas do Campo (Hollies of the Field) takes its name from a plant used for making tea that is commonly found growing on the hillsides of this town which occupies an undulating valley at an elevation of over 3,000 feet. Late in life, the sculptor Aleijadinho came to Congonhas and produced what many critics claim was his masterpiece, 12 statues of the Prophets carved in soapstone that adorn the terrace of a local shrine, the Santuário do Bom Jesus de Matosinhos.

Congonhas is connected by access road to the BR 040 highway, approximately 45 miles (72 km) from Belo Horizonte. Rich in iron ore deposits, Congonhas continues its evolution as a active mining community. As a result, much of its colonial aspect has been lost. Congonhas today is typical of country towns in the interior of the state, and as such, offers a view of Brazilian life not to be found in the big cities. With Congonhas only an hour or so by car or bus from B.H., a side trip there, even without the major attraction of the Aleijadinho statuary, would be worthwhile to capture the flavor of small-town life in Minas.

ANTÔNIO FRANCISCO LISBOA: In 1730 a slave named Isabel bore her Portuguese master, Manuel Francisco Lisboa, a son who, on the day of his baptism, was freed by his father and named Antônio. Manuel was a master-builder and church architect who encouraged the boy to develop his talents for carving in the workshops of local craftsmen. At the age of 47 the amiable and highly successful Antônio, whose work had already added great beauty to many churches of the region, was stricken by a crippling disease for which medical historians have been unable to provide a definitive diagnosis, their speculations running from a form of leprosy to rheumatoid arthritis. The disease deformed the artist's fingers and toes, and twisted the features of his face into a grotesque mask. It was due to this condition that Lisboa earned the nickname **Aleijadinho,** the little cripple. For almost another 40 years the artist continued to work, never slacking his pace, and creating some of his most powerful images with mallet and chisel strapped to his wrists by leather thongs. Despite the pain and mental anguish Lisboa suffered during his final years, art historians are astounded by the fact that as his own body deteriorated, the artist's carved figures became more and more robust and powerful, culminating in the work created in Congonhas while in his early 70s. Perhaps the choice of soapstone as the medium for the Prophets, and cedar for some 76 life-size Passion figures sculpted by Aleijadinho in his atelier, both comparatively soft materials, were the artist's only concession to the ravages of his disability. It is a mistake, however, to emphasize the artist's handicap in the evaluation of his work, which is considered to be as great as anything produced during his life-time by contemporary artists throughout the entire world.

O SANTUÁRIO DO BOM JESUS DE MATOSIHNOS: On the top of a hill, the Morro do Maranhão, the shrine of the Good Jesus of Matosinhos domi-nates the landscape of Congonhas do Campo. The church itself (1757), with its twin towers and exterior carvings, is undeniably baroque. Steps leading to the main portal cross an ample terrace, bordered by a stone wall along which are stra-tegically spaced the Profetas (Prophets) of Aleijadinho. Sloping down the hill away from the church is a broad stone patio, planted with tall, dramatic coconut palms, where six small devotional chapels house life-size wooden statues that de-pict scenes from the Passion of Christ. The interior of the church, heavily laden with carved arches, altars, and pulpits, all bathed in a hue of a golden tint, also contains work by Aleijadinho and Atraide. The whole ensemble was inspired by a shrine in Braga, Portugal, similar in detail but grander in scale.

The 12 Old Testament prophets were executed by Aleijadinho from 1800 to 1815. While taken as a whole the statues project a ballistic movement, their true power and uniqueness can only be fully grasped by studying each work individu-ally, to decipher its unique allegorical meaning. The Passion statues were all carved between 1796 and 1799. The construction of the chapels was plagued by economic delays for many decades, and only about half of the works were painted by Atraide and displayed during Aleijadino's lifetime. The remaining half were not completed until late in the 19th century.

OTHER SIGHTS: Congonhas has several other graceful churches of the peri-od. But beyond the shrine, the only reason to linger in the town is to explore the densely packed streets in search of souvenirs and some good home-cooking à la Mineira. The journey to Ouro Preto from Congonhas, while not that long, takes a good hour and 45 minutes by car through some lovely farming country, and even longer by bus, which stops often on the circuitous route.

Congonhas is at its most animated during the annual celebrations of **Semana Santa** (Holy Week), when its religious processions and enactment of the Crucifixion make the city one of the biggest tourist attractions in the state of Minas Gerais.

4. Ouro Preto

The title "Cultural Heritage of Mankind" was conferred on the city of Ouro Preto by UNESCO in 1980. Founded in 1711 as Vila Rica do Alberquerque. Ouro Preto today contains the largest homogeneous collection of baroque archi-tecture in Brazil. In a country oversaturated with baroque and colonial-era build-ings, that's saying a lot.

Ouro Preto is 62 miles (100 km) from Belo Horizonte, and may be reached by frequent buses. Direct bus service from Rio de Janeiro is also available, but should be booked several days in advance to assure a seat. Like Congonhas, Ouro Preto sits high in the mountains, at an elevation of over 3,000 feet, so the climate is somewhat mild, temperatures ranging from 2°C (37°F) to 28°C (82°F). The highest point, at over 5,600 feet, is the landmark **Pico de Itacolomi.** There is no valley to speak of in Ouro Preto. Human structures occupy all the available space on the tightly packed hills, which are etched with a network of winding and nar-row stone streets that follow the steep contours of the land across a dozen dimin-utive bridges over streams that empty from the surrounding heights, opening here and there into many small plazas, each of which is crowned with a graceful church.

WHAT TO SEE: Churches, churches, and more churches—each one packed with religious art and enriched by its own unique history and legend. Add to these the other historical buildings and museums, restaurants and inns, craft shops and events, and there's plenty to keep a visitor occupied and satisfied for days on end. Little noted is the fact that Ouro Preto is also a college town, filled with student *repúblicas,* similar to fraternity and sorority houses, where there is always a spare bed for a youthful comrade from abroad. At night the college students gather in the squares and in their cafés, and on occasion create a festive air when they serenade the city with their ballads.

The best way to see all the sights is in the company of a guide, one who is employed and trained by the city. These uniformed guides, who are hired from their offices at Praça Tiradentes 41 (tel. 551-2655), charge about $10 for four hours, and are excellent sources of information on the art, history, and lore of the city. A map, stylized but useful, can also be purchased at the guide office for about $1, showing all the main streets and the placement of the principal sights.

To visit the first two churches you will probably want to take a cab, as they are located on the fringes of town. Otherwise, unless health prohibits—the streets are often quite steep and the climbs can be arduous—most of the other places of interest are centered within walking distance of the main square, the Praça Tiradentes.

One of the early *bandeirantes* in the area, a Padre Faria, ordered a chapel built in 1701 in the vicinity of the earliest mines. The chapel, the **Capela do Padre Faria** is located in the oldest section of the early settlement that predates the founding of the city. The towerless church contains a bell that was rung, in prohibition of a local order, on Tiradentes's execution day. Inside, the church is extremely ornate, the main and two side altars both richly veneered in gold. The vestment cabinet is the oldest in the city, and the colors for the dome mural, *The Coronation of Mary,* painted in 1727, were all mixed from natural elements: the red from *sangue-de-boi,* (bull's blood), a kind of fruit: yellow from egg yolk: brown from a mixture of banana juice with the root of a vine. Water damage has all but destroyed other ceiling panels, a reality that underscores the terrible burden Brazil faces with maintaining its priceless art treasures in a country where resources for such projects are understandably scarce. Open 8 a.m. till noon daily, except Monday when all the churches in Ouro Preto are closed.

The nearby **Rua Santa Rita** is Ouro Preto's oldest street, with its original paving stones called *pé-de-muleque,* the Brazilian term for peanut brittle. Some early slave houses can be seen along this street, which is still one of the poorest sections of the city. Of special interest are the roadside excavations where some of the earliest gold diggings in the city were made. They remain as cavities cut in the sides of embankments, overgrown with vegetation but otherwise unaltered.

Built in 1723 entirely of granite from Mount Itacolomini, **Santa Efigênia** is also known as Our Lady of the Rosary, whose image (attributed to Aleijadinho) occupies a niche over the portal. Both Our Lady of the Rosary and Saint Efigênia (a Christian Nubian princess) were patrons of the slaves, whose church this was. Legend has it that slave women hid purloined gold dust in their hair, and then washed the mineral out in fonts at the church door, to provide a fund for artists who worked on the church. Open to visitors from 8 a.m. to noon daily except Monday.

Matriz de Nossa Senhora da Conceição is Ouro Preto's largest church, dating from 1727. It was designed by Manuel Francisco Lisboa, who also created the first altar on the right (one of eight side altars), beneath which his son, Aleijadinho, is buried. The church was not completed until the early 1800s, and the interior décor alternates between the carved wood of the baroque period and the later rococo style which made use of molded plaster. A side door in the church leads to the **Aleijadinho Museum,** which includes the artist's sculpture of São Francisco de Paula. The statue's head is of carved soapstone, and painted. To this day it is not understood how Aleijadinho got the paint to adhere to the cold, smooth surface of the stone. The museum and church are open from 8 to 11:30 a.m. and 1 to 5 p.m.

The **Igreja do Pilar** is the richest church in Ouro Preto, on the charming square in the middle of the city, dating from 1711. Over 1,000 pounds of gold, and almost the equivalent in silver, add an almost blinding glitter to the carvings, much of which were the creation of Aleijadinho's father, his uncle (Antônio Francisco Pombal), and the artist's principal mentor, Francisco Xavier de Brito.

The church of **São Francisco de Assis,** located near the town's principal square, the Praça Tiradentes, is considered the jewel of Ouro Preto. It was designed by Aleijadinho and commissioned by the local military command in 1765. The façade, with its great medallion in soapstone, is one of the finest of Aleijadinho's works of this kind, carved entirely by his own hands without the assistance of his students or associates. The ceiling painting in the central nave is a rococo creation by Atraide. The church has been closed for restorations since 1985, and is due to reopen sometime in 1988, though it would not be unanticipated to expect a delay in this target date for the completion of the work.

Praça Tiradentes was the principal plaza of old Vial Rica, as it is Ouro Preto's main square today. On one end is the old Governor's Palace; at the other, the former Legislative Chambers and Jail. Both buildings currently house museums. Until well into the 19th century the slave market and the public whipping post were both located in this square, which remains a picture of the past, with its stone pavement and border of colonial buildings. At the center of the square is a statue of Tiradentes, marking the spot where the martyr's severed head was displayed in a cage following his execution.

Born near the current town that bears his name, **Joaquim José da Silva Xavier** learned the trade of dentistry and denture-making from his godfather, and was thus nicknamed **Tiradentes,** the tooth-puller. The career he was to pursue, however, was in the state's militia, never rising above the rank of ensign, a position equivalent to second lieutenant. An ardent lover of freedom, Tiradentes espoused the republican cause at a time when all of Europe and the Americas were inflamed with a hatred of monarchic despotism. He helped to form a movement throughout Minas, centered in Ouro Preto, that came to be known as the Inconfidência Mineira, the "No-Confidence Movement of Minas." Along with numerous co-conspirators, Tiradentes planned a revolt against Portuguese rule, but the conspiracy was betrayed in 1789 by one of its own members. Tiradentes assumed total responsibility for the conspiracy, whose other members were imprisoned or exiled to Portugal and the Portuguese colonies in Africa. Tiradentes himself was hanged three years later in Rio de Janeiro, his body quartered, the separate pieces of his corpse carried to various locales in Minas where he had spoken vehemently against the Crown. His salted head was placed in Ouro Preto's main square, where after a short time it was stolen by friends. According to legend, the patriot's cranium was filled with gold dust and surreptitiously buried somewhere near the old Vila Rica, though the location was never revealed.

The **Museu de Mineralogia** (Mineral Museum) containing some 20,000 pieces, uncut gems and minerals, both precious and common, from the region has been installed in what was the **Paláçio do Governador** (Governor's Palace) in Minas Gerais from 1746 to 1897. The building was constructed in 1740 by Manuel Francisco Lisboa. In addition to the mineral collection, there is a gracious chapel in the palace that is worth visiting. Open daily from noon to 6 p.m.

The exhibition rooms of the **Museu dos Inconfidentes** are filled with cultural artifacts of the colonial period, from arms to implements of torture used to punish the slaves, from plate and furnishings to the ubiquitous samples of religious art and liturgical paraphernalia. The two most important exhibits are the Aleijadinho Room, with the articulated statue of St. George, which was mounted on horseback and used during public processions honoring the saint, and the monument to the Inconfidentes, an austere mausoleum containing the remains of many of the revolutionaries.

More Sights: Ouro Preto is not only a place to see, but also a place to be in. To be able to take in at a comfortable pace all the individual sights, as well as imbibe something of the general ambience, a two- to three-day visit is recommended. The town contains many other churches, some 13 in all, plus a dozen chapels and a score of colonial fountains, not to mention the many secular buildings of visual and historic importance as well.

As is the case with Congonhas, Easter Week in Ouro Preto is a time of great celebration and pageantry.

WHERE TO STAY: A number of the colonial era dwellings have been converted into *pousadas*, inns of the bed-and-breakfast variety. One choice to make in Ouro Preto as to accomodations is whether to stay close to the center of the town, within walking distance of many restaurants and other attractions, or in the outlying districts where your options will also include a number of resort-style hotels.

A state-run hotel (and therefore somewhat shabby) called the **Grande Hotel de Ouro Preto,** Rua Senador Pocha Lagoa 164 (tel. 031/551-1488) has one of the best locations in the small city. Only a block from the central plaza, the Praça Tiradentes, and within easy reach of the largest number of shops and restaurants, the Grande Hotel, at only $26 per night double and $20 for a single, is a choice to be reckoned with. The Grande Hotel is the only modern structure in the city, designed by Oscar Niemeyer—and not one of his successes by any means. Surrounded by inspirational architecture like that of Ouro Preto, the man seems to have missed the point. The hotel contains 17 rooms with baths, and the same number of duplex-style suites (a dubious bargain at $32 per night, considering that the first floor of these apartments is virtually unfurnished). The general décor of the place is uninspired, about as far from the elegant country furnishings and appointments of the city's intimate inns as utilitarian Salvation Army is from chic Bloomingdales. The hotel, I was told, will soon pass into private hands and undergo major renovation. (One learns to interpret such pronouncements in Brazil in the category of good intentions, rather than as statements of fact. This reaction is not one of bad faith, but rather based on an understanding of the country's precarious economy, where such plans requiring huge investments of money must await the absolutely perfect conditions, or all concerned risk losing their shirts.) The point is, that you might appear in Ouro Preto to find the Grande Hotel the same threadbare bargain it has always been, or gussied up and twice the price under new management. In either case, the location is superb.

On the other end of the comfort spectrum, and across the street from the spectacular Matriz de Nossa Sanhora de Conceição, is the **Luxor Pousada,** Praça Antônio Dias 10 (tel. 031/551-2244). This inn occupies an old town house, and has only 16 rooms, but they are first class all the way. The rooms are decorated in a colonial simplicity that is totally harmonious with Vila Rica tradition. All rooms have color TV, mini-bars, telephones, and separate baths. There is a small restaurant in the cellar where guests also eat their breakfasts, under a beamed ceiling and surrounded by a foundation wall of stone. Rates are $40 for a single, $55 for a double.

Unfortunately I didn't get to visit the **Pousada da Galeria Panorama Barroco,** Rua Conselheiro Quitiliano 722 (tel. 031/551-3366), because it had yet to open at the time I last visited the city. But I was so impressed with the letter that owners David and Lucia Peterkin sent me that I've decided to mention their small inn sight unseen. What impressed me was their commitment to the role of innkeepers, and the simple extras they offer with their rooms which demonstrate a genuine interest in the comfort of their guests. The inn has only six rooms in what the Peterkins describe as a renovated colonial house, where, they say, you will find "a comfortable bed, a substantial breakfast, a secure room, and a relaxed environment." The house is a ten-minute walk from the Praça Tiradentes, and at a level that provides a scenic view of the city from the veranda and rooms. There is also a telescope for stargazing and a library with books in English on local flora and fauna, gems, history, and anthropology. Use of their washing machine is extra, as are excursions they will organize for sightseeing or gem buying in their four-wheel-drive land cruiser. The owners did not include their prices, but they are undoubtedly comparable with rates charged at neighboring inns in the city.

The **Quinta dos Barões,** Rua Pandia Cologera 474 (tel. 031/551-1056), is small but delightful, on a quiet lane which rises above the center of Ouro Preto in a nearby suburb. This old baronial country house has seven extremely well-appointed rooms, furnished and decorated in period pieces. There is also a small restaurant in the old cellar. The inn is a short cab ride (or a long walk) from the center of Ouro Preto. For comfort and elegant surroundings, as well as peace and quiet, there are no better lodgings in the city. The rooms are priced at $38 to $40 for the standard, and $40 to $45 for the two deluxe accommodations.

The **Pouso do Chico Rey,** Rua Brigadeiro Musqueira 90 (tel. 031/551-1274), is another lovely little inn, this time on a side street very near the Praça Tiradentes. There are three rooms and three apartments, the difference being that only the latter have baths. The several attractive public rooms at various levels give the inn a genuine "house" feeling. Breakfast is included in the price of the rooms, which range from $14 to $20.

About a mile and a quarter outside of town in the São Cristóvão neighborhood, on the road back to B.H., is the **Recanto das Minas,** Rua Manganes 287 (tel. 031/551-3003). The hotel is reached by turning onto a dirt road at the sign, and traveling half a mile or so to the top of the hill. Of the 36 rooms, those with baths and TVs are $35 for two, and $25 for a single. Rooms without baths are $15. There is a restaurant and a small swimming pool.

The **Hotel da Estrada Real,** Rodovia dos Inconfidentes, km 87 (tel. 031/551-2112), about eight kilometers (five miles) outside the city in the hills off the highway, is the largest and fanciest hotel in Ouro Preto, in a beautifully landscaped resort-like setting on a scenic overlook. The hotel also has a fine restaurant, popular with guests and nonguests alike. Some of the 40 rooms are in separate bungalows. Rates for a standard room are $45 for one and $55 for two people, while deluxe rooms are priced at $50 to $60. The hotel also has a large pool and a tennis court.

WHERE TO EAT: One of the most popular restaurants of Ouro Preto is the **Casa do Ouvidor,** Rua Direita 42 (tel. 551-2141), located on the second floor. There is always a good crowd in here on a given day, a blend of locals and tourists. Most items on the à la carte menu range from $5 to $7. Brazilian drinks like caipirinhas are only about $1 each.

The **Casa de Pedra,** Rua Pandia Calogera 503 (tel. 551-2790), is a wine-and-cheese house, also serving fondue and other international dishes. This brand-new restaurant is directly across the street from the *pousada* Quinta dos Barões, where the small restaurant is also open to the public.

The **Taberna Luxor,** in the Luxor Pousada, has an excellent reputation.

Several other restaurants to consider are the **Restaurante de Estação,** Praça da Estação, in the old train station; **Taverna do Chafariz,** Rua São José 167 (tel.

551-2828); and the **Restaurante Vila Rica,** Praça Tiradentes 132 (tel. 551-2293) —all of which serve international dishes, as well as comida Mineira at prices in the $4 to $6 range. Normal hours for these restaurants are noon to midnight daily.

A SIDE TRIP TO MARIANA:

The neighboring town of Mariana is only about a 20-minute car ride from the Praça Tiradentes, leaving via the street that runs to the right of the Mineral Museum. Like Congonhas, Mariana is still a very active mining town, and while the town is the oldest in the state (1698), it, too, has lost much of its former colonial appearance. The town sits in a little valley, and the surrounding hills are today worked mostly for the iron deposits, as well as the veins of quartz and manganese.

The principal attraction is the cathedral, **A Sé de Mariana** (1709), Praça Cládio Manuel da Costa, containing an organ operated by hand bellows and work by Atraide (a native of the town) and the Lisboas, *père et fils.* Other works of these artists may be seen in the **Igreja de Nossa Senhora de Carmo** (1784) and the **Ireja de São Francisco** (1762), which are right next to each other on the Praça João Pinheiro.

On the same square is the **Casa de Câmara e Cadeia** (1784), the old council chambers and jailhouse, now the town hall, with some interesting portraits of Portuguese monarchs and Dom Pedro II.

On the road between Ouro Preto and Mariana you will pass the **Minas de Passagem,** the state's second-oldest gold mine. For an entrance fee of $2.50, you can tour the mine and its processing plant.

5. AROUND MINAS

There is so much more to this historic, economically powerful, and sophisticated state that cannot be adequately included in this edition of the guide. Several locales, given their significance, at least deserve honorable mention and brief descriptions.

SÃO JOÃO DEL REI:

Those who follow political developments in South America may remember reading about this town during Brazil's 1985 elections for the country's first civilian president in over 20 years. A native of São João, Tancredo Neves, won the election, but died before he could take office. In addition to being a town of historic importance, containing many relics of the colonial past, the town has become somewhat of a monument to Tancredo, in whom many Brazilians placed great hopes for democratic and economic reforms.

The tourist office in São João houses a small **museum** with the only known portrait of Aleijadinho. The **John Somers pewter factory** is also located here.

A MOONLIGHT WALK TO TIRADENTES:

While I was visiting Minas Gerais, the driver who accompanied me from the state tourist office, Turminas, mentioned that he was a native of São João. He told me of a very pleasant hike he has often taken in the company of friends after a night of drinking and fellowship in the local cafés, especially when the sky is clear and the moon bright and shining. They walk slowly along a path through the hills that connects São João to the nearby village of **Tiradentes,** about seven miles distant, timing it so that they arrive at dawn. A cure for whatever may ail you, says he. This may not be the most conventional way to visit Tiradentes, but with the orientation of a reliable local, it's certainly an option for anyone with the time and inclination. When I get to São João this excursion will be tops on my own list. Tiradentes, incidently, is said to be a very authentic 18th-century town, and today a center for crafts.

MORE MINAS: The diamond and gemstone towns are located to the north and east of B.H. **Diamantina,** 182 miles from the state capital, is the most important from a historical point of view. Here diamonds were discovered in the early 1700s, and as with the other great cities of the baroque period, much has been preserved from that time. **Teôfilo Otoni,** and **Governador Valadares** are the centers of the contemporary gem trade, and anyone serious about gems—whether commercially or academically—will naturally be drawn to these towns, which are on the way to Salvador, the Bahian capital.

Minas contains hundreds of prehistoric caverns, called *grutas* in Portuguese. The closest to Belo is **Lapinha,** 35 miles away, while the more famous caves at **Maquiné,** are about 75 miles distant. In both cases, visitors may descend into the several lighted chambers. The greatest of these caves, in the northern part of the state near Montalvania, contain primitive drawings and fossil finds said to rival in importance the great caves of Lascaux in France. But they have yet to be fully explored scientifically, and are not open to the public.

And Minas is still so much more than all this. It is the great Rio São Francisco, the river artery of interior travel and communication in Brazil for many generations before the construction of adequate roads, the hots springs at Caldas and other towns on the border of São Paulo, and much, much more.

CHAPTER VIII

BRASÍLIA AND GOIÁS

□ □ □

1. BRASÍLIA
2. GOIÁS

The land for Brazil's new capital, Brasília, was carved from Goiás, a central state in the heart of the country. Brasília, the Distrito Federal (Federal District), occupies a table land some 3,500 feet above sea level near the western border of Mainas Gerais. Both the state and the capital are worth visiting, the former for its wide-open spaces, scenic beauty, and medicinal hot springs; the latter as a phenomenon of contemporary civil engineering, a planned city of monumental scope that symbolizes Brazil's contradictory vision of its own future, a perplexing blend of daring and self-aggrandizement.

1. BRASÍLIA

When compared with the settlement of the United States, Brazil's experience could not have been less similar. Nor is there any reason to expect or demand a parallel development in two countries of such distinct cultural origins, not to mention climatic and geographical differences, merely because both are great in size and owe their respective existences to the same impulses of European mercantile expansion in the 16th century. Still, comparisons are inevitably made between these two New World colossi, and at least in academic circles, most often by Brazilian scholars themselves. Brazil, they point out, had no Manifest Destiny to spur exploration and settlement of its vast interior spaces, nor was there the equivalent of a Homestead Act to motivate settlers with the incentive of cheap land. For these and other reasons, settlement in Brazil was limited to the long but narrow strip of coastal lands, where even today 80% of the population make their homes within 50 miles of the sea. In place of a Manifest Destiny, the longstanding Brazilian vision—one that goes back two centuries or more—was to open up the interior by creating a new capital in the country's geographical center.

The *planalto* in Goiás, a plateau of rolling grasslands, had already been selected by a government commission in 1892 as the preferred site for the new capital. But the political will to make this vision a reality was missing until Brazilians in 1956 elected as their president a physician-turned-politician, the former mayor of Belo Horizonte and governor of Minas Gerais, Jucelino Kubitschek de Oliveira. During his campaign, Jucelino had promised Brazilians he would fulfill the long-delayed vision of the past: he pledged to build the capital during his

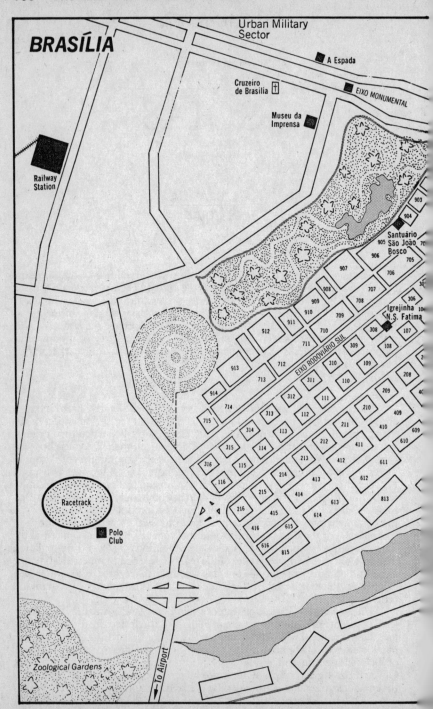

BRASÍLIA

Urban Military Sector

A Espada

Cruzeiro de Brasília

EIXO MONUMENTAL

Museu da Imprensa

Railway Station

903

904

905 Santuário São João Bosco

906

907

908

909

910

911

912

913

914

715

714

713

712

711

710

709

708

707

706

705

306

Igrejinha N.S. Fatima

308

309

310

311

312

313

314

315

316

116

115

114

113

112

111

110

109

108

107

208

209

210

211

212

213

214

215

216

415

414

413

412

411

410

409

609

610

611

612

613

614

615

616

813

815

Racetrack

Polo Club

To Airport

Zoological Gardens

EIXO RODOVIÁRIO SUL

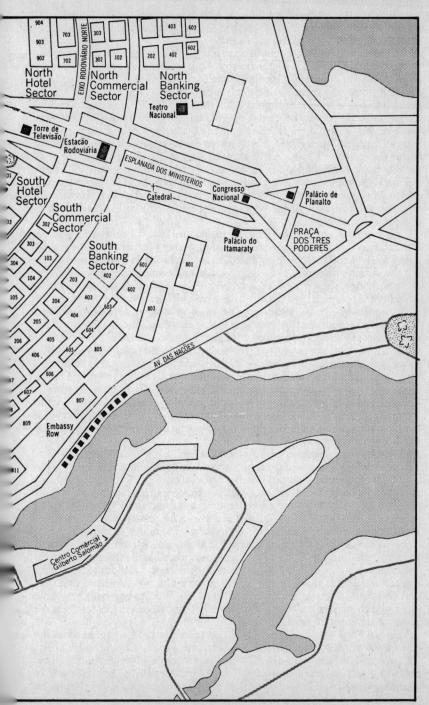

North Hotel Sector

EIXO RODOVIÁRIO NORTE

North Commercial Sector

North Banking Sector

Teatro Nacional

Torre de Televisão

Estação Rodoviária

ESPLANADA DOS MINISTERIOS

South Hotel Sector

South Commercial Sector

Catedral

Congresso Nacional

Palácio de Planalto

South Banking Sector

PRAÇA DOS TRES PODERES

Palácio do Itamaraty

AV. DAS NAÇÕES

Embassy Row

Centro Comércial Gilberto Salomão

term of office, despite the enormous costs and the seemingly insurmountable logistical obstacles, not the least of which was the lack of roads connecting the target site with the developed cities to its east.

Soon after Jucelino's election, construction of the new capital was begun, the first stage scheduled for completion by 1960, before the expiration of the new president's term of office. At the time, Brazil's presidents could only serve a single term, and the rush was entirely appropriate given certain historical precedents—it is not uncommon in Brazil for a project initiated by one administration to be abandoned by its successor. Even while a highway (BR 040) was being cut into the wilderness, heavy building materials were airlifted to the site by giant cargo planes, and buildings began to rise amid the isolation of the plains before the caravans of trucks could arrive to carry on the later stages of the project. Thousands of unskilled workers poured from the crowded slums of the big cities and the ruined backwaters of the northeastern badlands to grasp the employment opportunity of a lifetime. They soon re-created their shantytown existence on the periphery of the new city, as poverty in Brazil is the inevitable companion of progress.

Jucelino had adopted the layout of city planner Lúcio Costa, to construct an ultramodern metropolis of marble, glass, and steel in the form of a bow and arrow. (You will also hear the metaphor of an airplane used to describe the layout, but this is a later invention.) Along the bow would be block after block of apartment buildings facing interior pedestrian malls, with access roads connecting to neighboring *quadras* and to the principal avenues. There would be little need for traffic signals in Brasília, since most principal roads were to be expressways, linked by cloverleafs. And where these roads intersected, they would do so via underpaths and bridges. It was also, for some strange reason, to be a city virtually without sidewalks, despite the fact that distances between buildings—especially in the government and administrative areas—can be quite long. The arrow segment would divide the city into southern and northern sectors, and would be the line along which the government buildings and decorative monuments were to be constructed. For this task, Jucelino called upon his old collaborator from the Pampulha project in B.H., Oscar Niemeyer, to design the Congress, the presidential offices, the Palace of Justice, and a new cathedral, among other ambitious architectural projections.

Brasília was inaugurated on schedule. On April 21, 1960, the seat of the Brazilian government was officially moved from Rio de Janeiro and installed in the cold and futuristic buildings of Brasília, to the accompanying groans of those in the federal bureaucracy who were called upon to move there. Jucelino did his best to sugarcoat the transition, offering economic incentives in the form of doubled salaries and heavily subsidized rents. Resistance to the move remained strong for many years, particularly within the diplomatic community, as most embassies clung to Rio's golden strands until the dust of construction settled somewhat in the new capital, and residence in the city became bearable with the gradual establishment of services, restaurants, and cultural distractions. An additional inhibiting factor was that many of the buildings were built in such haste that they quickly began to deteriorate, as did roadways. Many had to be rebuilt before the city could claim to be truly ready to receive the tens of thousands of residents the government hoped to attract there.

When I first went to Brazil as a college student in 1964, opinions about the new capital were already polarized in the extreme. I fell in with the hostile camp. The photos I had seen of Brasília did not inspire my curiosity to visit the place, and so I didn't. It was not until 1987 that I finally traveled to Brasília, the only destination in Brazil I looked upon as an onerous obligation while in the process of researching this guide. In many ways I'm glad I waited so long, because in the ensuing quarter century Brasília has become a genuine city, not the sterile construction site I was urged to visit in the '60s, when I had no abstract interest in the modern architecture or the city plan. But I have also changed my mind somewhat about the look of the place. True, it still strikes me as a vision of an intergallactic settlement, but the buildings are more sympathetic and humane when seen three-dimensionally than when viewed in the flat medium of still photography or even moving pictures. I am now convinced that holographic photography is the only medium suitable for portraying the deeper human elements in Niemeyer's and Costa's visions that are embedded in the cold exteriors of their designs. In other words, I now realize that to appreciate the esthetic of Brasília—as opposed to the daring and folly of its mere conception—you have to go there, and that the trip is worthwhile on two accounts: first, to grasp the monumental vision and something of the yearning in the Brazilian soul for the fulfillment of a destiny forestalled; and second, because Brasília has a population of over 400,000 and is now a true city in its own right, with genuine urban nuances despite a layout that favors vehicular over pedestrian traffic. Furthermore, when you are in Brasília you get an unexpected bonus. For you are also in Goiás, one of the most inviting of all the Brazilian states, the attractions of which are discussed in the second section of this chapter.

GETTING TO BRASÍLIA: You can now **drive** from Rio de Janeiro on BR 040 to Brasília, and then on to Belém along the Belém–Brasília highway, which has only been paved in recent years. There is also a direct highway, BR 050, from São Paulo. **Buses** run daily from both Rio (20 hours) and São Paulo (15 hours) as well. The **Ponte Aérea** air shuttle links both São Paulo and Rio with Brasília on frequent daily flights of 2½ hours from either city. A passenger **train,** the Trem Bandeirante, connects the capital to São Paulo.

THE SIGHTS: It is not unusual for tourists to see all of Brasília in a single day. Many don't even bother to spend the night there, arriving at the airport on a flight that leaves Rio as early as 6:30 a.m. and returning that same evening after having seen all the obligatory sights. Tour companies all offer basically the same excursion, which may be booked directly at the airport without advance reservations. Or cars, with or without drivers, may be hired from the airport for the day. Anyone wishing to spend more time in the capital can easily—and cheaply—get around by public bus. Many buses, like those marked "Aeroporto," "Três Poderes/Universidade de Brasília," and "Avenida das Nações," make wide loops of the city and its environs, and in many ways are preferable in atmosphere to the sometimes-smarmy group tour.

The city is laid out very logically, once you catch on to the numbering system. There are no addresses per se. All locations are designated by block numbers in both the northern or southern sectors. These major directional sectors are further divided into subsectors, where specific activities are concentrated. Thus there are special sectors for shopping, hotels, sports and cultural activities, businesses, embassies, and banking. A quick glance at a map is suffcient to become oriented. I recommend the *Carta Turística de Brasília* put out by the Tourist Office.

It is possible to walk around the city, which—I stress again—is deceptively large, but not terribly convenient. There are few sidewalks, though local residents have cut paths through the grounds of various buildings and malls. Strollers must be very careful of the traffic, however, as motorists are not accustomed to seeing many pedestrians.

Eixo Monumental

Walking is somewhat easier along the Eixo Monumental (Monument Row), a five-mile-long strip running from the new combined bus/train station at one end of the central "arrow" to the **Praça dos Tres Poderes** (Plaza of the Three Powers) at the other. The strip is about 1,000 feet wide, separated by two roadways, along which all the principal ministry buildings and monuments are located.

Many of the buildings may be visited during business hours (Brasília is a formal town, so women visitors to official buildings must wear dresses, and men, sport jackets). The most interesting of these buildings are the **Palácio Planalto** (the presidential offices), the **Congresso Nacional** (the House and Senate Chambers), **Itamarati** (Foreign Ministry), and the **Catedral,** all designed by Niemeyer and all near the Praça dos Tres Poderes. Also of interest are the many modern sculptures in and near the praça, including *The Meteorite* by Bruno Giorgi above the Itamarati water mirror—it reflects the building's vaulted façade, and is a much-photographed symbol for the city. Itamarati, unlike the other offices, receives visitors only twice a day, at 10 a.m. and again at 4 p.m.

Brasília is also famous for its dried flowers, whose many varieties grow abundantly in the semi-arid scrublands beyond the metropolitan oasis. The flowers may be seen and purchased in an open-air market that functions weekdays on the plaza opposite the cathedral.

Observation Platform

Near the center of the esplanade is the old **Rodoviária,** the original bus station, across from the **National Theater,** which still serves as a terminus for city buses and where the tourist office maintains an information center and the Bureau of Indian Affairs (FUNAI) has a gift shop of Indian artifacts.

Directly to the south is the **Torre de Televisão,** a 600-foot television transmission tower with an observation platform at an altitude of 250 feet, from which there is an excellent panoramic view of the entire city. Access to the platform by elevator is free. A crafts fair is held at the base of the tower on Saturday, Sunday, and holidays. This event could be convenient for overnight guests, since the tower is within walking distance of the hotel sectors.

Memorial JK

At the far end of the Eixo Monumental, nearest to the new bus/train station, is the Memorial JK. Jucelino Kubitschek was also commonly referred to as *Jota Ka,* the Portuguese letters for the initials in his name. And this is his memorial, the latest addition to Monument Row, also designed by Oscar Niemeyer. Like so much of the architect's work, the memorial is deceptively simple on the outside and stunning within, suggesting the stylized burial chamber of an ancient Pharaoh. The monument was paid for by the *candangos,* the name given to the construction workers who built Brasília and who revered the former president. Jucelino died in an auto wreck somewhat mysteriously, believe many Brazilians, who are often given to mystical and conspiratorial speculations in the face of the bizarre coincidences that seem to bedevil the country's political and economic development.

Within the chamber is a photo gallery documenting Jucelino's career and the building of the capital, as well as a reproduction of his presidential library. Unfortunately, all the exhibits are labeled only in Portuguese. Withal, the former president is portrayed in larger-than-life terms, mythologized with imperial exaggerations as the great *Fundador,* the founder of Brasília. Every Rome must have its Romulus.

As if to deflate somewhat this overreaching for immortality, a sardonic rumor circulates the city. It is said that the progressive Niemeyer added a crescent cap to the platform tower where a statue of JK guards the entrance to the tomb, and that at a certain time of the year the sun casts its shadow through this crescent and forms a perfect hammer and sickle. Indeed such is the way it appears to the disinterested observer, though I include the tale here more as a sample of Brazilian wit at its best, than as a literal fact.

The Sword

Near the Memorial JK is the Setór Militar Urbano (Urban Military Sector), where outside the headquarters building on the Praça Duque de Caxias is a monument called **A Espada** (The Sword). The monument warrants attention both for its design and its acoustics. If you look closely at the monument's interior curve, you will notice that it is subtly, but inmistakably, shaped in the outline of an owl's head. To test the unique acoustic effect, you need a companion. If each of you take up positions at opposite ends of the monument's wide mouth, you may talk across the considerable distance in a conversational tone and understand perfectly what each other is saying.

O Santuário São João Bosco

Like so many modern structures which rely on the building materials of metal and glass, this box-shaped church conveys an initial impression of tawdriness and slipshod design. One is so used to admiring great churches in the set forms of medieval tastes—their enormity, their stonework combining the opposites of bulk and grace. Here again, as with so much of Brazil's modern architecture, the effect is reserved for the building's interior. The church is sheathed in small panes of stained glass, all in shades of blue. From inside the church, by day the walls seem like perfect reproductions of a starlit sky.

SIGHTS IN THE SUBURBS: Scrublands, called the cerrado, surround
Brasília, which is built by the banks of an artificial lake. Only when you get outside the city do you fully grasp the scale of the capital as an engineering feat, independent of personal views about "planned cities," and futuristic ones at that!

Even if your time in the city is limited, a drive along the perimeter of the 50-mile-long **Lake Paranoá** should not be missed. If you recross the bridge along the road that heads toward the airport and then turn in the opposite direction, you will soon be traveling with the lake on your left. In about 20 minutes you come to a shrine and overlook known as the **Ermida Dom Bosco.** The view of the city here from the opposite shore is quite spectacular, because it allows you to really capture the contrast between the self-contained island community and the sea of uninhabited plains that encircle it.

And while the shrine to Dom Bosco is not much in and of itself, the saint's story is worth retelling. A hundred years before the creation of Brasília the monk had a dream which revealed to him the map coordinates where "a great lake will be excavated that will flow forever." This, the faithful believe, was a prediction of the exact site where Brasília would be built.

Satellite cities

Brasília is also surrounded—at some distance—by the so-called satellite cities, suburban towns that were settled first by the construction workers for whom there were no accommodations in the new capital. By law, Brasília's population is not to exceed 500,000 inhabitants, and most of the housing there was planned for residents of middle and upper income levels. Thus 15 km (9 miles) from the city is the satellite city **Núcleo dos Bandeirantes.** From everything I had heard about the wild shantytown cities of the laborers, I had expected a giant slum, but I found a quiet and orderly suburban town.

Going beyond Núcleo dos Banderaintes for another half hour or so, you will come to **Catetinho,** the original campsite where a rustic house was built for Jucelino and other high-ranking visitors who came to Brasília on periodic inspection tours while work was still in progress. The grounds around the camp have been made into a park and picnic site, and the simple house, with its assortment of mementos, is also open to the public.

Some 75 miles from Brasília, and easily accessible by bus, is the town of **Cristalina,** which, as its name implies, is a center for gemstones in the state of Goiás. Most of the shops dealing in gems, jewelry, and precious metals are located on the Praça José Adamian and Rua da Saudade.

WHERE TO STAY IN BRASÍLIA: Practically every hotel in Brasília is located in either the southern or the northern hotel sectors (Setór Hoteleiro Sul/Norte). The two sectors face each other across the city's central esplanade, which runs from east to west and along which all the city's monuments and futuristic government buildings are located. All the hotels are within walking distance of each other, and their addresses—block and lot number—are superfluous. Even the distinction of north or south seems irrelevant, given the proximity of one zone to the other in the case of the hotel sector.

The **Nacional,** South Hotel Sector (tel. 061/226-8181), the oldest of the upper-bracket hotels, has a spacious lobby and public spaces, with dining rooms, bars, and a swimming pool deck off the main floor. The otherwise undecorated corridors are in plain wood paneling with carpets that have seen better days, but at least testify to the hotel's heavy traffic and popularity. The service is often friendly, and always courteous and correct, a feature which no doubt accounts for much of the hotel's repeat business and popularity with touring groups. Several shops, including a small branch of the jeweler H. Stern, are off the lobby. The hotel is one of the city's largest, with 350 rooms, ranging in price according to their décor and height in the building—and therefore the view they afford of the city . Standard rooms begin at $65 for one person, increasing to $70 for double occupancy. The deluxe rooms, with the better views, have all been recently redecorated with new furnishings, bath fixtures, and carpets. All rooms have the TV, mini-bars, and air conditioning features standard in hotels of this category.

The **Carlton,** South Hotel Sector (tel. 061/224-8819), is smaller but newer than the Nacional, and the building itself is more interesting architectually than most of the other hotels in Brasília, which tend to be slab-style high-rises. The lobby area occupies a one-story breezeway which joins the principal tower, where the rooms are located, with a smaller building which houses indoor parking and a host of public facilities, including an attractive rooftop pool. There are four bars in the Carlton, and the La Fontaine restaurant, which features international cuisine. Rooms are decorated in blond wood trim and beige tones, and are air-conditioned, with full bath, mini-bar, and color TV with satellite reception of the CNN American television network. Rates begin between $70 and $80. Other attractions include golf and tennis privileges at local clubs, sauna, hairdresser and barber services, boutiques, and a travel agency on the premises.

The newest of Brasília's five-star hotels, also in the South Hotel Sector, is the **São Marco** (tel. 061/226-2211). The rooms have small balconies, and next to each bathroom is a separate dressing area with a second sink. All told, there are 232 rooms and suites in the São Marco, some of which have small kitchenettes and rent on an apart-hotel basis. Normal daily rates, including breakfast, begin at

$65 for one, $75 for two, and other doubles go up to $85, depending on location. The rooftop restaurant and cocktail area are appealing, and the pool deck offers an excellent view of the city.

The **Eron** is another upper-category hotel, located across the way in the Hotel Sector North (tel. 061/226-2125). Slightly more care has gone into the décor (and perhaps maintenance) of the Eron's corridors and public areas than to those of its rivals in the same price range. The rooms, 187 in all, are only moderate in size, the furnishings clean-lined and modern. Rates, with breakfast, start at $62 to $72 for rooms of the standard type, while those with better views run about $10 more. All rooms have the usual amenities, including TV, mini-bar, and central air conditioning. The hotel's most unique feature, however, is the glass-sided elevator, compatible with the glass-and-steel appearance of the building, which runs up the front façade. On the 29th floor a rooftop restaurant encased in floor-to-ceiling windows offers a panoramic view and serves international cuisine. The public facilities include a pool, tennis court, a bar and Italian restaurant off the lobby, a discothèque, and a variety of shops for gifts and necessities.

The **Saint Paul,** South Hotel Sector (tel. 061/226-1515), offers very large rooms, furnished and decorated in the Scandinavian mode, with balconies. All rooms have TVs that offer in-house movies. The hotel is large, with 375 accommodations, and has a restaurant, bar, and nightclub on the premises, as well as a health club with sauna and a beauty shop. Single rooms are $62 and doubles run $69.

A slightly less expensive selection among the four-star hotels is the **Phenícia,** in the South Hotel Sector (tel. 061/224-3125). There are 130 airy and comfortable rooms, and the hotel offers a full range of services, including a restaurant. Single rates start at $55; doubles cost an additional $5.

The **Hotel das Américas,** in the South Hotel Sector (tel. 061/223-4490), is part of the Nações hotel chain, which has several hotels in the city, including the Alvorada, which is not air-conditioned. The atmosphere here is informal, and the many services include a good restaurant serving a luncheon buffet. Rooms are quite adequate and fully equipped, ranging in price from $45 to $50 for one or two persons.

The **Bristol,** South Hotel Sector (tel. 061/225-6170), has a single price range for all rooms, $40 to $45, but the best accommodations are in the corners of the building, which are slightly larger and have balconies. For $65 you can get a suite, which has a separate sitting room, two baths, and two verandas. The pool area is small, but seems like an agreeable place to sit and have a drink or take the sun.

Since everything in Brasília is organized into sectors, it will come as no surprise that there is also a special section of private homes whose owners rent out rooms—pensions. It is located in the South Sector on Quadras 703 through 705, quite close, incidentally to the hotel sector. The prices for these accommodations are definitely lower than for rooms in the hotel sector, and can even be negotiated. Since this service is informal, there are no phone numbers to call. You must simply show up in the area and make the necessary inquiries.

DINING IN BRASÍLIA:
Eating out is about the favorite pastime for residents of Brasília, and so an abundance of restaurants, specializing in many varieties of food, are available to choose from. Pick up the **"Guia Gastronômico de Brasília"** ("Gastronomic Guide to Brasília"), a pamphlet available from the tourist balcony at the airport or bus stations on your arrival in the city. Several score restaurants are listed according to type, with their addresses and phone numbers.

Around the City

While restaurants are located throughout the city, they also tend to be concentrated in specific *quadras*. First, here are a few places that are not in designated restaurant or entertainment areas, like the **Florentino,** at 402 South (tel. 223-7577), open daily from 11:30 a.m. until the last customer leaves late at night. The Florentino is one of the better restaurants in town, where you will eat French-style food, elegantly served, in the company of diplomats and politicians. The à la carte prices per course range from $7 to $15.

For Brazilian food, especially for those who still want a taste of Minas Gerais country cooking, there is the **Esquina Mineira,** at 704 North (tel. 274-9695), which is near one of the principal avenues, Via W3N (there's nothing like the warm, personal touch of a street with a name like an abbreviated ZIP Code!). Dishes are served in a rustic atmosphere on checkered cloth-covered tables, and are inexpensive: between $4 and $5. Open Tuesday through Saturday from 11:30 a.m. to midnight, and on Sunday from 11 a.m. till 5 p.m.

The **Restaurante da Torre** (tel. 223-8686) is a landmark in the city, and a favorite of both tourists and residents alike. The restaurant sits midway up the city's giant TV tower, and is open Tuesday through Sunday from noon to midnight. On Friday and Saturday, when it stays open later, there is live music and often a kind of modified samba show. Meals of an international variety cost $4 to $6 a plate, and the menu has an extensive listing of appetizers, referred to as *petiscos.* These can be anything from codfish balls to cold cuts and cheese cubes. The TV tower is close to the hotel sector, and hosts a Hippie or Craft Fair on its grounds every Saturday and Sunday during daylight hours.

An interesting alternative is the self-service **Comida Caseira** (which means home-cooking) at 104 North (tel. 225-7798). Hot and cold trays offer over 40 dishes daily, including many salads, and you pay by the weight of your meal—an average of 50¢ per 100 grams (3½ ounces). Open daily for lunch from 11:30 a.m. till 3 p.m., and for dinner from 7 p.m. till midnight.

The Centro Comércial Gilberto Salomão

Located across the lake on the South Peninsula not far from the airport is the main culinary and entertainment center of Brasília. On the weekends its spacious outdoor and open-air restaurants are filled to overflowing. And in addition to a number of fine restaurants, there are a variety of nightclubs and movie houses as well. To get there, just tell your driver you want to go the Gilberto Salomão. It's a ten-minute cab ride, and 30 minutes on the airport bus.

Among the better, non-weekend-oriented restaurants there is the **GAF** (tel. 248-1103), where you go for the food, not the action. Similar in style and quality to the Florentino, the GAF also serves nouvelle French cooking, at $6 to $15 a plate. The low range covers pasta or fish, and the more costly dishes are the better cuts of meat and shellfish. Open daily, except Sunday, from noon to 4 p.m. for lunch and from 8 p.m. until there are no customers remaining.

The **bierfass** (tel. 248-1519) is just what its name implies—a large and informal beer garden. The menu is extensive, but there are in fact only a few German dishes. The prices range from $6 to $10. The bierfass is an after-work as well as a weekend hangout, which opens daily at 6 p.m. and closes only when the action dies down. On Saturday and Sunday, the bierfass opens at noon.

Quadras 404/405 South

These blocks are lined with restaurants, one right after another, serving every imaginable variety of food from pizza to fried rice. Among those recommended by local residents are the German restaurant **Fritz** (tel. 223-4622), the

Chinese restaurant **Fon Min** (tel. 244-0193), **La Fornarina** (tel. 244-6333) for Italian food, the **Pizzarela** (tel. 225-1700), the **Recanto Goiano** (tel. 226-4580) for a Goianian variation on Brazilian country cooking, and two bars, **Fino's** and **Tasca**.

The Pamonha

This is the Brazilian version of the corn tamale, and not to be missed by lovers of cornmeal and native fast foods. Though usually filled with cheese or meat, there is also a sweet variety. Pamonha stands abound throughout the city. To find one, just ask a cabbie or doorman where to get the best pamonha in the city and I'm sure he will have several suggestions.

SHOPPING: There are several commercial sectors throughout the city. One principal complex not far from the Hotel Sector is the **Conjunto Nacional,** across from the National Theater. In addition to the many stores—including branches of Amsterdam Sauer and H. Stern—there are a number of Woolworth-style lunch counters, where for about $1.50 you can get the hot plate of the day. There are also movie theaters located in this shopping center.

The **Galeria dos Estados** is a 200-yard-long mall that links the central commercial district with the banking sector, and contains craft shops representing each of Brazil's 23 states. Stirred perhaps by a spirit of interregional competition, the crafts here are of generally high quality.

2. GOIÁS

The inhabitants of Goiás have a button that promotes their state. It says: *"Estado Solução"*—in a country where many states are considered *estados problemas,* the Goianos are saying, "Here in Goiás, we have found the solution." Of course, it helps that in all of this immense territory that cuts through the center of Brazil and occupies its core, there are only 5,000,000 inhabitants. No doubt the existence of wide-open spaces with plenty of elbow room for all explains the pride and euphoria of its citizens, and also adds to the allure of the state from the visitor's point of view. The climate, too, is near perfection. Rarely is it too hot or too cold.

Seen from the air, Goiás is a green land of low, bushy vegetation, rolling plains alternating with chains of small mountains. The state is cattle country, and the open land is a great range, reminiscent of the American West of the past century. In the towns, especially the small country towns, you are as likely to see the inhabitants on horseback as in Jeeps or pickup trucks. Along Goiás's western border with the neighboring states of Mato Grosso and Pará is one of Brazil's great rivers, the Araguaia, whose waters are filled with many fish, whose sandy banks furnish recreational beaches for hundreds of miles, and whose forested margins provide a haven for wildlife.

GOIÂNIA: The capital of Goiás is Goiânia, a city of over 700,000 residents, located some 125 miles from Brasília. Like Belo Horizonte, Goiânia was a planned city, inaugurated in 1933, and it, too, replaced its state's former colonial capital, Goiás Velho.

Goiânia is a city of many hospitable people, where a certain provincial isolation is compensated by lovely parks and widely available recreational and sporting facilities. The city also contains a number of very adequate hotels—better in most respects than those in Brasília with comparable ratings. Both lodgings and restaurants are also less expensive here than in the Federal District.

Nevertheless, Goiânia is not one of the state's primary attractions. Travelers wanting to visit the interior of Goiás should look on the state's capital city as a

transfer point. Those with VARIG air passes, for example, might stop over at Goiânia en route to destinations farther south—the Pantanal wildlife preserve or the
falls at Iguaçu—and use the city as a jumping-off point to visit the hot springs
region, the old colonial capital, or the river environment.

From Goiânia you can reach Goiás Velho and Aruanã, a principal town on
the Aragauia River, by car and bus, or even small plane if desired. Caldas Novas,
the health spa to the south where Brazilians flock from all over the country to take
the waters, can also be reached by road, or by regularly scheduled flights from
Goiânia's airport.

Staying Over in Goiânia

Goiânia's newest and best hotel is the **Castro Park,** Avenida República de
Líbano 1520 (tel. 062/223-7766), located in the city's western sector near the
Praça Tamandare. With the Castro Park, five-star luxury has come to Goiânia. In
addition to the 160 thoroughly modern rooms, the hotel offers a health club and
pool, delicatessen, tea room, nightclub, several bars, a coffeeshop, and a restaurant. The hotel's **Restaurante Ipé** offers excellent eating for reasonable prices.
Standard rooms are priced at $56 single and $62 double. Deluxe rooms are only
a few dollars more.

The **Hotel Bandeirantes,** Avenida Anhanguera 3278 (tel. 062/224-0066),
is located downtown in the oldest part of the city, where the blocks are more
tightly packed and a pleasant commercial atmosphere reigns. Rooms start at $27
for single and $34 for two. Also in the Centro is the **Hotel Umuarama,** Rua 4 no.
492 (tel. 062/224-1555), where prices are $26 for one, and $32 for double occupancy. Both are first-class hotels with four-star ratings, and offer many services.

For restaurants, you might try the following: **Cliff Piano Bar e Restaurante,**
Rua 23 no. 72 (tel. 241-7888), in the western sector: the **Pampaula Restau-
rante,** Rua 84 no. 497 (tel. 241-5607), in the southern sector; and the
Restaurante D'Ávila, Rua 2 no. 555 (tel. 225-8298), also in the western quarter.

GOIÁS VELHO: Founded in 1727, the pioneer settlement of Goiás (the
"Velho" is a recent addition, as in "Old Sacramento") quickly evolved into an
important regional center in west-central Brazil, and until 1937 remained the
capital of the territory, and later the state, which bears the same name. Like Ouro
Preto, whose history it parallels in many details, Goiás was a mining town during
days of the great Brazilian gold rush of the 18th century. Also like Ouro Preto,
the city of Goiás lacked the geographical setting—it was laid out in a small valley
and penned in by many hills and mountains—that would have allowed its transformation into a modern state capital. The planned city of Goiânia, 132 km (82
miles) away, was built to fulfill this role, and Goiás then ceased to be a center of
trade and political decision-making in the state, a factor that also contributed to
the preservation of its colonial appearance.

Unlike Ouro Preto, however, Goiás is a colonial-era town which has yet to
fully develop and exploit its architectural and cultural patrimony. While Ouro
Preto is hardly commercialized to the point of being unpleasant, the old section
of the city of Goiás is equally pristine and, for the time being, totally
noncommercialized. There are no fancy *pousadas* or boutiques. Tack shops and
general stores, *boutiquins* and small cafés exist in place of their gentrified
equivalents. The general flavor of Goiás is of a municipal center for the many
working farms and ranches in the wide-open spaces that surround the town. Riders on horseback and donkey carts are not part of some sideshow catering to
tourists—they are integral means of transportation still in use by local cowpokes
and tradesmen.

Most of the colonial structures are located in one large neighborhood in the city, which otherwise has the look of a typical town of the Brazilian interior—full of two-story stucco buildings in fading pastels, and narrow, wobbly streets, whatever their paving surface or lack thereof. Most of the colonial buildings, however, are whitewashed and of the dreamy baroque design that is the great human-made visual legacy of the 1700s throughout Brazil. There are, for example, seven baroque-era churches in Goiás. And while there is no hoopla associated with the historical legacy, the considerable number of old structures are lovingly preserved, many of them still in use as residences and others transformed into museums open to the public.

Goiás Velho is 90 miles (145 km) from Goiânia along Hwy. 070. Buses run frequently along this route, and then on from the old capital to the river towns along the Aragauia. There is also a dirt landing strip in Goiás, not far from the center of town. Over the years the poorer folk of town have built their simple wood-frame houses along both sides of the runway. And the strip has become front yard, playground, and soccer field for the local residents. To land there, the pilot must call ahead to the police chief and request that the local constabulary *limpar a pista*—clear the strip of toddlers, chickens, and stray mutts—so the plane can make its approach and land safely. It was most amusing to observe the police cars patrolling the margins of the runway as I was about to land there on a visit in a small plane that had been provided by the state government. The people lined the strip or stood watching from their doorways as we circled the field and came in for a landing. The arrival was something of an occasion at this infrequently used airport facility.

The Main Sights

One could just "be" in Goiás for several days, walking through the streets, absorbing the un-selfconscious historical atmosphere, riding on horseback or hiking in the backlands, and generally going native.

Those on a more restricted time schedule (as I was, unfortunately) will want to be sure to see the **Igreja de Nossa Senhora da Boa Morte,** built in 1779 and today a museum of sacred art. In addition to a fascinating collection of antique processional paraphernalia, all in handcrafted silver, the church is the principal repository of the work of José Joaquím da Veiga Valle (1806–1874), a sculptor who carved statues in wood. His favorite subjects were Our Lady and St. Sebastian—to whom there is much devotion in rural Goiás—and there are several examples of these figures, along with many others to be seen in the museum. The interior of the building is unusually appealing in its rustic simplicity. The altars are also of carved wood, utilitarian rather than elaborate, and the main chapel (where most of Veiga Valle's work is on display) is filled with soft, sacred music, piped in on tape. A little gift shop at the entrance to the museum sells record albums of both religious and native Indian music, and very plain but attractive earthenware.

The **Museu das Bandeiras,** off the Largo do Chafariz, is the secular counterpoint to the museum of sacred art. This plain, rectangular building was constructed in 1761 to house both the local legislature and the jail. On the ground floor, where the jail was located, the walls are nearly five feet thick, and entry to the cells was only through a trapdoor located in the 15-foot ceilings. The second floor, with a number of display cases containing artifacts of the early colonial period, was the venue of the local government. What recommends this building above all else is its remarkable state of preservation, allowing a clear view of both the method of construction and the nature of the building materials used at the time.

The **Paláçio Conde dos Arcos** (1755) housed the residence and the offices of the governors from the colonial through republican eras. The two-story building is a warren of rooms, atriums, and courtyards. Furniture of state, plate, and numerous wall hangings and photographs are on display throughout.

Food and Lodgings

There are few hotels in Goiás, but with the exception of Easter time, when the city fills up with visitors who come to attend the elaborate *Semana Santa* (Holy Week) festivities, the number of beds is sufficient to handle the normal tourist flow. Pensions and private homes take care of the overflow. The banks of the Bagagem and Bacalhau rivers are favorite sites for camping.

The **Villa Boa** (tel. 062/371-1000) is a state-run hotel, but one that is in excellent condition. The hotel has only 32 rooms, and sits on a hill. From the stately, building-length terrace you may look out at both the nearby city and the surrounding countryside of green-covered mountains. Each of the rooms has a small balcony, and at $15 single and $18 double including breakfast, they are a real bargain. The hotel also has a pool and a restaurant.

Three other hotels, with a total of 43 rooms among them, are the **Hotel Alegrama,** on Rua Morete Forgia (tel. 062/371-1947), which charges $5 for a room with bath and $3 without. The **Hotel Rio Vermelho,** Rua 2 no. 01 (tel. 062/371-1866), in the Jardim Vila Boa neighborhood, has rooms for as little as $1.50 without bath, and suites for $6 double. The **Hotel Serrano,** Avenida Dr. Deusdete Ferreira de Moura (tel. 062/371-1981), has single, double, and triple rates that are $3, $6 and $8.

There is a very good restaurant in the Hotel Vila Boa. Other recommended eating spots are the **Toka Churrascaria,** Rua Americano do Brasil 17 (tel. 371-1408), where you can savor the local beefsteaks for about $4 an order. The **Restaurante Dona Maninha,** Rua Dom Cândido 31 (tel. 317-1699), features inexpensive local cuisine, like empadão, galinhada, and arroz com pequi, the last a rice dish combined with *pequi,* a small and tasty yellow fruit. The **Restaurante Sobradinho,** Rua Prof. Alcides Jube 05 (tel. 371-1361), also serves the regional food of Goiáa.

CALDAS NOVAS: Traveling 110 (177 km) miles southeast of Goiânia, you

go to Caldas Novas for one reason: to take the waters. The natural hot springs attract tens of thousands of visitors annually to this town of 30,000 inhabitants which has more than 50 hotels. The trip from Goiânia takes about 2½ hours by car and slightly longer by bus. Some flights are also available, and may be booked not only through Goiânia, but also in major cities like São Paulo, Rio de Janeiro, and Brasília, where the Goiás company, Valetur, has officers or representatives.

Spa Hotels

Many claims are made as to the therapeutic properties of the hot mineral water, some amusing, including a restoration of sexual vitality. Whatever their ancillary benefits, the waters—naturally heated at temperatures between 37° C (99° F) and 51° C (124° F) are undeniably relaxing. One merely has to observe for a few minutes the blissful expressions on the faces of hundreds of satisfied customers to take the plunge at spas like the sprawling **Caldas Termas Clube,** Avenida Orcalano Santos 100 (tel. 062/453-1480), by far the largest of the city's watering places. The 100 or so rooms are simple and impeccably clean, as is befitting a resort dedicated to matters of health. Doubles cost $47, which includes breakfast and use of all the pools and facilities. The club also has two separate pools open to the public for a fee of $3.50 per day.

The **Tamburi,** Rua Eça de Queiroz 10 (tel. 062/453-1455), would seem to be the perfect choice for the couple or family arriving in Caldas Novas by private car. The hotel is small, with only 20 rooms, but there are some interesting features. Each room in the attractive two-story motel-type building has a carport beneath it, with a private staircase of beautifully polished wood leading up to quarters, which are quite large and decorated in the style of a Brazilian *fazenda* (farmhouse). The room's bathtub is fed by same thermal waters that fill the outdoor pools. Immense shuttered windows open onto the gardens and hot pools below. Nightly rates are $48 to $53, with breakfast.

On a slightly higher scale of poshness, and an apparent favorite of American diplomatic families resident in not-too-distant Brasília (230 miles), is the **Hotel Parque das Primaveiras,** Rua do Balneário 11 (tel. 062/453-1268). Of the 19 rooms, the simplest of which are priced at $85 for two, 8 are elegant suites which cost $120 per night, double occupancy. Each suite has a veranda with two hammocks, and inside is a small dip pool measuring 2½ yards square, where a guest can take the waters—piped in directly from the hot spring—in the privacy of his or her own room. There is a queen-size bed with quilt, and the other furnishings and décor bespeak the country elegance of craft and care. This small resort is totally self-contained and beautifully landscaped along the banks of the Riberao de Caldas, the source of the heated mineral water. On the grounds are two hot pools, and for variety, a cold pool as well, along with a sauna in a stone building heated only by the hot springs, and a rustic outdoor restaurant.

Camping

Eight kilometers (five miles) from Caldas Novas is a campsite in a rural setting, **Camping Lagoa Quente.** This site is the source of the hot springs, and the waters here are regularly at their hottest, around 50° C (120° F). Those who wish to camp must purchase their provisions in town, but there is a restaurant with simple but hardy fare. Campsites cost approximately $2 a night per person.

Eating in Caldas Novas

There are restaurants catering to all pocketbooks in Caldas Novas, including those at the major hotels. For pizza and Italian dishes in the $6 price range, there is the **Restaurante e Pizzaria Bella Nápoli,** Rua Machado de Assis Q.1 L.3 (tel. 453-1620). *Q* refers to the *quadra* or building number; *L* is the *loja,* or store number.

A good barbecue restaurant is the **Churrascaria Choupana,** Avenida Orcalino Santos, 40 (tel. 453-1775). The churrasco is served *rodízio* style and costs $6.

A restaurant with a typical Brazilian menu in the $4 range is the **Massa Dourada,** on Rua Major Vilas.

For a *rodízio*-style natural-foods restaurant serving salads, pancakes, and omelets for only $2 a round, try the **Restaurante A Caminho do Natural,** on Rua José Borges (tel. 453-1785).

The Pousada do Rio Quente

Also out of town, about seven miles away, is a very fine and extremely popular resort which, from the point of view of North Americans, is one of the best-kept secrets in South America. Use of the word *pousada* (inn) in the name of this resort, as if it were a quaint bed-and-breakfast, is a total misnomer. In fact what you will find is a vast complex, including a luxurious five-star hotel, a more modest but extremely appealing four-star facility, campgrounds, and bungalows, accommodating 2,500 guests a night (with an average daily occupancy all year of 2,000), and set in one of the most gorgeous natural and landscaped settings you will ever see.

The pousada has its own modern airstrip that will accommodate small jets carryings up to 50 passengers. Also on the sprawling grounds are half a dozen pool environments—including fountains and saunas—where you may soak or swim in the hot springs to your heart's content. A circular bar sits in the middle of one of the larger pools and serves drinks and appetizers. The sensation of floating up to your shoulders in the soothing, hot mineral waters while sipping a caipirinha, or a shot of cachaça with a beer chaser, is indescribably pleasurable. Just one, though, or you may find yourself sinking into oblivion. Other facilities at the pousada—which is also a ranch and farm, and raises its own meat and vegetables—are streams for boating and fishing, trails for hiking, a hang-glider takeoff platform, tennis courts, and live entertainment practically every night.

Reservations may be booked at offices in Rio (Rua Visconde de Pirajá 550; tel. 511-1443); São Paulo (Avenida Brig. Faria Lima 1575; tel. 211-8344), Brasília (Gal. Hotel Nacional, Lojas 30/31; tel. 224-7166), Belo Horizonte (Avenida Brasíl 1533; tel. 224-5199), and Goiânia (Avenida Tocantins 310; tel. 224-9400). The direct telephone number to the Pousada do Rio Quente is 062-421-2011. Prices for accommodations or campsites, including full board, are available on request.

RIO ARAGUAIA: A six-hour bus ride from Goiânia, costing only around $4, will take you through Goiás Velha to **Aruanã,** 185 miles away and the base town for a visit to the great Araguaia River. The 1,200-km- (740-mile-)long river separates Goiás from it's more westerly neighboring state of Mato Grosso, and to the north, the state of Pará. Fishing, camping, swimming, and observation of wildlife along the length of the river are the main attractions. From May to October the water level is at its lowest, exposing wide banks of pure white sand. Tents are set up all along the riverbank, with plenty of space and privacy for all comers, and the fishing is said to be about the best in the entire country. In Aruanã, you will find all the support for rental of boats—with or without guides—and all necessary camping equipment and fishing gear. Eight kilometers (five miles) from the village is the **Acampmento Sol,** where tents and full board can be had for a mere $10 per day.

North of Aruanã is the largest river island in the world, the 8,000-square-mile **Ilha do Bananal.** The island is divided between the tribal lands belonging to the Carajas and the Javaes Indians, and an 100,000-acre rain forest that has been designated a national park. Anyone wishing to visit the Indian lands must get the permission of the FUNAI offices (the Brazilian Bureau of Indian Affairs) in Brasília before being allowed to enter the reservation.

A SPECIAL EVENT IN PIRENÓPOLIS: Every year during the week preceding Pentecost Sunday, there is a very colorful celebration in the town of Pirenópolis, about 65 miles (105 km) from Goiânia. The pageant includes the famous **cavalhada,** a mock battle on horseback between Crusaders and Moors, with both groups dressed in lavish costumes. The event is a cross between a medieval jousting tournament and a latter-day rodeo.

CHAPTER IX

SÃO PAULO

□ □ □

São Paulo is Brazil's largest and economically most important city. Yet São Paulo always suffers the misfortune of being compared unfavorably with Rio de Janeiro, its older, more attractive urban sibling. Whole mythologies have grown up to help natives and residents of both cities, locked in fierce familial rivalry, define and protect their respective identities. A cascade of clichés pour from the mouths of Cariocas and Paulistanos alike, in their persistent, urgent attempts at self-definition and self-justification. The suspect generalizations that are the by-product of this squabbling are then taken in whole cloth and inserted in the pages of travel brochures and, unfortunately, find their way into travel articles and guidebooks as well. We are assured, according to these set scripts, that Rio is sensual, laidback, and perhaps slightly irresponsible. "When do those Cariocas work? They always seem to be on the beach," one frequently hears. São Paulo residents, on the other hand, are said to be driven and dynamic, if a bit dull. "Those Paulistanos don't know how to enjoy life. They're workaholics," so the other side claims. There are a dozen other facile characterizations, all of them self-serving or deprecating of the rival, but rarely on target. For someone standing in a neutral corner in either city, the people do not seem so different. They both seem to work and play hard; perhaps that's a general Brazilian quality. The conditions under which the inhabitants of the two cities, live, work, and play, however, are quite different. And in fact it isn't difficult to identify the major features that distinguish Brazil's two leading cities.

São Paulo's inferiority complex is based on its location—far from the nearest beach. The city, which is after all the largest in all of South America and therefore has something to feel superior about, has not been of particular interest to most international visitors, who come to Brazil on holiday adventures rather than commercial ventures.

Rio, the seashore city, is the destination of choice for the vast majority of Brazil's foreign tourists, while São Paulo, because of its industrial importance, gets hordes of international corporate visitors. This stand-off from the São Paulo point of view is unfair and unacceptable. The metropolis does not want to be known exclusively as a business destination, and so is starting to fight back with positive images of its attractions rather than with futile attempts to detract from Rio's undeniable beauty and favored status. São Paulo is beginning to bill itself as what it is: with around 9,000,000 inhabitants, the third-largest—and possibly the fastest-growing—city in the world. People who love big cities are therefore likely to find much to their taste when they visit this one.

1. ORIENTATION

São Paulo is the home of Brazil's urban scene in its highest development, and Rio in this sense is indeed somewhat provincial. Power and wealth are concentrated in São Paulo. Half of Brazil's industrial output comes from this single state—and most of this economic might encircles the city of São Paulo itself, as close and intimate as the rings around Saturn. In Osasco and the so-called ABC towns—Santo André, São Bernardo, and São Caetano—the giant multinational corporations have planted scores of factories from which a powerful labor movement has emerged in recent years as the heartbeat and conscience of Brazil's fledgling and precarious experiment with democracy.

Along with Minas Gerais and Rio Grande do Sul—though ever in the forefront—since the mid-19th century São Paulo has dominated Brazilian politics, first with its coffee wealth, and now with both coffee and industry. It is an oft-stated truism that São Paulo by itself would be as powerful as many contemporary European nations. But the one time São Paulo actually did try to exert its sovereignty over that of the nation—during the Revolution of 1932—it was soundly defeated. It may be a source of Brazilian pride to imagine an entity as powerful as the state of São Paulo standing alone today, able to compete with the best of the industrial giants. But the real challenge in Brazil is, and has always been, trying to overcome the patterns of uneven development that have plagued the nation during the entire 500 years of its existence. The inability of Brazilians to imagine São Paulo not as a separate nation, but as an inspiration and model for the rest of the country's internal development is reflected in the repetitious political instability that has characterized Brazilian governments since the end of the empire in 1889.

But São Paulo has also been a bit of a hot house. The state actually managed for a long time to determine who could settle within its boundaries and who couldn't. A great effort during the early part of this century was made to attract "white" Europeans—an instant labor force already accustomed to, and trained for, an industrial reality—and to stem the flow of Brazilians from the impoverished states in northeastern Brazil. Jorge Amado, whose writing taken as a whole is a kind of biography of Brazilian life and times of the 20th century—particularly life in the Northeast—portrays a touching migration scene in the as yet untranslated novel *Seara Vermelha*. In the scene, which takes place in the '30s, the São Paulo state government has set up a public-health station in the town of Pirapora, in the neighboring state of Minas Gerais. A train line then linked São Paulo to this southernmost river landing of the Rio São Francisco, the great inland commercial and passenger waterway serving to link the towns of the Brazilian interior since the earliest colonial times. Here in Piropora, in Amado's novel the doctors give free railway passage to the able-bodied and turn away the infirm from entering their state, which had already become a kind of promised land in the minds of the displaced peasants from the old semifeudal estates to the north.

Today, with a functioning, if not always state-of-the-art, network of roads and buses, such a policy of limited internal migration, never defensible, is also no longer possible in Brazil. In recent decades the *nordestinos* have literally invaded São Paulo (not to mention Bahia and the vast western and Amazon territories), extending in leaps the city's ever-widening periphery. They are indeed the force from which labor is recruited for the city's powerful industrial plants. Those for whom no jobs are available bide their time in the shantytowns, the ubiquitous poverty satellites typical of all of Brazil's modern cities, and survive by the skin of their teeth.

The city of São Paulo does not project poverty as its predominant image, however. Rather, one's eye runs along a skyline of gray concrete high-rise buildings, which seem to be replicated to infinity along the horizon. Dispersed among the high-rises throughout the city are a great variety of private homes, shopping centers, public parks, vest-pocket squares, and old neighborhoods of a smaller and more attractive scale, which invite closer inspection by true aficionados of inner-city life. Fortunately, São Paulo, which already sits at an altitude of over 2,500 feet above sea level, is also in many places a hilly city, a terrain feature which breaks up a certain feeling of architectural monotony.

São Paulo is not what you would call a pretty city. The urban rat race everywhere has long been motorized, and São Paulo is no exception. There can be monster traffic jams, and a lot of slow-motion driving, with (depending on the winds) the poor air quality that results from such concentrations of fuel exhaust. But neither is São Paulo a city where you go just to see skyscrapers, a few museums, the famous Butantã snake farm, or some other promotional attraction. It is a place to go and hang out, café-hop, shop, or walk the streets by day, eat out and boogie by night. There is an a quasi-bohemian Italian neighborhood with coffeehouses and pizza joints, scores of intimate *nordestino* hangouts—tiny hole-in-the-wall bars and outdoor cafés where you can go any time of day for great Brazilian draft beer and a quick snack—Japanese fairs and restaurants galore, and the same potential as elsewhere in Brazil to meet and spend time with such a group of convivial Brazilians as your time, luck, and initiative allow.

Until a recent trip, I had not been to São Paulo in more than 20 years. My recollections of that earlier visit being somewhat dim, I looked forward to rediscovering the city. I frankly concede I merely scratched the surface. In future revisions of this book this chapter on São Paulo is likely to expand in relation to the growing interest of international travelers to visit there. In that sense, those of us who visit São Paulo once, or several times, in the coming years will be discovering this enormous city together.

GETTING THERE: All roads in Brazil, by air or land—and such passenger trains as continue to run—lead to São Paulo. From Rio, the air shuttle (Ponte Aérea) takes you from inner city to inner city, from Santos Dumont Airport in downtown Rio to Congonhas in the midst of São Paulo. Flights leave every half hour from 6 a.m. until 10:30 p.m. and cost around $40 each way. You don't need a reservation unless you desire a specific flight. Ticketing arrangements for air travel in Brazil are relatively uncomplicated. The top hotels generally have, if not a ticketing representative among their lobby concessions, certainly a travel and tour agency. This agency will perform this service for you, sometimes only for a token fee.

Airport Transportation

The **airport bus** runs at 25-minute intervals during peak hours, and every 45 minutes or so in the dead of night, between São Paulo's two airports—Congonhas (domestic flights) and Garulhos (International flights)—and a downtown terminal at the Praça da República. A separate line operates directly between the two airports, with a brief layover at the Rodoviária, the city's principal bus terminal. The fare is $1.25 to $1.50.

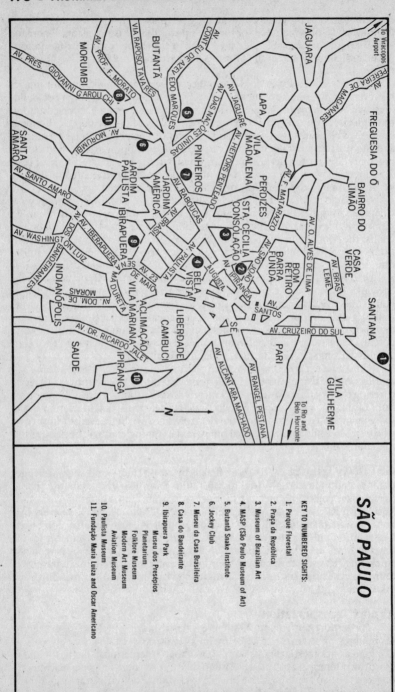

SÃO PAULO

KEY TO NUMBERED SIGHTS:

1. Parque Florestal
2. Praça da República
3. Museum of Brazilian Art
4. MASP (São Paulo Museum of Art)
5. Butantã Snake Institute
6. Jockey Club
7. Museu da Casa Brasileira
8. Casa do Bandeirante
9. Ibirapuera Park
   Museu dos Presépios
   Planetarium
   Folklore Museum
   Modern Art Museum
   Aviation Museum
10. Paulista Museum
11. Fundação Maria Luiza and Oscar Americano

Passenger Trains

The *Santa Cruz* is a passenger train connecting São Paulo and Rio in a journey of some 275 km (170 miles), which takes around nine hours. The train departs from Rio at 11:30 p.m., and the one-way fare is about $35. The sleeper fare is $110 for a single cabin and $185 for a double. Train service is also available to a point deep within the southwestern state of Mato Grosso do Sul, home of the Pantanal, the vast and—according to some concerned ecologists—the rapidly vanishing marshland retreat of the bulk of Brazil's remaining wildlife. The journey to Corumbá on the border with Paraguay, near the great river of the same name, takes about two days, accounting for a switch in trains in Baurú, in the interior of the state of São Paulo—and the usual delays.

The *Trem Bandeirante* leaves Brasília at 10:50 p.m. on Friday night and arrives in São Paulo at 7:20 p.m. the following evening. One-way fare is $70, and a full cabin costs approximately $200.

Car and Bus Travel

The quick car route to São Paulo from Rio is along the **Via Dutra** (BR 116), a toll road (token charge). The trip can be made safely in about six hours. The scenic route along the Rio–Santos highway (BR 101) follows the shoreline and is recommended for more relaxed touring. More description on this route can be found in Chapter VI. Express buses run frequently between Rio and São Paulo, and there is bus service to the economic capital from the most remote points throughout the country.

GETTING AROUND: All major entry points—airport, bus, and train stations—have **tourist information counters,** many open seven days a week, and they always have a full complement of specialists on hand to meet the arrival of all international flights. Ask these folk, who will certainly speak English and who are highly professional, helpful, and well informed, for their recommendations about maps, hotels, bus routes, and whatever other logistical information you need. If you want to get to your hotel by public bus, for example, these are the people to ask for a clear and detailed route.

As for maps, *São Paulo Is All,* a free and otherwise useful government map and guide you are likely to be given at a tourist information point, is not adequate for the following reason. Outside the old center city the map only shows the main arteries and thoroughfares, and not the hundreds of side streets you will need to search out in order to really get around. Furthermore, much of what you will want to see or do is outside the old center, even though you are likely to be staying in or near downtown, eating there at some point, and certainly visiting this section for one reason or another during your stay. Ask the tourist information people for a copy of the *Mapa Gastronômico de São Paulo (Guide to São Paulo's Restaurants).* The many restaurants listed and described on this map are also pinpointed by number on a detailed street layout which covers most—though not all—of São Paulo's neighborhoods. I would appreciate learning from any reader the name of an even-better and more detailed map of the city, with index, and information on where it may be purchased.

The **São Paulo Convention and Visitors Bureau,** Rua Colômbia 582 (tel. 280-2979), is an in-town option for tourist information, open Monday through Friday from 9 a.m. to 6 p.m. Operating two offices downtown for information in addition to the reception counters they staff at the airports and bus/train stations is the **State Secretary of Sports and Tourism.** The office at Avenida São Luís 115 (tel. 257-7248), is open weekdays from 8 a.m. to 6 p.m., while the sixth-floor office at Praça Antonio Prado 9 (tel. 229-3011), keeps hours on weekdays between 9 a.m. and 5 p.m.

Inner-City Transportation

São Paulo's **subway** system is in its infancy. There are two short lines currently in operation. The north-south line runs between the neighborhoods of Jabaquara and Vila Guilerme. An east-west line runs from one stop beyond the downtown Praça da República to Penha. Two other lines are currently being planned and constructed. The trains are new, the stations cavernous and clean, and the few trains crowded at all times of the day. But it's a good, cheap way to get around to a limited number of destinations.

Street crime is a problem for any big city, and São Paulo is no exception. City **bus** travel is only advised for those visitors who have some knowledge of Portuguese. **Taxis** are abundant, and your best bet is a radio cab. The fare is slightly more than the common cab, but you are less likely to be hustled.

One hears in São Paulo constant reference to a disturbing statistic: that every third inhabitant owns a car. Since São Paulo is both the Detroit and the Los Angeles of Brazil, this allegation is entirely plausible. City residents are close to the source of automobile manufacture, on the industrial edge of their city, and their geographically enormous metropolis is interconnected by many streets, avenues, freeways, and beltways. The automobile is clearly the favored mode of transportation, providing a strong argument in favor of taxi travel for all but the most intrepid and adaptable urban denizens, who might risk renting a car.

2. SIGHTS, ACTIVITIES, AND NIGHTLIFE

Discreet neighborhoods are the best places to begin for a tour of São Paulo. Here are a few starters. Those of you who explore different turf and discover something of interest, are encouraged to write and share your experiences.

The **Bexiga** is a neighborhood of Italian restaurants—dozens of them—and also a bohemian quarter of coffeeshops and other nightspots, from video theaters to punk rock clubs. The Bexiga is the unofficial name of an area centered on **Avenida 13 de Maio** (between Avenida Brig. Luís Antônio and Rua Santo Antônio) which overlaps the neighborhoods of Bella Vista and Morro dos Ingleses. The Bexiga Flea Market (see "Fairs and Markets," below) takes place there every Sunday between 7 a.m. and 1 p.m.

Liberdade is the neighborhood where Paulistanos of Asian descent and their culture, primarily Japanese, dominate the street scene. The neighborhood is clearly marked on all maps, and the principal thoroughfare is Rua Galvão Bueno. Here are numerous shops for bizarre and unusual Brazilian souvenirs, like stuffed and mounted piranhas with a gaping mouth full of sharp, carnivorous teeth. Many of the neighborhood's principal hotels, sushi bars, sweet shops, and restaurants are also on this serendipitous commercial street. An Oriental Crafts Fair takes place on the Praça da Liberdade, where there is a subway stop, every Sunday from noon to 10 p.m. (see "Fairs and Markets").

Rua Maracatines is a typical commercial block surrounded by a middle-class inner-city neighborhood, where factory outlets and large emporiums offer clothes, shoes, and leather goods at bargain prices. There is no earthly reason to single out the **Flor do Norte Lanchonete,** at the corner of Rua Miruna and Rua Maracatines, other than it is so typical of the blue-collar lunch stands you'll find on nearly every block of the city. If you did find yourself in this neighborhood looking for a good price on a pair of shoes, however, you could do worse for refreshment than stopping at this street-corner café with its counter and handful of outside tables, for a glass of freshly squeezed orange juice and a *salgado* of your choice—like a meat or shrimp pie, or a breaded chicken leg. Or if you want a stronger stimulant, do as some of the Brazilians do, have a *mé* (cachaça), the cane brandy that is Brazil's national drink, at about 15¢ a shot.

Avenida Ibirapuera, between República do Líbano (which runs along one side of Ibiraupera Park) and Avenida dos Bandeirantes, is strictly for after dark. A string of bars and clubs, like Moema Samba, at no. 2124 (tel. 549-3744), line the avenue. Most feature (generally) live samba music. The scene is dancing—these are not the honkytonk shows with scantily clad mulatto beauties.

Ibirapuera Park itself is a richly endowed and self-contained environment, offering a number of diversions. First of all, it's an immense green zone in a city of concrete. The shimmering leaves from a forest of eucalyptus trees shade acres of well-tended lawns and lakes. Scattered throughout the park are a number of important exhibition halls and popular attractions. São Paulo's biannual art show, the **Bienel**—an art event of international reknown—takes place in the **Pereira Pavilion** here in the park during odd years. The **Japanese Pavilion** is an exact replica of Japan's Katura Palace. The **Museu dos Presépios** (tel. 544-1329) displays its collection of crèches and Nativity scenes, and a **Planetarium** (tel. 544-4606) offers weekend shows (reputed to be quite good) at 4, 6, and 8 p.m., and on Tuesday and Thursday evenings there are also shows at 8 p.m. The price per entrance is around $1. The **Folklore Museum** (tel. 544-4212), the **Aviation Museum** (tel. 570-3915), and the **Modern Art Museum** (tel. 571-9818) are also on the grounds of the park.

MORE NIGHTLIFE: In addition to the scenes in the Bexiga and the Avenida Ibirapuera strip of samba clubs, there is a cluster of clubs and discothèques in the vicinity of the **Jardim América** neighborhood, some of which are exclusively singles spots on designated nights of the week. The **St. Paul,** Alameda Lorena 1717 (tel. 282-7697), which is closed Sundays, caters to three separate crowds during the week: over-30s on Monday and Thursday, younger singles on Tuesday and Wednesday, and couples on Friday and Saturday. The scene starts late, the bar is always crowded, and a supper menu is available. Other choices in the area are the **Up Down,** Rua Pamplona 1418 (tel. 285-1081); the **Area,** Rua dos Pinheiros 1275 (tel. 212-8698), with live music; and the **Roof,** Avenida Cidade Jardim 400, (tel. 212-3006), a rooftop *boate* (nightclub) on the 22nd floor.

OTHER SIGHTS: One of the favorite sights in all São Paulo, for kids and adults alike, is the **Butantã Snake Institute,** Avenida Vital Brasil 1500, in Butantã (tel. 211-8211), which charges a token admission and is open daily from 8 a.m. to 5 p.m. To be frank, the big attraction seems to be watching the snakes catch their live prey at feeding time. Small white mice—the really cute kind—circle the snake pits along the walls, stepping over so many motionless snakes as still as garden hoses, until one springs, encircles its prey, and so forth. Institute technicians also milk the snakes of their venom. This ritual, which takes place six times a day—at 10, 10:30, and 11 a.m., and at 3, 3:30, and 4 p.m.—is equally popular, and furthermore is a reminder of the institute's vital and serious mission. Antidotes to poisonous snakebites are produced here and are shipped on demand to hospitals around the world. In addition to the snake pit and the lovely tropical grounds, the institute has halls with exhibits, including live and stuffed venomous reptiles, spiders, and tarantulas.

CULTURAL SÃO PAULO: The great art collections of Brazil are in São Paulo. Art lovers and mavens can take a quick course in Brazilian art at the **MASP** (the São Paulo Museum of Art), Avenida Paulista (tel. 251-5644), wherein hang the works of the important Brazilian artists and sculptors, along with a rich selection of work by such masters as Raphael, Velásquez, Reubens, Rembrandt, Hals, Renoir, and Toulouse-Lautrec.

Examples of the work of two important 20th-century Brazilian painters, Portinari and Di Cavalcanti, can also be seen more intimately at the **Fundação Maria Luiza and Oscar Americano,** Avenida Morumbi 3700, in the neighborhood of Murumbi (tel. 240-0077). This former house of the industrialist/ philanthropist Oscar Americano and his socialite wife is today a tidbit-sized museum and park, with several beautiful collections, including first-rate paintings, plate, furnishings, and fascinating memorabilia of the Brazilian royal family. There is a token entrance fee, and the museum is open Tuesday through Sunday from 10 a.m. till 5 p.m. A small and genteel tea room serves *cha completo*—black tea with a variety of cakes, for $5.

Other Museums

The **Museu da Casa Brasileira** (Museum of the Brazilian Home), Avenida Brig. Faria Lima 774 (tel. 210-3727), is another former mansion, whose collection of furnishings and photographs gives a retrospective view of Brazilian domestic elegance over the centuries. The **Casa do Bandeirante** (Pioneer House), on Praça Monteiro Lobato (tel. 211-0920), is a short distance from the Butantã Snake Institute. The museum is a re-creation of the rustic and sparsely furnished frontier homestead (with house, outbuildings, and farm equipment) of an 18th-century pioneer family, or *bandeirantes*. The *bandeirantes* were companies of adventurers, each of which followed a single standard, or *bandeira*, who, in their quest for mineral wealth and slaves, explored all of Brazil, and in the earliest times settled the interiors of São Paulo and Minas Gerais.

FAIRS AND MARKETS: The Praça da República hosts a **Craft Fair** every Sunday from around 8 a.m. till late in the afternoon. The major traffic is in gemstones, jewelry, paintings, and leather goods. But there are also dozens of single-item vendors, novelty hawkers, and hurdy-gurdy men with trained birds instead of monkeys. This square is really an elegant little tropical garden, green and shady, full of winding sidewalks which suddenly become bridges and cross small bodies of water. A lot of buying and selling goes on, so there's a real market atmosphere—a very good place to buy souvenirs for yourself and your friends.

Another nearby option for shopping is the **Rua do Arouche,** which runs diagonally off the small square Praça da República toward Avenida Ipiranga, and is lined with shops selling shoes and leather goods, reportedly at good prices. The chic clothing shops are on **Rua Augusta** which crosses **Avenida Paulista,** which —if such a scattered urban sprawl as São Paulo can be said to have one—is the city's principal avenue.

The **Oriental Craft Fair** on the Praça da Liberdade, the heart of the city's Asian neighborhood, is held every Sunday from noon till 10 p.m. The booths offer a mix of items, from tooled leather belts and bags to practical kitchenware made from wood or bamboo. There are also artists and musicians, and a man who sells very imaginative papier-mâché puppets. The food stands are plentiful and sell an appealing variety of Asian street snacks.

Also in the daytime on Sunday is the **Bexiga Flea Market,** in the Bexiga square. You go to this not so much to buy—though there are many attractive and useful artifacts being recycled—but to experience the urban flea market environment in São Paulo.

A **flower and produce market** is held in Pacaembu Stadium, Praça Charles Miller, every Tuesday, Thursday, Friday, and Saturday. The sights and sounds of a Brazilian open-air food market are an education and a visual treat. Don't be shy about asking someone the name of an unfamiliar fruit or vegetable. You may even be invited to have a taste.

3. WHERE TO STAY IN SÃO PAULO

Perhaps because São Paulo caters to so many high-ranking corporate visitors, its hotels are among the best and the most expensive in Brazil. For the business traveler—or anyone else willing to pay the price—São Paulo's deluxe hotels offer the finest in rooms, services, facilities, and food. Many moderately priced hotels also offer fine accommodations and service.

DELUXE CHOICES: The place to stay for those who have the means and desire to purchase additional privacy and services, has to be in *top class* at the **São Paulo Hilton,** Avenida Ipiranga 165 (tel. 011/256-0033). The top three floors of the circular 33-story hotel are reserved for top-class clients, who use special elevator keys to arrive at their private floors, take breakfast and cocktails in a private lounge stocked with liquor, fresh coffee, food, and international newspapers and magazines—all yours for the asking—and are attended by a staff of charming hostesses from 7 a.m. till 10 p.m. every day. The top-class rooms, however, as attractive as they are, are not so different from the other accommodations in the 407-room Hilton. This is good news for anyone booked into the Hilton by a group or package tour, since they will also get the Hilton comfort and service, but at a reduced group rate. Standard rooms are priced between $155 and $170, while the superior rooms on the higher floors are $180 to $205 per night. Top-class rates are $210 to $235. Like all Brazilian five-star hotels, the Hilton is a self-contained environment, with several fine restaurants and bars, a steamroom and pool and an attached arcade of shops and boutiques for convenient shopping.

There are certain drawbacks to any hotel. For the Hilton it may be the location, the slightly shabby area of the old downtown, which is nonetheless still the one appealing visual hub of the city from an architectural point of view. At night the demimonde plays out its drama of low-grade sin and sleaze disturbingly—or, depending on your perspective—intriguingly near the enclave where the circular Hilton Tower stands as a recognizable landmark along the horizon of the cityscape. This scene of the backstreets has no immediate bearing on the comings and goings at the Hilton, most of which are by car or taxi. One is repeatedly warned, almost to the point of inducing a state of reckless curiosity, to foresake the paths of the Praça da República at night and not to wander among the crowds of prostitutes, toughs, and transvestites who decorate the street corners a block or two behind the Hilton.

A block or so from the Hilton at Avenida Ipiranga 344 is the Edifício Itália, São Paulo's tallest building. The view from the observation deck on the 41st floor is free and about the best in the city. You can get the same scenic view from the rooftop bar, or from one of two restaurants as well (tel. 257-6566).

For a hotel with a resort-like atmosphere half-an-hour from the center of town there is the **Transamérica,** located at Avenida Nações Unidas 18,591 (tel. 011/523-4511). The environs are modified industrial, but the point again here is what happens inside, not outside, the hotel. The Transamérica is a horizontal complex which opened in 1985 and is set on sprawling grounds with many outdoor sports facilities, including a putting green, jogging track, large outdoor pool with outdoor café, and a regulation soccer field. The hotel also offers several fine tennis courts, and as host to many national tennis tournaments, is considered the Forest Hills of Brazil. The Transamérica is truly an oasis for sports-minded executives who want to lodge close to the industrial scene. The hotel also provides many other comforts, including an elegant restaurant off the lobby, which is bordered by fresh flowers, changed daily. Accommodations, in beige and green color schemes, still have that just-out-of-the-package look, with queen-size beds, designer furnishings, and ceramic-tile baths. There are 211 rooms, all air-conditioned with TVs and mini-bars. The tariffs range from $130 to $150 for singles, and $150 to $170 for doubles.

One of the city's most elegant hotels is set on a hill behind the small Trianon Park, a botanical relic of the brush and tree species that once covered the land where all the city's human structures now stand. The sleek and well-toned **Hotel Mofarreg Sheraton,** Alameida (which means Lane) Santos 1437 (tel. 011/284-5544), looks like the ideal background for a fashion-magazine cover photo. The hotel's most striking feature is the lobby and atrium which sits beneath a many-paned skylight dome. The finely decorated rooms are spacious, trimmed in polished hardwood, with tasteful artwork and artifacts adorning the gallery-like walls. Deluxe rooms have two double beds and sitting areas with couch and armchairs. There are 284 rooms, with single rates between $155 and $195; doubles run $172 to $216.

The **Maksoud Plaza,** Alameida Campinas 150 (tel. 011/251-2233), is a rectangle of glass and steel built around a vast atrium that runs the full length of the 23-story building. The huge space is dominated by a great hanging sculpture of stainless steel and surrounded by balconies which are hung with living greenery. The four elevators travel up one side of the interior through transparent columns which view the atrium from three sides. Like the Sheraton, the Maksoud is in a neighborhood which conveys an atmosphere of chicness, calm, and security. There are seven restaurants at the Maksoud Plaza, representing the cuisine of several nationalities, including Scandinavian, French, Brazilian, and Japanese. The lobby bar specializes in drinks made from cachaça. The 416 rooms are entered from walkways that overlook the atrium. Accommodations are large and swank, with blond wood furnishings and beige broadlooms, and baths are equipped with separate temperature control for the showers. Rates are $150 to $190 for singles, and $155 to $200 for doubles.

The narrow, energetic Rua Augusta is promoted in most of the tourist literature as an attraction in itself. It is a long, commercial street crammed with shops, boutiques, and restaurants, and several of São Paulo's top hotels. The **Ca'd'Oro,** at no. 129 (tel. 011/256-8011), is a hotel cast in the tradition of European elegance of some bygone era. The building is set back from the street and guests enter the lobby under a canopy lined with the flags of many nations. The many alcoves off the lobby are filled with rococo statuary and prints of Renaissance figures. Also on the first floor is a cocktail area with highbacked upholstered chairs set before a large working fireplace. The adjacent room houses the hotel's popular and very formal Italian restaurant. There are two pools at the Ca'd'Oro, one set in a patio separating the main building from an annex, the other on the roof under a glass dome, with adjoining bar. There are 302 rooms split between the old and new wings, the former furnished in heavy old-world style, the latter with modern pieces. Rooms are priced between $117 and $134 for singles, and $150 to $170 for doubles.

São Paulo also has its **Caesar Park Hotel** at Rua Augusta, 1508 (tel. 011/285-6622), the choice for those who prefer quiet elegance over the splashiness of the newer deluxe properties. The lobby is small and dark, the many pigeon-holed shelves behind the reception desk more suggestive of a *fin-de-siècle* apothecary than a hotel. A certain snobbishness pervades the atmosphere, encouraged vicariously by the aloof posture of the reception personnel. Behind the lobby on the main floor are several boutiques, a French restaurant, and a sushi bar. On the roof is an open-air pool encircled by a wooden sunning deck, a bar, and a restaurant for more informal meals. The 180 rooms are furnished with queen-size beds, and plush oversize sofas. Room prices are $150 to $180 single and $170 to $200 double.

MEDIUM- TO UPPER-RANGE HOTELS: The **Augusta Hotel,** Rua Augusta 129 (tel. 011/283-5674), offers with its rooms every comfort—without the frills, of course—found in the expensive hotels: color TV, stocked mini-bar refrigerator, extra-large bathtub. But the hotel has no restaurant, or even a lobby to speak of. This is a hotel to sleep in, not lounge about as in the deluxe hotels that are loaded with bars, shops, sports facilities, and dozens of comfort-support services. The Augusta Hotel has only 41 rooms, the best of which are a very reasonable $29 to $39 for single and double occupancy respectively.

In the Liberdade neighborhood are a number of hotels that cater primarily to groups of Asian tourists and business travelers, but are a viable option for anyone who wants to soak up a little Asian atmosphere Brazil style. The **Nikkey Palace,** at Rua Galvão Bueno 425 (tel. 011/270-8511), is by far the best of the lot, a most charming and relatively small hotel with 100 rooms, delicately decorated in the austere good taste for which the Japanese are known. The hotel's Japanese restaurant has three separate environments: a salon with tables, a sushi bar, and half a dozen private rooms behind walls and sliding doors of rice paper. A thermal pool/sauna room is also typically Japanese in design. Rooms are simply but comfortably furnished, and offer all the amenities. A single costs $72 per night, and a double goes for $92.

The **Banri,** Rua Galvão Bueno 209 (tel. 011/270-8877), is modest, impeccably clean, and comfortable. Some of the 69 rooms have *furo* baths—Japanese-style bathtubs, higher than they are long, in which a bather kneels in chest-deep water. Less expensive rooms range in price from $24 to $32, and rooms with *furo* baths are slightly higher, at $27 to $35.

Around the corner on the Largo da Pólvora at no. 120 is the **Fiji Palace** (tel. 011/278-7466), midway in size and price between the other two selections in Liberdade. Standard rooms begin at $33 for one, and $37 for two; while deluxe rooms, larger and better furnished, range from $50 to $56.

Back in the downtown area is an elegant old street, not too far from the Praça da República, called Avenida Vieira de Carvalho. On this street are a number of still very fine hotels and restaurants to fit all budgets. At no. 99, at the top of the list, is the old **Hotel Bourbon** (tel. 011/223-2244). It's not easy to book a room in this 122-room hotel during the week, because the hotel is a traditional favorite of business travelers and has a clientele which keeps returning. One of the hotel's attractions is its moderately priced restaurants, serving quality meals costing an average of $10, not including drinks and service. Rooms are priced from $78 for a single to $92 for double occupancy.

The **Vila Rica,** Avenida Vieira de Carvalho 167 (tel. 011/220-7111), is a moderately priced option. The small scale of this 61-room hotel is one of its appealing attributes. Rooms cost between $46 and $54.

An even smaller, and genuinely inexpensive but totally acceptable, hotel is the **Amazonas,** Avenida Vieira de Carvalho 32 (tel. 011/220-4111), with only 32 rooms in all. You can get a single for as little as $15, and two can stay as cheaply as $21. Air-conditioned rooms, which are standard with all the other São Paulo hotels mentioned in this guide, are slightly higher, at $20 to $25 per night.

4. SÃO PAULO'S RESTAURANTS

The number-one pastime for residents of large cities is, and probably always will be, eating out. In response to this powerful popular demand for culinary variety, São Paulo embraces within its city limits literally thousands of restaurants. Which is the best? Who could ever possibly answer that question? Not this author, in any event. Like most restaurant devotees, my tastes change every day. Sometimes, no matter how good that much-touted French restaurant is, I'm just not in the mood for all that richness, or the pomp of being served by a small platoon of waiters, even when money is not the object.

For me, the best restaurant is the one where I'm enjoying the meal I feel like eating at the moment—assuming, of course, that the ingredients and preparation meet the high standards I've become accustomed to after years of eating out, and that the service is attentive and correct. This does not mean to say that every place listed is going to serve you some gourmet delight. Hardly! In most cases you'll get what you pay for—sometimes a little bit more, in others a little bit less. The size of your bill will in most cases reflect the amount of love and labor that have gone into your meal. In a few cases, where I was particularly satisfied, I will risk what comes close to an outright recommendation.

All that being said, you could visit São Paulo, never eat in one of the restaurants mentioned in this guide, and not register the slightest dissatisfaction with your culinary experience. That's one of the great advantages of any big city. People who eat out a lot develop pretty good tastes in restaurant food, and bad restaurants don't tend to stay in business very long. So, bon appétit—now we can eat. Enjoy, and write to tell me about all your favorites—especially the inexpensive ones. Everybody loves a deal.

I will begin my list with the restaurant I liked the best, for its charm, its service, and its food—particularly a delicious dessert of "hot" ice cream with fruit. **Tatini's** is located on the ground floor of a white-brick high-rise apartment building at Rua Batatais 558 (tel. 885-7601), a tree-lined street in the old and elegant neighborhood of Jardim Paulista. Many dishes from the selection of over a hundred on the menu are prepared at tableside. Proprietor Mario Tatini came to Brazil from Tuscany, and serves many pasta, seafood, and veal dishes inspired by that Italian region. A typical plate of fettuccine, for example, is likely to be overflowing with a sauce of many delectable ingredients like tomatoes, herbs, mushrooms, and fresh seafood. The final treat of the meal was a dessert called *sorvete quente,* or hot ice cream. The waiter prepares a special blend of cold fruits and cognac in a hot chafing dish, and spoons the mixture over fluffy vanilla ice cream. You could die! Meals are on the steep side—from $8 to $25 per entree—and the *sorvete quente* costs $6. Tip and drinks are extra. Tatini's is closed Monday, but is open for lunch on other weekdays between 11:30 a.m. and 3 p.m., and for dinner from 6:30 p.m. to 1 a.m. On Saturday and Sunday the restaurant stays open all day, and closes around 2 a.m. Reservations are advisable, and most major credit cards are accepted.

On a different scale, but likewise tasty when your mood turns to pizza, is the **Torre do Bexiga,** Rua 13 de Maio no. 848 (tel. 289-7364). Bexiga is the neighborhood for Italian restaurants, fringed with cafés and rock and video clubs that indicate the presence of a local bohemian and youth culture. Pizza at the Torre do Bexiga comes with dozens of unique and imaginative toppings: meats, cheeses, vegetables—and bananas. Pizza with bananas? That's what I said until I tasted it. Delicious! Open all week at normal lunch and dinner hours; prices are between $3 and $5 per pizza, depending on the toppings.

You won't find the term "Bexiga" on your map, incidentally. The word is a nickname (it means pockmarked!) for the neighborhood that spans parts of Bella Vista and Morro dos Ingleses, and is concentrated primarily on Rua 13 de Maio between Rua Santo Antônio and Avenida Brigadeiro Luís Antônio.

At no. 621 on Rua 13 de Maio is **La Távola** (tel. 288-5673), a large, lively, and popular restaurant specializing in fresh pasta dishes. combined with bits of sausage, beef, olives, vegetables, and herbs. Roast goat is also a favorite, as is *rondelli*—pasta filled with ricotta and mozzarella cheese. Flaming braziers are also much in evidence at La Távola, as waiters energetically put the finishing touches on dishes at tableside. Entrees range between $6 and $15, with a few more expensive dishes. The house red wine is robust and reasonable at $6 a bottle. Open seven days a week from 11:30 a.m. till 4 p.m. for lunch and from 6:30 p.m. till 1 a.m. for dinner.

The **Mexilão** is a moderately priced seafood restaurant of high repute at Rua 13 de Maio no. 626 (tel. 284-8887), roughly across the street from La Távola.

Several Greenwich Village–style coffeehouses are located at the beginning of the block, for example the **Café do Bexiga** at Rua 13 de Maio no. 76 and the nearby **Bar Café Socaite.**

For excellent Portuguese-style cuisine, and authentic fado singers straight from the banks of the Tagus in Lisbon, there is the **Alfama dos Marineiros,** Avenida Pamplona 1285 (tel. 285-0523). The broiled seafood platter, in addition to being a beautiful presentation of a fisherman's harvest, is fit for the palate of the most discerning diners. Giant shrimp, *sardinhas* (the Portuguese kind, which are much larger than the variety that gets canned), octopus, squid, and crayfish fill the serving dish to overflowing, at a cost of $36 for two. Affable proprietor Jerônimo Gomes imports the best fado talent from Portugal. There are fado shows four days a week, Wednesday through Saturday, beginning after 11 p.m. You can catch the show over drinks for an artistic cover charge of $10 per person, or have a meal and pay only a $5 cover. Reservations are desirable on show nights.

Having been for many years a resident of New York City, a certain snobbishness has crept into my own opinions about Chinese food. Only in Asia itself, I believed, or else in New York and San Francisco (because of their large populations of Chinese origin—and a very demanding clientele), could you find Chinese restaurant food that is consistently superb. What gets passed off for Chinese food elsewhere usually tastes as though it came out of a can. Such, at least, has been my experience—and I am not a particularly fussy eater. It seems then that, not unlike the rest of the world, I have overlooked its third-largest city for Chinese food—São Paulo. São Paulo has a very large Asian community, primarily Japanese. And therefore lovers of Japanese cooking are the ones who are really in for a treat here, if for no other reason than the sheer number of places to choose from—but I did find a Chinese restaurant that could survive in New York.

The **Sino Brasileiro,** Rua Doutor Alberto Torres 39, in Perdizes (tel. 67-4653), offers several regional varieties of Chinese cooking, from the bland and crunchy Cantonese to the fiery Szechwan. The hot-and-sour soup and the double-sautéed pork were excellent, as were the spring rolls and the shrimp with cashews. The restaurant is colorfully decorated, and occupies the downstairs rooms of a large and old stone house, conceivably once the mansion of a prosperous coffee family from the end of the last century. The Sino Brasileiro is open every day for lunch from noon till 4:40 p.m., and reopens for dinner, from 6:30 p.m. till midnight. Individual dishes cost between $4 and $5 each.

Feijoada is the midday meal eaten every Saturday all over Brazil, and São Paulo is no exception. And while the **Harvest** restaurant at the Hilton, Avenida Ipiranga 165 (tel. 256-0003), is a fancy French restaurant with a '20s ambience of frosted windows and draped walls, it also serves up what is probably the best feijoada lunch deal in the city. For around $10 you get a delicious meal, and all the caipirinhas (the crushed lime and cane-brandy cocktail) you can drink. The meal begins with small cups of black-bean soup. Then comes the feijoada, the various ingredients of which—several different cuts of pork, bacon, filet mignon, and sausage, plus the rice, beans, kale, and many condiments—are each served separately from shiny silver serving dishes.

Actually, the staff at the Hilton maintain that the tradition to serve up the ingredients of feijoada in separate dishes so that foreign visitors could see what they were eating originated at the São Paulo Hilton about ten years ago. Certainly this is the manner of service for feijoada at most of the better restaurants throughout Brazil today, especially those in the deluxe hotels. What this means is that in fact two distinct types of feijoada can be found in Brazilian restaurants today: that assembled piecemeal on your plate, and that ladled out like stew from one big cauldron. Ironically, a countermovement has begun at some restaurants to serve only the single-cauldron feijoada, saying that it is, after all, the traditional—and therefore the only correct—way to eat Brazil's favorite Saturday meal. I prefer to see the two as distinct dishes, one a kind of peasant stew about which it is better not to inquire as to why it tastes so good, and the other a buffet of choice cuts of pork and beef, with rice, black beans, and kale, Brazil's three main staples, which I personally could eat twice a day for the rest of my life, regardless of what else they are served with.

Less genteel, but tasty nonetheless, are the buffet-style Saturday feijoadas downstairs at the chic Hilton nightspot, the **London Tavern,** and only two blocks away at **Eduardo's,** Rua Nestor Pestana 80, at the Praça Franklin Roosevelt (tel. 257-0500). Eduardo's is one of those mid-priced, reliable Brazilian luncheon restaurants that open daily from 11 a.m. till 6 p.m., with a big menu. The Saturday feijoada is only $5.50, and other traditional dishes are not generally more than $6 to $8. Eduardo's has six locations throughout the city.

Anyone staying at a hotel on or near the Avenida Vieira de Carvalho will have numerous restaurant options nearby. On that very avenue at no. 122 is the **Rubaiyat** (tel. 222-8333), a churrascaria, with accompanying snackbar. The barbecue is not served *rodízio* style, and the grilled meat platters run between $8 and $10. The restaurant has an attached snackbar with a separate entrance, specializing in salgadinhos.

See Section 3, "Food and Drink," in Chapter II, for more information about, feijoada, churrasco, and salgadinhos.

The **Almanara,** Avenida Vieira de Carvalho 109, next to the Hotel Bourbon, is a bright-looking Arab fast-food restaurant for Middle -Eastern specialties. And the **O Gato Que Ri,** (Laughing Cat) restaurant, at no. 37/41 on the Largo do Arouche, where the permanent flower stands are located, is one of those wonderful and popular restaurants with white-tile walls and coarse white cotton tablecloths, where you can happily eat what can only be described as the Brazilian equivalent of American diner food. If you had one of these meals at a truck stop, you'd walk away smiling. Pasta, meat, and fish dishes cost $2 to $5, and the Laughing Cat keeps a lunch and dinner schedule from 11 a.m. to 3 p.m. and 6 p.m. till midnight, seven days a week.

5. A MOUNTAIN RETREAT IN CAMPOS DO JORDÃO

When Paulistanos want fresh air and cooler temperatures, they don't have to go far. The environs of São Paulo are mountainous, and the majestic Serra Mar (Ocean Range) runs the length the state's coastline, making any trip to the sea and excursion through the mountains as well. A favorite inland mountain spa, however—both during the summer vacation months of mid-December through February, and in the winter school holiday month of July—is Campos do Jordão, about a two-hour car ride from São Paulo heading east along the BR 116 highway in the direction of Rio. The three-hour bus ride from São Paulo costs about $2.

July is the coldest month in Campos do Jordão, when the mercury frequently hovers at the frost line overnight but warms up to a comfortable afternoon temperature of 50°F to 60°F on many days. Visually, this resort town is not so unlike its counterparts in New England, though architecturally it copies the alpine style, reflecting the European origins of many of its inhabitants. Narrow, winding roads climb the surrounding peaks, revealing around every curve the drive of a fine hotel or, at roadside, a chalet-style inn, all set among the towering evergreens of a dense conifer forest. By late March the few hardwood trees—mostly maples seemingly so out of place in this country of predominantly tropical vegetation—already display autumnal coloring and cover small patches of ground everywhere with their fallen leaves.

Campos do Jordão is entered through a formal portal which opens into the town's commercial center. Beyond this neighborhood, called Abernéssia, are the more swank sections of Juaguaribe and Capivari, where most of the shops, boutiques, and restaurants are located. Local crafts include products of the *malha* cottage industry—handmade pullovers and cardigans, a reminder of the town's frequent sweater-weather climate. But the greatest resource of the town is its pure mountain air, kept crisp and healthy at its protected mile-high altitude.

For further information, or to make reservations for Campos do Jordão directly in São Paulo, call **Campostur,** Rua 7 de Abril no. 404, sixth floor (tel. 255-1156).

WHAT TO SEE AND DO: The **Festival de Inverno** (Winter Carnival) occupies the entire month of July each year, when special events and festivities are scheduled for every day. Classical musicians flock to Campos do Jordão in July, and chamber music concerts are a big part of the scene.

The **Parque Florestal** is located in a remote corner of the town, along a mountain dirt road where cows graze freely among the trees on forested hillsides. The park has a trout hatchery, and many of these speckled beauties can be seen swimming in the local streams. There is also a working water-powered sawmill, and many separate picnic environments. You can rent horses at a stable near the park's entrance, and the local terrain and relatively open woods seem ideal for riding. Hiking and backpacking are also popular pastimes in the surrounding countryside.

The town also has a **mountain train** that makes hour-long excursions to a nearby village lower down the slopes, São José dos Campos.

A ski lift off a main square carries interested sightseers to a local mountaintop, the **Morro do Elefante,** for a panoramic view of the town and the surrounding Paraiba valley.

WHERE TO STAY AND EAT: There are over 50 hotels of differing categories in the region. Most hotels include full board with their rates, so guests tend to eat "at home" while in Campos do Jordão.

The **Hotel e Restaurante Vila Regina,** Avenida Emílio Lang Junior 443 (tel. 0122/63-1036), is typical of the upper-range inns in Campos do Jordão, with 22 modern and comfortable rooms. The daily rate for two is $117, which includes all three meals. The restaurant is decorated hunting lodge style, and specializes in baked trout along with a host of other international and Italian dishes. As an apéritif, try a negroni—a cocktail made from sweet vermouth, campari, and gin, served ice cold with lemon wedge. You may ask for a refill.

Other popular lodges are the town's two five-star inns, the **Vila Inglesa,** Rua Sen. Roberto Simonsenn 3500 (tel. 0122/63-1955), and the **Orotur Garden Hotel,** on Rua 3 (tel. 0122/62-2833), both of which are expensive and have long been watering holes of an elite clientele from São Paulo.

On the other end of the price spectrum are the **Cantinho de Portugal,** Rua Alexandre Sirim 127 (tel. 0122/62-1439), and the **Estoril,** Avenida Macedo Soares 241 (tel. 0122/63-1932).

Authorization to stay in the local youth hostel, the **Casa Azul,** may be obtained through the tourist office at the bus station.

Trout and fondue are the food specialties of the region. The **Sò Quijo,** Avenida Macedo Soares 642 (tel. 63-1910), is an attractive restaurant in a colonial-style building, which in addition to the regional specialties, also serves crêpes and steaks.

Willy's Confeitaria, Avenida Macedo Soares 183 (tel. 63-1015), has an informal café atmosphere, and serves meals and desserts.

For French cuisine there is the **Casa D'Irene,** Rua Raul Mesquita 83 (tel. 63-1115), offering pâté maison, escargot, rabbit, and steak au poivre.

THE SOUTH WILL RISE AGAIN:

A bit of U.S. Civil War history is preserved about 80 miles from São Paulo in **Americana,** a town founded and settled by Confederate refugees. There are still a number of descendants of the original families, and with many, English is still the language spoken at home. Their cemetery, located about six miles out of town on the Anhanguera highway, is filled with headstones bearing American surnames. Among the contributions to Brazilian culture of the *confederados,* as they were known, were improved agricultural techniques throughout the region, and the introduction of watermelons as a cash crop. *The Last Colony of the Confederacy,* by Eugene C. Harter, published in 1985 by the University Press of the University of Mississippi, is a fascinating account of the trials and tribulations of these defeated Confederates who chose exile in the tropics over life in the postwar South of the Reconstruction period.

6. THE SEASHORE: UBATUBA

A logical place to visit after a stay in Campos do Jordão, especially for those touring independently by car or bus, is the coastal town of Ubatuba. The drive down the winding sierra to the shore at this point—via Taubate and São Luís do Paraitinga—can be an unforgettable journey. Especially beyond this latter town, the roads curve through the hills like spirals, and become as narrow as logging trails in places. A perpetual mist hangs in these mountains, further slowing your forward progress to the pace of a caravan. After some three hours of occasionally breathtaking descent, you reach a flat coastal strip with 73 beaches, all incorporated into the municipal sphere of a resort town called Ubatuba.

The myriad beaches stretch over a distance of 72 km (45 miles) in both directions from Ubatuba, which has a year-round population of 35,000. The word *ubatuba,* incidentally is indigenous and literally means "place where the shafts grow," referring to the poles used by the earlier inhabitants to fashion their fishing spears. During Carnival—which always falls during the week before the Catholic penitential season of Lent—Ubatuba's population swells to some 400,000 souls. All these visitors during this particular time of the year, the majority of whom hail from Rio and São Paulo, come for the same singular reason: to escape Carnival. Clearly, Brazilians are not universally fond of their national festival.

By the same token, the Carnival time is not the time for foreign visitors to visit Ubatuba, which can be better appreciated as an off-season resort, when the vacation crowds have diminished and the hotel rates plummet to half of what is charged during the high season—December through February, and in July.

WHAT TO SEE AND DO: You could spend your entire time in Ubatuba trying to figure out which of the 73 beaches is the most perfect according to your own criteria. If, however, the sun should fail you on a given day, or if your peripatetic rhythms prevent you from staying prone in the tanning position for more than a few hours at a time, there are a number of touring and activity options which might be of appeal.

Of historical interest is the colonial-era town of **Parati** (see Chapter VI for a more detailed description of this town), only 70 km (43 miles) up the coast toward Rio. There are a number of **ruins** in the area: an old coffee plantation's slave quarters, Brazil's first glass factory, and a fort built at the turn of the century on nearby Anchieta Island, now a wildlife sanctuary, a ten-minute boat ride from the mainland.

A full range of **aquatic sports** from skindiving to sailing are also available. The tourist agency **Ubatur,** Rua Flamenguinho 17, on the Saco da Ribeira beach (tel. 0124/42-0388), offers tours, schooner excursions, equipment and a boat, and car-rental services.

WHERE TO STAY AND EAT: As with many Brazilian resort areas, you have the option of staying close to the center of activity or in relative seclusion, according to the dictates of your mood and constitution. The in-town hotel of choice has to be the **Ubatuba Palace Hotel,** Rua Coronel Domiciano 500 (tel. 0124/32-1500, or 011/280-8496 in São Paulo for reservations). This venerable 59-room hotel is a block from the Avenida das Praias, the town's principal oceanfront thoroughfare, where the evening promenade takes place and where nightlife is centered in the avenue's many cafés, restaurants, and beer gardens.

The rooms at the Ubatuba Palace all have deep-green louvered doors, and front on common balconies which offer a view of the town. Furnishings are comfortable and attractive in a *fazenda* (ranchhouse) style, right down to the pious placement of crucifixes over the queen-size beds. The hotel's several two-room suites are huge, with private balconies. Regular-season single-room rates are quite reasonable, at $67 for two, including breakfast, and the off-season price is a steal at $20 per person, including breakfast and your choice of either lunch or dinner.

It will require no hardship to eat in the Ubatuba Palace dining room, where the food ranging in price from $6 to $15, à la carte, is of genuine gourmet quality. The shrimp crêpe, with its creamy sauce, will melt in your mouth. The hotel also offers a very attractive pool and lounging area, and a steamroom.

Surrounding this hotel is a warren of small streets filled with craft shops and stores of every variety, laid out among the obligatory church-dominated plazas and small parks. The overall effect of municipal Ubatuba, however, is of an informal beach town where people in bathing costumes are in a constant parade either toward or away from the beachfront.

One choice for a more remote, resort-style hotel is the **Torremolinos,** Rua Domingos Della Mónica Barbosa 37, at Enseada beach (tel. 0124/42-625). There are 37 rooms in this modern, three-story beachfront hotel, which has the look of a Frank Lloyd Wright original. Most of the brightly decorated rooms face the ocean and open onto small balconies. Two pools—one for adults, the other for children—and a large tiled patio area with chaise lounges and umbrellas, separate the hotel from the sandy beach. The hotel has a restaurant and a poolside snackbar, and is about a 15-minute car ride from Ubatuba. The daily rates at the Torremolinos are comparable to those of the Ubatuba Palace, both during the *temporada* (high season) and the *baixa* (low season).

The nearby **Mediterrâneo,** also on Enseada beach (tel. 0124/42-0386), is true to its name, architecturally speaking. The grand white façade with the awninged windows is certainly imbued with a look of the European Riviera. Set against verdant rising hills and surrounded by tropical vegetation and lawns, the hotel looks out over the breaking sea. Steps from a large story-high terrace with pool lead down to the beach, where tables, chairs, and umbrellas have been placed for the convenience of the guests. The 30 rooms range from $100 to $50 a night for two, breakfast included, depending on the season.

For between $23 and $26 a night, for double occupancy and breakfast, you can stay off-season at the **Hotel Village Tropical,** also located at the edge of Enseada beach (tel. 0124/42-0055). The 24-room, two-story building has interior courtyards and open-air corridors filled with plants, like a Brazilian ranchhouse. There is also a beautifully planted *quintal* (yard) between the hotel and the beach, but no pool. High-season rates climb to between $50 and $55 per night.

ON TO SANTOS AND GUARUJA: Santos, located about 45 miles from São Paulo, is Brazil's largest and most active port city. Traditionally Santos, and now the nearby island of Guaruja, have been the principal beach resorts for the landlocked Paulistanos. Practically every weekend, the season and weather permitting, the urbanites flee São Paulo in droves and head for the beach, by car, train, bus, and even plane. Santos—one of Brazil's wealthiest cities, if somewhat industrialized—has the most modern facilities. In recent years, however, visitors have departed the in-town beaches of Santos for the more pristine strands of neighboring Guaruja. Buses leave regularly from the downtown bus station, and a free passenger ferry connects Santos with Guaruja, and buses shuttle bathers from there to the various beaches.

CHAPTER X

THE SOUTH

□ □ □

Iguaçu Falls is the second most popular destination for North American travelers in Brazil after Rio de Janeiro. No wonder! The falls are truly one of the world's great natural phenomena, and are understandably the main attraction in Brazil's southern region, but by no means the only one. Southern Brazil is totally distinct in its population, climate, geography, history, and culture from the rest of the country. The three states of Paraná, Santa Catarina, and Rio Grande do Sul are located along Brazil's most active border with its Spanish-speaking neighbors, touching as a whole the frontiers of Paraguay, Argentina, and Uruguay. Generations of conflict and several wars were fought before the existing boundaries of the region were agreed upon, as Uruguay was finally created by compromise as a buffer between South America's largest and most powerful nations, Brazil and Argentina.

The early settlers here, Spaniards and Portuguese, alternately lived in peaceful coexistence and fought each other for control of the territory, while the Jesuits built dozens of missions to protect the native peoples from annihilation and enslavement by both parties. The ruins of these missions in the Sete Povos district of Rio Grande, and Missiones in Argentina, are a striking testament to this historical period. To strengthen their hold in the south, the Portuguese further colonized the area with former mercenaries from their armies who came from the Azores Islands. These later arrivals mixed with the earlier Spanish and Portuguese settlers and formed the bedrock of the *gaucho* culture as it exists today. And while the Spanish presence in southern Brazil is now somewhat invisible, the influence can still be felt, especially when the population is compared with that of Brazil's other regions. During the 19th century great waves of German and Italian immigrants settled throughout the south. They, too, have left a strong mark on the region. Today their descendants are fully assimilated as Brazilians, and yet many families, particularly the Germans, remain bilingual and retain other cultural characteristics, notably their work ethic and a preference for alpine-style architecture.

Southern Brazil is both agrarian and industrial, prosperous, and highly developed. Modern cities are centers of textile and shoe manufacturing. Great expanses of prairie lands, *pampas,* primarily in Rio Grande do Sul, nourish the herds of cattle that provide the nation's main source of beef. Grains, soybeans, and coffee are grown in abundance throughout the region, both on small, private holdings and on enormous tenant-farmed estates. The interiors of Paraná and Santa Catarina are heavily forested, and home to Brazil's pulp and paper industries, while among the eastern hills of Rio Grande do Sul the vitaculture brought a century ago by the Italians flourishes, and today produces wine for all Brazil. As with the coastal lands to the north, the mountain range known as the Great Escarpment accompanies the shoreline, never far from the sea. But in the south the climate is temperate; frosts are frequent during the winter, but snow is rare. Summer, from November through May, is warm and dry along the shore, and humid in the subtropical interior.

1. IGUAÇU FALLS

THE RIVER IGUAÇU: Rising from an obscure spring on the outskirts of Curitiba, capital of Paraná state, the Iguaçu River flows from the high coastal plateau 4,000 feet above sea level, not immediately toward the nearby Atlantic, but inland, seeking the great valley that drains the Andes watershed to the south, merging its waters first with the mighty Paraná and ultimately with the Plata far to the south. The Iguaçu winds along its westerly course for nearly 800 river miles, and is fed by many streams hardly more impressive than that of its own source. As the Iguaçu approaches the Paraná, the final stretch of the river forms a border between Brazil and Argentina, cutting through the last great expanse of Atlantic rain forest that remains in South America. On both sides of the border, the forest —over 500,000 acres in all—has been converted to national park lands, providing a preserve for over 2,000 varieties of vegetation and habitat for a large population of native fauna, including 400 bird species and innumerable reptiles and insects. The awesome beauty and power of the forest cannot be deducted from a mere census of its animal and plant life, which meld into a visual symphony of color, texture, and sound that has to be experienced to be felt and appreciated.

About seven miles above its mouth (*foz*), the Iguaçu widens its bed to a span of some two miles, and here drops precipitously over a 200-foot-high cliff, forming an interconnected curtain of 275 cataracts. Mist rises from the bottom like boiling steam, and more than one moistened rainbow hovers in mid-air between the river bottom and the wide, curly lip of the enormous basin. Andorinhos, related to the sparrow, flock like pigeons throughout the canyon, and dart behind the sheets of falling water to perches on the rocky walls where they make their nests. There is something primordial, if not timeless, in the contrast between the placid upper river against its silent backdrop, the lush rain forest, and the naked, rocky canyon of the river below, seething with agitation from the tons of fallen water.

As the end approaches, the river achieves its moment of glory with an unanticipated and thunderous crescendo, only to be absorbed a few miles downstream in meek submission by the dominating currents of the much larger Paraná. During its last seven miles, the once-proud Iguaçu, having shed its dazzling forest plumage, is paraded like the condemned past the tawdry border towns and frontier markers of three nations—Argentina, Brazil, and Paraguay—which seem to mock both the river's moment of greatness and its ignominious end.

THE BORDER TOWNS: By far the most appealing of the three border towns is **Foz do Iguaçu** on the Brazilian side. Over the past decade Foz (as the town is called by locals) has grown in population from about 40,000 to 160,000 inhabitants, a boom resulting from the construction of the Itaipú Dam, the world's largest hydroelectric power station. A survey of the city's hotels, restaurants, and

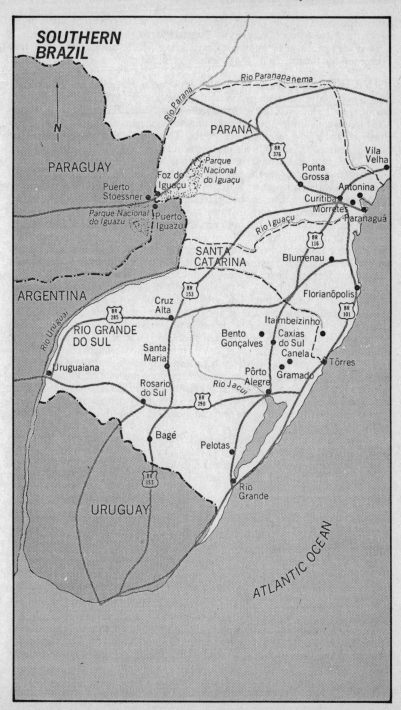

other attractions follows. On the Paraguayan side is **Puerto Stroessner,** about which there is also more to say below. **Puerto Iguazu,** on the Argentinian side, is a town very much in formation, given a boost by the inauguration of a new bridge linking the town with the Brazilian mainland.

IGUAÇU TRIVIA: The word *iguaçu* means "great waters" in the Guarani language, a prosaic understatement to say the least. The first European credited with having seen the falls was the Spaniard Don Alvar Nuñez Cabeza de Vaca, who in 1541 led an expedition from the coast of what is currently Santa Catarina state in Brazil to what is now Asunción in Paraguay. The redoubtable hidalgo (whose last name translates as Senor Cow's Head) rechristened the wonder as the Falls of Santa Maria, but the Guarani name has held firm.

Earlier in this century the pioneer Brazilian aviator Alberto Santos Dumont mounted a wooden tower to better observe the phenomenon. To reassure his nervous hosts—who owned the Brazil side of the falls at that time, but would have never dreamed of doing anything quite so bold as their guest—the melancholy Dumont cracked what was probably the only joke of his life, saying, "Heights don't intimidate me."

Eleanor Roosevelt is another historical personage whose reaction on first seeing the falls is much quoted. Moved no doubt by feelings of loyalty to her native New York, the First Lady was heard to muse, "Poor Niagara."

The Iguaçu Falls have a wet season and a dry season. The rains fall in the winter months, April through July, and so the volume of water crashing over the cliffs is greatest during that season, and the weather is mild, though it can be quite chilly in the vicinity of the falls themselves. During the autumn and summer months the temperatures climb to their subtropical warmest, with humidity and mosquitos to match, and the water flow is cut by a third during the driest periods. In 1977 the falls dried up for the only time in recorded history. And in 1983 the flooding was so severe that much of the vegetation surrounding the cataracts, as well as a network of catwalks that allow visitors a spectacular closeup view of the falls from numerous vantage points, were completely destroyed. Many moviegoers learned of Iguaçu for the first time in 1986 when they saw *The Mission,* which was filmed on the Argentine side.

Finally, a note on pronunciation. The accent at the bottom of the letter *c* in Iguaçu is called a *cedilha* (cedilla in Spanish). This letter always precedes the vowels *a, o,* or *u,* and is pronounced like an *s.* On occasion Brazilians employ the spelling Iguassu. The double *s* in Portuguese is also pronounced like a so-called soft *s.*

GETTING TO IGUAÇU: The falls are such a popular attraction—at least on the Brazilian side—that there is an international **airport** near Foz do Iguaçu receiving several daily 1¾-hour flights from Rio, via São Paulo, and from other points within Brazil as well. Round-trip air fare from Rio, for those who do not have a VARIG air pass, is approximately $130. A smaller airport on the Argentine side handles that country's domestic flights. There is regular service from Buenos Aires, and the flying time is an hour and a half.

There is also frequent **bus** service to Foz do Iguaçu from all major metropolitan centers throughout Brazil. The trip from Rio takes 23 hours, 12 hours from Curitiba. For those who wish to continue on to Asunción by land, regular bus service is also available. The trip takes about 4½ hours, with an additional two-hour delay for border crossing. Make sure that you have the appropriate documentation and visas if you wish to travel in Argentina or Paraguay beyond the border towns.

WHAT TO SEE: To view the falls and the region's other sights at a comfortable pace, a visit of at least two, and preferably three days is recommended. The first two days can be spent getting to know the falls from the Brazilian side, with side-trip excursions to the Itaipu Dam, the town of Foz do Iguaçu, and possibly Puerto Stroessner in Paraguay. The final day can then be reserved for a visit to the Argentine side, where you will want to spend a minimum of four to five hours wandering the various paths and catwalks both above and below the falls. The trip to and from the Argentine side will also consume a certain amount of time, which is why a full day for this excursion is suggested.

Getting to the Brazilian Side

Let's assume that you will be arriving at the international airport and staying at one of the dozens of hotels located in or around Foz do Iguaçu. By way of orientation, the airport sits at about the mid-point between the falls and the city, which are linked by a modern highway and are 16 miles apart. In addition to **taxis,** which will carry you to the city for about $10, there is an **executive bus** for about $1. The **local bus** costs only 15¢, but the driver will refuse to take you if you are loaded down with baggage. During the high season—the summer months and the July winter school holiday—buses run hourly from 8 a.m. to 6 p.m. between the city bus terminal (Avenida Jucelino Kubitschek) and the falls. In the off-season buses run every two hours. The one-way fare is about 30¢, plus an additional 30¢ to enter the **Parque Nacional do Iguaçu** (Iguaçu National Park). Operating hours for the park are 8 a.m. and 6 p.m. Keep in mind that the park entrance is still a good five miles from the area where the falls can be viewed. Some buses stop at the entrance to the park, while others continue on to the falls.

The tour of the Brazilian falls can very easily be self-guided. There is no need to incur the extra expense of a special agency tour. Spend the extra money on cab fare, if you want the most convenient transportation; for an added $2 per hour the driver will even wait for you.

The Park Museum

A brief visit to the museum, especially for those who wish to learn something of the forest's ecosystem, is worthwhile. Displays include cases of stuffed fauna native to the forest, including the tamanduá, a tropical anteater; the tapir, the largest of the South American mammals weighing more than 600 pounds (they resemble a swine, but are related to the rhinoceros), the paca, a large spotted rodent, also known as the water hare, as well as innumerable bird species, the most striking of which is the tucano with its curved beak and its cobalt-blue eyes. A separate room contains wood samples culled from the forest's many varieties of trees. The wood of the pinheiro, the giant pine of southern Brazil, is notable for its orange tint, strength, and lack of knots along the trunk, as the leafy growth, like that of a coconut palm, is confined in mature trees only to the crown. Placards and photographs document the history of the falls, though legends are only in Portuguese. There are some striking photos from the 1977 draught and the 1983 floods.

The Falls: Two Distinct Views

There is a primary distinction between the Brazilian and Argentine vistas of the Iguaçu Falls. Since most of the cataracts are on the Argentina side, the Brazilian view is more sweeping, more panoramic. Keep in mind that the full expanse of the falls is nearly 1½ miles in width. Only from the air, moreover, can all 275 cataracts that line the curving wall of the upper river be seen. The greater your distance from the falls, the more remote and abstract they appear, and their drama diminishes correspondingly. This is not to say that the falls seen from the Brazilian side are devoid of dramatic detail. Hardly! But the system of catwalks and paths on the Argentina side provides the visitor with a powerfully intimate experience, as you follow the outline of the river wall, alternately walking from the edge of one cataract to another. Each view has its compelling validity; and so both must be experienced for you to claim you have really seen the Iguaçu Falls.

The Brazilian View

A clearly marked stairway opposite the famous Hotel das Cataratas leads to a mile-long path that accompanies the river upstream. This walk offers a spectacular view of the falls across the lower river, which has narrowed at this point to channel width. The high ground to the land side is matted with dense forest growth, and if you're lucky (as was I, getting a good look at a colorful paca), you may sight a creature or two flitting through the underbrush. As you walk, a wider and wider horizon of crashing waters opens to view, until you reach the end of the trail near a tall elevator tower. The descent has been gradual, with many viewing stations along the way, but here you are actually below the first step of the Brazilian falls. A screened-in catwalk set on stone pillars leads through clouds of boiling mists to the very rim of a lower cataract, and the view here is a breathtaking experience. Depending on the time of year, you can expect to be soaked or merely dampened while walking on this catwalk. During steamy weather, the shower can be welcome and refreshing; otherwise, bring rain gear or rent an outfit from the enterprising vendors along the trail. The elevator lifts you back to road level. Before leaving the tower, however, the energetic may climb a metal ladder, hand over hand, to a viewing platform for a final appreciation of the wide canyon, and the "great waters" of the Iguaçu.

Excursions By Boat and Air

Once on the roadway you will see a stand operated by **Helisul,** offering seven-minute overflights of the falls by helicopter. The fee is roughly $30, slightly less if you pay in cruzados, assuming you have exchanged at a favorable parallel-market rate. Farther up the road is a concession offering **boat rides** on the upper river, which operates only under favorable conditions, depending on weather and volume of water.

Buses for the return trip to Foz leave from a nearby parking area, or you can return along the road, by foot, for refreshments at the Hotel das Cataratas and a walk around the spacious grounds. Be sure to notice the statue of Alberto Santos Dumont in the vicinity of the trail's end. The inscription on the pedestal implies that Petitsantos himself, the patron saint of Brazilian aviation, deserves credit for the idea of removing the lands surrounding Iguaçu from private hands and converting them into a public trust.

Macuco Safari

A 1½-hour-long guided tour of the forest environment is offered by a private company, Macuco Turis Safari. The concession is located beyond the park entrance going toward the falls. The 2.5-km (1½-mile) walk through the woods terminates at the edge of the river and includes a boat ride in the vicinity of the nearest falls. Unlike federal parks in the U.S. and Canada, access to the lands of the Iguaçu Park is limited. You cannot just walk about at will, but must have special permits or be accompanied by a park official. No camping, fishing, or hunting is allowed in the park. The Macuco tour is one of the few easily available means for actually penetrating, however superficially, the interior of the preserve.

Foz do Iguaçu

The city of Foz is itself an attraction. In fact, staying in town should be considered seriously by those who prefer urban over resort environments. The Hotel das Cataratas, the only hotel on the Brazilian side with a view of the falls, is in great demand. Indeed it's getting increasingly difficult to get a reservation at this favored locale unless the booking is made well in advance. Most tourists are placed in one of several first-class resort-style hotels that are located on the Rodovia das Cataratas (Highway of the Cataracts) that links the national park with the city.

The advantage of the city is its street life, as well as the numerous shops and restaurants. After a day of touring, the city offers the possibility of another, less structured excursion. Foz is small enough to walk around without getting lost while hunting for the restaurant that best fits your mood (as opposed to being limited to a single hotel dining room) and to search out the nightlife centered in a small but appealing selection of crowded cafés, bars, and discothèques. If you are lucky, there may even be a street fair going on during your visit. The fairs are animated by live music, and many stands selling excellent crafts and foods, representing all three nations.

The Argentine Side

When visiting the Argentine National Park, using the services of a tour company makes considerable sense, especially if your time is limited. Rather than hassle the logistics as an individual—not the least of which is the border crossing—you can leave all these details to the tour guide. By all means carry your passport with you when crossing into either Paraguay or Argentina. Visas are not generally required for day trips into these particular border areas, but in the case of Argentina this is not always so. Better check with an Argentine consulate before traveling to Iguaçu to avoid disappointment. Or consult with the consulate in Foz itself.

Until the completion of the Tancredo Neves Bridge, which links Foz with Puerto Iguazu, the crossing was made by ferry, and involved taking a bus or taxi to Porto Meira near Foz, crossing the river and negotiating Customs on both sides of the border, then taking another bus or cab to the Argentine park. Of course, the same was true for the return. Now you can go directly to the Argentine falls by a single means of transportation—a tour bus for example, or even by cab or rented car if you want to go it alone. Most hotels can help you book a tour to the Argentine side, and the better hotels usually provide the service themselves. Your only concern is to make sure there is sufficient time to walk freely along the many trails both above and below the falls, and to see everything you want to see, including the famous **Garganta do Diabo** (Devil's Throat), the largest single waterfall in the world in terms of its volume of water flow per second.

The entrance to the Argentine **Parque Nacional de Iguazu** is about 12 miles beyond the town of Puerto Iguazu. A good place to begin your exploration, however, is several miles beyond the entrance at **Puerto Canoas,** which is serviced by park buses. Here a one-kilometer (half-mile) catwalk leads to the edge of the Devil's Throat Falls, which straddles the imaginary frontier line in the river between Brazil and Argentina. Along this walk there are signs everywhere of the damage wrought by the devastating flood in 1983—the ruins of the original catwalk provide a particularly humbling reminder of nature's dark and angry side. Otherwise, on a given day, you are enveloped in the overwhelming beauty of the place, where so many strands of the great outdoors are woven into a single tableau. On one extreme there is the serenity of the shallow river beneath your feet, gently flowing among the dozens of fragmented islets that sustain the catwalk. On the other, and just as near at hand, is the din of the falls, as those same quiet waters unleash their latent energy by spilling over the U-shaped chasm and crash on the rocks below. Where there is vegetation, the setting is not manicured but well tended, a subtropical forest transformed into a cross between an English and a Japanese garden. Greens and earthy browns are the dominant hues, as all the flora seems to blend into a single continuous plant. As you pass beneath the tree-tops, a flock of a hundred parakeets will suddenly take to flight. And in their season (May and June) the air can be saturated with brightly painted butterflies (there are 500 known species in the forest). From the overlook at the Devil's Throat, the catwalk continues on for another mile and a half, back to the vicinity of the park's main parking lots, and here descends to the river bottom. Below there is a trail that takes you along the river's edge and across the several islands beneath the jungle canopy. Several pools beneath the more gentle falls are suitable for bathing, and meditating on the endless thundering echo of the cascading waters.

The Itaipu Dam

Itaipu is the artificial equivalent of Iguaçu. A dam, after all, is simply a variation on nature's waterfalls, a technique for concentrating the power of water and converting it to energy. Itaipu is an impressive achievement of Brazil's world-class civil engineering skills. When all the dam's 18 turbines are completed, it will provide the country with fully one-third of its electricity. Switch on a light in Rio or São Paulo, and then in your mind trace the illumination back to the molecules of water from the Rio Paraná that are squeezed through a massive concrete keyhole a few miles outside the town of Foz do Iguaçu. Enough concrete was used, it is said, to pave a two-lane road from Lisbon to Moscow.

The price tag for this binational effort—touted as a joint venture between Paraguay and Brazil—has risen into the billions, with Brazil picking up most of the tab as well as draining off most of the power. But the cost to nature has been even greater. The tradeoff for the power station involved flooding the Paraná valley above the dam, and obliterating **Sete Quedas** (Seven Falls), a natural wonder that the *Guinness Book of World Records* once listed as the greatest of all the world's waterfalls. The flooding also created an enormous lake, and transformed the ecosystem of the river valley for many miles above the dam—whether for good or for ill it is yet too early for environmentalists to determine conclusively.

To head off its environmental critics, whose voices in Brazil are muted at best, the Itaipu administrators have launched a massive public relations effort to draw the public to the site as a tourist attraction. A slick 35-mm color film and high-quality printed material make the case for the defense, the dam versus nature. Unless you are attuned to environmental issues, or to the impact of mass technology on nature, you would never suspect that there was even a potential problem if the technocrats involved in this and similar projects were not so eager to defend themselves. The issue for the tourist, however, is not necessarily to defend or support the dam, but whether or not it is worthwhile to visit as a bona fide attraction.

In its favor, the Itaipu film (available in several languages, including English) is a persuasive, if one-sided, documentary which focuses mostly on the fascinating technical challenges that accompanied the excavation and construction of the project. A bus tour takes visitors across the top of the dam, and to an overlook from which there is a closeup view of the waters as they rush through the locks. The tour is free, so there is no reason to engage a tour company, which is only performing the service of taking you to and from the site. Efficient public transportation, needed to support the project's 13,000 employees, runs frequently from nearby Foz to the administrative area, where the tour begins.

Itaipu is indeed a technological wonder, but in the end it is also just a partially completed dam, and therefore a gigantic construction site. The visitor is barraged with technical statistics, which seem impenetrable to a layperson—for example, you are informed that (as of 1986) over 600,000 visitors from 102 countries had passed through the portals of the dam's visitor center. In other words, it seems as if people are drawn to the place by all the hype and because the show is free, and then the numbers of past visitors are used to draw the latest arrivals. My strong advice would be that nontechnology buffs would be better served by spending more time at the falls and foregoing a visit to Itaipu.

Paraguay

Visiting Puerto Stroessner in Paraguay is also problematic. Not that it's difficult to cross to the border town, but why would one want to bother in the first place? For many Brazilians, the trip across the Ponte da Amizade (Friendship Bridge) is obligatory. Puerto Stroessner is a free port, and Brazilians shop there annually by the tens of thousands, mostly for electronic gadgets and appliances that are prohibitively expensive in their own country. In fact, according to one tourist official, more Brazilians are attracted to Iguaçu by the free port than by the falls. Fair enough. For North Americans, however, there are no bargains in Puerto Stroessner, even assuming you'd go all the way to Paraguay to buy your VCR. You'll get a better price in your local shopping mall than in Puerto Stroessner.

Nor does the town have the color and flavor—not to mention good food— that one associates with Mexican border towns in the American Southwest, for example. The town is filled with beeping automobiles fighting for a parking space and drab outlets selling geegaws—and not very interesting geegaws at that. More disturbing, however, is the presence of armed soldiers everywhere, a palpable reminder that you are entering the land where South America's most repressive dictatorship continues to rule after more than 30 years.

Paraguay's history is a sad one. The population is mostly Guarani, and it is said that most of Paraguay's citizens—rural peasants for the most part—still speak the Indian language and not Spanish. If this is so, it is heartening to learn that the aboriginal majority retains this critical ingredient of its culture despite a miserable existence under Presidente Stroessner, for whom the tacky border town could not be a more fitting memorial.

This being said, I have no doubt that traveling in Paraguay could be a very rewarding experience. Even my limited jaunt beyond Puerto Stroessner to nearby Puerto Franco served to see something of more typical Paraguayan townlife, beyond the inflated artificiality of the free port on the frontier. We were stopped once at a blockade where two young policemen tried to shake us down for money, which we refused to pay. No doubt this is a daily reality that any tourist might have to share with the average Paraguayan while traveling in the country.

For about five miles we drove along a brick-paved road that paralleled the Rio Paraná. There was an air of informality about the commercial center of Puerto Franco, a handful of stores and garages catering to obvious daily needs. The houses were simple, and all constructed of wood, horizontal plank siding with battens covering the joints. Windows were shuttered, but not glazed. Most of the dwellings were painted in flat, organic colors, and set on small plots of land planted with trees and flowering shrubs—not landscaped, but very agreeable to the eye. A well was visible in most yards, and hammocks could be seen through the open windows. Anyone who wanders as far as Puerto Franco, or beyond, should look for a roadside restaurant that serves empenadas—meat pies, the tastiest of which are made from manioc flour.

Três Fronteiras

The mark of the three frontiers is an unusual sight, but also not for everybody, especially if going there cuts into time that could be spent at the two national parks. At the point where the Rio Iguaçu flows into the Paraná, the corners of the three nations meet. Each country has erected a triangular marker painted in the colors of its national flag, and standing behind whichever one you choose to visit, all three obilisks can be seen simultaneously. The Brazilian marker is found at the end of a road outside Foz going away from the falls, while the Argentine marker is across the river on the outskirts of Puerto Iguazu. The Paraguayan marker is less accessible, at the end of a remote road beyond Puerto Franco.

Tour Bookings

The **Alvorada Turismo Ltda.** (tel. 0455/74-2577), a reliable tour company, has its offices in the Hotel San Martin, at Rodovia das Cataratas 17. The company offers many tour packages, at both individual and group rates. These include the nearby attractions, the falls, gambling casinos in both Argentina and Paraguay, as well as several overnight excursions to Asunción ($175), the Argentine mission ruins ($175), and a day trip which combines a visit to a gemstone mine and a mate (herbal tea) plantation in Paraguay.

WHERE TO STAY: There are over 120 hotels of all categories in and around Foz do Iguaçu. The best known, and most in demand, is the **Hotel da Cataratas,** located on the grounds of Iguaçu National Park (tel. 0455/74-2666). This is the only hotel on the Brazilian side with a view of the falls—and a commanding view it is. The hotel is also a classic of colonial design. The main section is shaped like a squared-off U, in rosy-pink stucco and white trim. There is an elegant covered veranda along the front of the building, spanning the entrance. The 200 rooms are large, and fitted in heavy ranchhouse furnishings of the Brazilian mission period. The front rooms face the falls and the rear rooms overlook the manicured grounds, which are all the more striking against the background of the encroaching rain forest. Both vistas are equally beautiful. All rooms offer heat or air conditioning, according to season. There is a swimming pool and some sports facilities on the grounds, where numerous animals can be seen walking about at their leisure, including emas or rheas, a close relative of the ostrich. Be forewarned: the emas have been known to eat guests' room keys and watches left loose on poolside tables. One drawback of the hotel is that you are as far away from the action in town as you can be, and there are no special recreational facilities here—no health club or sauna, no discothèque. Of course, this is not a problem for most guests, for whom Iguaçu is essentially an overnight destination. And after all, most international tourists come to see the falls, and that's why they stay at the Hotel das Cataratas. Reservations are an absolute necessity, made as far in advance of arrival as possible. This can be done through any VARIG office, since the airline owns and operates the hotel. Rooms range from $57 to $63 for singles, and $79 to $88 for doubles, depending on front or rear view.

The best in-town hotel is the brand-new five-star **Hotel Internacional Foz,** Rua Alm. Barroso 345 (tel. 0455/73-4240). The building is a round high-rise tower, where all 211 rooms are set spoke-like off circular corridors. The hotel has every facility, including restaurant, bar, and nightclub, as well as a barbershop and beauty parlor, gift shops, and a sauna. An outdoor pool area is at ground level, with a lawn for sunning and tent tops that shade a sitting area. The building is centrally located, but in a quiet corner of the town. Avenida Brasil, the town's principal avenue, is only a block away, and there you will find many shops and the offices of the major Brazilian airlines. The hotel is within walking distance of all restaurants and other in-town points of interest. The rooms are attractive, with color TVs, mini-bars, and full baths. Rates are $73 for a single, $87 for a double.

The area's other five-star facility is the **Hotel Bourbon,** located slightly more than a mile from town on the Rodovia das Cataratas, at km 2.5 (tel. 0455/74-1313). The building is a three-pronged star, three stories high, housing 181 rooms. The hotel's décor is very plush, but the rooms are spacious and comfortable. There is a large outdoor pool area, and the grounds are enormous, about a square mile in all. The hotel is ideal for those who want a resort atmosphere and still wish to be relatively close to town, which is within walking distance if you enjoy stretching your legs. Room prices begin at $72 for singles and $78 for doubles.

Closer to the entrance of Iguaçu National Park, at Rodovia das Cataratas 17 is the **Hotel San Martin** (tel. 0455/74-2577). A massive central chalet with exposed interior beams dominates the hotel's structure and houses its public spaces —lobby, restaurant, disco, game room, and gift shops. The 142 rooms are modern and appealing, with all the usual amenities, from television to full bath. The hotel's grounds, with swimming pool and outdoor barbecue area, do not overlook the river, but the left bank of the Iguaçu is within strolling distance from here. Rooms are priced at $36 for singles, $43 for doubles.

The **Foz Presidente Hotel,** Rua Xavier da Silva 918 (tel. 0455/73-1361), is located around the corner from the Hotel Internacional. The Presidente is what Brazilians refer to as a "family hotel"—clean, well run, inexpensive, and no frills. There are currently 73 rooms, but an additional floor is being added to expand the number of accommodations. The rooms are of good size and airy, with TVs and frigobars. A large backyard area, surrounded by a high wall, has a pool and sitting area. Rooms, depending on size, range from $12 to $17 for a single, and $16 to $21 for a double.

On the road leaving Foz in the direction of the state capital, Curitiba, is the **Rafahin Palace Hotel,** Rodovia BR 277, at km 727 (tel. 0455/73-3434). This is a medium-priced hotel, perfect for families traveling with small children. The 96-room hostelry is set on large, park-like grounds with sporting and playground facilities and a small but interesting zoo. The hotel boasts a barbecue restaurant that can accommodate 2,000 patrons, and serves churrasco *rodízio* style for a very reasonable $4.50 per person. Rooms are $38 for singles, $52 for doubles.

WHERE TO DINE: The typical fare in Iguaçu, as in all of southern Brazil, is churrasco, but there are several other interesting eating options as well. One of the more appealing places, both to eat and to hang out in the downtown section of Foz, is the **Centro Gastronômico Rafain,** Avenida Brasil 157 (tel. 73-5599). The Rafain family is well represented in both the local hotel and restaurant sectors, but the Centro Gastronômico has to be their flagship establishment. The very modern complex offers a range of environments: an interior dining room for sophisticated meals, several fast-food counters, and an outdoor café that remains open 24 hours a day. The restaurant is open from 11:30 a.m. till 3 p.m. for lunch, and from 6:30 p.m. till midnight for dinner. In addition to the à la carte menu, there is an above-average buffet served daily for about $7, offering two hot meat dishes, ten or more salad platters, rice and pasta, and a half a dozen tasty desserts, not to mention numerous fruits and compotes. Outside, in separate stalls, there is a pizza stand, bake shop, ice-cream parlor, and a pastel counter selling these meat, shrimp, and cheese pies, all open 18 hours a day. The open-air café serves sandwiches, hamburgers, and draft beer around the clock.

The **Churrascaria Cabeça de Boi,** Avenida Brasil 1325 (tel. 74-1168), is a cavernous barbecue palace serving locally produced meats from the owner's *fazenda* (ranch). Service is buffet style, and you may return to the groaning board as often as your personal capacity will tolerate. In addition to pork, lamb, fowl, and half a dozen cuts of beef, there are many salads and side dishes, including a large baked dourado to carve from. The golden-hued dourado is fished from the Rio Paraná and is considered a delicacy of the region. The meal costs $6 a head, and the restaurant, which holds 500 diners and provides live-music entertainment, is open for lunch from 11:30 a.m. till 4 p.m., and for dinner from 6:30 till 11 p.m. The Cabeça de Boi closes only on Christmas day.

Two other *churrascarias* worth mentioning are both located along the Rodovia das Cataratas. First is the **Churrascaria Charrua** (no phone), across from the Hotel Bourbon, where the barbecue is served *rodízio* style for $5 a person. Farther down the road toward the falls is the **Rafain Churrascaria das Cataratas,** at km 6.5 (tel. 74-2720), which provides a live samba show of music and dance. The restaurant can seat 1,500 diners and is self-service, with ten varieties of meats, other hot and cold platters, and a choice of 25 different desserts.

An unexpected novelty in dining here is the **Al Badiya,** Rua Alm. Barroso 893 (tel. 72-2026), an Arabian restaurant that serves its Middle Eastern delights *rodízio* style. (There is a large population of Arab descent in Foz, and if you're out for a drive around town, be sure to go past the very large and ornate mosque and cultural center that serves the Islamic community.) The round-robin meal includes ten typical dishes, and you more than get your money's worth for the $6 asking price. Open daily for lunch from noon till 3 p.m. and for dinner from 7 p.m. till midnight.

In the same enclave of shops with Al Badiya is the **Abaete** (tel. 74-3084). The restaurant has a very attractive red-brick interior, and serves both international and Brazilian dishes, including paella, codfish, shellfish, and the Bahian specialty vatapá.

SHOPPING: There are several shops along the Rodovia das Cataratas that are worth popping into to browse the wares. One complex is located at the kilometer 2.5 marker, and includes several interesting stores. The **Artesanato de Facas** (tel. 72-1340) sells handcrafted knives, including machetes, very reasonably priced from $5 to $15, leather sheaths included. Next door is the **Vale das Borboletas,** an art gallery, featuring the work of metal sculptor Haroldo Avarenga. The shop also sells better-than-average watercolors, mostly of flowers and other nature subjects indigenous to the region.

The **Artesanato e Chocolate Três Fronteiras** is the largest gift shop in Foz on the Rodovia das Cataratas, at km 11 (tel. 74-3002). The store is filled with bric-a-brac of the butterfly-tray variety, but the real attraction is the homemade chocolate, 70 delicious varieties—the bittersweet with cashews is particularly mouthwatering.

2. PARANÁ

The Brazilian state located immediately to the south of São Paulo is called Paraná. Along its wide western border with Argentina and Paraguay is the state's most famous attraction, the Iguaçu Falls. Paraná's eastern coast is limited to a mere 60 miles in width, encompassing the mouths of two tidal estuaries, the immense Bay of Paranaguá, and that of the smaller Bay of Guaratuba. The city of Paranaguá is Brazil's second-largest port and first in volume of agricultural exports. Two traditional products continue to dominate the state's agricultural production, coffee and *erva-mate,* the bitter herbal tea that has long been the favorite beverage of the southern populations. The capital city of Paraná, called Curitiba, like that of São Paulo, is located 60 miles inland, high on the *planalto,* where the coastal table lands flatten out to an altitude of over 4,000 feet above sea level. Visually, the Paraná countryside and coastal plains alike are stunningly beautiful. Even today the state justifies the praise it once received from a 19th-century visitor, the French botanist Saint-Hilaire, who referred to Paraná as the "earthly paradise of Brazil."

CURITIBA: Paraná's capital is a large city in miniature. All the ingredients of a genuine urban environment are there, limited in volume and spread, but true to proportion and scale. The city is tidy and compact, combining modern high-rises with monumental government buildings of an earlier era, the tree-lined streets and boulevards spaced with numerous parks, plazas, and promenades. The effect is more Swiss than Brazilian. To risk some generalizations about the population of Curitiba, the city's denizens seem to possess a rare blend of formality and warmth, spiced with a subtle humor that often escapes unexpectedly. Curitiba is a university town, and the seat of Paraná's government, as well as center for the state's professional and business life. Men typically go about in jacket and tie, and women are dressed formally in the fashion of the day. In all, Curitiba offers an atmosphere of urbane sophistication, combining provincial intimacy with animated street life, and a fair selection of historical and cultural attractions. Visitors touring Brazil more or less at leisure might find a layover in Curitiba for three or four days much to their taste.

What to See in Curitiba

Curitiba itself is the principal sight, a city that can be easily explored by foot from end to end. But there are several specific points of interest that are worth noting.

Since many of the city's tourist-grade hotels are located in the vicinity of the **Praça Osório,** this small park is a good place to begin a walking tour. Walk easterly along the pedestrian promenade called the Rua das Flores and turn left on Avenida Marechal Floriano Peixoto until reaching the **Praça Tiradentes,** the original hub from which Curitiba grew outward. The blocks bordering this square are narrower and more irregular than those in the newer parts of town, and it is among these streets that you will find the city's historic sector. A number of 18th-century public spaces and churches may be visited, including the **Romário Martins House,** the **Igreja São Francisco,** the city's two oldest buildings, and the **Praça Garibaldi,** also surrounded by historic buildings, and site of a craft fair every Sunday.

Continue on in a northerly direction from the Praça Garibaldi and turn right on Rua Carlos Cavalcanti. After several blocks you will come to the large park called the **Passeio Público,** a peaceful green zone in the heart of the city with boating on interconnected ponds, islands filled with monkeys, gardens, a zoo, and a small aquarium—even a bucolic park-restaurant called Pascuale. Return along Rua Presidente Faria to Rua das Flores.

Rua das Flores, a wide pedestrian mall several blocks long, is the evening gathering place for Curitiba's residents. Both sides of the promenade are lined with shops and cafés, not to mention the several florists and flower stands from which the mall derives its name. The cafés along the section of the strip called Avenida Luíz Xavier has been dubbed the **Boca Maldita** (Devil's Tongue) for it is here that the various currents of the city's population—politicians, bankers, artists, and intellectuals—meet and exchange ideas, argue politics, or bemoan world events from the Brazilian perspective.

Lodgings in Curitiba

As noted above, most of Curitiba's better hotels are located in the vicinity of the Praça Osório and Rua das Flores. The **Slaviero Palace Hotel,** Rua Senador Alencar Guimarães 50 (tel. 041/222-8722), is located on a block-long pedestrian alley of its own, two blocks from Rua das Flores. The 113-room hotel is modern and well maintained, offering rooms at half the normal rates on the weekends since Curitiba's hotels tend to be used primarily on weekdays by travelers doing business in the capital. The discounted room includes a free feijoada on Saturday. Both the rooms and interior spaces of this four-star hotel are pleasant and fully equipped. The Le Doyen restaurant serves good international food. Rates range from $40 to $50 for single accommodations, and $50 to $60 for doubles.

The **Hotel Del Rey,** Rua Ermelino de Leão 18 (tel. 041/224-3033), is a 142-room hotel with a curved exterior occupying the corner of Rua das Flores closest to the Praça Osório. While the interior looks as if Liberace were the decorator—the famed performer would have admired the outrageous and exaggerated plushness of the place—it would be hard to argue with the room prices of this four-star hotel with all the associated services, including a tea room, travel agency, bar, and restaurant. Prices for singles are $28 to $35, and doubles run $40 to $49.

On the same block several doors down is the **Curitiba Palace Hotel,** Rua Ermelino de Leão 45 (tel. 041/224-1222), a modern red-brick building. All rooms facing the street have balconies, and the rooms themselves are crisply decorated, with queen-size beds. As with most hotels in the region, rooms can be heated or air-conditioned, depending on the time of year. The Curitba Palace has 71 rooms in all, and appears to be a bargain at $24 to $32 single and $26 to $33 double. The hotel also has its own restaurant and inside parking facilities.

Directly on the square at Praça Osório 63 is the **Tourist Universo Hotel** (tel. 041/223-5816). This small hotel has only 48 rooms, but they are very serviceable and inexpensive. Single rooms with mock-colonial furnishings and gallery-white walls cost between $20 and $26, while doubles range between $22 and $29. The two-room suite is only $33. The rooms facing the front have large windows and are very bright. The house restaurant, called the Debret, serves an excellent Wednesday feijoada for $5.50.

Curitiba's only in-town five-star hotel is the **Araucária Flat Hotel,** Rua Doutor Faivre 846 (tel. 041/262-3030), located away from the center between the cross streets Rua Nilo Cairo and Rua Com. Macedo. All 84 units are suites, varying slightly in size, and have kitchen alcoves with separate sink, fridge, and hotplate burners. Daily rates are $47, $55, and $68, and weekly rates run $218, $249, and $308. The Araucária has the appearance of being a fashionable address in town, and houses one of the city's best (and most expensive) restaurants.

The **Hotel Paraná Suite,** Rua Lourenço Pinto 452 (tel. 041/223-8282) is near Avenida 7 de Setembro, where many office and government buildings are located on the outer ring of the urban center. The 110 suites each contain two separate rooms, plus a small kitchen. The standard accommodations cost $31 for one, $37 for two. Deluxe suites are air-conditioned, but otherwise the same, and range between $38 and $40.

AN OUT-OF-TOWN DELUXE CHOICE. The **Iguaçu Campestre** is a small, luxury motel outside the city on the BR 116, at km 396 (tel. 041/262-5315), on the road that connects Curitiba with São Paulo to the north. Each of the 47 rooms has its own walled-in outdoor garden and attached car port. As public transportation to the suburbs is infrequent, it would indeed be advisable to have a car while staying at the Iguaçu Campestre. If given adequate notice, however, the staff will pick you up at the Curitiba airport. This hotel is one of the few in Curitiba that has a swimming pool. Single rooms are $47; doubles, $51.

Dining in Curitiba

In town, a favorite hangout for professionals and politicians is the **Scupper,** Dr. Muricy 1089 (tel. 232-4324), which is essentially a seafood restaurant. The interior has a pub-like atmosphere, with a bar and various separate rooms for dining. Most meals cost between $6 and $10. Open for dinner only, from 7 p.m. to 2 a.m.

The **Restaurante Mali,** Rua Francisco Torres 427, despite its name is a neighborhood Japanese restaurant. The neighborhood in question is quiet and residential, and is within reasonable walking distance of the central hotel sector.

The Mali offers standard Japanese fare, including sushi, for between $6 and $10. Servings are large, however, and one plate generally will be sufficient for two people. Mali is open daily for lunch and dinner from noon to 3 p.m. and 6 p.m. till midnight.

The main gastronomic quarter in Curitiba is located in a suburb called Santa Felicidade. It was settled initially by Italian truck farmers, and today the wide principal avenue is lined with restaurants, most of which serve Italian food. A favorite of the locals is **Dom Antônio,** Avenida Manoel Ribas 6121 (tel. 272-1431). Dom Antônio, is enormous, an eclectic octagonal palazzo strung between two medieval-looking fortifications, complete with stone towers. The interior is cavernous, as up to 2,000 diners can be accommodated for the *rodízio di pasta*—a continuous round of 11 different homemade pasta and meat dishes. House wines are the product of the owner's own small farms. The *rodízio,* without beverage, is slightly more than $4 per person. Lunch is served from 11:30 a.m. to 3 p.m. and dinner is from 7 p.m. until the last customer goes home.

Similar in theme and style is the **Ristorante Siciliano Pinherão,** Avenida Manoel Ribas 5437 (tel. 272-1974). Part churrascaria, part pasta buffet, the restaurant can serve up to 500 guests simultaneously. The cost of the meal is about $4.50, and food is served throughout the day from 11:30 a.m. to 11 p.m.

The **Kamikaze,** Avenida Manoel Ribas 6354 (tel. 272-1575), has a reputation for serving the best Japanese food in the city. The owner, a former Zen master, recently arrived from Japan where he lived a contemplative monastic existence for many years, is particularly hospitable to Americans. The average meal, including sake or rice wine, is about $10. Dinner only, Tuesday to Friday from 7 p.m. to 2 a.m., and both lunch and dinner on weekends; closed Monday.

A TRIP TO PARANAGUÁ, MORRETES, AND ANTONINA: A visit to

the bay towns on the Paraná coast is an absolute must for anyone who has traveled as far as Curitiba. Paranaguá, Morretes, and Antonina are the three signal destinations on this excursion. From Curitiba, you can travel to the shore by rail or by highway. The best option is to do both, staying overnight in the sleepy port town of Antonina. If this is not possible, you can also visit all three locales in a single day—somewhat hurriedly—by bus alone, or even by combining bus and rail, assuming a bit of prior planning to ensure good transportation connections.

Take the early-morning **train** (leaving at 7 or 8:30 a.m.) from the railroad station *(ferrodoviária)* in Curitiba (on Avenida Afonso Camargo) to Paranaguá. The descent is one of the most dramatic and breathtaking railway rides you will ever experience. The construction of the track is considered to be as daring an engineering feat as any ever attempted in the world. As you descend the steep and rugged hills toward the sea, you pass over 41 bridges and viaducts, some of which seem suspended in mid-air, and through 14 tunnels carved from the mountainous rock. One ridge spans a river chasm some 350 feet wide, and the Viaducto do Carvalho hangs 2,000 feet above the valley floor. Make sure you pick a clear day for the descent, because in addition to the thrills, the scenery is unforgettable.

The trip down to Paranaguá by train takes 3 to 3½ hours and the number of passengers is limited, so either get to the station at least an hour before departure, or (preferably) buy your ticket a day in advance. For information on departure times and fares, call 234-8411. The same trip by car or bus can be as short as an hour and a half.

Paranaguá

You needn't spend much time in Paranaguá itself. The town is a sprawling, active port, and even though it's one of Brazil's oldest cities (founded in 1585), what remains of the past is too scattered about to visit conveniently. Besides, your time can be better spent in the two more interesting towns up the bay.

One popular attraction in Paranaguá is the **Archeology and Popular Art Museum,** Rua XV de Novembro 562, located in the small historical quarter. Open Tuesday through Friday from 1 till 5 p.m. and Saturday through Monday from noon to 5 p.m., the museum occupies a building that briefly housed a Jesuit high school from 1755 to 1759, when the Society of Jesus—trying to protect the Indians from extermination—was summarily expelled from Brazil by order of the Marques de Pombal, the most powerful prime minister and statesman Portugal has ever known.

The **waterfront market** in Paranaguá—which is a free port for Paraguay—can be very animated, and is worth a visit if time permits.

En Route to Morretes

For the return, take the bus to Morretes. You will begin the trip on BR 277, and turn off onto the charming **Estrada da Graciosa,** which traverses the marshy lowlands at the headwater of the Paranaguá estuary, continues along the foothills of the Marumbi mountains across the **Marumbi State Park,** and then connects with the BR 116 which goes on to Curitiba. There is good camping, hiking, and climbing throughout the region.

Morretes itself is at the headwater, where the Rio Nhundiaquara meets the tidal waters of the bay. The Paranaguá train also stops at Morretes, and on Sunday only, a special train runs from Curitiba via Morretes and on to Antonina.

In Morretes, walk around to savor the ambience of this quiet river town, and stop at the **Nhundiaquara Hotel,** Rua General Carneiro 13 (tel. 041/462-1228), for a glass of the aged and golden cachaça that is the town's principal product.

Also keep an eye out for announcements of musical events, especially **fandango** dances. The fandango is a regional favorite of the Paranaence coastal inhabitants, first introduced by the Spanish in colonial times, who for many years exercised considerable influence on the local culture.

Antonina

Heading back toward the bay along PR 408 for another ten miles (this is a state road; the PR stands for Paraná), you will come to Antonina, once a vital port in its own right but now virtually retired from the pages of active economic history. There is something magical about Antonina, the old wharf with its simple municipal market, the all-embracing presence of the upper bay, the well-worn buildings—a treasure of scale and antiquity.

Since the decline of its port, Antonina now functions as a weekend retreat for city folk, but the town remains a genuine backwater, not a resort. Even the infrastructure of the old port, which now stands dormant on the outskirts of the village, seems benign, like an industrial ghost town, more dignified and monumental in repose perhaps than it ever was as an active waterfront. Studies are now under way to determine how to ensure the preservation of the old port buildings and to what end they should be employed.

STAYING THE NIGHT. The best hotel in Antonina is the **Regency Capela Antonina,** Praça Cel. Macedo 208 (tel. 041/432-1357). The setting of this 37-room hotel is almost perfect: one side faces the bay and the other a quiet plaza and an old colonial church. The hotel grounds were once a Jesuit mission, and the current structures were constructed among the remaining ruins. Beyond the aesthetic, the practical accoutrements required by urban weekenders are not lacking. There is a good pool and fine tennis court. The overall impression of the hotel is of a comfortable, country boarding house. Some rooms face the water and have balconies. Weekend rates are $20 to $30; and weekdays, only $15 to $20.

EATING IN ANTONINA. Only on the Paranaense coast can you eat **barreado,** probably the best-kept culinary secret in Brazil. The dish was first prepared by the poor folk along the Paraná coast as a Carnival meal, one that would provide food for several days and require little tending while it cooked. Barreado is a kind of ragoût, a stringy beef stew. The secret to the dish's unforgettable taste, however, is in its unique preparation. The ingredients—beef, salt pork, and herbs—are placed in successive layers in a large urn-shaped clay pot. The pot is then "barreada," or sealed. First a banana leaf is tied across the opening, then the cover is placed on the mouth of the pot and hermetically sealed, using a paste of ashes and farinha (manioc flour). The pot is then placed in the oven of a wood stove and cooked at a low, steady temperature through the night. (Today, normal gas or electric ovens are usually used rather than wood fires; and in many homes—but not the better restaurants—pressure cookers substitute for the clay pots.) The finished barreado is served in bowls, with farinha, fried bananas, orange slices, and rice. And to drink, a fine glass of Morretes cachaça. The result is an unambiguous culinary rival of Brazil's other great national and regional specialties, feijoada and the moquecas of Bahia.

Many restaurants throughout the region serve barreado. But if you have only a single day or afternoon in Antonina, then there is only one choice, the **Barreado da Ieda,** Avenida Conde Matarazzo (tel. 432-1372). The restaurant is off the road, overlooking the bay, immediately past the Clube Nautico; look for a driveway on the left when heading in the direction of the old port from the center of Antonina. Dona Ieda caters mostly to the carriage trade, and is open only on weekends and holidays, beginning at noon and going into the evening as long as there is demand. The cost of the sumptuous meal is about $6.

If you have more time in Antonina, or if you visit the town during the week when Dona Ieda's is closed, there are several very appealing restaurants right on the old wharf. **Tia Rosinha,** Rua Cons. Antônio Prade 54 (tel. 432-1503), is a family-run place opposite the old municipal market. The restaurant specializes in seafood, but barreado is also a regular menu item. Tia Rosinha is open daily and closes in the early evening. The most expensive meal in the restaurant is about $6.

(The Nhundiaquara Hotel back in Morretes also serves a fine barreado with all the trimmings for only $2.75.)

VILA VELHA: A second day trip from Curitiba involves a visit to the **Vila Velha Park,** where the combined forces of time and nature have carved from glacial sandstone deposits some two dozen massive rock formations, many of which stand alone in open fields like monumental stabiles. There are several hiking trails in the park, a public swimming pool, and three deep craters filled with water, into one of which an elevator descends for a closeup look at the vegetation-covered walls and the placid bottom.

Vila Velha is reached by taking the road to Ponta Grossa, a large inland city about 75 miles west of Curitiba.

About 15 miles outside the capital city there is the old water-driven mill of a former *erva-mate* plantation. The mill is open to the public, and worth visiting to learn something of Paraná's rich mate economic cycle, and about the somewhat elaborate production and processing of the plant.

3. SANTA CATARINA

In its dimensions, Santa Catarina state is the reverse of Paraná, its neighbor to the north. Santa Catarina has a coastline 300 miles long and only the narrowest frontier with Argentina to the west. The state is also relatively small, like those of the northeast region of Brazil. In the northeast, however, the interiors of the states are parched with badlands. Santa Catarina's interior is a mixture of bucolic and prosperous farm country, rich hilly pastures, and great forest lands. In fact the state possesses the largest forested areas in all of southern Brazil.

The state's population derives primarily from three distinct ethnic groups, Acorian Portuguese, German, and Italian. Even today each group seems to dominate its respective region or regions, as if Santa Catarina were consciously organized into cantons, like Switzerland. The Acorians were the first to arrive, and then as now were primarily fishermen. Predictably, they settled on an island, the island of Santa Catarina, where today the state's capital, Florianópolis, is located. Throughout the 19th century Germans and Italians came in large numbers and settled on interior lands to farm. They established family holdings and duplicated the mixed farming methods they had brought with them from Europe. Some 60% of the state's population still lives in rural areas and is involved in agriculture.

Santa Catarina also has its urban side, and can claim the fourth-largest industrial output of all Brazil's 23 states. Cities like Joinville and Blumenau, founded as rural German colonies in the mid-19th century, have evolved into robust factory towns. In the large urban centers much of the German influence in local society has disappeared, blending into the general Brazilian reality, the few remaining visible signs of the culture reduced to its commercial components: beer festivals, restaurants, and cabaret entertainment. In the countryside the opposite is true: there is a healthy rural German-ness in the small towns and on the farms, where tradition is honored naturally, without fanfare or self-consciousness. The same can be said about the Açorian way of life in the fishing villages, and the Italian customs as they continue to be practiced in the valley of the Itajai and the wine district to the west. A traveler in Santa Catarina, therefore, who truly wishes to experience what the state tourist authority quite accurately portrays as its remarkable ethnic diversity, must avoid the cities and wander in the countryside.

As is typical along the Brazilian coast, the mountains are not far from the sea. And the rise is sudden, climbing over 4,000 feet at one point in the short distance of five miles. Much of the state's farmland is highly domesticated and picturesque, a subtropical version, yet similar in feeling to the European countryside. Here, too, as in Europe, there are winter frosts. The only town in Brazil that receives regular dustings of snow, São Joaquim, is in these hills.

Despite its inland attractions, most tourist movement in Santa Catarina is confined to the state's seashore, and so for this first edition of the guide I will concentrate on describing some representative beach areas. A traveler with limited time who is touring several locales in southern Brazil, for example, will almost certainly want to include Florianópolis, the state's island capital, in his or her itinerary. The only problem is that once you've been there, you are likely to have a typical reaction, wishing you could stay longer.

THE SANTA CATARINA SEASHORE: The island of Santa Catarina itself has 42 beaches, a strand for every taste, pocketbook, and age group. And the coast northward, toward the turnoff road for Blumenau, is dotted with fine seashore watering holes and fashionable beach resorts.

FLORIANÓPOLIS: The capital occupies the central third of Santa Catarina Island, which is 25 miles long from north to south, with a 6-mile girth at its widest point. The link to the mainland is made easily via two public bridges, one of which is Brazil's largest suspension bridge, of similar late 19th-century design to that of the Brooklyn, Manhattan, and Williamsburg bridges that span the East River in New York City.

The Sights

The island is a large beach community, with a limited urban atmosphere, uncrowded and slow-paced except during the summer months of January and February when it fills up with seasonal residents and visitors. In addition to the bay and ocean beaches, there is also a large lagoon, the **Lagoa da Conceição**, several exhilarating vistas from hillside overlooks like the **Morro das Sete Voltas**, and the preserved remains or ruins of three old fortifications from the colonial period. The shoreline is divided into three sections, the north, south, and east coasts.

After choosing a hotel, you can tour the island by public transportation, cab, or rented car. The most famous and fashionable beaches are those on the northern shore, **Jureré, Canasvieiras, Ponta das Canas,** and **Ingleses.** Many of the island's best hotels are found along these beaches, and there are many houses available for short-term rentals.

On the opposite (southern) end of the island are the more rustic and utilitarian beaches. Here you will find the still-active Acorian fishing community, and delight at the colorful, wedding-cake designs of the old houses and the simplicity of the churches, both so reminiscent of what their forebearers left behind in distant Portugal.

The most historic section, the birthplace of the Acorian colony, is **Ribeirão da Ilha**, on the bay side.

On the eastern shore, the stretch of the island most exposed to the sea is **Joaquina** beach, where national and international surf championships take place each year. On other nearby beaches, like **Barra da Lagoa,** you can watch the fishermen work their nets and pull large catches of mullet from the sea with the aid of many cooperative hands. Also near the eastern shore, the Lagoa da Conceição accompanies the coast for several miles, surrounded by a network of enormous dunes. There are many excellent seafood restaurants on the road that encircles the lagoon, where the specialty is a *sequência,* a succession of shrimp and other seafood platters that allow you to sample everything from the daily catch.

The road around the lagoon has several names, each of which designates a particular activity. **Avenida das Rendeiras** is lined with small wooden shacks where female descendants of the original Açorian islanders pursue the ancient handwork of their race, the creation of *renda de bilro,* bobbin-lace cloth for table coverings, clothes, or for whatever other use you may wish.

Each year on a weekend in mid-June the **Festa da Tainha** takes place on the Barra da Lagoa beach. *Tainha* means mullet, the most abundant of the fishes in these waters. Temporary restaurants are set up the length of the beach, where the mullet, shrimp, and other specialties are prepared in a variety of ways. The event also includes folkloric presentations like *brincadeira de boi,* a benign version of *farra do boi,* a somewhat barbaric ritual which is outlawed, but still widely practiced throughout Santa Catarina in local festivals. Originally a *farra do boi* was a game of running the bulls. For some years now, however, the game has degenerated. The bull, having come to symbolize a demon, is slowly tortured to death by the participants. The activity, which has Brazilian ecologists and local authorities up in arms, was once confined to Holy Week, but is now practiced frequently, and even accompanies other celebrations, like baptisms and birthdays.

Where to Stay

The most appealing lodgings in Florianópolis are the hotels and resorts that occupy favored positions along the beaches or in the hills. The **Jureré Praia Hotel** (tel. 0482/66-0459) has 63 cabañas, rented for a minimum of one week during the summer but available for overnights during the off-season, and then at a fair discount depending on your ability to negotiate. The cabañas are very unusual in design, made from hi-tech building materials: exposed steel I-beams, and arched metal roofs that look like segments cut from giant industrial drums. What could have been a design disaster somehow works very well, probably because all the building materials are first rate. The interiors also have modern furnishings, and feature large living rooms, dining areas with attached kitchenettes, and separate bedrooms. Each also contains a full bath, color TV, pots, pans, and full table service. Outside there is an attached car port in the front, and in the backyard, a patio with a brick barbecue grill. The spacious grounds overlook the protected Jureré beach, and are very well tended. The hotel has its own supermarket, restaurant, swimming pool, tennis court, and equipment for a full range of water sports. The daily price for a double is $55. Some of the units are larger, and will accommodate as many as ten people, according to the management.

The **Maria do Mar,** Rodovia Vigílio Várzea (tel. 0482/33-3009), is located in Saco Grande, a hillside neighborhood facing the northern bay, near the Praia de Cacupé. This is a new 60-room hotel, rustic in design, all in brick and timber, and occupying a beautiful natural hillside setting. The general environs of the Maria do Mar are sparsely populated, and the area seems perfect for long, leisurely walks. The rooms are attractive and reasonably priced: $38 for a single and $42 for two.

The *Centro* or downtown section of Florianópolis is located only a few minutes from the island's airport. The principal square is called Praça XV, notable for its century-old fig tree. A circular bench surrounds the tree, which serves as a kind of tribal function as a meeting place for locals, or a quiet spot for reading the daily paper. There are several first-class hotels in this area, and on the side streets that look out over the water.

The **Florianópolis Palace Hotel,** Rua Artista Bittencourt 02 (tel. 0482/22-9633), is several blocks inland from the Praça XV. The hotel is a classic of its kind, with 93 rooms, all decorated in the voluminous mission style, with large tile baths. The hotel has a thermal pool with Jacuzzi. Rates are $66 for a single and $77 for a double.

The **Castelmar Hotel,** Rua Felipe Schmidt 200 (tel. 0482/22-3228), on a hill several blocks from the water, has 96 suites, some with two bedrooms. The Castelmar has a very adequate restaurant, where for about $10 you can eat *catupiry,* a tasty cheese and shrimp casserole. All accommodations are relatively spacious, with separate sleeping and living areas; singles are priced between $43 and $54, while doubles cost $52 to $63. A middling walk around the curve of the bay from the hotel will bring you to a residential beach neighborhood along Avenida Jornalista Rubens de Arruda Ramos where there is constant late-night activity all week in a selection of restaurants, bars, and nightclubs along the strip.

The 100-room **Hotel Diplomat,** Avenida Paulo Fontes 800 (tel. 0482/23-4455), overlooks the old metal bridge that connects the city with the continent on the opposite shore. All rooms have queen-sized beds, and cost $56 for single occupancy and $69 for two.

A less expensive in-town alternative is the **Marambaia Hotel,** Avenida Rio Branco 172 (tel. 0482/23-2323). The hotel's 40 suites are large and airy, with good-sized kitchens. The cost for a single is $29, and two people will pay $37.

Where to Dine

On the lake, try the **Samuka,** Avenida das Rendeiras 1001 (tel. 32-0024), for a round-robin of shrimp dishes. Your meals begins with bolinhos de ciri (crab cake balls) and caldo de camarão (a stocky shrimp soup). Then come the platters: breaded shrimp, shrimp with garlic, and steamed shrimp, to name a few. The local pinga (sugarcane liquor) is clear white and goes very well with the meal or an apéritif. At the Samuka you can eat and drink to your total satisfaction for about $9 per person.

For in-town dining, there is the **Lindacap,** Rua Felipe Schmidt 178 (tel. 22-0558), with a panoramic view of the bay. The Lindacap is what residents consider a traditional restaurant. The specialty of the house is tainha, mullet served with ova, the fish's egg sack, which is fried in manioc flour, at $4. Other favorites are marreco (domesticated wild duck) at $4.50, and rabada ensopada (oxtail stew) for $3.50.

BEYOND FLORIANÓPOLIS: Roughly an hour from Florianópolis, heading north on highway BR 101, is a swank beach resort called the **Plaza Itapema,** at km 101 (tel. 0473/44-2212). The Plaza Itapema has 173 absolutely gigantic rooms and suites, each very tastefully decorated with enormous wood-decked verandas. To give you an idea, the single-room veranda measures about 20 by 12 feet, and those of the suites is 30 by 12 feet. The hotel has several pools and a wide-aproned outdoor café that overlooks the ocean beach. At one end of the property a bridge leads to a private island where there is a thermal pool and sauna. Other features are a boat marina, and a nine-hole golf course, with an additional nine holes to be completed by the end of 1988. Breakfast and dinner are included in the cost of accommodations: $70 for a room and $100 for a suite. The hotel is an excellent bargain for resort lovers who prize comfort and privacy.

About three miles up the highway, over a large hill, is the popular beachside spa **Camboriú.** There are 80 hotels both along the five-mile long beach and on the backstreets of this town of 40,000, which swells to a population of 400,000 during the summer vacation months. If you are looking for the summer scene along the Santa Catarina coast, Camboriú is the place. Typical of the medium-priced hotels facing the ocean is the **Marambaia Cassino Hotel,** Avenida Atlântica 300 (tel. 0473/66-0099), with 111 rooms priced between $25 and $33 a night.

BLUMENAU: About 30 miles inland from Camboriú is the industrial city of Blumenau, where much of the population can trace its ancestry from immigrant German stock. People you meet have names like Heide, Güenter, and Dieter, and look the part, except for the fact that they are also thoroughly Brazilian. For those who cherish beerfests, oompah bands, and Middle European cooking, Blumenau is worth a visit. The Oktoberfest occupies 15 days each year, during which beer is sold in the streets from *bierwagens*—barrels mounted between two bicycles.

The best German food (and view) can be had at the **Frohsinn** (tel. 22-2137), on the Morro do Aipin hill overlooking the river just outside of town. Another good choice is the **Cavalinho Branco,** Avenida Rio Branco 165 (tel. 22-4300), which serves very large portions.

An excellent and relatively inexpensive first-class hotel with all the facilities is the **Himmelblau,** Rua 7 de Setembro no. 1415 (tel. 0473/22-5800). The hotel has 145 rooms, and **Le Foyer,** one of the best restaurants in the city for French and international food, with entrees ranging from $5 to $8. Accommodations at the hotel are priced at $30 for singles and $37 for doubles.

4. RIO GRANDE DO SUL

A native of Rio Grande do Sul is called a *gaucho* (ga-*oo*-shoo). The same term is used to describe the very unique cowboy culture of the pampas, that great expanse of grasslands stretching across southern Brazil through Uruguay and into northern Argentina. Vast herds of cattle still roam throughout this rangeland, providing meat and leather for much of Brazil's domestic consumption and for export as well. And the cowboy, with his lonesome ways, still has a function here, despite being portrayed most often in his Sunday finery: dressed in baggy pantaloons and white linen shirt with red kerchief, and shod in high pleated boots with silver stirrups. As long as cattle roam freely, grazing in nature's pastures, there will be gauchos to round them up and drive them to market. The image of the solitary gaucho in the saddle, sipping chimarrão (sugarless mate tea) through a silver straw (a *bomba*) from a dried gourd called a *cuia* is not just a nostalgic re-creation of the past to entertain the tourist trade, but has a strong basis in reality, and accounts for the fiercely independent nature of the state's political history.

Border settlers, like those in Rio Grande do Sul, had to be active in defense of their territory until the respective Spanish and Portuguese authorities could finally settle on their permanent boundaries. Not surprisingly, the influence of the Spanish throughout Rio Grande do Sul is extensive, if subtle; even the Portuguese spoken here has a more clipped cadence, like castellano, very different from the lilting accent of the Cariocas in Rio. Originally the rangelands were divided into vast *latifúndios* (landed estates) and society was ruled by local *caudillos* (strongmen) and populists, some of whom, like Getúlio Vargas and João Goulart, rose to national prominence and power. Even today large landowners still wield the real power in the state. And while Rio Grande do Sol has also evolved in modern times to become the nation's most literate state, with considerable industrial might added to its traditional agrarian economy, a strong hint of gaucho individualism and hauteur still flavors the land.

The macho culture of the south was tempered—but by no means displaced—by the heavy influx of European immigrants in the last century, primarily Germans and Italians. The regions settled by these peoples are today the favorite attractions of visitors to the state. Which is not to say one should avoid the pampas. Hardly! Travelers with the time and inclination to explore the state could do no better than to wander at will among the villages of the range country, and travel all the way to São Borjas, birthplace of Vargas and Goulart, the state's western frontier with Argentina. Furthermore, a truly sentimental journey can be made among the ruins of the Jesuit Indian missions dating from the 17th century. The ruins, called the *Sete Povos das Missões Orientais* (the Seven Settlements of the Eastern Missions) are found in São Borjas, and in the surrounding district at São Nicolau, São Lourenço, São Miguel, São Luíz, São Ângelo, and São João. The most extensive and best preserved of the ruins is in São Miguel.

Nonetheless, the mainline of tourism in Rio Grande do Sul is in the Serra, the hill country, which is much closer to Porto Alegre, the state's capital and principal entry point for air and bus arrivals. Porto Alegre holds no major appeal for the casual tourist; it is a large and not particularly attractive city. But 70 miles inland, however, is some extraordinarily scenic landscape, rivaling anything you will see elsewhere in Brazil, a country whose reservoir of natural beauty seems at times infinite. Our tour will take us first to Gramado and Canela, the ideal base for either a brief or extended stay in the region. From there we explore the *colônias*, where descendants of Italian immigrants produce virtually all of Brazil's table wine. Visits to the wineries and sampling of the wares is much encouraged. Other excursions will include a day trip to Itaimbezinho, the "Grand Canyon of Brazil," a visit to an art treasure in Caxias do Sul, and a stopover in Torres, the state's most popular beach town.

PORTO ALEGRE: The capital of Rio Grande do Sul emerged from a settlement originally built below the confluence of five rivers, on the Rio Guaiba. Although Porto Alegre is a deep-water port, and one of Brazil's busiest, the open sea is over 150 miles distant, reached by crossing the Lagoa dos Patos, the largest freshwater lagoon in South America. The city was built on two levels: the upper town contains the oldest sections, while the waterfront and commercial district are on the lower level, much of it on landfill. A pleasant vantage point with a good view of the Guaiba estuary is on the **Morro de Santa Teresa.**

Porto Alegre is connected to other major Brazilian centers by regular air flights and bus service.

Where to Stay

The **Plaza São Rafael,** Avenida Alberto Bins 514 (tel. 0512/21-6100), is the only five-star hotel in the city. Both the suites and standard accommodations in the 284-room hostelry are large and well appointed, with attractive furnishings. The standard rooms also have separate alcoves with a table and seating area. The best rooms offer views of the river. Rates are $72 single and $82 double.

Also centrally located downtown is the **Alfred Porto Alegre Hotel,** Rua Senhor dos Passos 105 (tel. 0512/26-2555), a 94-room high-rise priced at $38 for a single and $46 for a double.

A bargain choice is the **Hotel Praça da Matriz,** Largo João Amorim do Alburquerque 72 (tel. 0512/25-5772). Located on a square lined with trees and government buildings, this is the perfect stop for an overnight in Porto Alegre if your tastes can accommodate the unadorned as well as the inexpensive simultaneously. The hotel occupies an old colonial house, and offers 22 large, clean rooms. The general atmosphere is seedy in a very graceful sort of way. The hotel's interior has many nooks and unexpected stairways, and some rooms open onto a catwalk of connected verandas overlooking an interior courtyard. Rooms are priced between $11 and $14.

Where to Dine

The Plaza São Rafael Hotel houses one of the city's best restaurants, **Le Bon Gourmet.** The service is French and formal, and the à la carte menu is changed every three months. The restaurant also features five daily platters priced between $7 and $10, and serves a churrasco, including nine varieties of meat with side dishes, for $7.

The **Alfred Coffee Shop,** in the hotel of the same name, is a pleasant rooftop restaurant with an excellent view of the city, ideal for lunch.

The **Portovelho,** Rua Andrade Neves 42 (tel. 25-6398), is a popular luncheon spot for businessmen and government officials. The lunch buffet features half a dozen hot dishes and another dozen cold platters and salads. Cost, with beverage, is about $5.

The **Churrascaria Sací** is located in the city's soccer stadium at Avenida Parque Cacique 891 (tel. 33-9090), and provides all you can eat for about $5.50.

A popular neighborhood restaurant is the **Restaurante Bon Ami,** Avenida Senador Salgado Filho 364, which serves typical meat, fish, and pasta dishes for between $3 and $4.

Souvenirs

For excellent craft items gathered from every corner of Rio Grande do Sul, try the **Artesanato Rio Grande do Sul,** Avenida Senador Salgado Filho 366, right next door to the Bon Ami. Here you will find both individual and craft art, painting, bolos, whips, sheepskin rugs, and panchos.

GRAMADO AND CANELA: These two picturesque mountain towns

stand side by side, high in the Serra Gaucha. Gramado can be reached by two routes: via Novo Hamburgo on BR 116, the faster and more industrialized highway, and via Taquara, the slower and more scenic way over state roads. The distance is roughly 75 miles along either route, adding another 5 miles for Canela. Originally both Gramado and Canela were immigrant colonies, the Germans arriving in the first quarter, and the Italians in the third quarter, of the 19th century.

Throughout their growth and development, both towns have shown a preference for Bavarian styling in their architecture, and so comparison with kindred towns in Europe has become inevitable, though the similarities are at best superficial. The area surrounding Gramado and Canela, which also includes the towns of Nova Petrópolis and São Francisco de Paula (which are of similar pedigree) is known as the Região das Hortâncias (Region of the Hydrangeas). Indeed the large and fragrant pom-pom–shaped flower seems to grow everywhere, both as ornamental bordering for roads and pathways and in wild clusters in the fields and woods. Gramado and Canela in particular are "in" spots, favorite summer and winter spas for the well-heeled. And Gramado hosts the very chic Brazilian National Film Festival every March, drawing to the town many of Brazil's top entertainment and film industry personalities, in addition to hordes of distinguished and sophisticated moviegoers.

The Sights

There are surprisingly many excursions that can be made around the Region of the Hydrangeas, including at least one "must-see" spot, the Canyon of Itaimbezinho.

AROUND CANELA. The **Parque Cascada do Caracol** is located five miles from Canela, and can be reached by a public bus called the "Caracol Circular," with four departures a day from the village. The park is a popular campsite, but the main attraction for day-trippers is a view of the narrow but dramatic cataract with a sheer drop of over 400 feet. At the entrance to the park you are likely to see several vendors standing behind large pots of boiling water. The pots are used to cook *pinhões*, the large pine nuts that are stripped from the volleyball-size cones of the towering *pinheiro*, the emblematic tree of the region. The boiled nuts are very tasty, similar in taste and consistency to roasted chestnuts.

There are two other points of interest in the vicinity of the falls. First is **Ferradura Point,** which is reached by traveling an additional five miles beyond the park along a dirt road to an overlook of the same canyon, which has descended to a depth of over 1,200 feet here. The Rio Caí, which can be seen at the bottom flowing between the narrow canyon walls, seems pencil-thin from this high perch. A trek down a woodsy path to see the **Araucária Milenar** (Thousand-Year-Old Pine) is also worthwhile. Whatever the actual age of the phenomenon (estimates are between 500 and 700 years), how often do you get a chance to see a tree 150 feet tall, with a circumference of almost 40 feet at the base of the trunk?

The **Parque Kurt Mentz** was donated to the town by a local figure from his own extensive holdings as a 500-acre conifer preserve. The main reason to visit this park is for its three *mirantes,* vantage points from which to view Canela in its lovely valley setting. The three hills have colorful names—Dedão (big toe), Pelado (naked), and queimado (scorched earth)—and endless vistas over wild, orchid-grown hills, apple orchards and vineyards.

AROUND GRAMADO. Like Campos do Jordão, the mountain retreat near São Paulo, Gramado is a town that caters to a year-round stream of weekend and seasonal visitors. Throughout the year the town hosts several important festivals and cultural events. The **Festa da Colônia** in January commemorates Gramado's Italian and German immigrant origins with traditional music and food. The annual **Brazilian Film Festival** takes place in March. The **Feira de Gramado** is the winter version of the Festa da Colônia, scheduled in June of each year. In September there is a major crafts fair, the **Feira Nacional de Artesanato**. And during July of even-numbered years Gramado hosts an **International Music Festival**.

Gramado is a pretty village, where several good hotels, restaurants, and shops are all within convenient walking distance of each other.

ITAIMBEIZINHO. The morning we left for Itaimbezinho, my host played down the side trip. We were going to some national park, about an hour and a half from Gramado, "through cowboy country." The trip was visually stimulating. We sped along over the hardtop that crossed over the undulating rangeland, where *fazendeiros* (ranchers) punched cattle for the country's meat market. The first town we came to was São João de Paula, a kind of regional depot for grains and meat bound for distribution elsewhere. As we neared the city, the sides of the road were festooned with huge flower-bearing hedges—ice-blue and pale-pink hydrangeas burned black by a recent frost which, though it was only late March, a cold front from Argentina had brought in its wake.

Beyond the municipality the road turned into a bumpy dirt surface. The landscape was simple and stunning, the way uniform grasslands and rolling hills can be, with groves of *pinheiros* (crown-topped pines) springing up here and there in the vicinity of solitary farmhouses, or away in fields where they provide shade for the grazing cattle. At one point we were startled by a wolf, which bolted across the road in front of us. After a further gut-wrenching drive of about 30 minutes, with my host making few concessions to the rocks and potholes, we drove through a one-road settlement, intriguingly rustic right down to its single visible symbol of world civilization, the ubiquitous Coca-Cola sign tacked to the side of a wood-frame building. A bit farther on, the road forked to the left, but we entered to the right under a sign which announced the **Parque Nacional de Aparados da Serra** (loosely translated as the National Park of the Sheered-Off Cliffs). We drove along for another several hundred yards over the unimproved road, surrounded by grass and scrub, parked the car, and walked into a field. In a few seconds I understood fully why we had come. It was not visible even a few feet behind us where we had parked, but I was suddenly standing on the edge of a vast, deep canyon, utterly spectacular in its scope and dimensions. Itaimbezinho —at that point only about 25 miles from the Atlantic coast—is almost four miles in length, between 2,000 feet and a mile and a quarter wide, and at its deepest point 1½ miles down to the stream-size river that runs the length of the canyon floor.

The canyon walls were covered with many species of trees and plants, one striking for the beach-umbrella size of its deep-green leaves. Perhaps the most extraordinary thing about the place—besides being able to drive within ten feet of its edge without barriers or warning signs—is the total lack of a commercializing presence there. The canyon is still in a totally pristine state. The park contains thousands of acres, and during our three hours there we only encountered four other carloads of visitors. The park, I was told, is primarily used by serious campers and backpackers. No one, however, traveling as far as Gramado, should fail to take this side trip, even if only as a half-day excursion.

Where to Stay

Between them Gramado and Canela boast some 60 hotels, ranging from sprawling first-class resorts to cozy Swiss-style boarding houses offering home-cooked meals.

IN CANELA. The best address in Canela, and perhaps in the entire region, is the **Laje de Pedra,** Avenida Presidente Kennedy (tel. 054/282-1530). The immense complex of horizontal halls and wings is perched at the edge of a mountain wall about 3,000 feet above sea level, and overlooks the valley of the Rio Caí. From several vantage points both within the hotel and on the grounds, the view of the valley seems to roll on to infinity, primitive and uncultivated in certain areas and quite settled in others. In every case it is breathtaking and superb. A favorite area for viewing the scenery is a spacious lounge off the main lobby, enclosed by floor-to-ceiling windows and warmed by a communal fireplace that is in regular evening use from March to August when the nighttime temperatures descend into the 40s and 30s, and sometimes lower.

After a day touring the countryside—where the opportunities for hiking and horseback riding should not be overlooked—the Laje de Pedra offers several choices for filling up the evening hours. If your visit is during the cool winter months, head first for the tea room—a *mate* tea room that is. The waiters will instruct you to place the ground and moistened *mate* leaves vertically in your *cuia*, leaving a space from top to bottom free in the gourd to receive the boiling water. You can refill the *cuia* up to a dozen times, with the fifth or sixth refilling said to be the most flavorful—that is, assuming you acquire a taste for *chimarrão* in the process. An option for the cocktail hour is Swiss-style *cave* for wine and fondue. This is wine country, after all. You can dine on the premises or in town, and then stay up half the night in the typical Brazilian fashion, partying in the hotel's swinging discothèque. Other facilities include a large park with woods and a pool, which is heated during times when temperatures are low. The rooms here are charming, and have small balconies; but make sure to request one that faces the scenic valley. Prices begin at $57 for singles and $65 for doubles.

The **Vila Suzana Parque Hotel,** Rul Cel. Theobaldo Fleck 15 (tel. 054/282-2020), is another of Canela's first-class lodgings. The hotel has 19 separate white stucco cabins, with bedrooms and living areas. Each also contains a working fireplace, and wood is provided gratis by the management. The bungalows can accommodate up to four people, and the cost is $60 a night, including an excellent breakfast, with several varieties of sausage and other hot dishes.

The **Grande Hotel Canela,** Rua Getúlio Vargas 300 (tel. 054/282-1285), is a family-run establishment in the old-world tradition. The lodge has 32 rooms in all, and is set on landscaped grounds overlooking a private pond, where fishing is allowed in season. A large lobby has a fireplace, fronted by comfortable armchairs. The Grande Hotel is not fancy, but has an appealing domestic atmosphere. Standard rooms are $22 double, and two-room suites are $33. The hotel does not charge the 10% service tax.

IN GRAMADO. The hotels in Gramado are all located on, or not terribly far from, the town's two main streets. Overlooking the town on a nearby hill is the **Hotel Serrano,** Rua Costa e Silva 1112 (tel. 054/286-1328), the most modern of Gramado's hotels, including convention facilities for up to 1,000 participants. The hotel is self-contained, with all the requisite four-star features from restaurant to swimming pool. The 84 rooms start at $40 to $45 for standard accommodations, and $60 to $70 for deluxe rooms.

The in-town four-star hotel is the **Hotel Serra Azul,** Rua Garibaldi 152 (tel. 054/286-1082), located right off Gramado's principal cross street, Avenida Cel. Diniz. This fully equipped hotel is an excellent choice for those who like to take their evening constitutional in the midst of boutiques and craft shops, and also for those attending the numerous screenings during the film festival—the principal theater is only a few doors from the lobby entrance of the Serra Azul. The chalet-style hotel has 90 rooms, ranging from $39 to $41 for singles, and $50 to $56 for doubles.

Gramado also has several excellent hotels in the less expensive price categories. The **Hotel das Hortênsias,** Rua Bela Vista 83 (tel. 054/286-1057), is one of the most attractive buildings in town, a cross between a Spanish mission and a Swiss inn. Located near the entrance to Gramado's beautiful public park in the heart of town, the hotel does not allow children under 12 and bars groups, to preserve the tranquil setting, they say. It's intimately small, with only 16 rooms, and the rate is $33 per night, for one or two persons alike.

The **Hotel Vovó Carolina,** Avenida Borges de Medeiros 3129 (tel. 054/286-1151), is right on Gramado's main street, a simple but very adequate hotel with 18 rooms for between $15 and $20, no service charge.

The **Parque Hotel,** Rua Leopoldo Rosenfeld 818 (tel. 054/286-1326), has 26 rooms, 13 of which are heated and have TVs; the other 13 are housed in separate cabins overlooking a small lake. The rates range from $15 to $18, also with no service charge.

Where to Dine

Most of the restaurants in the area are located in Gramado itself. Two excellent choices are owned, separately, by two brothers. The **St. Hubertus,** Rua da Carrière 974 (tel. 286-1273), specializes in fondue, but has a full selection of international dishes as well. A large curved window in the homey dining room looks out on a lake. An extra-large fireplace adds atmosphere and warmth in winter months. Entrees average around $10, and the fondue is $7. Open for lunch daily from noon to 2:30 p.m., and for dinner from 7 p.m. till midnight.

The **Gasthof Edelweiss,** on Rua da Carrière at the corner of Rua João Leopoldo Lied (tel. 286-1861), as the name implies, offers German specialties, as well as fresh trout. The restaurant also overlooks the Lago Negro, the town's so-called Black Lake, and is decorated with many excellent graphic artworks collected by owner Clécio Gobbi on his many trips to far corners of the world. With beer, a large platter of German viands goes for about $10. Open every day for lunch from 11 a.m. to 3 p.m., and for dinner from 7 to 11 p.m.

Visitors also might want to try a regional specialty called *café colonial,* a late lunch consisting of many small dishes, including pastries and meat pies. There are several restaurants in Gramado that serve *café colonial* exclusively.

Shopping

There are two products created in and around Gramado, both available in its many excellent shops, that are of exceptionally high quality: hand-knit sweaters and home-style chocolate.

Special Tours

Sergatur (Serra Gaucha Turismo Ltda.), Rua Garibaldi 152 (tel. 054/286-2087), offers accompanied tours throughout both the Region of the Hydrangeas and the wine country, (see the next section). The company provides transportation and a guide for three-hour city tours of Canela and Gramado for about $10, and the same for full-day tours of Itaimbezinho or the Wine Country, both of which cost around $30 per person.

THE WINE COUNTRY: Ideally, you will have several days to tour the wine country. If not, you can still see quite a bit of the area by taking a day trip from Gramado or Canela, either by private car or with an organized tour. You will begin by heading toward Caxias do Sul, the "capital" of the wine region and one of the state's principal industrial cities.

Along the way, be sure to stop over in **Nova Petrópolis,** a community that retains much of its German flavor, especially on farms in the outlying districts where Portuguese is still the second language of the inhabitants. Whether or not you stop, the drive is a particularly scenic one, with many enchanting views of mountain passes, clusters of houses and outbuildings, and fields cultivated up and down the hillsides.

A traveler seeking lodgings here ought to inquire at the **Recanto Suiço,** Avenida XV de Novembro no. 2195 (tel. 054/281-1229). This is a real country inn, with only ten rooms, in an alpine-style home that would not be out of place practically anywhere east of the Rhine. The rooms are very personalized and charming, and the daily rate of $35 includes all three meals—a combination of Swiss and Brazilian home-cooking, according to the owner.

Caxias do Sul

The most important reason for stopping in Caxias do Sul, the third-largest city in Rio Grande do Sul, is for a quick pilgrimage to **São Pelegrino,** at the intersection of Avenida Rio Branco and Avenida Itália, to see the amazing work of the Italian artist Aldo Locatelli (1915–1962). The interior of the church is lush with Locatelli's dynamic murals. Locatelli was a vivid colorist, and a modernist in every way, so each scene in the larger-than-life panels of the artist's Stations of the Cross explodes with emotion. The ceiling murals also—especially of the Creation and the Last Judgment—are paradigms of the expressionist vision. This collection of Locatelli's work is truly one of the great hidden treasures of modern art to be found anywhere in Brazil.

The art of wine making is also not overlooked in the environs of Caxias do Sul, where an annual **Festa da Uva** (Wine Festival) draws tens of thousands of participants to the city in late February and early March to celebrate the annual harvest. The rest of the year many **adegas** (wineries) are open to the public for tours of the facilities and, of course, a little *digustação* (sampling of the produce). Outside of Caxias at km 143 on the Rodovia BR 116 is the **Château Lacave.** Tastings and tours are scheduled at 9, 10, and 11 a.m., and at 2, 3, 4, and 5 p.m.

Five miles from Caxias do Sul is a resort worth knowing about, especially for anyone interested in visiting the region during the wine festival. The **Samuara,** located on RS 122, the road to Farroupilha, at km 10 (tel. 054/221-7733), is an 81-room resort occupying 1,000 acres of parkland, complete with its own private lake for boating and fishing. A large pool (enclosed in glass and heated in the winter) is centered on a wide patio overlooking the countryside. Rooms are $38 for singles and $45 for doubles. Good bargains in footwear can be had in nearby Farroupilha, center of the state's shoe industry.

Bento Gonçalves

The next stop on our tour of the wine country is the town of Bento Gonçalves, founded by Italian immigrants who began to settle in the region after 1875. These original colonists came from wine-growing backgrounds, and brought with them all the necessary skills to transplant that tradition in the hills of the Serra Gaucha. Their descendants are today the backbone of the Brazilian wine industry, most of which is centered in these few towns of the wine country. Bento is one of the most productive and charming of these towns. A visit to Bento's small but lovingly tended museum, the **Museu do Imigrante,** Rua Erny Dreher, can provide an informed introduction to the experience of Italians who came to Brazil.

For food and lodgings in Bento, try the following:

The **Ipiranga** restaurant, Rua Vis, de São Gabriel 403 (tel. 252-3278), is typical of the *galetos* (barbecue houses) found throughout the state. Begin your meal with a healthy, stocky chicken soup, Brazil's famous canja, and then try the churrasco. The meat served here is excellent. With a good bottle of wine, dessert, and coffee, the meal will cost around $15 for two. Open daily from 11:30 a.m. to 1:30 p.m. for lunch, and from 7 to 11 p.m. for dinner.

A good hotel choice in town is the **Hotel Dall 'Onder,** Rua Erny Dreher 197 (tel. 054/252-3555), located in the *cidade alta,* the upper section of this town built on many hills. The hotel is relatively large, with 150 rooms that cost between $19 and $21 for one, and from $26 to $32 for two.

Degustação

The 1,350 wine-growing families throughout this district participate in a cooperative called the **Cooperative Venícola Aurora,** Rua Olavo Bilac 500 (tel. 252-4111). The winery offers 40-minute tours and wine-tasting in its cellars, with a 20% discount on all purchases. From December through March the hours are 8 to 11 a.m. and 3:15 to 5:15 p.m. Monday through Friday, and till 5 p.m. on Saturday and Sunday; from April to November, morning hours only. Here, as in all the wineries, ask to sample the best wines, in the case of the Aurora, the merlot and the cabernet franc, in either white or red.

A third *adega* to visit, if you desire additional background for your survey of the region's wines, is in the town of Garibaldi. The **Forestier** complex is located off Rodovia RS 470 at km 62.2 (tel. 262-1811). As you enter the grounds, all around you are plantings of experimental vines. The tour includes a 20-minute video, followed by wine sampling.

TORRES: The most popular beach resort on the coast of Rio Grande do Sul is the municipality of Torres. The beaches are very crowded during the summer season and all but deserted during the six cold months of the off-season. There are many hotels in all price ranges, and camping is also popular the length of the coast. In all candor, however, neither the beach nor the big cities are the reasons one comes to Rio Grande do Sul.

CHAPTER XI

SALVADOR, BAHIA

□ □ □

Mention Salvador, Bahia, to the average Brazilian and you are likely to elicit an unexpected outpouring of sentiment and national pride. The state of Bahia, and Salvador, its capital city, are as deeply symbolic to Brazilians as Plymouth Rock is to many Americans. And like the Puritan colony, Bahia was not the only cradle of its nation's formative culture, but it was the most significant. Bahia is also the gateway to Brazil's legendary northeast, while Salvador is the region's main entrance and still its most fascinating city.

1. ORIENTATION

Beyond its role as a national symbol, Bahia's story and reality could not be more distinct from that of Yankee New England. Bahia, for example, was settled almost 100 years before the Puritans established their colony. The state's name was bestowed by Cabral's expeditionaries, who anchored in the harbor on November 1, 1501, and christened it Bahia de Todos os Santos (All Saints Bay), in honor of the feast being celebrated that day on the Catholic liturgical calendar. In time the name was shortened by popular usage to simply Bahia, often referring to both state and city at the same time. The initial settlement on the right bank of the bay, then as now called Salvador, was established in 1549, by which time tiny Portugal with a population of barely two million souls, made its decision to colonize the new continent and defend it from the predatory intentions of the French and the Dutch, who had never reconciled to the papacy's decision in the Treaty of Tordesillas to divide South America exclusively between the Spanish and the Portuguese.

By the late 1600s—the time that Daniel Defoe was writing some of the first novels in the English language—Salvador was already well known to European readers of the day, ever-hungry for adventurous accounts of fortune seekers in the New World "plantations," and of seadogs and piracy on the high seas. In the story of *Robinson Crusoe*, Defoe's best-known book, the hero, an English seaman and adventurer, is living the life of a prosperous tobacco planter in Portuguese Bahia early in the 17th century. Just prior to his famous shipwreck on an uninhabited island, Crusoe has embarked from Bahia as a principal investor on a spec-

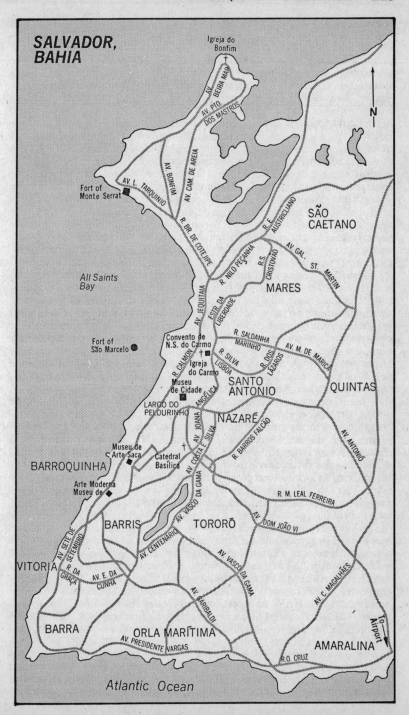

SALVADOR, BAHIA

Igreja do Bonfim

N

AV. BEIRA MAR

AV. PTO. DOS MASTROS

AV. BONFIM

AV. CAM. DE AREIA

Fort of Monte Serrat

AV. L. TARQUINIO

R. BR. DE COTEJIPE

SÃO CAETANO

R. E. AUSTRICLIANO

All Saints Bay

AV. JEQUITAIA

R. NILO PEÇANHA

ESTR. DA LIBERDADE

R. S. CRISTOVÃO

AV. GAL. ST. MARTIN

MARES

Fort of São Marcelo

Convento de N.S. do Carmo

R. CALMON

R. SALDANHA MARINHO

R. SILVA LISBOA

R. DOS LAZAROS

AV. M. DE MARICA

Igreja do Carmo

Museu de Cidade

AV. ANGÉLICA

SANTO ANTONIO

QUINTAS

LARGO DO PELOURINHO

AV. JOANA ANGÉLICA

NAZARÉ

Museu de Arte Sacra

AV. COSTA E SILVA

R. BARROS FALCÃO

AV. ANTONIO

BARROQUINHA

Catedral Basílica

Arte Moderna Museu de

AV. VASCO DA GAMA

R. M. LEAL FERREIRA

BARRIS

AV. VASCO DA GAMA

TORORÓ

AV. DOM JOÃO VI

AV. SETE DE SETEMBRO

R. DA GRAÇA

AV. CENTENARIO

VITORIA

AV. E. DA CUNHA

AV. VASCO DA GAMA

AV. C. MAGALHÃES

To Airport

AV. GARIBALDI

BARRA

ORLA MARÍTIMA

AMARALINA

AV. PRESIDENTE VARGAS

R. O. CRUZ

Atlantic Ocean

ulative voyage to the Ivory Coast of Africa, directly across the ocean at that longitude, to trade sugar and tobacco for slaves and gold.

While Defoe's story is the imaginary portrait of a failed "slaver," he might just as well have written of the many more successful ventures in that trade. The Portuguese, already hampered by their small numbers, nevertheless displayed a special distaste for physical labor when they inhabited the colonies of their new empire. And so their dependency on slaves—both natives and Africans—to work their fields was even greater than their counterparts in the colonies to the north. In the long run, enslavement of the Indians proved problematic. To some extent the "noble savages" were protected by the missionaries, but as a last resort to subjugations, they could slip off into the deep and still-familiar forest and hope to evade the hunters. But the Africans were trapped. In time, some slaves also escaped into the "bush" and created independent villages, but for most, the choices were to work or die. It did not take long under these conditions for the slaves to outnumber their masters, but neither element was so dominant in Bahia as to obscure the other. Both currents were strong, and they survive today as very separate realities in Salvador—the European descendants still represent power and privilege; the blacks, marginal in economic terms, are creators of a viable subsistence economy and a rich popular culture that has only been integrated commercially around its smoother edges.

Visually, Salvador today reflects this division. On the 30-minute drive into town from the very modern airport, it is easy to observe the city's social organization. Along the outer rings are the squatters' camps, called *invasões* (invasions), dwellings that are no more than hovels, filled with dark-skinned refugees from yet another cycle of droughts and failed harvests somewhere in the interior. The city's middle parts are suburbs of the working poor, tightly packed wood or brick bungalows, the streets and public spaces like bus stops, so exclusively occupied by blacks that you might as easily imagine you are in Nigeria as in Brazil. Even the details of the street scenes can be at times as patently African—for instance, when you see a file of turbaned women, balancing water cans and bundles on their heads, disappear from the main road down some dirt pathway into their village. The inner city, however, suggests not Africa, but Lisbon. Here the Portuguese masters of the colonial era built their mansions, their sturdy counting houses and massive fortifications, their scores of elaborately ornamented churches. And it is here today—as well as along the nearly 70 miles of Salvador's shoreline—that their descendants have built their villas and their modern city, in the midst of an architectural preserve that includes over 20,000 structures built before 1800. that Nowhere else in the Americas can you see, almost routinely, so many churches and other structures that date from the 1600's, and astoundingly, even the 1500's.

While the contrast between the city's two dominant and coexisting cultures may be stark in strict economic terms, the common ground they occupy is also great. In the areas of religion, food, music, art, and popular celebrations, both influences are strongly felt, and it is through these activities that the population of Salvador has achieved a kind of cultural synthesis, a common trunk that thrives despite the dissimilar roots that feed it. Catholicism and *candomblé,* the drum beat and the ballad, African street food and Iberian shellfish stews, folk art and fine art—all overlap their boundaries in Salvador, where at its best, tolerance and compromise, not bigotry and confrontation, are the operative ingredients of the day-to-day social contract.

Salvador's relative social harmony can perhaps be attributed to several factors. Food, fish and fresh fruit in particular, seem super-abundant. By outward appearances, even the poor seem well fed and physically robust. But there are also in Salvador certain intangibles of life that are available and free to all, not the least of which are the perpetually sunny climate, the miles of excellent public beaches, and the tradition of street celebrations, spontaneous and organized, dozens of which occur throughout the year. "That man is the richest," observed Thoreau, "whose pleasures are the cheapest."

Religion, also, is of central importance in the daily lives of many Bahians. Catholicism began as the colony's official religion, and has left a remarkable artistic legacy in Salvador. The city is justifiably proud of its many fine churches, which represent a collective monument to the energy, spiritualism, and high esthetic expression achieved during both the early colonial and the baroque eras. In the shadows of the state religion, however, the slaves managed to preserve and enrich their own spiritual traditions. It was coincidently the case that their particular animist faith—today known as *candomblé*—and Catholicism were both religions that revered many saintly personages. The slaves therefore were able to cleverly disguise the practice of their traditional beliefs. Each of their spirits and gods was identified with either the diety of Catholicism or with one of the many saints. So when a slave—or later, a descendant of slaves—was seen to pray to Saint Ann or Saint George, for example, what was not perceived was that he or she was also seeking communion with the African spirits that had been "syncretized" with the holy figures of the dominant religion. The open practice of "pure" *candomblé*—which had never ceased to be practiced behind closed doors in the slave quarters or the shantytowns—was not legally permitted until early in this century. Today in Salvador alone, it is said that the temples of *candomblé* number some 4,000, and are now almost as popular with the descendants of the masters as with those whose forebears were in bondage.

The tourist, too, in Salvador, will find that the best the city has to offer is there, either for the taking or at a price that is more than reasonable. The beaches, the historical sites, the city streets, the outdoor markets, the open-air cafés, the island-studded bay, the moveable feast of sights, sounds, and flavors—this is the Salvador that more and more international visitors are discovering every year, the great "secret" that Brazilians themselves have known since the city was first founded almost 450 years ago.

GETTING TO SALVADOR: Salvador is one of six Brazilian cities (along with Rio, São Paulo, Manaus, Belém, and Recife) that can be reached by direct flight on VARIG Airlines from the United States. Salvador-bound flights embark from Miami only. As of this writing there is one nonstop flight to Salvador each week, on Sunday. (Confirm this and all scheduling information directly with the airline or with your travel agent at the time of travel. Schedules, as well as fares, change frequently.) There are several direct flights daily from Rio to Salvador. The two cities are about 700 ground miles apart, and flying time is roughly an hour and a half, at a cost of approximately $250 round trip. There is ample bus service from Rio to Salvador, via both interior and coastal routes, a trip that will take a minimum of 24 hours and cost between $30 and $45, depending on whether you travel by express "sleeper," or on the local carrier.

SALVADOR'S GEOGRAPHY: Salvador's geographic layout is similar to Rio's, but also the mirror opposite. Both are cities built at the mouth and along the shores of immense bays. But while Rio occupies the lower bank of the estuary and curves around to the ocean beaches to the south, Salvador was built on the upper bank and has expanded up the northern seashore. Also, both cities combine coastal strips and high grounds. But in Salvador, the two levels—at least in the oldest part of town—are more distinct, forming a lower city of wharfs, warehouses, and commercial buildings, and an upper city which sits on a cliff 250 feet above the waterfront, connected to it by steep inclines called *ladeiras,* and by the

Elevador Lacerda, a complex of municipal elevators that carries passengers quickly between the two levels. With only 1.5 million inhabitants, Salvador is also considerably smaller than Rio, and easier to get around in. The beaches in Salvador, too, begin in the bay where, in most cases, swimming is not recommended, and stretch out for many miles along the ocean on a strip called the **orla.** The great arch of land that surrounds the bay, beyond Salvador's city limits, is called the **recôncavo,** and it was here that the plantation system first took root in Brazilian colonial times.

GETTING AROUND SALVADOR: Buses are the principal means of mass transit in Salvador. The destinations and routes of the various lines are clearly marked on the windshields of public buses. With the aid of a good city map, you may reliably depend on the **buses** to get around the city. They feel safe, and while drivers speed right along, there are many stops and the routes tend to be circuitous, and so they are not the fastest way to get around the city.

For those with limited time in the city, **taxis** are the most efficient way to cover ground quickly. Fares are cheaper than in Rio, and drivers less likely to hassle you about running on the meter.

SALVADOR'S CLIMATE: Throughout the year, average temperatures hover between the 70s and the high 80s. Cool sea breezes ensure pleasant days even when the mercury climbs higher during the hottest summer days. Tropical rainstorms are possible anytime of year in Salvador. Most typically there will be a sudden and tempestuous downpour for an hour or so, and then the sun will return and reclaim all signs of moisture within minutes. On occasion—during the winter months—ocean squalls, like tropical monsoons, will close the city in for several days of gloomy, rainy weather. If there is one region in Brazil, however, where you can almost count on having some sun during your vacation there, it is the northeast. And Salvador is no exception to this general rule.

TOURIST INFORMATION: The state tourist board is called **Bahiatursa,** which has several information centers at key points throughout Salvador. Bahiatursa's main branch is in the Palácio Rio Branco (tel. 071/254-7000), off the Praça Tomé de Souza, adjacent to the Lacerda Municipal Elevator, open from 8 a.m. to 6 p.m. Other branches can be found at the airport (tel. 240-1244), which is open from 8 a.m. to 10 p.m., and in the lower city at the Mercado Modelo, Praça Cairú (tel. 241-0242), open from 8 a.m. to 6 p.m. Bahiatursa can furnish you with practical, up-to-the-minute information on such matters as available tours, English-language guides, cultural events, and so forth.

The agency also sells a map of the city for about $1, which is adequate to gain an overview of the urban layout. But if you plan to do any serious exploration, buy a copy of the more detailed **Planta de Salvador,** put out by the Brazilian tour guide company Quatro Rodas, available at bookstores and newsstands.

2. WHAT TO SEE AND DO

Salvador's most important sights and activities can be divided into five distinct groupings, each of which occupies a specific neighborhood or area within the city or on the bay, and represents either a full- or half-day excursion. First are the 30 miles of beaches along the *orla* and beyond. Second are the historical and religious sights, found primarily in the vicinity of the Pelourinho, the colonial district overlooking the bay from the edge of the cliff in the upper city. Third is the Itapagipe Peninsula, for a taste of the city's bayside ambience, including visits to Bonfim, the city's most important active church, and Monte Serrat, one of its oldest fortifications. Fourth is the neighborhood of Barra, between the *orla* and the city, with many medium-priced hotels and restaurants, and a center of café society and nightlife. Fifth is Itaparica, an incomparable island across the bay. There are, in addition, various events, points of interest, museums, and so forth scattered throughout other sections of the city, each of which will be described separately.

THE ORLA: *Orla* in Portuguese means hem, and the area given this name in Salvador is precisely that seam of land on the city's northern coast that joins with some 15 miles of ocean frontage. Along this strip are found virtually all of Salvador's best hotels and its finest beaches. Most visitors who book their lodgings in Salvador in advance of arrival are likely to find themselves staying somewhere along the *orla*.

The **coastal beaches** begin where the neighborhood of Barra ends, and lead all the way to Itapoã, near the city limits. The rule of thumb in Bahia as far as good beaches is concerned is that the farther out you go, the better they get and the longer it takes to reach them, especially during weekend traffic jams. By this criterion, the good beaches begin more or less with **Pietá,** and include **Placaford** and finally **Itapoã** itself. The really super beaches today are considered to be even farther up the coast, from **Buraquinho** to **Praia do Forte.** Between them is **Arembepé,** once an international watering hole for the '60s counterculture, which was frequented by giants of rock 'n' roll like Joplin and Jagger; now it has returned to its more sedate existence as a coastal resort and fishing village.

The beaches closer to the city, like **Ondina** and **Rio Vermelho,** may not be the largest or the most pristine, but they offer in places some lovely natural pools ringed by rock formations where bathing can be very intimate.

There is much nightlife in bars and restaurants throughout the quaint streets of these chic residential neighborhoods that overlook the water.

Along the entire run of strands lining the *orla,* the beaches continue to be shared by solitary fishermen, who work the shallows with their nets, or farther out, fish from sailing rafts of lashed logs, called *jangadas,* dozens of which can be seen at any given time bobbing just beyond the breakers.

HISTORICAL SALVADOR: The greatest concentration of historical buildings in Salvador—a city where around every corner you are capable of stumbling upon a rare and ancient architectural gem—is found in the **Pelourinho.** Like so much of historical Brazil, the Pelourinho has been sanctified by UNESCO as an "international treasure, the most important area for colonial architecture in the Americas." It is good to keep in mind that while Salvador bloomed radiantly during the Belle Époque of Brazil's baroque period (essentially the gold cycle of the 1700s), the city—Brazil's capital until 1763—was already the flower of the South Atlantic during the 1600s. And of all Brazil, only here in Salvador will you see the roman numerals XVI and XVII (denoting the 1500s and 1600s) so frequently associated with extant structures.

A tour of the Pelourinho district can begin at the **Praça da Sé,** a large public square adjacent to its smaller neighbor, the **Terreiro de Jesus,** from which you actually enter the Pelourinho. The Praça da Sé has its own architectural charm, bordered by the 18th-century former Palace of the Archbishop and the Igreja da Sé, but the real show on this square is its animated street scene. Someone is always performing here: a backcountry poet selling his work in a rudely printed chapbook; a magician who will wrap your watch in a handkerchief, smash it with a stone, and return it to you whole; or a pitchman swearing on his mother's grave that the weird gadget he is hawking "really works" and that you can't live without it. How will you resist the photographers who want to shoot your picture with one of those old box cameras that stand on skinny tripod legs like bashful cranes in a marsh?

From here you can approach the Pelourinho in one of two ways, entering the Terreiro de Jesus directly, or via a short backstreet digression to visit Salvador's famous "church of gold," considered by many the most striking of all Brazil's baroque accomplishments. For the latter option, walk from the Praça da Sé up Rua Geudes de Brito, past the monumental gate of the Saldanha Palace, now housing the School of Arts and Crafts, and on to Rua São Francisco. Turning left here, proceed to the **Praça Anchieta** where you will find the **Igreja e Convento de São Francisco** (Church and Cloister of St. Francis), open all week during business hours, but closed Sunday afternoon. The church's uncomplicated façade contrasts mightily with the elaborately carved interior, where every chisled surface is sheathed in brilliant gold. A wainscoting of *azuleijos* (blue and white Portuguese tiles) lines the walls, each panel illustrating a signal episode from the life of St. Francis of Assísi. On the altar is an unexpected sight: a large, sensual carving of the *candomblé* goddess Iemanjá, syncretized with the Virgin Mary, is mounted on the prow of the main pulpit, a familiar gesture of Catholicism's compromise in Bahia with its pagan rival. A statue of St. Peter of Alcântara on the right lateral altar was one of Dom Pedro II's favorite works of sacred art. The cloisters themselves, covered walkways around an interior courtyard, may be visited by men in the company of a monk, but women may only view the tiled and colonnaded retreat through a wrought-iron gate.

Next to the convent church is the equally stunning **Igreja da Ordem Terceira de São Francisco** (Church of the Third Order of St. Francis), built in 1703. The exterior of this church is as unique and prized in Brazilian architecture as the glittering interior of its next-door neighbor. The intricately carved stone façade was covered with stucco for generations, and only discovered accidently by workmen a few years back. The discovery is viewed as one of Brazil's greatest art finds, ever. A room inside the church filled with life-size statues is worth visiting.

Walk through the Praça Anchieta and you will enter the Terreiro de Jesus, one of the oldest squares of the original city, with some of its oldest churches, including the **Catedral Basílica,** originally a Jesuit church, dating from the mid-1600s and final resting place of Mem de Sá, the Portuguese Governor-general who drove the French from Rio de Janeiro. The basilica is open Tuesday to Saturday from 9 to 10:30 a.m. and 2 to 5 p.m. and on Sunday from 9 to 10 a.m. The *terriero* (sacred ground) itself is heavily shaded by broad-leafed almond and poinciana trees, and in its midst stands the city's original public water source, though the cast-iron fountain imported from France is of a later period.

The walk through the Pelourinho district—a lengthy succession of narrow, cobbled streets, opening every several blocks into small interior *largos* (squares) —should take about two hours, especially if you wander all the way to the Praça de Santo Antônio and stop frequently along the way to admire the buildings, singly or ensemble, browse the shops and side streets, and take such refreshment as is necessary. The pavement is of rough stones, and the descent is steep in places, but to get the entire flavor of the old neighborhood, it's wise to go the distance. Begin by entering Rua Alfredo Brito, past the old medical college which today houses the Afro-Brazilian Museum and its collection of *candomblé* art and artifacts. In a few minutes you will come to the irregularly shaped **Largo do Pelourinho,** an archetype of the colonial square of its day with its fine old houses. Here stood the *pelourinho,* the public whipping post where slaves were punished in full view of the approving gentry. Legend has it that the victims of this cruelty were succored at the nearby Igreja do Rosário, the Slave's Church, a sweet sampler of the baroque style in its own right.

The Pelourinho circuit is much tramped by visitors to Salvador, but it is still best to stick to the straight and narrow of the route and avoid the backstreets and alleys, where the darkened doorways of the poor are not a pretty sight and muggers have been known to intimidate tourists and fleece them of their purses and cameras. A more probable danger faces the gullible who fall victim to the sting of a hustler; he offers to change money at a rate you can't refuse, then disappears with your cash through the doorway of a respectable building, never to be seen again. Overall, it should be stressed that Salvador seems a safe place to stroll endlessly and at will, avoiding only the most obvious cul-de-sacs of poverty, and staying alert at points where tourists concentrate and make obvious and tempting targets.

Also on the Largo do Pelourinho are the SENAC cooking school and cultural center, about which more below, and the **Museu da Cidade** (City Museum), where scenes from *candomblé* ceremonies are displayed wax-museum style, with mannequins dressed in ritualistic garb and posed in a variety of trance-like postures. Continuing on to the bottom of the square, to a point where five lanes converge, go straight on along Rua Luís Viana, and climb the incline toward the **Largo do Carmo,** where in the mid-1600s the city's Créole population finally defeated and forced the surrender of the Dutch, who had by then occupied Salvador for some years. On the way, a set of stairs to the left leads to the **Igreja do Passo,** perched above the lower city and offering a wide view of the bay. On the largo itself is the **Igreja da Ordem Terciera do Carmo** (1585) with its museum, one of the city's several repositories of fine sacred art, also containing an illustrated key to the sycretization of the Christian saints with their counterparts among the African deities. Next door is the **Igreja e Convento de Nossa Senhora do Carmo,** where the convent now houses one of the smartest and most appealing of the city's luxury hotels (described in detail in Section 3, below).

Here ends the obligatory tour of the Pelourinho, but the walk on to the plaza at the end of the slope is much recommended, for a more unstructured contemplation of the quieter zones of this neighborhood, where nonetheless steady restoration of all the charming little buildings is rapidly transforming the place into the Brazilian equivalent of a gentrified bohemia. Preservationism, universally, knows no middle ground between gentrification and decay. The single lane changes names several times as you descend, from Rua do Carmo to Rua Joaquim Távora, and finally Rua Direita. At the end of this final stretch is the **Praça de Santo Antônio,** a shady, quiet corner of the city bordered by delightful cottages—nos. 6, 7, and 8, in coral pink, pale blue, and earthy yellow—have a storybook quality about them. The plaza dead-ends at the **Forte do Santo Antônio,** one of the many colonial fortifications that defended early Salvador from the encroachments of its foes, and where today a Popular Cultural Center has been installed that provides space for craftspeople and dancers, and for the *capoeira* studio of Mestre João Pequeno.

A Note on Capoeira

Wherever you travel in the city, whether on the beach or in the local square, you are bound to see boys, young and old, practicing what appears to be an acrobatic form of kung fu. This is called *capoeira,* and while it is a martial art, it is also an art form. According to legend, this form of foot fighting was brought to Brazil by the slaves. But since slaves were not allowed to fight among themselves, the masters outlawed the practice. To circumvent the ban, the men, so that they might both preserve the form and themselves, began to choreograph the steps, and over time transformed *capoeira* into a dance of ritualistic confrontation. The object is to not deliver the blows, but to sweep close to the opponent's head and body with the many varieties of kicks and feints. Each "fight" is between two dancers only, who are accompanied by the rhythmic music of a drum, a tambou-rine, and a *berimbau* (a gourd and bow strung with a single strand of wire), and by the chanted verse of a melancholy song, often related to a *briga de amor* (a fight over a woman).

Capoeira can be viewed at tourist shows, in the *capoeira* academies them-selves, which often have weekly performances as a means of fundraising, and best of all, on the streets. Bahiatursa can provide the names of academies and the scheduling of their performances.

THE ITAPAGIPE PENINSULA: This is a large codicil of land beyond the port jutting into Salvador's upper bay. Tourists have long been coming here to visit its most famous parts, Monte Serrat and Bonfim, but have seldom been taught to consider the peninsula as a whole as a place for a day's outing and explo-ration, rather than just a quick in-and-out by cab to visit the requisite sights.

The best time for a pilgrimage to the peninsula is on Saturday, and we begin our tour—at dawn if possible—with the colorful **Feira D' Agua de Meninos,** also known as the Open Air Market of São Joaquim, about three miles up the bay from the Mercado Modelo in the lower city. While the market is mounted daily (6 a.m. to 6 p.m.; on Sunday till 1 p.m.), Saturday is the universal shopping day, and so finds the *feira* at its most animated. But why at dawn? For the same reason one went to the old Les Halles in Paris at daybreak—not for onion soup alone, but to witness the market as it awakens from the torpor of inactivity and is filled not with shoppers, but with porters carrying tons of produce to the individual stalls.

Nowhere else in Salvador will you see gathered in a single place such a cross section of inhabitants so typical of the northeast, a people cast in as many shades of bronze and ebony as any artist could imagine, much less distinguish. Many a wary *caboclo,* as the country folk are called, will stare back at you, puffing slowly on his or her pipe, as intensely as you stare at them. Most producers arrive with their goods by truck, and some still come by cart and on donkeys. But many more come by sea, on coastal sloops called *saveiros,* and beach or tie up in the little coves adjacent to the market grounds.

Here is the way to tour the bay, if you are bold. Bargain with the master of a sloop, someone going up the bay toward the colonial towns of Cachoeira or Maragogipe on the opposite shore, and ask him to carry you as a passenger. Then find a sloop making the return voyage, or take a swing through the *recôncavo* and come back to Salvador by bus.

With so much fruit and raw meat, the market has its rank and squishy sec-tions, to be savored or avoided according to personal taste. There are also many stalls filled with sacks of colorful spices, household items you won't find in either department stores or souvenir shops but which deserve the status of genuine folk craft, and pottery—dozens of tented shops selling brittle plate and knickknacks, underglazed, and underfired, which you won't be able to resist but which will probably break long before you get home, or soon thereafter.

When you tire of the market, continue up the shoreline to the favorite of all the in-town beaches, in the vicinity of the **Praça da Boa Viagem.** The weekend scene here is very democratic and appealing, and there are dozens of beach-shack restaurants to satisfy hunger and thirst. Farther on along the shore you will arrive at the point of the peninsula, where the old 16th-century fort of Monte Serrat (not open to the public) commands the high ground and offers a wide, breezy view of both upper and lower bay. The nearby **Igreja do Monte Serrat,** farther out on the point, is a lovely miniature that dates from the 1500s and has the rude, hand-hewn pews to prove it.

From here the land makes a 90° bend and continues up the bay, and we will follow Rua Rio São Francisco (which becomes Rua Plínio de Lima) uphill toward the most fascinating of all Salvador's religious shrines, **Nosso Senhor do Bonfim,** a landmark in the daytime by virtue of its hillside perch, and by night as well, its outline traced in the light of a thousand bulbs.

To Catholics, Bonfim is Christ the Lord; to the fetishists he is Oxala, prince of the gods. The Church of Bonfim somehow evolved into the great crossroads of both faiths. Once a year, in early January (see "The Festivals of Bahia," below), Bonfim is actually the focus of a major rite of the *candomblé.* Lest we forget the significance of Bonfim to the average Bahian, everywhere in the city, encircling people's wrists or fastened to the rear-view mirrors of taxis and buses, are thin streamers in various shades of pastel printed with the legend, "*Lembrança do Bonfim*" ("souvenir of Bonfim"). This ribbon is a good-luck charm common to adherents of both religions, and its presence is also much in evidence throughout the church, looped around crucifixes and candlesticks (which are electric, on the main altar) and pinned to the very walls.

The faithful pray to Bonfim to be delivered from harm or illness. Promises are made, and fulfilled. A woman is seen carrying her baby, walking on her knees from the main entrance the full distance of the long central aisle, all the way to the altar. Other believers add their requests for special favor in the form of letters—often with accompanying photographs of loved ones for whom they wish to intercede—to the thousands of similar appeals that form a thick covering on the walls and ceiling of the Room of Miracles, to the rear of the church on the right-hand side. Also suspended everywhere in this room are the ex votos—plaster and plastic models of limbs and organs, offered in thanks for miraculous cures. One man has pasted a note with some photocopied pictures, asking the Lord to help his brother stop drinking. There are few smiles on the faces in these photographs; people have their tough, everyday faces. The most devout—or perhaps just the most affluent—commission miracle painters, a profession unique to the city, to capture their hour of need on canvas, and these, too, are found hanging throughout this bizarre gallery of human hope.

Outside the church in the plaza are the milling squads of *capitães da areia* (beach urchins), so called by novelist Jorge Amado, a resident of the city and principal chronicler of its popular and sacred myths. The children are attracted by the thousands of tourists who visit Bonfim yearly, and are seeking alms for the here and now, while others inside plot their strategies for eternity. Across the street, toward the water, is a line of shops, including a juice bar that serves fresh-squeezed beverages in large plastic bags taped around long, thin straws. A road along the bay leads from here to the very desirable back-harbor neighborhood of Ribeira, a place to fantasize about when imagining where in Salvador you might want to live in your future life.

A WALK THROUGH BARRA: Barra, on the opposite end of the bay from Itapagipe, might be characterized as a kind of Bahian Greenwich Village. Barra began as a neighborhood of wealthy planters, and in its decline became a bohemian quarter. Today it has been restored to some of its past glory, and is a favorite address of the professional set, young and not-so-young alike. Barra is also a neighborhood attuned to the sensibilities of tourists, as its numerous hotels can attest, and is furthermore the city's most concentrated zone of nightlife.

Anyone staying in or near Barra, might want to consider all or part of the following walking-tour itinerary. Begin in Barra at the **Forte de Santo Antônio da Barra,** a fortress originally built in the early 1600s to defend against the Dutch invasion. Today the fort houses the Hydrography Museum, and can be entered on Tuesday, Wednesday, Friday, and Saturday from 11 a.m. to 5 p.m. From here, the walk will take you via **Avenida 7 de Setembro** (with several detours) as far as you wish to go into the heart of the city. Consult a map before you begin, and carry it with you to verify distances and landmarks along the way. The entire walk as outlined here could easily consume four or five hours.

From the Largo da Barra you begin a steady climb up Avenida 7 de Setembro past many of the city's better small hotels. The first detour is a brief stroll off to the right up **Rua da Graça,** a pleasing residential block where you'll see several old mansions with grounds that are overgrown with large trees, vines, and other vegetation similar to what you might see in an interior town of Louisiana. Look also for the façades of houses decorated with Portuguese tiles that portray colonial and plantation scenes. Continuing back up Avenida 7 de Setembro you will come to the **Museu Carlos Costa Pinto,** at no. 2490 (tel. 247-6081), open daily except Tuesday from 1 to 7 p.m. The museum is a modern house with a collection of fine furnishings and jewelry—including the *balangadãs,* gold and silver trinket jewelry of the slaves—that once belonged to a wealthy Brazilian family.

The next major point of interest along the avenida is **Campo Grande,** a large, formal park with a monumental column as its primary landmark. Behind the park, on Rua Forte de São Pedro, is the modern **Teaetro Castro Alves,** a venue for theater, dance, and popular concerts. Beyond the park Avenida 7 de Setembro curves inland, rising to the upper city, while Avenida do Contorno hugs the shore and leads to the lower city. The next stretch of the walk along Avenida 7 de Setembro takes you past a wide variety of shops and offices, until arriving at the **Praça da Piedade,** where you may continue on in one of two directions.

If you wish to walk toward the harbor—to the Lacerda Municipal Elevator, for example—continue to follow Avenida 7 de Setembro to the **Praça Castro Alves,** monument and tomb of the romantic poet. From here you enter **Rua Chile,** a street of shops, once the most fashionable commercial zone in the city. Walk until you come to the **Palácio Rio Branco,** originally the Governor's House, some portions of which dates to 1549, and now a museum and headquarters of Bahiatursa. The Palácio has been through many transformations, renovations, and expansions since the colonial governors first resided on this spot, and the bulk of the building is really *fin-de-siècle,* constructed around 1900. Whatever its age, the building is an impressive edifice, and very much worth a visit. Despite a fantastic mix of styles, the rooms open to the public reflect a grandness and splendor of detail found in the great palaces of European royalty. Among the attractive details are several striking panel paintings recently uncovered from beneath successive layers of thick oil paint. From here you can descend to the lower city by elevator or go on to the historic district.

If on arriving at the Praça da Piedade, however, you wish to explore something of the inner city, simply follow **Avenida Joana Angêlica,** a principal thoroughfare through the neighborhood of **Barroquinha.** There are many pleasant discoveries to be made as you wander among the unpretentious backstreets of this old commercial district. Turning left on **Rua da Independência,** which turns into **Rua do Gravatá,** walk until reaching the **Praça dos Veteranos** and then enter onto **Rua 28 de Setembro.** This route will lead you to within a block of the Praça da Sé, and you will have seen a perfectly charming part of Salvador that few tourists ever bother to visit, yet it's only several blocks away from the more frequented historical zone.

THE BAY: All Saints Bay has a life of its own, independent of the hustle and bustle of the city. There are supposedly 34 islands in the bay, with **Itaparica** by far the most important. Itaparica is a summer and weekend colony for Salvadorans, serviced frequently by passenger and car ferries. But even on Itaparica you can see how different, and exquisitely so, life on the bay islands is from the urban intensity that is Salvador. Itaparica is treated as a separate destination, below, where you will find details on the island's villages, beaches, hotels, and restaurants. But a day trip is also strongly recommended for those on limited schedules, who nevertheless have a yen to get out on the bay as well as to see something of life outside the city.

Ferries to Itaparica

To keep it simple, I will outline two separate day-trip excursions to the island of Itaparica. In both cases, you will get to spend two hours cruising the bay—an hour each way—which is by far the cheapest, least formal way of observing both harbor life and the outline of the city skyline from the vantage point of the bay itself.

TO BOM DISPACHO. The São Joaquim Ferry leaves from its slip adjacent to the grounds of the Agua de Meninos market. This ferry, which costs about 50¢ or less each way for passengers, also carries motor vehicles, and disembarks at **Bom Dispacho** on the island of Itaparica. The ferry is large, loud, and unadorned except for a stand-up bar and a blaring TV in the main compartment. Most passengers hang dreamily over the rails when the weather is fair, and watch the endless harbor activity during the 50-minute crossing. The first ferry in the morning leaves at 6 a.m., and boats run hourly until 10 p.m. to midnight on weekends and holidays.

When you arrive at the Bom Dispacho terminal, you will have several transportation choices for touring the island. Most efficient and expensive are the private cars, about $10 an hour. The advantage here is that you will get a driver who is probably an Itaparica native and who can give you an excellent orientation in two to three hours, including a stop for lunch and a swim. The *kombi* is a VW van that carries half a dozen passengers to fixed destinations, like Mar Grande, or the town of Itaparica, for anywhere from $3 to $5. The public bus is a rickety affair, used mostly by the simpler folk, but it goes everywhere and is a wise and reasonable choice for the more self-reliant.

TO MAR GRANDE. Another boat, a passenger launch, leaves from a pier next to the Mercado Modelo, every hour on the hour beginning about 8 a.m., for the town of Mar Grande; the final boat returns late in the afternoon. In fact the launch's schedule is not fixed, and is subject to a variety of factors. It seldom sails, for example, before the boat is full. Ask the master when the last boat returns on the day of your crossing. And remember, if you miss it, you can always return via nearby Bom Dispacho. The one-way fare is less than $1, and the trip takes about an hour each way.

The advantage of the Mar Grande launch is that you arrive directly at the dock of the island's most fashionable beach town, and need travel no further for your pleasures if you so choose. Mar Grande has lovely beaches, and several excellent restaurants.

Bay Excursions

Several companies offer full- and half-day excursions aboard fully equipped schooners (written *escuna* in Portuguese) that cruise the bay and call at the islands. The ship **Bahia de Todos os Santos** leaves from the Mercado Modelo pier. For fares and schedules contact the Companhia de Navegação Bahiana directly on the dock, or make your booking through Bahiatursa.

Other companies that offer regular schooner excursions, for groups or private charter, are **L.R. Turismo**, Avenida 7 de Setembro no. 3959 (tel. 235-0981), and **Kontik-Franstur**, Praça da Inglaterra 2 (tel. 242-0433).

Many of the smaller *saveiro* sloops moored in the vicinity of the Mercado Modelo are also available for private rental. Arrangements are made directly with the skippers of these craft.

Ilha de Maré

An overnight excursion can be made to the Ilha de Maré, in the upper bay, on a small boat that leaves from Ribeira (Praça Gen. Osório) sometime in the morning between 9 and 11 a.m. The boat makes calls on the island at the hamlets of Itamoabá, Praia Grande (a basket-weaving center), and Santana (known for its lace), and returns the following morning from Santana before dawn. There are no tourist facilities on the island, but you can bargain with a local for a bed or camp on the beach.

MORE MUSEUMS: The **Museu de Arte Sacra** (Museum of Sacred Art), Rua do Sodré 276 (tel. 243-6310), is probably the most important collection of art—religious or secular—in the city. The museum is housed in the former 17th-century convent of the Barefoot Carmelites, and is a veritable cornucopia of religious-inspired art, much of it the old carved-wood images the Portuguese brought with them from the mother country. Of the domestic work, there is a gilded reliquary by Aleijadinho. The collection is open to the public Tuesday through Saturday from 10 to 11:30 a.m. and 2 to 5:30 p.m.

Across from the Museum of Sacred Art is **Tempostal,** a private museum devoted to postcards and stamps, open only on Saturday and Sunday from 2 to 6 p.m.

The **Museu de Arte da Bahia,** Avenida 7 de Setembro no. 2340 (tel. 235-9492), is an eclectic collection of paintings and furnishings from both Europe and Brazil, set in a restored colonial mansion. Open Tuesday through Saturday from 2 to 6 p.m.

The **Museu de Arte Moderno** (Modern Art Museum) is attached to the **Solar do Unhão** (tel. 243-6174), a complex of colonial-era buildings that includes a popular restaurant, with entertainment, on Avenida do Contorno. The museum houses no permanent collection, but is open during exhibitions, as scheduled. There is a *son et lumière* focused on the buildings on many evenings.

The **Museu do Recôncavo Wanderlei de Pinho,** about 25 miles outside Salvador via highway BR 324, is an old plantation converted into a museum. In Brazilian lore, the term *Casa Grande e Senzala* (the Master's House and the Slaves' Quarters) is of more than passing anthropoligical significance. It recalls a way of life that predominated in Brazil's plantation-based economy of large landed estates until late in the 19th century. Indeed, that way of life has not entirely passed, as land-starved peasants in land-rich Brazil can bear witness even today. The Museum of the Recôncovo preserves well both the glory and the shame of the plantation reality. (The museum, closed for extensive renovations since 1985, was due to reopen in 1988; check with Bahiatursa for new schedule.)

Map and history buffs might enjoy browsing through the stately halls of the **Museu do Instituto Geográfico e Histórico,** Avenida 7 de Setembro no. 94A (tel. 241-2453), located on the Praça da Piedade and open Monday through Friday from 2 to 5 p.m.

THE FESTIVALS OF BAHIA: Salvadorans celebrate often, and not only in private. Their best parties are public and take place in the streets, some even on the water. The feasting begins on New Year's Day with the impressive boat procession of the **Festa do Nosso Senhor do Bom Jesus dos Navigantes** (Our Lord Patron of Sailors). Hundreds of boats, led by the archbishop himself, who accompanies the image of Christ, are festooned with flowers and banners, and sail from the cove opposite Conceição da Praia Church in the lower city to the beach of Boa Viagem on the Itapagipe Peninsula. Rental boats are available to follow the procession by water.

January 6, the **Festa dos Reis** (Feast of the Magi) is a cause for some pre-Lenten street dancing. The third Sunday of January is reserved for one of the city's most traditional celebrations, the **Festa do Nosso Senhor do Bonfim.** This festival actually begins on the preceding Thursday, when priestesses of the *candomblé*, dressed in full regalia, wash the white steps of Bonfim Church, which are considered the sacred stones of the god Oxala. The great Carnival-like parade to Bonfim takes place on Sunday, and on Monday the **Festa da Ribeira** brings to a close this particular cycle of outdoor celebrations, although the more modest **Festa de São Lázaro** on the last Sunday in January is the official end of the month's wild festivities.

Can February be far behind? By no means! After barely a breather, one of the great popular spiritual manifestations of the year is orchestrated on February 2, the **Festa de Iemanjá,** goddess of the sea and principal mother figure in the pantheon of *candomblé* dieties. This is a festival of fishermen who are seeking the protection of the goddess from storms and shoals in the practice of their craft. All of the trappings of the *candomblé* accompany this colorful water pageant—priests, priestesses, and devotees in their vestments and symbolic costumes, processions, drums, chanting, candles. Offerings deemed appropriate to one as vain as Iemanjá is thought to be, from cosmetics to jewelry, are floated out to sea all along the beach from Rio Vermelho to Itapua in the hope they will find favor with Salvador's most beloved goddess.

Two Sundays before Carnival, which usually takes place in February, the **Festa do Rio Vermelho** pays special homage to St. Anne, mother of the Blessed Virgin. And then all hell breaks loose in Salvador as **Carnival** has come again, and is celebrated like nowhere else in Brazil. The Carnival of the slaves, incorporating music and dance that originated in the rites of the *candomblé*, was imported from Salvador and melded seamlessly throughout the country with the ancient pre-Lenten festivities that stemmed from Christian traditions. The practice of Carnival in Salvador, moreover, has not been completely commercialized, as in Rio. The spontaneous singing and dancing through the streets, behind sound trucks carrying live bands, is still more central to the event than the formal parades and competitions of the *blocos* and *escolas de samba* or the celebrations in private clubs.

Holy Week in Salvador is more of a religious festival than a party, though Eastertime is also a major secular holiday weekend throughout Brazil and the country comes to a complete halt. With so many churches, the processions in Salvador are endless, and particularly medieval throughout the city's historic district.

On May 10, Salvadorans publicly celebrate the feast day of their patron saint, **St. Francis Xavier,** a tradition in the city that dates from the late 17th century.

June is the month of bonfires and fireworks, the apostolic feasts honoring **Sts. John and Peter.** June is also significant on the calendar of the *candomblé*, when all the gods are honored in rites spread over a 12-day period.

Finally a hiatus, until November, when the pre-Carnival festivities begin the celebratory cycle anew. The next-to-last Sunday in November is the public **Feast of São Nicodemo de Cachimbo,** then **St. Barbara's Day** on December 4, and the **Feast of the Immaculate Conception** on December 8, a major street event on the waterfront, especially in the vicinity of the Igreja Nossa Senhora da Conceição da Praia.

After Christmas begins the **Festa da Boa Viagem** once again, culminating on New Year's Day with the boat procession of Nosso Senhor dos Navigantes. And in Salvador, for the rest of the year, the beat goes on.

NIGHTLIFE: The show at the **SENAC**, Largo do Pelourinho 19 (tel. 242-5503), is a dignified introduction to Bahian folkloric culture, including *candomblé* and *capoeira*. Earnest young artists and performers put on the show here, and their respect for the experiences they portray is communicated, even if these abstractions of culture are never as good as the real thing when witnessed at their most spontaneous and least self-conscious. Similar shows are at the **Solar do Unhão,** on Avenida do Contorno (tel. 245-5551), and the **Tenda dos Milagres,** Avenida Amaralina 553 (tel. 248-6058). *Tenda dos Milagres,* by the way, is the title of Jorge Amado's epic tale of Afro-Brazilian life on the streets of Bahia, available in English from Avon Books.

The hot spot for singles recently was the **Bar Ad Libitum,** Rua João Gomes 88, off the Largo de Santana (Praça Marechal Aguiar) in the beach neighborhood of Paciência, not far from Barra. All the deluxe and first-class hotels have nightclubs or discothèques, some of which, like the **Hippopotamus** in the Bahia Othon Palace and the **Charles Night** in the Itapuã Praia Hotel, are private clubs, usually open to tourists by invitation.

Many headliners, often natives of the city or region, play Salavador frequently. Names to look for are Gilberto Gil, Gal Costa, Maria Bethânia, and Caetano Veloso. A new sensational home-grown talent to watch for is singer Margareth Menezes, who often plays clubs and cabarets, but has recently broken through to the concert level.

There are numerous good bars scattered around town with music nightly by pianists or small combos. Notable is the **Bistro do Luís,** Rua Cons. Pedro Luís 369 (tel. 247-5900), in the fashionable Rio Vermelho neighborhood on the *orla*. The bistro is co-owned by Lisbon Luís Guedes and his American wife, Patricia, and is popular with luminaries of the Bahian art, music, and literary scenes. Habitués are said to include the artists Carybé and Carlos Bastos, whose works hang with those of many other painters, salon-style, about the premises.

Bars and clubs in the Barra neighborhood include the **Bistro Porto 507,** Avenida 7 de Setembro no. 507 (tel. 237-3821), which has live music on weekends. For music and dancing, there is **Close-Up,** Rua Prof. Fernando Luís 12 (tel. 245-5763). The **Clube 45,** Rua Barão de Sergy 196 (tel. 235-0604), has an animated pub-like atmosphere. Barra is the one place in town where the nightspots are concentrated along both the Avenida 7 de Setembro and its side streets, and so café- and bar-hopping is convenient here.

Most of the other good clubs are located along the 15-mile stretch of the *orla,* from Barra to Itapua.

Candomblé

The preservation of *candomblé* and its related sects that exist throughout Brazil represents one of the great struggles and achievements of a people threatened with cultural annihilation in the modern age. To be sure, the African-derived religions have suffered many modifications since the first slaves were transported to Brazil. Over time these animist practices borrowed freely from both the dominant state religion, Catholicism, and from the myths and sensibilities of the indigenous peoples as well. Nonetheless, it is humbling to recollect just how much of the original African content is retained in the rites despite the overwhelming repression and the strong currents of assimilation to which the slaves and their ancestors were subjected: snatches of chanted language, like Yoruba, passed surreptitiously from one generation to another; the names and attributes of the various deities; the drum and percussion rhythms, so intimately related to the religion, and which have no peer in musicology; the transcendent body movements of the celebrants when possessed by their gods, which in the secular culture gave birth to the samba; the cuisine, special dishes prepared to satisfy the most demanding spirit.

Too often *candomblé* and *macumba* ceremonies are exploited by the tourism industry in Brazil, and served up to visitors as if they had no more significance than a TV variety show. It is precisely the color, music, and movement of the legitimate ceremonies, in fact, that encourage this tendency to view and present these practices to tourists as a form of entertainment. As a result, the rituals attended by most "outsiders" have a staged and artificial quality, as if their only purpose were to put on a good show for the foreigners, who in exchange are charged a healthy entrance fee.

There are at least two ways—beyond traditional research in libraries and museums—in which the visitor may make a more authentic connection with *candomblé,* if so motivated. The first is obvious: befriend a believer, and convince him to quietly sponsor you as a guest during one of the regular services. The second is to go privately to a *terreiro*, as the temples are called, and meet the *mãe de santo* or the *pai de santo* (priest or priestess), and ask them if you can tour the facilities, interesting in and of themselves. Many of these clerics (for want of a better term) will also be happy to throw the shells and read your fortune, one of the many services they provide their parishioners, though this will cost you a donation and you will probably need an interpreter if you don't speak Portuguese.

SHOPPING IN SALVADOR: The streets of Salvador are filled with vendors.
Half the people on the streets are out walking somewhere, while the other half seem to be selling something: handmade jewelry, "silver" charms, T-shirts, rosewood carvings, *balangandãs* (copies of the baubles given in the past to favored female slaves), leather goods, percussion instruments, and of course, gemstones—raw, polished, strung, or set in rings, bracelets, or brooches. Some vendors sell, more or less officially, from stalls in the various plazas like the Praça da Sé, the Praça da Piedade, or the Praça Castro Alves, and many others spread their wares at curbside, while jewelry makers carry their goods pinned to cardboard placards and approach you as you stroll by. You can probably do all the shopping you require, for personal mementos and presents, without ever entering a store. And remember—never accept the first price. Try to pay half, or at most, two-thirds of the offered price.

For craft items of better quality, try the **Instituto Mauá**, Avenida 7 de Setembro no. 261, in Barra (tel. 235-5440). This nonprofit organization is charged with the mission of protecting and supporting the state's traditional crafts, samples of which—including pots, lace, and baskets—are assembled here from various centers of handcraft manufacture from all over Bahia. There is no bargaining at the Instituto Mauá: all items have clearly marked price tags.

The **Mercado Modelo**, overlooking the harbor on the Praça Cairú, is a big disappointment as a craft market. It seems to exist today solely for tourists, and the quality of the goods is no better than that found on the streets, while the prices are considerably higher. The one advantage of the Mercado Modelo is that all the geegaw-style souvenirs are assembled here under a single roof. While you might reasonably forgo shopping at the Mercado Modelo, the building's two restaurants should not be ignored. The second-floor café with the large outdoor veranda is one of the more pleasant places to lunch, snack, or drink, while observing the lively harbor scene.

Many vendors will approach you with items crafted from silver—or a metal they claim to be silver. Unless you are expert in distinguishing true silver from its alloys, you're better off going to a legitimate shop, like **Gerson** in the Pelourinho at Rua do Carmo 26 (tel. 242-2133), which specializes in silver service and jewelry. The shop occupies several floors of a lovingly restored colonial building, and hostesses circulate continually, offering trays of fresh-squeezed juices while you browse. Gerson also has branches in Barra next to the Hotel Praia Mar, at the airport, and in **Iguatemi**, Salvador's principal shopping center, located on the Praça da Mariquita, Rio Vermelho.

H. Stern is also well represented in the city, with shops at the airport, the shopping center, and in the Othon and Meridien Hotels.

If there is one city in Brazil where art collectors might have some luck in acquiring first-rate **contemporary paintings**, it is Salvador, long a bohemian haven for practicing painters. The naive street art can be found displayed in the various plazas mentioned above. Galleries and artist studio shops also abound, particularly in Barra. The enigmatic **Carybé**, a kind of latter-day Debret, is an Argentine who through his anthropological drawings has become the chief interpreter of Bahia's folk culture, and has a studio at Rua Medeiros Neto 9. The equally popular **Mirabeau Sampaio**, sculptor and draftsman, has an atelier at Rua Ary Barboso 12.

3. WHERE TO STAY

Hotel construction in Salvador has yet to catch up with the city's rising popularity as a destination for a new generation of international visitors, mostly traveling from the demanding European and North American markets. One result is that hotel resources sometimes seem strained, and service can suffer. Standards in Salvador are not quite on a par with those of more tourist-sensitized Rio or more sophisticated São Paulo. One senses that Salvadorans are trying to adjust to a new dimension in tourism, and that the necessary fine-tuning will follow this adjustment. All upper- and medium-bracket hotels listed here, unless noted to the contrary, furnish mini-bars, telephones, and TVs in their air-conditioned rooms.

THE UPPER BRACKET: While by no means the most expensive accommodations in town, the **Pousada Convento do Carmo**, Largo do Carmo 1, in Pelourinho (tel. 071/242-3111), because of its unique charm and setting, must be listed with the city's best hotels. In 1975 the nuns' cells in this former Carmelite cloister were converted into a 70-room *pousada* or inn. Grand Inn might be a more suitable description, since a building of this enormous scale in its own time—300 years ago—would have been a public house of considerable dimensions. When examining the "cells," one is struck by the generosity of the space, an image somewhat at odds with the preconceived notion that the contemplative orders led ascetic lives in cramped quarters. The chest-high window casements run nearly to the ceiling, easily 15 feet high. They are bordered with green shutters, all fitted with the vintage hand-forged hardware of their era. The wide door to the cell is encased in stone, and finish-molded with some noble hardwood. The floors have wide planking, perhaps handsawed rather than milled, and the massive timber beams visible everywhere in the corridors were definitely hewn, first by hand and then by age.

If the plastered and whitewashed walls of the room and the Shaker-like simplicity of its furnishings seem spartan at first sight, never was self-denial accompanied by so much pure style. The scale of the beds ought to be discreetly increased, however, to better accommodate *Homo sapiens* who pamper themselves with such comforts at home. The Convento do Carmo has one of the city's more reliable restaurants, the Forno e Fogão, and a stone-paved courtyard with a pool and plantlife set in the old cloister yard where the sisters once meditated and read their offices. Best of all, as a guest in the Convento you are located in the bull's-eye of the historic district, which is also a living tableau of the present. Standard double rooms start at $50.

With the exception of the **Hotel da Bahia**, Praça 2 de Julho no. 2 (tel. 071/237-3699), all of Salvador's other luxury hotels are on the *orla*, the strip of suburban ocean beaches. The Hotel da Bahia is across from the Campo Grande park, mid-way between downtown and the neighborhood of Barra. The attractive ten-story Mediterranean-style building was completely renovated in 1984, and upgraded in the process to a five-star hotel. In addition to the attractive standard rooms, white in décor with dark-wood furnishings, the hotel has a variety of luxury rooms with large verandas, and two duplex suites, complete with wooden decks and private dip pools. The high-ceilinged lobby has stuffed leather chairs, several boutiques, and a travel agency. The large pool and patio on the second level overlook the park, where on occasion public fairs are staged, like the Spring Festival in early October with music, plus craft and food stands. Standard and superior rooms, differing only in view, range from $60 to $71 for a single, and $66 to $79 for a double.

The **Salvador Praia Hotel**, Avenida Presidente Vargas 2338 (tel. 071/245-5033), is in Ondina, the first of the ocean beach neighborhoods, along a stretch of coast that is more rocky than sandy. Nevertheless, the Salvador Praia is blessed with a small private sand beach on its own grounds. The hotel has 164 rooms, painted in languid shades of café au lait, with polished wood furniture and original oil paintings. Each bath is tiled in marble from floor to ceiling, with a stall shower but no tub. Outside, overlooking the beach is a large pool and sundeck area adjacent to an equally spacious shaded terrace. The hotel's breakfast room sparkles, and has some strange, but quite good, surreal art. Nightly rates are $60 to $68 for a single and $65 to $72 for a double.

A stone's throw from the Salvador Praia is the delightful **Bahia Othon Palace Hotel**, Avenida Presidente Vargas 2456 (tel. 071/247-1044). The Othon Palace lobby is one of grand conception, quite consciously a vaulted cathedral, but the lines are more square than curved, and the materials are thoroughly contemporary. Near the entrance, two floors are offset, with shops on each level. A succession of high arches deliberately creates the effect of a cloister yard and leads to the reception area. The building itself is brown-tinted, the two 12-story wings meeting in a V, a design that provides all 277 rooms with views of the sea. The pool area is built on a platform that slightly overhangs a rocky stretch of the shoreline, where the elevation is no more than 15 feet above the water. A trail leads to a nearby beach.

The rooms are very large, and the walls are decorated with tiles. The cabinetry and bed alike are curvaceous and shiny, like Oriental furniture. The headboards are rattan, and the floors are of polished stone. Each room has a small balcony with teak floorboards, and lattice shutters. Blue-tile baths have tubs with shower curtains. The hotel's bright coffeeshop with blue-checkered cloth-covered tables overlooks the pool, and serves a full lunch for about $6. Accommodations are classified in three categories—standard, deluxe, and super-deluxe —and are priced $70 to $77, $84 to $93, and $93 to $103, for singles and doubles respectively.

The **Enseada das Lajes**, Avenida Oceânica 511 (tel. 071/237-0095), is a former private villa tucked away on a hill called the Morro da Paciência, and now converted into a small hotel of distinction by the same family that had once resided there. Each of the nine guest rooms has walls of polished red brick and wood plank floors, but no two rooms are furnished or decorated alike. Each is large and light, and contains several stunning antique pieces. One bathroom has a sunken tub and a separate shower with a curtain of lace. Venerable brass fixtures operate the plumbing. There is no lobby to speak of, but several large public spaces, including an atrium garden, an inviting lounge, and a glass-enclosed veranda restaurant with rattan tables and chairs and a superb view of the sea. The hotel has a pool and patio, lovely grounds set on a sloping hillside, and access to several quiet, rocky coves on the shore below. Rooms are between $135 and $165.

Salvador's premier beach hotel, the **Meridien**, Rua Fonte do Boi 216 (tel. 071/248-8011), is the next luxury establishment along the beach, in Rio Vermelho, immediately following the Paciência. With 277 rooms, the Meridien is Salvador's largest hotel, and chic in the French mold, boasting of both a superior restaurant, the rooftop St. Honoré, and a popular discothèque, Régine's. All the hotel's rooms face the sea, since the tall high-rise building occupies the point of a small peninsula. The décor in the rooms is subtle—peach is the dominant shade—and the furnishings, like the maroon jug-shaped lamps, are modern and tasteful. Original art decorates the walls, and all rooms have small balconies with long views of neighboring beaches. Other facilities include a large pool and patio, sauna, and tennis courts. Singles begin at $76 and doubles at $85.

About 15 miles from downtown in Itapoã, the **Hotel Quatro Rodas**, Rua do Passárgada (tel. 071/249-9611), sits on 14 acres of beach land thickly planted with coconut palms. The lobby and public rooms are large and elaborately decorated with plants and old farm equipment. There is a happy hour in the piano bar every night at 6 p.m. A small working watermill provides both the theme and the centerpiece for the hotel's restaurant. Outside, there is a small natural lake on the grounds, and boats for the guests to paddle. The beach itself, considered Salvador's best, is about a five-minute walk over a path that cuts beneath the palms. The 200 accommodations all look out on the sea over a landscape of dunes and beach vegetation. Standard rooms have twin beds, and deluxe accommodations have two large double beds. Rooms are spacious and clean-lined, with whitewashed walls and carpeted floors. Baths are also large, and have tubs with showers. There are three tennis courts on the grounds, and a large swimming pool and sunning area. Rooms are $74 to $82 for standards, and $87 to $97 for deluxe.

THE MIDDLE BRACKET: At the **Grande Hotel da Barra**, Avenida 7 de Setembro no. 3564 (tel. 071/247-6011), half the 117 rooms are classified as standards and occupy an older building off the street. The deluxe rooms are in a newer building nearer the water, attached by glass-enclosed walkways to the hotel's older components. The standard rooms are large, with enough space for several extra armchairs, and have big baths, tiled in blue from floor to ceiling. The deluxe accommodations are newer and smaller, and they all have balconies with views of either the sea or a very private interior courtyard pool. Rates are $45 to $50 for the standard rooms, and $51 to $56 for the deluxe.

Nearby is the pleasant and sturdy **Praiamar**, Avenida 7 de Setembro no. 3577 (tel. 071/247-7011), with a nice diagonal view of the old Barra Fort. Rooms are of medium size, and all very dayroom bright with bedspreads and other highlights in orange and with solid furnishings. Added to green carpets and floral-patterned tiles in the baths, it sounds garish, but the decorators somehow carry off their statement with good effect. A single room costs $34, and a double, $38.

The **Marazul**, Avenida 7 de Setembro no. 3937 (tel. 071/235-2110), is across the street from both the Porto da Barra beach and another old fort, the Forte de Santa Maria. The hotel is relatively new, with 125 rooms in a nine-story modern building of glass and molded concrete. A terrace at mezzanine level with a small but stylish pool on a raised teak deck overhangs the street, but looks through the tops of palms to the water beyond. The rooms are no-nonsense modern, with large double beds, and built-in hardwood furniture, all in light earth tones (except for the dark-brown blackout curtains). The baths are fully tiled, and in the ceiling is a single recessed light. Room prices are the same as the Praiamar, $34 single and $38 double.

The **Bahia Park Hotel**, on Praça Augusto Sévero in Rio Vermelho (tel. 071/248-6588), has 56 rooms, each with its own large stenciled number. Shades of brown dominate the décor in the rooms. The bedboard is unusual—detached from the bed, it hangs from the wall. The rooms' stark design and use of abstract paintings is appealing, and the bathrooms have marble sinks, tile floors, and large stall showers. The rooftop terrace is very simpatico; it has only a dip pool, but a spectacular view of Rio Vermelho and its environs. One major defect of the Bahia Park is that roughly half the rooms in effect have no windows, because the glass is covered by a metallic façade fixed to the building's front, creating not only an intrusive feature, but one that is totally unnecessary architecturally or functionally. Standard rooms are $36 to $42, and the deluxe room is $60. The hotel does not charge the 10% service tax.

On the downtown side of the Avenida 7 de Setembro at no. 2209 is the **Hotel Bahia do Sol** (tel. 071/247-7211), between Barra and Campo Grande, along the so-called Vitoria Corredor. The building has wooden shutter shades, a feature quite typical of apartment buildings in the tropics. The shades shut out the light but allow ventilation, a nice feature for people who like to sleep without air conditioning. The walls of the 90 rooms are papered, while bright heavy-textured fabric is used for the bedspreads. The furniture is modular, constructed of hardwood, with white Formica surfaces. The baths are large with attractive turquoise-colored tile walls, seashell pedestal sinks, and mirrors framed in wood. Off the lobby is an atrium garden and a restaurant bar set in the rear of the building, distant from the street. Rooms cost between $36 and $42 a night.

The next-door **Vila Velha**, Avenida 7 de Setembro no. 1971 (tel. 071/247-8722), is an older hotel, but well maintained and newly redecorated. The rooms are mid-sized but have large bathrooms with powder-blue tiles and marble-topped sinks. The rooms don't face the front or back, but the sides of the building, and all have good lateral views. Rates are the same as the Bahia do Sol, between $36 and $42 a night.

THE BUDGET RANGE: There are several inexpensive beach hotels on the *orla*, along the city's outer strands. Two that are run by the same management as the Bahia Park in Rio Vermelho are the **Hotel Itapoã**, Rua Dias Gomes 04 (tel. 071/249-9988), and the **Hotel Praia Dourada**, Rua Dias Gomes 10 (tel. 071/249-9639), both in Praia Placaford.

Students and impecunious writers favor the cheaper hotels—by no means fleabags—that are located in the old city, like the **Hotel Pelourinho**, at Rue Alfredo de Brito 20, in the Largo do Pelourinho (tel. 071/242-4144), and off such inner-city plazas as the Praça Anchieta and the Terreiro de Jesus.

4. DINING OUT

BAHIAN CUISINE: Bahian food is the most unique and varied of all regional cooking in Brazil. The use of many spices and herbs along with coconut milk and an African palm oil called **dendê** make it so. The cuisine of Bahia owes much to African tradition, and to the improvisational abilities of the early slaves, whose choice of ingredients were limited to a catch from the sea or the master's unwanted leftovers. Out of this adversity has come a great school of cooking.

Many a restaurant meal in Salvador will begin with **casquinha de siri**, a concoction of white crabmeat mixed with dendé (palm oil), onions, and tomatoes, and served in its own shell with a sauce, and topped with sprinkles of grated parmesan cheese. **Moquecas**, fish or shellfish stews cooked in earthern pots, are the city's culinary emblem. Moquecas should be made with the freshest ingredients from the sea, and are flavored by hot chiles and dendé, but are seldom overly spicy right from the kitchen. **Molho de pimenta**, a hot sauce of chile paste and dendé, is always present on the table, and can be added according to taste for those who savor truly "hot" food. Cooked with coconut milk instead of dendé, a moqueca becomes an **ensopada**.

Bahians have two favorite chicken dishes, the first a stew called **xim xim** (pronounced "shing shing"), with ingredients that vary from cook to cook. The preparation can include ground peanuts, coconut, mint, fish, or squash, but the sauce is always thick, and the chicken well stewed and flavorful. **Galinha do molho pardo** is a freshly killed chicken served in a brown gravy from its own blood. This dish is a popular offering to the gods in *candomblé* rituals, where animal sacrifice is a central element in the liturgy. From here the dishes become even more exotic, like **efó**, beef tongue and shrimp stew, and **sarapatel**, a pork dish in which innards like tripe and other unmentionables are stewed in the pig's blood. Bahian-style **feijoada**, with red instead of black beans, should also not be overlooked.

As is usual throughout all Brazil, side dishes also play an important role in every Bahian meal. Commonly served as accompaniments are rice, **farofa de dendé** (manioc flour fried in palm oil), and **vatapá**, a very tasty porridge made primarily from bread, ground cashews and peanuts, dried shrimp, dendé, and the usual flavorings.

Bahian desserts are rich and much in demand. The most delicate are **quindim** and **papo de anjo**, egg yolk custards, the first with coconut, served doused in sticky syrup. **Cocadas** are coconut candies, white or dark depending on whether regular or burnt brown sugar is used in their preparation.

Street food is sold everywhere in Salvador by Bahianas, women in traditional costume—wide skirts and lacy white blouses, turban-headed and bejeweled. These vendors once had to be sanctioned by their respective *candomblé* temples, where as devotees the young women were initiated into the culinary secrets of the sect. They learned how to make those bean-cake fritters called **acarajé**, which you will see boiling in oil on their improvised braziers. A dried bean called fradinho, similar to a black-eyed pea, ground and mixed with dendé is the basic recipe. Salvadorans have as many opinions about who makes the perfect acarajés, as New Yorkers have about where to buy the best pizza. You can eat the acarajé by itself, or have it served stuffed with vatapá and shrimp and seasoned with hot pepper sauce. Some Salvadorans hold that the best acarajés are sold on the Praça de Santana, across from the Ad Libitum bar. The perfect beverage with this snack is **caldo de cana**, freshly squeezed sugarcane juice, which is also sold at this same location.

SALVADOR'S RESTAURANTS: Since Bahian food is bound to represent a

whole new taste for many visitors, it would be wise to sample the fare first at the **Casa da Gamboa**, Rua da Gamboa de Cima 51 (tel. 245-9777), where you will be assured of fine ingredients and fastidious preparation. This whitewashed old town house on a hill would be a perfect setting for any meal in Salvador, but ask to be seated near a window looking out over the bay, if possible. Order the moqueca of your choice, and the xim xim too, if in company, along with vatapá, rice, and farofa, and then settle back with an apéritif, say a fruit *batida* (fresh-squeezed mango, passion fruit, or maracujá) with cachaça cane brandy. Sample as many desserts as you have appetite for, and one or more of proprietor Dona

Conceição's homemade liquors. If you decide you've enjoyed the experience, you will have many other opportunities in the city to satisfy and widen your newly acquired tastes. Depending on your selections and bar bill, the meal will cost you between $10 and $15 per person. The Casa da Gamboa is open for lunch from noon till 3 p.m. and for dinner after 7:30 p.m. until midnight; closed Sunday.

Your next Bahian meal, then, should be at the **SENAC**, an acronym for Serviço de Educação Nacional de Artes Culinarias, the state-run restaurant school where young chefs get their training. The SENAC occupies a grand old building at Largo do Pelourinho 13/19 (tel. 242-5503), and serves its meals buffet style in a formal atmosphere, a reproduction of a dining room for heads of state. More than a dozen regional dishes are kept hot in steam trays on a central table, and guests can serve themselves at will. There is a separate table with over 20 desserts, including sweets and fresh fruit. Here you can sample the more exotic offerings, like efó or sarapatel, relatively risk-free in small doses. Drinks are served by waiters and are charged for separately. After the meal, for about $6 per person, you can stay for the folklore show staged outdoors in the yard behind the building. SENAC is open for lunch from noon to 3 p.m.,and for dinner from 7 to 10:30 p.m. Patrons may order the seia, coffee or hot chocolate with sweets, alone for $2 between 5 and 8 p.m.

A block from the SENAC building is the Convento do Carmo, with its **Forno e Fogão** restaurant, Largo do Como 1 (tel. 242-3111), serving international food as well as a selection of Bahian dishes like moquecas. Once the refectory of the Carmelites, placed in the cellar among the arched underpinnings and stone foundations, the restaurant maintains, with its plain blue linen and pewter service, the hotel's theme of understated elegance. The chefs strive to capture the imagination of diners with offerings like camarão à moda do chefe—sautéed shrimp with fish, fruit, corn, and mushrooms, served flambéed in cognac. Dessert might be slices of mango or papaya with fresh lime, or a gossamer-light quindim custard. Prices at the Forno e Fogão are very reasonable, often no more than $15 for two, with drinks. Open daily from midday to midnight.

There's a small French restaurant in Ondina, the **Chaillot**, Avenida Presidente Vargas 3305 (tel. 237-4621), in a renovated house facing the sea from across the main avenue of the *orla*, that just may be the best restaurant in the city. Owner Caio Mario Gatti moved the family business from Petrópolis, outside of Rio, to the Bahian capital a few years back. Caio, a quiet bear of a man, creates the dishes and supervises the cooking in his restaurant, and judging from the results, he's not one to rest on his reputation or past laurels. As you sit at the zany bar near an open window being refreshed by cool sea breezes, on zebra-striped banquettes before tables that look like sawed-off temple columns, Caio may suggest a round of cajú amigos. This batida is made with the juice and pulp of the cashew fruit, with a healthy dose of cachaça, only available when that delectable fruit is in season during the Brazilian springtime. To dine, you descend a set of stairs into the dining room, and begin the meal with boca de carangueijo, the forelegs of the mangrove crab, fried in batter and dipped in fresh mayonnaise. The moqueca de badejo, a local fish similar to sea bass, is likely to be the most delicate fish stew you will sample in Salvador. A second course of filet molho de roquefort (filet mignon in roquefort sauce) is equally superb. For dessert, melt-in-your-mouth mousse de coco—coconut mousse, what else! Entrees are less than $10 each, remarkably reasonable for meals of truly gourmet quality. Open daily for lunch from noon to 3 p.m., and for dinner from 8 p.m. to midnight, later on weekends.

The **Restaurante Bargaço**, Rua P. Quadra 43 (tel. 231-5141), in Jardim Armação (after Pituba beach on the *orla*), began as a simple beach-neighborhood fish house. Today the restaurant can boast the most chic clientele in the city.

Upper-class Salvadorans from cabinet ministers on down dine regularly on the fine seafood of the Bargaço. Most of the tables are at an outdoor covered patio. For appetizers there are generous portions of crab and lobster meat, grilled shrimp and raw oysters, at about $7 a platter. The principal entrees are several varieties of ensopadas, mariscadas, and fish stews simmered in coconut milk, which arrive at the table still bubbling and cost an average of $13. The Bargaço is on a backstreet in the vicinity of the city's Convention Center complex, and it's not easy to find on your own. But most cab drivers will know how to get there. Open daily for lunch and dinner at the usual hours.

A less pretentious seafood restaurant, and just as good, is the popular seaside **Marisco**, Rua Euricles de Matos 123, in Paciência. Lobster dishes are $9, and shrimp costs $6.50. Fresh fish, sautéed, baked, or grilled in a variety of styles, costs $4 to $9 a serving. Octopus stew runs $7, and the crab Créole is $5. Caipirinhas and batidas cost between 50¢ and 75¢ a drink. You sit on a veranda at a table with a rumpled cloth and begin your meal with a heaping mound of casquinhas fried in batter and plenty of cold beer. But the ensopada is the real treat, a ceramic pot filled to overflowing with fish, clams, octopus, shrimp, and crabmeat, for about $12. Open all week from 11:30 a.m. to 3 p.m. for lunch, and from 7 p.m. to midnight for dinner.

Also near the Convention Center is the **Praiano**, Avenida Otávio Mangabeira (tel. 231-5988), in the Boca do Rio stretch of the *orla*, opposite the old Air Club field, now fallow real estate awaiting the right moment for development. The Praiano is a typical beach-side seafood restaurant with an informal open-air dining patio and another 60 or so linen-covered tables in a more formal inside dining room. The restaurant's menu is extensive, including all the local fish specialties—the most expensive items cost about $8—along with beef, chicken, even turkey dishes, for an average price of around $5. Open daily during normal lunch and dinner hours.

For fine cuts of beef, Salvadorans favor **Baby Beef,** next to the giant Hipermercado Paes Mendonça, on Avenida Carlos Antonio Magalhães (tel. 244-0811). Filet, T-bone, beefsteak, pork, and lamb are the specialties, all for a very affordable $5 to $6 in a sophisticated atmosphere. Paes Mondonça also operates a chain of fast-food joints throughout Salvador, featuring the usual fare borrowed from the kitchens of the Metropolis: grilled-cheese sandwiches, hot dogs, burgers, fries, even potato salad—all with a distinct Brazilian twist, of course. Locations include Barra, and Praça Cairú, near the Mercado Modelo.

For French cooking, and one of the best views of both town and sea in Salvador, there is the rooftop **St. Honoré**, in the Meridien Hotel, Rua Fonte do Boi 216 (tel. 248-8011). While not quite on a scale of conception or performance with the equivalent category of restaurant in Rio or São Paulo, the St. Honoré comes close enough, and has an atmosphere that is refreshingly relaxed, rather than stiffly formal as is commonly the case where French service is imposed. Surprisingly, the St. Honoré is not that expensive, so if you want to treat yourself to some genuine designer food as a break from *comida baiana*, this is a recommended spot to consider. Open for dinner only, from 7 p.m. to midnight, and later when attending the weekend set.

The **Solar do Unhão**, on Avenida do Contorno (tel. 245-5551), is the popular restaurant/cabaret set in this colonial *engenho* (sugarcane mill). The atmosphere is right, the food Bahian and international, and the show begins around 11 p.m.

After their having made such a grand contribution to Salvador's heritage, it would be unthinkable not to recommend a restaurant of the old master class, to wit, the **Cozinha Portuguesa**, Avenida 7 de Setembro no. 699, on the mezzanine (tel. 241-2641).

Another beef and new cuisine restaurant that has become a very popular gathering spot in the city is **Tiffany's**, on Rua Barão de Sergy, in Barra (tel. 247-4025).

5. EXCURSIONS AROUND BAHIA

Bahia is such a vast state, with so many attractions beyond the city limits of Salvador, that in future years the state's appeal may come to justify a guidebook of its own, just for the visitors from abroad. Brazilians already tour Bahia in its entirety, and have been doing so for years. For the moment, we will confine ourselves to brief descriptions of three locales, all within an hour or so of the capital city: the incomparable island of Itaparica, the Praia do Forte beach resort on the northern coast, and the old sugarcane capital of Cachoeira, nestled in an upper estuary of the Bay of All Saints.

ITAPARICA: This is the largest island in the Bay of All Saints, straddling its mouth between the two opposing points of the mainland, Salvador to the east, and rural coastal Bahia to the west. Itaparica was once a center of Brazilian whale fishing, but in recent years the island alternates between its off-season role as a backwater of fishing communities and small agricultural holdings, and its high-season function as a spa for escapees from Salvador who are well enough heeled to possess summer homes on this little corner of Eden. Itaparica also has a fledgling, but growing, infrastructure of tourist facilities. The ideal vacation in Salvador, especially for the first-timer, is to split the time between the city and the island. The ferry service (see "The Bay" in Section 2, above, for details on ferry service to Itaparica) is so regular, and the crossing sufficiently brief—less than an hour— that you can easily consider a form of commuting between the two destinations.

Itaparica is long and relatively narrow, about 18 miles from tip to tip, with major settlements on each end, **Vila Itaparica** to the north and **Cacha Pregos** to the south. A third center of summer action, **Mar Grande**, is in the middle of the island, a settlement with its eye turned perpetually toward the Salvador skyline across the bay. Strung between these principal towns are fishing hamlets, beaches, and colonies of summer cottages: some extravagant, others quite simple. Inland, a large portion of the native population lives on small farms, and works the soil producing crops of mandioca, along with bananas, breadfruit, mango, cashews, and numerous other fruits typical of tropical Bahia. The interior network of rutted dirt roads is hard on motor vehicles, but the inhabitants travel distances on the backs of horses and burros, and occasionally a bicycle is seen among the throngs of folk who most often walk from place to place.

On the opposite shore, the *contra costa* is close to the western continent and linked by a bridge. Here are located forgotten villages, like **Baiacú**, whose jet-black inhabitants, their dugout canoes and houses of mud and wattle, suggest the disorienting image of an isolated African hamlet. And indeed, perhaps this and similar communities are the remnants of **quilombos**, the free towns established as early as the mid-1600s by runaway slaves. Uprisings accompanied the institution of slavery in Brazil from its inception. The greatest of all the *quilombos*, called **Palmares,** was established in the neighboring state of Alagoas, and it endured for a century, finally brought to heel only in 1869. The great leader of Palmares, Zumbi, is today an honored national figure in Brazil, particularly among adherents of the country's incipient civil rights, or Black Consciousness movement.

Where to Stay in Itaparica

My personal first choice is always the **Galeão Sacremento**, in Mar Grande (tel. 071/833-1021). The Galeão is the perfect retreat for a quiet weekend on the island during the off-season (anytime really other than December through early

March, and on major holiday weekends throughout the year). The hotel's best rooms are in Tudor-style towers, and the grounds are large and shady, under a canopy of palms and flowering vines, and right on the beach as well. The hotel has its own good restaurant, and offers a number of activities *pour le sport*, including horseback riding and windsurfing. Standard rooms range in price from $42 to $48, and deluxe tower rooms are $52 to $60.

Two other hotel options for the island are both in Villa Itaparica, ne miniature city on the northern tip that has a mysteriously medieval air about .t. Nc doubt the presence of several extent churches and chapels that are among the oldest in Brazil contributes to this feeling. In fact, the entire island is studded with antiquities and ruins, and Itaparica's relatively small size makes it ideal for unstructured exploration, adding an element of wonder and surprise to private discoveries.

A budget choice is the **Hotel Icaraí**, Praça da Piedade 03 (tel. 071/831-1110), with 17 simple rooms, located on one of the most charming sites in the town, overlooking a delightful square and the waterfront. Rooms are approximately $10 double.

The islands' aging first-class hotel is the **Grande Hotel de Itaparica**, Avenida Beira Mar (tel. 071/831-1120). The hotel grounds hug Itaparica's northern point, and the two-winged colonial-style structure houses 87 rooms, all with verandas. Outdoor facilities include an illuminated tennis court and a swimming pool. The less expensive rooms cost between $27 and $30; deluxe accommodations run $37 to $41. Campers may pitch their tents for free on the **Praia da Areia**, a beach on the bay side between Villa Itaparica and Mar Grande.

Where to Eat

The best food on the island can be found at the **Philippe Restaurant**, Praça de São Bento 53 (tel. 833-1060). A transplanted Frenchman and former employee of the island's Club Med (a playground for wealthy Brazilians and Argentines that studiously avoids promoting to the North American market) offers both local and French-inspired dishes, priced between $7 and $15 per entree.

There are simple seafood restaurants all over the island, usually right on the shores of the sandy beaches. Nowhere on Itaparica are you ever far from a cold beer and a plate of fresh-caught shrimp sautéed in garlic and oil.

PRAIA DO FORTE: Several years ago, before the coastal Coconut Road (BA 099) was paved, the beach at Praia do Forte, a once-quiet fishing village, was the lone weekend preserve of those who had the dune buggies or four-wheel-drive vehicles needed to get there. And while the beach has undergone some development since those halcyon days, mostly the region remains protected by an ecologically minded foundation which holds title to the shore and its surrounding lands, the former estate of a Portuguese nobleman. Garcia D'Ávila once ruled virtually all of northeastern Brazil, and the ruins of the family castle, built in 1552—the only example of Renaissance architecture that remains in the country—are not far from the beach and definitely worth a visit.

There are several inns and a brand-new resort on the beach itself. The resort, the **Hotel Praia do Forte**, formerly the Club Robinson, recently underwent a change of ownership. Anyone wishing to book a room in this very special hotel should do so through Bahiatursa. Rooms cost $100 a night for two.

CACHOEIRA: Cachoiera is another of Brazil's colonial towns that has been declared a national monument. Once a major port and financial center for the sugarcane plantations, the town is located in the *recôncavo*, about 40 miles from Salvador. In 1624 the Portuguese colonials retired to Cachoiera, which became the *de facto* capital of Bahia during the two-year-long Dutch occupation of Salvador. The small provincial city is a showcase of colonial-era architecture, whose most remarkable buildings date from as early as the 16th and 17th centuries.

Many hotels and travel agencies in Salvador offer day trips to Cachoeira, some of which transport visitors there via the bay on converted commercial schooners. Check with Bahiatursa for details.

CHAPTER XII

THE NORTHEAST

□ □ □

The Brazilian Northeast is a land of legends. "*O nordeste,* that's the real Brazil," say the citizens of the country's comfortable and developed south, whenever the topic of the northeast comes up. And you might respond, "But isn't the nordeste the land of the dreaded *sertão*—the arid badlands, where sometimes there is no rain for an entire year, and cattle and people routinely die of starvation?" "Yes, of course, but do you know," you are instructed, "that despite the misery of the northeast, the underdevelopment, the high infant mortality, and all the other ills of the region, a quarter of the Brazilian population still lives there, though it is only 10% of the national territory. True, people leave all the time whenever the droughts are particularly prolonged, but at the first sign of rain, they all go back." Strange, this nordeste.

It was in the nordeste that the Portuguese staked their first claims in Brazil, planted their sugarcane, imported their slaves, slaughtered male Indians, and mated with their women. The mixed-race culture of the *caboclos* is what remains of that legacy. In the black-haired, bronze-faced *caboclos* you see a reflection of the earliest indigenous peoples. The amalgamation of their race and culture with that of their conquerers is their compromise with history, one that has endured in the *sertão* for over 4½ centuries. Yes, you think, this *is* the real Brazil.

The region's inhabitants, the *sertanejos,* are also often referred to as the *flagelados* (the flagellants), with the unmistakable inference that their status as Brazil's sacrificial lambs is at least partially self-inflicted. And indeed, to modernists everywhere, even native Brazilians, the *caboclos* seem inscrutable, and their punishing way of life incomprehensible. And yet, the *sertanejo* is stubbornly committed to the unforgiving desert where he makes his home. No other people anywhere, moreover, has embraced more fully the mystical elements of Catholicism. Out of this mysticism have sprung the greatest of all Brazilian legends, including the millenarian tragedies like the seige and destruction of the *flagelado* stronghold, Canudos, by the modernizing forces of the First Republic; and *coronelismo* (strongman rule) and *cangaceiros* (banditry), which go hand in hand, spawning such historic figures as Lampião and Padre Cícero, one a legendary gunslinger, the other a demagogue-priest, both mad as hatters, and as typical a human product of the *sertão* as the scrawny *caatinga* growth that covers the waterless backlands.

But the culture of the *caboclo* is only half the reality of northeastern Brazil. The rest of the story is told along the *literal,* the extensive coastal plains that run from one end of the great Brazilian bulge to the other. While never prosperous like the south, the northeastern coastal cities were the setting for great political and intellectual movements which have their strong echos in the Brazil of the present, as well as their historical and literary romance. Recife was the center of several bloody rebellions, providing its share of names for Brazil's pantheon of national heroes, like Frei Caneca, a republican priest who was executed under the first Brazilian Empire in the early 19th century. The northeast has also provided the nation with some of its greatest statesmen and poets, like Rui Barboso and Castro Alves.

It is within the seven cities of this chapter—each the capital of a state—that we will confine our current tour, surveying an attraction of the northeast that has only just begun to catch the eye of the international traveler: a coastline that can boast of possessing some of the world's finest and most unspoiled beaches. Despite being in the equatorial zone, the northeastern coast is blessed with perpetually cooling breezes from the sea. The sunshine is equally constant, giving credence to the region's claim of year-round summer weather. But the beaches are not the only appealing features of the northeastern coast. The cities themselves—some small and provincial, others genuinely metropolitan and urbane—are each special in a multiplicity of ways. The time to visit the nordeste, moreover, is now. Hotel and resort development has increased geometrically in the region over the past five years. But the coastline is so long, so rich with beachfront, that the atmosphere remains for the time being minimally touristic, and very fun-loving.

1. ARACAJÚ

Aracajú is the capital of **Sergipe,** the next state up the northern coast from Bahia. Aracajú is connected to Salvador by adequate roads, and the 200 miles between the two cities can be driven in five or six hours. VARIG and other Brazilian domestic airlines have regular, conveniently scheduled flights that originate in Salvador and make the daily run up the coast from capital to capital. This is a situation in which having the VARIG air pass makes a lot of sense, allowing you to get to know as many of the northeastern cities as you wish—each between 20 and 40 minutes apart by air—in a short space of time.

WHAT TO SEE: The name Aracajú means "the land of the cashew trees" in the Indian dialect native to the area. The city occupies the western bank of the Rio Sergipe, about ten miles upstream from the river's mouth. Also within the city limits are 18 miles of beaches that stretch off along the oceanfront to the south. But in truth, the state's entire coastline is one continuous beach, and the farther you go from the city, the more unspoiled and uncrowded are the strands.

The beach closest to the city proper is called **Atalaia Velha,** right on the outskirts of town, with its 1½-mile-long walkway by the shore, crowded with beer gardens and restaurants where much of Aracajú's nightlife is centered. Aracajú's main square is the **Praça Olímpio Campos,** a formal park and garden, dominated at one end by the city's old cathedral.

The **Centro de Turismo,** across from the plaza (tel. 079/222-9023), is in an old government building where the former offices have been turned into show

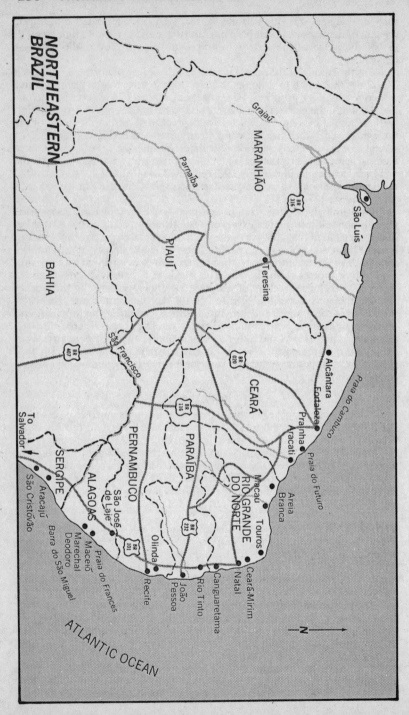

rooms for a wide variety of handmade items, including lace, carvings, pottery, and paintings—all of very good quality. At the other end of the shopping spectrum is the **Mercado Tales Ferraz,** Rua José do Prado Franco, a lively open-air market right along the wharves of the river. An old pavilion shelters grain and vegetable stands, vendors of raw cashews and coils of sticky chewing tobacco, as well as items of folk craft made from straw, clay, wood, and leather.

WHERE TO STAY: The brand-new **Parques dos Coqueiros,** Praia da Atalaia (tel. 079/223-2445), a stylish resort overlooking palms and the sea, is only five minutes from the airport. Laid out horizontally, this large attractive central building with a slanted red-tile roof contains the public spaces, a ground-floor open-sided coffeeshop, and a second-floor restaurant surrounded by a wall of windows. On the flanks are two wings of rooms—74 in all, but with plans to expand to 188—with verandas that open onto an enormous flagstone patio where a large pool encircles an island of potted palm trees. The rooms have beds with fringed spreads and sturdy hardwood furniture. In each closet a folded hammock is stored, ready to be mounted on hooks built into the veranda. The whole place has the snazzy look of an Arizona resort, but the prices are more modest. Lunch in the coffeeshop, with its unobstructed poolside view, and of the beach some several hundred yards beyond that, will cost about $5 for one of five daily offerings, fresh fish or *tutu mineiro,* for example. Nightly rates for rooms are $70 for a single, and $80 for a double.

The **Hotel das Dunas,** Avenida Presidente José Sarney, (tel. 079/223-6990), is located across the street from the nearby Robalo beach—right on the dunes, as the name implies, so there is only a bit of scrub vegetation around. But the sea air and constant breeze are wonderfully refreshing, and the sound of water breaking on the nearby shore couldn't be more relaxing. All 50 rooms are housed in bungalows with covered patios off the front door, where guests can recline on *espreguiceiras* (deck chairs) and face the sea. Rooms have double beds, large shuttered windows, and stone floors—which are perfect considering the amount of sand that gets tracked on them. Rooms are priced at $26 for a single and $30 for a double.

Closer to town is the **Hotel Beira Mar,** on Avenida Rotary (tel. 079/223-1921), off the Praia Atalaia Velha. The most comfortable of the hotel's 75 rooms are the deluxe accommodations. These are spacious, with tables and chairs in a separate anteroom, and glass-enclosed (and therefore air-conditioned) verandas, though the windows may also be opened for natural ventilation. Baths are large with pink tubs. Standard rooms, while a bit smaller, are also quite nice. The hotel's facilities include a courtyard pool and patio, and a bar said to be a popular nightspot. Deluxe rooms are $68 to $82, and standards cost between $52 and $61.

Also on the Praia Atalaia Velha is the **Aracajú Praia Hotel,** Avenida Santos Dumont (tel. 079/223-2521). All 66 rooms have ocean views, stone floors, and naïve paintings decorating the walls. Wooden catwalks connect the lobby to the hotel's other buildings and to a large pool area with an outdoor snackbar covered native style by an umbrella-shaped roof of straw. The inside restaurant offers a good selection of domestic wines, and fresh bread baked on the premises, a rarity in Brazil—which is by no means a knock on the country's commercial breads, consistently tasty and fresh no matter where you travel in Brazil. Rooms here cost $40 to $44 per night.

WHERE TO EAT: Downtown, there are several appealing choices for dining, starting with the **Cacique Cha,** Praça Olímpio Campos (tel. 222-5688). The restaurant is located in the city's main plaza, a formal and shady little park. The interior of the Cacique Cha is inviting. Tables have smart maroon-colored cloths, and the walls are covered with a technically interesting mural of the social-realist school portraying, in a series of panels full of feeling and movement, and tortured story of the nordeste, and painted in the '40s by the artist Jenner Augusto. The menu is varied, with many *pratos típicos*, like galinha do molho pardo and carne de sol. Most entrees are in the $3 to $5 range, and the restaurant is open daily from 10 a.m. until as late as there are customers to serve.

Across the street, in the courtyard of the Centro de Turismo building, is the **Rendendê** (tel. 224-3140), another restaurant serving typical regional dishes. Specialties include fritada de camarão (oven-cooked shrimp casserole, covered with beaten eggs), carne de sol na manteiga de garrafa (sun-dried beef with a sauce of clarified butter), and the side dish, pirão de leite (a gruel of manioc meal and milk). Entrees average around $5, and the restaurant is open for lunch from 11:30 a.m. till 3 p.m., and for dinner from 7 till 11 p.m.

The **Restaurante Panorama,** Praça Tobías Barreto 510 (tel. 222-3231), is located on the 13th floor of the Centro Médico Odontológico Building. As the restaurant's name implies, you get a view with your meal—and what a view it is! The building is close enough to the river's edge so that you see the ocean waves breaking at the mouth of the inlet, all of downtown and the waterfront, and the soccer stadium and the red-tile roofs of the many one- and two-story residences and commercial buildings spread across the floor of the city. The food is as good as the view, with such entrees as pitu de sergipe (crayfish stewed in coconut milk), large shrimp sautéed in garlic and oil, and fritada de aratú (a shrimp omelet-like soufflé). One of the side dishes is rich, creamy, lumpless mashed potatoes, a unaccountable favorite throughout the entire northeast region. Prices range from $5 to $10 per platter. The Panorama is open daily from 11:30 a.m. till midnight.

On the strip of the old section of the Atalaia beach is the **Taberna do Tropeiro,** Avenida Oceânica 6 (tel. 223-1466), another superb eatery where you can dine royally. To begin, try the pitu no espeto (crayfish on the skewer) and patinho de carangueijo (breaded mangrove crab leg). And don't forget the *pinga*. No cocktail goes better with this food than a shot or two of good, smooth cachaça. Notable among the main-course offerings are the shrimp salad, a platter of cold shrimp smothered in raw vegetables, hard-cooked eggs, hearts of palm, lettuce, and tomato; and also the breaded shrimp with a plate full of banana and pineapple (also breaded), palmito, hard-boiled eggs, rice, and mashed potatos. A meal for two with all the trimmings will cost $15 to $20. The restaurant opens at 10 a.m. and stays open until the last customer vacates the premises.

Street Food

All along the strip outside the O Tropeiro, and in many other sections of the city as well, you will see the hot coal braziers of the street vendors who are preparing **queijo coalho,** chunks of barbecued goat's-milk cheese served on wooden skewers. Try it—it's delicious!

A Suburban Park and Overlook

A 20-minute ride from downtown will bring you to the city park, the **Parque do Governador,** set in the foothills with a *mirante* (overlook) and a nice view of all Acarajú in the distance. There is a popular churrascaria here serving grilled meats and other typical dishes at low prices, in the $4 to $6 range. Open Tuesday through Sunday from 11 a.m. till 11:30 p.m.

EXCURSIONS FROM ARACAJÚ: At the mouth of the Rio Sergipe sits the **Ilha Santa Luzia,** also known as the **Barra dos Coqueiros** (Coconut Reef). The island is easily accessible by commercial ferry from the Terminal Hidroviário, located near the Telles Ferraz market, which makes the 15-minute crossing frequently for a princely sum of about 5¢.

The island can be visited as a day trip, to explore the little village and find a secluded stretch of ocean beach, or for a longer stay at the **Hotel da Ilha** (tel. 079/262-1221). The hotel complex is located on the ocean side of the island, and has acres of grounds with numerous sporting facilities and a pristine beach 2½ miles long with nothing but coconut palms. The hotel's 90 rooms are in chalets dispersed among the grounds, under their own canopy of palms and other colorful trees like the *mamona,* the castor-bean tree with its star-shaped leaves and large puffy red flowers. The rooms are extra-large, with a step down to a separate seating area containing rustic wood chairs, a couch, and a mini-bar. Other attractive details are the double beds with cream-colored sheets, shuttered windows, and large paintings mounted on the bright white walls, with orange-painted wood trim around the doorway. Rooms are $45 to $50 nightly, including breakfast.

Other meals must be purchased in the hotel's restaurant, which though catering to a captive audience, is reasonably priced. The other eating options are the **barracas,** the beach-shack food stands at the end of the beach in Ponta da Ilha, that sell seafood and beer.

The Hotel da Ilha also has its own large pool and sunning area, children's playground, and stable horses for guests who like to saddle up. Room rates are $45 single and $50 double.

São Cristóvão

A 45-minute car or bus drive southwest of Aracajú brings you to São Cristóvão, Sergipe's original capital and Brazil's fourth-oldest city, founded in 1590. The city has many architectural treasures, in particular the large stone square and **Convent of São Francisco** and the **Museum of Sacred Art and History.** São Cristóvão today is also known for its **casas de doces,** cottage-industry bakers who produce and sell from their houses a variety of sweets called queijadas. The little bags of sweets with names like doce de jenipapo, doce batata, argolinha, and bolachinhas sell for 25¢ to 50¢ and can be purchased at Rua do Rosário 70 and Praça Lauro de Freitas 87.

TOURS AND INFORMATION: The **Papagaios** agency, Avenida Hermes Fontes 838 (tel. 224-7518), in the capital's Salgado Filho neighborhood, conducts tours of Aracajú and its environs. The state tourist information bureau is **Emsetur** (Empresa Sergipana de Turismo), which may be consulted at their airport information counter, or in their main offices at Avenida Barão de Maruim 593, in downtown Aracajú (tel. 222-2426 or 222-1150).

2. MACEIÓ

Maceió is the capital of **Alagoas,** the next state as we travel northeasterly up the coast, approximately 120 miles from Aracajú by road and only a short hop by plane. The story of how the state got its name is prosaic in the extreme. An early explorer, Pero Vaz da Caminha, commenting on the number of large inland lakes along the future state's coastline, included the following sentence in his report to the Crown: *"Encontrei um lugar onde ha lagoas"* ("I have found a place where there are lakes"), and thus *"ha lagoas"* became Alagoas. Or so the story goes.

The state today is rare in what was once an entire region whose lands were saturated with sugarcane plantations. Sugarcane remains Alagoas's principal agricultural crop. The great green shoots of the cane are seen growing everywhere as you travel around the immediate environs of Maceió, and the very presence of the plants still embodies something of the atmosphere of Brazil's agrarian beginnings.

With about 400,000 inhabitants, the capital at Maceió is almost twice the size of Aracajú, and is one of the fastest-growing tourist destinations in Brazil. The state's coastline is a continuous and beautiful beach some 150 miles long. Among the cognoscenti, moreover, the beaches of Maceió are considered the best in all Brazil—though it's difficult to see how one would make such a judgment in a country where equally gorgeous beaches can be found from the mouth of the Amazon all the way to the Uruguayan border.

WHAT TO SEE: Maceió, like Salvador, has an *orla,* a strip of in-town beaches where most of the city's tourist-quality hotels and restaurants are concentrated. The best of these, as would seem logical, are the strands that are farthest from the inner city, which remains an active and colorful sugar port with some of the historical flavor of the days when it first evolved in the mid-1600s as a plantation and sugar mill.

The prime beaches are **Pajuçara, Ponta Verde, Jatiúca,** and **Praia de Cruz das Almas.** Maceió occupies the tip of a curved peninsula, the ocean beaches on one shore and the great lagoon, **Lagoa do Mundaú,** on the other, immediately to the south of Maceió's downtown area. Beyond the lagoon is the **Região do Sul** (the southern beach zone), and to the north of the city, going in the direction of Pernambuco state, are the beaches of the **Região do Norte,** both of which will be described under "Excursions from Maceió."

The In-Town Beaches

The major attraction of these beaches, beyond the obvious pleasures of sand and sea, is the sidewalk promenade that accompanies the contours of the shoreline. The wide pedestrian way, raised slightly above the sand and shaded by innumerable tropical trees, doubles as a jogging track by day and a center of nightlife when the sun goes down. All along the promenade, spaced every hundred yards or so, are sidewalk cafés—large stylized Indian huts with conical straw roofs, uniform in design according to a city plan. Each café, however, has its own regulars and its particular scene, one that often includes live music, and always tables full of friends in animated conversation.

On the southern fringe of the city's urban zone and waterfront begins the old surburban fishing village of **Pontal da Barra,** along the shores of the Lagoa do Mundaú. The village has a small and lovely town square, surrounded by old, low buildings and cottages. At the cottage windows, women weave their lace and display their artistic works for sale. Many rustic, but excellent, restaurants line the shores of the lagoon, specializing in seafoods purchased from the daily catch from its waters.

Boat and canoe excursions can be booked here for the popular cruises on the enormous lagoon, with its many islands and canals, and numerous other towns upstream along its banks.

WHERE TO STAY: Maceió's only five-star hotel, the **Matsubara,** Avenida Roberto Brito 1551 (tel. 082/231-6178), is a paradigm of discreet good taste, and may just possibly be the best small luxury hotel in Brazil. Every detail of design and organization in the Matsubara seems to have been consciously selected to blend and harmonize with its immediate surroundings, as well as with the overall image of the hotel. The building—an interconnected series of white blocks with protruding windows trimmed in brown—is a study in the creative applications to architecture of plain and solid geometry. All the forms are there, but their arrangement is never repetitious or banal. The hotel is located across from the Praia de Cruz das Almas, the farthest strand from the city, just now being developed by the hotel sector.

The Matsubara's bright atrium lobby is not huge by any means, but the space is ingeniously divided by barriers, mixed levels, plants, mirrors, and columns to create several distinct environments: a circular arrangement of green leather chairs; an informal café with rose-colored table linen, on a raised platform in a smart wood-dominated setting of its own; an excellent mezzanine restaurant behind an elegant wall of glass. The hotel has 110 accommodations spread among its six stories and various wings, all of which have balconies, some quite generous depending on the category of the room. Décor in the rooms, light shades of blues and greens, maintains the standard of elegance set by the hotel in its public spaces. The best carpets, classically striped fabrics, fine wood, and decorative modern art are used to highlight the bedroom, while the bath is lined in speckled brown granite tile and has a sauna-type ceiling of tongue-and-groove wood battens.

The hotel's grounds occupy a somewhat narrow strip, but they stretch from oceanside way back to the lower slopes of a palm-tree-covered hill. Behind the hotel are a large serpentine pool, two tennis courts, and basketball and volleyball facilities. And in the front courtyard is another pool which faces the beach. Both pools are set on patios ringed with recliners, and are served by their own bars. Another rare treat is the terrific steamroom in the health club area.

Nightly rates vary depending on room classification. The superior room—the least expensive—costs between $80 and $90 a night, for single and double occupancy. The deluxe runs $90 to $100, and so on up the scale to include special deluxe, and junior, family, or presidential suites. A half-board rate is also available, featuring a daily selection of ten different dishes from the hotel's restaurant menu.

Maceió is blessed with a second fine hotel, the **Hotel Jatiúca,** Lagoa de Anta 220 (tel. 082/231-2555), more of a resort really, and only 20 minutes from town, right on a point overlooking Jatiúca beach. A long driveway leads to a separate lobby building, with a courtyard restaurant and pool to the rear. And laid out over the 15-acre grounds under a cover of much vegetation are four long two-story buildings with the hotel's 96 rooms, and half a dozen other structures housing various facilities, all of which are interconnected by a network of covered brick pathways. The path, which also has walls of louvered shutters that open and close, crosses a small lagoon at one point as it meanders over the grounds down to the sand. No roadway need be crossed to reach the water, as is the case with the city's other hotels. In a rose stucco building near the edge of the sand is the cocktail bar and a restaurant, with banquettes along the walls, and large mullioned windows that slide open the better to take in the seascape and the ocean air. Rooms at the Jatiúca are large, bright, and simply but tastefully decorated, and each opens onto a balcony. The hotel's rates are between $81 and $90 for a standard single and double, and for the suite, $134 per night.

A very popular hotel all year round is the much simpler **Punta Verde,** Avenida Álvaro Otacílio 2933 (tel. 082/231-4040), a ten-story tower with 78 rooms across from the beach of the same name. Like most beaches on the stretch of coast from Maceió to above Recife, Punta Verde has a reef line that follows the outline of the shore, about 200 yards out. At low tide a natural pool is formed between the coral rock and the land, and fishermen easily catch the trapped octopus at that time. The Hotel Punta Verde has rates that begin at $25 and go up to $60 double for the best rooms, which are large and face the sea. The hotel has a pool and restaurant, but limited facilities otherwise. What it does have is super-friendly service, fair comfort, and a great location opposite one of Maceió's most popular beaches by day and its nighttime promenade after dark.

The **Hotel Enseada**, Avenida Dr. Antônio Gouveia 171 (tel. 082/231-5134), is across from the Praia de Pajuçara. The hotel has one wall that slopes like a stepladder, and all rooms in the unusually shaped nine-story building are built around a floor-to-ceiling atrium. The 104 rooms are large, modern, and well furnished. The hotel faces the Pajuçara beach where a reef a mile and a half offshore forms a vast natural pool, neck high at its deepest point at low tide. Standard rooms are priced from $48 to $52, and the deluxe rooms go for $52 to $58. If you stay for a weekend or longer, however, the hotel discounts the rates up to 40%.

WHERE TO EAT: Two excellent choices are the Matsubara's **Blooming Garden** or the **Restaurante das Alagoas** in the Hotel Jatiúca.

On a backstreet not far from the Hotel Punta Verde is the **Candelária**, Rua Cláudio Ramos 315 (tel. 231-2253), an Argentine restaurant specializing in grilled meats and Italian food. You can dine very well on the mixed grill, a variety of barbecued meats and sausage, at the Candelária for less than $7 a person. Open for lunch from 11:30 a.m. to 3 p.m., and for dinner from 7 p.m. to midnight.

On the road that runs along the bank of the lagoon in Barra do Pontal there are many small restaurants with unpretentious exteriors and superior kitchens. A good choice is the **Bar do Alípio**, Avenida Alípio Barbosa 321 (tel. 221-5186), where the nearby lagoon is a steady and reliable supplier of fresh seafood. The camarão moda da casa is shrimp poached in a broth of herbs and coconut milk. Particularly good is the carne de sol, tender and tasty slices of sun-dried beef with side dishes of rice and pirão, a kind of grits made from mandioca. The prices, to the relief of many locals, are ridiculously low: between $2 and $4 a platter.

EXCURSIONS FROM MACEIÓ: Outside of Maceió there are good beaches to both the north and south of the city. Also worth visiting is the far shore of the lagoon, with its small houses and the look of a rural bayou culture, subsisting on fishing and small-scale agriculture. Here on the far shore was the old state capital, also the birthplace of Brazil's first president, Marechal Deodoro da Fonseca, whose name it now bears.

The South Region

The road to the Região do Sul is a pleasant ramble on the lakeside, passing homes and occasional bars—like the Bar do Walter—about nine miles from Maceió, where you can sit under a grove of trees drinking a cold beer and watching the comings and goings on the lagoon.

Around 15 miles from the city is the turnoff to the left for a prized ocean beach, the **Praia do Francês** (Frenchman's Beach). You'd think a name like that would refer to some recent resident, a well-liked or eccentric expatriate who had perhaps built the first home or restaurant on the beach. But the derivation is more remote, harking back to a national slight committed centuries ago by French smugglers who were raiding the coast of Alagoas for valuable brazil wood. Today the beach is a favorite weekend retreat for residents and vacationers alike. By contrast, weekdays at Frenchman's Beach are tranquil and all but deserted. The beach is wide and long, with clean white sand and tepid waters, and natural pools at low tide.

Six miles farther south is **Barra do São Miguel**, where Brazil's first bishop, Dom Pero Fernandes Sardinha, had the misfortune to be captured by a tribe of nonbelievers. These people of the Caetés sacrificed the poor bishop and, one assumes, as was customary in such cases, consumed him. There is a very swank little hotel here on the beach, the brand-new and inexpensive **Village Barra Hotel,** (tel. 082/272-1207). The construction materials used here are both first-rate and imaginative. For example, jangada logs are used as exposed support posts for a variety of structures. Rates are as little as $26 for a standard single to $36 for two people in a "super-deluxe" room.

Marechal Deodoro

To visit the old colonial capital, founded in 1612, we must head back toward Maceió for a bit and turn off away from the Praia do Frances exit toward the interior, heading up the opposite shore of the lagoon. All told, Marechal Deodoro is about 40 miles from the new capital. The banks of the lagoon here are remarkably hilly in places, so the town has several dramatic prospects with views high above the water. Most streets have never been modernized, and remain narrow and paved with stone. President Deodoro, who expelled Dom Pedro II and proclaimed the Republic of Brazil in 1889 with himself as first "president," was born here in a respectable, but by no means luxurious house. Deodoro is never spoken of in Brazil. He seems somewhat of a national embarrassment, best forgotten as the perpetrator of the country's first military coup. His home is now a modest museum, but not without its fascinations, including the family furnishings and memorabilia—mostly photographs and news clippings related to the marshal's career, first in the military, later as a statesman.

The Northern Region

The Região do Norte covers a route that runs close to the ocean. One of several popular watering places is the **Balneário Paripueira,** 20 miles north of Maceió. The population zones to the north are closer to the ocean than they are immediately south of Maceió. These are old residential beaches with a standard blend, albeit Brazilian style, of year-rounders and summer folk. There is nothing built up or touristy about the area though. The small towns retain a rural character, and the beaches are shared by fishermen and bathers, snackbars and bathing beauties—in all, an appealing combination.

An old coastal ranch, the **Bosque Fazenda,** Barra de Santo Antônio (tel. 082/221-5581) now serves as a hotel with 30 simple stucco cabins filled with country furniture and hammocks. The Bosque Fazenda has a good restaurant, where guests who have full board take all their meals, and there are even real cattle and horses about. Best of all, the beach is just down the hill a quarter mile or so. Double-occupancy rooms are $28 a night, with breakfast.

3. RECIFE

After having been expelled from Salvador in 1625, the Dutch re-invaded Brazil to the north, hoping to establish a foothold in the rich, sugar-producing lands above Bahia, thus marrying the supply side of that precious commodity with its distribution, which as the major maritime power of the day, the Netherlands already dominated. In 1630 forces of the Dutch West India Company occupied the colonial city Olinda, the old capital of Pernambuco. But they built their own capital four miles to the south in a little village, called Recife, where the natural features of the coastline were more suitable to good defenses and a deep, working harbor.

By the mid-1630s the Dutch controlled most of the fertile coastal plains from the mouth of the Rio São Francisco—which divides Sergipe from Alagoas —all the way to Maranhão, almost to the mouth of the Amazon in the north. The invaders administered the conquered territory and maintained a monopoly on the trade in sugar, slaves, and dyewoods, but permitted the colonials free trade in all other commodities, and extended liberal credits to planters for the rebuilding of plantations and mills that had decayed or had been destroyed during the years of fighting.

The Dutch settled in for a long stay, as this was the height of their colonial expansion in both the New World and in Africa. Dutch settlements had also been established throughout the Caribbean and the Hudson Valley in New York, as well as along the coast of Angola, where they sought to gain control of the slave trade and the labor supply so necessary to their newly won sugar-producing lands in Brazil. From their base in Recife, the curious Dutch, under the leadership of the intelligent and energetic viceroy, Johan Maurits of Nassau-Siegen, began the first systematic and scientific study of the tropics. The Dutch colony was depicted on the excellent canvasses of Albert Eckhout; Willem Piso isolated tropical diseases and concocted remedies for them; naturalist Georg Marcgraf collected flora, fauna, and geological samples. The Dutch adorned Recife with an aviary and both zoological and botanical gardens, and built the New World's first weather station and observatory in their colonial capital.

The native Brazilian population, however, had never reconciled to the Dutch presence. Much of the conflict rested on religious scruples. The Dutch were Protestants, and the Portuguese Brazilians, Catholics. And never was sectarian hatred between the two faiths at a more fevered pitch than during those very years, when Europe was consumed by the near apocalyptic fires of the Thirty-Years' War. But Portugal, having been absorbed by Spain through an accident of royal succession, was powerless to expel the invaders, and the renowned Spanish infantry was occupied in the service of the Holy Roman Emperor on the battlefields of Germany.

The native population, however, began to coordinate a guerrilla operation to effect the expulsion through their own efforts. And while their motives were fired by religious zeal, this was also the first major step taken by the colonials toward the creation of a unified Brazilian nation. The combined forces of patriots from Salvador, Rio de Janeiro, and Pernambuco, with troops representing all three races in equal proportion, defeated the Dutch regulars in several important battles and laid seige to the city of Recife. With the Netherlands suffering reverses in the European war, the motherland could not come to the aid of its colony. The Dutch were forced to surrender Recife in 1654 and leave Brazil, never to return again. But when the Crown of Portugal was restored to the House of Bragança, and the Portuguese found themselves in an ironic alliance with the Netherlands against Spain, a Brazilian expedition was organized which sailed to Angola and successfully liberated Luanda from the Dutch occupation there.

The Dutch had found Recife a mere village of 150 huts, and left it a city of over 2,000 houses, inhabited by Brazil's first truly commercial class, one in which the seeds of republicanism would one day grow to challenge the monarchist sentiments prevalant among the landed gentry. Of the Dutch legacy, little is visible in Recife today other than a few fortifications they built, different in no obvious way from the forts of their Portuguese contemporaries. The one indelible mark the Dutch left on Recife, however, was their choice of a building site. They had chosen a kind of terrain familiar to them from their homeland—land etched with waterways, including inlets, marshes, canals, and two rivers—and used their engineering skills to link into a single entity a peninsula, an island, and the mainland. The modern city of Recife occupies all three of these geographies, which are connected by such a large number of bridges that local boosters promote the city as the "Venice of Brazil."

WHAT TO SEE: With a population of over 1.5 million people, Recife is Brazil's fourth-largest city. Its name derives from the word *arrecife,* referring to the ubiquitous rocky reefs that lie not only off this city's shores, but off those of much of the northeastern coast. The municipality itself has a historic district set on its central peninsula, and on the mainland is the suburb of Boa Viagem, where the best hotels and beaches are found. The colonial city of Olinda is Recife's main attraction. Several excursions to more remote coastal beaches are also quite popular.

Pátio de São Pedro

This large, inner-city square in the Santo Antônio district dating from the early 18th century has yet to be beautified, a fact that may explain why it remains a popular meeting spot for Recife's youth, its artists and intellectuals. The broad cut stone façade of the São Pedro dos Clérigos church with its imposing portal of carved rosewood (1782), and the square's other buildings of similar vintage and girth, create an atmosphere of shadows and forms reminiscent of town life as portrayed on the canvases of old masters. This is particularly so at night, when the square is filled with the mirthful laughter and chatter of its denizens who occupy the tables at several outdoor cafés. In one corner of the square is a stage, set high on scaffolding, where on weekends musicians jam and poets proclaim their latest pieces. The Pátio is also a center for handcrafts, with numerous shops both on the square and its surrounding side streets.

Many of Recife's other architectural treasures are located within walking distance of the Pátio de São Pedro, including the Dutch-built **Five-Points Fort** (1630), now a museum, the **Basílica de Nossa Senhora de Carmo** (1687) on Avenida Dantas Barreto, and the **Capela Dourada** (the Golden Chapel of the Church of Santo Antônio) on Rua do Imperador.

Museu do Homem do Nordeste

The Museum of Inhabitants of the Northeast, on Avenida 17 de Augusto (tel. 268-2000), is a complex containing several separate collections located on the outskirts of town near the zoo and the botanical gardens. The **Museu de Açúcar** (Sugar Museum) section documents Brazil's great sugar cycle, the first episode in the country's long-standing single-crop economy. The collection contains models of *engenhos* (mills), early processing equipment, and artifacts relating to sugar's domestic usage—the evolution of the sugar bowl so to speak. Located quite appropriately in the same building is the **Museu Joachim Nabuco.** Nabuco, a lawyer and native of the Pernambuco backcountry, was Brazil's most outspoken abolitionist. The interdependence of the sugar economy and the institution of slavery is self-evident. Preserved in the museum are examples of the instruments of torture used to bend recalcitrant slaves to the fulfillment of their role in the manifest vision of the sugar barons. Equally interesting is the **Museu de Antropologia** (Anthropology Museum), with its display of chapbook poetry and literature. This *literatura de cordel* represents the popular view of local history and heroes, in popular literary language. These crudely printed, but often delightfully illustrated, self-published pamphlets are still hawked in markets and squares throughout the northeast by earnest bards and balladeers.

Boa Viagem

Avenida Boa Viagem is to Recife what Avenida Atlântica is to Rio de Janeiro and the *orla* is to Salvador: a shoreline drive on a long stretch of ocean frontage with the city's most enviable beachside residences, its best hotels, and the center of its conventional nightlife. On the weekends, however, the strands of Boa Viagem do not discriminate, and become the playground for all of Recife's citizens, as a glorious and colorful democratic hodge-podge flocks to the nearby shore and every square inch of sand, from the sidewalk to the waves of the washing tide, is packed with bodies.

Those who have the time and the means head for the more remote strands on the outskirts of the city, to the southern beaches of Piedade, Venda Grande, Candeias, and Barra de Jangada, or the northern beaches of Rio Doce, Janga, Pau Amarelo, and Maria Farinha. As a general rule, the farther you travel from the city center, the cleaner and more deserted are the beaches, and the more dense their cover of palm trees.

All the beaches of Pernambuco, like those of Alagoas to the south, possess natural pools at low tide because of the rocky offshore ledge along the entire coastline that traps the ebbing water. And all the beaches have their populations of fishermen who ply the waters in their native log-lashed rafts, *jandagas*, and who are often willing to carry passengers for a reasonable fee.

Olinda

Every bit as striking and well preserved as Ouro Preto is Pernambuco's old colonial capital of Olinda, founded in 1537 and only four miles north of Recife. Unlike Ouro Preto, however, which remains a self-contained and viable municipal entity, Olinda has become a *dormitório* (bedroom community) for nearby Recife, as well as a center of fine dining, art and handcrafts, and nightlife. Notwithstanding the city's narrowed social and economic role, Olinda has not succumbed to theme-park status by any means. There's just too much authenticity, too many original structures scattered over its one square mile of hilly terrain overlooking the south Atlantic, for example, for the town to reflect only the glitter of its modern inhabitants.

Olinda is small enough to explore in its entirety by foot, an exercise made doubly enjoyable by restrictions placed on automobile traffic along its tight, winding lanes. The tour begins at the **Praça do Carmo,** where the stately, impoverished **Igreja do Carmo** (1588), the first Carmelite church in Brazil, sits on a mound a hundred feet above the square, undergoing a slow and expensive restoration. Considering the sheer volume of the country's historic real estate, it is admirable what Brazilians have already managed to preserve under their perennially belt-tightening economy. Now that Olinda has been declared a National Monument, however, the restoration must go forward at an even faster pace to satisfy criteria imposed by the government. But since much of the town is already amazingly well preserved, the restoration task is not as overwhelming as in other areas we'll visit farther on up the coast, like São Luís do Maranhão.

Running off the square is Rua do São Francisco, where the **Convento da Nossa Senhora das Neves** (1585) has lovely panel paintings. It was the first Franciscan church in Brazil, and one of the few churches in Olinda open to the public during normal daytime hours. The street ends at Rua Bispo Coutinho, opening onto the Alto da Sé, a wide hill with a dramatic view of town and sea. The **Igreja da Sé** (1537) was the first seat of an archbishopric in Brazil. The nearby bishop's palace houses the **Museu de Arte Sacra,** with its collection of paintings of the city as well as some of the country's oldest examples of sacred art. It's open Tuesday to Friday from 8 a.m. to noon and 2 to 6 p.m., and on weekends from 2 to 6 p.m. The **Convento da Conceição** at the far end of the street remains an active convent, and may be visited by applying at the gate.

The **Alto da Sé** itself, a large cone of a hill, is Olinda's outdoor party spot and permanent craft fair. Every evening and on Sunday afternoons, the Alto begins to swell with people who come to shop, eat from the food stalls, and dance while they listen to musicians playing regional music. A spiritist temple, the **Tenda do Edu,** is off to one side on the Alto, and is worth a visit if for no other reason than for the contrast it provides to the predominantly Catholic viewpoint of Olinda's historic reality. Opposite the working convent is the **Largo da Misericórdia**, with a former academy, **Santa Getrudes**, and the Misericórdia church, with its golden wood carved panels and Portuguese *azuleijo* tiles with their allegoric illustrations. A further landmark of this square is the **Bica de São Pedro**, a public fountain from colonial days.

On **Rua Bernado Vieira de Melo** are the ruins of the old colonial senate where in 1710 the street's namesake, in a great, though premature, historic gesture, called for the establishment of a republic. The context was the so-called Peddler's War, an armed conflict pitting the sugar aristocracy of Olinda against the rising commercial bourgeoisie of Recife. Here you also find the **Mercado Rebeira,** an arts and crafts market.

The building of the **Museu de Arte Contemporânea,** Rua 13 de Mayo, has a history more interesting than the art collection it now houses. Built as a jail to confine clergy who ran afoul of the Inquisition in its later, tamer years of the 18th century, the building has the further dubious distinction of having been a slave market. The Inquisition in Brazil was never established as an institution, and its influence was minimal, directed primarily against licentious priests and New Christians—Jews forced to convert to Catholicism who were required to make periodic displays of their adherence to the "true faith." The museum is open daily from 9 a.m. to noon and 2 to 6 p.m.

The final "official" site on the walking tour is the **Monastery of São Bento** (1582), on Rua de São Bento, a continuation of Rua Bernado de Melo Vieira. The church is worth a visit to see the unique terracotta images, as is the monastery, which once sheltered Brazil's first law school. Interconnecting all the religious monuments are hundreds of houses, many from the 1600s, with their cartoon façades of stucco, heavily framed doors and windows, and balconies with wooden railings, among other charming architectural features.

WHERE TO STAY: Most visitors to Recife, either by choice or because they are placed there by predetermined hotel packages, stay on the beach at Boa Viagem. Olinda now also has a first-class beach hotel to add to its several inns and pensions.

For students and other youthful travelers to the city there are newly established **youth hostels** that charge only $4 per night with breakfast.

Inquiries about hostel and hotel availability, as well as general tourist information, should be made at **Empetur,** Rua Cruz Cabuga 535, in the Santo Amaro neighborhood (tel. 081/231-7744), which also maintains information counters at the airport and bus station.

Staying in Recife

The **Recife Palace,** Avenida Boa Viagem 4070 (tel. 081/325-4044), is a new 300-room luxury hotel equipped with all the five-star facilities, including a nightclub and a fine French restaurant. The hotel belongs to the same group that owns and runs the Rio Palace Hotel in Copacabana, and like its Rio counterpart, the Recife Palace caters equally well to tourists and business travelers who demand the best when away from home. The deluxe room, for example, is extra-large, creating a sense that the sleeping and sitting areas occupy very distinct spaces. The care with the hotel's construction and design can be seen even in the corridors, with their wooden ceilings and hardwood table tops suspended from the walls, decorated with attractive lamps and hand-thrown pottery. The service is also a cut above—discreet and professional. Nightly rates for standard rooms are $85 for a single, $90 for a double; for deluxe rooms, $95 to $100.

Sitting back a block off the beach is the **Miramar,** Rua dos Navigantes 363 (tel. 081/326-7422). The Miramar is comprised of a U-shaped block of three buildings overlooking a large, sumptuous courtyard pool. The hotel is well run and super-comfortable, and has all the facilities required of a luxury hotel. The 156 rooms are decorated in soft yellows and light wood trim. Deluxe rooms have balconies with louvered double doors and white wood patio furniture. In addition to the separate coffeeshop, bar, and nightclub, the hotel possesses the respected Gávea restaurant. Room prices start at $75 to $80 for standard single or double respectively.

The **Othon Palace,** Avenida Boa Viagem 3722 (tel. 081/326-7225), occupies a 17-story tower with 264 rooms, directly across from the beach. Narrow wood-paneled and carpeted corridors open into spacious deluxe rooms where table tops and luggage racks are slabs of stone, suspended legless from the walls. Potted plants and cream-colored walls add warmth to the room, with its curved glass doorway leading to a balcony. Other features are built-in bar with TV, and extra-large baths tiled in brown from floor to ceiling. The standard rooms are slightly smaller, while their connecting corridors are correspondingly wider. The small rooftop pool and its deck seem to overhang the beach below. A second small pool occupies an interior courtyard, and the veranda off the entrance serves as an outdoor café and restaurant. Standard rooms range from $52 to $57, and deluxe accommodations are priced at $64 to $71.

The **Mar Hotel,** Rua Barão de Souza Leão 451 (tel. 081/341-5433), located a block and a half from the Boa Viagem beach, has one of the most elaborate and gorgeous poolside environments of any hotel in Brazil. The pool is a mosaic of fountains and falls, separate compartments of water on split levels, plus islands and isthmuses of mottled flagstone with potted palm trees. The hotel's rooms are on the small side, but have balconies. Quilted bedspreads, modern armchairs, and rich, mineral-blue carpets add elegance to the rooms. There are good-size tubs in the marble-highlighted baths. The hotel, with its jet-age lobby in stainless steel and black leather, also has variety in its eating environments, including a sushi bar and a restaurant called the Mont Blanc, specializing in Swiss-German cuisine. Rooms rent for $76 to $84 for the standard accommodations, and for $91 to $101 for the deluxe.

An especially attractive hotel in the moderate price range is the **Castelinho Praia,** Avenida Boa Viagem 4520 (tel. 081/326-1186). The former *casarão* (mansion) is a stone building with a red-tile roof and a large covered front porch with a red-painted railing. The Castelinho Praia has only 41 rooms: the standard accommodations are in the old main house, and the deluxe rooms are spread among several two-story outbuildings with views of either a backyard court or the patio pool deck which also faces the ocean. The rooms lack the extra attention to detail of the more pricey establishments, being smaller and less elegantly furnished, but they are comfortable and modern in every way. The baths receive natural lighting from the corridors. Rates run $40 to $45 for standard rooms and $45 to $50 for the deluxe.

The **Hotel Savaroni,** Avenida Boa Viagem 3772 (tel. 081/325-5077), has a pleasant and informal lobby restaurant with dried flowers on the tables. A compact, but appealing pool and sunning deck on the second floor has tables with bright-yellow umbrellas and a wide view of the sea. The hotel's rooms are entered through an alcove with a built-in carpeted bench and table. The same carpet motif continues on to the sleeping area, and the entire front wall is a large window, a section of which can be opened. The room is filled with light during the day, and has blackout and soundproofing curtains for nighttime. The bathroom has a round stall shower with a transparent curtain, and a frosted-glass wall that lets in light from the corridors. The 70 rooms are priced from $37 to $42 for the standard accommodation, and $42 to $48 for the deluxe.

The **Vila Rica,** Avenida Boa Viagem 4308 (tel. 081/326-5111), has 102 rooms reached from corridors with brown-carpeted walls, and Day-Glo purple carpets on the floor. And if that doesn't get your attention, try the polka-dot-painted tubs in the bathroom. Furnishings are slightly worn, but the single beds are regulation size and comfortable. The standard room views only neighboring buildings. The hotel is across from a nice stretch of the Boa Viagem beach, and the service, despite the idiosyncrasies of the hotel's décor, is especially friendly and helpful. The least expensive rooms cost between $45 and $50, with promotional prices during certain months lowering the cost to as little as $31 for double occupancy.

The **Voyage,** Rua Barão de Souza Leão 349 (tel. 081/341-7491), is an inexpensive hotel, next to the Hotel Mar and close to the beach. The 100 rooms are housed in five two-story block buildings, with a mid-sized pool and sun veranda occupying an interior patio. The rooms are functional and modern, and baths have a seat built into the wall and stall showers. Rates are $26 to $28 for the least expensive rooms.

Staying in Olinda

The only luxury hotel in Olinda is the **Quatro Rodas,** Avenida José Augusto Moreira 2200 (tel. 081/431-2955). In reality the Quatro Rodas is also the only genuinely resort-style hotel in all of Recife, with its location right on the beach, and such aquatic and sporting activities as windsurfing, sailing on catamarans, tennis, and of course, freshwater swimming in the large pool. The hotel has a giant lobby, lush with plants, rustic antiques, and old farm equipment, the same theme that is duplicated in each of the chain's hotels. Facilities off the lobby include a live-music bar, a restaurant, and an outdoor barbecue snackbar. Superior and deluxe rooms differ only slightly in size, but are otherwise the same in details and furnishings. All rooms face the sea, and have balconies with crescent-shaped window lights above the door and either two double beds or one king-size bed. Rates for the superior room are $74 single and $84 double, while deluxe rooms cost $87 to $97.

WHERE TO EAT: Good restaurants are scattered throughout the large metropolitan area, but the greatest concentrations of eating spots are in Boa Viagem and Olinda. Northeastern cooking and seafood top the list of specialties in most restaurants.

Eating in Recife

The straw-covered cabañas of the **Maria Bonita Tropical Bar,** Rua Jack Ayres, opposite the Shopping Center Recife, (tel. 355-5402), make a pleasant setting for open-air dining. The eclectic menu offers a variety of items ranging from chicken Stroganoff to more typical Brazilian dishes like crab stew. Prices also fluctuate considerably, from $2 to $9, depending on the entree. Thursday to Saturday there is live music after 10 p.m. The name Maria Bonita refers to a bandit heroine and moll of the infamous Virgolino Ferreira da Silva, the gunslinger who terrorized the northeast with his gang, and who is known popularly as Lampião in recognition of his lightening tendency to shoot first and ask questions later. Open daily for dinner only, after 6 p.m.

The **Restaurante Lobster,** Rua Bruno Veloso 200 (tel. 326-7593), is located in Boa Viagem, at the corner of Avenida Concelheiro Aquiar. An elegant eating space, the large rectilinear room is made extra-bright by white walls and large windows. The featured dish is the clawless Brazilian lobster, costing about $12. Dinner is accompanied nightly by piano music. Open seven days a week for lunch and dinner, from 11 a.m. to midnight.

The **Ceia Regional,** Rua Prof. Andrade Bezerra 1462 (tel. 241-8958), offers an unusual repast. *Ceia* means supper, and the meal offered by this tourist-oriented restaurant is precisely a sampling of regional dishes that might make up the evening supper of a typical rural northeastern family. For $10 you are served a round of platters, enough for two people, with colorful names like munguza (a cream of cornmeal soup), paçoca (farofa with sun-dried beef), macaxeira (a variety of boiled cassava root), and ihname (taro-root yam). It's interesting to try once as an unusual culinary experience. The restaurant is located near the end of the Estrada de Belém highway, near the Convention Center in the direction of Olinda. Open daily for dinner, after 7 p.m.

A more sophisticated option for experimenting with regional dishes is the **Marruá,** Rua Ernesto de Paula Santos 183 (tel. 326-1656), a block off the beach in Boa Viagem. One specialty is the barbecued mixed grill, a variety of meats and sausages served on a skewer. International entrees may be ordered à la carte from the menu, and regional dishes are served buffet-style, from terracotta chafing dishes. Open daily for lunch and dinner beginning at noon.

The **Vivenda Bar,** Avenida Domingos Ferreira 2766 (tel. 326-3960), is a supperclub and dance hall, located on the outskirts of Recife. A live band plays regional and popular music Thursday through Saturday usually beginning after 11 p.m., and on Friday there is a floor show as well. Every night customers in the downstairs bar are serenaded by a singing guitar player. Open Tuesday through Saturday, after 7 p.m.

Eating in Olinda

L'Atelier, Rua Bernado Vieira de Melo 91 (tel. 429-3099), occupies a restored colonial house whose façade can be sampled as an aesthetic appetizer before entering to eat. Diners sit in several rooms and alcoves on the first floor amid the tapestries and wall hangings produced by the two owner/craftsmen who live above the store. A backyard veranda contains additional tables, and there's a second level with a swimming pool, which guests sometimes use, especially during the wilder parties. L'Atelier serves the new French cooking—which is to say, well-crafted small portions—and is quite simply "the best restaurant in the northeast," says Brazil's premier travel guide, *Quatro Rodas.* But even more impressive is the lavish praise bestowed on the two French entrepreneurs, and reprinted on their brochure as a jacket blurb by the respected Brazilian sociologist Gilberto Freyre. Entrees are priced between $10 and $15, expensive for this region, but well compensated by the quality of the food and the atmosphere. Open daily for dinner from 7 p.m.

The building housing the **Morisco,** Rua João Alfredo 07 (tel. 429-1390), is equally charming, while the restaurant itself is more traditional in the Luzo-Brazilian mold. The 400-year-old timber-framed stucco building is a masterpiece of rustic detail, with hand-hewn and planed wood trim and railings everywhere polished smooth by centuries of use. The elegant dining area, divided among several rooms, contrasts pleasingly with the backyard *choparia* (beer garden) with its shiny apple-red metal café tables and chairs. The menu is international, featuring steaks and seafood in the $6 to $10 range. Open daily for both lunch and dinner, after 11:30 a.m.

On the beach in Olinda is the **Sinhá Maria,** Avenida Beira Mar 953, set in a cottage facing the long-settled oceanfront of the old colonial town. The specialties here are fresh-caught fish like pescada, a species of South Atlantic hake, broiled and served whole. Also tasty is the shrimp casserole. Meals are a bargain at $4 to $5 per entree. Open daily from 11 a.m. through to midnight.

NIGHTLIFE: A special event takes place every Friday night in Olinda, an all-night dance party called **Noites Olindences** at the Clube Atlântico on the town's main plaza (tel. 429-3616). The party begins at 11 p.m., and the music changes hourly, embracing dance forms as varied as the merengue, waltz, and forró, the slinky, sensual northeastern dance.

CARNIVAL: Carnival time in both Recife and Olinda are said to rival in spirit and authenticity, if not scale, the pre-Lenten festivities in both Rio and Salvador.

EXCURSIONS FROM RECIFE: About 20 miles north of Recife is the old colonial town of **Igaraçu,** settled in 1535 and full of architectural relics of its own, including the **Igreja Santos Cosme e Damião,** reputed to be the first church ever built in Brazil. Other notable attractions in the town are the country's first Masonic Temple, and a mile to the south on the Recife road, the **Engenho Monjope,** an early sugar plantation, preserved and open to the public.

Another 10 miles farther north is the island of **Itamaraca,** connected to the mainland by a causeway and bridge. A sign on the Itamaraca side boasts that "Adam and Eve spent their vacations on this island," which is prized for its 50 miles of beautiful beaches. Itamaraca now has a first-class tourist hotel to attract international visitors who come to Recife. The **Orange Praia Hotel,** Avenida do Forte (tel. 081/341-4000), has 54 large rooms which command a view of the beach and Fort Orange, a fortification built by the Dutch during their occupation of the coast. Rooms are priced as low as $33 to $38, $48 to $58 for the fancier accommodations. The hotel has many resort facilities, a big pool, sailing boats, and a lighter-than-air plane for those guests who wish to soar above it all.

An interesting side trip off the island can be taken to an old settlement called **Villa Velha.** Traveling toward the water over six miles of very bad road, you ride through an old plantation where tenant farmers in rustic cottages still live closer to the rhythms of colonial life than to modern ways. At the end of trail is an old harbor town with a few buildings, one of which is now a restaurant.

West of Recife some 75 miles distant is the town of **Fazenda Nova,** which visitors to the region during Holy Week will want to make sure to visit. Outside the town is a vast open-air arena, a scaled-down reproduction of ancient Jerusalem, where a full-blown **Passion Play,** including the crucifixion of Christ, is reenacted every year.

A few miles from this Nova Jerusalem is the state craft capital, the town of **Caruaru,** with its famous weekend market for pottery, terracotta figurines, and other handmade items in wood, leather, and straw.

4. JOÃO PESSOA

Funny-shaped **Paraiba** state seems to have spilled over the map of Brazil from the overturned inkpot of a tipsy cartographer. Paraiba's capital, João Pessoa, 70 miles north of Recife, is odd for another reason. It is the only state capital in Brazil named for a mere mortal, a politician of modern vintage. Pessoa, president of Paraiba—an office equivalent in those days to that of governor—ran as vice-presidential candidate on the 1929 ticket with Getúlio Vargas, and the two suffered defeat. When Pessoa was felled by an assassin's bullet the following year, the incident was used to justify the military coup that brought Vargas to power. And the fallen politician's star was enshrined in the eternal firmament of Brazil's national mythology, his name replacing that of the old colonial capital, once known successively as Filipeia, Frederikastaat, and most recently, Paraiba do Norte. On the flag of Paraiba is Presidente Pessoa's one-word reply to the entreaties of the political opposition to gain his support—"*Nego*" ("I refuse").

Paraiba is an agricultural state, at least in those regions where rainfall makes agriculture possible, producing cash crops of sugar, pineapples, tobacco, and taro root. The state's interior dovetails into the arid *sertão* (as do the interiors of all the northeastern states), and here a subsistence living for both man and cattle makes do with strange succulents like those that sustain life on any desert. The poverty of the interior, however, is not reflected in the markets of the coastal towns like João Pessoa. One could devote a lifetime to the study of the many wonderous fruits alone. The names of these fruits are here included for those who wish to initiate this study by the art of random sampling: abacaxi, abacate, araca, araticum, banana maçã, banana anã, banana preta, banana comprida, joboticaba, cajú, cajá, cajarana, coco, goiaba, graviôla, groselha, imbu, jaca dura, jaca mole, jambó, manga rosa, manga espada, manguito, mamão, maracujá, melão, mangaba, oliviera, pinha, pitanga, sapoti, sapota, and tamarindo.

WHAT TO SEE: João Pessoa spreads literally over a flat coastal plain, with few tall buildings and many streets of private houses both modest and imposing, where the town's 300,000 inhabitants reside. First and foremost João Pessoa is a delightful beach town. There are—for the moment—few hotels and few tourists from abroad, though Brazilians seeking a quiet resort have certainly discovered the city's charms.

A chain of sweeping coves called *enseadas* form an ocean beachfront 15 miles long. Closest to the downtown and suburban hotel sector is **Tambaú,** which anchors one end of the urban beach and flows southward to the more unpopulated strands, like **Cabo Branco,** where a lighthouse marks the overlook at **Ponta do Seixas** (Gravel Point), the easternmost landfall in the Western Hemisphere (longitude 34° 47′ 38″, latitude 07° 09′ 28″). Stalls line the overlook pathways where artisans sell craft goods not seen thus far in our journey up the northeastern coast—whale-bone carvings and jewelry of coral and shells. Beyond this point are the more remote beaches of **Penha** and **Bessa,** with their palms and shanty restaurants, and finally **Poço,** already in the neighboring municipality of Cabedelo.

About 15 minutes upriver from the ocean along the Rio Sanhaua is downtown João Pessoa, with a small but impressive core of colonial structures. The one imperative sight is the **Igreja de São Francisco,** a section of which dates from 1591, while the church itself is gloriously late baroque, built in 1779, and is without doubt one of the most beautiful churches in all Brazil. From inside, the cloister looks down over sloping greenery on the old port, never developed much beyond the colonial period. In front of the church, walk down the **Ladeira de São Francisco,** João Pessoa's oldest street, to the **Praça São Pedro,** where you will see the city's first hotel, the Globo (still functioning). From here the rough backstreets continue down to the old waterfront.

WHERE TO STAY: Shaped like a giant wagon wheel let fall at the edge of the beach, the luxury **Hotel Tambaú,** Avenida Alm. Tamandaré 229 (tel. 083/226-3660), is part of the VARIG-owned Tropical chain. The walls of the hotel in places serve as a buttress against the crashing sea. For those rooms over the beach, there is a two-foot step down onto attached verandas to prevent water from entering the room proper when seas are rough. The 175 rooms are divided into several classifications. Those designated deluxe have brick walls, floors of granite, and a second sink outside the bathroom, which has a stall shower. Most rooms in the two-story circular building open onto the interior court, which has several pools, including one devoted exclusively to water polo. Also within the circle are formal gardens, where standard rooms occupy separate but attractive quarters. Rates are $50 to $56 for standard rooms, $65 to $73 for superior rooms, and $70 to $78 for deluxe.

The **Hotel Brisa Mar,** Avenida Sen. Ruy Carneiro 577 (tel. 083/226-5400), is João Pessoa's newest hotel, a long block from the beach up one of the seashore's principal avenues. The attractive white block building contains 65 rooms with balconies, and an excellent restaurant serving well-prepared regional and international food. The Brisa Mar also has an attractive medium-sized pool and sun patio. The rooms are large and comfortable at this medium-priced three-star hotel, and range in price from $23 to $26 for standard accommodations and $32 to $36 for the deluxe.

The **Manaira Praia Hotel**, Avenida Flavio Ribeiro 115 (tel. 083/226-1550), has 50 rooms and is organized motel style, similar in design to something you might see in Miami Beach. The luxury and standard rooms differ only in view (toward or away from the beach), and beds are on the smallish size. The hotel also has a small pool. Rates are $28 to $32 for the standard rooms, and $40 to $43 for the deluxe.

The **Sol Mar,** Avenida Sen. Ruy Carneiro 500 (tel. 083/321-4304), was playing host to Jorge Bem, one of Brazil's most popular singers in the '60s, when I visited there recently. Bem and his entourage were in João Pessoa on a concert date, and they seemed to be enjoying both the city and the hotel. In the case of the Sol Mar, there is a big difference between the hotel's standard and deluxe accommodations. The deluxe rooms are large, with verandas, and are accessed through wood plank doors, the bottoms of which are louvered while the upper sections open into a window, Dutch-door style. The baths receive natural light from an outside walkway. The standard rooms are smaller, furnished more simply, without carpets and with black-and-white rather than color TVs. The Sol Mar also has its own pool and restaurant. Deluxe rooms are priced between $38 and $40 nightly, and standards cost $26 to $30.

WHERE TO EAT: In the historic section, downtown, is the **Cordon Bleu,** Rua Duque de Caxias 73 (tel. 221-5783), an art gallery, piano bar, and restaurant. In an atmosphere of mounted photographs and paintings, and soft piano music, diners occupy tables on both the ground floor and the mezzanine in the old colonial building, and select their meals from either an à la carte menu or a buffet of many dishes. Typical meals include lobster at $10, shrimp at $6, fish plates at $5, and meats like steak au poivre or loin of pork at $6. The menu is extensive, the clientele formally dressed, and the service attentive. Open daily for lunch and dinner from 11:30 a.m. to 3:30 p.m. and from 6 p.m. to midnight.

The **Cha Wan Casa de Cha,** Avenida Epitácio Pessoa 2200 (tel. 224-7640), is a charming tea house suitable for lunch, supper, or a snack anytime. After raising her ten children, in early 1987 the very warm and dynamic Dona Alaide realized her lifelong dream of opening a genuine tea room. She personally selected the perfect house, and supervised all the decorating, choosing rose-colored undercloths for tables, covered with white embroidered lace and hand-woven linen placemats. The room has touches of Oriental décor everywhere, including the costumes of the waitresses. Full tea service is $4, including tea, bread, toast, jellies, salgadinhos (a platter of diminutive meat and cheese pastries), and petits-fours. Patrons are serenaded by piano and violin music. Open from the Queen's teatime at 4 p.m., until 1 a.m. seven days a week.

For live music and supper there's the **Gulliver Pub,** Avenida Olinda 1590 (tel. 226-5734). The pub is tucked away in a small house on a backstreet behind the Brisa Mar Hotel. The Gulliver was created by its co-owner, Saulo Barreto, who studied architecture at the University of Edinburgh in Scotland. Saulo wanted to reproduce in his hometown both the style and the mood of a genuine pub, and he has succeeded. The square, three-sided bar with leather-covered stools, the antique prints of royalty, and great scenes from the history of the U.K., all contribute to the effect he sought to create. The pub is open Wednesday through Saturday from 7 p.m. till 1 a.m. sharp, and Saulo alternates between his role as bartender, slicing fruit for his customers' drinks, and chanteur, joining the band for a set of ballads in French, English, and Portuguese.

TOURIST INFORMATION: The state tourist information bureau is **PB-TUR,** Avenida Getúlio Vargas 301 (tel. 083/221-7220), downtown.

5. NATAL

Natal, a city of 500,000 inhabitants and capital of the state of **Rio Grande do Norte,** is quite simply the new fun capital of the nordeste, with the best beaches, the best food, and the best hotels. In fact, more new hotels have been built in Natal in recent years than in any other Brazilian city. And the building boom continues. Slated for completion along a newly developed six-mile stretch of beachfront immediately to the south of the city are 18 new hotels, a number of which are already open for business.

Natal has a long history of receiving foreign visitors. The city was an obligatory refueling point for aviation pioneers who flew the first mail runs between Europe and South America. And during World War II, thousands of Americans were stationed at a large airbase outside the city, called the "Victory Trampoline," a major logistical link in the resupply route for Allied forces in North Africa.

WHAT TO SEE: Natal has three major zones of interest: the city itself with its satellite beaches, and the more remote coastal beaches, both to the north and the south. The one feature that characterizes Natal more than any other is the presence of giant sand dunes that embrace the town and continue on the length of its coastline. Considering its configuration, Natal itself must have been built on dunes very similar to those you will see along the virgin shoreline. The city begins at the water's edge on a spit of land between the Atlantic and the **Rio Potengi,** and climbs steeply upward to the downtown commercial and administrative center.

Along the river on the lower town is the waterfront, and Natal's oldest neighborhood, **Ribeira.** Nearby is the **Igreja de Santo Antônio,** known as the Rooster's Church, built in 1766. The next neighborhood going up the river is **Alecrim,** where every Friday from dawn till Saturday afternoon there is a popular outdoor fair covering ten square blocks. The point where the river meets the sea is occupied by the **Forte dos Três Magos** (Fort of the Three Wise Men), which is open to the public. The fort was built and occupied by the Portuguese in 1598 as part of their system of coastal defenses to discourage the marauding of their European rivals. The official settlement of the town occurred the following year, on Christmas Day, and thus the name Natal.

On the ocean side of the fort in the lower town are Natal's oldest beaches, the **Praia do Forte, Praia do Meio, Praia dos Artistas,** (a center for nightlife), and **Praia de Areia Preta,** with its many restaurants overlooking the rocky shore. From here the **Via Costeira** begins at the **Praia Mãe Luíza** and travels for several miles along the coastal highway lined with new hotels to **Ponta Negra,** one of the most popular of Natal's outlying beaches.

The beaches continue along the southern shore, but the road jogs inland here and then back along the sea, through several traditional summer beach communities like **Piragi do Norte.** Across the Potengi River to the north is another string of beaches, more primitive, with mountainous snow-white dunes that begin at the shore and travel inland for many miles. Both of these regions will be described under "Excursions from Natal."

WHERE TO STAY: The visitor to Natal has three basic choices for accommodations in the city proper. First are the hotels at the foot of the downtown section, along or close to the traditional beaches and the centers of nightlife and shoreside dining. Next are the new, self-contained resort hotels along the Via Costeira, with their miles of unspoiled beaches, yet still only a few minutes' ride from downtown by bus or taxi. Finally, there is an executive-style hotel in the upper city, where many more fine restaurants are located, as well as a number of bargain accommodations, less expensive because they aren't on the beach.

One of Natal's nicest hotels is the **Novotel Ladeira do Sol,** Rua Fabricio Pedroza 915 (tel. 084/221-4204), on the ramp leading from the Praia dos Artistas to the upper town. The split-level lobby has a tile floor and a seating area with black, soft-leather couches and armchairs. On the lower level is a bar and cocktail lounge, and in the mezzanine, a restaurant where a delicious buffet is served at lunchtime daily. The brand-new hotel has 62 rooms in standard and deluxe categories. The standard room has a double bed with a quilted spread, and light-yellow carpets on the floor. There is also a couch that can serve as an extra bed, and a pair of captain's chairs. These rooms face an interior open-air walkway. The deluxe rooms are similarly furnished, and all have balconies with hooks for hammocks, provided by the hotel on request. Other features are an imaginative interior garden and a two-level pool with a waterfall effect and a large patio. Rates are $40 to $42 for the standard rooms and $42 to $48 for the deluxe.

The well-placed **Hotel Três Magos,** Avenida Pres. Cafe Filho 822 (tel. 084/222-2055), overlooks both the old fort and the Praia do Meio beach. This first-class hotel is bargain-priced for the moment, but plans for complete renovation spurred by competition from the newer hotels along the Via Costeira are sure to increase the rates. The 91 rooms are distributed among several two- and four-story buildings with curved exterior lines in white stucco. Deluxe rooms, all in white with stone floors, open either on the interior courtyard with an extra-large pool or have ocean views, seen through a curtain of swaying *coqueiros* from their balconies. Standard rooms have smaller beds, but are otherwise the same, and some standards on the higher floors have the best views in the hotel. Other facilities include a restaurant and a nightclub. Double occupancy for a standard room is $40, and for a deluxe, $55; less 10% in either case for a single.

The **Luxor Hotel de Natal,** Avenida Rio Branco 634 (tel. 084/221-2731), is an unusual and attractive circular structure in a somewhat nondescript downtown neighborhood that is close to the city's financial and governing centers, and to the colorful waterfront. The deluxe rooms are extremely well decorated and not as expensive as their appearance might suggest. An imaginative use of partitions divides the space into sleeping and bath areas, and into a separate seating alcove with a table and chairs. The floors are finely carpeted in deep blue, and the ceilings and table surfaces are coconut green. Quality cotton spreads in striped patterns with pom-pom fringe cover the beds. In addition to the full bath with a large shower, there is a second sink and closet dressing area behind the partition. The La Tour rooftop restaurant is surrounded by windows and offers an excellent view of the city and its port, and of the small patch of nearby historic buildings. A deck on a lower level contains a pool with a waterfall. The three categories of rooms are priced at $35 to $39, $41 to $45, and for the hotel's best accommodations, $47 to $52.

Closest to the city along the Via Costeira is the **Barreira Roxa Praia Hotel,** Via Costeira, at km 05 (tel. 084/222-1093). This spacious 40-room hotel is actually a school run by the state to train hotel staff for Natal's growing tourism sector. The best rooms have large balconies that look out beyond the large pool area to the ocean. Like all the hotels on this new strip, the Barreira Roxa sits directly on the beach, although much of the coast here alternates between rocky ledges and patches of sand. The hotel has a full complement of facilities, including restaurant, bar, and a lobby gift shop. Rooms are a bargain at $32 for a single, $35 for a double.

Next in line is the **Marsol,** Via Costeira 1567 (tel. 084/221-2719), where the 60 rooms occupy two stories. First-floor rooms open on stone- and brick-paved patios, with a colorful hammock, plus table and chairs, only 100 feet from the water's edge. Rooms have clean-lined, bunk-style beds with hardwood frames, and stone floors. The hotel's lobby and other public spaces occupy a central pagoda with a high ceiling of exposed timbers and a red-tile roof which opens onto a deck with two pools, one for children. The beach is a very private strand about 300 feet wide, the sand covered in places with natural growth typical of the local ecology. Standard rooms fronting the road cost $35 to $40, while the deluxe ocean-facing accommodations run $55 to $60.

The **Imira Plaza,** Via Costeira 4077 (tel. 084/222-4105), bills its location as the Parque das Dunas, in recognition of the surrounding hills of sand. The lobby of this 46-room hotel opens onto an atrium bar and coffeeshop. A terraced walkway, with a waterfall wall, wanders through a rock garden of pools filled with aquaculture plants. The rooms all face the sea and Dutch doors (the top sections have shutters that open) lead to large balconies perched over the dunes. The rooms contain two large beds with broad-striped cotton spreads. Baths with large open showers and marble-topped sinks have ceilings of cedar boards, which exude their inimitably fresh aroma. A pool area at the edge of the dunes drops off to the long and narrow beach below. Rates are uniform for all rooms: $60 for a single, $70 for two occupants.

The **Hotel Vila do Mar,** Via Costeira 4223 (tel. 084/222-3755), comes closest of all the new hotels on the strip to creating a full-blown resort atmosphere. Two separate buildings, each with its own reception area, are linked by a wide, stone patio of salmon-colored bricks cut into the dunes, with a swimming pool bridged by a wooden walkway. The lobby in the main building has a greenhouse façade and a sloping glass roof, and looks out on the breaking waves. The sea—a mere 100 feet distant—is always in view from most points within the complex. Close to the pool is a separate structure with a bar and several shops. Another building is a breakfast room with a mock thatch roof, straw fastened deftly to more reliable red roofing tiles. The main building and the annex together contain 154 rooms with small balconies, some of which face the water. With the built-in hardwood furniture and large box-frame bed, the rooms are designed for space and beachside comfort. Handmade baskets and pottery add a touch of intimacy to the décor, and baths are equipped with hairdryers and shampoo. Rates begin at $50 to $55.

The top floor of the small **Jacumã Hotel,** Via Costeira, at km 11 (tel. 084/236-2128), suggests a native pyramid sitting atop the dunes amid the palms and the deep greens of the scrubby beach vegetation. A central veranda off the lobby surrounds a restaurant with cushioned seats of bamboo. The 34 rooms all have balconies, and are attractively priced at $30 to $34 for the standard rooms and $36 to $40 for the deluxe.

Cheek-by-jowl with the Praia da Ponta Negra is the **Natal Mar Hotel,** Via Costeira 8101 (tel. 084/236-2121), in a superb location on this prized beach. The hotel has two blocks of rooms with a central area occupied by a smallish pool and a seaside patio circled by white umbrella-covered tables and contoured modular recliners. The deluxe room is of suite size, with a large table and chairs occupying a partitioned space opposite which is a circular cut-out in the wall with a coffee table and more seating. These rooms have double beds and verandas that view the sea. And the tile baths offer the novelty of double sinks and windows of their own. The deluxe room is $62 nightly, and standard rooms, of similar décor but smaller, are $48 to $50 if they face the water and $38 to $44 when overlooking the dunes.

A Note on Pool-Hopping

Wherever you decide to stay in Natal, there's no reason why you can't spend as much time as you like poolside at any hotel of your choice. Protocol requires that you order a drink or two, or a meal, if you take up table and pool space at a given hotel. But this is a reasonable and inexpensive way to experience a variety of different resort environments along the Via Costeira.

WHERE TO EAT: When it comes to meals in Natal, often the best food and prices are found in the dining rooms of the many top hotels. Other fine restaurants can be found throughout the downtown area, and at the beaches along the coast to the north or south of the city. Restaurants located in the environs will be described in the "Excursions from Natal" section, below.

Natureza, Avenida Hermes da Fonseca 569, serves deliciously prepared dishes that are typical of the *sertão*. The restaurant is located opposite the Maria Auxiliador Colégio school on an avenue lined with restaurants in the Petrópolis section of the city. Some of the rich but tasty items include arroz de leite, a brown rice pudding served hot, and balão de dois, white rice and navy beans cooked together with onions and coconut milk, served with a topping of melted goat's milk cheese. The homemade sausages are also highly recommended, and for an apéritif with a gentle kick, try the batida de coco—coconut and cachaça. The average entree at the Natureza is in the $5 range. Open every day except Tuesday for lunch and dinner.

Raizes, at the corner of Avenida Campos Sales and Rua Mossoro (tel. 222-7338), in the Petrópolis section, offers in addition to its full à la carte menu, a *cafe sertanejo,* a *rodízio* of cheeses, juices, and cakes, plus tapioca and coffee, tea, or milk, for $4; and for $8, a *ceia nordestino,* a *rodízio* of 35 items, including homemade liquors, covering just about all the foods that are typical of the northeast region. Raizes is open daily for lunch and dinner, closing in the afternoon from 3 p.m. to 6 p.m.

In the nearby Tirol neighborhood, occupying a colonial-style house surrounded by a garden of lush tropical plants, is **Xique Xique,** Avenida Afonso Pena 444 (tel. 222-4426). There are several dining rooms inside, each decorated with the original art of a local artist, notably the landscapes and folkloric scenes of Milton Navarro. The specialties here are strictly international platters, meats and seafood, the menu ranging from $5 to $10 a dish. Open Monday through Saturday for lunch and dinner.

Also in Tirol is an unpretentious hole-in-the-wall called **O Crustáceo,** Rua Apodi 414 A, near the Avenida Prudente de Morais. It's not much to look at on the inside, but the food, billed as home-cooked seafood—shrimp, oysters, lobster, crab, and fish at $3 to $5 a serving—is good and you can't beat the price. This is also a great place to sit and drink beer while consuming large quantities of *pastel de camarão,* little turnovers filled with shrimp cooked in a superb sauce of onions and tomatoes, a steal at about 50¢ each. Open from 11 a.m. to midnight every day.

NIGHTLIFE: Among several others, Natal has two particularly interesting supper clubs, one a hangout of the town's upper crust, the other a more touristic joint with a quasi-amateur, but amusing, floor show.

The **Chaplin,** Avenida Pres. Cafe Filho 27 (tel. 222-0217), has one of the best locations in the city, at the circle where the roads to the city and those leading to the traditional and the new beaches all meet, at the end of the Praia dos

Artistas. Outdoors on a partially covered veranda is a *choparia,* an informal café. Indoors is a pub and a swank restaurant for formal dining and dancing. The service is formal, and the entrees run $10 and $15 for most items.

The **Zás Trás,** in Tirol at Rua Apodi 500 (tel. 222-6589), in contrast, is a popular cavern, seating up to 1,000 patrons, most of whom are Brazilian tourists there for the show, and to hear the *repentista,* a singer who makes up the verse as he goes along, managing to make a crack or compliment about every table and many individuals in the audience with his song that goes on for 45 minutes. Natives of Natal come to the Zás Trás when the show is over, around 11 p.m., to dance the *forró* to live music. Meals here are basic and not expensive, from $4 to $6.

On the outskirts of town, in the village of Ponta Negra near the beach of the same name, is the **Bar do Buraco,** a new "in" nightspot for drinking, eating, and disco dancing.

EXCURSIONS FROM NATAL: North of the city, across the Rio Potengi, are the most extraordinary beaches and dunes, without a doubt among the very best in all Brazil. The best way to make your first visit there is by renting a dune buggy with a driver and getting a full introduction to the attractions of the region over the course of an entire day. The rental cost for a buggy and driver is about $35 for a six-hour excursion. And here is what you will get for your money:

A Dune Buggy Adventure

The driver will pick you up at your hotel in the morning, say, between 8:30 and 9 a.m. The open dune buggy is most comfortable with a maximum of three people, including the driver. One passenger rides shotgun next to the driver, the other occupies a kind of rumble seat, in theory big enough for two, but actually bearable for one person alone. Since the buggy is a convertible with no top, be sure to apply plenty of sun screen, and above all, wear a hat to protect your head from Natal's tropical sun.

Your driver now speeds through the city and then up along the river to the bridge where you cross the Rio Potengi, and turns off toward **Redinha.** If the day is really scorching, ask him to stop at a roadside stand so you can buy a cooling drink of agua de coco, coconut water, served in its green shell with a straw. When you finish drinking, ask the vendor to slice the shell in quarters so you can eat the soft, unripened meat on the inside, a kind of coconut custard (this has the reverse name, coco de agua). Reaching the beach of Redinha you notice that you are merely on the other side of the river, viewing the port and the old fort from the opposite bank. Many small children are wading in the water on the river end of the beach, which curves northward and confronts the ocean head-on, continuing for many miles up the coast. The little village of Redinha, with its quaint buildings and country chapel, serves as a backdrop to the beach, where an animated urban beach crowd takes its pleasures on the weekends amid racing dune buggies, motorcycles, food stalls, and a classy-looking restaurant, the **Porto Belo,** overlooking the sand.

For additional excitement, there are kayaks for shooting the waves, rented for $2 an hour, and a contraption called a **triócolo a vela,** a land-sail tricycle built of metal tubing in the triangular shape of a dragster, with a mast and mainsail. The single front wheel can turn, manipulated by foot pedals, and the vehicle is said to reach speeds nearing 40 mph on flat, hard sand. Getting the knack of the thing is easy for anyone who has sailed; otherwise you can give it a whirl in the company of an attendant, also for about $2 per hour.

But the real excitement begins when you head for the **Genipabú,** for a roller-coaster ride of buggy-surfing by way of the giant dunes. The ride is a set piece, and should only be attempted with an experienced driver who knows the itinerary. Up and down the slopes of the dunes you race, making one hairpin turn after another. At one point the driver stops the buggy on a hill high above Lake Genipabú, a totally unexpected body of fresh water set among the dunes like the cone of an extinct volcano. A few tents line the margin of the shore below, campers who have come by way of an access road to this relatively isolated spot, only a 15-minute walk to the beach. After a few more thrilling slalom runs comes the pièce de résistence, a final dramatic descent down a 200-foot-high slope onto the beach at Genebapú.

Boys lead jackasses and small horses by the bridle, and will rent them if you wish to saddle up and wander the beach or explore the dunes further at a slower pace. But it's time for lunch, and there are four bars and restaurants on this beach, including the **Restaurante Pontal Genipabú,** (tel. 222-8926), where you can dine on gourmet-quality food. The restaurant, which occupies a rocky bluff on a point at the beginning of the beach, was once the summer home of its owner, Alvamar Barbosa, a civil engineer who converted it to a restaurant. Tables line the veranda of the old ranchhouse, and beyond the railing is a patio and dip pool set among the rocks, and a covered dance floor where young girls in scanty bikinis dance the *forró* with their beaus, a sight to behold. The meal begins with a delectable appetizer, a tapioca crêpe. A pancake is made from tapioca flour and comes with a variety of seafood fillings—the crab combines particularly well with the flavor of the root-derived pastry. For the main course, shrimp in crème of coconut milk is heavenly, and the filet moda do chefe is inspired. The latter is rolled steak filled with a sautéed blend of tomatoes, palmito (hearts of palm), and herbs. A number of side dishes, including a delicious paçoca, accompany the meal. In the kitchen, the chef demonstrated for me how to make paçoca *sertão* style. He used an apparatus called a *pilão,* a thigh-high mortar, into which he placed ground carne de sol (beef jerky), farinha de tapioca (tapioca flour), feijão verde (cooked black-eyed peas), and coentro (fresh coriander leaves). The mixture was then pulverized with a pestle the size of a baseball bat, and sautéed in a bit of oil like any farofa. The result was the spectacular paçoca of the northeast.

After lunch, the journey up the coast continues on to the beach at **Pitangui.** To get there, the buggy must cross the relatively narrow Ceara Mirim river, but there is no bridge. The ancient art of ferrymen is alive and well on the Ceara Mirim, however. Cars and buggies alike drive to the edge of the bank and board individual rafts, called *balsas,* that are polled to the other side by two men. From here to the beach you follow the dune route, past an occasional fisherman's house, planted like a lonely wooden cactus in a desert of white sand, with a few scrawny *cocquiero* seedlings the owner hopes will one day grow into mature crop-bearing trees. In the distance, a lone rider or two on horseback paces slowly from somewhere in the interior toward the beach for some unknown purpose. Suddenly you come upon a second, even more isolated lake, where it is possible— indeed desirable—to stop for a dip in the transparent green water among the tiny fish. This is the crescendo of a magnificent outing. The ride back retraces the route as far as Genipapú. From there you drive along the beach to Redinha, and return on the road to Natal by late afternoon.

Buggy Rental

For a buggy with a professional driver, contact the **APCBA** (Independent Association of Buggy Owners), Rua João Pessoa 267, Room 267 (tel. 222-7306). The association has a list of over 50 qualified drivers, and will be happy to recommend someone who is safe and reliable. Or contact directly **Beto & Ângela,** Avenida Alexandrino de Alencar 1094 (tel. 223-4727). The couple, who are members of the association, have a fleet of cars. Ask for Beto to accompany you personally, if possible. He's a former banker turned beachcomber, excellent company, and an extremely responsible driver.

A Sunset Harbor Cruise

A transplanted Frenchman and former professional diver named Jean Paul offers a sunset cruise along the Rio Potengi on his boat, the **Verona**. The cruise embarks from a pier on Avenida Contorno at 4:30 p.m., runs to the mouth of the river taking in a close view of the port, then returns almost to the bridge to watch the setting sun, making its way back to the pier by starlight around 6 p.m. Beer and soft drinks are available from the boat's locker, and Jean Paul sets the proper mood with his tapes of Mozart and Gershwin, while quoting from Antoine de Saint Exupéry (who along with Lindbergh and other early pioneers of aviation once landed his hydroplane on this same river and later eulogized this very sunset). The cost of the cruise is $5: drinks are extra. For reservations, call 231-7979.

Região do Sul

South of Natal are a string of beaches—part summer and weekend colonies, part rural fishing villages—that are completely different in appearance and function than the more primitive and recreational beaches to the north. Also distinct from the north, the road here runs close to the sea, and so the ride with its many lovely views of coves and coastal boating is an end in itself, not merely a drab conduit to carry you to your favorite beach.

A popular destination here is **Pirangi do Norte,** not only a lovely beach but home to the world's largest cashew tree, a veritable phenomenon of nature. The tree, which can be visited in a little park of its own, has spread its branches in serpentine fashion along the ground, so that it occupies the terrain of a good-sized house lot.

It's easy to imagine wanting to prolong your stay in Pirangi, and the beach has just the right hotel to satisfy such an impulse, the **Hotel Village do Sol** (tel. 084/222-9005). Two former employees of a petroleum multinational—an Englishman named Alan and an Argentine named Adolfo—have realized their escape from the bondage of corporate ambition and built their paradise in the form of a chic, modern 20-room hotel in the tropics. A dozen bungalows are spaced on a well-landscaped and gently rising dune, surrounding a pool with patio and a very reputable restaurant. Each apartment has two rooms with three beds in all, and the price for a double is a giveaway at $25 a night.

The **Marina Badaué,** (tel. 222-9366) company offers a cruise of the southern waters off Pirangi and its neighboring beaches.

NATAL TOURIST INFORMATION: Natal has a **Centro de Turismo** at Rua Adebal de Figueiredo 980, in Petrópolis (tel. 084/231-6729), open every day except Sunday from 2 to 8 p.m. In addition to an information counter hosted by the state tourism bureau, the Tourism Center contains **Emproturn** (tel. 084/221-3751), arts and crafts galleries, and a restaurant.

6. FORTALEZA

The state of **Ceara** is a living metaphor for the contradictions besetting modern Brazil. Within the borders of the state, all the extremes of the country's paradoxical development are reflected. Ceara's interior remains backward. The *sertanajos* there still look more to the next world for solace to their misery than to the possibilities of real gain or satisfaction in the present world. The traditions of religious fanaticism are woven deeply into the fabric of rural Ceara, and the roots of that phenomenon run deep. Even as the troops of the first Republic were obliterating one manifestation of millenarian power in Canudos, another was rising in the interior of Ceara, in the city of Juazeiro do Norte. In 1889 a woman received communion from a priest and the water was said to have turned to blood within her mouth. This and subsequent "miracles" were attributed to a simple parish curate, Padre Cícero Romão Batista. Padre Cícero went on to exert a powerful and reactionary influence over state and national politics for many years thereafter. And the shadow of his rule has yet to vanish from the barren core of the northeastern region.

On the modern end of the political spectrum is the new, forward-looking urban experience of cities like Fortaleza, Ceara's capital of 1.3 million inhabitants. In a burst of hope and a vote for change in the present, the citizens of Fortaleza recently elected a female mayor, a member of the most radical of Brazil's parties that is today functioning within the country's political mainstream, the PT, or Worker's Party. And while the socialist mayor has had her share of difficulties dealing with the city's old guard, and has had to learn the art of horse-trading with the powerful and the meek as well, her election underscores a certain reality about this equatorial capital. Fortaleza has evolved into northeastern Brazil's most genuinely urban city, one where the savvy pragmatism of an urban middle class has neutralized certain trends and qualities that characterize even the larger and more prosperous of its sister cities in the region: the patrician provincialism of Salvador, and the suburban spread of Recife, for example.

WHAT TO SEE: Fortaleza, like the other coastal cities of the region, has its perennial sunshine and sensual beach life, but it also has a special inner-city rhythm. Much of the street life takes place along the main drag of the in-town **Iracema** and **Meireles** beaches on Avenida Presidente Kennedy. The polluted waters here don't attract many bathers, but the beach is in constant use, primarily by joggers, walkers, and exercise activists. The sidewalks along the avenue are lined with hotels, cafés, restaurants, and nightspots. This is the playground for the city's residents, and for tourists and conventioneers who seem to be drawn here in great numbers throughout the year. At the far end of the beach the *jangada* fishermen land their rafts every afternoon and unload the day's catch.

Around the point is the closest good swimming at the **Praia do Futuro,** and farther south is the fishing village and weekend resort of **Prainha.**

The sweetest swimming within a reasonable distance is to the north, in **Cambuco.** The more remote beaches—some of which can only be reached by four-wheel-drive vehicle or even burro—like **Jericoacoara,** are many hours to the north, and are visited as overnight excursions from Fortaleza.

HOTELS: Along the Beira Mar, the in-town beachfront, the best address is the **Esplanada Praia Hotel,** Avenida Presidente Kennedy 2000 (tel. 085/224-8555). The Esplanada is five-star luxury in all its details. The 238 rooms in the 20-story hotel all face seaward, and in the shade of your private balcony you can sway to your heart's content in a rustic linen hammock, cooled by the steady breeze from the east despite the tropical heat. A pair of louvered sliding doors separate the balcony from the room with its modern décor and king-size bed. The hotel has a large deck with a pool on a platform that protrudes out over the sidewalk from the second floor. The Moringa Restaurant as well as the Esplanada's bar and night-club are popular ports of call on most nights during the week. Rates are surprisingly low for what you get: double rooms cost $50 to $55, and singles run $45 to $50.

The **Hotel Praia Centro,** Avenida Monsenhor Tabosa 740 (tel. 085/221-1122), looks like a five-star hotel but its rates are those of a mid-range establishment. Perhaps it is because of the location of this striking high-rise, a large black square trimmed in white, propped up on a foundation of pillars. The Praia Centro may have a slight complex at not being across from the Iracema beach (despite the fact that you can't swim there) and at being tucked off on a secondary avenue a block from the sea. The explanation is likely implausible, but one need not plumb the mystery to enjoy this attractive hotel. The rooms are spacious almost to a fault, simply but flawlessly decorated. The hotel towers over the homes and businesses in its own neighborhood, and from the rooftop restaurant or the adjacent pool deck area there is a commanding view of the entire city, near and far. The cost for two people is $46 to $49, depending on room size and location. Singles pay $31 to $43. The hotel also runs a regularly scheduled and complementary shuttle bus to points along the Iracema and Futuro beaches.

Also in the medium range is the **Hotel Beira Mar,** Avenida Presidente Kennedy 3130 (tel. 085/224-4755), centrally located on the beachfront and close to most of the nightlife action. The Beira Mar has 97 rooms and maintains itself at near-capacity occupancy throughout the year since the management markets heavily to tourist and convention groups. As a result there is always a diverse, lively crowd on hand. The large outdoor patio in the courtyard is used for colorful shows and pageants, while guests view the events seated at tables around the swimming pool. Rooms are large and are decorated in modern and traditional designs. They are divided into standard rear units and standard and deluxe units that face the sea. Singles are priced at $32, $35, and $37, and doubles are $38, $42, and $43.

In the budget range, the **Hotel Praia Mar,** Avenida Presidente Kennedy 3190 (tel. 085/244-2455), is a three-star hotel with only 34 rooms, some of which are cavernous and will accommodate up to four guests, all in separate beds. Some of the accommodations for single or double occupancy have king-size beds, and all rooms are furnished with simple elegance, and include such touches as potted plants, ceramic objects, and original art. The Praia Mar also has a bar and coffeeshop. The rate is $24 for singles, $26 for doubles, $33 for triples, and $39 for quadruples.

On the Praia do Futuro

Only five miles from town the beaches are relatively undeveloped, except for occasional clusters of summer homes and oases like that of the resort **Hotel Praia Verde,** Avenida Dioguinho 3860 (tel. 085/234-5233), on the Praia do Futuro. The Praia Verde is a self-contained luxury hotel set right on the beach, about a hundred yards from the water. The walled-in complex consists of a square of two-story buildings built around an inner courtyard playground, with a mini-zoo— several cages of tropical birds and small animals. Other interior environments include a large patio with two circular swimming pools. Deluxe rooms occupy the ground floor, and super-deluxe accomodations are on the second level. Both have hammock-equipped verandas. Rooms are spacious with king-size beds, and are decorated in pale-yellow tones and blond wood trim. Baths are also large, with walls in light-brown tiles, marble sink tops, and wood-framed mirrors.The 146-room Praia Verde also has its own restaurant, the Termidor, and an American bar. Rates for first-level rooms are $60 for singles, $75 for doubles, super-deluxe rooms cost $70 to $80.

EATING IN FORTALEZA: The excellent **Restaurante Mirante** is in the Hotel Praia Centro, Avenida Monsenhor Tabosa 740 (tel. 211-1122). This rooftop restaurant is a good choice for lunch, to take in the daylight view of the city. As for the meal, try the filet Praia Centro, a cut of prime beef braised at tableside in butter and cognac, to which thin slices of ham are added, making a very succulent dish. Add a good Brazilian claret and a dessert like coconut pudding, and the bill—with gratuity—comes to around $12 per person.

Many restaurants and cafés can be found along the oceanfront Avenida Presidente Kennedy. A popular eatery and nightspot with live music is the **Choppileque,** at no. 2560. Seating is under the roof of an open-air veranda, and the food is straightforward and tasty, with many seafood specialties, and for lighter meals, pizza. Fortaleza is so cosmopolitan that a bar like Choppileque can stage live music all week long, from 7 p.m. till 5 a.m., and expect to draw a good crowd every night.

Close to the source where the day's catch is sold each afternoon by the returning *jandadeiros* is the **Peixada do Meio,** Avenida Presidente Kennedy 4632 (tel. 224-2719). The house specializes in rich stews of shrimp, oysters, octopus, and lobster.

PRAIHNA: The Praihna beach is approximately 20 miles south of Fortaleza, and parallels the old capital of Ceara, **Aquiraz,** which is located about a mile inland. Unlike the beaches right outside the city, which are endless expanses of flat sand and scrub growth, Prainha, long a summer colony, dates from an earlier era and is more appealing to the eye with its groves of coconut palms, old stucco buildings, and vintage cottages. The old capital of Aquiraz is unusual on the northeastern coast, where most of the early cities were built upstream along riverbanks as protection against coastal pirates. The town is agreeably sleepy, with several small squares, old churches, and narrow backstreets.

For lodgings at Prainha, a hundred yards from the beach is an ideal weekend hideaway, the **Prainha Solar Hotel,** on Rua Central (tel. 085/361-1000, ext. 156; or 239-1254 in Fortaleza for reservations), opposite the area's center of lacemaking. Most of the 15 rooms here are beach house informal, but there are a couple of larger rooms on the second floor of a separate building overlooking the swimming pool that have balconies with hammocks, louvered doors and windows, and old-fashioned ceiling fans. With the doors and shutters open, the rooms are well ventilated with the most refreshing sea breezes. The best rooms are $10 and $12 a night.

An even simpler, but larger beach hotel nearby is the **Aquiraz Praia Hotel,** a four-floor walk-up with 36 very simple rooms, and a few "suites." The rooms cost $8 a night for two people.

FORRÓ: Dancing the *forró* is the passion of all northeasterners. Every Wednesday night, thousands flock to the outskirts of Fortaleza where the large *forró* dance halls are located. The word is of uncertain derivation. Local myth has it that decades ago an American firm invited to Brazil to help install and manage local utilities would host a weekly dance "for all," a weird combination of sounds to the Brazilian ear yielding *forró* (the double *r* in Portuguese sounds like an *h*, sometimes raspy, sometimes not). While colorful, the story is no doubt apocryphal, a more likely derivation being the Brazilian slang word *forrobodó*, meaning riot, disorder, and ultimately, popular ball.

On the main inland road between Aquiraz and Fortaleza is **Obá Obá,** Avenida Washington Soares 3199 (tel. 239-2820), near the Convention Center, about a 15-minute ride from the capital. The expression *obá* incidentally, is the Brazilian equivalent of "wow." The dance hall, which is also a restaurant, sits on grounds planted with ornamental tropical fruit trees, the pride of the owner, behind high stucco walls. The 400 rustic plywood tables and chairs are distributed beneath a high-roofed, open-air A-frame. In addition to the *forró* every Wednesday night, there is dancing Friday through Sunday, and shows, sometimes with major national headliners.

The other extremely popular *forró* spot is the **Clube do Vaqueiro,** out of town on the main highway, the BR 116, where the event is also scheduled for Wednesday nights only.

A CASINO: While not advertised openly as such, the **Clube Guarany,** Rua Carlos Vasconcelos 390 (tel. 244-5847), is a small-scale, but genuine gambling casino, operating in the same semi-legal penumbra as the black market currency exchange. Housed in an old mansion, the casino also has a bistro restaurant and piano bar. But the grand hall is a casino, pure and simple, with roulette, craps, baccarat, and twenty-one. Gamblers are treated well here, with free drinks and canapés—and the best rate of exchange for your cruzados in the city.

CRAFTS AND MARKETS: Fortaleza is a center for both folk and artistic crafts. Popular with tourists and residents alike is the **Mercado Central,** a closed market occupying an entire block on Rua General Bezarril, downtown. The *mercado* has been operating since 1930 and shelters 600 stalls. Around the perimeter are dozens of hardware stores for those who wish to see what Brazilian tools are like or who wish to purchase a *facão,* as the large machete-like knives are called. Inside is a honeycomb of shops selling fabrics, ready-to-wear clothes, lace towels and tablecloths, and what are reputed to be the best hammocks in Brazil. An attractive and sturdy linen hammock can be purchased for about $12 from the **Depósito O Sousa,** stall numbers 505 and 515 (tel. 231-9713). Hammocks are called *redes* in Portuguese, and they come in a variety of qualities. The detail to look for is how the end loops are joined to the body of the cloth—the better hammocks are woven at this point, not sewn. The Mercado Central is open Monday through Saturday from 7 a.m. to 6 p.m.

Many of the better crafted objects, whether lace *(filé),* straw *(palha),* ceramics *(cerámica)* or macramé *(cipó),* are sold in individual shops along **Avenida Monsenhor Tabosa,** near the Hotel Praia Centro, between Rua Idelfonso and Avenida Dom Manuel. Two locations for artist-run shops are the government-sponsored **Centro de Turismo,** Rua Senador Pompeu 350, open during the high season on Saturday from 7 a.m. to 6:30 p.m. and on Sunday from 8 a.m. to 1 p.m., and the **Central Cearense de Artesanato Luíza Távora,** on Avenida Santos Dumont, Monday through Saturday open from 9 a.m. to 6 p.m. year round, and on Sunday as well during the high season. The Luíza Távora Center is a huge and remarkable structure: a tent-like roof, suspended by log rafters and purloins, with two large stucco wings that contain separate compartments for craftspeople selling primarily goods of leather, wood, and cloth. One man does those bottled sand paintings you see in all the markets and souvenir shops in the northeast, and which at first sight seem as though they must be trompe l'oeil, some illusion of what they would seem to be. But here you can watch one of these amazing artisans creating the image inside the bottle one grain of sand at a time—not only the set landscapes of house and palm trees, but commissioned works, like wedding portraits that he copies from photographs his clients provide.

THE NORTHERN BEACHES: Quite close to the city is the **Praia do Cambuco,** a 30-minute ride north of Fortaleza. For a token fee, you sit under an umbrella on chairs provided by the local beachside restaurant while a waiter brings your chilled beer in a Styrofoam container, and vendors circulate selling such delicacies as home-roasted cashew nuts. The swimming here is good, and other activities include a variety of excursions by buggy, horseback, or *jangada,* all of which may be rented on the beach. For a more formal meal, there is the **Restaurante Sal e Sol,** right on the beach.

The new "in" side trip for the more adventuresome tourists is a stay—

overnight or longer—at **Jericocoara.** The state tourist bureau organizes overnight trips to this remote beach in four-wheel-drive minibuses, which cover the distance from Fortaleza in about seven hours. The itinerary includes "sand skiing" on the dunes, watching the sunset, then a moonlight walk and an evening of *forró.* The tour leaves the city at 7 a.m. on Saturday and returns Sunday night. For information, call 224-7660 during weekday business hours and 239-3407 on the weekends.

TOURIST INFORMATION: You'll find **EMCETUR** information counters at the airport (tel. 227-2117); the bus station, **Terminal Rodoviário Eng. João Thomé,** Avenida Borges de Melo 1630 (tel. 227-4614); the Centro de Turismo, mentioned above (tel. 231-4411); and along Avenida Presidente Kennedy at a kiosk near the Iracema Monument.

7. SÃO LUÍS

São Luís, capital of the state of Maranhão, is the final stop on this swing through the capitals of Brazil's northeastern states. About 330 miles from Fortaleza, São Luís is an island city, founded and settled by French explorers in 1612, occupied later by the Dutch, and finally secured through battle by the Portuguese. Maranhão is the transitional state of the nordeste: its interior is more fertile, like Goiás which it borders to the south, and more forested like vast Amazónia to the west, to which it can also legitimately be said to be the gateway.

In its heyday, the second half of the 18th century, the port of São Luís was responsible for half of Brazil's exports. Since that golden age the economic health of Maranhão and its capital, São Luís, has steadily disintegrated. Subsistence agriculture is the characteristic economy of the countryside in this large state, second in size to Bahia among all the northeastern states. Electrification remains a dream for much of the state's rural population—a nightmare for others who have seen the other face of modernity and would prefer to preserve the simplicity of their ways, inconveniences notwithstanding. Political power in Maranhão, as in all of rural Brazil, still resides in the hands of the land barons, and the family of the country's current president, José Sarney, is one of the most powerful in the state. The capital city of São Luís today is threadbare, decrepit, and thoroughly charming—the way a ruined tropical backwater ought to be in the imagination, a place where you might still expect to see old colonials in rumpled white suits and panama hats fanning themselves in the shade of the town square. In reality the city is poor, its historic buildings—of which there are scores—crumbling, many almost beyond repair.

Why go to São Luís then? Not for the beaches, when you could choose those of Natal, Fortaleza, Maceió, or Aracajú, which are far superior. Not for its pampered resort life which also cannot compete with the facilities of the region's other cities, nor for some tidy vision of the past frozen in the skillful preservation of is historic quarter, because that task has yet to be accomplished in São Luís. São Luís does not live by tourism, and therein you might find sufficient motivation for a visit. The very lack of polish, the lack of self-consciousness among its citizens in the presence of visitors, the spontaneity of the state's folkloric traditions—and the general appeal of a city that is no more than it pretends to be—these are the reasons that some might find compelling enough to include São Luís on their itinerary.

WHERE TO STAY: Visitors to São Luís have a choice of staying in the city itself, or at lodgings located on one of the nearby beaches. All hotels listed below include breakfast with their daily rates, and are air-conditioned and equipped with televisions and mini-bars.

Two Downtown Deluxe Choices

Located on the Praia Calhau, the best of the beaches close to São Luís, is the **Hotel Quatro Rodas** (tel. 098/227-0244). One of the city's two luxury hotels, the Quatro Rodas occupies a point of land at the tip of a coastal forest near the water's edge. The 107 rooms have been newly redecorated, adding marble surfaces to the night tables and vanities. Double glass doors let in plenty of light, and lead to a wide but shallow balcony, some with views of the estate-size grounds, while others peer over dunes into the rain forest. The grounds are formally planted, and etched with a network of paths and sidewalks, some of which go down to the sea. For freshwater swimming there is a large pool, spanned by a bridge. At the lobby entrance a working replica of a colonial fountain has been installed, and within there is a large copper still, an *alambique*, like those used throughout rural Brazil for the production of *cana*. The deluxe rooms, with couches, which open onto the courtyard and pool area, cost $85 to $95, while rooms classified as superior are priced at $70 to $80.

The **Vila Rica,** Praça Dom Pedro II 299 (tel. 098/222-4455), has an excellent location for those who wish to be right in the city. The Praça Dom Pedro II is one of the oldest squares in the city, and by far the grandest, built on a hill that looks out over the bay. The buildings bordering the square represent an eclectic architecture. Some are colonial, others art nouveau, and still others faceless and modern. As is often the case in these older sections of Brazil's colonial cities, this square leads directly to another, the Praça Benedito Leite, the unrivaled popular center of São Luís. Both *praças* look on the Catedral da Sé, a section of which dates to the 1600s.

The Hotel Vila Rica was constructed on one slope of this high ground, so that when you enter the lobby you are already on the third floor of the five-story building. Of relatively modern vintage, the hotel's interior conveys a feeling of homey elegance. With 223 rooms the Vila Rica is deceptively large. Rooms have a two-tone décor, with clothes trees and beds that are covered with spreads in geographic patterns. A balcony looks out over the very private, tree-shaded grounds onto the harbor beyond. The baths have extra-large sink tops in speckled marble, and wall tiles with asymmetrical mosaic patterns in black and gray. Other details that catch the eye in the rooms are the full-length mirrors and closet doors made of cane. At the rear of the building, on the ground floor is a patio with a large circular pool and an arresting terrace bar. Most rooms are $63 for singles and $75 for double occupancy, while those rooms with direct access to the pool are $65 and $80 per night.

A Downtown Budget Hotel

The **Hotel Central,** Avenida Dom Pedro II 251 (tel. 098/222-2737), is the oldest hotel in the city. Though no longer housed in its original building, the new structure of World War II vintage occupies the same site, facing the very agreeable Praça Benedito Leite. The hotel's four-story building with its yellow façade is somehow reminiscent of Lisbon, and curves around the corner that links the two adjacent squares. The Central has a history of being a commercial hotel, transient quarters for visiting businessmen and traveling salesmen, a role it no doubt continues to play, though in a slightly different context. The rooms are simple but comfortable, and fully equipped, and a reasonable bargain at $18 to $20 a night.

The Beach Hotels

The most frequented beaches in São Luís are those on the island, closest to downtown. They are **Ponta d'Areia, São Marcos, Calhau,** and **Olho d'Agua.**

The greatest concentration of hotels is near Ponta d'Areia, about two miles from the city.

The newest of these hotels is the **Praia Mar,** Avenida São Marcos, Quadra Commercial 04 (tel. 098/227-4477). The Praia Mar is a solid and well-designed first-class hotel, though in a somewhat woebegone location. The interior of the hotel is a complete environment, with a good restaurant, a bar with a dance floor, and an attractive pool area. And the rooms are comfortable and modern. The nearby beach has little appeal, and there is no place to walk once you are at the hotel and night closes in. Still, transportation is readily available, and the city and better beaches not very distant. The rooms are priced between $45 and $55 per night.

The **Pousada Tia Maria,** Avenida Nina Rodrigues 1 (tel. 098/227-1534), is a former private house in an affluent residential neighborhood. The inn has 11 rooms in two categories. The simplest rooms are equipped with only beds and other necessary furnishings, and are perfectly adequate, especially considering the rate of $10 single and $14 double, including breakfast. There are also four superior rooms that are air-conditioned and equipped with televisions and mini-bars. These have a large wood-trimmed window and shutters with moveable slats and look out on a covered veranda with tile walls. They are priced slightly higher, from $14 to $18.

The **Hotel Ponta d'Areia,** Avenida dos Holandeses 13 (tel. 098/277-2737), has 46 rooms, and is typical of the utilitarian two-star hotel as it exists in Brazil. Nothing fancy, and with little ambience, the hotel has a pool and an inexpensive restaurant open 24 hours a day, serving meals for an average of $3 a dish. Singles are $23; doubles, $25.

WHAT TO SEE: Today's major transient population in São Luís is maritime. Five miles from the city is the modernized port of Itaqui, terminal for the huge Alcoa complex, Alumar, grown to prosperity in recent years by the development of the Carajas mining site that embraces the interior lands of three states, including Mananhão. Copper, iron ore, and bauxite—some of which is smelted into aluminum near São Luís, the rest exported—are among the metallic riches currently being extracted from this ore-soaked region. The deep port attracts many ships, and in São Luís, especially around the **Praça Beneditio Leite,** you can hear the babble of many tongues, as sailors from Korea and Scandinavia, Poland and the Philippines, mix with the democratic gaggle of peasants, bureaucrats, craftspeople, and vendors who already crowd the square.

In the old days the guests at the Hotel Central would place their chairs on the sidewalk outside the hotel, and take the evening air. Today there is a restaurant/bar with outdoor tables for the same purpose. And by 5 or 6 p.m. all of São Luís seems to gather here. You have to sit still in a city like São Luís to catch its pulse, to coexist with it, not just as a consumer of its most obvious attractions—however meritorious they may be—but as a participant in the rhythms of its day-to-day existence. As you sit in the café of the Hotel Central at the close of day, suddenly you are no longer looking for a good reason to visit São Luís.

Historic São Luís

The blocks off the Praça Benedito Leite that run down the sloping hillside toward the waterfront are where the oldest buildings of the city are located. Few are restored, many unpainted, and several unlikely to survive another generation without a massive injection of preservationist consciousness and the funds implicit in that state of mind. The visual result of this decay is a somewhat more anthropological experience than is witnessed in other locales. To wander through these streets is to be left with a vision of the past no less profound—and perhaps more so—than in Ouro Preto or Olinda, however unclaimed it may be by the present populace.

Here you will also find the small **Feira da Praia Grande,** the old public market. Sheltered under a round canopy of timbers and roofing tiles, and open at the sides, the shops and stalls radiate spoke-like from the center. While very much a miniature, this market is among the most interesting to be seen in any of Brazil's larger cities, seeming to function for the moment exclusively for the local citizenry. The displays in the market are the first palpable sign that you are approaching the more homespun culture of the Amazon region, with its less frazzled roots still somewhat connected to the original indigenous inhabitants. The hand-carved household items are less finished than elsewhere, but perhaps more functional; the fruits and vegetables, those of the rain forest, rather than the fertile coastline.

Government House

On the Praça Dom Pedro II is the **Palácio dos Leões,** seat of the state government and official residence of its governor. Certain rooms of the palace are open to public inspection Monday through Friday from 3 to 6 p.m. A hostess (who speaks some English) guides you through various halls and reception rooms, pointing out the origins of the furnishings and artifacts, paintings and engravings, and providing a capsule history of Maranhão.

WHERE TO EAT: Many of the better and most popular restaurants in São Luís are located at the beaches. The **Restaurante Carne do Sol** is located off the Ponta d'Areia beach, opposite the somewhat exaggerated memorial to one Bandeira Tribuzi, a politician and poet who wrote the state's official anthem. The restaurant serves sun-dried beef, tasty and tender, said to be the best for miles around.

The **Pousada Tia Maria,** Avenida Nina Rodrigues 1 (tel. 227-1534), also has an excellent kitchen and its restaurant is open to the public as well as the inn's guests. It serves mostly seafood dishes for between $5 and $7 each, and specialties include caldeirada, a stew of shrimp in their shells cooked in pirão, a porridge of *aipim* flour, similar to *mandioca*. Other dishes are ova, hake fish eggs, and steamed sururu, a bivalve in the mussel family.

The **Frango Dorado,** Estrada de São Marcos 33 (tel. 227-4797), is a barbecued-chicken house in the São Marcos beach neighborhood, about 3½ miles from São Luís proper. The house specialty is chicken grilled over coals, and topped with melted parmesan cheese, for about $3. But an excellent dish as an alternative is the fritada de batipuru, a kind of ratatouille omelet made of dried shrimp, green pepper, tomato, and a variety of local greens that give the dish its unforgettable taste, for about $3.50. The filling may be ordered separately—não fritada, a large portion costing about $2. On Saturday the restaurant serves a full feijoada for $3.50. Open daily from 11 a.m. till 11 p.m.

The **Hibiscus,** on Avenida dos Franceses (tel. 223-2830), is in the neighborhood of Vila Palmeira about 15 minutes from downtown. The Hibiscus is a popular spot for business luncheons among local professionals and executives who wish to dine well but inexpensively. And on Friday and Saturday nights there is live music during the dinner hours. An excellent offering on the menu is a filet of fish with *cuxa,* a green sauce, for $3.50, and also the grilled chicken with a tomato sauce for $2.50. Open daily for lunch from noon to 3 p.m., and for dinner from 7 p.m. to midnight.

A POPULAR NIGHTSPOT: Every day from Tuesday through Sunday there is live music and dancing at the **Tom Marrom,** Avenida Colares Moreira 10, on the outskirts of São Luís in the São Francisco neighborhood. This is another place in

São Luís where the upper crust meets the demimonde. Sailors, bar girls, executives with their wives or dates—even families—all congregate here to dance, drink, and hang out.

A SIDE TRIP TO ALCÂNTARA: The principal side trip from São Luís is to cross the bay to the old colonial city of Alcântara. An excursion by catamaran costs $12, including transfers to and from your hotel, and a local guide. You leave at 9 a.m. and return at about 4 p.m. The crossing of the São Marcos Bay takes about an hour each way, leaving you five hours to explore the ruins and preserved historic sites, which are in a much better state of repair than those in the city.

Alcântara is the former state capital, settled in the early 1600s. When slavery was abolished in the late 19th century, the town was all but abandoned and many of the old buildings fell into ruin. Still well preserved, however, are a number of churches, colonial mansions, and the Praça Gomes Castro, the town square with its *pelourinho,* the old whipping post.

For information, inquire at **Taguatur Turismo, Ltda.,** Praça Benedito Leite, Loja 1 (tel. 222-0100).

FESTIVALS: The Maranhense are a festive people. They celebrate the feast days of their ancestors with a special zeal, and a great respect for tradition. The most unique of their yearly festivals is **Bumba-Meu-Boi** (or simply bumba-boi, as the simple people call it), which is observed throughout the state (and much of the northeast as well). The merrymaking originated as an informal distraction among slaves on the cattle ranches during colonial times. Today a set piece has evolved, like a morality play, which tells the story of a couple, Francisco and Catarina. Catarina is pregnant and craves a taste of beef tongue. To oblige his wife, Chico (short for Francisco) steals the master's prize bull, but is caught by the overseer in the act of slaughter. Chico is then condemned to death if the bull should die from the wound he has inflicted on it. Hearing of his plight, the whole village rallies to Chico's support, and bull and man are both given new leases on their lives, creating the theme of resurrection and rebirth retold yearly with colorfully costumed players, dancers, musicians, and a bull. In the remote areas, the bull is ultimately sacrificed at the end of the festival, perhaps to symbolize Chico's ultimate triumph.

For while bumba-meu-boi (literally, "whack my bull") is celebratory in spirit, and dramatic and musical in effect, the event also has its social and political significance as a satire of the opulent landed rich and testimony to the injustices suffered by the poor who are bound to them in peonage.

The festival has its season and goes on for days, but the principal event occurs on the eve of St. John's Day, June 23, when the dramatic legend is reenacted.

TOURIST INFORMATION: The state's tourist bureau is **MARATUR,** which staffs an information counter at the airport, and has main offices in São Luís at Rua 14 de Julho no. 88 (tel. 221-1231).

CHAPTER XIII

THE AMAZON AND THE PANTANAL

□ □ □

1. BELÉM
2. MANAUS
3. THE PANTANAL

Before traveling to the Amazon, it might be advisable to ask yourself the following questions: "Why am I going there?" "What do I expect to see and do?" To be frank, many people will get more out of "exploring" the Amazon from the comfort of their own armchairs, persuing the vast body of literature that has been written about the region over the years, than they will out of actually going there. Let me explain this somewhat paradoxical perspective. The very idea of the Amazon conjures up fantasies of adventure in the remote and un-spoiled rain forest, and a vision of Indian cultures clinging precariously to pre-Columbian, if not prehistoric, ways of life. The casual tourist to the Amazon region gets to experience little of this reality—a reality, moreover, at least where the Indians are concerned, that is rapidly vanishing from the historic scene.

To be sure, there are still vast unexplored areas in the rain forest and among the seemingly infinite number of tributaries that empty into the basin's major rivers. But these are accessible only to those with the time, money, desire, and skills necessary for such expeditions far from the lifelines of civilization. An amusing account of a recent expedition by writer and amateur explorer Red-mond O'Hanlon appears in issue 20 of *Granta* magazine (Winter 1986). Outfit-ted by a professional, and in the company of experienced guides, O'Hanlon treated himself to a true adventure, the discovery of a new river route to the jun-gle mountain of Neblina. On the way the author's macho companion from home —in great physical shape compared with the paunchy O'Hanlon—is defeated by the jungle, the insects, the solitude. In mid-adventure the companion goes "bonkers," begins screaming "Where is my tomato ketchup?" and must be evac-uated. And therein lies the moral of the tale. Few people, even the seemingly fit, are suited to the real adventures the Amazon still has to offer. Indeed, the greatest expeditionaries in the Amazon region through the years were studious natural-ists, not men or women cut in the Roughrider mold, although, come to think of it, TR himself did once hazard an exploration there, and the Brazilians named a previously undiscovered river after him for his efforts.

What, then, can the casual tourist hope to get out of a visit to the Amazon? Most visitors opt for a stay in one of the region's major cities, like Manaus or Belém, and fan out from there, under careful supervision, availing themselves of a range of boat trips and overnights of varying duration into the nearby jungle. Few of these tours involve roughing it, and some house their guests in first-class accommodations, built on floating platforms or in clearings not far from the riverbank. As for wildlife, you don't see much under these circumstances, though the existence of so many bird and animal species in the rain forest ensures you of seeing something. In my own neck of the woods, a Cub Scout recently asked a woodsman/historian why the men on Benedict Arnold's expedition to Québec had to eat tallow candles for four days after their food supplies ran out, when they had guns to hunt with. The answer was that when you have so many people traipsing through the woods, making so much noise, you're not likely to see any critters in that area for weeks to come. The same answer applies to those who go on organized tours in the Amazon with great expectations of seeing the animal wildlife there.

Ruling out true adventure and intimate familiarization with the virgin forest—other than under the most controlled, even pampered conditions, except in rare cases—most tourists go to the Amazon to experience the cities for their unique river-town moodiness, and their settings, with the jungle as a mysterious, and for the most part impenetrable, background. Even at that, even while staying at the best luxury hotels, all but the most intrepid travelers are likely to undergo some discomfort resulting from the climate, the bugs, the funky— albeit undeniably tasty—food, and the general informality of the tourist apparatus. Sound discouraging? It need not be so. To be forewarned is to be forearmed. There is still ample justification for a visit, assuming your trip is well planned, and you know what to expect.

The city of Belém is a delightful relic, from which several unique side trips can be taken. Manaus, oasis of civilization that it is, is an astounding phenomenon, a semi-modern metropolis in the jungle, virtually disconnected from the rest of Brazil. Even today the only reliable way of getting to Manaus is by plane or boat, because trans-Amazonian roads are both primitive and seasonal at best. This chapter, then, is an introduction to these urban destinations on the edges of the forest, and in the final section, to the wetland wildlife preserve of the Pantanal in the south of Brazil. For those adventuresome folk with a genuine taste for roughing it, I will include the names of one or two outfitters who accompany visitors to the more remote areas. In the main, however, the chapter is addressed to the average tourist whose interest in the Amazon I must assume is kindred to my own, that of an armchair adventurer.

AMAZÔNIA ORIENTATION: Amazônia should not be confused with Amazonas, Brazil's largest state, of which Manaus is the capital. Amazônia is a vast basin of forests and wetlands occupying roughly half of the South American continent, embracing not only a substantial chunk of Brazil—estimates ranging as high as 57%—but also parts of the Guyanas, Suriname, Venezuela, Colombia, Bolivia, Ecuador, and Peru. Within Brazil itself, Amazônia embodies all of Amazonas, the remote states and territories of Acre, Rondônia, Roraíma, and Amapá, and parts of Pará and Maranhão as well. Amazon is also the name given to the system of rivers and tributaries that stretches some 4,000 nautical miles from its several outlets on the Atlantic Ocean to its source, Lago Lauricocha, at an altitude approaching 13,000 feet in the Peruvian Andes, but only 90 miles from the Pacif-

ic coastline. Until it crosses into Brazilian territory, the river is called Marañon, and thereafter the Solimões, itself fed by major and minor tributaries until joining the Rio Negro several miles upstream of Manaus at the famous Encontro das Aguas (the Meeting of the Waters). The Solimões is a "live" river, full of silt and microorganisms that give the river its "whitish" color. The Rio Negro is a "dead" river, much less hospitible to waterlife, and is dark and clearer. When the two meet, they run parallel for several miles until the two tones blend and form the pale-brownish Amazon, as it is called from here until it empties into the Atlantic.

From below Manaus until Santarém to the east, the river is so wide in places that from midstream neither bank can be seen. Here at the "narrows," the Amazon tapers and reaches its deepest point, 225 feet during the high-water season. The Amazon system, from source to mouth, is the longest river in the world, just barely outdistancing the Nile, and the largest river basin on earth by a substantial margin, containing 20% of the planet's fresh water. The forest is also believed to possess fully 10% of all the world's species of life forms, including countless invertibrate, 2,500 fish, and 50,000 plant species. And even more remarkable is the theory that as many as 85% of these species have yet to be identified and documented.

Among the European explorers, it was possibly Columbus himself, on his third voyage in 1498, who first set foot on the shores of South America and who noted in his journal that the presence of fresh water far into the Caribbean was evidence of a great river (the Orinoco in Venezuela), and "a very great continent, until today unknown." First of the Europeans actually to enter the Amazon from the Atlantic end was the great Genoan navigator's former subaltern, Vicente Pinzon, captain of the *Nina* on the 1492 voyage. Pinzon, returning with a fleet of his own in 1500, penetrated some 50 miles up one of the mouths of the Amazon. It was not until over 40 years later, however, that a European was finally to sail the length of the river. In 1541 an expedition left Quito, commanded by Francisco Pizarro's brother, Gonzalo, in search of precious spices. A year later, his forces decimated by battles with both the Indians and the elements, the younger Pizarro gave his lieutenant general, Francisco de Orellana, permission to take a party of men by ship and forage downstream for food to relieve the expedition. Orellana, who disregarded his orders, continued all the way to the Atlantic and returned to Spain. The account of this journey was recorded by his scrivener, Friar Gaspar de Carvajal, who chronicled, among many other hair-raising adventures, a battle with female warriors (or Amazons), a hallucination brought on by the heat, no doubt—at least scholars give little credence to the tale. But the name stuck.

Is the Amazon Disappearing?

A great deal of controversy surrounds the development occurring throughout the Brazilian Amazon, and the impact of these activities on the region's ecology. At the core of the conflict may ultimately rest those two endlessly irreconcilable world views: the romantic and the pragmatic. To some—whether or not they actually wish to visit the region—the continued existence of the Amazon represents an almost transcendental vision. One instinctively rebels against the disappearance of the earth's remaining unsettled forests. To others, the Amazon represents the future, at best a solution to the problem of scarce land, but also a fulfillment of aspirations of national greatness, or merely the restless quest for the grail of instant riches—gold, oil, diamonds, whatever the land will yield.

Nature seems to have her own point of view, perhaps the most compelling. As the forest is cut—to make room for towns, mines, sprawling cattle spreads, factory farms, and the civil construction of dams and roads—the fertility of land seems to diminish very rapidly. You would think that land capable of sustaining the dense and varied growth of the Amazon forest would be capable of producing good hay for grazing or some kind of cash crop. This seldom appears to be the case. The topsoil of the forest floor is thin, easily eroded, and —strangest of all considering the plethora of decaying organic matter—low in nutrients. When land is cleared, often with the highest of motives—to give land to settlers, and to produce food for the national belly—it often refuses new plantings and turns to dust. Perhaps Nature is trying to tell us something. Or, as some would undoubtedly respond, we just haven't found the right technological key to maintain the growing cycle.

The controversy rages on, but on one point there is some modicum of concensus. Not a great deal of the Amazon Valley has thus far been developed or destroyed. The real issue here seems to be exactly how fast the forest is disappearing, not how much still remains. And about this there are endless debates. An excellent account of the state of the Amazon is a paperback book by Roger D. Stone, *Dreams of Amazônia* (Penguin, 1986).

Classic Amazon Literature

Eggheads and armchair travelers (the original couch potatoes) may find useful the following book list: Alexander von Humbolt's *Personal narrative of travels to the equinoctial regions of the New Continent during the years 1799–1804* (published between 1814 and 1829); William H. Edward's *A Voyage up the River Amazon* (1847), Alfred Russell Wallace's *A Narrative of Travels on the Amazon and Rio Negro* (1853), Henry Walter Bates's *The Naturalist on the River Amazons* (1863), and Richard Spruce's *Notes of a Botanist on the Amazon and Andes* (1908).

SPECIALTY TOURS: There are a number of organizations and agencies that offer specialty tours, most involving few deprivations, in selected regions of Brazil, including Amazônia. These may be tours for naturalists or birdwatchers, history and cultural tours, outdoors or trekking tours—even insider urban tours. A listing of the best facilitators in the specialty markets can be found in the next chapter.

1. BELÉM

There are only three Brazilian cities that may be reached on nonstop flights from the United States: Rio de Janeiro, Manaus, and Belém. The VARIG Belém-bound flight leaves from Miami on Sunday evenings and arrives in Belém six hours later, nonstop. As long as this flight continues in service, Belém can be considered a Brazilian destination in and of itself, three hours closer in flying time than Miami to Rio. A traveler's itinerary in Belém might justifiably consist of several days for getting to know the city, and several days to explore the environs, like the island of Marajó or Macapá, capital of Amapá, a city slightly to the north and west of Belém that straddles the equator.

Belém is really a splendid little city. Located barely 80 miles upriver from the Atlantic, Belém was never far removed from the major shipping lanes of the ocean. Since its founding in 1616, Belém has prospered steadily in its role as depot for the natural wealth extracted ever since from Amazônia and distributed from its docksides to the markets of the world. When you talk of nature's plenty, the Amazon forest and its rivers are unsurpassed for providing great stores of fish, fruits, berries, nuts, wood, and innumerable derivatives, not the least of which are some remarkable handcrafts. The city was christened Saint Mary of Bethlehem of Grand Pará, because on the day the site was first consecrated by the formal act of its founder, Francisco Caldeira Castelo Branco, the church liturgical calendar indicated the feast of Santa Maria de Belém (Belém is the Portuguese for the town of Christ's birth).

Belém was built on the shores of the Guajará estuary which empties into the Rio Pará, the southernmost arm of the mighty Amazon from which it is separated by the country-sized delta island of Marajó. The Amazon's main branch is reached by boat, along a serpentine water route that never flows far from the edge of the forest. Much closer to Belém than the River Amazon is the Rio Tocantíns, another of Brazil's giant internal waterways, springing from Goiás and joining with the Rio Pará in the immense Bay of Marajó that opens to the sea. **Pará** is also the name of the state of which Belém is the capital, a territorial land mass larger than most European countries, including France, Italy, and the British Isles. Most typically one hears the city referred to in its long form as Belém do Pará, as if to emphasize the distinction between this secular Bethlehem and its namesake in the Holy Land.

Architecturally, Belém is one of the most delightful and diverse of all Brazilian cities with colonial roots. In Belém, moreover, which has a perfectly wonderful historic quarter, it's not just what remains of the colonial period that catches the eye. Belém's days of splendor were actually much later, dating from Victorian times and running through the turn of the century. These years covered the Brazilian rubber boom, an economic miracle of relatively short duration that rested on an arbitrary fact of nature. The latex-producing trees called *Hevea* brasiliensis existed in great numbers only in the Amazon forest. Owing to the forest's peculiar ecological ground rules, rubber trees do not grow there in clusters, but individually, often hundreds of feet from one another. Thousands of gatherers, each of whom tended massive plots, were required to tap the widely scattered trees. Despite a tremendous security effort to retain the country's rubber monopoly, seedlings were soon smuggled out of Brazil and domesticated in the far more efficient plantations of the British East Asian colonies.

But the short-lived rubber wealth transformed the cities of the Amazon, particularly Belém. From a prosperous backwater, Belém evolved into the genuine urban belle of the Amazon river towns. The stately *mangueiras* (mango trees) that line the avenues and plazas were planted then, their bushy forms and wide leaves providing excellent shade in a city where the average yearly temperature is 80°. Public buildings and private houses followed the rapidly changing fashions of those days, from neoclassical to art nouveau to *fin-de-siècle*, with a fair dose of glass and cast-iron construction for bandstands, park gazebos, and markets. There are also many palazzos in the Italianate style remaining in Belém as testimony to the tastes and fortunes of the city's old rubber barons. Added to the buildings of the rubber-boom era are the many examples of what Brazilians call "pure Portuguese" architecture—colonial houses and commercial buildings with their characteristic billowy windows and portals, iron railings, and tile façades. And the ubiquitous baroque of the sacred structures, with unique equatorial signatures, is by no means lacking. Each shaded street in the center of Belém and each stark, sunny alley in the historic quarter along the waterfront is a visual treat for the professional stroller and amateur building buff.

The crown jewel of structures in Belém is the Teatro da Paz, a world-class monument to the human arts. The markets of Belém, like the nonstop Ver-O-Peso on the waterfront, are also in a class by themselves. In contrast to the urban scene is the life of the river and the people who live on its margins and depend on it for their livelihood. Many varieties of boat excursions are available for getting as close to the river culture as you may wish. And once you have exhausted the attractions of Belém and its environs, there are still the horizons of Marajó and Macapá to explore.

WHERE TO STAY: Belém is not blessed with a surplus of good hotels, which means that any rapid increase in the city's popularity as a destination will stand to place a severe strain on the availability of acceptable lodgings. For those who wish to visit the city during the time of its major festival, Círio, which takes place in mid-October, it's advisable to make your reservations far in advance. All hotels listed here have air-conditioned rooms with full baths, telephones, TVs, and mini-bars, with breakfast included in the rates.

By far the best hotel in Belém is the **Hilton,** Avenida Presidente Vargas 882 (tel. 091-223-6500). The 384-room Hilton occupies a 19-story tower off Belém's principal square, the Praça da República, where the elegant old theater stands in its proud shell of white marble. The standards set by Brazil's Hilton hotels in facilities, décor, and services are only rarely duplicated by a handful of its competitors. In Belém, the Hilton has no competitor. And naturally, the Hilton's rates reflect its dominant position among the city's hotels, though in comparison with Rio's price scale, the cost of a room at the Belém Hilton is about middling.

In addition to the extremely comfortable rooms, the Hilton serves excellent food in several restaurants and bars, and offers the perfect environment on its outdoor veranda for observing the scene and streetlife around the nearby Praça da República. The rooms are spacious and outfitted with large double beds, a generous seating area, and a TV that receives a U.S. satellite channel. Until December 1988 the least expensive single and double in the Hilton will be $98 and $118, respectively, per night, and the most expensive, $137 and $164. Thereafter, assuming the Hilton follows its own pattern of the past several years, rates will go up in increments of $2 to $3 every six months.

Built on a slightly lower order of magnitude is the **Equatorial Palace Hotel,** Avenida Braz de Aquiar 612 (tel. 091-224-8855). The hotel fronts a residential and chic commercial street shaded by a vaulted arch of mango trees and made agreeably quiet by the one-way traffic. This is an elegant hotel, and much more personal than the Hilton, but possessing far fewer facilities as well. What the hotel can boast, however, is a fine dining room, as reputable as any in the city, and beautifully appointed with its polished plank floor and cedar-boarded ceiling. On the hotel's roof is a very intimate pool and patio area similar to something you might find in the backyard of a well-off friend. While the Hilton may have the "ideal" room from the standpoint of maximum travel comfort, the accommodations at the Equatorial Palace are warmer and more homey. The Equatorial has 211 rooms: standard rooms are priced between $57 and $63 for single and double occupancy, and deluxe rooms run $66 to $74. Rates for groups of 15 or more people are $36 to $40 per individual.

Six miles from the center of town is the **Novotel,** Avenida Bernardo Sayão 4804 (tel. 091-229-8011). The Novotel seems to cater to groups of visitors whose stay in Belém is a week or more, and offers special package rates to these guests. The Novotel also provides transportation to and from the airport, an incentive owing perhaps to the hotel's location on the city outskirts. It's location, right at the edge of the river, is also the hotel's most arresting feature. Another very agreeable facility is the courtyard with two pools and a large wooden deck that looks out on the river, where the pageant of passing boats is endless and fascinating. While rated a four-star establishment, the Novotel provides only a three-star room, either ascetic or spartan, depending on your viewpoint. Outside, at the Novotel's own pier, a launch seems to be ever in attendance, about to embark on one of the many water excursions the hotel offers its guests. Rates are $46 to $51 for a standard room and $55 to $63 for a deluxe.

The **Hotel Excelsior Grão Pará,** Praça da República 718 (tel. 091-222-3255), was once the best hotel in Belém, and is still reliable as well as moderately priced. The small, utilitarian lobby reveals how tastes in the design of first-class hotels have changed with the years. Instead of the posh lobby boutiques of the newer establishments, a lone salesgirl sits behind a table attending to the sale of jewels and stones. The Excelsior's 136 rooms are a mixed bag. The rooms in the rear of the hotel are musty and dark, while those that face the square are superb. Front rooms have double doors of frosted glass that open onto, not a balcony, but a wrought-iron railing. The baths are large and comfortably old-fashioned, also with double windows which open to allow wide views as well as good circulation of air. Front rooms cost $32 to $36, and those in the rear run $28 to $32.

Away from the waterfront, going toward the Church of Nazaré, is the **Hotel Regente,** Avenida Gov. José Malcher 485 (tel. 091-224-0755). This very moderately priced hotel has 149 large rooms, with glass-fronted walls and modern baths. The beds, however, are on the small side. The hotel has an excellent backyard pool, behind a very private high wall, and an appealing mezzanine bar. Rooms in the rear are $20 to $22, and those facing the front go for $30 to $35.

Farther out on the same avenue is the **Hotel Sagres,** Avenida Gov. José Malcher 2927 (tel. 091-228-3999). The interior of the Sagres looks something like a cruise ship. The rooms are not cabin-size, though, but large and very ship-shape in appearance with clean wood-trimmed lines and gallery-white walls. The rooftop pool, where the nautical theme is even more pronounced, offers the best panoramic view of Belém. Rooms are all of one type, with rates at $28 for a single and $34 for a double.

WHERE TO DINE: Belém's cuisine is genuinely aboriginal, as directly traceable to the longstanding diet of the continent's pre-Columbian inhabitants as that of Bahia is known to derive from various African cultures. In both cases, of course, other influences have contributed to the evolution of the dishes served today. But the use of certain basic ingredients, like **tucupi** (fermented juice from the manioc root), **maniva** (the leaf of the manioc plant), and **jambú** (a green similar to Italian broccoli)—as is the case with *dendé* in Bahia—ensures that the respective cuisines retain much of their original character.

La em Casa, Avenida Gov. José Malcher 982 (tel. 223-2293), is to Belém what the Casa da Gamboa is to Salvador. When you experiment with food as novel to the palate as the aboriginal food of Amazônia, it's best to find a restaurant that takes particular care in its choice of ingredients and with their final preparation. Some of the specialties served at La em Casa are pato no tucupi (slices of roast duck stewed in tucupi sauce, with jambú leaves), manicoba (often referred to as the feijoada of the Amazon, a stew of minced maniva leaves with jerked beef, smoked pork, tongue, sausage, calves' and pigs' feet, tripe, and pigs' ear and tail, served with feijão da colônia, (small white beans), and pirarucu (a gigantic river fish, salted like cod, and served in a variety of presentations). La Em Casa occupies an open-air veranda of a private house belonging to Dona Ana Maria Martins, a local society figure who opened the restaurant, and who personally supervises the kitchen. The restaurant is moderately priced—$5 to $8 per entree —and serves only regional food. A second restaurant at the same site is the enclosed and air-conditioned **O Outro,** where fine cooking in the international mold is the specialty. Both restaurants are open daily for lunch and dinner.

Attached to the Forte do Castelo is the restaurant **O Círculo Militar,** on Praça Frei Caetano Brandão (tel. 223-4374), a former officer's club, but long open to the public. The old fort sits on the waterfront in the oldest section of Belém. In the restaurant, try to occupy a table by the window. Even at night, when visibility is necessarily curtailed, the sounds of life from the river continue. The constant putter-sputter signals the one-stroke engines of the flat-bottomed riverboats, spiritual kin to the *African Queen,* that glide by in endless procession, illuminated only by the night sky and their running lights. River fish and forest game are the mainstay of the Círculo's menu, which extends to many varieties of standard Brazilian dishes as well, like filet mignon or roast chicken. One delicacy is the casquinho de buçuã, a blend of farofa and tortoise meat, for about $3.50 a serving. I must point out that many game meats—like tortoise and manatee—are illegally hunted throughout the Amazon, to the degree that the existence of these species is gravely endangered. Nonetheless, the habit of eating tortoise is deeply rooted in the region, and manatee, the large Amazon sea mammal, is a staple among the river dwellers in the bush. One result of this habit and demand is that these foods are still served by even respectable restaurants in Belém, although often requested discreetly and referred to euphemistically. Most meals at the Círculo are in the $10 range. The restaurant is open for both lunch and dinner.

The **O Theatro** restaurant at the Hilton is expensive, but recommended for its innovative dishes, like lobster and caviar topped with hollandaise sauce. The **churrascaria** at the Equatorial Palace Hotel is less expensive but equally recommended.

Augustu's, Avenida Almirante Barroso 439 (tel. 226-8317), is a popular restaurant near the Hotel Sagres.

Snack foods and more informal meals are available throughout the city, but particularly at the tent-covered popular restaurants found throughout the stalls of the public markets. One favorite street food is tacaca, a very strong-flavored porridge laced with shrimp and tucupi. Ice cream made with unique Amazon fruits is also widely available in Belém. New fruits to look for at the market and taste are açaí, popunha, muricí, sapotí, buçuri, mangaba, taperebã, cupuaçu, and uxí.

WALKING AROUND BELÉM:
A walking tour of Belém can begin at the **Praça da República** with a visit to the **Teatro da Paz.** Construction on this unabashedly classical temple was begun in 1869, and follows the Empire style then in fashion, inspired by a romantic rediscovery in the West of the ruins of Greek and Roman antiquity. The building houses several richly detailed spaces—rehearsal halls, foyers, a terrace, and salon for the entr'acte—but the theater itself outsparkles the undeniable loveliness of these other components. The auditorium is horseshoe-shaped, with three levels of boxes, a pit, a balcony, and high above, a gallery called Paradise. The décor is original in most details, notably the woven-straw armchairs and a spectacular floral wallpaper that from afar seems remarkably abstract. On a wall near the entrance are commemorative plaques memorializing great artists who have performed here. In 1918 the local press club so honored the presence of the Russian prima ballarina Anna Pavlova.

Of further interest in the Praça da República itself are the **Bar do Parque,** an outdoor café on a raised platform, and the miniature "crystal palace," the **gazebo** built of cast iron and glass.

Going from the Praça da República in the direction of the bay, descend along **Rua do Santo Antônio** toward the waterfront. Note the striking example of the art nouveau building named "F. de Castro," the one with the trendy América boutique. Continue on to the **Praça Mercês,** with its church; although much altered from the original, it still has its rude flooring of terracotta tiles. There are several buildings on the square in the "pure Portuguese" style, their façades sheathed in tiles. A block or two from the square is the wide boulevard along the pier, **Avenida Castilhos França,** and the vast stone apron where the public markets, including the permanent stalls of the Ver-O-Peso, are located.

The **Ver-O-Peso market** is a warren of stands, many of which remain open 24 hours a day, selling fruits and vegetables, snack foods, and many strange objects that have been salvaged from the creatures of the river or forest, or that have been prepared by human hands to dispel ill fortune or disease in all the many forms they can assault us. The market's name literally means "see the weight," but a more accurate translation might be "watch the scale," a local reference no doubt to the universal consumer complaint of the green grocers' heavy thumbs. Endless streams of porters carry produce from the boats at dockside, which come and go all day and night, to their appropriate stalls and vendors.

Among the sights are the fetish potions used in the rites of the Afro-Umbanda religion, hundreds of vials for giving or repelling the evil eye, to induce virility, or for seduction. One little bottle had a printed label which in translation reads: "Strong potion to seduce your secret love and dominate her affections." On some stalls scores of little bags of powder are suspended by strings, each one a herbal remedy for whatever ails you, the traditional medicines being at least affordable to most of Belém's denizens, unlike modern pharmaceuticals which are only for the affluent. There are withered roots and leaves for purposes not indicated by signs or labels, dried starfish and sea horses, deer's hooves and alligators' teeth, cocks' tails and the hard tongues and scales of the *pirarucu* fish, used as emory boards.

Emerging from this spectacle of strange smells and sights, you come to the great old market itself, a cast-iron marvel, painted marine gray and imported piece by piece from England, including the stately steeples that adorn each of its four corners. Inside is the fish fair. Here you will see the biggest, smelliest, ugliest fish in existence, all culled from the rivers of this land. Note the *mero,* a finny creature the size of a St. Bernard, with a huge round head to match.

Here and there on the dockside you might see green bundles of some rolled material, a yard or so in length, and tied like fasces, those symbols of a Roman magistrate's authority. These are giant leaves called *guarumã* — simply the "wrapping paper" people buy to carry their fish in.

From the Ver-O-Peso, we now enter the **Cidade Velha,** the older part of the city, stretching away from downtown and generally accompanying the shoreline of the bay. Immediately off the waterfront is the **Praça Frei Caetano Brandão,** also called the Largo da Sé because of the **Catedral,** an 18th-century church but completely restyled in the past century. It is from here that the procession for Círio begins during Belém's most important celebration. On the same square is the **Igreja do Santo Alexandre,** commissioned in the early 1800s by Jesuits, and built by unskilled Indian laborers, resulting in a primitive baroque effect most notable in the crude decorative touches, like the childlike carved flowers on the façade.

Leave the square along the **Travessa da Vegia,** a narrow lane left very undisturbed since the colonial days. The street contains many period houses with smooth façades and balconies with iron grillwork. At the other end you come out onto Rua Siqueira Mendes and another square, the **Praça do Carmo,** which seems like a study of so many village squares found in any given town of the Brazilian interior. The layout of the garden is formal but modest, with stone-demarcated paths bordering sparse patches of grass and a few plants. What gives the square its stature and ancient quality, however, are the century-old mango trees that envelop the space in a blanket of shade.

At the far end of the praça is the **Igreja do Carmo,** a mixture of baroque and neoclassical design. From the church floor to the beginning of the great vault, the details like the main and side altars are all heavily carved in busy, intricate baroque. The vault and its paintings are of a latter period. One unsatisfactory explanation has it that the difference reflects the long delay and passage of time between the laying of the cornerstone and the church's finished form. But how came it that the altars were installed before the roof was on?

The old city covers a wide area, and has by far the highest concentration of colonial homes, buildings, and churches in all Belém. Yet practically whatever street you turn onto as you wander through this city seems to offer some vision of the past, one that is nonetheless generally well integrated into the present. Perhaps the presence of so many tree-lined streets provides a common denominator for the many ages that are so inexplicably—though not self-consciously—preserved in this city.

An Evening Walk

An interesting excursion to tie in with a dinner at the Círculo Militar is a visit to the **Feira do Açaí,** which begins in the evening and goes on till dawn. From outside Castelo Fort, near the entrance to the restaurant, descend the **Ladeira do Forte,** which is said to be the oldest paved street in the city. On the ladeira you will pass two popular and informal nightspots right next door to each other, the **Canto da Ladeira** and the **Teatro Paço da Ladeira.** When you arrive on the pier, you'll see the comings and goings of many boats, and troops of stevedors in the process of unloading the cargo and neatly stacking on the dock hundreds of baskets of açaí fruit. The açaí is an olive-size black berry from which locals make a syrupy juice, very popular as a flavoring in ice cream. Coming away from the fort, you pass near the cathedral again and into two other squares with interesting atmospheres of their own: the **Praça do Relógio,** with its monumental clock tower, and the **Praça Dom Pedro II,** with its statues of lions on pedestals and therefore known popularly as the Praça dos Leões.

THREE MORE SIGHTS: There are three additional and important sights in Belém not far from downtown, going toward the suburbs and the airport. First is the **Basílica de Nossa Senhora da Nazaré,** Praça Justo Chermont, a church built in 1908 that sparkles with marble and stained glass, and is another of Belém's relics from the rubber boom.

Not far from the basilica is the **Museu Paraense Emílio Goeldi,** Avenida Magalhães Barata 376 (tel. 224-9233), a very special zoo and Indian museum. The museum has been in existence since 1866 when it was created to perform a naturalistic inventory of Amazonian resources, embracing the flora, fauna, rocks and minerals, geography, history, and indigenous cultures, and to mount exhibitions for the public. The Goeldi Museum continues to carry out the same mandate to this day. Surrounding the museum building are a zoo and an array of structures where the staff does its research. In the zoo, you will get what may be your only chance to see a manatee, the nearly extinct sea mammal of the Amazon, as well as cats, birds, monkeys, snakes, and other creatures native to the region. The museum itself contains a well-organized collection of Indian artifacts—weapons, headgear, funeral urns—photographs of contemporary tribes, and a reproduction of a typical Indian hut. Open Tuesday through Sunday from 8 a.m. to noon and 2 to 6 p.m.; on Saturday only the zoo is open.

Finally, there is the **Bosque Rodrigues Alves,** on Avenida Almirante Barroso, a park occupying a square block on the outskirts of the city where the original vegetation of rain forest is preserved. Open from 8 a.m. to 5 p.m.; closed Monday.

AN UNUSUAL NIGHTSPOT: A totally unique nightclub environment is the **Gemini Drive-In,** Rodovia BR 316, at km. 02 (tel. 235-0793). Not far from town, along the same highway that links Belém ultimately with northeastern Brazil, is this concept discothèque offering "a world of options" in music and dancing. Four separate spaces cater to different tastes and sounds, including blues, rock, Brazilian pop, and country and western.

CRAFTS: Belém ships its high-quality pottery all over the world. Called **marajoara,** the style of the local ceramic crafts is derived from techniques and designs first produced by the Marajo Indians. An interesting morning or afternoon excursion can be made to the **Vale do Paracuri,** a suburb of Belém beyond the air force base, named for the small river that traverses it. You will need a guide or an astute cab driver to find this very rustic neighborhood with its unmarked and unpaved roads. The Paracuri River (really a stream) is the source of the mud from which scores of cottage artisans who live here make their pots. With every high tide, canoes ascend the Paracuri and dump mounds of mud along the riverbanks where the small factories are located. I entered one of the larger establishments, the **Olaria Rosemiro,** where some 30 potters and other workers are employed (*olaria* means pottery factory). The structure they occupy is wood-framed and thatch-roofed in part, and open along the sides. The workers follow a defined division of labor: some scoop the mud from the shore and pound it into blocks, while others feed the blocks into a kind of mill to purify it and produce clay. Potters sit behind their foot-powered wheels and throw the variety of pieces —great jars, vases, bowls—that are the stock-in-trade of the house. Still others glaze the pots and fire them for the artists who by hand paint the old Indian designs on the finished surfaces.

In Belém, near the Praça da República, the state tourist bureau **Paratur,** Praça Kennedy (tel. 224-9633), maintains a craft shop where *marajoara* pottery may also be bought, in addition to Indian-made goods and other items in leather, straw, and wood. Paratur also maintains a tourist information center at this same location.

RIVER EXCURSIONS: River excursions from the port of Belém fall into two categories: local sightseeing tours, and river journeys to other destinations. A number of companies offer day trips in and around the harbor of Belém, often with visits up meandering *igarapés* or *igapós* (seasonally or permanently flooded creeks) for a peek at stilt houses and local village life, rubber and Brazil-nut trees, and the like. Such local excursions are organized by **Telstar Turismo,** at the Novotel, Avenida Bernardo Sayãs 4804 (tel. 229-8011); **Lusotur,** Avenida Braz de Aquiar 612 (tel. 224-8855); and **Gran-Pará Turismo,** Avenida Presidente Vargas 676 (tel. 224-3233).

Many companies operate cruises between Belém and other Amazon cities like Manaus, Macapá, and Soure in Marajó. The most comfortable boats are operated by **ENASA,** a government company, with main offices at Avenida Presidente Vargas 41 (tel. 223-3011), and ticket purchases directly on ENASA's pier off Avenida Castilhos França. The journey upstream to Manaus takes about six days, and only part of the time—owing to the width of the river—does the ship travel in sight of land. First-class passage in the company's flagship starts at $370 for a bunk in a four-person cabin. Hammock space in the less fancy ships can be had for $40, including meals—but you must supply the hammock. The discomfort, crowding, and poor sanitary conditions are free.

CÍRIO: Círio is Belém's most important festival. It takes place the second Sunday of October every year, and attracts as many as a million visitors to the city. The festival is both sacred and secular. The religious component involves a procession, accompanying a statute of Belém's patron saint, Our Lady of Nazaré, from the cathedral to the basilica. To local residents Círio is also a kind of Thanksgiving, a family day of feasting on traditional foods. The festivities go on for two weeks, until at the end of October the image of the saint is returned to her permanent niche.

AN EXCURSION TO MARAJÓ: An interesting two-day side trip can be made to the nearby country-size island of Marajó. The best way to make the trip is to fly one way and return by boat, economizing a bit on time, yet availing yourself of a pleasant river crossing as well. A seat on a small plane can be booked in the early morning at the in-town airstrip, the Aeroporto Júlio César, for about $120 one way (less for each additional passenger up to four people). The half-hour flight is highly worthwhile, as you soar above the mata, the forest green, etched everywhere with rivulets and creeks.

The asphalt landing strip in **Soure,** capital of Marajó, is somewhat of a luxury for so small a town in the Brazilian interior, but in compensation for this unexpected symbol of the island's development, there are no cabs or buses to take you to the town's only hotel. For this reason—unless you are absolutely resigned to go it alone under all circumstances—it's advisable to book at least a portion of your Marajó visit through a tour company, like one of those listed above. If you do, you'll be met by a car belonging to the **Pousada Marajoara,** Quarta Avenida (tel. 091-741-1472), which provides perfectly adequate quarters for your overnight on Marajó. It's within walking distance of the waterfront, the center of town life, and has comfortable rooms, a swimming pool, and a good restaurant.

Many visitors to Marajó prefer to stay on one of the water buffalo ranches, like the **Bonjardim,** two hours farther into the island by boat from Soure. Great herds of water buffalo are raised on Marajó, and the first of this species apparently came to the island by accident, the result of a shipwreck. Bonjardim is a working spread, but also something of a dude ranch, with many outdoor activities programmed, like horseback riding, roundups, fishing and nature walks, and excellent home-cooking—much of the food provided in the form of butter, cheese, and meat by the same buffalos. The Bonjardim has a booking office in Belém at Rua Tiradentes 392 (tel. 091-222-1380).

Those who stay in Soure may also visit a **water buffalo ranch** on a tour organized by the pousada. The trip involves a ride on a comfortable riverboat with a bar, to a typical ranch where you will be met at the dock by local cowpokes driving buffalo carts to carry you up to the house. You will then be served a few dairy snacks made from buffalo milk and treated to a rather stupid display of animal abuse that is passed off as a kind of rodeo.

My personal recommendation would be to forgo the ranch tour and spend your day at the remarkable **Araruana** beach. The pousada also organizes tours to this nearby beach, but they are of too limited duration given the beauty of the spectacle that awaits you. Your best bet would be to rent a bicycle in town and make the trip on your own. As you near the water, you will first have to cross the mangrove swamp on the half-mile-long wooden walkway that connects the access road to the beach. The *mangueiros* (mangroves) are those remarkable trees which have adapted to the ecologies of delta lands and savannas, flooded or dry depending on the season. The root systems grow in swirls above the ground, and so the thousands of trees seem like dainty ladies holding up their skirts as they cross through a puddle. Here in the mud, among the twisted roots, the funny, side-stepping *carangueijo* crab makes his home, and is gathered as a favorite food by rich and poor alike.

As you near the beach, you will get your first view of the roiling, boiling water. The surf is not high but amazingly agitated, like the ocean during a hurricane, owing to the location of the beach some 50 short miles below the mouth of the Amazon, where the inland and the ocean seas crash against each other.

The sun here, and throughout the region, is very hot, the bathing good, and the water warm and shallow a long way out. On the weekends the shanty restaurants are open, selling food and beverages. But there is no other development, and you can wander far down the beach for all the privacy you want. Stay away from the edge of the treeline, however. The insects are large and rapacious.

For the evening, you have basically two choices: You can stay at the pousada and participate in the organized follies, where guests are called upon to join a performer on the dance floor for a little jig and are then given certificates for being good sports, and so forth. Or you can go to the town square, opposite the dock where the ENASA boat is docked, and hang out in one of the two **outdoor cafés**, mixing with the locals and snacking on the savories. The little town is really quite charming, especially its main avenue lined with bulky mango trees, and the formal garden and walkway that accompanies the bank of the river. Soure is not old, having been laid out at the end of the last century by the same architect who designed Belo Horizonte, but it feels absolutely timeless.

If you choose to return by boat, you should already have made arrangements in Belém prior to coming to Marajó. The ENASA liner boards around 10 p.m. for the return, at which time you can retire to your cabin or party all night in the discothèque, and arrive in Belém sometime early the following morning.

A SIDE TRIP TO MACAPÁ: Another popular side trip from Belém is to the capital city of the Brazilian territory of Amapá, usually on a regularly scheduled flight with VARIG or another of the country's airlines, although a 12-hour boat trip is also available on the ENASA line.

The main attraction in Macapá is a more dramatic version of what you will see and hear at the beach on Marajó. Travelers come all the way to Macapá to witness the **pororoca,** the thundering sound made when the draining waters of the Amazon crash into the rushing tide of the Atlantic. The best time to experience the phenomenon is when the Amazon is high, roughly from July through December.

TOURIST INFORMATION IN BELÉM: The state tourist bureau, **Paratur,** maintains a tourist information center on Praça Kennedy (tel. 091-224-9633), providing visitors with maps, brochures, and timetables for river trips, both short and long.

2. MANAUS

Manaus is the capital of the state of **Amazonas,** built up from an obscure river village only at the end of the last century as a result of the rubber boom. Amazonas state has a population of perhaps 1.2 million inhabitants, and yet represents some 20% of Brazil's national territory. After the fall of the Brazilian rubber market, Manaus foundered for half a century. To revive the city, Manaus was designated a free port by the Brazilian government in 1967, and since then government policy has encouraged the growth in the city of extensive assembly plants by major multinational firms, primarily in the consumer electronics field.

Manaus grew up on the hilly left bank of the Rio Negro, which is carved by an endless chain of creeks called *igarapés,* where water enters or recedes depending on the time of year. In July the river is at its highest, and December, its lowest, a difference of as much as 35 feet most years, sometimes more. Floating houses and stilt dwellings are the adaptations made by those who live near the riverbank in response to flood season. And while the city is some 1,000 water miles from the Atlantic, its general elevation is only 20 feet above sea level. With few historic buildings and a pattern of hodgepodge industrial development over the past 20 years, Manaus is not what you would call a pretty city. What Manaus does have in its favor is its location on the great river, and—despite the hive-like activity of its port and industrial suburbs—an eerie sense of isolation from the mainstream of civilization. Its distance from other regional centers in Brazil puts the Amazonian capital and its vast, sparsely populated surrounding territories somewhat in the same position as Alaska in the U.S. But of course the comparison does not extend to the climate. Manaus is hot and humid. The year-round mean temperature is 85° Fahrenheit, with September through November being the hottest months.

A stay of two or three days in Manaus is sufficient to see the city and a few of the better-known sights on the river, like the truly impressive "meeting of the waters," where the different-colored Rio Solimões and Rio Negro run parallel before mixing into the muddy brown of the Amazon. Manaus, of course, is also the major port of entry for visitors who wish to travel extensively on the river, taking advantage of the dozens of excursions and adventure tours that originate from the city, which are usually booked long in advance of arrival through specialty travel agents at home. The names of several respected travel agencies and tour operators active in these areas, with brief descriptions of their itineraries, are given in Chapter XIV.

WHERE TO STAY: Manaus does not have an abundance of good hotels, and because of the generally higher cost of living in the city, you should expect to pay more here than for hotels of comparable quality in other Brazilian cities. Unless otherwise noted, all rooms listed here are air-conditioned, and are equipped with TVs and mini-bars, and have breakfast included in the daily rate.

The Deluxe Bracket

By far the best hotel in Manaus—and one of the most luxurious resorts in all Brazil—is the **Hotel Tropical,** Estrada da Ponta Negra (tel. 092/238-5757). For those who wish to be in the Amazon but remain insulated from its rough edges, the Hotel Tropical provides the perfect environment. The hotel even organizes all its own tours, including several options for overnights in the forest at the Tropical's very own first-class floating lodge. Located near the airport approximately a half-hour ride from the city, the Tropical sits on the bank of the Rio Negro, with its own access to one of Manaus's most popular beaches, and on acres of private, beautifully landscaped grounds that contain a small zoo, a playground, an enormous central courtyard with swimming pool, and tennis courts. Everything about the Tropical is voluptuous, including the somewhat oversize *fazenda*-style furnishings. Several of the public spaces are genuinely elegant, including a formal restaurant, the very masculine bar in polished hardwood and leather, and several lounges and seating areas off the lobby. The rooms have wood floors with Persian-style throw rugs, floor-to-ceiling armoires, and lantern sconces on the walls. Baths have bright tiles painted with floral motifs, and contain separate tub and stall shower. The standard and deluxe rooms differ only in their location within the hotel. Rates for single occupancy range from $85 to $119, and for doubles, $95 to $133.

Away from the river, about 15 minutes from the city in Adrianópolis, one of its most affluent suburbs, is the **Da Vinci Hotel,** Rua Belo Horizonte 240-A (tel.

092/233-6800). The 81-room Da Vinci is only four years old, and while it has a classification of only three stars from Brazil's Federal Tourist Authority, the hotel is the living example of the inconsistency of that classification system, one that is based on a mechanistic checklist of facilities and is apparently blind to aesthetic considerations. The Da Vinci is only a shade less grand in its appointments than the Matsubara in Maceió. The Da Vinci is a hotel, not a plush resort like the Tropical, but it still provides the most elegant digs in Manaus.

There are four categories of rooms, distinguished by location, size, and to some degree, furnishings. The least expensive standard room does not suffer a decline in either comfort or the tastefulness of its décor. The room has a double bed, armchair, and deep-brown carpeted floors, and is of high-quality workmanship in its furnishings and finish. The regular deluxe room adds a balcony with plenty of elbow room, covered by a sloping tile roof, and sports two modern rocking chairs. A large set of double doors—part louvered slats, part mullioned window panes—separates the room from the balcony. The deluxe room also contains a couch, and all rooms display dried floral arrangements that have been fashioned into unique wall hangings.

A lovely sunken lobby is imaginatively divided into several discreet seating environments, each with individually styled armchairs, love seats, and tables—all of rattan and cane. Borders of living plants and vases of dried flowers, grasses, and leaves complete the effect. Both the bar and the restaurant off the lobby convey an air of sophistication, and outside there is a large pool area with two dozen patio tables with chairs, shaded by umbrellas. The standard rooms cost $53 to $65, or $60 to $72 if they face the pool. The regular deluxe rooms run $68 to $80, while an extra-large executive deluxe room is priced at $83 to $95.

The Upper Bracket

Right in town, close to both the free-port shopping district and the floating dock and market is the 171-room **Hotel Amazonas**, Praça Adelberto Valle (tel. 092/234-7679). Deluxe accommodations at the Amazonas are high-ceilinged rooms with good-sized balconies offering views of the active waterfront and the Rio Negro. The standard rooms are smaller and face the rear, with views over the back commercial streets. All rooms are furnished with cabinetry and surfaces in modern, straight-lined designs, with two single beds in the deluxe rooms and a double bed in the standards. The hotel has a large second-floor restaurant with voluminous black columns, heavy handmade, country-style tables and chairs, and a small courtyard pool with a hardwood deck and separate bar. Standard single and double rooms rent for $60 to $70, and deluxe rooms are priced at $85 to $90.

The **Imperial Hotel**, Avenida Getúlio Vargas 227 (tel. 092/233-8744), is a ten-story apartment-style building with 100 rooms, located on one of Manaus's principal avenues. Rooms are of good size, approximately 12 feet by 15 feet, and comfortably furnished, some with large double beds, a couch, and a lace-covered table with chairs, while others have two single beds and an armchair. The hotel's second-floor restaurant is a pleasant room where food is served both à la carte and buffet style, and there is live music on Friday and Saturday nights. Behind the hotel is a mid-size backyard, with a pool and a tile deck. Rates begin at $55 to $60 for standard rooms, and are $65 to $70 for deluxe accommodations.

Next door to the Imperial is the 80-room **Plaza Hotel**, Avenida Getúlio Vargas 215 (tel. 092/234-2032), open since 1986. The deluxe rooms are small and set up like a pullman suite to maximize the use of limited space. Some rooms have a single bed and a couch that opens to a second bed; other rooms are larger with double beds, tables, and chairs. The closets have doors that slide up and down like rolltop desks, and the bathrooms are also small, but equally well organized with marble corner sinks whose surfaces are large. The general décor of the hotel is attractive, and the corridors are wide, carpeted, and well painted—not dazzling, but well done. An atrium lobby leads to a mezzanine restaurant. The Plaza has no swimming pool. Rooms rent for $60 single and $75 double. Rates include the 10% service charge.

The Middle Bracket

The best of the middle-bracket hotels is the **Lord,** Rua Macílio Dias 217 (tel. 092/234-9741), though it has a few serious flaws, some of which are being corrected by the gradual renovation of the accommodations. The six-story building with a pseudo-modern façade occupies a corner (with Rua Quintino Bocaiúva) on an active commercial street closed to traffic and recently converted to a pedestrian shopping mall. Many consumer shops selling crafts and electronic goods line the street. Rooms on the upper floors look out over the surrounding rooftops, and are pleasant enough, though the individual air conditioners make a terrible noise, forcing you to open the windows at night, which is not necessarily unpleasant. The bathrooms, however, are a bit of a disaster. Sinks have only cold-water taps, and the showers are fitted with electric shower heads, which are not only dangerous but work indifferently at best. The hotel is well situated, quite near the central section of the waterfront, and has a reasonably spacious lobby—something lacking in most hotels of its class in Manaus. The attached bar is pleasant, and the restaurant is an adequate space, but the breakfast is all but inedible—a most unusual criticism to be leveled at any hotel in culinary-conscious Brazil. Standard rooms have no TVs, and cost $42 to $48; deluxe rooms cost $50 to $55.

A block from the Lord is a street with several of the city's older medium-priced hotels. The **Hotel International,** Rua Dr. Moreira 168 (tel. 092/234-1315), is the best of the lot. The deluxe rooms in this 39-room hotel are large, and breezy when the windows are open, although all rooms are also equipped with individual air conditioners. The rooms contain two good-sized beds, and the floors are carpeted. Baths are tiled with decorative *azuleijos*. The furnishings are definitely well used, but not in bad shape by any means. Rates start at $25 to $30 for the standard rooms, and at $28 to $35 for the deluxe.

At no. 302 on the same block is the 50-room **Hotel Central** (tel. 092/234-2197). The rooms are spacious enough, with windows, double beds, and good old-fashioned baths with porcelain fixtures. Rates are $25 to $30. And in a pinch there's the **Solomão Hotel** at no. 119 (tel. 092/232-8479), with 28 very small rooms with undersize beds, also costing $25 to $30.

A Budget Hotel

The **Kyoto Plaza Hotel,** Rua Dr. Moreira 232 (tel. 092/232-6552), with 15 rooms, is more of a *pensão* than a hotel. Rooms are small, without windows but otherwise adequate. Some rooms have single beds, others doubles, and all are air-conditioned. Rates are $15 to $20 a night.

WHERE TO EAT: The regional food in Manaus is the same as that in Belém. Such dishes as pato no tucupi (duck in fermented manioc sause) and tacaca (the funky tapioca porridge served in a gourd, primarily as a street food) are readily available throughout the city. But the mainstay of the local diet is fish—*pirarucu, tambaquí,* and *tucunaré* are the most popular, but the list only begins with these. Despite the high cost of living in Manaus, restaurant food is not appreciably more expensive than elsewhere in Brazil.

One very popular fish restaurant, and one of the most expensive in Manaus, is the **Caçarola,** Rua Maurés 188 (tel. 233-3021), located on the outskirts of town in a modest suburb. The Caçarola has the atmosphere of a neighborhood outdoor café, nothing fancy; indeed, the chairs and tables are a bit rickety. But the restaurant has won its reputation on the basis of its kitchen, not its décor. All the typical fish dishes are served, in a variety of presentations, and the steak is also excellent. Most of the à la carte entrees cost between $10 and $15. Open daily for lunch and dinner, the restaurant takes a break between 3 and 6 p.m.

Manaus has two restaurants named **Panorama,** both with their attractions. **Panorama** number one, at Rua Recife 900 (tel. 232-3334), has no vista at all to speak of. The attractive brick-and-timber open-air lean-to actually occupies a corner on a busy intersection in the Adrianópolis neighborhood. The food here, both the fish and the meat dishes, is excellent, and in the $6 to $8 range. Especially recommended are the farofa de tambaquí, the caldo verde (a Portuguese country soup), and the caldeirada (a boullabaise of river fish served with *pirão*, manioc grits). The second **Panorama,** Boulevard Rio Negro 199 (tel. 232-3177), is in the riverside Educandos neighborhood, and has an excellent view overlooking the Rio Negro. This is a simpler restaurant, serving meals in the $4 to $6 range, an excellent place to eat or to hang-out for the "panorama." Hours for both are from 11 a.m. to 3 p.m. and 6 p.m. to midnight.

Many of Manaus's favorite restaurants are located outside the city, along various suburban access roads. The **Palhoça,** Estrada da Ponta Negra (tel. 238-3831), is such a place. A large, open-sided shed with a straw roof, the Palhoça serves a good mixed-grill barbecue for about $5.

Two restaurants in an area called Parque 10 are worthy of note. **La Barca,** Rua Recife 684 (tel. 236-8544), is a white stucco building, trimmed in dark hardwood and open on three sides, that looks like the veranda of a hacienda. This is probably the most sophisticated restaurant in Manaus. The tables are attractively set for elegant dining, and the menu is extensive, listing over 100 plates, including many *iscas* (side dishes and appetizers). Best of all, meals are reasonably priced, from $5 to $10. Open Monday through Saturday for lunch and dinner, but on Sunday for lunch only.

The **Timoneiro,** Rua Paraiba 07 (tel. 236-1679), is also in Parque 10. For native décor, this is the most attractive restaurant in Manaus. The large space is saturated with authentic artifacts of the Amazon Indian cultures, as well as taxidermic oddities like mummified alligators, strange fish, tortoise shells, and jaguar pelts. Bird cages in the parking lot are filled with chatty parrots and arraras. Specialties here are tambaquí barbecue, tucunaré stew, and filet of pirarucu. International platters are also available. Fresh fruits of the Amazon are recommended for dessert, especially the capuacu, tucuma, pupunha, and graviola. The liquor made from graviola is strong and smooth, and makes an excellent apéritif. Prices are very reasonable, from $4.50 to $6 for most dishes. Open for dinner seven days a week, and for lunch only on weekends, when live music is also featured.

NIGHTLIFE: The **Gafieira Carioca,** Estrada do V8 2222 (tel. 236-9930), is a dance hall, as the term *gafieira* implies. The large covered space has many tables, a dance floor, and a bandstand where a ten-piece combo with plenty of brass holds forth. Open Thursday, Friday, and Saturday only, from 10 p.m. till 3 a.m.

The **Espaço Aberto,** Avenida Pedro Texeira 300, Loja 6, is located in the Kissia Shopping Center in Planalto. Open Thursday through Sunday, this is *the* hot spot for young people in Manaus. On Friday and Saturday the club jumps to rock music; otherwise there is a singer with guitar. The artistic cover is about $2 per person.

A NOTE ON BUGS: There are many small, flying insects that will penetrate the otherwise hermetic security of even the city's finest hotels. Come to the Amazon prepared to tolerate a certain amount of insect annoyance. If you are prone to allergic reactions from insect bites, bring plenty of repellent or other appropriate medications. To lessen the impact of insects, most overnight river excursions are on sites along the Rio Negro, where the relatively antiseptic ecological conditions keep the bug population to a minimum. The flora is also less disturbed along the Negro, while the Solimões is known for its fishing.

THE SIGHTS AND THE RIVER: One of the most popular nonriver sights in Manaus is the old **Teatro Amazonas,** an opera house that was opened in 1896, a cultural by-product of the city's newfound rubber wealth. The building is a synthesis of various styles, including baroque, neoclassical, and art nouveau. The structure beneath the façade is of cast iron which along with all the other building and finishing materials, was imported from Europe. Renovations have been in progress on both the exterior and interior of the theater for some time, but it remains partially open to the public.

Near the theater is the **Praça do Congresso,** a popular zone for evening promenades.

The **Municipal Market** at dockside is an impressive cast-iron building, similar to the Belém market. And much of what can be seen in the Ver-O-Peso can be seen here as well.

INPA (Instituto Nacional de Pesquisas da Amazonia), the National Institute of Amazonian Research, on the Estrada do Aleixo, is a government research facility outside Manaus that is worth visiting. It is necessary to enter through the main gate and get permission from the security police. Once inside the forested grounds, you immediately hear the music of the jungle, since the many trees provide a kind of urban refuge for great numbers of birds. INPA is also like a large college campus, with many buildings where scientists pursue the various branches of naturalistic studies relevant to gaining a greater understanding of the Amazon. You can see many different animals here as well, like the manatee and the *ariranha,* a very funny and animated Amazonian otter. Don't be surprised at the large numbers of Americans you see within the grounds. They are here serving on staff, sharing their ecological training in exchange for a rare opportunity for practical study in the world's largest remaining forest reserve.

A River Day Trip

The eight-hour river excursion organized by **Amazon Explorers,** Rua Quintino Bocaiúva 189 (tel. 092/232-3052), came highly recommended. I boarded the double-decker boat around 8 a.m. from the floating pier. (This pier is a considerable engineering accomplishment in itself, for it must not only accommodate many sizes of ships and boats, but also accompany the rise and fall of the river's seasonal water levels.) The company's excursion boat has a top deck, part of which is open to the sun, the other part covered by a permanent roof, with canvas side flaps for nighttime and inclement weather. Down below there is a bar and galley, four heads, and a souvenir stand selling T-shirts, hats, and suntan lotion.

As the boat glides from its slip into the **Rio Negro,** you get your first view of the city from the water. Most of the buildings sit on the high ground, well back from the river embankments. Since the river was low when I made the trip, I could see the outlines of the creeks and the high-water marks on the pilings and stone retaining walls. The stilt houses (*palafitas*) stand like circus clowns on stilts high above the water. Boats are everywhere on the move, mostly canoes, some propelled by paddles, others by outboard motors. There are also the *barcos regionais,* the typically long and narrow barges with superstructures covering the entire deck. Like so many *Merrimacks,* these floating houses of the river traders seem to ride right on the surface of the water.

For the first few miles as you head downstream, you pass half a dozen giant platforms moored in midstream—floating gas stations. The shore is lined with sawmills; millions of board feet of sawed lumber stockpiled on land, millions more uncut in the form of saw logs floating in the river on the edges of the banks. Roughly an hour later you begin to pick up the silty coloring of the **Rio Solimões** as it joins the dark Rio Negro and flows alongside without mixing, as if each river still occupied its own separate channel: the "living" river and the "dead" river. This "meeting of the waters" stretches on for several miles, until the rivers have finally melded into the yellowish Amazon. But here you reverse course and begin to run up the Solimões, hoping to sight a few dolphins (*botos*) and sure enough— as if responding to a predetermined script—the rose- and gray-colored *botos* begin to surface and submerge as they accompany the lazy perambulation of the slow-moving boat.

There are several versions of the **legend of the botos.** The one you are most likely to hear is the sentimental myth, packaged for touristic consumption. The sociological version is both more realistic and more disturbing. First the roman- tic tale: On the nights of the full moon, when there is sure to be some festive celebration in the illuminated villages deep in the forest, the dolphins transform themselves into handsome young men and seduce the young maidens. Pregnan- cy follows, and the dolphin is held to be the unassailable culprit. The legend may have arisen, social scientists now believe, as a way to explain the high incidence of pregnancy among young girls who most often live in relative isolation from their potential suitors, and who were more likely the victims of incest. The dolphins also figure in a more naturalistic, and less controversial, theory. All dolphins are believed to have originated as saltwater creatures. Their presence in the fresh wa- ter of the Amazon may indicate that South America was two land masses, and the basin was a sea that once connected the Atlantic and the Pacific.

The vegetation you see along the banks of the Solimões as you sail on for almost two hours is all secondary growth. It can even be said to be sparse in places. You pass no settlements, but there are scattered farms at decent intervals at the edges of the shore. At each of these homesteads, a system of wooden pipes can be seen running from the water and disappearing over the embankment. These are the hollow branches of the *imbambeira,* a deciduous tree, linked together to make a conduit for carrying water to the fields and houses. For any real experi- ence of the dense jungle, it would be necessary to travel many more hours above Manaus, you are told by your guide.

At a clearing where there is a single residence, you make your first stop. Past the dwelling, past a small garden plot where scrawny chickens are scratching the ground, past a few banana and mango trees, you follow a wooden boardwalk into the forest to a platform built over an *igapo,* a creek bed that is permanently flooded. Growing in the water are the giant lily pads, the *Victória régia,* today very much a symbol of the Amazon despite their being named to honor an En- glish monarch. That crackling sound you hear beneath the lilies is the gnawing of piranhas and other small fish that feed on the plants and give them their perfo- rated appearance. Here, several hundred yards beyond the riverbank, **the jungle** begins to reappear. Wildlife is abundant, especially birds and butterflies. But you can see small alligators as you approach the platform, especially if you are quick of eye, as they slide off the mud banks into the safety of the water. Kingfishers dive for fish. Many other birds—blues, yellows, reds—dart among the branches or bounce along the water's edge as they feed, in what must be a particular treat for bird fanciers familiar with the names and habits of the various species. Flocks of black birds (called *anuns*) flit through the bulrushes and swamp cane as you retrace your steps to the river. When domesticated, they are said to talk as well as parrots.

For your second stop you visit a small village populated by migrants from the northeast. A *caboclo* (rural Brazilian) demonstrates how to tap a rubber tree. He tells you that he goes out at night with a head lantern like a miner's hat and taps all his trees. Then in the morning he gathers up the latex, which is rendered slowly in a little smokehouse over a fire using only green wood. When the substance coagulates, it is joined into large balls called *pelas,* which are collected by boat at riverside, along with the other produce like cacão, mandioca, and fruits grown by the little community. The *coboclo* is also an artisan, and some people buy his model canoes, delicately carved from rose wood. Others buy petrified piranhas or native-style jewelry. You'll walk into the village, a cluster of little wood buildings, including a diminutive clapboard chapel, to look at the cacão trees. The flowers grow almost stemless right from the trunk, and mature into a large green fruit with a funny shape like a pleated balloon. You'll also see the *castanheira* with its coconut-size *ouriço,* which when opened expels anywhere from 25 to 30 Brazil nuts.

From here you begin the return trip. Lunch is served on the boat, a delicious home-cooked fish stew and a variety of side dishes. You can drink little cocktails of Amazon fruit juices with cachaça. A while later you stop at a swimming spot and everyone takes a cooling dip in the river, with much giggling and guffawing about the danger of piranhas. In fact, the fierce little fish seldom attacks humans, you are told, but a cow unfortunate enough to fall from a floating pen during the flood season can be consumed in seconds. You are back in Manaus by 3 p.m. The cost of the excursion is about $30 per person.

Informal Day Trips

Below the market, on any given day there are dozens of boats tied up along the shore (or at the piers when the water is high) whose owners will take you on the river and cover pretty much the same attractions as the large companies. No lunch is served on these boats and there is no deck to walk around on, but you also aren't required to follow any formal program. The skipper will take you wherever you want to go—and may even have a few suggestions of his own. His fee should be no more than half of what the excursion boats charge.

Overnight River Trips

Dozens of tour operators in Manaus, like Amazon Explorers, offer overnights in the jungle, usually at special "lodges" or "villages," located five or six hours from the city up the Rio Negro. Typically, these excursion packages offer one or two nights in comfortable accommodations, with hammocks for beds and a variety of daytime and evening programs. These include walks into the jungle, canoe trips up streams and creeks, and an alligator hunt, where flashlights are used to "freeze" the reptiles, which are then captured and released unharmed. A package of three days and two nights runs around $300 per person, and two days and one night, around $175. Cheaper overnights are also available through numerous other tour operators in Manaus. These generally involve accommodations that are considerably more rustic than those offered by operators on the upper end of the market.

Pousada dos Guanavenas

This is an independent first-class forest hotel about 150 miles from Manaus. The hotel, which has won several major architectural awards, was completely built with regional materials, and occupies a clearing near the riverbank. To get there, guests first travel to Itacoatiara by bus, and continue on by boat. Guests may also make special arrangements to arrive by sea plane. The hotel offers various packages from three to seven days. Each package includes full board and several guided jungle expeditions. The Guanavenas has offices in Manaus at Rua Ferreira Pena 755 (tel. 092/233-5350). Rates are available on request or through your travel agent.

An Ecological Safari

One of the more interesting excursions out of Manaus for the ecologically minded traveler, but suitable for the general public as well, is a seven-day river tour aboard an 80-foot boat called the *Tuna*. The *Tuna* has every comfort, including ten first-class, double-occupancy, air-conditioned cabins, each with private bath. Other features include a well-equipped kitchen, dining room, lounge, bar, and a library well stocked with titles about the Amazon's ecosystem. The *Tuna* cruises far up the Rio Negro, making calls at several research stations, where there are scientific lectures and videotape presentations. The safari costs $805 per person. A mini-safari of four days is also available for $435.

Agencies

The names of U.S. travel agents and organizations that book specialty tours to Brazil, including adventure tours throughout the Amazon like the "ecological safari," are listed in the next chapter.

3. THE PANTANAL

THE SOUTHERN WETLANDS: Five years ago, no one among world travelers but the most committed naturalists and birdwatchers had ever heard of the Pantanal, a vast wildlife preserve occupying segments of two southern Brazilian states as well as sections of two bordering South American nations. **O Grande Pantanal** (the Great Wetlands), as the region is known, stretches over an area roughly 400 miles long and 200 miles wide, forming an ecological bridge among the states of Mato Grosso and Mato Grosso do Sul and the countries of Bolivia and Paraguay. Like the Amazon River Valley, the Pantanal is also a great basin through which numerous rivers drain en route to the Rio de la Plata and the Atlantic Ocean to the south. Largest of these is the Rio Paraguay, which forms Brazil's southern frontier with its South American neighbors.

But the comparison with the Amazon stops with this hydrographic analogy. The Pantanal is not a forest but a plain, combining swamps and grazing lands during the dry season, April through November, and largely flooded during the rains, from December through March, when fishing is said to be as good as anywhere on the planet. The region is shared by huge populations of wildlife and the cattle herds belonging to ranchers with spreads of baronial proportions. During the rains, both cattle and wildlife take refuge on the pockets of high ground that are never covered by water. During these days the lion lies down with the lamb. Or more accurately, the jaguar and the deer cohabit in the thick undergrowth of these elevated mounds.

Tourists who visit the Pantanal are often those whose attention has been drawn in recent years to nature and to those conditions that threaten the stability and existence of species and natural habitats. This new consciousness has spawned a generation of amateur naturalists who come to the Pantanal to see the birds—of which there are some 600 species—and the animals like deer, capibaras, monkeys, rheas, alligators, and occasionally the more stealthful jaguar, which is relatively easy to sight on the open terrain. Most tourists come during the dry season, when access to the Pantanal is greatest, unless of course they wish to fish. Ideally, the visitor will be able to travel the entire length of the **Transpantaneira,** a raised dirt highway that crosses the Pantanal from **Poconé** (outside of Cuiabá, capital of Mato Grosso) to **Corumbá** in Mato Grosso do Sul, a river city on the border with Bolivia.

The best way to visit the Pantanal is on a guided tour with one of the ecologically sophisticated tour agencies that are mentioned in the next chapter. As an alternative to this, a traveler touring Brazil somewhat more hurriedly—taking advantage of the VARIG Air Pass, for example, in order to visit as much of the country as possible in a relatively short time—may still sample the fringes of the Pantanal by stopping over at Cuiabá.

CUIABÁ: The capital of Mato Grosso grew up as a gold-rush town during the 1700s and remained relatively undeveloped until recently, when agricultural prosperity in the state transformed Cuiabá from a frontier town to a modern city. In the process the town lost most of its character and charm, and cannot be considered a destination in and of itself. It's not, however, a bad place to hang-out for a couple of days, and to use as a base for a few brief forays into the nearby countryside, including the edges of the Pantanal.

Tourist Information

The state tourist office, **Turismat,** is located on the Praça da República (tel. 065/322-5363).

Where to Stay

The four-star **Mato Grosso Palace Hotel,** Rua Joaquim Murtilho 170 (tel. 065/32-9254), is one of the best in Cuiabá. The hotel is located around the corner from the city's principal square, the Praça da República. The 100-room Palace Hotel has very comfortable rooms and other facilities, like a restaurant and bar, but no swimming pool. Rates are $38 to $49 for standard rooms, and $52 to $65 for the deluxe rooms.

The town's other four-star establishment is the **Aúrea Palace Hotel,** Rua General Melo 63, (tel. 065/322-3637). The hotel has some character, but the rooms here are small, as are the beds, and the whole place could use a paint job. There is a small pool on ground level. Rates are $38 for a single and $44 for a double.

A budget choice is the **Hotel Mato Grosso,** Rua Comandante Costa 2522 (tel. 065/321-9121). The interior of this hotel is interesting in that the rooms are off an open-air corridor, which aids in ventilation. Rooms with fans cost $7 to $13; with air conditioners, $8 to $14. Add a TV and the charge is $10 to $15.

Where to Dine

The **Restaurante O Regionalíssimo,** Rua 13 de Julho, at the corner of Rua Senador Metello (tel. 313-2217), is located on the Casa do Artesão, the city's restored colonial jail house, now a center for some of the best crafts to be found anywhere in Brazil. The state of Mato Grosso has a large Indian population, and much of the work in clay and straw comes from the hands of these artisans. The restaurant, which occupies the ground floor of the building, serves a tasty feijoada, Mato Grosso style, including unique side dishes like farofa de banana, and for dessert, doce de limão, a compote of lime peels and sugar. The cost is about $5, less beverage. During much of 1988, and perhaps 1989, the restaurant will be occupying temporary quarters at the Restaurante do Servidor Público in front of the Palácio Paiaguas, on an avenue known locally as C.P.A., where most of the government buildings are located.

Excursions from Cuiabá

Two colonial-era towns not far from Cuiabá retain much of their old-fashioned charm. One is **Chapada de Guimarães,** gateway to the stunning table-lands that begin some 40 miles from the capital; the other is **Poconé,** entry point to the *transpantaneira* highway about 60 miles to the south of Cuiabá. Both places would be excellent locales for stays of indeterminate duration for those who are seeking the authenticity and quietude of small-town life in the Brazilian interior. Both are served by several country-style hotels and pensions. The main attraction around Guimarães is the rolling landscape, which is excellent for camping or hiking. From Poconé, of course, you enter the Pantanal.

There is a check point at the beginning of the *transpantaneira* where a guard will hand you a brochure explaining the ground rules of a visit to the preserve. You read, for example, that there is absolutely no hunting allowed. Indeed, there would be little sport in the hunt, especially for the jacaré (alligators), large numbers of which sunbathe in streams by the sides of the highway. The road itself is wide, and of a rough dirt surface. Every mile, or so it seems, you cross a rude bridge of planks over the endless arroyos and streams that carry the seasonal rains to the larger rivers that are also plentiful throughout the area. Already a few miles within the great marsh, you sight a dozen bird species, including the emblematic bird of the Pantanal, the *tuiuiú,* a red-collared white stork with a jet-black bill and a six-foot wing span.

After about 20 miles you come to the first of several ranch hotels, the **Pousada das Araras** (tel. 065/322-4570), a working ranch of 20,000 acres that receives guests. The proprietor has built a brick bunkhouse with half a dozen very simple rooms. A veranda, installed with several hammocks, wraps around the building. Anyone in a restful mood might easily spend a few days on the ranch, fishing or horseback riding with the staff, or nature walking in search of birds and animals to add to your sightings. Just swinging on a hammock in the veranda, you are bound to see the flocks of colorful macaws overfly the ranchhouse screeching *arara, arara*—the source of their name in Portuguese. The cost per night at the ranch is $20 per person, including three meals.

From here it is a day's journey to **Porto Jofre,** where you enter Mato Grosso do Sul, where you may continue south to the Rio Paraguay and the Bolivian border if you choose. The deeper you travel into the Pantanal, the more creatures you will see, it is said.

CHAPTER XIV

SPECIALTY TOURS

□ □ □

Most people who visit Brazil book their tickets and package tours through their local travel agents. The services they receive are, in general, quite adequate, since the majority of North Americans going to Brazil do not venture much beyond the beaches of Rio de Janeiro. For those who wish to travel more extensively in Brazil, however, there are a number of organizations and agencies that cater to a range of special interests, including adventure, urban culture, study and nature tours, and much more. In addition to these specialists, and a description of what they offer, I have also listed the major charter companies and travel clubs that provide some of the most economical flights to Brazil.

ESCORTED TOURS TO RIO AND BEYOND: One of the best escorted-tour companies is **Brazil Nuts,** 81 Remsen St., Brooklyn, NY 11201 (tel. 718/834-0717), offering a variety of escorted tours for small groups that focus on Brazil's popular culture. An eight-day/seven-night tour of Rio covers all the obligatory sights, and threads its way through the city's nightlife, visiting a different "nontouristy" music club every night. Another Brazil Nut 13-day package takes in Rio, Buzios, and Salvador. The company also takes a group to Carnival in Rio every year, one of their most popular packages.

For adventure and nature travel, Brazil Nuts works with **Expeditours,** Rua Visconde de Pirajá 414, in Rio (tel. 021/287-9048), which escorts groups to both the Amazon and the Pantanal. If you are in Rio already and want someone to show you the city, or organize an excursion to the Costa Verde or the Costa do Sol, drop by Expeditour's Ipanema office and they will make all the necessary arrangements for you.

NATURE TOURS: In the early 1980s **Focus Tours,** Rua Grao Mogol 502, Belo Horizonte, MG 30330 (tel. 031/223-0358; telex 031-3823 RAPT BR), inaugurated the concept of "conservation tourism" in Brazil. Founder Douglas Trent, a Michigander, is himself a trained ecologist. The majority of the company's tours are custom-designed, and concentrate on taking groups to various "natural destinations." Among these are the Amazon, the Pantanal, the Atlantic forest regions, the *cerrado* of central Brazil, and the *sertão* of the northeast. A typical tour might begin in the Amazon, with a few days on a rustic ranch with high concentrations of macaws and other bird species. From there the group flies to Brasília, visiting the heart of the *cerrado* at dawn to catch the height of animal activity. Then it's on to the Pantanal and a trip along the entire length of the *transpantaneira* highway, also taking in the lush gallery forest on the edge of Brazil's central plain outside Cuiabá. A visit to Iguaçu is next, including both sides of the falls and the little-visited national parks in both countries. Last stop might be the Itatiaia National Park outside Rio, and then a few days on the beaches of Ipanema for some fun in the sun. Focus Tours donates a portion of tour proceeds to a number of private Brazilian conservation organizations, a campaign which is endorsed by the National Audubon Society.

ADVENTURE TOURS: Though it specializes in Amazon adventures, **CanoAndes,** 310 Madison Ave., New York, NY 10017 (tel. 212/286-9415), also organizes trekking, rafting, wildlife, and cultural expeditions for all levels, from novice to expert. CanoAndes offers a one-day white-water rafting expedition only hours from Rio, and the company is an American agent for the Ecological Safari in the Amazon, the week-long river trip aboard the boat *Tuna.*

SPECIAL-INTEREST TOURS: Those with specialized interests should consider **Brazilian Views,** 201 E. 66th St., Suite 21G, New York, NY 10021 (tel. 212/472-9539), the brainchild of Suzanne Barner, who lived in Brazil for 35 years. Her company offers expertly guided tours for those whose interest is in horticulture, birdwatching, fiber arts/needlework, history, and gems, among other subjects. On one of Brazilian Views' two-week gemstone tours, the group spent a week visiting mines and mining towns in Minas Gerais and Goiás, as well as the major mineralogy museums in Belo Horizonte and Ouro Preto, before settling into Rio for some insider touring of the retail jewelry businesses there.

MUSEUM TOURS: In this category, **Jacqueline Moss Museum Tours,** 131 Davenport Ridge Lane, Stamford, CT 06903 (tel. 203/322-8709), has led art, architecture, and folk art tours to Brazil in past years, and plans to do so again if there is the necessary demand. The 23-day tour took in eight Brazilian cities, and focused on sights of cultural significance.

EDUCATIONAL AND STUDY TOURS: For something a bit more demanding mentally, **International Study Tours Ltd.,** 225 W. 34th St., Suite 613, New York, NY 10122 (tel. 212/563-1202), specializes in "educational travel for those who seek knowledge and understanding of a foreign culture beyond the scope of the usual sightseeing tour." The tour programs are created in conjunction with Brazilian universities, and include lectures and field trips, and the presentation of certificates to participants. Participating universities are in Rio, Salvador, São Paulo, Ouro Preto, Brasília, Niterói, and Belém.

Some U.S. universities and cultural institutions that offered educational tours to Brazil in 1988 are:

The **New York University School of Continuing Education,** 331 Shimkin Hall, Washington Square, New York, NY 10003 (tel. 212/998-7133), offered a two-week cultural program called "Brazil: Carnival and Beyond," to Bahia, Belo Horizonte, Brasília, and Rio—with seats for the Carnival parade.

The **American Museum of Natural History Discovery Tours,** Central Park West at 79th Street, New York, NY 10024 (tel. 212/769-5700), offered an Amazon Wildlife Adventure tour.

The **National Trust for Historic Preservation,** 1785 Massachusetts Ave. NW, Washington, DC 20036 (tel. 202/673-4138), offered a tour entitled "Brazil: New World in the Tropics," with a focus on colonial and modern architecture in a three-week swing through six Brazilian cities.

PACKAGE TOURS AND CHARTERS: In cooperation with VARIG Airlines, **South American Fiesta,** P.O. Box 456, Ridge, NY 11961 (tel. 516/924-6200), offers 15 different package tours to destinations throughout Brazil.

The following **private companies** offer special vacation packages to Brazil —primarily to Rio de Janeiro—and may be booked through your travel agent: PanAm Fantasy Holidays, American Express South America Vacations, Council Charter, Tourlite, Marnella Tours, and Abreu Tours.

TRAVEL CLUBS: The **BACC (Brazilian American Cultural Center),** 20 W. 46th St., New York, NY 10036 (tel. 212/730-0515, or toll free 800/222-2746 outside New York City), offers inexpensive charter fares to Rio from Miami, New York, and Los Angeles.

The **Skyline Travel Club,** 666 Old Country Rd., Suite 205, Garden City, NY 11530 (tel. 516/222-9090, or toll free 800/645-6198), offers cheap flights to Rio out of New York.

USEFUL WORDS AND PHRASES IN BRAZILIAN PORTUGUESE

□ □ □

1. PRONUNCIATION GUIDE

2. VOCABULARY

3. MENU TERMS

Obviously, a mere vocabulary list at the end of a travel guide can give only limited insight into a foreign tongue, especially one as unfamiliar to most English speakers as Brazilian Portuguese. For both practical and cultural reasons, however, it is worth the traveler's while to bone up a bit on Portuguese before visiting Brazil. Few Brazilians outside the tourist orbit speak English. And even then the level of fluency is very uneven. There are times, moreover, in any foreign locale when the best way to get your point across is in *their* language rather than your own. But even more important to the success of your Brazilian adventure are the points you score by extending yourself—making an effort to communicate in the host language. Such efforts, even when only symbolic, can go a long way toward neutralizing cultural chauvinism and smoothing the way for you, especially in cases where English may be resented as much as it is spoken.

1. PRONUNCIATION GUIDE

The following notes on pronunciation are meant as a bridge—a few sturdy planks—across what may at first appear a language gap too wide to span. Both English and Portuguese writing systems use the Roman alphabet (the ABCs). But the two languages sometimes apply very different sound values to the same letters. Some of these major distinctions are described below.

VOWELS: As is the case with English and other Western languages, Portuguese uses the five vowel *symbols* provided by the alphabet to represent more than five distinct vowel *sounds*. An **o** in Portuguese can stand for two very different sounds in words that are spelled the same except for their accents. For example, *avô*, with the *o* sound similar to "row," means grandfather, while *avó*, with the sound of the *ou* in "cough," means grandmother. And though the words *céu* (sky, heaven) and *seu* (the pronoun "your" in its masculine singular form) are not written the same way, their *e* sounds are also pronounced differently. The *e* in *céu* is similar to that of the word "bet," as is also the case of the *e* in *café*. One of the easiest ways to pinpoint an American accent in Portuguese is when you hear someone pronounce *café* where that *e* sounds like the *ai* in "bait." *Seu*, on the other hand, *is* pronounced with the *ai* sound as in the word "bait."

Portuguese makes liberal use of **nasal vowels,** indicated either by the presence of a tilde, as in *lã* (wool) or an *m,* as in *bém* (well). (That *m* becomes an *n* when the word is pluralized, as in *bens*—worldly goods—but it remains a nasal vowel.) The proper pronunciation is a lot closer to "bangs" than to "Ben's." The way this sound is made in the mouth is similar to how we make the *ng* sound in English, as in the word "sing." In the case of the nasal vowel, however, the tongue does not make contact with the roof of the mouth, and the air from the sound escapes through the nostrils, not from between the lips. The letters **ng** will be used to indicate the approximate pronunciation of Portuguese words using nasal vowels in the vocabulary list that follows. To get the correct sound in Portuguese, however, start out as if you were going to pronounce an *ng* sound. Then tense the tongue and don't let it touch the top of your mouth. It's easy.

The **nasal dipthong** (a dipthong is a pair of vowels together) is also common in Portuguese, as in the words *pão* (bread), *cidadão* (citizen), and *não* (no). The sound is like that of "cow"—but nasalized. To practice the sound, try adding an *ng* to "cow" and you'll come close. Other common nasal dipthongs are *ãe,* as in the proper name Magalhães (Magellan's real name!), and *õe,* as in *ladrões* (thieves). The *ãe* is pronounced like the affirmation "aye" and the *õe* like the sound in "boy"—but remember that both are nasalized.

The vowel *o* when occurring at the end of a word, even when pluralized, sounds like the *oo* in "moo." Thus Rio is pronounced *"Ree*-oo," as in the vowels of "tree" and "zoo." The vowel *e* in word final position is pronounced like *ee* as in "knee." Thus *bife* (beef) is pronounced *"bee*-fee," as in the vowels of "bee" and "fee." There are two exceptions to this rule. The first is when an *o* or *e* at the end of a word receives the stress, for example in accented words like *café* or *avô*. The other is when someone is speaking with artificial formality. We do this in English too, when we pronounce "the" like "thee," rather than the way we say it in normal, un-self-conscious speech, with the same sound as in the word "love."

CONSONANTS: The **c cedilla** is pronounced like a soft *s* as in the word *praça* (*"prah*-sa.").

Cariocas (natives of Rio) pronounce the letters *t* and *d* that preceede the vowels *e* and *i* like *ch* and *j*. The pronunciation can be illustrated with a single word, *diferente* (different), which is pronounced "jiff-eh-*rehn*-chee."

Portuguese has several ways to represent the **sh** sound, like *ch* in "Chico" (the diminutive of Francisco), which is pronounced *"She*-coo." The *sh* sound is also represented in Portuguese by the letter *x,* as in *Mexico,* pronounced *"Meh*-she-coo." In fact, practically any *s* preceded by a vowel and followed by a consonant is shush-ed in the Carioca dialect, as in *as casas* (the houses), pronounced "ahsh *cahz*-ahss."

The letter **j** in Portuguese has the same sound as the second syllable of the words "measure" or "pleasure," represented by the letters *su;* or as the *zs* in the name Zsa Zsa. This is not a sound that normally occurs in beginnings of words in English.

A **single r** in Portuguese is flapped, as in Spanish. If you say the word "fodder" fast, the double *d* is close to the Portuguese single *r*. The **double r,** or the *r* at the beginning of a word followed by a vowel, in Brazilian Portuguese is generally pronounced like our English *h*. Thus *carro* (car) is pronounced *"cah*-who," and Rio is actually pronounced *"Hee*-yoo." In some parts of Brazil, as in Portugal, the double *r* or single initial *r* is trilled, the way upper-class British pronounce the *r*.

Portuguese, like Spanish and Italian, has a **nya** sound, represented by *nh* as in *piranha*, pronounced "pee-*rahn*-ya," and a **lya** sound represented by *lh*, as in *brilhante* (brilliant), pronounced "bril-*yahn*-chee."

There are many more subtleties to Brazilian speech patterns than can be outlined in these brief introductory comments. With these hints in mind, however, you will have the key to some pronunciations that appear all the more puzzling when you compare them with the written word. After that, the best guide to pronouncing and understanding Portuguese will be your own ear.

2. VOCABULARY

Good morning	**Bom dia**	bong *gee*-ya
Good night	**Boa noite**	bwa *noy*-chee
How are you?	**Como vai?**	*coh*-moo vie
Everything ok?	**Tudo bem?**	too-doo bang
fine, great	**tudo bem**	too-doo bang
Let's get going	**Vamos embora**	*vah*-moose eng-*boh*-rah
bye	**tchau**	chow
so long	**até logo**	ah-*teh loh*-goo
What time is it?	**Que horas são?**	key *oh*-rass sowng
It's (five) o'clock	**são (cinco) horas**	sowng *seeng*-coo *oh*-rass
How much is . . . ?	**Quanto é . . . ?**	qwahn-too eh . . . ?
Where are you going?	**Onde vai?**	*own*-gee vie
Where is . . . ?	**Onde esta . . . ?**	*own*-gee eh-*stah*
the subway	**o metrô**	oo meh-*troe*
the bathroom	**o banheiro**	oo bahn-*yay*-roo
the room	**o quarto**	oo *qwahr*-too
the meal	**a comida**	ah coe-*me*-dah
I want . . .	**Quero . . .**	*care*-roo . . .
I would like . . .	**Queria . . .**	*care*-*ree*-ah . . .
Pardon me	**Com licença**	cong lee-*sehn*-sa
Excuse me	**Desculpe**	desh-*cul*-pee
yes	**é**	eh
no	**não**	now
I don't know	**Não sei**	now say
Do you know?	**Você sabe?**	voe-*say sah*-bee
please	**faz favor**	fiez fah-*vohr*
thank you (male)	**Obrigado**	owe-bree-*gah*-doo
thank you (female)	**Obrigada**	owe-bree-*gah*-dah
Do you have . . . ?	**Tem . . . ?**	tang . . . ?

I don't speak . . .	**Não falo . . .**	now *fah*-loo . . .
Do you speak . . . ?	**Você fala . . .?**	voe-*say fah*-lah . . .
Portuguese	**português**	poor-too-*gays*
English	**inglês**	eeng-*glays*

MORE VOCABULARY: For the words that follow, unless otherwise noted, adjectives are shown in their masculine singular form. Since, in general, an adjective must agree with the noun it modifies in both gender and number, masculine adjectives ending in *o* become feminine adjectives by changing the *o* to *a*, and are pluralized by adding *s* to the masculine or feminine singular form. The adjectives ending in *e* are the same for masculine and feminine, and are pluralized by adding *s*.

N. B. the double oo in my phonetic transcription has the same value as the vowels in such diversely spelled English words as boo, Lew, two, true and you. I will on occasion insert these other spellings to avoid any possible ambiguity.

the (masc. sing., plural)	**o, os**	oo, oos
the (fem. sing., plural)	**a, as**	ah, ahs
a (masc., fem.)	**um, uma**	oong, OOmah
some (masc., fem.)	**uns, umas**	oongs, OOmahs
good (masc., fem.)	**bon, boa**	bong, BOWah
bad (masc., fem.)	**mal, mala**	mao, MAHlah
cheap	**barato**	bahRAHtoo
expensive	**caro**	CAHroo
old	**velho**	VEHLyoo
new	**novo**	NOvoo
big	**grande**	GRAHNgee
small	**pequeno**	pehKAYnoo
early	**cedo**	CEHdoo
late	**tarde**	TAHRaee
hot	**quente**	KENchee
cold	**frio**	FREEyou
left	**esquerda**	eshCAREdah
right	**direita**	geeRAYtah
straight ahead	**em frente**	ang FRENchee
here	**aquí**	ah KEY
there	**aí**	Ah EE
over there	**alí**	ah LEE
yonder	**lá**	lah
today	**hoje**	O zsee (like Zsa Zsa)
yesterday	**ontem**	ONG tang
tomorrow	**amanhã**	ah mahn YAH (nasal)
the day	**o dia**	oo GEE yah
the week	**a semana**	ah seh MAHN ah

the weekend	o fim de semana	oo fing gee. . . .
the year	a ano	oo AH noo
the month	o mês	oo mace
Monday	segunda-feira	say GOON dah FAY rah
Tuesday	terca-feira	TARE sah. . . .
Wednesday	quarta-feira	GWAH tah
Thursday	quinta-feira	KEEN tah
Friday	sexta-feira	SAYSH tah. . . .
Saturday	sabado	SAH bah doo
Sunday	domingo	doe MING goo

1 **um/uma** (oong/oomah)
2 **dois/duas** (doysh/doo-ash)
3 **tres** (traysh)
4 **quatro** (QWAH true)
5 **cinco** (SING coo)
6 **seis** (SAYSH)
7 **sete** (SEH chee)
8 **oito** (OY two)
9 **nove** (NO vee)
10 **dez** (DAYSH)
11 **onze** (OWN zee)
12 **doze** (DOE zee)
13 **treze** (TREH zee)
14 **quatorze** (qwa TOR zee

15 **quinze** (KEEN zee)
16 **dezesseis** (dez ah SAYSH)
17 **dezessete** (dez ah SEH chee)
18 **dezoito** (dez OY too)
19 **dezenove** (dez ah NO vee)
20 **vinte** (VEAN chee)
21 **vinte e um** (VEAN chee oong)
30 **trinta** (TREEN tah)
40 **quarenta** (qwa RENH tah)
50 **cinquenta** (sing QWEN tah)

60 **seissenta** (say SEHN tah)
70 **setenta** (say TEHN tah)
80 **oitenta** (oy TENH tah)
90 **noventa** (no VENH tah)
100 **cem** (sang)
101 **cento e um** (SENH too ee oong)
500 **quinhenta** (keen YEHN tah)
1,000 **mil** (mil)

3. MENU TERMS

And now, here's a very brief guide to some of the menu terms you will probably encounter as you eat your way around Brazil.

FOOD AND DRINK

a comida   the food/meal
a bebida   the drink
o cardápio/menu   the menu
a conta   the bill
a nota   the receipt
mal passado   rare
bem passado   well done
ao ponto   medium
o gelo   the ice
a agua mineral   the mineral water

com gaz   carbonated
sem gaz   regular
a refrigerante   soda pop
a chá   the tea
o café   the coffee
o leite   the milk
o vinho   the wine
  tinto   red
  branco   white
a cerveja   the beer

MEATS

carne   meat
bife   beef
carneiro   lamb
porco   pork
frango   chicken

coelho   rabbit
bode   goat
peru   turkey
presunto   ham
linguiça   sausage

galinha chicken
costeletas chops

vitela veal

SEAFOOD

peixe fish
frutos do mar seafood
bacalhau codfish
linguado sole
lagosta lobster
camarão shrimp

siri crab
caranguejo marsh crab
lula squid
polvo octopus
ostras oysters

SIDE DISHES, CONDIMENTS, AND DESSERTS

pão bread
manteiga butter
queijo cheese
sopa soup
canja chicken soup
sobremesa dessert
ovos eggs
bacon bacon
sal salt

pimenta do reino pepper
mostarda mustard
açúcar sugar
sanduiche sandwich
molho sauce
torrada toast
azeite oil
  de azeitona olive oil
vinagre vinegar

VEGETABLES

batata potato
puré mashed potatoes
batatas fritas french fries
batata doce sweet potato
salada mixta mixed salad
alface lettuce
tomate tomato
cebola onion
azeitona olive

alho garlic
pepino cucumber
cenoura carrot
legumes vegetables
vagens green beans
ervilhas peas
feijão preto black beans
arroz rice
champignon mushrooms

FRUITS

limão lemon/lime
maça apple
abacaxi pineapple
melancia watermelon
melão melon
morangos strawberries
pera pear

pêssego peach
uvas grapes
cerejas cherries
figos figs
suco juice
suco de laranja orange juice

Index

Note: Common terms such as "Igreja" (Church), "Museu" (Museum), and "Praia" (Beach), have been transposed if they occur at the beginning of a name. To find a place or attraction, look under the next significant word (e.g., "Igreja do Carmo" can be found under "Carmo, Igreja do"). Places named after a person can be found under that person's last name (e.g., "Museu Carlos Costa Pinto" can be found under "Pinto (Carlos Costa), Museu").

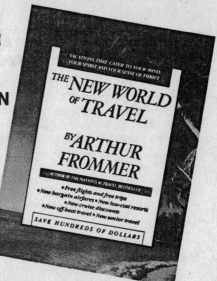

NOW, SAVE MONEY ON ALL YOUR TRAVELS!
Join Frommer's™ Dollarwise® Travel Club

Saving money while traveling is never a simple matter, which is why, over 27 years ago, the **Dollarwise Travel Club** was formed. Actually, the idea came from readers of the Frommer publications who felt that such an organization could bring financial benefits, continuing travel information, and a sense of community to economy-minded travelers all over the world.

In keeping with the money-saving concept, the annual membership fee is low—$18 (U.S. residents) or $20 U.S. (Canadian, Mexican, and foreign residents)—and is immediately exceeded by the value of your benefits which include:

1. The latest edition of any TWO of the books listed on the following pages.

2. A copy of any Frommer City Guide.

3. An annual subscription to an 8-page quarterly newspaper *The Dollarwise Traveler* which keeps you up-to-date on fastbreaking developments in good-value travel in all parts of the world—bringing you the kind of information you'd have to pay over $35 a year to obtain elsewhere. This consumer-conscious publication also includes the following columns:

Hospitality Exchange—members all over the world who are willing to provide hospitality to other members as they pass through their home cities.

Share-a-Trip—requests from members for travel companions who can share costs and help avoid the burdensome single supplement.

Readers Ask . . . Readers Reply—travel questions from members to which other members reply with authentic firsthand information.

4. Your personal membership card which entitles you to purchase through the club all Frommer publications for a third to a half off their regular retail prices during the term of your membership.

So why not join this hardy band of international Dollarwise travelers now and participate in its exchange of information and hospitality? Simply send $18 (U.S. residents) or $20 U.S. (Canadian, Mexican, and other foreign residents) along with your name and address to: Frommer's Dollarwise Travel Club, Inc., Gulf + Western Building, One Gulf + Western Plaza, New York, NY 10023. Remember to specify which *two* of the books in section (1) and which *one* in section (2) above you wish to receive in your initial package of member's benefits. Or tear out the next page, check off your choices, and send the page to us with your membership fee.

FROMMER BOOKS
PRENTICE HALL PRESS
ONE GULF + WESTERN PLAZA
NEW YORK, NY 10023

Date_____

Friends:
Please send me the books checked below:

FROMMER'S™ $-A-DAY® GUIDES

(In-depth guides to sightseeing and low-cost tourist accommodations and facilities.)

☐ Europe on $30 a Day $14.95	☐ New Zealand on $40 a Day $12.95
☐ Australia on $30 a Day $12.95	☐ New York on $50 a Day $12.95
☐ Eastern Europe on $25 a Day $12.95	☐ Scandinavia on $50 a Day $12.95
☐ England on $40 a Day $12.95	☐ Scotland and Wales on $40 a Day $12.95
☐ Greece on $30 a Day $12.95	☐ South America on $30 a Day $12.95
☐ Hawaii on $50 a Day $13.95	☐ Spain and Morocco (plus the Canary Is.)
☐ India on $25 a Day $12.95	on $40 a Day $13.95
☐ Ireland on $30 a Day $12.95	☐ Turkey on $25 a Day $12.95
☐ Israel on $30 & $35 a Day $12.95	☐ Washington, D.C., & Historic Va. on
☐ Mexico (plus Belize & Guatemala)	$40 a Day $12.95
on $25 a Day $13.95	

FROMMER'S™ DOLLARWISE® GUIDES

(Guides to sightseeing and tourist accommodations and facilities from budget to deluxe, with emphasis on the medium-priced.)

☐ Alaska $13.95	☐ Cruises (incl. Alask, Carib, Mex, Hawaii,
☐ Austria & Hungary $14.95	Panama, Canada, & US) $14.95
☐ Belgium, Holland, Luxembourg $13.95	☐ California & Las Vegas $14.95
☐ Brazil (avail. Nov. 1988) $14.95	☐ Florida $13.95
☐ Egypt $13.95	☐ Mid-Atlantic States $13.95
☐ France $14.95	☐ New England $13.95
☐ England & Scotland $14.95	☐ New York State $13.95
☐ Germany $13.95	☐ Northwest $13.95
☐ Italy $14.95	☐ Skiing in Europe $14.95
☐ Japan & Hong Kong $13.95	☐ Skiing USA—East $13.95
☐ Portugal, Madeira, & the Azores $13.95	☐ Skiing USA—West $13.95
☐ South Pacific $13.95	☐ Southeast & New Orleans $13.95
☐ Switzerland & Liechtenstein $13.95	☐ Southwest $14.95
☐ Bermuda & The Bahamas $13.95	☐ Texas $13.95
☐ Canada $13.95	☐ USA (avail. Feb. 1989) $15.95
☐ Caribbean $13.95	

FROMMER'S™ TOURING GUIDES

(Color illustrated guides that include walking tours, cultural & historic sites, and other vital travel information.)

☐ Australia $9.95	☐ Paris $8.95
☐ Egypt $8.95	☐ Thailand $9.95
☐ Florence $8.95	☐ Venice $8.95
☐ London $8.95	

TURN PAGE FOR ADDITONAL BOOKS AND ORDER FORM.

FROMMER'S™ CITY GUIDES

(Pocket-size guides to sightseeing and tourist accommodations and facilities in all price ranges.)

☐ Amsterdam/Holland	$5.95	☐ Montreal/Quebec City	$5.95
☐ Athens	$5.95	☐ New Orleans	$5.95
☐ Atlantic City/Cape May	$5.95	☐ New York	$5.95
☐ Boston	$5.95	☐ Orlando/Disney World/EPCOT	$5.95
☐ Cancún/Cozumel/Yucatán	$5.95	☐ Paris	$5.95
☐ Dublin/Ireland	$5.95	☐ Philadelphia	$5.95
☐ Hawaii	$5.95	☐ Rio (avail. Nov. 1988)	$5.95
☐ Las Vegas	$5.95	☐ Rome	$5.95
☐ Lisbon/Madrid/Costa del Sol	$5.95	☐ San Francisco	$5.95
☐ London	$5.95	☐ Santa Fe/Taos (avail. Mar. 1989)	$5.95
☐ Los Angeles	$5.95	☐ Sydney	$5.95
☐ Mexico City/Acapulco	$5.95	☐ Washington, D.C.	$5.95
☐ Minneapolis/St. Paul	$5.95		

SPECIAL EDITIONS

☐ A Shopper's Guide to the Caribbean	$12.95	☐ Motorist's Phrase Book (Fr/Ger/Sp)	$4.95
☐ Beat the High Cost of Travel	$6.95	☐ Paris Rendez-Vous	$10.95
☐ Bed & Breakfast—N. America	$8.95	☐ Swap and Go (Home Exchanging)	$10.95
☐ Guide to Honeymoon Destinations		☐ The Candy Apple (NY for Kids)	$11.95
(US, Canada, Mexico, & Carib)	$12.95	☐ Travel Diary and Record Book	$5.95
☐ Manhattan's Outdoor Sculpture	$15.95	☐ Where to Stay USA (Lodging from $3	
		to $30 a night)	$10.95

☐ Marilyn Wood's Wonderful Weekends (NY, Conn, Mass, RI, Vt, NH, NJ, Del,Pa) $11.95

☐ The New World of Travel (Annual sourcebook by Arthur Frommer previewing: new travel trends, new modes of travel, and the latest cost-cutting strategies for savvy travelers) $12.95

SERIOUS SHOPPER'S GUIDES

(Illustrated guides listing hundreds of stores, conveniently organized alphabetically by category)

☐ Italy	$15.95	☐ Los Angeles	$14.95
☐ London	$15.95	☐ Paris	$15.95

GAULT MILLAU

(The only guides that distinguish the truly superlative from the merely overrated.)

☐ The Best of Chicago (avail. Feb. 1989)	$15.95	☐ The Best of New England (avail. Feb. 1989)	$15.95
☐ The Best of France (avail. Feb. 1989)	$15.95	☐ The Best of New York	$15.95
☐ The Best of Italy (avail. Feb. 1989)	$15.95	☐ The Best of San Francisco	$15.95
☐ The Best of Los Angeles	$15.95	☐ The Best of Washington, D.C.	$15.95

ORDER NOW!

In U.S. include $1.50 shipping UPS for 1st book; 50¢ ea. add'l book. Outside U.S. $2 and 50¢, respectively.

Allow four to six weeks for delivery in U.S., longer outside U.S.

Enclosed is my check or money order for $_____

NAME _____

ADDRESS _____

CITY _____ STATE _____ ZIP _____